Lecture Notes in Artificial Intelligence   8445

Subseries of Lecture Notes in Computer Science

LNAI Series Editors

Randy Goebel
University of Alberta, Edmonton, Canada
Yuzuru Tanaka
Hokkaido University, Sapporo, Japan
Wolfgang Wahlster
DFKI and Saarland University, Saarbrücken, Germany

LNAI Founding Series Editor

Joerg Siekmann
DFKI and Saarland University, Saarbrücken, Germany

Lecture Notes in Artificial Intelligence   8445

Subseries of Lecture Notes in Computer Science

LNAI Series Editors

Randy Goebel
University of Alberta, Edmonton, Canada
Yuzuru Tanaka
Hokkaido University, Sapporo, Japan
Wolfgang Wahlster
DFKI and Saarland University, Saarbrücken, Germany

LNAI Founding Series Editor

Jörg Siekmann
DFKI and Saarland University, Saarbrücken, Germany

Aristidis Likas   Konstantinos Blekas
Dimitris Kalles (Eds.)

Artificial Intelligence: Methods and Applications

8th Hellenic Conference on AI, SETN 2014
Ioannina, Greece, May 15-17, 2014
Proceedings

 Springer

Volume Editors

Aristidis Likas
Konstantinos Blekas
University of Ioannina
Department of Computer Science and Engineering
45110, Ioannina, Greece
E-mail: {arly, kblekas}@cs.uoi.gr

Dimitris Kalles
Hellenic Open University
School of Science and Technology
26335, Peribola, Patras, Greece
E-mail: kalles@eap.gr

ISSN 0302-9743   e-ISSN 1611-3349
ISBN 978-3-319-07063-6   e-ISBN 978-3-319-07064-3
DOI 10.1007/978-3-319-07064-3
Springer Cham Heidelberg New York Dordrecht London

Library of Congress Control Number: 2014938030

LNCS Sublibrary: SL 7 – Artificial Intelligence

Typesetting: Camera-ready by author, data conversion by Scientific Publishing Services, Chennai, India

Printed on acid-free paper

Springer is part of Springer Science+Business Media (www.springer.com)

Preface

This volume contains the papers presented at the 8th Hellenic Conference on Artificial Intelligence (SETN 2014), the official meeting of the Hellenic Artificial Intelligence Society (EETN). The SETN 2014 conference took place in Ioannina, Greece, during May 15–17, 2014, and was organized by the Department of Computer Science and Engineering, University of Ioannina, Greece, in collaboration with the Hellenic Artificial Intelligence Society.

SETN was first held in 1996 (University of Piraeus) and then in 2002 (Aristotle University of Thessaloniki). Since then it has occurred biannually: at the University of the Aegean (2004, 2008), the University of Crete (2006), the NCSR Demokritos (2010), and the University of Central Greece (2012). Over the years, SETN has become one of the premier events for the discussion and dissemination of research results in the field of AI, produced mainly by Greek scientists from institutes both in Greece and around the world. The two major goals of the conference are (a) to promote research in AI, one of the most exciting and active research areas in computer science and engineering and (b) to bring together scientists and engineers from academia and industry to discuss the challenging problems encountered and the solutions that could be adopted. In addition, SETN conferences aim at increasing international participation. This year we had submissions from all over the world: USA, Australia, UK, Germany, Italy, France, Austria, Denmark, Norway, Czech Republic, China, and Tunisia among others.

The technical program of SETN 2014 included three plenary talks from distinguished keynote speakers:

- *Planning for Complex Physical Systems*, Lydia E. Kavraki, Rice University, USA.
- *Making Educational Software more Reactive to Users: How AI Can Help*, George D. Magoulas, University of London, UK.
- *Multisensory Data-Driven Systems to Promote Safe Exercising in Chronic Conditions*, Fillia Makedon, University of Texas at Arlington, USA.

The conference attracted paper submissions by 229 authors from 21 countries (11 European). The decision for each submitted paper was based on the evaluation of at least two reviewers. The reviews were performed by an international Program Committee consisting of 107 members as well as from 11 additional reviewers. The review process was very selective and, as a result, 34 out of 60 papers submitted as regular (10-14 pages) were accepted. In addition, five submissions were accepted as short papers (6 pages). Finally, another 15 papers were accepted and presented in the following four special sessions:

- *Action Languages: Theory & Practice*, organized by Alexander Artikis, Marco Montali, Theodore Patkos, and Stavros Vassos.

- *Computational Intelligence Techniques for Biosignal Analysis and Evaluation*, organized by Chrysostomos Stylios and Lenka Lhotska.
- *Game Artificial Intelligence*, organized by Antonios Liapis, Spyridon Samothrakis, Georgios N. Yannakakis, and Stavros Vassos.
- *Multimodal Recommendation Systems and Their Application to Tourism*, organized by Constantine Kotropoulos and Pavlos Efraimidis.

All the 54 papers presented at the conference are included in this proceedings volume. An indication of the scientific quality is that the *International Journal of Artificial Intelligence Tools* (IJAIT) agreed to publish a special issue with extended versions of selected papers presented at the conference.

The SETN 2014 program also included the following four tutorials:

- *Accessing 3D Object Collections* (Instructor: Ioannis Pratikakis).
- *Community Detection and Evaluation in Real Graphs*, (Instructors: Christos Giatsidis, Fragkiskos D. Malliaros, and Michalis Vazirgiannis).
- *Engineering Competitive Multi-Agent Systems* (Instructors: Alexander Artikis and Jeremy Pitt).
- *Game Artificial Intelligence*, (Instructors:Antonios Liapis and Georgios N. Yannakakis).

The editors would like to thank all those who contributed to the implementation of SETN 2014. In particular, we would like to express our gratitude to the Organizing Committee (and especially to Nikolaos Tziortziotis) for implementing the conference schedule in a timely and flawless manner, the Steering Committee for its assistance and support, the Program Committee and the additional reviewers who did valuable work under a tight time schedule, and the three distinguished keynote speakers for their kind participation.

We would also like to thank our financial sponsors: the University of Ioannina, Greece, the Hellenic Open University, Greece, and Klidarithmos Publications. We owe special thanks to Springer as well as to the Springer team and, especially, to Alfred Hofmann, Anna Kramer, and Frank Holzwarth for their continuous help and support in preparing and publishing this volume of LNCS/LNAI. Last but not least, we are indebted to all authors who considered this conference as a forum for presenting and disseminating their research work, as well as to all conference participants for their active engagement and their contribution to the success of SETN 2014.

May 2014   Aristidis Likas
                                                    Konstantinos Blekas
                                                       Dimitris Kalles

Organization

SETN 2014 was organized by the Department of Computer Science and Engineering of the University of Ioannina, Greece, and the Hellenic Artificial Intelligence Society (EETN).

General Chairs

Aristidis Likas   University of Ioannina, Greece
Konstantinos Blekas   University of Ioannina, Greece
Dimitris Kalles   Hellenic Open University, Greece

Steering Committee

Vangelis Karkaletsis   NCSR Demokritos, Greece
Ilias Maglogiannis   University of Pireaus, Greece
Vassilis Plagianakos   University of Thessaly, Greece
Constantine Spyropoulos   NCSR Demokritos, Greece
Ioannis Vlahavas   Aristotle University of Thessaloniki, Greece
George Vouros   University of Pireaus, Greece

Organizing Committee

Nikolaos Tziortziotis   University of Ioannina, Greece
Grigoris Tzortzis   University of Ioannina, Greece
Antonis Ioannidis   University of Ioannina, Greece
Evaggelos
  Kourakos-Mavromichalis   University of Ioannina, Greece
Konstantinos Tziortziotis   University of Ioannina, Greece

Program Committee

Christos-Nikolaos
  Anagnostopoulos   University of the Aegean, Greece
Andreas Andreou   Cyprus University of Technology, Cyprus
Ion Androutsopoulos   Athens University of Economics and Business,
                            Greece
Grigoris Antoniou   University of Huddersfield, UK
Avi Arampatzis   Democritus University of Thrace, Greece
Antonis Argyros   University of Crete and FORTH, Greece

Manolis Koubarakis	National and Kapodistrian University of Athens, Greece
Costas Koutras	University of Peloponnese, Greece
Konstantinos Koutroumbas	National Observatory of Athens, Greece
Antonios Liapis	IT University of Copenhagen, Denmark
Jorge Lobo	Universitat Pompeu Fabra, Spain
George Magoulas	University of London, UK
Manolis Maragoudakis	University of the Aegean, Greece
Nikolaos Mavridis	New York University, Abu Dhabi, UAE
Loizos Michael	Open University of Cyprus, Cyprus
Phivos Mylonas	National Technical University of Athens, Greece
Mark Nelson	IT University of Copenhagen, Denmark
Nikos Nikolaidis	Aristotle University of Thessaloniki, Greece
George Nikolakopoulos	Lulea University of Technology, Sweden
Christophoros Nikou	University of Ioannina, Greece
Georgios Paliouras	NCSR Demokritos, Greece
Michail Panagopoulos	Ionian University, Greece
Christos Papatheodorou	Ionian University, Greece
Konstantinos Parsopoulos	University of Ioannina, Greece
Ioannis Partalas	Laboratoire d'Informatique de Grenoble, France
Theodore Patkos	FORTH, Greece
Nicos Pavlidis	Lancaster University, UK
Pavlos Peppas	University of Patras, Greece
Diego Perez	University of Essex, UK
Georgios Petasis	NCSR Demokritos, Greece
Sergios Petridis	NCSR Demokritos, Greece
Vassilis Plagianakos	University of Central Greece, Greece
Dimitris Plexousakis	University of Crete, Greece
George Potamias	FORTH, Greece
Ioannis Pratikakis	Democritus University of Thrace, Greece
Mike Preuss	TU Dortmund, Germany
Ioannis Refanidis	University of Macedonia, Greece
Regis Riveret	Imperial College London, UK
Ilias Sakellariou	University of Macedonia, Greece
Spyridon Samothrakis	University of Essex, UK
Kyriakos Sgarbas	University of Patras, Greece
Andreas Stafylopatis	National Technical University of Athens, Greece
Efstathios Stamatatos	University of the Aegean, Greece
Stefano Bromuri	University of Applied Sciences Western Switzerland
Kostas Stergiou	Aristotle University of Thessaloniki, Greece

Giorgos Stamou	National Technical University of Athens, Greece
Chrysostomos Stylios	Technological Educational Institute of Epirus, Greece
Anastasios Tefas	Aristotle University of Thessaloniki, Greece
Michalis Titsias	Athens University of Economics and Business, Greece
Julian Togelius	IT University of Compenhagen, Denmark
Panos Trahanias	University of Crete, Greece
Ioannis Tsamardinos	University of Crete, Greece
George Tsihrintzis	University of Piraeus, Greece
Grigorios Tsoumakas	Aristotle University of Thessaloniki, Greece
Nikolaos Tziortziotis	University of Ioannina, Greece
Grigorios Tzortzis	University of Ioannina, Greece
Nikolaos Vassilas	Technological Educational Institute of Athens, Greece
Stavros Vassos	Sapienza University of Rome, Italy
Michalis Vazirgiannis	Athens University of Economics and Business, Greece
Maria Virvou	University of Piraeus, Greece
Konstantinos Vlachos	National Technical University of Athens, Greece
Ioannis Vlahavas	Aristotle University of Thessaloniki, Greece
Nikos Vlassis	University of Luxembourg, Luxembourg
Dimitrios Vogiatzis	NCSR Demokritos, Greece
Michael N. Vrahatis	University of Patras, Greece
George Vouros	University of Piraeus, Greece
Dimitris Vrakas	Aristotle University of Thessaloniki, Greece
Stefanos Zafeiriou	Imperial College London, UK
Michalis Zervakis	Technical University of Crete, Greece

Additional Reviewers

Christos Berberis	International Hellenic University, Greece
Anestis Fachantidis	Aristotle University of Thessaloniki, Greece
Theodoros Giannakopoulos	NCSR Demokritos, Greece
Ioannis Kavakiotis	Aristotle University of Thessaloniki, Greece
Aris Kosmopoulos	NCSR Demokritos, Greece
Remous-Aris Koutsiamanis	Democritus University of Thrace, Greece
Anastasia Krithara	NCSR Demokritos, Greece
Christos Rodosthenous	Open University of Cyprus, Cyprus
Eleftherios Spyromitros-Xioufis	Aristotle University of Thessaloniki, Greece
Giorgos Stamatelatos	Democritus University of Thrace, Greece
Chrysostomos Zeginis	University of Crete, Greece

Table of Contents

Main Conference Regular Papers

Main Conference Short Papers

Special Session: Action Languages

Special Session: Computational Intelligence Techniques for Biosignal Analysis and Evaluation

Special Session: Game Artificial Intelligence

Special Session: Multimodal Recommendation Systems and their Application to Tourism

Performance-Estimation Properties of Cross-Validation-Based Protocols with Simultaneous Hyper-Parameter Optimization

Ioannis Tsamardinos[1,2], Amin Rakhshani[1,2], and Vincenzo Lagani[1]

[1] Institute of Computer Science, Foundation for Research and Technology Hellas,
Heraklion, Greece
[2] Computer Science Department, University of Crete, Heraklion, Greece
{tsamard,vlagani,aminra}@ics.forth.gr

Abstract. In a typical supervised data analysis task, one needs to perform the following two tasks: (a) select the best combination of learning methods (e.g., for variable selection and classifier) and tune their hyper-parameters (e.g., K in K-NN), also called *model selection*, and (b) provide an estimate of the performance of the final, reported model. Combining the two tasks is not trivial because when one selects the set of hyper-parameters that seem to provide the best estimated performance, this estimation is optimistic (biased / overfitted) due to performing multiple statistical comparisons. In this paper, we confirm that the simple Cross-Validation with model selection is indeed optimistic (overestimates) in small sample scenarios. In comparison the Nested Cross Validation and the method by Tibshirani and Tibshirani provide conservative estimations, with the later protocol being more computationally efficient. The role of stratification of samples is examined and it is shown that stratification is beneficial.

1   Introduction

A typical supervised analysis (e.g., classification or regression) consists of several steps that result in a final, single prediction, or diagnostic model. For example, the analyst may need to impute missing values, perform variable selection or general dimensionality reduction, discretize variables, try several different representations of the data, and finally, apply a learning algorithm for classification or regression. Each of these steps requires a selection of algorithms out of hundreds or even thousands of possible choices, as well as the tuning of their hyper-parameters[1]. *Hyper-parameter optimization* is also called the *model selection* problem since each combination of

---

[1]   We use the term "hyper-parameters" to denote the algorithm parameters that can be set by the user and are not estimated directly from the data, e.g., the parameter K in the *K-NN* algorithm. In contrast, the term "parameters" in the statistical literature typically refers to the model quantities that are estimated directly by the data, e.g., the weight vector w in a linear regression model $y = w \cdot x + b$. See [2] for a definition and discussion too.

A. Likas, K. Blekas, and D. Kalles (Eds.): SETN 2014, LNAI 8445, pp. 1–14, 2014.
© Springer International Publishing Switzerland 2014

hyper-parameters tried leads to a possible classification or regression model out of which the best is to be selected.

There are several alternatives in the literature about how to identify a good combination of methods and their hyper-parameters (e.g., [1][2]) and they all involve implicitly or explicitly searching the space of hyper-parameters and trying different combinations. Unfortunately, trying multiple combinations, estimating their performance, and *reporting the performance of the best model found leads to overestimating* the performance *(i.e., underestimate the error / loss)*, sometimes also referred to as overfitting[2]. This phenomenon is called the problem of *multiple comparisons in induction algorithms* and has been analyzed in detail in [3] and is related to the *multiple testing* or *multiple comparisons* in statistical hypothesis testing. Intuitively, when one selects among several models whose estimations vary around their true mean value, it becomes likely that what seems to be the best model has been "lucky" in the specific test set and its performance has been overestimated. Extensive discussions and experiments on the subject can be found in [2].

The bias should increase with the number of models tried and decrease with the size of the test set. Notice that, when using Cross Validation-based protocols to estimate performance each sample serves once and only once as a test case. Thus, *one can consider the total data-set sample size as the size of the test set.* Typical high-dimensional datasets in biology often contain less than 100 samples and thus, one should be careful with the estimation protocols employed for their analysis.

What about the number of different models tried in an analysis? Is it realistic to expect an analyst to generate thousands of different models? Obviously, it is very rare that any analyst will employ thousands of different algorithms; however, most learning algorithms are parameterized by several different hyper-parameters. For example, the standard 1-norm, polynomial Support Vector Machine algorithm takes as hyper-parameters the cost C of misclassifications and the degree of the polynomial d. Similarly, most variable selection methods take as input a statistical significance threshold or the number of variables to return. If an analyst tries several different methods for imputation, discretization, variable selection, and classification, each with several different hyper-parameter values, the number of combinations explodes and can easily reach into the thousands.

Notice that, model selection and optimistic estimation of performance *may also happen unintentionally and implicitly* in many other settings. More specifically, consider a typical publication where a new algorithm is introduced and its performance (after tuning the hyper-parameters) is compared against numerous other alternatives from the literature (again, after tuning their hyper-parameters), on several datasets. The comparison aims to comparatively evaluate the methods. However, *the reported performances of the best method on each dataset suffer from the same problem of multiple inductions and are on average optimistically estimated.*

In the remainder of the paper, we revisit the Cross-Validation (CV) protocol. We corroborate [2][4] that CV *overestimates* performance when it is used with hyper-parameter

---

[2]   The term "overfitting" is a more general term and we prefer the term "overestimating" to characterize this phenomenon.

Algorithm 1: K-Fold Cross-Validation $\underline{CV}(D)$
Input: A dataset $D = \{\langle x_i, y_i \rangle, i=1, ..., N\}$
Output: A model M
            An estimation of performance (loss) of M

Randomly Partition D to K folds F_i
Model $M = f(\cdot, D)$ // the model learned on all data D
Estimation $\widehat{L_{CV}}$:
$$\widehat{e}_i = \frac{1}{N_i}\Sigma_{j\in F_i}\, L(y_j, f(x_j, D_{\backslash i}))\,, \quad \widehat{L_{CV}} = \frac{1}{K}\Sigma_{i=1}^{K}\widehat{e}_i$$
Return $\langle M, \widehat{L_{CV}} \rangle$

---

optimization. As expected overestimation of performance increases with decreasing sample sizes. We present two other performance estimation methods in the literature. The method by Tibshirani and Tibshirani (hereafter TT) [5] tries to estimate the bias and remove it from the estimation. The Nested Cross Validation (NCV) method [6] cross-validates the whole hyper-parameter optimization procedure (which includes an inner cross-validation, hence the name). NCV is a generalization of the technique where data is partitioned in train-validation-test sets. We show that both of them are conservative (underestimate) performance, while TT is computationally more efficient. To our knowledge, this is the first time the three methods are compared against each other on real datasets. *The excellent behavior of TT in these preliminary results makes it a promising alternative to NCV.*

The effect of stratification is also empirically examined. Stratification is a technique that during partitioning of the data into folds for cross-validation forces the same distribution of the outcome classes to each fold. When data are split randomly, on average, the distribution of the outcome in each fold will be the same as in the whole dataset. However, in small sample sizes or imbalanced data it could happen that a fold gets no samples that belong in one of the classes (or in general, the class distribution in a fold is very different from the original). Stratification ensures that this doesn't occur. We show that stratification decreases the variance of the estimation and thus should always be applied.

2   Cross-Validation without Hyper-Parameter Optimization (CV)

K-fold Cross Validation is perhaps the most common method for estimating performance of a learning method for small and medium sample sizes. Despite its popularity, its theoretical properties are arguably not well known especially outside the machine learning community, particularly when it is employed with simultaneous hyper-parameter optimization, as evidenced by the following common machine learning books: Duda ([7], p. 484) presents CV without discussing it in the context of model selection and only hints that it may underestimate (when used without model selection): "The jackknife [i.e., leave-one-out CV] in particular, generally gives good estimates

because each of the n classifiers is quite similar to the classifier being tested ...".
Similarly, Mitchell [8](pp. 112, 147, 150) mentions CV but in the context of
hyper-parameter optimization. Bishop [9] does not deal at all with issues of performance
estimation and model selection. A notable exception is the Hastie and co-authors [10]
book that offers the best treatment of the subject, *upon which the following sections are
based*. Yet, CV is still not discussed in the context of model selection.

Let's assume a dataset $D = \{ \langle x_i , y_i \rangle, i=1, ..., N \}$, of identically and independently
distributed (i.i.d.) predictor vectors x_i and corresponding outcomes y_i . Let us also
assume that we have *a single method* for learning from such data and producing a
single prediction model. *We will denote with $f(x_i , D)$ the output of the model produced by the learner f when trained on data D and applied on input x_i . The actual
model produced by f on dataset D is denoted with $f(\cdot, D)$*. We will denote with $L(y, y')$
the loss (error) measure of prediction y' when the true output is y. One common loss
function is the zero-one loss function: $L(y, y') = 1$, if $y \neq y'$ and $L(y, y') = 0$, otherwise.

Thus, the average zero-one loss of a classifier equals 1-accuracy, i.e., it is the probability of making an incorrect classification. K-fold CV partitions the data D into K
subsets called folds $F_1 , ..., F_k$. We denote with $D_{\backslash i}$ the data excluding fold F_i and N_i
the sample size of each fold. The K-fold CV algorithm is shown in Algorithm 1.

First, notice that *CV returns the model learned from all data D, $f(\cdot, D)$. This is the
model to be employed operationally for classification*. It then tries to estimate the
performance of the returned model by constructing K other models from datasets $D_{\backslash i}$,
each time excluding one fold from the training set. Each of these models is then applied on each fold F_i serving as test and the loss is averaged over all samples.

Is $\widehat{L_{CV}}$ an unbiased estimate of the loss of $f(\cdot, D)$? First, notice that each sample x_i is
used once and only once as a test case. *Thus, effectively there are as many i.i.d. test
cases as samples in the dataset*. Perhaps, this characteristic is what makes the CV so
popular versus other protocols such as repeatedly partitioning the dataset to train-test
subsets. The test size being as large as possible could facilitate the estimation of the
loss and its variance (although, theoretical results show that there is no unbiased estimator of the variance for the CV! [11]). However, test cases are predicted with different models! If these models were trained on independent train sets of size equal to the
original data D, then CV would indeed estimate the average loss of the models
produced by the specific learning method on the specific task when trained with the
specific sample size. As it stands though, since the models are correlated and have
smaller size than the original:

*K-Fold CV estimates the average loss of models returned by the specific learning me-
thod f on the specific classification task when trained with subsets of D of size $|D_{\backslash i}|$*

Since $|D_{\backslash i}| = (K-1)/K \bullet |D| < |D|$ (e.g., for 5-fold, we are using 80% of the total sample
size for training each time) and *assuming that the learning method improves on aver-
age with larger sample sizes* we expect $\widehat{L_{CV}}$ to be conservative (i.e., the true
performance be underestimated). How conservative it will be depends on where the
classifier is operating on its learning curve for this specific task. It also depends on the
number of folds K: the larger the K, the more $(K-1)/K$ approaches 100% and the bias
disappears, i.e., leave-one-out CV should be the least biased (however, there may be

still be significant estimation problems, see [12], p. 151, and [4] for an extreme failure of leave-one-out CV). When sample sizes are small or distributions are imbalanced (i.e., some classes are quite rare in the data), we expect most classifiers to quickly benefit from increased sample size, and thus $\widehat{L_{CV}}$ to be more conservative.

3 Cross-Validation with Hyper-Parameter Optimization (CVM)

A typical data analysis involves several steps (representing the data, imputation, discretization, variable selection or dimensionality reduction, learning a classifier) each

---

Algorithm 2: K-Fold Cross-Validation with Hyper-Parameter Optimization (Model Selection) $\underline{CVM}(D, \boldsymbol{a})$

Input: A dataset $D = \{ \langle x_i , y_i \rangle, i=1, ..., N \}$
A set of hyper-parameter value combinations $\boldsymbol{a}$
Output: A model M
An estimation of performance (loss) of M

Partition D to K folds F_i
Estimate $\widehat{L_{CV}}(a)$ for each $a \in \boldsymbol{a}$:
$$\widehat{e_i(a)} = \frac{1}{N_i}\sum_{j \in F_i} L(y_j, f(x_j, D_{\setminus i}, a)) , \quad \widehat{L_{CV}}(a) = \frac{1}{K}\sum_{i=1}^{K} \widehat{e_i(a)}$$
Find minimizer a^* of $\widehat{L_{CV}}(a)$ // "best hyper-parameters"
$M = f(\cdot, D, a^*)$ // the model from all data D with the best hyper-parameters
$\widehat{L_{CVM}} = \widehat{L_{CV}}(a^*)$
Return $\langle M, \widehat{L_{CVM}} \rangle$

Algorithm 3: $\underline{TT}(D, \boldsymbol{a})$
Input: A dataset $D = \{ \langle x_i , y_i \rangle, i=1, ..., N \}$
A set of hyper-parameter value combinations $\boldsymbol{a}$
Output: A model M
An estimation of performance (loss) of M

Partition D to K folds F_i
Estimate $\widehat{L_{CV}}(a)$ for each $a \in \boldsymbol{a}$:
$$\widehat{e_i(a)} = \frac{1}{N_i}\sum_{j \in F_i} L(y_j, f(x_j, D_{\setminus i}, a)) , \quad \widehat{L_{CV}}(a) = \frac{1}{K}\sum_{i=1}^{K} \widehat{e_i(a)}$$
Find minimizer a^* of $\widehat{L_{CV}}(a)$ // "best hyper-parameters"
Find minimizers a_k of $e_k(a)$ // the minimizers for each fold
Estimate $\widehat{Bias} = \sum_{k=1}^{K}(e_k(a^*) - e_k(a_k))$
$M = f(\cdot, D, a^*)$, i.e,. the model learned on all data D with the best hyper-parameters
$\widehat{L_{TT}} = \widehat{L_{CV}}(a^*) + \widehat{Bias}$
Return $\langle M, \hat{L}_{TT} \rangle$

with hundreds of available choices of algorithms in the literature. In addition, each algorithm takes several hyper-parameter values that should be tuned by the user. A general method for tuning the hyper-parameters is to try a set of *predefined* combinations of methods and corresponding values and select the best. We will represent this set with a set a containing hyper-parameter values, e.g, $a = \{ \langle$no variable selection, K-NN, K=5$\rangle$, $\langle$Lasso, $\lambda = 2$, linear SVM, C=10$\rangle \}$ when the intent is to try K-NN with no variable selection, and a linear SVM using the Lasso algorithm for variable selection. The pseudo-code is shown in Algorithm 2. The symbol $f(x, D, a\ )$ now denotes the output of the model learned when using hyper-parameters a on dataset D and applied on input x. Correspondingly, the symbol $f(\cdot, D, a\ )$ denotes the model produced by applying hyper-parameters a on D. The quantity $L_{CV}(a)$ is now parameterized by the specific values a and the minimizer of the loss (maximizer of performance) a^* is found. The final model returned is $f(\cdot, D, a^*)$, i.e. , the models produced by values a^* on *all data* D. On one hand, we expect CV with model selection (hereafter, *CVM*) to underestimate performance because estimations are computed using models trained on only a subset of the dataset. On the other hand, we expect *CVM* to overestimate performance because it returns the maximum performance found after trying several hyper-parameter values. In Section 7 we examine this behavior empirically and determine (in concordance with [2],[4]) that indeed when sample size is relatively small and the number of models in the hundreds CVM overestimates performance. Thus, in these cases other types of estimation protocols are required.

4   The Tibshirani and Tibshirani (TT) Method

The TT method [5] attempts to *heuristically and approximately* estimate the bias of the CV error estimation due to model selection and add it to the final estimate. For each fold, the bias due to model selection is estimated as $e_k(a^*) - e_k(a_k)$ where, as before, e_k is the average loss in fold k, a_k is the hyper-parameter values that minimizes the loss for fold k, and a^* the global minimizer over all folds. Notice that, if in all folds the same values a_k provide the best performance, then these will also be selected globally and hence $a_k = a^*$ for $k=1, ..., K$. In this case, *the bias estimate will be zero.* The justification of this estimate for the bias is in [5]. *Notice that CVM and TT return the same model (assuming data are partitioned into the same folds)*, the one returned by f on *all data* D using the minimizer a^* of the CV error; however, the two methods return a different estimate of the performance of this model. *It is also quite important to notice that TT does not require any additional model training and has minimum computational overhead.*

5   The Nested Cross-Validation Method (NCV)

We could not trace who introduced or coined up first the name Nested Cross-Validation (NCV) method but the authors have independently discovered it and using it since 2005 [6],[13],[14]; one early comment hinting of the method is in [15].

Algorithm 4: K-Fold Nested Cross-Validation $\underline{NCV}(D,\ \boldsymbol{a})$
Input: A dataset $D = \{\langle x_i\ ,\ y_i \rangle,\ i=1,\ \dots,\ N\}$
             A set of hyper-parameter value combinations $\boldsymbol{a}$
Output: A model M
             An estimation of performance (loss) of M

Partition D to K folds F_i
$\langle M,\ \sim \rangle = CVM(D,\ \boldsymbol{a})$
Estimation $\widehat{L_{NCV}}$:
$$\hat{e}_i = \frac{1}{N_i}\Sigma_{j\in F_i}\ L(y_j, CVM(x_j, D_{\setminus i}))\ ,\quad \widehat{L_{CV}} = \frac{1}{K}\Sigma_{i=1}^{K}\ \hat{e}_i$$
Return $\langle M,\ \widehat{L_{NCV}} \rangle$

A similar method in a bioinformatics analysis was used as early as 2003 [16]. The main idea is to consider the model selection as part of the learning procedure f. Thus, f tests several hyper-parameter values, selects the best using CV, and returns a *single model*. NCV *cross-validates* f to estimate the performance of the average model returned by f just as normal CV would do with any other learning method taking no hyper-parameters; it's just that f now contains an internal CV trying to select the best model. NCV is a generalization of the Train-Validation-Test protocol where one trains on the Train set for all hyper-parameter values, selects the ones that provide the best performance on Validation, trains on Train+Validation a *single model* using the best-found values and estimates its performance on Test. Since Test is used only once by a single model, performance estimation has no bias due to the model selection process. The final model is trained on *all data* using the best found values for a. NCV generalizes the above protocol to cross-validate every step of this procedure: for each Test, all folds serve as Validation, and this process is repeated for each fold serving as Test. The pseudo-code is shown in Algorithm 4. The pseudo-code is similar to CV (Algorithm 1) with CVM (Cross-Validation with Model Selection, Algorithm 2) serving as the learning function f. *Notice, that NCV returns the same final, single model as CV and TT (assuming the same partition of the data to folds)*. Again, the difference regards only the estimation of the performance of this model. NCV requires a quadratic number of models to be trained to the number of folds K (one model is trained for every possible pair of two folds serving as test and validation respectively) and thus it is the most computationally expensive protocol out of the three.

6   Stratification of Folds

In CV folds are partitioned randomly which should maintain *on average* the same class distribution in each fold. However, in small sample size sizes or highly imbalanced class distributions it may happen that some folds contain no samples from one of the classes (or in general, the class distribution is very different from the original).

In that case, the estimation of performance for that fold will exclude that class. To avoid this case, "in stratified cross-validation, the folds are stratified so that they contain approximately the same proportions of labels as the original dataset" [4]. Notice that leave-one-out CV guarantees that each fold will be unstratified since it contains only one sample which can cause serious estimation problems ([12], p. 151, [4]).

7 Empirical Comparison of Different Protocols

We performed an empirical comparison in order to assess the characteristics of each data-analysis protocol. Particularly, we focus on three specific aspects of the protocol performances: bias, variance of the estimation and the effect of stratification.

7.1 The Experimental Set-Up

Original Datasets: Five datasets from different scientific fields were employed for the experimentations. The computational task for each dataset consists in predicting a binary outcome on the basis of a set of numerical predictors (binary classification). In more detail the **SPECT** [17] dataset contains data from Single Photon Emission Computed Tomography images collected in both healthy and cardiac patients. Data in **Gamma** [18] consist of simulated registrations of high energy gamma particles in an atmospheric Cherenkov telescope, where each gamma particle can be originated from the upper atmosphere (background noise) or being a primary gamma particle (signal). Discriminating biodegradable vs. non-biodegradable molecules on the basis of their chemical characteristics is the aim of the **Biodeg** [19] dataset. The **Bank** [20] dataset was gathered by direct marketing campaigns (phone calls) of a Portuguese banking institution for discriminating customers who want to subscribe a term deposit and those who don't. Last, **CD4vsCD8** [21] contains the phosphorylation levels of 18 intra-cellular proteins as predictors to discriminate naïve CD4+ and CD8+ human immune system cells. **Table 1** summarizes datasets' characteristics.

Sub-Datasets and Hold-out Datasets: Each original dataset D is partitioned into two separate, stratified parts: D_{pool}, containing 30% of the total samples, and the hold-out set $D_{hold-out}$, consisting of the remaining samples. Subsequently, for each D_{pool} 50 sub-datasets are randomly sampled with replacement for each sample size in the set {20, 40, 60, 80, 100, 500 and 1500}, for a total of 5 $\times$ 7 $\times$ 50 sub-datasets $D_{i, j, k}$ (where i indexes the original dataset, j the sample size, and k the sub-sampling). For sample sizes less than 100 we enforce an equal percentage among the two classes, in order to avoid problems of imbalanced data. Most of the original datasets have been selected with a relatively large sample size so that *each $D_{hold-out}$ is large enough to allow a very accurate (low variance) estimation of performance*. In addition, the size of D_{pool} is also relatively large so that each sub-sampled dataset *to be approximately considered a dataset independently sampled from the data population of the problem*. Nevertheless, we also include a couple of datasets with smaller sample size.

Table 1. Datasets' characteristics. D_{pool} is a 30% partition from which sub-sampled datasets are produced. $D_{hold-out}$ is the remaining 70% of samples from which an estimation of the true performance is computed.

Dataset Name	# Samples	# Attributes	Classes ratio	$|D_{pool}|$	$|D_{hold-out}|$	Ref.
SPECT	267	22	3.85	81	186	[17]
Biodeg	1055	41	1.96	317	738	[19]
Gamma	19020	11	1.84	5706	13314	[18]
CD4vsCD8	24126	18	1.13	7238	16888	[21]
Bank	45211	17	7.54	13564	31647	[20]

Bias and Variance of each Protocol: For each of the data analysis protocols *CVM*, *TT*, and *NCV* both the stratified and the non-stratified versions are applied to each sub-dataset, in order to select the "best model/hyper-parameter values" and estimate its performance $\hat{L}$. For each sub-dataset, the same split in $K = 10$ folds was employed for the stratified versions of *CVM*, *TT* and *NCV*, so that the three data-analysis protocols always select exactly the same model, and differ only in the estimation of performance. For the NCV, the internal CV loop uses $K=9$. The bias is computed as $L_{hold-out}$ - $\hat{L}$. Thus, *a positive bias indicates a higher "true" error* (i.e., as estimated on the hold-out set) than the one estimated by the corresponding analysis protocol *and implies the estimation protocol is optimistic*. For each protocol, original dataset, and sample size the mean bias, its variance and its standard deviation over the 50 sub-samplings are computed and reported in the results' Tables and Figures below.

Performance Metric: All algorithms are presented using a loss function L computed for each sample and averaged out for each fold and then over all folds. The zero-one loss function is typically assumed corresponding to 1-accuracy of the classifier. However, we prefer to use the Area Under the Receiver's Operating Characteristic Curve (AUC) [22] as the metric of choice for binary classification problems. One advantage is that the AUC does not depend on the prior class distribution. This is necessary in order to pool together estimations stemming from different datasets. In contrast, the zero-one loss depends on the class distribution: for a problem with class distribution of 50-50%, a classifier with accuracy 85% has greatly improved over the baseline of a trivial classifier predicting the majority class; for a problem of 84-16% class distribution, a classifier with 85% accuracy has not improved much over the baseline. Unfortunately, the AUC cannot be expressed as a loss function $L(y, y')$ where y' is a single prediction. Nevertheless, all Algorithms 1-4 remain the same if we substitute $\hat{e}_i = 1 - AUC(f(\cdot, D_{\setminus i}), F_i)$, i.e., the error in fold i is 1 minus the AUC of the model learned by f on all data except fold F_i, as estimated on F_i as the test set.

Model Selection: For generating the hyper-parameter vectors in a we employed three different modelers: the Logistic Regression classifier ([9], p. 205), as implemented in Matlab 2013b, that takes no hyper-parameters; the Decision Tree [23], as implemented also in Matlab 2013b with hyper-parameters MinLeaf and MinParents both within $\{1, 2, \ldots, 10, 20, 30, 40, 50\}$; Support Vector Machines as implemented in the libsvm software [24] with linear, Gaussian ($\gamma \in \{0.01, 0.1, 1, 10, 100\}$) and polynomial (degree $d \in \{2,3,4\}$, $\gamma \in \{0.01, 0.1, 1, 10, 100\}$) kernels, and cost parameter

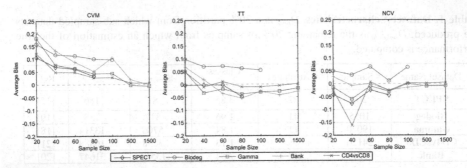

Fig. 1. Average loss bias for estimation protocols stratified CVM, TT, and NCV that include model selection. CVM is clearly optimistic and systematically overestimates performance for sample sizes less or equal to 100. TT and NCV do not substantially and systematically overestimate on average, although results vary with dataset.

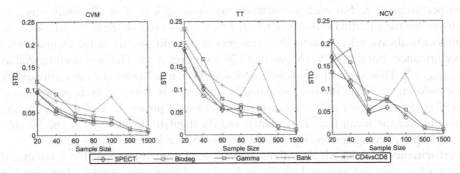

Fig. 2. Standard deviation of bias over the 50 sub-samplings. CVM has the smallest variance but it overestimates performance. TT and NCV exhibit similar stds.

$C \in \{0.01, 0.1, 1, 10, 100\}$. When a classifier takes multiple hyper-parameters, all combinations of choices are tried. Overall, 271 hyper-parameter value combinations and corresponding models are produced each time to select the best.

7.2   Experimental Results

Fig. 1 shows the average loss bias of CVM, TT, and NCV showing that indeed *CVM overestimates performance* for small sample sizes (underestimates error) corroborating the results in [2],[4]. *TT and NCV do not substantially and systematically overestimate, although results vary with dataset.* **Table 2** shows the bias averaged over all datasets, where it is shown that CVM often overestimates the AUC by more than 5 points for small sample sizes. TT seems quite robust with the bias being confined to less than plus or minus 1,7 AUC points for sample sizes more than 20. We perform a t-test for the null hypothesis that the bias is zero, which is typically rejected: all methods usually exhibit some bias whether positive or negative. Nevertheless, in our opinion the bias for TT and NCV is in general acceptable. The non-stratified versions of the protocols have more bias in general. Fig. 2 shows the standard deviation (std) of CVM, TT, and NCV. CVM exhibits the smallest std (and thus variance) but in our opinion it should be avoided since it overestimates performance. **Table 3** shows the averaged std of the bias over all datasets. We apply the O'Brien's modification of Levene's statistical test [25] with the null hypothesis that the variance of a method is the same as the corresponding variance for the same sample size as the NCV. NCV and TT show almost statistically indistinguishable variances. Thus, *within the scope of our experiments and based on the combined analysis of average bias, average variance, and computational complexity the TT protocol seems to be the method of choice.* The non-stratified versions also exhibit slightly larger variance and again, *stratification seems to have only beneficial effects.*

8   Related Work, Discussion and Conclusions

Estimating performance of the final reported model while simultaneously selecting the best pipeline of algorithms and turning their hyper-parameters is a fundamental task for any data analyst. Yet, arguably these issues have not been examined in full depth in the literature. The origins of cross-validation in statistics can be traced back to the "jackknife" technique of Quenouille [26] in the statistical community.

In machine learning, [4] studied the cross-validation without model selection (the title of the paper may be confusing) comparing it against the bootstrap and reaching the important conclusion that (a) CV is preferable to the bootstrap, (b) a value of K=10 is preferable for the number of folds versus a leave-one-out, and (c) stratification is also always preferable. In terms of theory, Bengio [11] showed that there exist no unbiased estimator for the variance of the CV performance estimation, which impact hypothesis testing of performance using the CV.

To the extent of our knowledge the first to study the problem of bias *in the context of model selection* in machine learning is [3]. Varma [27] demonstrated the optimism of the CVM protocol and instead suggests the use of the NCV protocol. Unfortunately, all their experiments are performed on simulated data only. Tibshirani and Tibshirani [5] introduced the TT protocol but unfortunately they do not compare it against alternatives and they include only a proof-of-concept experiment on a single dataset. Thus, the present paper is the first work that compares all three protocols (CVM, NCV, and TT) on multiple real datasets.

Based on our experiments we found evidence that the TT method is unbiased (slightly conservative) for sample sizes above 20, has about the same variance as the NCV (the other conservative alternative), and does not introduce additional computational overhead. Within the scope of our experiments, *we would thus suggest analysts to employ the TT estimation protocol.* In addition, we corroborate the results in [4] that stratification exhibits smaller estimation variance and we encourage its use.

We would also like to acknowledge the limited scope of our experiments in terms of the number and type of datasets, the inclusion of other steps into the analysis (such as variable selection), the inclusion of other procedures for hyper-parameter optimization that dynamically decide to consider value combinations, varying the number of folds K in the protocols, using other performance metrics, experimentation with

Table 2. Average Bias over Datasets. P-values produced by a t-test with null hypothesis the mean bias is zero ($P<0,05*$, $P<0,01**$). NS stands for Non-Stratified. CVM systematically overestimates performance. TT and NCV slightly underestimate performance for larger sample sizes.

	CVM	NS-CVM	TT	NS-TT	NCV	NS-NCV
20	0,1551**	0,1892**	0,0525**	0,1142**	-0,0007	-0,032*
40	0,0891**	0,0993**	0,0085	0,0172*	-0,054**	-0,1102**
60	0,0749**	0,0825**	0,0045	0,0136*	0,0083	0,0111
80	0,0507**	0,0563**	-0,0176**	-0,0097	-0,0228**	-0,0338**
100	0,0681**	0,0731**	-0,0036	0,0079	0,0131*	0,0183**
500	0,0072**	0,0073**	-0,025**	-0,0261**	-0,0054*	-0,0055*
1500	-0,0005	0,0002	-0,0139**	-0,0136**	-0,0034**	-0,003*

Table 3. Average bias STDs over Datasets. P-values produced by a test with null hypothesis that the variances are the same as the corresponding variance of the NCV protocol ($P<0,05*$, $P<0,01**$). NS stands for Non-Stratified. NCV and TT have indistinguishable variances and are conservative. CVM has smaller variance but overestimates performance.

	CVM	NS-CVM	TT	NS-TT	NCV	NS-NCV
20	0,1134**	0,119**	0,1826	0,1989**	0,1616	0,2055**
40	0,0751**	0,0808**	0,1194**	0,1298*	0,1571	0,1784
60	0,0659*	0,0727	0,0916	0,1017	0,0828	0,0936
80	0,0497**	0,0526**	0,0757	0,0804	0,0731	0,0871*
100	0,0651*	0,0697	0,0917	0,0903	0,0826	0,0845
500	0,028	0,0237	0,0341	0,0351	0,0285	0,0308
1500	0,0119	0,014	0,018**	0,0192**	0,0125	0,0143

regression methods and o`thers which form our future work on the subject in order to obtain definite answers to these research questions.

We also note *the concerning issue* that the variance of estimation for small sample sizes is large, again in concordance with the experiments in [2]. The authors in the latter advocate methods that may be biased but exhibit reduced variance. However, we believe that CVM is too biased no matter its variance; implicitly the authors in [2] agree when they declare that model selection should be integrated in the performance estimation procedure in such a way that test samples are never employed for selecting the best model. Instead, they suggest as alternatives limiting the extent of the search of the hyper-parameters or performing model averaging. In our opinion, neither option is satisfactory for all analysis purposes and more research is required.

References

1. Anguita, D., Ghio, A., Oneto, L., Ridella, S.: In-Sample and Out-of-Sample Model Selection and Error Estimation for Support Vector Machines. IEEE Trans. Neural Networks Learn. Syst. 23, 1390–1406 (2012)
2. Cawley, G.C., Talbot, N.L.C.: On Over-fitting in Model Selection and Subsequent Selection Bias in Performance Evaluation. J. Mach. Learn. Res. 11, 2079–2107 (2010)
3. Jensen, D.D., Cohen, P.R.: Multiple comparisons in induction algorithms. Mach. Learn. 38, 309–338 (2000)

4. Kohavi, R.: A Study of Cross-Validation and Bootstrap for Accuracy Estimation and Model Selection. In: International Joint Conference on Artificial Intelligence, pp. 1137–1143 (1995)
5. Tibshirani, R.J., Tibshirani, R.: A bias correction for the minimum error rate in cross-validation. Ann. Appl. Stat. 3, 822–829 (2009)
6. Statnikov, A., Aliferis, C.F., Tsamardinos, I., Hardin, D., Levy, S.: A comprehensive evaluation of multicategory classification methods for microarray gene expression cancer diagnosis. Bioinformatics 21, 631–643 (2005)
7. Duda, R.O., Hart, P.E., Stork, D.G.: Pattern Classification, 2nd edn. (2000)
8. Mitchell, T.M.: Machine Learning (1997)
9. Bishop, C.M.: Pattern Recognition and Machine Learning (Information Science and Statistics) (2006)
10. Hastie, T., Tibshirani, R., Friedman, J.: The Elements of Statistical Learning. Elements 1, 337–387 (2009)
11. Bengio, Y., Grandvalet, Y.: Bias in Estimating the Variance of K-Fold Cross-Validation. Statistical Modeling and Analysis for Complex Data Problem, 75–95 (2005)
12. Witten, I.H., Frank, E.: Data Mining: Practical Machine Learning Tools and Techniques, 2nd edn. Morgan Kaufmann Series in Data Management Systems (2005)
13. Lagani, V., Tsamardinos, I.: Structure-based variable selection for survival data. Bioinformatics 26, 1887–1894 (2010)
14. Statnikov, A., Tsamardinos, I., Dosbayev, Y., Aliferis, C.F.: GEMS: A system for automated cancer diagnosis and biomarker discovery from microarray gene expression data. Int. J. Med. Inform. 74, 491–503 (2005)
15. Salzberg, S.: On Comparing Classifiers: Pitfalls to Avoid and a Recommended Approach. Data Min. Knowl. Discov. 328, 317–328 (1997)
16. Iizuka, N., Oka, M., Yamada-Okabe, H., Nishida, M., Maeda, Y., Mori, N., Takao, T., Tamesa, T., Tangoku, A., Tabuchi, H., Hamada, K., Nakayama, H., Ishitsuka, H., Miyamoto, T., Hirabayashi, A., Uchimura, S., Hamamoto, Y.: Oligonucleotide microarray for prediction of early intrahepatic recurrence of hepatocellular carcinoma after curative resection. Lancet 361, 923–929 (2003)
17. Kurgan, L.A., Cios, K.J., Tadeusiewicz, R., Ogiela, M., Goodenday, L.S.: Knowledge discovery approach to automated cardiac SPECT diagnosis. Artif. Intell. Med. 23, 149–169 (2001)
18. Bock, R.K., Chilingarian, A., Gaug, M., Hakl, F., Hengstebeck, T., Jiřina, M., Klaschka, J., Kotrč, E., Savický, P., Towers, S., Vaiciulis, A., Wittek, W.: Methods for multidimensional event classification: a case study using images from a Cherenkov gamma-ray telescope. Nucl. Instruments Methods Phys. Res. Sect. A Accel. Spectrometers, Detect. Assoc. Equip. 516, 511–528 (2004)
19. Mansouri, K., Ringsted, T., Ballabio, D., Todeschini, R., Consonni, V.: Quantitative structure-activity relationship models for ready biodegradability of chemicals. J. Chem. Inf. Model. 53, 867–878 (2013)
20. Moro, S., Laureano, R.M.S.: Using Data Mining for Bank Direct Marketing: An application of the CRISP-DM methodology. In: Eur. Simul. Model. Conf., pp. 117–121 (2011)
21. Bendall, S.C., Simonds, E.F., Qiu, P., Amir, E.D., Krutzik, P.O., Finck, R., Bruggner, R.V., Melamed, R., Trejo, A., Ornatsky, O.I., Balderas, R.S., Plevritis, S.K., Sachs, K., Pe'er, D., Tanner, S.D., Nolan, G.P.: Single-cell mass cytometry of differential immune and drug responses across a human hematopoietic continuum. Science 332, 687–696 (2011)
22. Fawcett, T.: An introduction to ROC analysis (2006)

23. Coppersmith, D., Hong, S.J., Hosking, J.R.M.: Partitioning Nominal Attributes in Decision Trees. Data Min. Knowl. Discov. 3, 197–217 (1999)
24. Chang, C.-C., Lin, C.-J.: LIBSVM: A library for support vector machines. ACM Trans. Intell. Syst..... 2, 1–39 (2011)
25. O'brien, R.G.: A General ANOVA Method for Robust Tests of Additive Models for Variances. J. Am. Stat. Assoc. 74, 877–880 (1979)
26. Quenouille, M.H.: Approximate tests of correlation in time-series 3 (1949)
27. Varma, S., Simon, R.: Bias in error estimation when using cross-validation for model selection. BMC Bioinformatics 7, 91 (2006)

An Incremental Classifier from Data Streams

Mahardhika Pratama[1,*], Sreenatha G. Anavatti[1], and Edwin Lughofer[2]

[1] School of Engineering and Information Technology, The University of New South Wales,
Canberra, Australia
pratama@ieee.org, s.anavatti@adfa.edu.au
[2] Department of Knowledge-Based Mathematical Systems, Johannes Kepler University,
Linz, Austria
edwin.lughofer@jku.at

Abstract. A novel evolving fuzzy rule-based classifier, namely parsimonious classifier (pClass), is proposed in this paper. pClass can set off its learning process either from scratch with an empty rule base or from an initially trained fuzzy model. Importantly, pClass not only adopts the open structure concept, where an automatic knowledge building process can be cultivated during the training process, which is well-known as a main pillar to learn from streaming examples, but also incorporates the so-called plug-and-play principle, where all learning modules are coupled in the training process, in order to diminish the requirement of pre- or post-processing steps, undermining the firm logic of the online classifier. In what follows, pClass is equipped with the rule growing, pruning, recall and input weighting techniques, which are fully performed on the fly in the training process. The viability of pClass has been tested exploiting real-world and synthetic data streams containing some sorts of concept drifts, and compared with state-of-the-art classifiers, where pClass can deliver the most encouraging numerical results in terms of the classification rate, number of fuzzy rule, number of rule base parameters and the runtime.

Keywords: pClass, Parsimonious Classifier, Evolving Fuzzy Classifier, Fuzzy System, Neural Network.

1 Introduction

Classification problems constitute a centric constituent of most real-life applications, in which this field has drawn many research efforts at least since several decades ago. Arguably, many classifiers have been devised in [1]-[3], where most of them are mature in the offline environment, which does not necessitate swift model updates. Nevertheless, these classifier encompass a computationally prohibitive training phase, as the iterative learning scenario or the multi-pass learning step ought to be committed, where a retraining step benefiting from an up-to-date dataset, whenever a new knowledge is observed, should be enforced. Apart from a considerable computational cost, these classifiers impose the so-called catastrophic forgetting of previously valid

---

* Corresponding Author.

A. Likas, K. Blekas, and D. Kalles (Eds.): SETN 2014, LNAI 8445, pp. 15–28, 2014.
© Springer International Publishing Switzerland 2014

knowledge due to its fixed learning capacity, where the previously sound rules are omitted with a set of totally new rules. These classifiers are also less flexible or adaptive to cope with regime shifting and drifting properties of the system being solved as the number of fuzzy rules or nodes is pre-fixed. Moreover, the knowledge building process is not automated, so that the classifiers cannot reflect the degree of nonlinearity and deal with the possible non stationary of learning environments.

Evolving system, which emphasizes an evolvable architecture according to the knowledge being injected and affirms a low computational power and memory demand, has traversed uncharted territories of contemporary classifiers. This field has transformed to be a zealous research field, which has produced several cutting-edge research works notably in confronting non-stationary data streams and time-critical applications. The underlying construct of the evolving system was pioneered with several works in the scope of fuzzy systems to regression problems in [4]-[9]. Henceforth, these works were amended to conform with the classification problems [11]-[15] and the evolving system concept was extended to other machine learning variants [16]-[20]. Notwithstanding rich literatures of the evolving system, this area deserves more thorough investigations to deliver more reliable evolving systems. The major deficiency of existing evolving systems is rudimentary where several noteworthy learning constituents are absent in the learning module, i.e., rule pruning, rule recall, dimensionality reduction, etc, to which all of them play a precarious role to boost the classifier's performances.

This paper presents a novel evolving fuzzy rule-based classifier, termed Parsimonious Classifier, which can be perceived as a substantial extension of GENEFIS-class of [21], [22]. pClass address technical flaws of GENEFIS-class, which are detailed in the sequel as follows:

- GENEFIS-class endures a rule growing demerit, where the novelty of streaming data is extracted with an unrealistic assumption of uniformly distributed streaming data of DS method and excludes spatial and temporal proximities of the datum with other data points. Consequently, it is incompetent to posit the rule focalpoints in the strategic zone of the input space, while being vulnerable with noisy streaming data and imbalanced training samples. To remedy this bottleneck, another rule growing adornment, namely Extended Recursive Density Estimation (ERDE) method, is put forward, where it is inspired by the notion of data potential of Angelov et al [4]. Nonetheless, this construct is enhanced in such a way to be in line with the generalized fuzzy rule type of pClass, whereby the original version is solely fit to accommodate the conservative spherical clusters.

- The rule pruning module of GENEFIS-class, namely Extended Rule Significance (ERS) method, stems from the statistical contributions of fuzzy rules, akin to DS method in pinpointing the paramount training samples to be deemed as extraneous fuzzy rules. Accordingly, the ERS method is solely effective in pointing out the superfluous fuzzy rules, without being able to capture obsolete or outdated fuzzy rules due to the change of data distribution. To get rid of this shortcoming, a supplementary rule pruning strategy is amalgamated termed Potential + (P+) method, in order to seize obsolete fuzzy rules. The P+ method is derived from the so-called potential concept of [4]. Even so, the original version of [4] is revamped as the rule pruning cursor and is refurbished in such a way to be commensurate with the working framework of pClass.

- The drawback of GENEFIS-class and other evolving classifiers is unappealing to sort out the cyclic drift phenomenon, wherein the past data distribution re-appears in the current learning context. A completely new fuzzy rule is usually generated to conquer this data distribution, which does not coincide with the strict sense of flexible and adaptive system as the fuzzy rules scrapped in the earlier training observations due to signifying obsolete trait cannot be revived. This can evoke a detrimental loss of the adaptation history conferred to these fuzzy rules. To this end, the rule recall mechanism is assembled herein, which enables to resurrect the pruned fuzzy rules in the past training episodes as their significances substantiate with the current trend of data distribution.
- The curse of dimensionality problem is usually obviated with the input pruning mechanism in the existing evolving classifiers, which can induce instability owing to a changing structure of input attributes. Furthermore, the input attributes can prevail in the future, so as to cover some parts of the feature space in the future. Unfortunately, these input features cannot be resumed due to permanent forgetting of these input attributes. As a causal relationship, pClass makes use of the soft input feature reduction approach by means of the input weighting method. In what follows, the significance of input features is monitored by the Fisher Separability Criterion (FSC) method in the empirical feature space to which the input weights are allocated. The idea of the feature weighting mechanism using the FSC method was synergized in the evolving system context by [10], [11]. Yet, the FSC method is scrutinized in the feature space. In this paper, we exacerbate the work of [23] delving the FSC method in the empirical feature space to be workable in the online learning situation.

The materials of this paper are organized as follows: Section 2 outlines the network architectures of pClass, Section 3 details algorithmic development of pClass, Section 4 elaborates numerical examples in various real-world and synthetic datasets, encompassing discussions to performances of benchmarked algorithms. Section 5 deliberates the contributions and the research gap, conceived in this paper. Conclusions and future works are presented in the last section.

2   Architecture of pClass

pClass can be contrasted with omnipresent evolving classifiers in term of the fuzzy rule variant, wherein the premise part is constructed by a multivariate Gaussian function spurring non axis-parallel ellipsoidal cluster. As such, pClass can reap some merits which can handle data with different operating regions per input variables or can demonstrate a scale-invariant property, while forming an ellipsoidal cluster arbitrarily revolved in any direction, which is in turn convenient to be utilized, when the training samples are not scattered in main input variable axis. In principle, this fuzzy rule type characterizes a fruitful property, precluding the loss of input variable interactions owing to t-norm operator in charge in the inference scheme [5],[12]. In essence, the fuzzy rule of pClass can be formally expressed as follow:

$$R_i : \text{IF } X \text{ is Close to } \varphi_i \text{ Then } y^i = x_e \Omega_i$$

Note that Ω_i is a weight vector, which can be formed as Multi-Input-SingleOutput(MISO) $\Omega_i = [w_{i0}, w_{i1}..., w_{ip}]^T \in \Re^{(p+1)\times 1}$ or as Multi-Input-Multi-Output(MIMO) structure, expressed as follows:

$$\Omega_i = \begin{bmatrix} w_{i0}^{1}, w_{i0}^{2},..., w_{i0}^{k},.., w_{i0}^{K} \\ w_{i1}^{1}, w_{i1}^{2},..., w_{i1}^{k},..., w_{i1}^{K} \\ \cdots\cdots\cdots\cdots\cdots\cdots\cdots\cdots\cdots \\ w_{ip}^{1}, w_{ip}^{2},..., w_{ip}^{k},..., w_{ip}^{K} \end{bmatrix} \tag{1}$$

where K is the number of classes, whereas $x_e = [1, x_1, x_2,..., x_p] \in \Re^{1\times(p+1)}$ is an extended input vector to include the intercept of the consequent hyper-planes with the number of input dimensions p.

The fuzzy rule expression can evoke the rule transparency to slump, given the fact that the input attributes cannot be directly associated with particular linguistic labels (fuzzy sets), which constitutes a paramount feature to render tangible rule semantics. Nonetheless, this issue was overcome in our previous works of [6], [21], [22], where two avenues to dig up the fuzzy set representations of a non axis-parallel ellipsoidal clusters are offered. The first mode is undertaken with the help of eigen-values and eigen-vector of a non diagonal covariance matrix subject to the maximal cosine of the angles spanned between the rule's eigenvector and all axes, which can land on an exact fuzzy set representation of the ellipsoidal rule. Unfortunately, the first approach draws a costly computational complexity, which is not suitable for an instantaneous model update requirement as a reciprocal relationship of probing the eigen-values and eigen-vector in every training episode. Hence, the second method is composed to explore the plausible expression of the Gaussian membership function via the axis-parallel intersection of the ellipsoids. The later can pry the fuzzy sets in a fast manner, albeit inaccurate in the case of large coverage span of the ellipsoid rotated around 45 degree. We do not elaborate these two methods in details for the sake of simplicity. As such, pClass fuzzy rule is capable of synchronizing highly flexible clusters and interpretability of rule semantics. The decision making process is formulated in the high dimensional space in tandem as follows:

$$O^k = \frac{\sum_{i=1}^{R} \varphi_i y_i^{k}}{\sum_{i=1}^{R} \varphi_i} = \frac{\sum_{i=1}^{R} \exp(-(X - C_i)\Sigma_i^{-1}(X - C_i)^T)y_i^{k}}{\sum_{i=1}^{R} \exp(-(X - C_i)\Sigma_i^{-1}(X - C_i)^T)} \tag{2}$$

where stands for a local sub-model or consequent parameter of i-th rule to k-th class and $X = [x_1, x_2,..., x_p] \in \Re^{1\times p}$ denotes an input vector. Meanwhile, $C_i \in \Re^{1\times p}$ labels a center of i-th multivariate Gaussian function and $\Sigma_i^{-1} \in \Re^{p\times p}$ epitomizes an inverse covariance matrix of i-th rule. R signifies the number of fuzzy rules.

pClass algorithm can be consummated in any classifier's architectures, including Multi-Input-Multi-Output (MIMO), Multi-Model (MM) and Round Robin (RR) architectures [13], [14]. Nevertheless, we just take into account the MIMO architecture for the sake of a fair comparison with other classifiers as the MIMO architecture is more ubiquitous than those of other two in the machine learning literatures. By extension, the MIMO architecture is presumed to deal with the class overlapping problem more satisfactorily than the MM architecture as it is invigorated by an independent rule consequent per a class label. In a nutshell, the final classification decision in form of class O is composed by:

$$O = \arg\max_{k=1,...,K}(O^k)$$ (3)

A more accurate classification boundary can be concocted in comparison with the MM architecture in the region in which the classes overlap, as the standalone decision boundary per class can be crafted, thus leading to more reliable classification results. In this paper, we exclude to exploit the zero-order classifier's architecture, which does not likely work out to incur dependable classification results in many cases, as it foresees the class label rather than the classification surface.

3   Algorithmic Development of pClass

3.1   Automatic Fuzzy Rule Generation

gClass makes use of three cursors, termed datum significance (DS) method [21], [22], extended recursive density estimation (ERDE) method and generalized adaptive resonance+ (GART+) theory, to fathom the quality of the datum. The DS method is blueprinted to pry the datum statistical contribution, in turn supplies a contribution of a hypothetical fuzzy rule in the future. The ERDE method [15] is used to figure out the position of the focalpoint in the input space, whether or not it lies on a strategic position in the input space with respect to the all training samples. Meanwhile, GART+ [25],[26] deters the so-called cluster delamination phenomenon [24]. That is, one cluster contains two or more data clouds, inevitably worsening the logic of the input space parition and rule semantic. In a nutshell, three rule growing criteria are expressed as follows:

$$V_{P+1} \geq \max_{i=1,...,P}(V_i)$$ (4)

$$V_{win} \geq \rho_1 \sum_{i=1}^{P} V_i$$ (5)

$$ERDE_{P+1} \geq \max_{i=1,...,P}(ERDE_i) \, or \, ERDE_{P+1} \leq \min_{i=1,...,P}(ERDE_i)$$ (6)

where V_{P+1} indicates the volume of a hypothetical new rule (the R+1st) and V_i denotes the volume of the i-th rule, whereas $ERDE_{P+1}$ stands for the ERDE of the newest datum [8]. ρ_1 labels a predefined constant, whose value is stipulated in the range of [0.1,0.5] [27]. More specifically, the density of the datum can be recursively elicited as follow:

$$ERDE_N = \sqrt{\frac{U_N}{U_N(1+a_N) - 2b_N + c_N}} \tag{7}$$

$$U_N{}^i = U_{N-1}{}^i + ERDE_{N-1} \quad , \quad a_N = C_i\,\Sigma_i^{-1}\,C_i^T \quad , \quad b_N = ERDE_{N-1}C_i\alpha_N \quad ,$$

$$\alpha_N = \alpha_{N-1} + \Sigma_i^{-1}X_{N-1}{}^T \quad c_N = c_{N-1} + ERDE_{N-1}X_{N-1}\,\Sigma_i^{-1}\,X_{N-1}.$$

One can perceive that ERDE method, mounted in gClass, is tantamount with the one in eClass of [4]. Nevertheless, we dissent with this argument as three differences are at hand. We apply the different fuzzy rule exemplar with eClass and utilize the inverse multi-quadratic function in lieu of the Cauchy function. Apart from that, we reinforce the ERDE method with a weighting factor, to hamper a large pair-wise distance problem due to outliers [34]. The volume of the non axis-parallel ellipsoidal cluster can be concocted by the determinant operator. Nevertheless, it is a heuristic approach, so that it is less accurate. A volume of hyper-ellipsoidal cluster arbitrarily rotated in any positions can be quantified more accurately as follow:

$$V_i = \frac{2 * \prod_{j=1}^{u}(r_i \,/\, \lambda_{ij}) * \pi^{u/2}}{\Gamma(u/2)} \tag{8}$$

$$\Gamma(p) = \int_0^{\infty} x^{p-1}e^{-x}dx \tag{9}$$

where r_i the Mahalanobis distance radius of the i-th fuzzy rule, which defines its (inner) contour (with default setting of 1) , λ_{ij} is the j-th eigenvalue of the i-th fuzzy rule and Γ is the gamma function. To expedite the execution of (9), a look up table can be a priori generated and used during the training process. Conversely, the Bayesian concept is explored to accord the winning category, which is effective to grasp the winning rule owing to the prior probability, when two or more rules dwell an input zone, which is in the similar proximity to the datum. The posterior, prior probabilities as well as the likelihood function are mathematically illustrated respectively as follows:

$$\hat{P}(R_i|X) = \frac{\hat{p}(X|R_i)\hat{P}(R_i)}{\sum_{i=1}^{P}\hat{p}(X|R_i)\hat{P}(R_i)} \tag{10}$$

$$\hat{P}(R_i) = \frac{\log(N_{i,o}+1)}{\sum_{o=1}^{m}\log(N_{i,o}+1)} \tag{11}$$

$$\hat{P}(X|R_i) = \frac{1}{(2\pi)^{1/2}V_i^{1/2}}\exp(-(X-C_i)\Sigma_i^{-1}(X-C_i)^T) \tag{12}$$

where $N_{i,o}$ stands for the number of samples covered by i-th cluster falling in the o-th class. Note that, equation (12) is a refurbished version of prior probability formula of [26], in order to allow the newly born cluster to win the competition and to evolve its shape as such clusters are usually populated with a lower number of samples than the older clusters.

3.2   Initialization of A Newly Born Fuzzy Rule and Premise Part Adaptation

The parameters of a new fuzzy rule should be organized, after encountering all criteria of evolving a new fuzzy rule. This step should be performed carefully, in order to warrant a favorable input space partition especially to land on a firm conclusion of ε-completeness [28]. On the one hand, the premise parameters of the extraneous fuzzy rule can be enacted as follows:

$$C_{R+1} = X_N \tag{13}$$

$$dist_j = \min_{i=1,..,p} (x_j - c_{i,j}), \Sigma_{R+1} = dist^T dist \tag{14}$$

Note that this setting is contrast with our previous work in GENEFIS of [21], [22], wherein the initial contour and shape of the ellipsoidal cluster is the axis-parallel ellipsoidal cluster. In what follows, we initialize the rule premise as the ellipsoidal cluster arbitrarily rotated in accordance with the inter-relations among input variables. On the other hand, the output parameters of the new fuzzy rule are enacted as follows:

$$W_{R+1} = W_{winner} \tag{15}$$

$$\Psi_{R+1} = \omega I \tag{16}$$

where $\Psi_{R+1} \in \Re^{(P+1) \times (P+1)}$ stands for the inverse covariance matrix of the output fuzzy rule and the constant ω is set up as a positive big value. The setting of the covariance matrix of rule consequent is desirable, as it can mimic the true solution via the batch learning scheme, mainly when it is managed as a positive definite big constant. This was articulated and proven mathematically in [28]. On the contrary, the new weight vector is designated as the rule consequent of the winning rule. The rule consequent of the winning rule can be expected to delineate an identical trend of the new rule, thus being able to attain the convergence more promptly.

If the training observation cannot concur with the rule generation conditions, or the new knowledge conveys a marginal conflict with the existing ones, the rule premise adaptation is activated to refine the position and coverage of the existing rules as follows:

$$C_{winner}{}^N = \frac{N_{win}{}^{N-1}}{N_{win}{}^{N-1} + 1} C_{win}{}^{N-1} + \frac{(X_N - C_{win}{}^{N-1})}{N_{win}{}^{N-1} + 1} \tag{17}$$

$$\Sigma_{win}(N)^{-1} = \frac{\Sigma_{win}(N-1)^{-1}}{1-\alpha} + \frac{\alpha}{1-\alpha} \frac{(\Sigma_{win}(N-1)^{-1}(X_N - C_{win}{}^{N-1}))(\Sigma_{win}(N-1)^{-1}(X_N - C_{win}{}^{N-1}))^T}{1 + \alpha(X_N - C_{win}{}^{N-1})\Sigma_{win}(old)^{-1}(X_N - C_{win}{}^{N-1})^T} \tag{18}$$

$$N_{win}{}^N = N_{win}{}^{N-1} + 1 \tag{19}$$

where $\alpha = 1/(N_{win}{}^{N-1} + 1)$. Equation (18) is appealing to cater in the truly online learning scenario, as it is capable of boiling down the training time, as the inverse covariance matrix is updated directly (no need for an eventual unstable inversion operation). Equation (17) represents the update of winning rule center in accordance with the incremental mean.

3.3   Rule Pruning Procedure

pClass is mounted by two rule pruning cursor, discovering the superfluous or outdated fuzzy rules. The first method is on a par with GENEFIS [21], [22], which emanates from the Extended Rule Significance (ERS) method. The subject of investigation of this method is inactive fuzzy rules, owning marginal leverages to the overall system output. More specifically, the ERS method can be mathematically expressed as follow:

$$\beta_i = \sum_{o=1}^{m}\sum_{j=1}^{2u+1} y_{ij}{}^o \frac{V_i{}^u}{\sum\limits_{i=1}^{P} V_i{}^u} \tag{20}$$

where V_i stands for the volume of i-th rule obtained by equation (8), thus representing the contribution of input part of the i-th rule, whereas y_{ip} constitutes a hyperplane of i-th fuzzy rule and in the case of MIMO architecture $y_{ip} = \sum_{k=1}^{K} y_{ip}{}^k$ pointing out the total contribution of output part of i-th fuzzy rule. β_i denotes the statistical contribution of fuzzy rules.

If $\beta_i < \hat{\beta} - \beta_\sigma$, where $\hat{\beta}, \beta_\sigma$ are the average and standard deviation of fuzzy rule statistical contributions, the fuzzy rule looms to the classifier's output during its lifespan, it can be pruned without an adverse loss of accuracy. Clearly, the ERS method is expedient as the fuzzy rules holding a tiny zone of influence and a minor local sub-model do not affect substantially to the overall system outputs. The second approach is obtained by the enhanced version of the potential theory of [4], [29], termed Potential + (P+) method. The primary goal of the P+ method is to seize the obsolete or outdated fuzzy rules, which are no longer valid to delineate the up-to-date data trend. The P+ method is mathematically formulated as follow:

$$\chi_i = \sqrt{\frac{(N-1)\chi_{n-1,i}{}^2}{(N-1)\chi_{n-1,i}{}^2 + (N-2)(1-\chi_{n-1,i}{}^2) + \chi_{n-1,i}{}^2 d_i{}^n}} \tag{21}$$

where χ_i labels the potential of the i-th fuzzy rule whereas $d_i{}^n$ epitomizes the Malanobis distance between i-th rule to the newest datum. If $\chi_i < \hat{\chi} - \chi_\sigma$, where $\hat{\chi}, \chi_\sigma$ stand for the average and standard deviation of fuzzy rule contributions, the fuzzy rules can be subsumed as obsolete fuzzy rules. Hence, the fuzzy rule can be temporarily deactivated without catastrophic effect of classification accuracy, but can be regenerated in the future subject to the rule recall mechanism condition, deliberated in the next sub-section. Note that our contribution in P+ method is in which the potential method is exacerbated in such a way to serve the generalized fuzzy rule. Another pivotal facet is where the P+ method is advocated by the inverse multi-quadratic function rather than the Cauchy function. It is worth-stressing as well that the P+ method is revamped to act as the rule pruning module.

3.4   Rule Recall Mechanism

The fuzzy rules, which are written off owing to the obsolete trait, can be possibly invoked in the future, as they are deemed convenient to portray the current data trend. Intrinsically, this phenomenon can ensue in the presence of the cyclic drift, for instance: weather data streams, etc, where the old data distribution in particular reactivates in the current training episode. In what follows, the classifier should be endued by the rule recall mechanism, in which the fuzzy rules pruned in the earlier training episodes, can be regenerated in the future, given that their validity is confirmed with the current data trend. The trivial analogy of this learning module can be found in the human learning principles, where human being can retrospect the obsolete knowledge whenever it is pertinent with the current knowledge [30]. It is worth-mentioning that it will be counterproductive, if this issue is impaired with the use of a completely new fuzzy rule, as adaptations given to the pruned fuzzy rules in the past training episodes are catastrophically eroded.

To deal with this issue, the rules pruned by (21) are firstly impounded with a contingency to be revived in the future, when the following condition is satisfied.

$$\max_{i*=1,..,R*} (\chi_{i*}) > \max_{i=1,..,R+1} (\varphi_i) \tag{22}$$

This condition asserts that the already pruned fuzzy rule is more compatible than that of the current datum as it incurs a higher density. The pruned fuzzy rule should be reactivated, rather than evolving the datum as an supplementary fuzzy rule, which is resolved as follow:

$$C_{R+1} = C_{i*}, \Sigma_{R+1}^{-1} = \Sigma_{i*}^{-1}, \Psi_{R+1} = \varpi, \Omega_{R+1} = \Omega_{winner} \tag{23}$$

It is worth-stressing that the rules pruned in the past training episodes are solely exploited to enumerate their density. Even so, they are eradicated in any learning mechanisms or inference mechanisms, thereby still being able to guarantee the abatement of the computational complexity.

3.5   Fuzzily Weighted Generalized Recursive Least Square (FWGRLS) Procedure

The weight vectors of pClass are polished up with the so-called Fuzzily Weighted Generalized Recursive Least Square (FWGRLS) method, which poses a local learning version of Generalized Recursive Least Square (GRLS) method of [31]. The merit of FWGRLS method over the standard Recursive Least Square (RLS) method is capable of maintaining the weight vectors to hover around a small bounded range, thus substantiating the model's generalization and the compactness and parsimony of the rule base.

On the one side, as the rule consequents fluctuate in the small finite range, a likelihood of the unstable adaptations can be alleviated, thus aggravating the model's generalization. On the other side, the compactness and parsimony of the rule base can be fostered, as it is easier for the inconsequential fuzzy rules to be apprehended by the ERS method (20). Formally speaking, the FWGRLS method can be written as follows:

$$\psi(n) = \Psi_i(n-1)F(n)(\frac{R(n)}{\Lambda_i(n)} + F(n)\Psi_i(n-1)F^T(n))^{-1} \tag{24}$$

$$\Psi_i(n) = \Psi_i(n-1) - \psi(n)F(n)\Psi_i(n-1) \tag{25}$$

$$\Omega_i(n) = \Omega_i(n-1) - \varpi\Psi_i(n)\nabla\xi(\Omega_i(n-1)) + \Psi(n)(t(n) - y(n)) \tag{26}$$

$$y(n) = x_{en}\Omega_i(n) \text{ and } F(n) = \frac{\partial y(n)}{\partial\Omega(n)} = x_{en} \tag{27}$$

where $\Lambda_i(n) \in \Re^{(P+1)\times(P\times 1)}$ stands for a diagonal matrix, whose diagonal element consists of the firing strength of fuzzy rule φ_i and the covariance matrix of the modeling error is shown by $R(n)$ which is managed as an identity matrix for the sake of simplicity. Meanwhile, ϖ is a predefined constant specified as $\varpi \approx 10^{-15}$ and $\nabla\xi(\Omega_i(n-1))$ stands for the gradient of the weight decay function. The weight decay function can be any non-linear function to which the exact solution of the gradient is unavailable. In consequence, it is expanded to the n-1 time step, whenever the gradient information is inconvenient to be elicited. For our case, we make use of the quadratic weight decay function $\xi(y_i(n-1)) = \frac{1}{2}(\Omega_i(n-1))^2$ as it is capable of shrinking the weight vector proportionally to its current values.

3.6   Online Feature Weighting Algorithm

An online feature weighting mechanism is assembled in the pClass, in order to smoothly rule out the curse of dimensionality or combinatorial rule explosion shortcoming in dealing with a system with a massive number of the input features. This approach has been exemplified by [10], [11], where the input weights are obtained by the FSC in the feature space. As vindicated by [23], the FSC is more convenient to be inquired in the empirical feature space with the kernel trick approach. This is mainly attributed by which the within class scatter matrix and the between class scatter matrix do not attract a continuous adjustment in the every training episode. Importantly, the construct of FSC in the empirical feature space is amended in such a way to be appropriate with the online learning demand of the evolving system. The point of departure is the introduction of the within class scatter matrix and between class scatter matrix S_b, S_w as follows:

$$tr(S_b) = \sum W - \frac{1}{N}\sum K \tag{28}$$

$$tr(S_w) = tr(K) - \sum W \tag{29}$$

Note that the symbol ΣW means the sum of matrix W in every dimension $\sum_{i,j} W$.

$$W = \frac{1}{N}diag(K_{ii}/N_i), i = 1,...,K \tag{30}$$

$$K = \begin{bmatrix} K_{11}, K_{12}, ..., K_{1k}, ..., K_{1K} \\ K_{21}, K_{22}, ..., K_{2k}, ..., K_{2K} \\ .... \\ K_{K1}, K_{K2}, ..., K_{Kk}, ..., K_{KK} \end{bmatrix} \tag{31}$$

where K represents a kernel-Gram-matrix. One may comprehend, that $K_{11} \in \Re^{N_1 \times N_1}$ demonstrates a kernel-Gram-sub-matrix, emanating from data in class 1, whereas $K_{12} \in \Re^{N_1 \times N_2}$ constitutes a kernel-Gram-sub-matrix, originating from data in class 1 and 2 and so on. The kernel class separability is then gauged as follows:

$$J = \frac{\sum W - \sum K \Big/ N}{tr(K) - \sum W} \tag{32}$$

The key to render the FSC in the empirical feature space usable in the environment is to construct the kernel-Gram matrix recursively via the use of Cauchy kernel as follows:

$$K_{k\hat{k}}^{N} = \frac{(N-1)}{(N-1)(\vartheta_N + 1) + \theta_N - 2\varsigma_N} \tag{33}$$

$$\vartheta_N = \sum_{p=1}^{P} (x_p(N)^k)^2 , \quad \theta_N = \theta_{N-1} + \sum_{p=1}^{P} (x_p(N-1)^{\hat{k}})^2 , \quad \varsigma_N = \sum_{p=1}^{P} x_p(N)^k v_N ,$$

$$v_N = v_{N-1} + x_{N-1}^{\hat{k}}$$

$x_p(N)^k$ is the p-th element of the N-th training sample falling into class k. θ_0 and V_0 can be initialized as zero before the process runs. One can apply another kernel type in lieu of the Cauchy function. However, the Cauchy function is desirable as it constitutes a Taylor series approximation of Gaussian kernel, thus resembling Gaussian function, but sustaining a recursive operation. We can work out the input weight vector with the use of Leave-One-Feature-Out (LOFO) approach of [10], in which the FSC in (32) is quantified P times $J = [J_1, J_2, ..., J_P]$. More specifically, the input weight of a particular input attribute is elicited, when this input attributes is masked. This adds up to conceive the discrimination power of each input attribute, where the input weights are assigned as follow:

$$\lambda_p = 1 - \frac{J_p - \min_{p=1,..,P} (J_p)}{\max_{p=1,..,P} (J_p) - \min_{p=1,..,P} (J_p)} \tag{34}$$

3.7   Experimentation

pClass is numerically validated with the use of 4 data streams, where all of which contain various concept drifts. Two data streams, namely sin and circle are picked from the so-called Diversity for Dealing with Drift (DDD) of [32], whereas we explore the data streams developed by [33] termed SEA dataset. The last data streams are spurred with the use of weather dataset. The efficacy of pClass is benchmarked with eClass of [13], GENEFIS-class of [22] and OS-ELM of [33], in terms of classification rate, number of fuzzy rules and rule base parameters and runtime. All classifiers are embedded by the Multi-Input-Multi-Output (MIMO) classifier's architecture to build the classification boundary as lodged in [13], in order to support fair comparisons. The so-called 10-fold periodic hold-out process is employed as the experimental procedure, in which the final experimental results are relinquished from the average results of the 10-fold process. This experimental procedure is partitioned into 10 standalone sub-processes, in which each sub-process comprises the training and testing phases. The data proportion is commensurate for both phases and the empirical study is capped off when all sub-processes have been consumed. Generally speaking, the 10-fold periodic hold-out procedure is appealing to be vetted, as it simulates the training and testing processes in the real time.

Table 1. Consolidated results of benchmarked system in three datasets

algorithm		sin	line	SEA	Weather
pClass	classification rate	**0.82±0.2**	**0.91±0.07**	**0.88±0.02**	**0.8±0.01**
	Rule	**3.3±1.2**	**2.5±0.71**	**2.1±0.74**	**3.8±2.5**
	Time	0.15±0.01	0.15±0.0009	2.97±0.5	1.27±0.18
	Rule base	**39.6**	**30**	**42**	342
eClass	classification rate	0.81±0.5	0.89±0.06	0.87±0.03	0.8±0.05
	Rule	4±1.14	4.4±0.51	9.2±2.2	5.6±1.72
	Time	**0.1±0.02**	0.1±0.009	6.1±1.5	1.13±0.3
	Rule base	44	39.6	104.2	**151.2**
GENEFIS-class	classification rate	0.81±0.2	0.9±0.07	0.87±0.001	0.8±0.02
	Rule	5.4±2.2	3.6±0.7	2.9±1	4.4±1.64
	Time	0.32±0.3	0.14±0.01	3.02±0.26	1.13±0.14
	Rule base	58.8	43.2	58	396
OS-ELM	classification rate	0.8±0.2	0.91±0.08	0.61±0.001	0.74±0.06
	Rule	50	25	100	80
	Time	0.25±0.02	**0.04±0.02**	**0.006±0.01**	**0.56±0.7**
	Rule base	500	250	600	2160

Referring to Table 1, pClass can on the one hand outperform other benchmarked classifiers, where it can dispatch the most reliable classification rates, while retaining the most compact and parsimonious rule base, verified by the number of rule base parameters and fuzzy rules. On the other hand, OS-ELM can beat pClass in the realm of the execution time. It is conceivable as OS-ELM is a semi random algorithm, where no rule premise adaptations are solicited. This leverage can in turn expedite the training process significantly. Nonetheless, pClass can indemnify this downside with other three aspects, which can approbate the learning potency of pClass over that of OS-ELM.

3.8   Conclusion

A novel evolving classifier, namely Evolving Classifier (eClass), is proposed. pClass adopts a holistic concept of evolving system and even extends it to the plug and play process. pClass is fitted out by the open structure aptitude, where the network topology is dynamic and the soft feature reduction algorithm is coupled, enabling to handle the curse of dimensionality issue on the fly. pClass has been numerically validated with a series of streaming data benefiting from 4 data streams and comparisons with state-of-the-art classifiers. In what follows, pClass can land on the most encouraging numerical results, where it can excel other algorithms in terms of the classification rate, number of fuzzy rule and rule base parameters, whereas its runtime is comparable with its counterparts. The subject of investigation in the future is the integration of meta-cognitive and scaffolding theories popular in the cognitive psychology literatures, in order to boost the adaptive nature of pClass.

References

1. Vapnik, V.N.: The Statistical Learning Theory. Springer, New York (1998)
2. Haykin, S.: Neural Networks: A Comprehensive Foundation, 2nd edn. Prentice Hall Inc., Upper Saddle River (1999)
3. Wu, X., Kumar, V., Quinlan, J.R., Gosh, J., Yang, Q., Motoda, H., MacLachlan, G.J., Ng, A., Liu, B., Yu, P.S., Zhou, Z.-H., Steinbach, M., Hand, D.J., Steinberg, D.: Top 10 algorithms in data mining. Knowledge and Information Systems 14(1), 1–37 (2006)
4. Angelov, P., Filev, D.: An approach to online identification of Takagi-Sugeno fuzzy models. IEEE Transactions on Systems, Man, and Cybernetics, Part B: Cybernetics 34, 484–498 (2004)
5. Lemos, A., Caminhas, W., Gomide, F.: Multivariable Gaussian Evolving Fuzzy Modeling System. IEEE Transactions on Fuzzy Systems 19(1), 91–104 (2011)
6. Pratama, M., Anavatti, S., Angelov, P., Lughofer, E.: PANFIS: A Novel Incremental Learning. IEEE Transactions on Neural Networks and Learning Systems (2013) (online and in press)
7. Angelov, P., Filev, D.: Simpl_eTS: A simplified method for learning evolving Takagi-Sugeno fuzzy models. In: IEEE International Conference on Fuzzy Systems (FUZZ), pp. 1068–1073 (2005)
8. Angelov, P.: Evolving Takagi-Sugeno Fuzzy Systems from Data Streams (eTS+). In: Angelov, P., Filev, D., Kasabov, N. (eds.) Evolving Intelligent Systems: Methodology and Applications. IEEE Press Series on Computational Intelligence, pp. 21–50. John Willey and Sons (April 2010) ISBN: 978-0-470-28719-4
9. Lughofer, E.: FLEXFIS: A Robust Incremental Learning Approach for Evolving TS Fuzzy Models. IEEE Transactions on Fuzzy Systems 16(6), 1393–1410 (2008)
10. Lughofer, E.: On-line incremental feature weighting in evolving fuzzy classifiers. Fuzzy Sets and Systems 163(1), 1–23 (2011)
11. Pratama, M., Anavatti, S., Lughofer, E.: pClass: An Effective Classifier to Streaming Examples. Submitted to IEEE Transactions on Fuzzy Systems, Under Review (June 7, 2013)
12. Pratama, M., Anavatti, S., Lughofer, E.: Evolving Fuzzy Rule-Based Classifier Based on GENEFIS. In: Proceedings of the IEEE Conference on Fuzzy Systems, Hyderabad, India (2013)
13. Lughofer, E., Buchtala, O.: Reliable All-Pairs Evolving Fuzzy Classifiers. IEEE Transactions on Fuzzy Systems 21(4), 625–641 (2013)

14. Angelov, P., Lughofer, E., Zhou, X.: Evolving fuzzy classifiers using different model architectures. Fuzzy Sets and Systems 159(23), 3160–3182 (2008)
15. Rong, H.-J., Sundarajan, N., Huang, G.-B.: Extended Sequential Adaptive Fuzzy Inference System for Classification Problems. Evolving System 2(2), 71–82 (2011)
16. Pang, S., Ozawa, S., Kasabov, N.: Incremental Linear Discriminant Analysis for Classification of Data Streams. IEEE Transactions on System, Man and Cybernetics-Part: Cybernetics 35(5), 905–914 (2005)
17. Sateesh Babu, G., Suresh, S.: Meta-cognitive neural network for classification problems in a sequential learning framework. Neurocomputing 81(1), 86–96 (2012)
18. Suresh, S., Dong, K., Kim, H.: A sequential learning algorithm for self-adaptive resource allocation network classifier. Neurocomputing 73(16-18), 3012–3019 (2010)
19. Huang, G.-B., Saratchandran, P., Sundararajan, N.: An efficient sequential learning algorithm for growing and pruning RBF (GAP-RBF) networks. IEEE Transaction on Systems., Man, Cybernetics., Part-B: Cybernetics 34, 2284–2292 (2004)
20. Huang, G.-B., Saratchandran, P., Sundararajan, N.: A generalized growing and pruning RBF (GGAP-RBF) neural network for function approximation. IEEE Transaction on. Neural Networks 16, 57–67 (2005)
21. Lemos, A., Caminhas, W., Gomide, F.: Adaptive fault detection and diagnosis using an evolving fuzzy classifier. Information Sciences 220, 64–85 (2013)
22. Pratama, M., Anavatti, S., Lughofer, E.: GENEFIS: Towards An Effective Localist Network. IEEE Transactions on Fuzzy Systems, http://dx.doi.org/10.1109/TFUZZ.2013.2264938 (online and in press)
23. Pratama, M., Er, M.-J., Li, X., Oentaryo, R.J., Lughofer, E., Arifin, I.: Data Driven Modelling Based on Dynamic Parsimonious Fuzzy Neural Network. Neurocomputing 110, 18–28 (2013)
24. Lughofer, E.: A Dynamic Split-and-Merge Approach for Evolving Cluster Models. Evolving Systems 3(3), 135–151 (2012)
25. Vigdor, B., Lerner, B.: The Bayesian ARTMAP. IEEE Transactions on Neural Networks 18(6), 1628–1644 (2007)
26. Yap, K.S., Lim, C.P., Au, M.T.: Improved GART Neural Network Model for Pattern Classification and Rule Extraction with Application to Power System. IEEE Transaction on Neural Network 22(12) (2011)
27. Pratama, M., Anavatti, S., Garratt, M., Lughofer, E.: Online Identification of Complex Multi-Input-Multi-Output System Based on GENERIC Evolving Neuro-Fuzzy Inference System. In: Proceedings of the Symposium Series on Computational Intelligence, Singapore (2013)
28. Lee, C.C.: Fuzzy logic in control systems: Fuzzy logic controller. IEEE Transaction. Systems., Man, Cybernetics, pt. I, II 20, 404–436 (1990)
29. de Barros, J.-C., Dexter, A.L.: On-line Identification of Computationally Undemanding Evolving Fuzzy Models. Fuzzy Sets and Systems 158, 1997–2012 (2007)
30. Bartett, F.C.: Remembering: A study in Experimental and Social Psychology. Cambridge Press University Press, Cambridge (1932)
31. Xu, Y., Wong, K.W., Leung, C.S.: Generalized Recursive Least Square to The Training of Neural Network. IEEE Transaction on Neural Network 17(1) (2006)
32. Minku, L.L., Yao, X.: DDD: A New Ensemble Approach for Dealing with Drifts. IEEE Transactions on Knowledge and Data Engineering 24(4) (2012)
33. Liang, N.-Y., Huang, G.-B., Saratchandran, P., Sundararajan, N.: A fast and accurate online sequential learning algorithm for feedforward networks. IEEE Transactions on Neural Networks and Learning Systems 17(6), 1411–1423 (2006)
34. Wang, L., Ji, H.-B., Jin, Y.: Fuzzy Passive-Aggressive Classification: A Robust and Efficient Algorithm for Online Classification Problems. Information Sciences 220, 46–63 (2013)

Sequential Sparse Adaptive Possibilistic Clustering

Spyridoula D. Xenaki, Konstantinos D. Koutroumbas,
and Athanasios A. Rontogiannis*

IAASARS, National Observatory of Athens, GR-152 36, Penteli, Greece
{ixenaki,koutroum,tronto}@noa.gr

Abstract. Possibilistic clustering algorithms have attracted considerable attention, during the last two decades. A major issue affecting the performance of these algorithms is that they involve certain parameters that need to be estimated accurately beforehand and remain fixed during their execution. Recently, a possibilistic clustering scheme has been proposed that allows the adaptation of these parameters and imposes sparsity in the sense that it forces the data points to "belong" to only a few (or even none) clusters. The algorithm does not require prior knowledge of the exact number of clusters but, rather, only a crude overestimate of it. However, it requires the estimation of two additional parameters. In this paper, a sequential version of this scheme is proposed, which possesses all the advantages of its ancestor and in addition, it requires the (crude) estimation of just a single parameter. Simulation results are provided that show the effectiveness of the proposed algorithm.

Keywords: possibilistic clustering, parameter adaptivity, sparsity, sequential processing, k-means, fuzzy c-means.

1 Introduction

Clustering is a well-established data analysis method, where the aim is to locate the physical groups involved in the problem at hand (clusters) formed by a number of entities (usually each entity is represented by a set of measurements that constitute the corresponding *feature vector*). Various clustering philosophies have been proposed during the last five decades. Among them are the *hard clustering* philosophy, where each entity belongs exclusively to a single cluster, the *fuzzy clustering* philosophy, where each entity is allowed to be shared among more than one clusters and the *possibilistic clustering* philosophy, where what matters is the "degree of compatibility" of an entity with a given cluster.

Several clustering algorithms that follow one of these philosophies have been previously reported. The most celebrated among them are the k-means (hard case), e.g. [12], the fuzzy c-means, FCM (fuzzy case), e.g. [1], [2], and several

* This research has been co-financed by the European Union (European Social Fund - ESF) and Greek national funds through the Operational Program "Education and Lifelong Learning" of the National Strategic Reference Framework (NSRF) - Research Funding Program: ARISTEIA - HSI-MARS - 1413.

A. Likas, K. Blekas, and D. Kalles (Eds.): SETN 2014, LNAI 8445, pp. 29–42, 2014.
© Springer International Publishing Switzerland 2014

possibilistic c-means algorithms, PCM (possibilistic case), e.g. [7], [8], [10], [16], [11]. These algorithms are suitable for recovering compact and hyperellipsoidally shaped clusters and they represent each cluster by a single vector, called *cluster representative*, which lies in the space of the feature vectors. The determination of the cluster representatives is carried out via the minimization of suitable cost functions. Also, all of them require knowledge of the number of clusters underlying in the data set (which, of course, is rarely known in practice). However, the k-means and the FCM differ from PCM algorithms in that the former two *impose* a clustering structure on the data set (that is they split the data set into the given number of clusters, independently of the fact that the data set may contain more or less physical clusters than that number), while the latter, in principle, leads the cluster representatives to regions that are "dense in data points". Thus, in this case, the scenario where two or more cluster representatives are led to the same "dense in data" region in space, may arise.

Focusing on PCM algorithms, they have attracted considerable attention in the recent years. Optimization of different cost functions gives rise to different PCMs (e.g. [7], [8]). A significant issue with these cost functions is that they involve a set of parameters (one for each cluster), usually denoted by η, which need to be accurately estimated before the algorithm starts and they are kept fixed during its execution. Poor estimation of these parameters (often) leads to poor clustering performance (especially in more demanding data sets). Usually, these parameters are estimated by utilizing the results of the FCM that needs to be executed first. However, the resulted estimates are not always accurate. For example, if FCM is not fed with the correct number of clusters, the resulting estimates for η's are expected to be poor.

Recently, in [14] a novel PCM algorithm, termed adaptive PCM (APCM), has been proposed, where the parameters η are adapted during its execution. In addition, APCM has, in principle, the ability to automatically detect the true number of clusters, provided that it is fed with an overestimated value of this number. A further extension of APCM, called sparse APCM (SAPCM), is introduced in [15], where sparsity is imposed on the *degrees of compatibilities* of the data vectors with the clusters, in the sense that each data vector is forced to be compatible with only a *few* (or even *none*) of the clusters. SAPCM inherits the characteristics of APCM and, in addition, it has the ability to locate the clusters more accurately, since points that lie "away" from a given cluster are prevented from contributing to the adjustment of its associate parameters.

Both APCM and SAPCM require (a) a certain parameter, denoted by β, that is used in the initialization of the parameters η, (b) an overestimation of the number of clusters and (c) (only for SAPCM) a certain parameter, λ, that controls sparsity. Although these algorithms exhibit, in principle, some degree of robustness in the choice of the previous parameters, parameter fine tuning is unavoidable. To deal with this issue, a sequential version of SAPCM, termed *SeqSAPCM*, is proposed here, which requires neither an overestimated value of the number of clusters, nor the definition of any parameter like β. The only paramater that needs to be defined is the one that controls the sparsity, i.e. λ.

The paper is organized as follows. In section 2, the SAPCM is described, while in section 3, the proposed SeqSAPCM algorithm is presented in detail. Section 4 contains simulation results that allow the assessment of the performance of the proposed algorithm. Finally, section 5 concludes the paper.

2 The Sparse Adaptive Possibilistic c-Means (SAPCM) Algorithm

Let

$$X = \{\boldsymbol{x}_i \in \Re^\ell, i = 1, ..., N\}$$

be a set of N, l-dimensional data vectors that are to be clustered. Let also

$$\Theta = \{\boldsymbol{\theta}_j \in \Re^\ell, j = 1, ..., m\}$$

be a set of m vectors that will be used for the representation of the clusters formed in X. In what follows, $\| \cdot \|$ denotes the Euclidean norm. Let $U = [u_{ij}]$ be an $N \times m$ matrix whose (i, j) element stands for the so called *degree of compatibility* of $\boldsymbol{x}_i$ to the jth cluster, denoted by C_j, and represented by the vector $\boldsymbol{\theta}_j$. Let also $\boldsymbol{u}_i^T = [u_{i1}, ..., u_{im}]$ be the vector containing the elements of the ith row of U.

According to [7] the u_{ij}'s in the classical (non-sparse) PCM algorithms should satisfy the conditions, (a) $u_{ij} \in [0,1]$, (b) $\max_{j=1,...,m} u_{ij} > 0$ and (c) $0 < \sum_{i=1}^N u_{ij} < N$. However, in SAPCM, the last two conditions are removed, since a point may not be compatible with anyone of the clusters (removal of condition (b)). A consequence of the removal of condition (b) is that the case $\sum_{i=1}^N u_{ij} = 0$ for a cluster C_j becomes possible in the extreme scenario where the degrees of compatibility of all points with C_j are zero. Thus, condition (c) is also removed.

SAPCM results from the minimization of the following cost function

$$J(\Theta, U) = \sum_{i=1}^N [\sum_{j=1}^m u_{ij} \|\boldsymbol{x}_i - \boldsymbol{\theta}_j\|^2 + \sum_{j=1}^m \eta_j (u_{ij} \ln u_{ij} - u_{ij}) + \lambda \|\boldsymbol{u}_i\|_p^p] \quad (u_{ij} > 0) \text{ }^1$$

$$(1)$$

where $\|\boldsymbol{u}_i\|_p$ is the p-norm of the vector $\boldsymbol{u}_i$ and $p \in (0, 1)$. The first two terms constitute the classical possibilistic cost function proposed and explained in [8], while η_j is a measure of how much the influence of a cluster is spread around its representative. The last term is the sparsity inducing term.

Minimization of $J(\Theta, U)$ with respect to $\boldsymbol{\theta}_j$ leads to the following updating equation

$$\boldsymbol{\theta}_j = \frac{\sum_{i=1}^N u_{ij} \boldsymbol{x}_i}{\sum_{i=1}^N u_{ij}} \tag{2}$$

On the other hand, taking the derivative of $J(\Theta, U)$ with respect to u_{ij}, we obtain

$$\frac{\partial J(\Theta, U)}{\partial u_{ij}} \equiv \eta_j f(u_{ij}) = \eta_j (\frac{d_{ij}}{\eta_j} + \ln u_{ij} + \frac{\lambda}{\eta_j} p u_{ij}^{p-1}), \tag{3}$$

---

[1] The positivity of u_{ij} is a prerequisite in order for the $\ln u_{ij}$ to be well-defined.

where $d_{ij} = \|x_i - \theta_j\|^2$. Obviously, $\frac{\partial J(\Theta, U)}{\partial u_{ij}} = 0$ is equivalent to $f(u_{ij}) = 0$. For the latter, the following propositions hold.

Proposition 1: $f(u_{ij})$ *may* become zero *only* for $u_{ij} \in (0, 1]$.[2]

This happens since *only* in this case the second term in the right-hand side of eq. (3) is negative (the other two are always positive).

Proposition 2: The unique minimum of $f(u_{ij})$ is $\hat{u}_{ij} = \left[\frac{\lambda}{\eta_j} p(1-p)\right]^{\frac{1}{1-p}} (\in (0,1])$.

This results from the direct minimization of $f(u_{ij})$ with respect to u_{ij}.

Taking into account the previous two propositions and provided that there exists at least one point $u_{ij}^0 \in (0, 1]$ (e.g., $u_{ij}^0 = \exp(-d_{ij}/\eta_j)$) for which $f(u_{ij}^0) > 0$, it can be deduced that $f(u_{ij}) = 0$ has two solutions, if $f(\hat{u}_{ij}) < 0$ and one solution, if $f(\hat{u}_{ij}) = 0$. In any other case, $f(u_{ij}) = 0$ has no solutions. In any case all solutions (if they exist) lie in $(0, 1]$. Also, the following proposition holds.

Proposition 3: If $f(u_{ij}) = 0$ has two solutions, the largest of them is the one that minimzes $J(\Theta, U)$.

This results by proving that $f(u_{ij})$ is positive (negative) on the left (right) of the largest solution.

Based on the above propositions, we proceed to the solution of $f(u_{ij}) = 0$ as follows. First, we check whether $f(\hat{u}_{ij}) > 0$. If this is the case, then $f(u_{ij}) > 0$, for all $u_{ij} > 0$, thus J is increasing with respect to u_{ij}. Therefore, setting $u_{ij} = 0$ (i.e., *imposing sparsity*), J is minimized with respect to u_{ij}. If $f(\hat{u}_{ij}) = 0$, we set $u_{ij} = \hat{u}_{ij}$. If $f(\hat{u}_{ij}) < 0$, $f(u_{ij}) = 0$ has two solutions in $(0, 1]$. In order to determine the largest of the solutions of $f(u_{ij}) = 0$, we apply the bisection method (e.g. [3]) in the range $[\hat{u}_{ij}, 1]$, which is known to converge very rapidly to the optimum u_{ij}, that is, in our case, to the largest of the two solutions of $f(u_{ij}) = 0$.

After the above analysis, the SAPCM algorithm can be stated as follows.

The SAPCM algorithm

$-\ t = 0$

$-$ **Initialization** of θ_j's: $\theta_j \equiv \theta_j(0)$, $j = 1, ..., m$, using the **Max-Min** alg. ([9])

$-$ **Initialization** of η_j's: Set $\eta_j = \dfrac{\min_{\theta_s \neq \theta_j} \|\theta_j - \theta_s\|^2 / 2}{-\log \beta}$, $\beta \in (0, 1)$, $j = 1, ..., m$

$-$ **Repeat:**

  - $t = t + 1$

  - **Update** U: As described in the text

  - **Update** Θ: $\theta_j(t) = \sum\limits_{i=1}^{N} u_{ij}(t-1)x_i \Big/ \sum\limits_{i=1}^{N} u_{ij}(t-1)$, $j = 1, ..., m$

  - *Possible cluster elimination part*:

    * **Determine:** $u_{ir} = \max_{j=1,...,m} u_{ij}$, $i = 1, ..., N$

    * **If** $u_{ir} \neq 0$ **then** Set $label(i) = r$ **else** Set $label(i) = 0$ **end**

    * **Check** for $j = 1, ..., m$: **If** $j \notin label$ **then** Remove C_j **end**

---

[2] Due to space limitations the proof of this and the following propositions are omitted.

- **Adaptation** of η_j's: $\eta_j(t) = \frac{1}{n_j(t)} \sum_{x_i:u_{ij}(t)=\max_{r=1,\ldots,m} u_{ir}(t)} \|x_i - \mu_j(t)\|$,
  with $\mu_j(t) = \frac{1}{n_j(t)} \sum_{x_i:u_{ij}(t)=\max_{r=1,\ldots,m} u_{ir}(t)} x_i, \, j = 1,\ldots,m$

- **Until:** the change in θ_j's between two successive iterations gets very small

Some comments on the algorithm are now in order.

- *Initialization:* In SAPCM, the initialization of θ_j's for an overestimated number of clusters is carried out using a fast approximate variation of the Max-Min algorithm proposed in [9] (see also [14]). This is done in order to increase the probability of each θ_j to be placed initially close to a "dense in data" region[3]. Denoting by X_{re} the set of the initial cluster representatives, η_j's are initialized as follows. First, the distance of each $\theta_j \in X_{re}$ from its closest $\theta_s \in X_{re}$ {θ_j}, denoted by $d_{\min}(\theta_j)$, is determined and then η_j is set to $\eta_j = \frac{d_{\min}(\theta_j)/2}{-\log \beta}$, where $\beta \in (0,1)$ is an appropriately chosen parameter (see *Initialization of η_j's* part in the description of the SAPCM algorithm). As it has been verified experimentally, typical values for β that lead to good initializations are in the range $[0.1, 0.5]$. The experiments showed also that β depends on how densely the natural clusters are located; smaller values of β are more appropriate for sparsely located clusters, while larger values of β are more appropriate for more densely located clusters.

- *Adaptation:* In SAPCM, this part refers to (a) the adjustment of the number of clusters and (b) the adaptation of η_j's, which are two interrelated processes. Here, let *label* be a N-dimensional vector, whose ith component is the index of the cluster that x_i is most *compatible* with, i.e., the cluster C_j for which $u_{ij} = \max_{r=1,\ldots,m} u_{ir}$. Let also n_j denote the number of the data points x_i, that are most compatible with the jth cluster and μ_j be the mean vector of these data points. The adjustment (reduction) of the number of clusters is achieved by examining if the index j of a cluster C_j appears in the vector *label*. If this is the case, C_j is preserved. Otherwise, C_j is eliminated (see *Possible cluster elimination* part in the SAPCM algorithm). Moreover, the parameter η_j of a cluster C_j is estimated as the mean value of the distances of the most compatible to C_j data vectors from their mean vector μ_j and *not* from the representative θ_j, as in previous works (e.g. [7], [17]) (see *Adaptation of η_j's* part in the SAPCM algorithm). It is also noted that, in the case where there are two or more clusters, that are equally compatible with a specific x_i, then x_i will contribute to the determination of the parameter η of *only* one of them, which is chosen arbitrarily.

- *Sparsity:* Taking into account that $d_{ij}/\eta_j \geq 0$ and utilizing proposition 2, for $\ln \hat{u}_{ij} + \frac{\lambda}{\eta_j} p \hat{u}_{ij}^{p-1} > 0$, i.e., $\lambda > \max_{i,j} (\frac{-\ln(\hat{u}_{ij})\hat{u}_{ij}^{1-p} \eta_j}{p})$, no point is allowed to be compatible with any one of the clusters. On the other hand, for $\lambda \simeq 0$ almost no sparsity is imposed, that is, almost all points will be compatible with all clusters up to a non-zero degree of compatibility. Therefore, λ is required

---

[3] In contrast, random initialization may lead several representatives to the same physical cluster, leaving other clusters without a representative.

to be chosen carefully between these two extremes. In addition, for $p \to 0$ or $p \to 1$ no sparsity is imposed, since eq. (3) has always a single solution in both cases. A requirement for sparsity to enter into the scene is to have $p \in (0,1)$, but with p away from both 0 and 1.

3   The Sequential SAPCM (SeqSAPCM)

We proceed now with the description of the sequential SAPCM, which involves in its heart the SAPCM. Note that in the framework of SeqSAPCM, the SAPCM algorithm does not initialize by itself the parameters θ and η. It rather takes as input the initial estimates of these parameters. To denote this explicitly we write

$$[\Theta, H] = SAPCM(X, \Theta^{ini}, H^{ini}, \lambda) \tag{4}$$

In words, the algorithm takes as input, initial estimates of the cluster representatives (included in Θ^{ini}) and their corresponding parameters η (included in H^{ini}) and returns the updated set of (a) representatives (Θ) and (b) their corresponding parameters η (H). Also, recall that λ is the parameter that controls sparsity.

Unlike SAPCM, in SeqSAPCM the number of clusters increases by one at a time, until the true number of clusters is (hopefully) reached. From this point of view, if SAPCM, as described in Section 2, can be considered as a *top-down* technique in the sense that it starts with an overestimated number of clusters and gradually reduces it, SeqSAPCM can be considered as a *bottom-up* approach in the sense that it starts with two clusters and gradually increases them up to the true number of clusters.

The algorithm works as follows. Initially, the two most distant points of X, say x_s and x_t, are determined and serve as initial estimates of the first two cluster representatives, θ_1 and θ_2, denoted by θ_1^{ini} and θ_2^{ini}. Thus, at this time it is $m = 2$ and $\Theta^{ini} = \{\theta_1^{ini}, \theta_2^{ini}\}$. The initial estimation of each one of the parameters η_1 and η_2 (η_1^{ini}, η_2^{ini}) that correspond to the first two clusters, is computed as the *maximum* of the following two quantities:

- $d_{\max}$, which is the maximum among the distances between each data vector $x_i \in X$ and its nearest neighbor $x_i^{nei} \in X$, i.e.,

$$d_{\max} = \max_{i=1,\dots,N} d(x_i, x_i^{nei})$$

- d_{slope}^j, which is determined as follows: The distances of θ_j^{ini} from its q nearest neighbors in X [4], d_s^j, $s = 1, \dots, q$, are computed and plotted in increasing order. The neighboring point of θ_j^{ini} where the resulting curve exhibits the maximum slope, say the rth one, is identified and d_{slope}^j is set equal to d_r^j (the distance between θ_j^{ini} and its rth neighbor).

---

[4] Typically, q is set to a value around 10.

Thus $\eta_j^{ini} = \max\{d_{\max}, d_{slope}^j\}$ and $H^{ini} = \{\eta_1^{ini}, \eta_2^{ini}\}$. Then, we run the SAPCM algorithm (4) and after its convergence, $\boldsymbol{\theta}_1$ and $\boldsymbol{\theta}_2$ are placed to the centers of dense regions, while η_1 and η_2 take values that characterize the spreads of these regions around $\boldsymbol{\theta}_1$ and $\boldsymbol{\theta}_2$, respectively. We have now $\Theta = \{\boldsymbol{\theta}_1, \boldsymbol{\theta}_2\}$ and $H = \{\eta_1, \eta_2\}$.

We proceed next by identifying the point in X that will be used as initial estimate of the next representative as follows. For each $\boldsymbol{x}_i \in X$ we compute its distances from the points of Θ and we select the minimum one. Then, among all N minimum distances we select the maximum one and the corresponding point, say $\boldsymbol{x}_r$ is the initial estimate of the next representative ($\boldsymbol{\theta}_3$), that is $\boldsymbol{\theta}_3^{ini} \equiv \boldsymbol{x}_r$. In mathematical terms, $\boldsymbol{x}_r$ is the point that corresponds to the distance $\max_{i=1,...,N}(\min_{j=1,...,m} d(\boldsymbol{x}_i, \boldsymbol{\theta}_j))$. Also, η_3^{ini} is computed as the previous ones. Next, the SAPCM algorithm is employed with $H^{ini} = \{\eta_1, \eta_2, \eta_3^{ini}\}$ and $\Theta^{ini} = \{\boldsymbol{\theta}_1, \boldsymbol{\theta}_2, \boldsymbol{\theta}_3^{ini}\}$ and executed for three clusters now. After its convergence, all $\boldsymbol{\theta}_i$'s are found to the centers of "dense in data" regions and we have $\Theta = \{\boldsymbol{\theta}_1, \boldsymbol{\theta}_2, \boldsymbol{\theta}_3\}$ and $H = \{\eta_1, \eta_2, \eta_3\}$. The algorithm terminates when no new cluster is detected between two successive iterations.

The algorithm can be stated as follows:

The SeqSAPCM algorithm

- **Normalize** the data set X to the $[0, 10]^l$ space[5].
- **Set** λ to an appropriate value.
- **Determine** the two most distant points in X, say $\boldsymbol{x}_s$ and $\boldsymbol{x}_t$ and use them as initial estimates of the first two representatives $\boldsymbol{\theta}_1$ and $\boldsymbol{\theta}_2$ (i.e., $\boldsymbol{\theta}_1^{ini} \equiv \boldsymbol{x}_s$, $\boldsymbol{\theta}_2^{ini} \equiv \boldsymbol{x}_t$)[6].
- **Initialize** η_1 and η_2 ($\eta_1^{ini}, \eta_2^{ini}$) as described in the text.
- $[\Theta, H] = SAPCM(X, \{\boldsymbol{\theta}_1^{ini}, \boldsymbol{\theta}_2^{ini}\}, \{\eta_1^{ini}, \eta_2^{ini}\}, \lambda\}$
- **Repeat**
  - (A) Use as initial estimate of the next cluster the point $\boldsymbol{x}_r \in X$ that corresponds to the distance $\max_{i=1,...,N}(\min_{j=1,...,m} d(\boldsymbol{x}_i, \boldsymbol{\theta}_j))$ and set $\boldsymbol{\theta}_{new}^{ini} = \boldsymbol{x}_r$.
  - **Compute** the η_{new}^{ini} as described in the text
  - $[\Theta, H] = SAPCM(X, \Theta \cup \{\boldsymbol{\theta}_{new}^{ini}\}, H \cup \{\eta_{new}^{ini}\}, \lambda)$
- **Until** no new cluster is detected

Some comments on the proposed SeqSAPCM are in order now.

- The initialization of the representatives is carried out so that to increase the probability to select a point from each one of the underlying clusters. It is

---

[5] This is a prerequisite that stems from the fact that u_{ij} decreases rapidly as the distance between $\boldsymbol{x}_i$ and $\boldsymbol{\theta}_j$ increases. However, it should be noted that things work also for any value around 10.

[6] In order to avoid high computational burden, this step is carried out approximately using the method described in [4].

noted that, in contrast to SAPCM where the initialization of the representatives is carried out via the **Max-Min** algorithm, in SeqSAPCM a single step of the **Max-Min** (step (A) in the SeqSAPCM algorithm) is executed each time a new representative is to be initialized.

- The initialization of the parameters η for each new cluster may seem a bit tricky. Its rationale is the following. For data sets whose points form well separated clusters, d_{max} is, in general, a good estimate for η_{new}^{ini} of each new cluster. In this case, since the initial estimates of the representatives are clusters points[7], d_{max} is a reasonable value for controlling the influence of a cluster around its representative. Note also, that in this case d_{slope}^j is close to d_{max}. On the other hand, when there are points in the data set that lie away from the clusters (e.g. outliers), the algorithm is likely to choose some of them as initial estimates of cluster representatives. However, a small initial value of η for these representatives will make difficult their movement to dense in data regions. In this case η is set initially equal to d_{slope}^j which, in this case, turns out to be significantly larger than d_{max}. Experiments show that d_{max} is a small value for η in this case, while d_{slope}^j leads to better cluster estimations.
- It is worth mentioning that previously determined η_j's (and $\boldsymbol{\theta}_j$'s) *may* be adjusted in subsequent iterations, as new clusters are formed.
- The SeqSAPCM algorithm, actually requires fine tuning only for the sparsity promoting parameter λ. On the other hand, SAPCM requires additional fine tuning for the initial number of clusters as well as for the parameter β that is used for the initialization of η's.
- A generalization of the proposed scheme may follow if, instead of adding a single representative at each time, we seek for more than one of them at each iteration. In principle, this may reduce the required computational time.

4   Experimental Results

In this section, we assess the performance of the proposed method in several experimental synthetic and real data settings. More specifically, we compare the clustering performance of SeqSAPCM with that of the k-means, the FCM, the PCM, the APCM and the SAPCM algorithms[8]. To this end, we need to evaluate a clustering outcome, that is to compare it with the true data label information. This is carried out via three different measures. The first is the so-called Rand Measure (RM), described in [12], which can cope with clusterings whose number of clusters may differ from the true number of clusters. A generalization of RM is the Generalized Rand Measure (GRM) described in [6], which further takes into account the *degrees of compatibility* of all data points to clusters. Note that in k-means algorithm, the RM does not differ from GRM, since each vector belongs exclusively to a single cluster. Thus, the GRM is not considered in the k-means case. Finally, the classical Success Rate (SR) is employed, which measures the percentage of the points that have been correctly labeled by each algorithm.

---

[7] Ususally, they are "peripheral" points of the clusters.

[8] In order to make a fair comparison, all algorithms are initialized as SeqSAPCM.

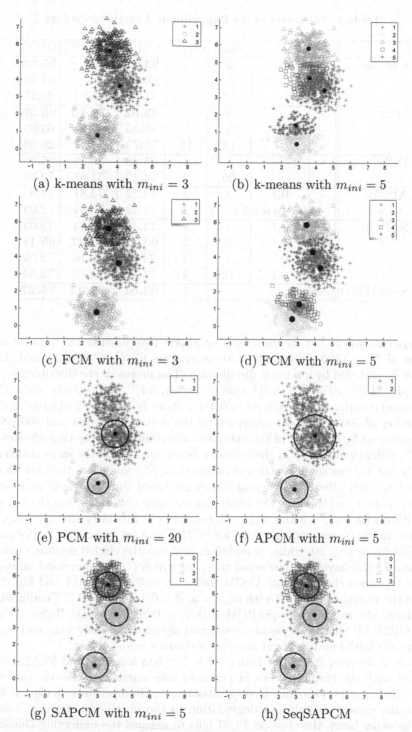

Fig. 1. Clustering results for **Experiment 1**. Bolded dots represent the final cluster representatives. Note that in PCM only the truly "different" clusters are taken into account.

Table 1. The results of the **Experiment 1** synthetic data set

	λ	β	m_{ini}	m_{final}	RM(%)	GRM(%)	SR(%)
k-means	-	-	3	3	**93.62**	-	**95.36**
	-	-	5	5	80.82	-	62.00
	-	-	12	12	71.97	-	28.27
FCM	-	-	3	3	**93.62**	79.10	**95.36**
	-	-	5	5	81.36	67.81	63.00
	-	-	12	12	71.72	59.51	29.00
PCM	-	-	5	1	35.48	35.48	45.45
	-	-	20	2	74.32	51.67	72.09
APCM	-	0.1	3	2	74.32	73.81	72.09
	-	0.1 to 0.5	5 to 12	2	74.32	73.81	72.09
SAPCM	0.3	0.1	3	2	74.32	73.94	72.09
	0.3	0.1	5	3	**93.39**	**90.27**	**95.18**
	0.3	0.5	5	2	74.32	74.16	72.09
	0.3	0.1	12	2	74.32	74.16	72.09
SeqSAPCM	0.28	-	-	3	**93.51**	**90.03**	**95.27**

Experiment 1: Let us consider a synthetic two-dimensional data set consisting of $N = 1100$ points, where three clusters C_1, C_2, C_3 are formed. Each cluster is modelled by a normal distribution. The means of the distributions are $c_1 = [4.1, \ 3.7]^T$, $c_2 = [2.8, \ 0.8]^T$ and $c_3 = [3.5, \ 5.7]^T$, respectively, while their (common) covariance matrix is set to $0.4 \cdot I_2$, where I_2 is the 2×2 identity matrix. A number of 500 points are generated by the first distribution and 300 points are generated by each one of the other two distributions. Note that clusters C_1 and C_3 differ significantly in their density (since both share the same covariance matrix but C_3 has significantly less points than C_1) and since they are closely located to each other, a clustering algorithm could consider them as a single cluster. Figs. 1 (a), (b) show the clustering outcome obtained using the k-means algorithm with $m_{ini} = 3$ and $m_{ini} = 5$, respectively. Similarly, in Figs. 1 (c), (d) we present the corresponding results for FCM. Fig. 1 (e) depicts the performance of PCM for $m_{ini} = 20$, while, in addition, it shows the circled regions, centered at each θ_j and having radius equal to η_j, in which C_j has increased influence. Fig. 1 (f) shows the results of APCM with $m_{ini} = 5$ and $\beta = 0.1$ and Fig. 1 (g) shows the results of SAPCM with $m_{ini} = 5$, $\beta = 0.1$ and $\lambda = 0.3$. Finally, Fig. 1 (h) shows the results of SeqSAPCM with $\lambda = 0.28$. Moreover, Table 1 shows RM, GRM, SR for the previously mentioned algorithms, where m_{ini} and m_{final} denote the initial and the final number of clusters, respectively.

As it is deduced from Fig. 1 and Table 1, when k-means and FCM are initialized with the (rarely known in practice) true number of clusters ($m = 3$), their clustering performance is very satisfactory. However, any deviation from this value causes a significant degradation to the obtained clustering quality. On the other hand, the classical PCM fails to unravel the underying clustering structure, due to the fact that two clusters are close enough to each other and the algorithm does not have the ability to adapt η_j's in order to cope with this situation. In this data set, the APCM algorithm also fails to detect all naturally formed clusters and unites clusters C_1 and C_3 thus leading to a two-cluster clustering result for several values of β. On the other hand, for a large enough value of λ ($\lambda = 0.3$) and a proper overestimation of the initial number of clusters (m_{ini}), SAPCM heavily imposes sparsity so that the remotely located from the mean of the C_3 cluster points are not taken into account to the estimation of the parameters of cluster C_3 (θ_3 and η_3), thus leading to smaller values for η_3. As a consequence, the unification of C_3 with its neighboring (denser) C_1 cluster is prevented. However, as it is deduced from Table 1, the parameters (λ, β, m_{ini}) of SAPCM have to be fine tuned, in order for SAPCM to be successful. This is not the case for SeqSAPCM, which produces very accurate results after cross validating just a single parameter (λ).

Experiment 2: Let us consider a synthetic two-dimensional data set consisting of $N = 5000$ points, where fifteen clusters are formed (data set S_2 in [5]), as shown in Fig. 2. All clusters are modelled by normal distributions with different covariance matrices. As it is deduced from Table 2, k-means fails to unravel the underlying clustering structure, even when it is initialized with the actual number of natural clusters ($m_{ini} = 15$). On the other hand, FCM works well when it is initialized with the true number of clusters ($m_{ini} = 15$), providing very satisfactory results. However, any deviation from this value causes, again, a significant degradation to the obtained clustering quality. The classical PCM fails independently of the initial number of clusters. In this data set, the APCM and the SAPCM algorithms work well after fine-tuning their parameters and properly selecting m_{ini}. Finally, by simply selecting $\lambda = 0.1$, SeqSAPCM is able to capture the underlying clustering structure very accurately.

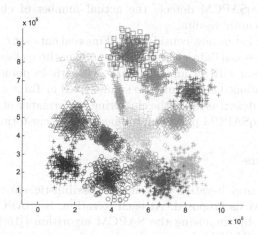

Fig. 2. The data set in **Experiment 2**. Colors indicate the true label information.

Experiment 3: Let us consider the real *Iris* data set ([13]) consisting of $N = 150$, 4-dimensional data points that form three classes, each one having 50

Table 2. The results of the **Experiment 2** synthetic data set

	λ	β	m_{ini}	m_{final}	RM(%)	GRM(%)	SR(%)
k-means	-	-	15	15	97.24	-	81.68
	-	-	20	20	**98.23**	-	**84.84**
	-	-	25	25	97.61	-	78.48
FCM	-	-	15	15	**99.23**	80.09	97.00
	-	-	20	20	98.40	75.36	87.50
	-	-	25	25	97.46	71.30	75.02
PCM	-	-	15	3	62.05	20.43	20.40
	-	-	25	6	78.67	22.02	39.22
APCM	-	0.1	10	10	93.28	90.98	67.16
	-	0.1	20	14	98.38	95.71	91.18
	-	0.1	25	15	**99.23**	**96.88**	**97.00**
SAPCM	0.1	0.1	10	10	93.28	91.07	67.22
	0.1	0.1	20	14	98.39	95.84	91.18
	0.1	0.1	25	15	**99.24**	**96.94**	**97.04**
SeqSAPCM	0.1	-	-	15	**99.23**	**96.94**	**97.02**

points. In *Iris* data set, two classes are overlapped, thus one can argue whether the true number of clusters m is 2 or 3. As it is shown in Table 3, k-means and FCM provide satisfactory results, only if they are initialized with the true number of clusters ($m_{ini} = 3$). The classical PCM fails to end up with $m_{final} = 3$ clusters independently of the initial number of clusters. On the contrary, the APCM and the SAPCM algorithms, after appropriate cross validation of their parameters and a proper overestimated initial number of clusters, produce very accurate results. Finally, SeqSAPCM detects the actual number of clusters, providing constantly very accurate results.

Experiment 4: Let us now consider the *Wine* real data set ([13]) consisting of $N = 178$, 13-dimensional data points that stem from three classes, the first with 59 points, the second with 71 and the third one with 48 points. The results of the previously mentioned algorithms are summarized in Table 4. Again the same conclusions can be drawn as far as the clustering performance of the algorithms is concerned, with SeqSAPCM providing the best overall clustering quality results.

5   Conclusions

In this paper a novel iterative bottom-up possibilistic clustering algorithm, termed SeqSAPCM, is proposed. At each iteration, SeqSAPCM determines a single new cluster by employing the SAPCM algorithm ([15]). Being a possibilistic scheme, SeqSAPCM does not *impose* a clustering structure on the data set but, rather, *unravels* sequentially the underlying clustering structure. The proposed algorithm does not require knowledge of the number of clusters (not even a crude estimate, as SAPCM and APCM do), but only fine tuning of a single parameter λ that controls sparsity (which is data dependent). SeqSAPCM

Table 3. The results of the *Iris* (**Experiment 3**) real data set

	λ	β	m_{ini}	m_{final}	RM(%)	GRM(%)	SR(%)
k-means	-	-	2	2	77.63	-	66.67
	-	-	3	3	**83.22**	-	**83.33**
	-	-	10	10	72.84	-	36.00
FCM	-	-	2	2	77.63	69.15	66.67
	-	-	3	3	**83.68**	**71.56**	**84.00**
	-	-	10	10	75.97	59.96	37.33
PCM	-	-	2	1	32.89	32.89	33.33
	-	-	3	2	77.63	50.45	66.67
	-	-	10	2	77.63	51.99	66.67
APCM	-	0.2	2	2	77.63	77.63	66.67
	-	0.2	5	3	78.20	77.66	72.00
	-	0.3	5	3	**89.23**	**87.78**	**90.67**
	-	0.3	10	5	83.02	78.06	68.00
SAPCM	0.1	0.1	2	2	77.63	77.63	66.67
	0.1	0.1	5	4	83.57	82.70	78.67
	0.1	0.2	5	3	**88.59**	**88.69**	**90.00**
	0.1	0.2	10	4	83.57	82.72	78.67
SeqSAPCM	0.15	-	-	3	**88.59**	**88.73**	**90.00**

Table 4. The results of the *Wine* (**Experiment 4**) real data set

	λ	β	m_{ini}	m_{final}	RM(%)	GRM(%)	SR(%)
k-means	-	-	3	3	68.55	-	51.69
	-	-	5	5	69.66	-	56.74
	-	-	8	8	69.56	-	40.45
FCM	-	-	3	3	71.05	64.91	68.54
	-	-	5	5	71.68	65.37	54.49
	-	-	8	8	70.15	63.40	35.96
PCM	-	-	3	1	33.80	33.80	39.89
	-	-	15	1	33.80	33.80	39.89
APCM	-	0.2	2	2	68.33	68.42	60.11
	-	0.2	5	2	68.33	68.42	60.11
	-	0.1	5	3	**92.42**	**91.61**	**94.38**
	-	0.1	8	4	89.94	87.72	87.08
SAPCM	0.01	0.1	2	2	67.72	67.91	60.11
	0.01	0.1	5	3	67.70	65.01	60.11
	0.01	0.05	5	3	**93.18**	**92.75**	**94.94**
	0.01	0.05	8	4	89.27	87.77	86.52
SeqSAPCM	0.08	-	-	3	**93.31**	**91.25**	**94.94**

outperforms the classical k-means and FCM when the latter are not fed with the actual number of clusters. In addition, it has almost the same clustering performance with SAPCM, when the latter is equipped with the optimal values for its parameters, which are three (initial estimate of the number of representatives, the parameter β for the initialization of η's and the paramater λ that controls sparsity) against one in SeqSAPCM (λ).

The automatic selection of the sparsity inducing parameter λ and a convergence analysis of the proposed SeqSAPCM are subjects of current research.

References

1. Bezdek, J.C.: A convergence theorem for the fuzzy Isodata clustering algorithms. IEEE Transactions on Pattern Analysis and Machine Intelligence 2(1), 1–8 (1980)
2. Bezdek, J.C.: Pattern Recognition with Fuzzy Objective Function Algorithms. Plenum (1981)
3. Corliss, G.: Which Root Does the Bisection Algorithm Find? Siam Review 19, 325–327 (1977)
4. Egecioglu, O., Kalantari, B.: Approximating the diameter of a set of points in the Euclidean space. Information Processing Letters 32, 205–211 (1989)
5. Franti, P., Virmajoki, O.: Iterative shrinking method for clustering problems. Pattern Recognition 39(5), 761–765 (2006)
6. Hullermeier, E., Rifqi, M., Henzgen, S., Senge, R.: Comparing Fuzzy Partitions: A Generalization of the Rand Index and Related Measures. IEEE Transactions on Fuzzy Systems 20, 546–556 (2012)
7. Krishnapuram, R., Keller, J.M.: A possibilistic approach to clustering. IEEE Transactions on Fuzzy Systems 1(2), 98–110 (1993)
8. Krishnapuram, R., Keller, J.M.: The possibilistic c-means algorithm: Insights and recommendations. IEEE Transactions on Fuzzy Systems 4(3), 385–393 (1996)
9. Mirkin, B.: Clustering for Data Mining: A Data Recovery Approach. Chapman Hall. London (2005)
10. Pal, N.R., Pal, K., Keller, J.M., Bezdek, J.C.: A Possibilistic Fuzzy c-Means Clustering Algorithm. IEEE Transactions on Fuzzy Systems 13, 517–530 (2005)
11. Treerattanapitak, K., Jaruskulchai, C.: Possibilistic exponential fuzzy clustering. Journal of Computer Science 28, 311–321 (2013)
12. Theodoridis, S., Koutroumbas, K.: Pattern Recognition, 4th edn. Academic Press (2009)
13. UCI Library database, http://archive.ics.uci.edu/ml/datasets.html
14. Xenaki, S.D., Koutroumbas, K.D., Rontogiannis, A.A.: Adaptive possibilistic clustering. In: Proceedings of the IEEE International Symposium on Signal Processing and Information Technology, ISSPIT (2013)
15. Xenaki, S.D., Koutroumbas, K.D., Rontogiannis, A.A.: Sparse adaptive possibilistic clustering. In: Proceedings of the IEEE International Conference of Acoustic Speech and Signal Processing, ICASSP (2014)
16. Yang, M.-S., Wu, K.-L.: Unsupervised possibilistic clustering. Pattern Recognition 39, 5–21 (2006)
17. Zhang, J.-S., Leung, Y.-W.: Improved Possibilistic C-Means Clustering Algorithms. IEEE Transactions on Fuzzy Systems 12, 209–217 (2004)

A Rough Information Extraction Technique
for the Dendritic Cell Algorithm
within Imprecise Circumstances

Zeineb Chelly and Zied Elouedi

LARODEC, University of Tunis, High Institute of Management of Tunis, Tunisia
zeinebchelly@yahoo.fr, zied.elouedi@gmx.fr

Abstract. The Dendritic Cell Algorithm (DCA) is an immune inspired classification algorithm based on the behavior of Dendritic Cells (DCs). The performance of DCA depends on the extracted features and their categorization to their specific signal types. These two tasks are performed during the DCA data pre-processing phase and are both based on the use of the Principal Component Analysis (PCA) information extraction technique. However, using PCA presents a limitation as it destroys the underlying semantics of the features after reduction. On the other hand, DCA uses a crisp separation between the two DCs contexts; semi-mature and mature. Thus, the aim of this paper is to develop a novel DCA version based on a two-leveled hybrid model handling the imprecision occurring within the DCA. In the top-level, our proposed algorithm applies a more adequate information extraction technique based on Rough Set Theory (RST) to build a solid data pre-processing phase. At the bottom level, our proposed algorithm applies Fuzzy Set Theory to smooth the crisp separation between the two DCs contexts. The experimental results show that our proposed algorithm succeeds in obtaining significantly improved classification accuracy.

Keywords: Dendritic Cell Algorithm, Information Extraction, Imprecise Reasoning, Classification.

1 Introduction

The Dendritic Cell Algorithm (DCA) [1] is a recent immune inspired algorithm derived from behavioral models of natural Dendritic Cells (DCs). Lately, DCA has caught the attention of researchers due to the worthy characteristics expressed by the algorithm as it exhibits several interesting and potentially beneficial features for binary classification problems [2]. However, as the DCA is still a new foundation, it is necessary to conduct further investigations to address and resolve the DCA limitations by proposing new models of the standard algorithm. This will be the main goal of the current research paper. Back to literature, DCA has been successfully applied to various real world binary classification domains. However, it was noticed that DCA is sensitive to the input class data order [3]. It was shown that the DCA misclassifications occur exclusively at the transition

A. Likas, K. Blekas, and D. Kalles (Eds.): SETN 2014, LNAI 8445, pp. 43–56, 2014.

boundaries. Hence, DCA makes more mistakes when the context changes multiple times in a quick succession unlike when the data are ordered between classes; class 1 and class 2. Thus, to obtain high and satisfactory classification results, the DCA was only applied to ordered data sets where all class 1 are followed by all class 2. Such a drawback is the result of an environment characterized by a crisp separation between the DC semi-mature context and the DC mature context. However, the reality is connected to uncertainty and imprecision by nature. Such imperfection may affect the classification performance of the DCA leading the algorithm being sensitive to the input class data order. Therefore, one idea was to combine theories managing imprecision, mainly Fuzzy Set Theory (FST), with the DCA to deal with imprecise contexts. In this sense, in [4], a first work named the Fuzzy Dendritic Cell Method (FDCM) was developed to solve the DCA issue as being sensitive to the input class data order. FDCM is based on the fact of smoothing the mentioned crisp separation between the DCs' contexts since we can neither identify a clear boundary between them nor quantify exactly what is meant by "semi-mature" or "mature". This was handled by the use of FST. Yet, FDCM was a user-dependent algorithm as its parameters have to be set by the user. Thus, in [5] a modified version of FDCM was developed named the Modified Fuzzy Dendritic Cell Method (MFDCM), where the parameters of the system were automatically generated using a fuzzy clustering technique. This can avoid false and uncertain values given by the ordinary user.

While investigating MFDCM and more precisely its crucial first algorithmic step, the data pre-processing phase, we have noticed that this phase which is divided into feature selection and signal categorization is based on the use of the Principal Component Analysis (PCA) technique. Formally, MFDCM uses PCA to automatically select features and to categorize them to their specific signal types; as danger signals (DS), as safe signals (SS) or as pathogen-associated molecular patterns (PAMP). MFDCM combines these signals with location markers in the form of antigens to perform antigens classification. Investigating the algorithm data pre-processing phase is important as it represents the main step of any knowledge discovery process (KDD). Back to MFDCM, we notice that using PCA for the MFDCM feature reduction step presents a drawback as it is not necessarily true that the first selected components will be the adequate features to retain. Furthermore, applying PCA destroys the underling meaning (the semantics) behind the features present in the used data set which contradicts the characteristic of the DCA and MFDCM as it is important to know the source (feature) of each signal category. Adding to these issues, an informed guess has to be made as to how many variables should be kept for the PCA data reduction process. This may introduce a potential source of error. As for the signal categorization phase, it refers to the process of appropriately mapping the selected features into each signal category of the algorithm; either as DS, as SS or as a PAMP signal. In the MFDCM data pre-processing phase, the categorization process is based on the PCA attributes ranking in terms on variability. However, this categorization process could not be considered as a coherent and a reliable categorization procedure. Many KDD techniques were proposed in literature to achieve the task of data pre-processing. However, most of them tend to destroy the underlying semantics of the features after reduction or require additional information about the given data set for thresholding [6]. Thus, it seems necessary and clearly desirable to think about a more adequate information extraction technique, for the MFDCM data pre-processing phase, which can in one hand extract features using information contained within the data set and in other hand capable of preserving the meaning of the features. Rough Set Theory (RST) [6] can be used as such a tool to discover data dependencies and to reduce the number of attributes contained in a data set using the data alone, requiring no additional information. In this sense, in [7], a new DCA model based on a rough data pre-processing technique has been developed. The work, named RC-DCA, is based on the Reduct and the Core RST main concepts for feature selection and signal categorization. It was shown that using RST, instead of PCA, for the DCA data pre-processing phase yields better performance in terms of classification accuracy. However, it is important to note that RST was only applied to the standard DCA which is sensitive to the input class data order. Thus, in this paper, we propose to hybridize the works of [5] and [7] in order to obtain a robust dendritic cell stable classifier within imprecise circumstances. Our hybrid model, named RC-MFDCM, is built as a two-leveled hybrid immune model. In the top-level, RC-MFDCM uses RST as a robust information extraction technique to ensure a more rigorous data pre-processing phase. In the second level, RC-MFDCM uses fuzzy set theory to ensure a non-sensitivity to the input class data order. This is achieved by handling the imprecision occurring within the definition of the DCs contexts.

2   The Dendritic Cell Algorithm

The initial step of the DCA is the automatic *data pre-processing phase* where feature selection and signal categorization are achieved. More precisely, DCA selects the most important features, from the initial input database, and assigns each selected attribute its specific signal category (SS, DS or PAMP). To do so, the DCA applies PCA as explained in the previous section. The DCA adheres these signals and antigens to fix the context of each object (DC) which is the step of *signal processing*. The algorithm processes its input signals in order to get three output signals: costimulation signal (Csm), semi-mature signal $(Semi)$ and mature signal (Mat). A migration threshold is incorporated into the DCA in order to determine the lifespan of a DC. As soon as the Csm exceeds the migration threshold; the DC ceases to sample signals and antigens. The migration state of a DC to the semi-mature state or to the mature state is determined by the comparison between cumulative $Semi$ and cumulative Mat. If the cumulative $Semi$ is greater than the cumulative Mat then the DC goes to the semi-mature context which implies that the antigen data was collected under normal conditions. Otherwise, the DC goes to the mature context, signifying a potentially anomalous data item. This step is known to be the *context assessment phase*. The nature of the response is determined by measuring the number of DCs that are fully mature and is represented by the Mature Context Antigen Value (MCAV). $MCAV$ is applied in the DCA final step which is the *classification procedure* and used to assess the degree of anomaly of a given antigen. The closer the $MCAV$ is to 1, the greater the probability that the antigen is anomalous. By applying thresholds at various levels, analysis can be performed to assess the anomaly detection capabilities of the algorithm. Those antigens whose $MCAV$ are greater than the anomalous threshold are classified as anomalous while the others are classified as normal. For the DCA pseudocode, we kindly invite the reader to refer to [1].

3　Rough Set Theory for Information Extraction

1)Preliminaries of Rough Set Theory: In rough set theory, an *information table* is defined as a tuple $T = (U, A)$ where U and A are two finite, non-empty sets, U the *universe* of primitive objects and A the set of attributes. Each attribute or feature $a \in A$ is associated with a set V_a of its value, called the *domain* of a. We may partition the attribute set A into two subsets C and D, called *condition* and *decision* attributes, respectively. Let $P \subset A$ be a subset of attributes. The indiscernibility relation, denoted by $IND(P)$, is an equivalence relation defined as: $IND(P) = \{(x, y) \in U \times U : \forall a \in P, a(x) = a(y)\}$, where $a(x)$ denotes the value of feature a of object x. If $(x, y) \in IND(P)$, x and y are said to be *indiscernible* with respect to P. The family of all equivalence classes of $IND(P)$ (Partition of U determined by P) is denoted by $U/IND(P)$. Each element in $U/IND(P)$ is a set of indiscernible objects with respect to P. Equivalence classes $U/IND(C)$ and $U/IND(D)$ are called *condition* and *decision* classes. For any concept $X \subseteq U$ and attribute subset $R \subseteq A$, X could be approximated by the R-*lower* approximation and R-*upper* approximation using the knowledge of R. The lower approximation of X is the set of objects of U that are surely in X, defined as: $\underline{R}(X) = \bigcup\{E \in U/IND(R) : E \subseteq X\}$. The upper approximation of X is the set of objects of U that are possibly in X, defined as: $\overline{R}(X) = \bigcup\{E \in U/IND(R) : E \cap X \neq \emptyset\}$ The boundary region is defined as: $BND_R(X) = \overline{R}(X) - \underline{R}(X)$. If the boundary region is empty, that is, $\overline{R}(X) = \underline{R}(X)$, concept X is said to be R-*definable*. Otherwise X is a rough set with respect to R. The positive region of decision classes $U/IND(D)$ with respect to condition attributes C is denoted by $POS_c(D)$ where: $POS_c(D) = \bigcup \overline{R}(X)$. The positive region $POS_c(D)$ is a set of objects of U that can be classified with certainty to classes $U/IND(D)$ employing attributes of C. In other words, the positive region $POS_c(D)$ indicates the union of all the equivalence classes defined by $IND(P)$ that each for sure can induce the decision class D.

2)Reduct and Core for Feature Selection: Rough set theory defines two important concepts that can be used for information extraction which are the CORE and the REDUCT. The CORE is equivalent to the set of strong relevant features which are *indispensable* attributes in the sense that they cannot be removed without loss of prediction accuracy of the original database. The REDUCT is a combination of all strong relevant features and some weak relevant features that can sometimes contribute to prediction accuracy. These concepts provide a good foundation upon which we can define our basics for defining the importance of each attribute. In RST, a subset $R \subseteq C$ is said to be a D-*reduct* of C if $POS_R(D) = POS_C(D)$ and there is no $R' \subset R$ such that $POS_{R'}(D) = POS_C(D)$. In other words, the REDUCT is the minimal set of attributes preserving the positive region. There may exist many reducts (a family of reducts) in a information table which can be denoted by $RED_D^F(C)$. The CORE is the set of attributes that are contained by all reducts, defined as: $CORE_D(C) = \bigcap RED_D(C)$; where $RED_D(C)$ is the D-reduct of C. In other words, the CORE is the set of attributes that cannot be removed without changing the positive region meaning that these attributes cannot be removed from the information system without causing collapse of the equivalence-class structure. This means that all attributes present in the CORE are indispensable.

4   RC-MFDCM: The Two-Leveled Hybrid Approach

In this section, we present our newly proposed fuzzy rough DCA version within imprecise framework. Our two-leveled hybrid model incorporates, firstly, the theory of rough sets to ensure a robust data pre-processing phase. This task is performed in the RC-MFDCM top-level. RC-MFDCM incorporates, secondly, the theory of fuzzy sets to generate a stable classifier dealing with imprecise contexts. This task is performed at the RC-MFDCM bottom level.

4.1   Top-Level : Data Pre-processing Phase

The data pre-processing phase of our RC-MFDCM includes two sub-steps which are feature selection and signal categorization; both based on the RST concepts.

RC-MFDCM Information Extraction Process. For antigen classification, our learning problem has to select high discriminating features from the original input database which corresponds to the antigen information data set. We may formalize this problem as an information table, where universe $U = \{x_1, x_2, \ldots, x_N\}$ is a set of antigen identifiers, the conditional attribute set $C = \{c_1, c_2, \ldots, c_N\}$ contains the different features of the information table to select and the decision attribute D of our learning problem corresponds to the class label of each sample. As RC-MFDCM is an extension of DCA and since DCA is applied to binary classification problems, then our RC-MFDCM is also seen as a binary classifier and thus, the input database has a single binary decision attribute. The decision attribute D, which corresponds to the class label, has binary values d_k: either the antigen is collected under safe circumstances reflecting a normal behavior (classified as normal) or the antigen is collected under dangerous circumstances reflecting an anomalous behavior (classified as anomalous). The condition attribute feature D is defined as follows: $D = \{normal, anomalous\}$.

For information extraction, RC-MFDCM computes, first of all, the positive region for the whole attribute set C for both label classes of D: $POS_C(\{d_k\})$. Based on the RST computations, RC-MFDCM computes the positive region of each feature c and the positive region of all the composed features $C - \{c\}$ (when discarding each time one feature c from C) defined respectively as $POS_c(\{d_k\})$ and $POS_{C-\{c\}}(\{d_k\})$, until finding the minimal subset of attributes R from C that preserves the positive region as the whole attribute set C does. In fact, RC-MFDCM removes in each computation level the unnecessary features that may affect negatively the accuracy of the RC-MFDCM. The result of these computations is either one reduct $R = RED_D(C)$ or a family of reducts $RED_D^F(C)$. Any reduct of $RED_D^F(C)$ can be used to replace the original antigen information table. Consequently, if the RC-MFDCM generates only one reduct $R = RED_D(C)$ then for the feature selection process, RC-MFDCM chooses this specific R which represents the most informative features that preserve nearly the same classification power of the original data set. If the RC-MFDCM generates a family of reducts $RED_D^F(C)$ then RC-MFDCM chooses randomly one reduct R among $RED_D^F(C)$ to represent the original input antigen information table. This random choice is argued by the same priority of all the reducts in $RED_D^F(C)$. In other words, any reduct R from $RED_D^F(C)$ can be used to replace the original information table.

These attributes which constitute the reduct will describe all concepts in the original training data set. Using the REDUCT concept, our method can guarantee that attributes of extracted feature patterns will be the most relevant for its classification task. An illustrative example related to the REDUCT and the CORE generation can be found in [6]. Once the reduct is generated, our proposed solution moves to its second data pre-processing sub-step which is signal categorization.

RC-MFDCM Signal Categorization Process. All along this sub-step, our method has to assign for each selected attribute, produced by the previous step and which is included in the generated REDUCT, its definite and specific signal category. The general guidelines for signal categorization are presented in the list below [1]:

- **Safe signals:** Their presence certainly indicates that no anomalies are present. High values of SS can cancel out the effects of both PAMPs and DSs.
- **PAMPs:** The presence of PAMPs usually means that there is an anomalous situation.
- **Danger signals:** Their presence may or may not show an anomalous situation, however the probability of an anomaly is higher than under normal circumstances.

From the previous definitions, both of the PAMP and safe signals are positive indicators of an anomalous and normal behavior while the DS is measuring situations where the risk of anomalousness is high, but there is no signature of a specific cause. In other words, PAMP and SS have a certain final context (either an anomalous or a normal behavior) while the DS cannot specify exactly the final context to assign to the collected antigen. This is because the information returned by the DS is not certain as the collected antigen may or may not indicate an anomalous situation. This problem can be formulated as follows: Both PAMP and SS are more informative than DS which means that both of these signals can be seen as indispensable attributes. To represent this level of importance, our method uses the CORE RST concept. On the other hand, DS is less informative than PAMP and SS. Therefore, our method applies the rest of the REDUCT attributes, discarding the attributes of the CORE chosen to represent the SS and the PAMP signals, to represent the DS.

As stated in the previous sub-step, our method may either produce only one reduct R or a family of reducts $RED_D^F(C)$. The process of signal categorization for both cases are described in what follows.

The Process of One REDUCT: In case where our model generates only one reduct; it means that $CORE_D(C) = RED_D(C)$. In other words, all the features that represent the produced reduct R are indispensable. For signal categorization and with respect to the ranking of signal categories that implies the significance of each signal category to the signal transformation of the DCA which is in the order Safe, PAMP, and Danger, our method processes as follows: First of all, RC-MFDCM calculates the positive region $POS_C(\{d_k\})$ of the whole core $CORE_D(C)$. Then, our method calculates the positive regions $POS_{C-\{c\}}(\{d_k\})$ that correspond to the positive regions of the core when removing each time one attribute c from it. Our method calculates the difference values between $POS_C(\{d_k\})$ and each $POS_{C-\{c\}}(\{d_k\})$ already calculated. The removed attribute c causing the highest difference value $POS_C(\{d_k\}) - POS_{C-\{c\}}(\{d_k\})$ is considered as the most important attribute in the CORE. In other words, when removing that attribute c from the CORE then the effectiveness and the reliability of the core will be strongly affected. Therefore, our method selects that attribute c to form the Safe signal. The second attribute c_r having the next highest difference value $POS_C(\{d_k\}) - POS_{C-\{c_r\}}(\{d_k\})$ is used to form the PAMP signal. And finally, the rest of the CORE attributes are combined and affected to represent the DS as it is less than certain to be anomalous.

The Process of a Family of REDUCTs: In case where our model produces more than one reduct R, a family of reducts $RED_D^F(C)$, our method uses both concepts: the core $CORE_D(C)$ and the reducts $RED_D^F(C)$. Let us remind that $CORE_D(C) = \bigcap RED_D(C)$; which means that on one hand we have the minimal set of attributes preserving the positive region (reducts) and on the other hand we have the set of attributes that are contained in all reducts (CORE) which cannot be removed without changing the positive region. This means that all the attributes present in the CORE are indispensable. For signal assignment and based on the positive regions calculation, our method assigns the convenient attributes from the CORE to determine the SS and PAMP following the same reasoning as our method produces only one reduct. As for the DS signal type categorization, our solution chooses first of all, randomly, a reduct $RED_D(C)$ among $RED_D^F(C)$. Then, our method combines all the $RED_D(C)$ features except the first and the second attributes already chosen for the SS and PAMP and assigns the resulting value to the DS.

Once the selected features are assigned to their suitable signal types, our method calculates the values of each signal category using the same process as the standard DCA [1]. The output is, thus, a new information table which reflects the signal database. In fact, the universe U of the induced signal data set is $U = \{x'_1, x'_2, \ldots, x'_N\}$ a set of antigen identifiers and the conditional attribute set $C = \{SS, PAMP, DS\}$ contains the three signal types; i.e., SSs, DSs and PAMPs. The induced signal database which is the input data for the next proposed model steps contains the values of each signal type for each antigen identifier.

4.2   Bottom-Level : Fuzzy Classification Phase

The second level of our RC-MFDCM hybrid model is composed of five main sub-steps and is based on the basics of fuzzy set theory.

1)Fuzzy System Inputs-Output Variables: Once the signal database is ready, our RC-MFDCM processes these signals to get the semi-mature and the mature signal values same as DCA and as previously explained in section 2. To do so and in order to describe each of these two object contexts, we use linguistic variables. Two inputs (one for each context) and one output are defined. The semi-mature context and the mature context, denoted respectively C_s and C_m, are considered as the input variables to the fuzzy system. The final state "maturity" of a DC, S_{mat}, is chosen as the output variable. They are defined as:

$$C_s = \{\mu_{C_s}(c_{s_j})/c_{s_j} \in X_{C_s}\}$$

$$C_m = \{\mu_{C_m}(c_{m_j})/c_{m_j} \in X_{C_m}\}$$

$$S_{mat} = \{S_{mat}(s_{mat_j})/s_{mat_j} \in X_{S_{mat}}\}$$

where c_{s_j}, c_{m_j} and s_{mat_j} are, respectively, the elements of the discrete universe of discourse X_{C_s}, X_{C_m} and $X_{S_{mat}}$. μ_{C_s}, μ_{C_m} and $\mu_{S_{mat}}$ are, respectively, the corresponding membership functions.

2)Defining the Term Sets: The term set $T(S_{mat})$ interpreting S_{mat} which is a linguistic variable that constitutes the final state of maturity of a DC, can be defined as: $T(S_{mat}) = \{Semi - mature, Mature\}$. Each term in $T(S_{mat})$ is characterized by a fuzzy subset in a universe of discourse $X_{S_{mat}}$. Semi-mature might be interpreted as an object (data instance) collected under safe circumstances, reflecting a normal behavior and Mature as an object collected under dangerous circumstances, reflecting an anomalous behavior. Similarly, the input variables C_s and C_m are interpreted as linguistic variables with:
$T(Q) = \{Low, Medium, High\}$, where $Q = C_s$ and C_m respectively.

3)Membership Function Construction: In order to specify the range of each linguistic variable, we have run the RC-MFDCM and we have recorded both semi-mature and mature values which reflect the (Semi) and (Mat) outputs generated by the algorithm. Then, we picked up the minimum and maximum values of each of the two generated values to fix the borders of the range which are:

$$min(range(S_{mat})) = min(min(range[C_m]), min(range[C_s]))$$

$$max(range(S_{mat})) = max(max(range[C_m]), max(range[C_s]))$$

The parameters of our RC-MFDCM fuzzy process, the extents and midpoints of each membership function, are generated automatically from data by applying the fuzzy Gustafson-Kessel clustering algorithm. Each cluster reflects a membership function. The number of clusters is relative to the number of the membership functions of each variable (inputs and output).

4)The Rule Base Description: A knowledge base, comprising rules, is built to support the fuzzy inference. The different rules of the fuzzy system are extracted from the information reflecting the effect of each input signal on the state of a dendritic cell. This was previously pointed in the itemized list in the RC-MFDCM signal categorization phase section. The generated rule base is the following:

1. If (C_m is Low) and (C_s is Low) then (S_{mat} is Mature)
2. If (C_m is Low) and (C_s is Medium) then (S_{mat} is Semi-mature)
3. If (C_m is Low) and (C_s is High) then (S_{mat} is Semi-mature)
4. If (C_m is Medium) and (C_s is Low) then (S_{mat} is Mature)
5. If (C_m is Medium) and (C_s is Medium) then (S_{mat} is Semi-mature)
6. If (C_m is Medium) and (C_s is High) then (S_{mat} is Semi-mature)
7. If (C_m is High) and (C_s is Low) then (S_{mat} is Mature)
8. If (C_m is High) and (C_s is Medium) then (S_{mat} is Mature)
9. If (C_m is High) and (C_s is High) then (S_{mat} is Mature)

5)The Fuzzy Context Assessment: RC-MFDCM is based on the "Mamdani" composition method and the "centroid" defuzzification mechanism [8]. Once the inputs are fuzzified and the output (centroid value) is generated, the cell context has to be fixed by comparing the output value to the middle of the S_{mat} range. In fact, if the centroid value generated is greater than the middle of the output range then the final context of the object is "Mature" indicating that the collected antigen may be anomalous; else the antigen collected is classified as normal.

5   Experimental Setup

To test the validity of our RC-MFDCM model, our experiments are performed on two-class databases from [9]. The used databases are described in Table 1. We try to show that using the RST information extraction technique, instead of PCA, is more adequate for our proposed RC-MFDCM data pre-processing phase. Thus, we will compare the results obtained from RC-MFDCM to the ones obtained from the PCA-MFDCM version where the latter algorithm applies PCA for information retrieval. We will, also, compare our RC-MFDCM algorithm to our first work proposed in [10], named RST-MFDCM, which is also based on the use of RST for information extraction. First of all, let us remind that both RC-MFDCM and PCA-MFDCM assign different features for different signal types; a specific feature is assigned to be either as SS or as DS or as a PAMP signal. Now, the work of [10], RST-MFDCM, differs from our newly proposed RC-MFDCM algorithm and from PCA-MFDCM in the manner on how it categorizes features to their signal types (SS, DS and PAMP). More precisely, the main difference between RST-MFDCM and both RC-MFDCM and PCA-MFDCM is that RST-MFDCM assigns only one attribute to form both SS and PAMP as they are seen as the most important signals. As for the DS categorization, RST-MFDCM combines the rest of the reduct features and assigns the resulting value to the DS. Like RC-MFDCM, RST-MFDCM generates all the possible reducts and proposes solutions to handle both cases (generating one reduct or a family of reducts) for data pre-processing.

Table 1. Description of Databases

Database	Ref	♯ Instances	♯ Attributes
Sonor	SN	208	61
Molecular-Bio	Bio	106	59
Cylinder Bands	CylB	540	40
Chess	Ch	3196	37
Ionosphere	IONO	351	35
Sick	Sck	3772	30
Horse Colic	HC	368	23
German-Credit	GC	1000	21
Labor Relations	LR	57	16
Red-White-Win	RWW	6497	13

In [10], RST-MFDCM was compared to the MFDCM version when applying PCA. It was shown that applying RST, instead of PCA, leads to better classification results. The latter version of MFDCM based PCA, just like RST-MFDCM, assigns the same feature for both SS and PAMP. It is, also, based on the same signal categorization process for the DS signal as RST-MFDCM. So, to distinguish this version from the initial mentioned PCA-MFDCM version, we will named it as PCA'-MFDCM. Based on the [10] work, we aim to show that assigning for each selected feature a specific signal category, a process performed by our proposed RC-MFDCM and PCA-MFDCM, leads to a better classification performance than assigning the same attribute to both SS and PAMP, a process performed by both RST-MFDCM and PCA'-MFDCM. We will, also, show that using the RST information extraction technique, instead of PCA, in case of assigning different features to different signal categories is more adequate for our proposed RC-MFDCM data pre-processing phase.

For data pre-processing and for all the mentioned rough MFDCM works, including RC-MFDCM and RST-MFDCM, and for the PCA MFDCM based approaches, including PCA-MFDCM and PCA'-MFDCM, each data item is mapped as an antigen with the value of the antigen equal to the data ID of the item. The migration threshold of an individual DC is set to 10. To perform anomaly detection, a threshold which is automatically generated from the data is applied to the MCAVs. Items below the threshold are classified as class one and above as class two. For each experiment, the results presented are based on mean MCAVs generated across 10 runs. We evaluate the performance of the algorithms in terms of number of extracted features, sensitivity, specificity and accuracy which are defined as: $Sensitivity = TP/(TP + FN); Specificity = TN/(TN + FP); Accuracy = (TP + TN)/(TP + TN + FN + FP)$; where TP, FP, TN, and FN refer respectively to: true positive, false positive, true negative and false negative.

6 Results and Analysis

In this section, we show that using the theory of rough sets as an information extraction technique, instead of PCA, is more convenient for the MFDCM data pre-processing phase as it improves its classification performance. We will, also, show that assigning for each selected feature a specific signal category leads to a better performance than assigning the same attribute to both SS and PAMP. This is confirmed by the results displayed in Table 2.

First of all, from Table 2, we can notice that both RC-MFDCM and RST-MFDCM have the same number of selected features. This is explained by the fact that both models are based on the same feature selection phase. They generate all the possible reducts and choose the one having the smallest set in terms of number of extracted features. Indeed, from Table 2, we can notice that the number of features selected by the rough MFDCM approaches, both RC-MFDCM and RST-MFDCM, is less than the one generated by the standard MFDCM when applying PCA; PCA-MFDCM and PCA'-MFDCM. This can be explained by the appropriate use of RST as an information extraction technique. In fact, RC-MFDCM, by using the REDUCT concept, keeps only the most informative features from the whole set of features. For instance, when applying our RC-MFDCM method to the CylB data set, the number of selected features is only 7 attributes. However, when applying the PCA-MFDCM to the same database, the number of the retained features is set to 16. We can notice that PCA preserves additional features than necessary which leads to affect the PCA-MFDCM classification task by producing less accuracy in comparison to the RC-MFDCM results. On the other hand, RC-MFDCM based on the REDUCT concept, selects the minimal set of features from the original database and can guarantee that the reduct attributes will be the most relevant for the classification task. Based on these selected attributes, the accuracies of the algorithms are calculated. From Table 2, we notice that the classification accuracy of our RC-MFDCM is notably better than the one given by PCA-MFDCM for almost all the data sets. We can, also, notice that the RST-MFDCM classification results are better than the ones given by PCA'-MFDCM. Same remark is noticed for both the sensitivity and the specificity criteria. For instance, when applying the RST-MFDCM to the CylB database, the classification accuracy is set to 97.26%. However, when applying the PCA'-MFDCM to the same database, the accuracy is set to 93.75%. When applying the RC-MFDCM algorithm to the same data set, the classification accuracy of the algorithm is set to 98.42%. However, when applying the PCA-MFDCM to the same database, the accuracy is set to 96.48%. Thus, from this part, we can conclude that the rough information extraction technique is an interesting pre-processor that would be better applied to our proposed fuzzy rough DCA version instead of applying the principal component analysis.

Table 2. Comparison Results of MFDCM Approaches

DB	Sensitivity(%) MFDCM				Specificity(%) MFDCM				Accuracy(%) MFDCM				♯ Attributes MFDCM			
	PCA	RC	PCA'	RST	PCA	RC	PCA'	RST	PCA	RC	PCA'	RST	PCA	PCA'	RC	RST
SN	89.18	91.89	85.58	90.09	83.50	95.87	79.38	85.56	86.53	93.75	82.69	87.98	28	28	20	20
Bio	56.60	83.01	50.94	66.03	54.71	84.90	49.05	58.49	55.66	83.96	50.00	62.26	24	24	19	19
CylB	96.00	98.00	92.50	97.00	96.79	98.39	94.55	97.43	96.48	98.24	93.75	97.26	16	16	7	7
Ch	95.26	98.92	94.66	98.20	95.61	99.60	94.95	99.21	95.43	99.24	94.80	98.68	14	14	11	11
IONO	95.23	96.82	94.44	96.03	97.77	98.66	95.55	98.22	96.86	98.00	95.15	97.43	24	24	19	19
Sck	97.83	98.26	96.53	97.40	97.03	97.99	95.08	96.89	97.08	98.01	95.17	96.92	22	22	20	20
HC	94.90	98.14	92.59	96.75	88.81	96.05	85.52	92.10	92.39	97.28	89.67	94.83	19	19	14	14
GC	90.87	92.33	84.67	87.95	92.28	92.69	90.63	90.35	91.90	92.60	89.00	89.70	17	17	17	17
LR	90.00	95.00	70.00	90.00	91.89	97.29	78.37	94.59	91.22	96.49	75.43	92.98	10	10	5	5
RWW	99.18	99.63	98.18	99.26	99.12	99.56	98.74	99.31	99.16	99.61	98.32	99.27	10	10	6	6

Secondly, from Table 2, we can clearly see that in all databases, RC-MFDCM and PCA-MFDCM outperform the classification accuracy generated by RST-MFDCM and PCA'-MFDCM. For instance, the classification accuracies of RST-MFDCM and PCA'-MFDCM when applied to the IONO database are set to 97.43% and 95.15%, respectively, which are both less than 98.00% and 96.86% generated respectively by RC-MFDCM and PCA-MFDCM. This is explained by the fact that RST-MFDCM and PCA'-MFDCM differ from both RC-MFDCM and PCA-MFDCM in the signal categorization phase. More precisely, both RC-MFDCM and PCA-MFDCM assign different features to different signal categories; a specific feature is assigned for each of the SS and the PAMP signals. However, RST-MFDCM and PCA'-MFDCM use the same attribute to assign it for both SS and PAMP. From these results, we can conclude that it is crucial to assign for each signal category a specific and different feature.

Up to now, we have shown, first, that RST is a more convenient information extraction technique to hybridize with our proposed fuzzy rough DCA version and, second, it is crucial to assign different features to different signal categories. On these fundamental points, our proposed RC-MFDCM algorithm is developed. As we have just shown that our RC-MFDCM outperforms the RST-MFDCM version as well as the MFDCM PCA based versions, in what follows, we will compare the performance of our RC-MFDCM to other well known machine learning classifiers. In fact, since we are focusing on the supervised learning taxonomy and more precisely on the algorithms classification task, we will compare the RC-MFDCM classification results with the standard DCA when applying PCA (PCA-DCA), RC-DCA, PCA-MFDCM, the Support Vector Machine (SVM), the Artificial Neural Network (ANN) and the Decision Tree (DT). Please, note that PCA-DCA, RC-DCA and PCA-MFDCM are based on the concept of assigning different features to different signal categories. The comparison made is in terms of the average of accuracies on the databases presented in Table 2. The parameters of SVM, ANN and DT are set to the most adequate parameters to these algorithms using the Weka software.

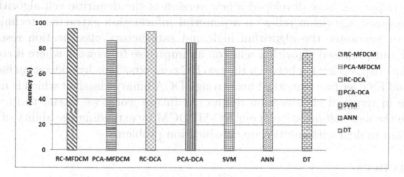

Fig. 1. Classifiers' Average Accuracies

Figure 1 shows that PCA-DCA when applied to the ordered data sets, has better classification accuracy than SVM, ANN and DT confirming the results obtained from literature. Indeed, Figure 1 shows that when applying RST instead of PCA to the standard DCA, the classification accuracy of RC-DCA is notably better than PCA-DCA. It, also, shows that RC-DCA outperforms the mentioned classifiers including SVM, ANN and DT. This confirms the fact that applying RST as an information extraction technique is more convenient for the DCA data pre-processing phase. Furthermore, from Figure 1, we can notice that applying the fuzzy process to the DCA leads to better classification results. We can see that the classification accuracy of PCA-MFDCM is better than the one generated by PCA-DCA. This confirms that applying a fuzzy process to the DCA is more convenient for the algorithm to handle the imprecision within the definition of the two DCs contexts. The fact of coping with this imprecision leads the algorithm to be a more stable classifier. From these remarks, we can conclude that if we hybridize both RST and the fuzzy process, we will obtain a better performance of the classifier. We can clearly notice that our hybrid RC-MFDCM developed model outperforms both PCA-MFDCM, which only applies FST, and RC-DCA which only applies RST. In addition, our RC-MFDCM hybrid model outperforms the rest of the classifiers including PCA-DCA, SVM, DT and ANN.

These encouraging RC-MFDCM results are explained by the appropriate set of features selected and their categorization to their right and specific signal types. RC-MFDCM uses the REDUCT concept to select only the essential part of the original database. This pertinent set of minimal features can guarantee a solid base for the signal categorization step. The RC-MFDCM good classification results are, also, explained by the appropriate categorization of each selected attribute to its right signal type based on both the REDUCT and the CORE concepts. Adding to these interesting notes, RC-MFDCM is coping with the crisp version of the standard DCA as it relies within an imprecise framework. The DCA imprecise context is handled by the use of fuzzy sets. Such hybridization led to the generation of a more stable classifier.

7   Conclusion and Future Work

In this paper, we have developed a new version of the dendritic cell algorithm. Our proposed algorithm relies on a powerful information extraction technique that can guarantee the algorithm high and satisfactory classification results. Indeed, our proposed algorithm relies on an imprecise framework where it copes with the crisp separation between the two DC contexts. This hybridization based RST and FST let to a smoothed fuzzy rough DCA binary classifier which is more reliable in terms of classification results. As future work, we intend to further explore the new instantiation of our RC-MFDCM by extending the ability of the algorithm to deal with multi-class classification problems.

References

1. Greensmith, J., Aickelin, U., Cayzer, S.: Introducing dendritic cells as a novel immune-inspired algorithm for anomaly detection. In: Jacob, C., Pilat, M.L., Bentley, P.J., Timmis, J.I. (eds.) ICARIS 2005. LNCS, vol. 3627, pp. 153–167. Springer, Heidelberg (2005)
2. Greensmith, J., Aickelin, U., Twycross, J.: Articulation and clarification of the dendritic cell algorithm. In: Bersini, H., Carneiro, J. (eds.) ICARIS 2006. LNCS, vol. 4163, pp. 404–417. Springer, Heidelberg (2006)
3. Greensmith, J., Aickelin, U.: The deterministic dendritic cell algorithm. In: Bentley, P.J., Lee, D., Jung, S. (eds.) ICARIS 2008. LNCS, vol. 5132, pp. 291–302. Springer, Heidelberg (2008)
4. Chelly, Z., Elouedi, Z.: FDCM: A fuzzy dendritic cell method. In: Hart, E., McEwan, C., Timmis, J., Hone, A. (eds.) ICARIS 2010. LNCS, vol. 6209, pp. 102–115. Springer, Heidelberg (2010)
5. Chelly, Z., Elouedi, Z.: Further exploration of the fuzzy dendritic cell method. In: Liò, P., Nicosia, G., Stibor, T. (eds.) ICARIS 2011. LNCS, vol. 6825, pp. 419–432. Springer, Heidelberg (2011)
6. Jensen, R.: Data reduction with rough sets. In: Encyclopedia of Data Warehousing and Mining, pp. 556–560 (2009)
7. Chelly, Z., Elouedi, Z.: Rc-dca: A new feature selection and signal categorization technique for the dendritic cell algorithm based on rough set theory. In: Coello Coello, C.A., Greensmith, J., Krasnogor, N., Liò, P., Nicosia, G., Pavone, M. (eds.) ICARIS 2012. LNCS, vol. 7597, pp. 152–165. Springer, Heidelberg (2012)
8. Broekhoven, E., Baets, B.: Fast and accurate center of gravity defuzzification of fuzzy system outputs defined on trapezoidal fuzzy partitions. In: Fuzzy Sets and Systems, pp. 904–918 (2006)
9. Asuncion, A., Newman, D.J.: UCI machine learning repository (2007), http://mlearn.ics.uci.edu/mlrepository.html
10. Chelly, Z., Elouedi, Z.: A new hybrid fuzzy-rough dendritic cell immune classifier. In: Tan, Y., Shi, Y., Mo, H. (eds.) ICSI 2013, Part I. LNCS, vol. 7928, pp. 514–521. Springer, Heidelberg (2013)

An Autonomous Transfer Learning Algorithm for TD-Learners

Anestis Fachantidis[1], Ioannis Partalas[2], Matthew E. Taylor[3], and Ioannis Vlahavas[1]

[1] Department of Informatics, Aristotle University of Thessaloniki
{afa,vlahavas}@csd.auth.gr
[2] Laboratoire LIG, Université Joseph Fourier
ioannis.partalas@imag.fr
[3] School of Electrical Engineering and Computer Science, Washington State University
taylorm@eecs.wsu.edu

Abstract. The main objective of transfer learning is to use the knowledge acquired from a source task in order to boost the learning procedure in a target task. Transfer learning comprises a suitable solution for reinforcement learning algorithms, which often require a considerable amount of training time, especially when dealing with complex tasks. This work proposes an autonomous method for transfer learning in reinforcement learning agents. The proposed method is empirically evaluated in the keepaway and the mountain car domains. The results demonstrate that the proposed method can improve the learning procedure in the target task.

1 Introduction

In recent years, a wealth of *transfer learning* (TL) methods have been developed in the context of *reinforcement learning* (RL) tasks. Typically, when an RL agent leverages TL, it uses knowledge acquired in one or more (*source*) tasks to speed up its learning in a more complex (*target*) task[1].

Although the majority of the work in this field presumes that the source task is connected in an obvious or natural way with the target task, this may not the case in many real life applications where RL transfer could be used. These tasks may have different state and action spaces or even different reward and transition functions. One way to tackle this problem is to use functions that map the state and action variables of the source task to state and action variables of the target task. These functions are called *inter-task mappings* [1].

While inter-task mappings have indeed been used successfully in several settings, we identify two shortcomings. First, an agent typically uses a hand-coded mapping, requiring the knowledge of a domain expert. If human intuition cannot be applied to the problem (e.g. transferring knowledge for robotic joint control between robots with different degrees of freedom), selecting an inter-task mapping may be done randomly requiring extensive, costly experimentation and time not typically available in complex domains or in real applications. Second, even if a correct mapping is used, it is fixed and applied to the entire state-action space, ignoring the important possibility that different mappings may be better for different regions of the target task.

A. Likas, K. Blekas, and D. Kalles (Eds.): SETN 2014, LNAI 8445, pp. 57–70, 2014.

In this paper we propose a generic method for the automated on-line selection of inter-task mappings in transfer learning procedures. The key insight of the proposed method is to select the inter-task mapping for a specific state-action of the target task based on the corresponding source task state-action values.

The main contributions of this work are to 1) Present a novel method for value-based mapping selection, providing its theoretical foundations and an empirical comparison of two different mapping selection criteria; 2) Alleviate the problem of predefining a mapping between a source and target task in TL procedures by presenting a fully automated method for selecting inter-task mappings; 3) Introduce and evaluate a novel algorithm that implements the proposed method.

Experimental results demonstrate success of the proposed algorithm in two RL domains, Mountain Car and Keepaway. Some part of the Keepaway results presented here has been presented also in a workshop [2]. The extensive results and the analysis in this work support the method's key insight on the appropriate mapping selection criteria for value-based mapping selection methods.

2   Background

2.1   Reinforcement Learning

Reinforcement Learning (RL) addresses the problem of how an agent can learn a behaviour through trial-and-error interactions with a dynamic environment [3]. In an RL task the agent, at each time step t, senses the environment's state, $s_t \in S$, where S is the finite set of possible states, and selects an action $a_t \in A(s_t)$ to execute, where $A(s_t)$ is the finite set of possible actions in state s_t. The agent receives a reward, $r_{t+1} \in \Re$, and moves to a new state s_{t+1}. The general goal of the agent is to maximize the expected return, where the return, R_t, is defined as some specific function of the reward sequence.

2.2   Transfer Learning

Transfer Learning refers to the process of using knowledge that has been acquired in a previously learned task, the *source task*, in order to enhance the learning procedure in a new and more complex task, the *target task*. The more similar these two tasks are, the easier it is to transfer knowledge between them. By similarity, we mean the similarity of their underlying Markov Decision Processes (MDP) that is, the transition and reward functions of the two tasks as also their state and action spaces.

The type of knowledge that can be transferred between tasks varies among different TL methods. It can be value functions, entire policies as also a set of samples from a source task used from a batch RL algorithm in a target task [1]. In order to enable transfer learning across tasks with different state variables (i.e., different representations of state) and action sets, one must define how these tasks are related to each other. One way to represent this relation is to use a pair $\langle X^S, X^A \rangle$ of inter-task mappings [1], where the function $X^S(s_i)$ maps one target state variable to one source state variable and $X^A(a)$ maps an action in the target task to an action in the source task (see Table 1 for an example of states mapping).

3 Multiple Inter-task Mappings in TD Learners

This paper proposes a value-based transfer method which is also able to autonomously select the appropriate inter-task mapping. As this transfer method applies to TD-learners it doesn't require any information about the environment, such as a model of its transition or reward functions, therefore being a more computationally efficient method capable for on-line selection of the appropriate mappings.

We assume that an RL agent has been trained in the source task and that it has access to a function Q_{source}, which returns an estimation of the Q value for a state-action pair of the source task. The agent is currently being trained in the target task, learning a function Q_{target} and senses the state s_τ. In order to transfer the knowledge from the source task, the method selects the best state-action mapping $X_{best} = \langle X^S_{best}, X^A_{best} \rangle$, under a novel criterion described next in this text, and adds the corresponding values $Q_{source}(X^S(s_\tau)), X^A(a_\tau))$ from the source task via the selected mapping to the target task values $Q_{target}(s_\tau, a_\tau)$. In our proposed method the best mapping is defined as the mapping that returns the state-action values that had the maximum mean value in the source task compared to the state-action values returned by the other mappings, that is

$$X_{best} = \arg\max_X \sum_{a \in A_{source}} \frac{Q_{source}(X^S(s_\tau), a)}{|A_{source}|}$$

There are alternate ways to select the best mapping based only on the Q-values of the source task, such as selecting the mapping with the maximum action value, but such a choice would imply that a source task action is correctly mapped beforehand and also that the best action for the source task policy is also the best for the target task policy. In order to avoid such assumptions, we use instead the maximum mean Q-Value as our transfer heuristic. Moreover, we analytically argue on the natural meaning and correctness of such a choice.

Specifically, as our value-based transfer method belongs to a family of methods such as Q-value reuse [1], we note two things. Every transfer method that shapes a target task Q-function using a source task's Q-values, is based on two main assumptions:

- The most meaningful and correct inter-task mapping is known beforehand and is used to map the state and action variables of the target task's Q-function to the source task's Q-function.
- Using this inter-task mapping, a greedy (max Q-value) target task policy derived exclusively from the (mapped) source task Q-function, is meaningful in the target task and assists towards its goal.

Simply said, the second assumption implies that given a correct mapping, a high value state-action pair in the source task is expected to be of high value in the target task too. Since our proposed method belongs to this family of methods but with the major difference that we don't manually set (and presume) the best mapping, but instead aim to find it, the first assumption is not met and should at least be relaxed.

Concretely, not necessarily meeting the first assumption means that a target task policy derived by greedily (max $Q(s, a)$) using the source task Q-function is also not necessarily meaningful. This means that selecting mappings for the current target task state based on the maximum source task Q-value implies not only that the actions are correctly mapped but that they are also the best for the target task policy.

To relax these assumptions we don't presume the immediate and greedy next-step use of the source task policy (implied when one uses the maximum $Q^\pi(s, a)$ for the agent's next step) and instead we use the value $V^\pi(s)$ of that source task state but under a different source task policy, the *random next-step* policy. In this policy the agent chooses a random action for the current state and then uses π for the next step and after that.

The random next-step policy protects us from the violation of the assumptions stated above, if we would greedily use the source task Q-function (max Q-value). It is actually **a parsing policy of the source task's state-action values**. Considering this policy leads us to transferring based on the mean Q-value returned by each mapping for the agent's next step.

Specifically, consider the state value function $V^\pi_{source}(s)$ in the source task. Although known from basic MDP theory, we analytically calculate the following in order to demonstrate the natural meaning of the mean Q-value choice:

$$V^\pi_{source}(s) = E_\pi\{R_t | s_t = s\}$$

Based on the conditional expectation theorem and conditioning on all possible actions, the above is equal to:

$$= \sum_\alpha E_\pi\{R_t | s_t = s, \alpha_t = \alpha\} P\{\alpha_t = \alpha | s_t = s\}$$

The probability term above is the policy $\pi(s, \alpha)$, so:

$$= \sum_\alpha E_\pi\{R_t | s_t = s, \alpha_t = \alpha\} \pi(s, \alpha)$$

Since the expectation term above, is $Q^\pi(s, \alpha)$ the above is equal to:

$$= \sum_\alpha Q^\pi(s, \alpha) \pi(s, \alpha)$$

Since under our policy the next action in a state s is chosen randomly (uniformly): $\pi(s, \alpha) = \frac{1}{|A_{source}(s)|} = \frac{1}{k}$ so

$$V^\pi_{source}(s) = \frac{1}{k} \sum_\alpha Q^\pi(s, \alpha) \tag{1}$$

And so using a random policy just for the next step and then assuming following π as usual, implies that the value of the state s when following our modified policy, equals the mean Q-value of the state s (RHS of Equation 1). As we mentioned above using the next-step random policy protects our proposed method from an "assumption over assumption" pitfall.

The above insight is implemented in our proposed TL algorithm, Value-Addition. Algorithm 1 shows the pseudo-code of the transferring procedure.

Algorithm 1. Value-Addition procedure: Multiple Mappings in TD Learners

1: **procedure** VALUE-ADDITION($s_\tau, X, Q_{target}, Q_{source}$)
2:     $bestMeanQValue \leftarrow 0; bestMapping \leftarrow 0$
3:     $N \leftarrow |X|$ ▷ the number of mappings considered
4:     **for** $i \leftarrow 1 \ldots N$ **do**
5:         $s \leftarrow X_i^S(s_\tau)$
6:         $meanQValue \leftarrow 0$
7:         **for all** $a \in A_{source}(s)$ **do**
8:             $meanQValue \leftarrow meanQValue + Q_{source}(s, a)$
9:         $meanQValue \leftarrow meanQValue/|A_{source}(s)|$
10:        **if** $meanQValue > bestMeanQValue$ **then**
11:            $bestMeanQValue \leftarrow meanQValue$
12:            $bestMapping \leftarrow i$
13:    $\chi_S \leftarrow X_{bestMapping}^S$
14:    $\chi_A \leftarrow X_{bestMapping}^A$
15:    $s \leftarrow \chi_s(s_\tau)$
16:    **for** $a \in A_{source}(s)$ **do**
17:        $Q_{target}(s_\tau, \chi_A^{-1}(a)) \leftarrow Q_{target}(s_\tau, \chi_A^{-1}(a)) + Q_{source}(s, a)$

On lines 3–12, the algorithm finds the best mapping for the current target task state s_τ from instances that are recognized in the target task.

After the best mapping is found, the algorithm adds the Q-values from the source task to the Q-values from the target task (lines 13–16). Through the inverse use of the best action mapping, χ_A^{-1} the algorithm updates the value of the equivalent target task action. Note that if a target action is not mapped to a source action, the algorithm does not add an extra value. Finally, the updated Q-values in the target task can be used for a regular TD update, action selection, etc.

4 Domains

4.1 Keepaway

Keepaway [4], is a subset of the RoboCup robot soccer domain, where K keepers try to hold the ball for as long as possible, while T takers (usually $T = K - 1$) try to intercept the ball (Figure 1). The agents are placed within a fixed region at the start of each episode, which ends when the ball leaves this region or the takers intercept it.[1]

The task is modelled as a semi-Markov decision process (SMDP), as it defines macro-actions that may last for several time steps. The available macro-actions for a keeper with ball possession are *HoldBall* and *Pass-k-ThenReceive*, where k is another keeper. A keeper executing *HoldBall* remains stationary. A keeper executing *Pass-k-ThenReceive* performs a series of actions in order to pass the ball to team-mate k and then executes the *Receive* sub-policy: If no keeper possesses the ball and he is the closest keeper to the ball then he executes macro-action *GoToBall*, otherwise he executes macro-action *GetOpen* in order to move to an open area. *Receive* is also executed by keepers when they don't possess the ball.

---

[1] For more information please refer to the original paper [4].

The features that describe the state of the environment for a keeper K_1 that possesses the ball are: a)
the distances of all agents to the center of the field, b)
the distance of all other players to K_1, c) the distances
of K_1's team-mates to the closest opponent, and d) the
minimal angles between K_1's team-mates and an opponent with the vertex at K_1.

The task becomes harder as extra keepers and takers are added to the fixed-sized field, due to the increased number of state variables on one hand, and the
increased probability of ball interception in an increasingly crowded region on the other.

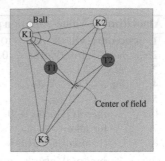

Fig. 1. 3 vs. 2 Keepaway

4.2 Mountain Car

Our experiments use the mountain car domain [5]. The standard 2D task (MC2D) requires an under-powered car to drive up a hill. The state is described by two continuous
variables, the position $x \in [-1.2, 0.6]$, and velocity $v_x \in [-0.07, 0.07]$. The actions are
{Neutral, Left, Right}, and the goal state is $x >= 0.5$, with a reward of -1 on each time
step. The 3D mountain car (MC3D) task extends the 2D task by adding an extra spatial
dimension [6]. The state is composed by four continuous variables. The coordinates x
and y are in $[-1.2, 0.6]$, and the velocities v_x and v_y are in $[-0.07.0.07]$. The actions
are {Neutral, West, East, South, North}, the goal is $x, y >= 0.5$ and the reward is -1
on each time step.

5 Experiments

5.1 Transferring with Value-Addition in Mountain Car 3D

First, an agent is trained in the Mountain Car 2D task (source task). The algorithm
that is used for training in the source task as also in the target task, is the Sarsa(λ)
using linear tile-coding (CMAC) with 14 tilings. The learning rate α is set to 0.5. The ϵ
parameter is set to 0.1, which is multiplied by 0.99 at each episode, and λ to 0.95. These
settings are the default in the Mountain Car package and they are the best found so far.
While acting in the source task, the agent is recording the weights of its CMAC function
approximator for each tiling and action. The resulting data file captures the state of the
source task function approximator and is the knowledge we need to transfer and use in
the target task. Finally, in the source task the agent was trained for 1600 episodes.

For the MC3D task we use the same settings as above except for α which is set to
0.2. We select this setting as it was found to yield very good results [7]. For both the
MC2D and MC3D tasks we set the maximum steps of an episode to 5000. If the agent
exceeds the maximum number of steps without reaching the goal state, then the episode
ends and the agent is placed at the bottom of the hill.

In this experiment, Value-Addition uses a pool of 7 mappings that we manually set
before the experiment's execution. The first four mappings we set are considered intuitive since they map position state variables of the MC2D to position state variables

Table 1. An intuitive inter-task mapping in Mountain Car mapping correctly same-type state variables and similar effect action variables

3D variable	2D variable	3D action	2D action
x	x	Neutral	Neutral
y	-	West	Left
v_x	v_x	East	Right
v_y	-	South	-
		North	-

in MC3D and consequently the velocity state variables of MC3D to the velocity state variable of MC2D. See Table 1 for an example of an intuitive mapping. For the other three mappings, the first one maps in an intuitively correct way the action variables but not the state variables. The second one maps the states intuitively but maps actions in a different way (as an example, it maps the action Neutral of MC2D to the action East in MC3D) Finally the third mapping maps both state and action variables in a non-intuitive way.

For comparison, various other algorithm were tested besides Value-Addition. Each algorithm was selected in order to examine some specific hypothesis of this study: i) A standard Sarsa(λ) agent without transfer, in order to evaluate the quality and feasibility of transfer using Value-Addition; ii) an agent implementing transfer learning using random mappings from the pool of the 7 mappings described earlier, in order to demonstrate the importance of using the correct mapping; iii) an agent using the single most intuitive mapping with the Q-Value Reuse algorithm [1], in order to demonstrate the ability of Value addition to achieve similar performance to a transfer algorithm that has been given beforehand a correct mapping and is not able to autonomously change that selection - and finally iv) an agent using Value-Addition but transferring from the mapping that has the maximum action value (see Section 3) in order to evaluate the proposed criterion of using instead, the mean state-action value.

Figure 2 depicts the results of this experiment using the time-to-threshold metric. The x axis shows various thresholds representing the steps needed by the agent to find the goal (exit) and the y axis represents the corresponding training time needed to achieve these goals. Each curve averages the results from 15 runs of it's corresponding algorithm.

The Value-Addition shows a statistically significant (at $p < 0.05$) performance increase from the no-transfer case. Using a random mapping implements negative transfer since it's performance is worse than the no-transfer case. Clearly this shows the importance of correctly selecting an inter-task mapping. Moreover, Value-Addition in its standard set-up performs better than value addition using the mapping that has the maximum action value (at $p < 0.05$). This finding confirms the method's key intuition described in section 3, for selecting a mapping based on its average state-action value and not on their maximal one. Even more interestingly value addition demonstrates better (not stat. sig.) performance than the single-mapping algorithm (Q-Value Reuse). This finding is important since as it is mentioned above, the single mapping algorithm was using an intuitively-correct mapping given to it beforehand whereas Value - Addition had to discover it.

Furthermore, we conducted an analysis on the mappings selected by Value-Addition in MC3D. Table 2 shows how many times Value-Addition used each of the 7 mappings

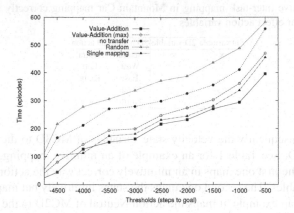

Fig. 2. Time-to-threshold metric for different thresholds in the 3D MC

Table 2. The seven available mappings for Value-Addition in MC, the percentage of the total time and the average state in which they were selected

Mapping	Mapping Description	Percentage	mean x	mean y	mean vx	mean vy
0	intuitive	25.1	-0.427	-0.453	-0.003613	0.00346525
1	intuitive	34.7	-0.458	-0.141	0.00311873	-0.00271896
2	intuitive	0	-	-	-	-
3	intuitive	0	-	-	-	-
4	intuitive actions	40.2	-0.473	-0.451	0.001659	0.00245182
5	intuitive states	0	-	-	-	-
6	not intuitive	0	-	-	-	-
All		100	-0.456816	-0.344	0.000842	0.0009142

(described earlier in this section). The four rightmost columns of the table show the mean state values of the states where each mapping was used. Also, the last row represents the general case independently from the mapping selected. We can observe how each mapping's mean state value differentiates from that of "all mappings" mean state value showing that Value-Addition selects mappings also in relation to the specific state the agent is. As an example, mapping #4 is used more in west and south positions of the state space because it's mean x and y values are smaller that the corresponding ones of "All".

Interestingly, the mappings analysis shows that the mappings selected were at a 59.8% those considered as intuitive and correct for MC . Moreover, Value-Addition may also select a mapping that maps state variables in a non intuitive way (i.e. a velocity state variable to a position state variable), but it never selects a non-intuitive action mapping (it finds the intuitive ones). The proposed method is more sensitive on the action mappings differences than that among state mappings. This behaviour is explained by the fact that different state mappings may have the same average action value but different action mappings tend to have different average action values thus resulting to a behaviour particularly able to differentiate and select among action mappings.

5.2 Transferring with Value-Addition in Keepaway

This section evaluates the proposed approach in Keepaway. The dimensions of the Keepaway region are set to 25m × 25m and remains fixed for all source and target tasks. The algorithm that is used to train the keepers is the SMDP variation of Sarsa(λ) [3]. Additionally, we use linear tile-coding for function approximation with settings shown to work well in the Keepaway domain [8].[2]

To evaluate the performance of the proposed approach in Keepaway we also use the time-to-threshold metric. In Keepaway this threshold corresponds to a number of seconds that keepers maintain ball possession. In order to conclude that the keepers have learned the task successfully, the average performance of 1,000 consecutive episodes must be greater than the threshold. We compare (1) the time-to-threshold without transfer learning with (2) the time-to-threshold with transfer learning **plus the training time in the source task**. Finally, an important aspect of the experiments concerns the way that the mappings are produced. For the Keepaway domain, the production of the mappings can be automatic. More specifically, any K^t vs. T^t task can be mapped to a K^s vs. T^s task, where $K^s < K^t$ and $T^s < T^t$, simply by deleting $K^t - K^s$ team-mates and $T^t - T^s$ opponents of the keeper with ball possession. The actual number of different mappings is:

$$|X| = \binom{K^t - 1}{K^s - 1}\binom{T^t}{T^s} = \frac{(K^t - 1)!T^t!}{(K^s - 1)!(K^t - K^s)!T^s!(T^t - T^s)!}$$

Transfer into 4 vs. 3 from 3 vs. 2. This subsection evaluates the performance of the proposed approach on the 4 vs. 3 target task using a threshold of 9 simulated seconds. We use the 3 vs. 2 task as the source and experiment with different number of training episodes, ranging from 0 (no transfer) to 3,200.

Table 3 shows the training time and average performance (in seconds) in the source task, as well as time-to-threshold and total time in the target task for different amount of training episodes in the source task. The results are averaged over 10 independent runs and the last column displays the standard deviation. The time-to-threshold without transfer learning is about 13.38 simulated hours.

We first notice that the proposed approach leads to lower time-to-threshold in the target task compared to the standard algorithm that does not use transfer learning. This is due to the fact that the more the training episodes in the source task the better the Q-function that is learned. Note that for 800 episodes of the 3 vs. 2 task, the keepers are able to hold the ball for an average of 8.5 seconds, while for 1600 episodes their performance increases to 12.2 seconds. As the number of the training episodes in the source task increase the time that is required to reach the threshold decreases, showing that our method successfully improves performance in the target task.

The total time of the proposed approach in the target task is also less than the time-to-threshold without transfer learning in many cases. The best performance is 8.21 hours,

---

[2] We use 32 tilings for each variable. The width of each tile is set to 3 meters for the distance variables and 10 degrees for the angle variables. We set the learning rate, α, to 0.125, ϵ to 0.01 and λ to 0. These values remain fixed for all experiments.

Table 3. The table shows the training time and average performance in the source task, as well as time-to-threshold and total time in the target task. The best time-to-threshold and total time are in **bold**.

	3 vs. 2		4 vs. 3		
#episodes	train time	performance	time-to-thr.	total time	st. dev.
0	0	-	13.38	13.38	2.02
100	0.11	4.38	13.19	13.30	1.77
200	0.23	4.67	12.59	12.82	2.10
400	0.72	6.71	12.08	12.80	1.70
800	1.73	8.52	10.28	12.01	0.97
1600	4.73	12.20	3.48	**8.21**	1.16
2500	8.42	16.02	4.16	12.44	0.60
3200	12.17	16.84	**2.76**	14.95	0.28

which corresponds to a reduction of 38.6% of the time-to-threshold without transfer learning. This performance is achieved when training the agents for 1600 training episodes in the source task. This result shows that rather than directly learning on the target task, it is actually faster to learn on the source task, use our transfer method, and only then learn on the target task.

In order to detect significant difference among the performances of the algorithms we use paired t-tests with 95% confidence. We perform seven paired t-tests, one for each pair of the algorithm without transfer learning and the cases with transfer learning. The test shows that the proposed approach is significantly better when it is trained with 800 and 1600 episodes.

Scaling up to 5 vs. 4 and 6 vs. 5. We also test the performance of the proposed approach in the 5 vs. 4 target task. The 5 vs. 4 threshold is set to 8.5 seconds. The 3 vs. 2 task with 1,600, 2,500 and 3,200 training episodes and the 4 vs. 3 task with 4,000 and 6,000 training episodes are used as source tasks. Table 4 shows the training times, time-to-threshold and their sum for the different source tasks and number of episodes averaged over 10 independent runs along with the standard deviation.

In all cases the proposed approach outperforms the no-transfer case. It is interesting to note that the best time-to-threshold is achieved, when using 3 vs. 2 as a source task, with fewer episodes than when using 4 vs. 3 as a source task. This means that a relatively simple source task may provide *more* benefit than a more complex source task. In addition, the 3 vs. 2 task requires less training time, as it is easier than the 4 vs. 3 task. We perform 5 paired t-tests, one for each case of the proposed approach against learning without transfer. The proposed method achieves statistically significantly higher performance (at the 95% confidence level) in all cases.

Additionally, we also considered the 6 vs. 5 task, where the threshold is set to 8 seconds. As source tasks, we use the 3 vs. 2 tasks with 1600 and 3200 training episodes, the 4 vs. 3 task with 4000 training episodes and the 5 vs. 4 task with 3500 and 8000 episodes. Table 5 shows the results in a similar fashion to the previous table.

The best total time is achieved when a 3 vs. 2 task (trained for 3200 episodes) is used as the source task, reducing the total time roughly 68%. As in the case of 5 vs. 4, we again notice that when a simpler source task is used, both the time-to-threshold and the total training time decrease. This is an indication of the role of the use of the multiple mapping functions. The 6 vs. 5 game is decomposed to 25 5 vs. 4 instances to 100 4

Table 4. Average training times (in hours) for 5 vs. 4. The results are averaged over 10 independent trials. The best time-to-threshold and total time are in **bold**.

source task	#episodes	tr. time	time-to-thr.	total time	st. dev.
-	0	0	26.30	26.30	2.85
3 vs. 2	1600	4.73	15.54	20.27	3.24
3 vs. 2	2500	8.42	8.88	17.31	3.23
3 vs. 2	3200	12.17	**3.43**	**15.60**	1.24
4 vs. 3	4000	7.52	10.07	17.59	1.49
4 vs. 3	6000	12.32	9.26	21.58	1.92

Table 5. Average training times (in hours) for 6 vs. 5. The results are averaged over 10 independent trials. The best time-to-threshold and total time are in **bold**.

source task	#episodes	tr. time	6 vs. 5	total	st. dev.
-	0	0	45.66	45.66	4.77
3 vs. 2	1600	4.73	31.77	36.50	3.87
3 vs. 2	3200	12.17	**2.50**	**14.67**	0.27
4 vs. 3	4000	7.52	33.34	40.86	3.78
5 vs. 4	3500	5.17	45.38	50.55	2.92
5 vs. 4	8000	16.08	28.43	44.51	2.39

vs. 3 instances and to 100 3 vs. 2 instances. In the second case the algorithm searches among a larger number of source instances and it is more likely to get better Q−values as more situations are considered in the phase of the source values transfer. Note that in the case of 5 vs. 4 (3500 episodes) as the source task, there is no improvement. These results demonstrate that the proposed approach scales well to large problems, especially when a small task is used as the source.

Besides the benefit of using multiple mappings with Value Addition compared to a single predefined mapping which requires domain knowledge, we further investigate if there are also performance benefits of using multiple mappings with Value-Addition in Keepaway. We compare the proposed approach with a variation that uses only one mapping function. We use the mapping function that corresponds to the first K_s keepers and T_s takers as they are ordered increasingly to their distance from the ball. This way we select the agents that are nearest to the learning agent and we shall refer to it as *nearest agents* (NA) mapping. We must mention here that the NA mapping is similar to the one that is used in [1].

We compare the two methods in the 4vs3 target task using the 3vs2 task as source. Table 6 shows the training times spent in 4vs3 task for different amounts of training episodes in the source task along with the total time averaged over ten independent repetitions. The last column shows the corresponding results of the proposed approach Multiple Mappings (MM) for comparison purposes.

The first observation is that in all cases MM outperforms NA. An interesting outcome is that NA in all cases did not succeeded to reduce the total training time. Additionally, in the case of 800 episodes we have negative transfer. We perform three paired t-tests between NA and MM for the different cases of training episodes in the source task. At a confidence level of 95% the tests show that MM performs significantly better than NA. The results indicate that using only a single mapping function is not adequate to enhance the learning procedure in the target task.

Table 6. Average training times for 4vs3 of the NA algorithm for different number of training episodes in the source task averaged over 10 repetitions

3vs2		4vs3-NA	4vs3-MM
#episodes	tr. time	total time	total time
0	0	13.38	13.38
800	1.73	15.52	12.01
1600	4.73	16.92	8.21
2500	8.42	18.63	12.44

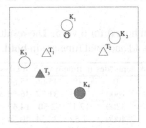

Fig. 3. Example of the NA mapping in the 4vs3 task

An example that justifies this observation is given in Figure 3. The non-shaded agents are those considered by the NA mapping. In this case, K_1 can pass either to K_2 or K_3. Note that these keepers are blocked by takers T_1 and T_2 and ball interception is very likely. However K_4 is quite open, and a pass to K_4 would seem the appropriate action in this case. This shows that NA mapping is not always the best mapping in the source task and **that a single mapping can lead to inferior behaviour**.

6 Related Work

An approach that reuses past policies from solved source tasks to speed up learning in the target task is proposed in [9]. A restriction of this approach is that the tasks (source and target) must have the same action and state space. In contrast, our method allows the state and action spaces to be different between the target and the source task.

Advice based methods have been proposed in the past [10,11]. [10] proposed a method that uses a list of learned rules from the source task as advices to the target task. The authors introduce three different utilization schemes of the advice. [11] export rules in first-order logic and translate them into advices.

A method presented in [1] and named *Transfer via inter-task mappings*, initializes the weights of the target task with the learned weights of the source task using mapping functions. The method depends strongly on the approximation function that is used in both tasks, as the function that transfers the weights is altered according to the approximation method. Additionally, a different approach is introduced in the same work which is named *Q-Value Reuse*. This method is similar to the way that we add the Q-values from the source task to the target task. The main difference is that in our method, we allow the use of multiple mappings and there is no need for a single mapping given beforehand by a domain expert.

An automatic method for constructing the mapping functions using exhaustive search on the set of all possible mappings was proposed in [7]. The main disadvantage of this method is that the computational complexity grows exponentially to the number of the state variables and actions.

In [12], each possible inter-state mapping is considered as an expert and with the use of a multi-armed bandit algorithm the agent decides which mapping to use. This method shows significant improvement but its performance is surpassed in the long run as it continues to explore always taking "advice" from low return experts.

Another promising method that has been proposed [13] is capable of learning a continuously parametrized function representing a stochastic mapping between the state spaces of two MDP's (soft homomorphism). However, this work doesn't handle action mappings and requires the explicit learning of a model in the source task and an on-line learning process of the mapping function, in the target task.

Finally there are other TL methods which are focused on *learning* a mapping and not on computationally discovering it like Value-Addition does. In an example of a work that aims to learn a mapping between arbitrary tasks [14], the authors use a data-driven method to discover a mapping between two tasks in a new dimensional space using sparse coding. However, the authors do not consider allowing multiple mappings and their method applies to model based RL agents as opposed to this work which applies to any value-based RL algorithm.

7 Conclusions

Concluding, this work presented a novel method for autonomous multiple-mappings selection in TL. Results in Mountain Car 3D and on several instances of Keepaway have shown that Value-Addition can successfully select and use multiple mappings and improve learning via transfer. Using different mappings in different state space regions was significantly beneficial in Keepaway. This result further indicates that in some domains the use of multiple mapping is not only a step towards a more autonomous transfer of knowledge, but that it can also help to achieve better performance compared to a single mapping, even if that mapping is considered an intuitively correct one. Furthermore the results presented in this work provide similar conclusions, regarding the efficacy of value function transfer, to those presented by Taylor et al. [1]. However, we emphasize that the proposed method is able to succeed without requiring that a human provides a single inter-task mapping, but instead may autonomously select multiple mappings from a large set, successfully improving the autonomy of TD transfer learning.

Two limitations of the proposed method are that: 1) it requires a set of mappings to be given beforehand, then it is able to select the best of them. However, this set can theoretically be exhaustive and it can be generated in an automatic way and 2) since Value-Addition belongs to a family of value-based transfer methods it assumes the similarity of two state-action pairs if both of these have high values in their parent tasks. However, as discussed in Section 3, this assumption is partially relaxed through the use of the mean-value transfer criterion.

The above let us conclude with some ideas for future work. First, new methods to autonomously construct or learn the inter-task mappings should be explored, second, for less related transfer domains, TL algorithms should exploit other MDP similarity features to identify the correct mappings such as the task's dynamics etc. Finally, more work is needed to further investigate as to where and how multiple mappings transfer should be chosen compared to single-mapping methodologies, even if a correct mapping is known beforehand.

Acknowledgments. The authors thank the reviewers for their comments and insights. This work was supported in part by NSF IIS-1149917.

References

1. Taylor, M.E., Stone, P., Liu, Y.: Transfer learning via inter-task mappings for temporal difference learning. Journal of Machine Learning Research 8, 2125–2167 (2007)
2. Fachantidis, A., Partalas, I., Taylor, M.E., Vlahavas, I.: Transfer learning via multiple inter-task mappings. In: Sanner, S., Hutter, M. (eds.) EWRL 2011. LNCS, vol. 7188, pp. 225–236. Springer, Heidelberg (2012)
3. Sutton, R.S., Barto, A.G.: Reinforcement Learning, An Introduction. MIT Press (1998)
4. Stone, P., Sutton, R.S., Kuhlmann, G.: Reinforcement learning for RoboCup-soccer keep-away. Adaptive Behavior 13(3), 165–188 (2005)
5. Singh, S.P., Sutton, R.S.: Reinforcement learning with replacing eligibility traces. Machine Learning 22(1-3), 123–158 (1996)
6. Taylor, M.E., Jong, N.K., Stone, P.: Transferring instances for model-based reinforcement learning. In: Daelemans, W., Goethals, B., Morik, K. (eds.) ECML PKDD 2008, Part II. LNCS (LNAI), vol. 5212, pp. 488–505. Springer, Heidelberg (2008)
7. Taylor, M.E., Kuhlmann, G., Stone, P.: Autonomous transfer for reinforcement learning. In: 7th AAMAS, pp. 283–290 (2008)
8. Stone, P., Kuhlmann, G., Taylor, M.E., Liu, Y.: Keepaway soccer: From machine learning testbed to benchmark. In: Bredenfeld, A., Jacoff, A., Noda, I., Takahashi, Y. (eds.) RoboCup 2005. LNCS (LNAI), vol. 4020, pp. 93–105. Springer, Heidelberg (2006)
9. Fernández, F., Veloso, M.: Probabilistic policy reuse in a reinforcement learning agent. In: 5th International Joint Conference on Autonomous Agents and Multiagent Systems, pp. 720–727 (2006)
10. Taylor, M.E., Stone, P.: Cross-domain transfer for reinforcement learning. In: 24th International Conference on Machine Learning, pp. 879–886 (2007)
11. Torrey, L., Shavlik, J., Walker, T., Maclin, R.: Skill acquisition via transfer learning and advice taking. In: Fürnkranz, J., Scheffer, T., Spiliopoulou, M. (eds.) ECML 2006. LNCS (LNAI), vol. 4212, pp. 425–436. Springer, Heidelberg (2006)
12. Talvitie, E., Singh, S.: An experts algorithm for transfer learning. In: 20th IJCAI, pp. 1065–1070 (2007)
13. Sorg, J., Singh, S.: Transfer via soft homomorphisms. In: Proceedings of the 8th International Conference on Autonomous Agents and Multiagent Systems, AAMAS 2009, vol. 2, pp. 741–748 (2009)
14. Ammar, H.B., Tuyls, K., Taylor, M.E., Driessen, K., Weiss, G.: Reinforcement learning transfer via sparse coding. In: International Conference on Autonomous Agents and Multiagent Systems, AAMAS (June 2012)

Play Ms. Pac-Man Using an Advanced Reinforcement Learning Agent

Nikolaos Tziortziotis, Konstantinos Tziortziotis, and Konstantinos Blekas

Department of Computer Science & Engineering, University of Ioannina
P.O.Box 1186, Ioannina 45110 - Greece
{ntziorzi,cs091771,kblekas}@cs.uoi.gr

Abstract. Reinforcement Learning (RL) algorithms have been promising methods for designing intelligent agents in games. Although their capability of learning in real time has been already proved, the high dimensionality of state spaces in most game domains can be seen as a significant barrier. This paper studies the popular arcade video game Ms. Pac-Man and outlines an approach to deal with its large dynamical environment. Our motivation is to demonstrate that an abstract but informative state space description plays a key role in the design of efficient RL agents. Thus, we can speed up the learning process without the necessity of Q-function approximation. Several experiments were made using the multiagent MASON platform where we measured the ability of the approach to reach optimum generic policies which enhances its generalization abilities.

Keywords: Intelligent Agents, Reinforcement Learning, Ms. Pac-Man.

1 Introduction

During the last two decades there is a significant research interest within the AI community on constructing intelligent agents for digital games that can adapt to the behavior of players and to dynamically changed environments [1]. Reinforcement learning (RL) covers the capability of learning from experience [2–4], and thus offers a very attractive and powerful platform for learning to control an agent in unknown environments with limited prior knowledge. In general, games are ideal test environments for the RL paradigm, since they are goal-oriented sequential decision problems, where each decision can have long-term effect. They also hold other interesting properties, such as random events, unknown environments, hidden information and enormous decision spaces, that make RL to be well suited to complex and uncertain game environments.

In the literature there is a variety of computer games domains that have been studied by using reinforcement learning strategies, such as *chess*, *backgammon* and *tetris* (see [5] for a survey). Among them, the arcade video game Ms. Pac-Man constitutes a very interested test environment. Ms. Pac-Man was released in early 80's and since then it has become one of the most popular video games of all time. That makes Ms. Pac-Man very attractive is its simplicity of playing

A. Likas, K. Blekas, and D. Kalles (Eds.): SETN 2014, LNAI 8445, pp. 71–83, 2014.

in combination with the complex strategies that are required to obtain a good performance [6].

The game of Ms. Pac-Man meets all the criteria of a reinforcement learning task. The environment is difficult to predict, because the ghost behaviour is stochastic and their paths are unpredictable. The reward function can be easily defined covering particular game events and score requirements. Furthermore, there is a small action space consisting of the four directions in which Ms. Pac-Man can move (up, down, right, left) at each time step. However, a difficulty is encountered when designing the state space for the particular domain. Specifically, a large amount of features are required for describing a single game snapshot. In many cases this does not allow reaching optimal solutions and may limit the efficiency of the learning agent. Besides, a significant issue is whether the state description can fit into the memory, and whether optimization can be solved in reasonable time or not. In general, the size of the problem may grow exponentially with the number of variables. Therefore working efficiently in a reinforcement learning framework means reducing the problem size and establishing a reasonable state representation.

To tackle these disadvantages several approximations, simplifications and/or feature extraction techniques have been proposed. In [6] for example, a rule-based methodology was applied where the rules were designed by the human and their values were learned by reinforcement learning. On the other hand, neural networks have been also employed for value function approximation with either a single or multiple outputs [7,8]. Further search techniques have been applied to developing agents for Ms. Pac-Man, including genetic programming [9], Monte-Carlo tree search [10,11] and teaching advising techniques [12].

In this study we investigate the Ms. Pac-Man game since it offers a real time dynamic environment and it involves sequential decision making. Our study is focused on the designing of an appropriate state space for building an efficient RL agent to the MS. Pac-Man game domain. The proposed state representation is informative by incorporating all the necessary knowledge about any game snapshot. At the same time it presents an abstract description so as to reduce computational cost and to accelerate learning procedure without compromising the decision quality. We demonstrate here that providing a proper feature set as input to the learner is of outmost importance for simple reinforcement learning algorithms, such as SARSA. The last constitutes the main contribution of our study and it suggests the need of careful modeling of the domain aiming at addressing adequately the problem. Several experiments have been conducted where we measured the learning capabilities of the proposed methodology and its efficiency in discovering optimal policy in unknown mazes. It should be emphasized that, although different Pac-Man simulators have been applied within the literature and a direct head-to-head comparison of the performance is not practical, we believe that our method yields very promising results with considerable improved performance.

The remaining of this paper is organized as follows: In section 2 we give a brief description of the Ms. Pac-Man game environment. Section 3 describes the background of the reinforcement learning schemes and presents some preliminaries about the general temporal-difference (TD) scheme used for training the proposed Ms. Pac-Man agent. The proposed state space structure is presented at section 4 while the details of our experiments together with some initial results are illustrated in section 5. Finally, section 6 draws conclusions and discusses some issues for future study.

2   The Game of Pac-Man

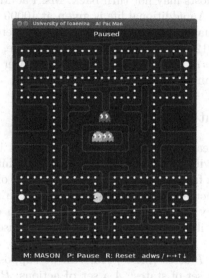

Fig. 1. A screenshot of the Pac-Man game in a typical maze (*Pink maze*)

Pac-Man is an 1980s arcade video-game that reached immense success. It is considered to be one of the most popular video games to date. The player maneuvers Ms. Pac-Man in a maze that consists of a number of dots (or pills). The goal is to eat all of the dots. Figure 1 illustrates a typical such maze. It contains 220 dots with each of them to worth 10 points. A level is finished when all the dots are eaten ('win'). There are also four ghosts in the maze who try to catch Ms. Pac-Man, and if they succeed, Pac-Man loses a life.

Four power-up items are found in the corners of the maze, called power pills, which are worth 40 points each. When Ms. Pac-Man consumes a power-pill all ghosts become edible, i.e. the ghosts turn blue for a short period (15 seconds), they slow down and try to escape from Ms. Pac-Man. During this time, Ms. Pac-Man is able to eat them, which is worth 200, 400, 800 and 1600 points, consecutively. The point values are reset to 200 each time another power pill is eaten, so the player would want to eat all four ghosts per power dot. If a ghost is eaten, it remains hurry back to the center of the maze where the ghost is reborn. Our investigations are restricted to learning an optimal policy for the maze presented at Fig. 1, so the maximum achievable score is $220 \times 10 + 4 \times 40 + 4 \times (200 + 400 + 800 + 1600) = 14360.$ [1]

In the original version of Pac-Man, ghosts move on a complex but deterministic route, so it is possible to learn a deterministic action sequence that does not require any observations. In the case of Ms. Pac-Man, randomness was added to the movement of the ghosts. Therefore there is no single optimal action sequence and observations are necessary for optimal decision making. In our case ghosts moved randomly in 20% of the time and straight towards Ms. Pac-Man in the remaining 80%, but ghosts may not turn back. Ms. Pac-Man starts playing the game with three lives. An additional life is given at 10000 points.

It must be noted that, although the domain is discrete it has a very large state space. There are 1293 distinct locations in the maze, and a complete state consists of the locations of Pac-Man, the ghosts, the power pills, along with each ghosts previous move and whether or not it is edible.

3   Reinforcement Learning

In the reinforcement learning (RL) framework an agent is trained to perform a task by interacting with an unknown environment. While taking actions, the agent receives feedback from the environment in the form of rewards. The notion of RL framework is focused on gradually improving the agent's behavior and estimating its *policy* by maximizing the total long-term expected reward. An excellent way for describing a RL task is through the use of Markov Decision Processes.

A *Markov Decision Process* (MDP) [13] can be supposed as a tuple $(\mathcal{S}, \mathcal{A}, P, R, \gamma)$, where $\mathcal{S}$ is a set of states; $\mathcal{A}$ a set of actions; $P : \mathcal{S} \times \mathcal{A} \times \mathcal{S} \to [0, 1]$ is a Markovian transition model that specifies the probability, $P(s, a, s')$, of transition to a state s' when taken an action a in state s; $R : \mathcal{S} \times \mathcal{A} \to \mathbb{R}$ is the reward function for a state-action pair; and $\gamma \in (0, 1)$ is the discount factor for future rewards. A *stationary policy*, $\pi : \mathcal{S} \to \mathcal{A}$, for a MDP is a mapping from states to actions and denotes a mechanism for choosing actions. An *episode* can be supposed as a sequence of state transitions: $< s_1, s_2, \ldots, s_T >$. An agent repeatedly chooses actions until the current episode terminates, followed by a reset to a starting state.

The notion of *value function* is of central interest in reinforcement learning tasks. Given a policy π, the value $V^\pi(s)$ of a state s is defined as the expected discounted returns obtained when starting from this state until the current episode terminates following policy π:

$$V^\pi(s) = E\left[\sum_{t=0}^{\infty} \gamma^t R(s_t) | s_0 = s, \pi\right] . \tag{1}$$

---

[1] In the original version of the game, a fruit appears near the center of the maze and remains there for a while. Eating this fruit is worth 100 points.

As it is well-known, the value function must obey the *Bellman's equation*:

$$V^{\pi}(s) = E_{\pi}\left[R(s_t) + \gamma V^{\pi}(s_{t+1})|s_t = s\right],\tag{2}$$

which expresses a relationship between the values of successive states in the same episode. In the same way, the state-action value function (Q-function), $Q(s,a)$, denotes the expected cumulative reward as received by taking action a in state s and then following the policy π,

$$Q^{\pi}(s,a) = E_{\pi}\left[\sum_{t=0}^{\infty}\gamma^t R(s_t)|s_0 = s, a_0 = a\right].\tag{3}$$

In this study, we will focus on the Q functions dealing with state-action pairs (s,a).

The objective of RL problems is to estimate an optimal policy π^* by choosing actions that yields the optimal action-state value function Q^*:

$$\pi^*(s) = \arg\max_a Q^*(s,a).\tag{4}$$

Learning a policy therefore means updating the Q-function to make it more accurate. To account for potential inaccuracies in the Q-function, it must perform occasional exploratory actions. A common strategy is the ϵ-greedy exploration, where with a small probability ϵ, the agent chooses a random action. In an environment with a capable (reasonably small) number of states, the Q-function can simply be represented with a table of values, one entry for each state-action pair. Thus, basic algorithmic RL schemes make updates to individual Q-value entries in this table.

One of the most popular TD algorithms used in on-policy RL is the SARSA [4] which is a *bootstrapping* technique. Assuming that an action a_t is taken and the agent moves from belief state s_t to a new state s_{t+1} while receiving a reward r_t, a new action a_{t+1} is chosen (ϵ-greedy) according to the current policy. Then, the predicted Q value of this new state-action pair is used to calculate an improved estimate for the Q value of the previous state-action pair:

$$Q(s_t, a_t) \leftarrow Q(s_t, a_t) + \alpha\delta_t,\tag{5}$$

where

$$\delta_t = (r_t + \gamma Q(s_{t+1}, a_{t+1}) - Q(s_t, a_t))\tag{6}$$

is known as the one step temporal-difference (TD) error. The term α is the learning rate which set to some small value (e.g. $\alpha = 0.01$) and can be occasionally decreased during the learning process.

An additional mechanism that can be employed is that of *eligibility traces*. This allows rewards to backpropagate to recently visited states, allocating them some proportion of the current reward. Every state-action pair in the Q table is given its own eligibility value (e) and when the agent visits that pairing its eligibility value set equal to 1 (*replacing traces*, [14]). After every transition all eligibility values are decayed by a factor of $\gamma\lambda$, where $\lambda \in [0, 1]$ is the trace decay parameter. The TD error forward proportional in all recently visited state-action pairs as signalised by their nonzero traces according to the following update rule:

$$Q_{t+1}(s, a) \leftarrow Q_t(s, a) + \alpha\delta_t e_t(s, a) \qquad \text{for all } s, a \qquad (7)$$

where

$$e_{t+1}(s, a) = \begin{cases} 1 & \text{if } s = s_t \text{ and } a = a_t \\ 0 & \text{if } s = s_t \text{ and } a \neq a_t \\ \gamma\lambda e_t(s, a) & \text{otherwise} \end{cases} \qquad (8)$$

is a matrix of eligibility traces. The purpose of eligibility traces is to propagate TD-error to the state-action values faster so as to accelerate the exporation of the optimal strategy. The specific version, known as SARSA(λ) [4], has been adopted for the learning of the Ms. Pac-Man agent.

4   The Proposed State Space Representation

The game of Ms. Pac-Man constitutes a challenging domain for building and testing intelligent agents. The state space representation is of central interest for an agent, since it plays a significant role in system modeling, identification, and adaptive control. At each time step, the agent has to make decisions according to its observations. The state space model should describe the physical dynamic system and the states must represent the internal behaviour of system by modeling an efficient relationship from inputs to actions. In particular, the description of the state space in the Ms. Pac-Man domain should incorporate useful information about his position, the food (dots, scared ghosts) as well as the ghosts. An ideal state space representation for Ms. Pac-Man could incorporate all these information that included in a game snapshot, such as:

 - the relative position of Ms. Pac-Man in the maze,
 - the situation about the food (dots, power pills) around the agent,
 - the condition of nearest ghosts.

Although the state space representation constitutes an integral part of the agent, only little effort has been paid in seeking a reasonable and informative state structure. As indicated in [6], a full description of the state would include (a) whether the dots have been eaten, (b) the position and direction of Ms. Pac-Man, (c) the position and direction of the four ghosts, (d) whether the ghosts are edible (blue), and if so, for how long they remain in this situation. Despite its benefits, the adoption of such a detailed state space representation can bring several undesirable effects (e.g. high computational complexity, low convergence rate, resource demanding, e.t.c), that makes modeling of them to be a difficult task.

According to the above discussion, in our study we have chosen carefully an abstract space description that simultaneously incorporate all the necessary information for the construction of a competitive agent. More specifically, in our approach the state space is structured as a 10-dimensional feature vector, $s = (s_1, s_2, s_3, s_4, s_5, s_6, s_7, s_8, s_9, s_{10})$ with discrete values. Its detailed description is given below:

- The first four (4) features $(s_1, \ldots, s_4)$ are binary and used to indicate the existence (1) or not (0) of the wall in the Ms. Pac-Man's four wind directions (north, west, south, east), respectively. Some characteristic examples are illustrated in Fig. 2; state vector $(s_1 = 0, s_2 = 1, s_3 = 0, s_4 = 1)$ indicates that the Pac-Man is found in a corridor with horizontal walls (Fig. 2(a)), while state values $(s_1 = 1, s_2 = 0, s_3 = 1, s_4 = 0)$ means that Ms. Pac-Man is located between a west and east wall (Fig. 2(b)).

- The fifth feature s_5 suggests the direction of the nearest *target* where it is preferable for the Ms. Pac-Man to move. It takes four (4) values (from 0 to 3) that correspond to north, west, south or east direction, respectively. The *desired target* depends on the Ms. Pac-Man's position in terms of the four ghosts. In particular, when the Ms. Pac-Man is going to be trapped by the ghosts (i.e. at least one ghost with distance less than eight (8) steps is moving against Ms. Pac-Man), then the direction to the closest *safer* exit (*escape direction*) must be chosen (Fig.2(d)). In all other cases this feature takes the direction to the closest dot or frightened ghost. Roughly speaking, priority is given to neighborhood food: If a edible (blue-colored) ghost exists within a maximum distance of five (5) steps, then the ghost's direction is selected (Fig.2(a)). On the other hand, this feature takes the direction that leads to the nearest dot (Fig.2(c,f)). Note here that for calculating the distance as well as the direction between Ms. Pac-Man and *target*, we have used the known A* search algorithm [15] for finding the shortest path.

- The next four features $(s_6, \ldots, s_9)$ are binary and specify the situation of any direction (north, west, south, east) in terms of a *direct* ghost threat. When a ghost with distance less that eight steps (8) is moving towards pac-man from a specific direction, then the corresponding direction takes the value of 1. An example given in Fig.2(d) where the Ms. Pac-Man is approached threateningly by two ghosts. More specifically, the first ghost approaches the agent from the east $(s_7 = 1)$ and the other from the south direction $(s_8 = 1)$.

- The last feature specifies if the pac-man is trapped (1) or not (0). We assume that the Ms. Pac-Man is trapped if there doesn't exist any possible escape direction (Fig.2(e)). In all other cases the Ms. Pac-Man is considered to be free (Fig.2(a, b, c, d, f)). This specific feature is very important since it informs the agent whether or not it can (temporarily) move in the maze freely.

Table 1 summarizes the proposed state space. Obviously, its size is quite small containing only $4 * 2^9 = 2048$ states. This fact allows the construction of a computationally efficient RL agent without the need of any approximation scheme. Last but not least, the adopted reasonable state space combined with the small action space speed up the learning process and enables the agent to discover optimal policy solutions with sufficient generalization capabilities.

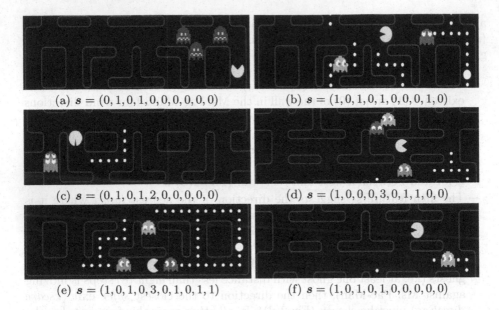

(a) $s = (0, 1, 0, 1, 0, 0, 0, 0, 0, 0)$ (b) $s = (1, 0, 1, 0, 1, 0, 0, 0, 1, 0)$

(c) $s = (0, 1, 0, 1, 2, 0, 0, 0, 0, 0)$ (d) $s = (1, 0, 0, 0, 3, 0, 1, 1, 0, 0)$

(e) $s = (1, 0, 1, 0, 3, 0, 1, 0, 1, 1)$ (f) $s = (1, 0, 1, 0, 1, 0, 0, 0, 0, 0)$

Fig. 2. Representative game situations along with their state description

Table 1. A summary of the proposed state space

Feature	Range	Source
$[s_1\ s_2\ s_3\ s_4]$	$\{0, 1\}$	Ms. Pac-Man view
s_5	$\{0, 1, 2, 3\}$	target direction
$[s_6\ s_7\ s_8\ s_9]$	$\{0, 1\}$	ghost threat direction
s_{10}	$\{0, 1\}$	trapped situation

5   Experimental Results

A number of experiments has been made in order to evaluate the performance of the proposed methodology in the Ms. Pac-Man domain. All experiments were conducted by using the MASON multiagent simulation package [16] which provides a faithful version of the original game. Due to the low complexity of the proposed methodology and its limited requirements on memory and computational resources, the experiments took place on a conventional PC (Intel Core 2 Quad (2.66GHz) CPU with 2GiB RAM).

We used three mazes of the original Ms. Pac-Man game illustrated in Figs. 1 and 3. The first maze (Fig. 1) was used during the learning phase for training the RL agent, while the other two mazes (Fig. 3) were applied for testing. In all experiments we have set the discount factor (γ) equal to 0.99 and the learning rate (α) equal to 0.01. The selected reward function is given at Table.2. It must be noted that our method did not show any significant sensitivity to the above reward values; however a careful selection is necessary to meet the requirements

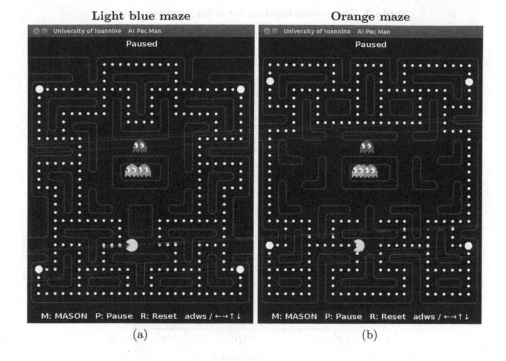

Fig. 3. Two mazes used for evaluating the proposed RL agent

of the physical problem. In addition, we assume that an episode is completed either when all the dots are collected (*win*) or the Ms. Pac-Man is collided with a non-scared ghost. Finally, the performance of the proposed approach was evaluated in terms of four distinct metrics:

- Average percentage of successfully level completion
- Average number of *wins*
- Average number of steps per episode
- Average score attained per episode

The learning process follows a two-stage strategy. At the first phase, the agent is trained without the presence of ghosts. In this case the agent's goal is to eat all the dots and terminates the level with the minimum number of steps. During the second phase the agent is initialized with the policy discovered previously and the ghosts are entered into the same maze. Likewise, the agent's target is to eat all the dots, but now with the challenge of the 'non-scared ghosts avoidance'.

Figure 4 illustrates the depicted learning curve during the first phase, i.e. mean number of steps (after 20 different runs) that the agent needs to finish the episode by eating all the dots of the maze (Fig. 1). In order to study the effectiveness of the eligibility trace (Eqs. 7, 8) to the RL agent, a series of initial experiments were made with three different values $(0, 0.2, 0.8)$ of the decay parameter λ. According to the results, the value of $\lambda = 0.8$ had shown the best performance,

Table 2. The reward function for different game events

Event	Reward	Description
Step	−0.5	Ms. Pac-Man performed a move in the empty space
Lose	−35	Ms. Pac-Man was eaten by a non-scared ghost
Wall	−100	Ms. Pac-Man hit the wall
Ghost	+1.2	Ms. Pac-Man ate a scared ghost
Pill	+1.2	Ms. Pac-Man ate a pill

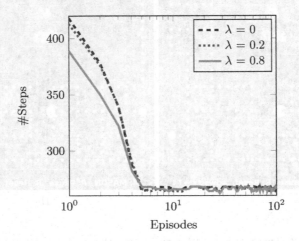

Fig. 4. Learning progress of the agent at the pink maze without ghosts

since it allows reaching optimal policy solution very quickly (260 steps in less than 100 episodes). We have adopted this value in the rest experiments. Note here that in all three cases the discovered policy was almost the same. Another useful remark is that the received policy is perfect, i.e. eating all 220 dots of the maze in only 260 steps (only 15% moves in positions with no dots).

The learning performance of the second phase is illustrated in Fig. 5 in terms of the (a) percentage of level completion and (b) number of wins (successful completion) in the last 100 episodes. As shown the method converges quite rapidly at an optimal policy after only 800 episodes. The Ms. Pac-Man agent manages to handle trapped situations and completes successfully the level at a high-percentage. We believe that the 40% of the level completion suggests a satisfactory playing of the pacman game.

Table 3. Testing performance

Maze	Level completion	Wins	# Steps	Score
Pink maze (Fig. 1)	80% (±24)	40%	348.7 (±153)	2292.3 (±977)
Light blue maze (Fig. 3(a))	70% (±24)	33%	319.4 (±143)	2538.4 (±1045)
Orange maze (Fig. 3(b)	80% (±20)	25%	360.8 (±155)	2515.7 (±1011)

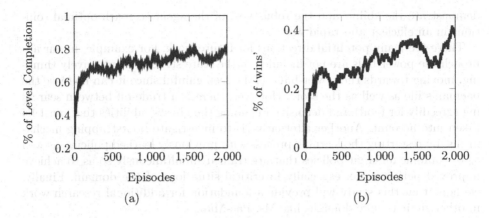

Fig. 5. Learning progress of the agent at the pink maze with ghosts

Table 4. Ms. Pac-Man game score

Mazes	Average Scores	Max Score
Pink maze (Fig. 1)	9665	20860
Light blue maze (Fig. 3(a))	12753	38840
Orange maze (Fig. 3(b)	11587	27620

In order to measure the generalization capability of the proposed mechanism, we have tested the policy that was discovered during the learning phase into two unknown mazes (Fig. 3). Table 3 lists the performance of the fixed policy in three mazes, where the statistics (mean value and std) of the evaluation metrics were calculated after running 100 episodes. That is interested to note here is that the agent had shown a remarkable behavior stability to both unknown mazes providing clearly significant generalization abilities. Finally, the obtained policy was tested by playing 50 consecutive games (starting with 3 lives and adding a live at every 10000 points). Table 4 summarizes the depicted results where we have calculated the mean score together with the maximum score found in all three tested mazes. These particular results verify our previous observations on the generalization ability of the proposed agent that is managed to build a generic optimal policy allowing Ms. Pac-Man to navigate satisfactory at every maze.

6 Conclusions and Future Directions

In this work we have presented a reinforcement learning agent that learns to play the famous arcade game Ms. Pac-Man. An abstract but informative state space representation has been introduced that allows flexible operation definition possibilities through the reinforcement learning framework. Initial experiments demonstrate the ability and the robustness of the agent to reach optimal solutions in an efficient and rapid way.

There are many potential directions for future work. For example, in our approach the power-bills are not included in the state structure. Intuitively thinking, moving towards the power-bills can be seen gainful since it can increase the pacman's life as well as the score. However, there is a trade-off between searching (greedily for food) and defensive (avoiding the ghosts) abilities that must be taken into account. Another alternative is to investigate bootstrapping mechanisms, by restarting the learning process with previously learned policies, as well as to combine different policies that are trained simultaneously so as to achieve improved performance, especially in critical situations of the domain. Finally, we hope that this study will provide a foundation for additional research work in other similar game domains like Ms. Pac-Man.

References

1. Galway, L., Charles, D., Black, M.: Machine learning in digital games: A survey. Artificial Intelligence Review 29, 123–161 (2008)
2. Sutton, R.: Learning to predict by the method of temporal differences. Machine Learning 3(1), 9–44 (1988)
3. Kaelbling, L.P., Littman, M.L., Moore, A.W.: Reinforcement learning: A survey. Journal of Artificial Inteligence Research 4, 237–285 (1996)
4. Sutton, R.S., Barto, A.G.: Reinforcement Learning: An Introduction. MIT Press, Cambridge (1998)
5. Szita, I.: Reinforcement learning in games. In: Reinforcement Learning, pp. 539–577 (2012)
6. Szita, I., Lorincz, A.: Learning to play using low-complexity rule-based policies: Illustrations through ms. pac-man. Journal of Artificial Intelligence Research 30, 659–684 (2007)
7. Lucas, S.M.: Evolving a neural network location evaluator to play ms. pac-man. In: Proc. of IEEE Symposium on Computational Intelligence and Games (CIG 2005), pp. 203–210 (2005)
8. Bom, L., Henken, R., Wiering, M.A.: Reinforcement learning to train ms. pacman using higher-order action-relative inputs. In: Proc. of IEEE Intern. Symposium on Adaptive Dynamic Programming and Reinforcement Learning (ADPRL), pp. 156–163 (2013)
9. Alhejali, A.M., Lucas, S.M.: Evolving diverse ms. pac-man playing agents using genetic programming. In: Proc. of IEEE Symposium on Computational Intelligence and Games (CIG 2010), pp. 53–60 (2010)
10. Samothrakis, S., Robles, D., Lucas, S.: Fast approximate max-n monte-carlo tree search for ms. pac-man. IEEE Trans. on Computational Intelligence and AI in Games 3(2), 142–154 (2011)
11. Nguyen, K.Q., Thawonmas, R.: Monte carlo tree search for collaboration control of ghosts in ms. pac-man. IEEE Trans. on Computational Intelligence and AI in Games 5(1), 57–68 (2013)
12. Torrey, L., Taylor, M.: Teaching on a budget: Agents advising agents in reinforcement learning. In: Intern. Conferecene on Autonomous Agents and Multi-agent Systems (AAMAS), pp. 1053–1060 (2013)

13. Puterman, M.L.: Markov Decision Processes: Discrete Stochastic Dynamic Programming. Wiley (2005)
14. Singh, S., Sutton, R.S., Kaelbling, P.: Reinforcement learning with replacing eligibility traces, pp. 123–158 (1996)
15. Hart, P.E., Nilsson, N.J., Raphael, B.: A formal basis for the heuristic determination of minimum cost paths. IEEE Transactions on Systems, Science, and Cybernetics SSC-4(2), 100–107 (1968)
16. Luke, S., Cioffi-Revilla, C., Panait, L., Sullivan, K., Balan, G.: Mason: A multiagent simulation environment. Simulation 81(7), 517–527 (2005)

Multi-view Regularized Extreme Learning Machine for Human Action Recognition

Alexandros Iosifidis, Anastasios Tefas, and Ioannis Pitas

Department of Informatics, Aristotle University of Thessaloniki,
Box 451, 54124 Thessaloniki, Greece
{aiosif,tefas,pitas}@aiia.csd.auth.gr

Abstract. In this paper, we propose an extension of the ELM algorithm that is able to exploit multiple action representations. This is achieved by incorporating proper regularization terms in the ELM optimization problem. In order to determine both optimized network weights and action representation combination weights, we propose an iterative optimization process. The proposed algorithm has been evaluated by using the state-of-the-art action video representation on three publicly available action recognition databases, where its performance has been compared with that of two commonly used video representation combination approaches, i.e., the vector concatenation before learning and the combination of classification outcomes based on learning on each view independently.

Keywords: Extreme Learning Machine, Multi-view Learning, Single-hidden Layer Feedforward networks, Human Action Recognition.

1 Introduction

Human action recognition is intensively studied to date due to its importance in many real-life applications, like intelligent visual surveillance, human-computer interaction, automatic assistance in healthcare of the elderly for independent living and video games, to name a few. Early human action recognition methods have been investigating a restricted recognition problem. According to this problem, action recognition refers to the recognition of simple motion patterns, like a walking step, performed by one person in a scene containing a simple background [1, 2]. Based on this scenario, most such methods describe actions as series of successive human body poses, represented by human body silhouettes evaluated by applying video frame segmentation techniques or background subtraction. However, such an approach is impractical in most real-life applications, where actions are performed in scenes having a complex background, which may contain multiple persons as well. In addition, actions may be observed by one or multiple, possibly moving, camera(s), capturing the action from arbitrary viewing angles. The above mentioned problem is usually referred to as 'action recognition in the wild' and is the one that is currently addressed by most action recognition methods.

The state-of-the-art approach in this, unrestricted, problem describes actions by employing the Bag-of-Features (BoF) model [3]. According to this model, sets of shape and/or motion descriptors are evaluated in spatiotemporal locations of interest of a video

A. Likas, K. Blekas, and D. Kalles (Eds.): SETN 2014, LNAI 8445, pp. 84–94, 2014.

and multiple (one for each descriptor type) video representations are obtained by applying (hard or soft) vector quantization by employing sets of descriptor prototypes, referred to as codebooks. The descriptors that provide the current state-of-the-art performance in most action recognition databases are: the Histogram of Oriented Gradients (HOG), the Histogram of Optical Flow (HOF) and the Motion Boundary Histogram (MBH). These descriptors are evaluated on the trajectories of densely sampled video frame interest points, which are tracked for a number of consecutive video frames. The normalized location of the tracked interest points is also employed in order to form another descriptor type, referred to as Trajectory (Traj).

Since different descriptor types express different properties of interest for actions, it is not surprising the fact that a combined action representation exploiting all the above mentioned (single-descriptor based) video representations results to increased performance [3]. Such combined action representations are usually obtained by employing unsupervised combination schemes, like the use of concatenated representations (either on the descriptor, or on the video representation level), or by combining the outcomes of classifiers trained on different representation types [4], e.g., by using the mean classifier outcome in the case of SLFN networks [5]. However, the adoption of such combination schemes may decrease the generalization ability of the adopted classification scheme, since all the available action representations equally contribute to the classification result. Thus, supervised combination schemes are required in order to properly combine the information provided by different descriptor types.

Extreme Learning Machine (ELM) [6] is a, relatively, new algorithm for fast Single-hidden Layer Feedforward Neural (SLFN) networks training, requiring low human supervision. Conventional SLFN training algorithms require adjustment of the network weights and the bias values, using a parameter optimization approach, like gradient descent. However, gradient descent learning techniques are, generally, slow and may lead to local minima. In ELM, the input weights and the hidden layer bias values are randomly chosen, while the network output weights are analytically calculated. By using a sufficiently large number of hidden layer neurons, the ELM classification scheme can be thought of as being a non-linear mapping of the training data on a high-dimensional feature space, called ELM space hereafter, followed by linear data projection and classification. ELM not only tends to reach a small training error, but also a small norm of output weights, indicating good generalization performance [7]. ELM has been successfully applied to many classification problems, including human action recognition [8–11].

In this paper we employ the ELM algorithm in order to perform human action recognition from videos. We adopt the state-of-the-art BoF-based action representation described above [3], in order to describe videos depicting actions, called action videos hereafter, by multiple vectors (one for each descriptor type), each describing different properties of interest for actions. In order to properly combine the information provided by different descriptor types, we extend the ELM algorithm in order to incorporate multiple video representations in its optimization process. An iterative optimization scheme is proposed to this end, where the contribution of each video representation is appropriately weighted. We evaluate the performance of the proposed algorithm on three publicly available databases, where we compare it with that of two commonly adopted video representation combination schemes.

The proposed approach is closely related to Multiple Kernel Learning (MKL) [16–18]. MKL methods aim at the determination of an "improved" feature space for non-linear data mapping. This is usually approached by employing a linear combination of a set of kernel functions followed by the optimization of an objective function by employing the training data for the determination of the kernel combination weights. A recent review on MKL methods can be found in [19]. Our work differs from MKL in that in the proposed approach the feature spaces employed for nonlinear data mapping are determined by employing randomly chosen network weights. After obtaining the data representations in the high-dimensional ELM space, we aim at optimally weighting the contribution of each data representation in the outputs of the combined network outputs.

The remainder of the paper is structured as follows. In Section 2, we briefly describe the ELM algorithm. The proposed Multi-view Regularized ELM (MVRELM) algorithm is described in Section 3. Experimental results evaluating its performance are illustrated in Section 4. Finally, conclusions are drawn in Section 5.

2 Extreme Learning Machine

ELM has been proposed for single-view classification [6]. Let x_i and c_i, $i = 1, ..., N$ be a set of labeled action vectors and the corresponding action class labels, respectively. We would like to employ them in order to train a SLFN network. For a classification problem involving the D-dimensional action vectors x_i, each belonging to one of the C action classes, the network should contain D input, H hidden and C output neurons. The number of the network hidden layer neurons is, typically, chosen to be higher than the number of action classes, i.e., $H \gg C$. The network target vectors $t_i = [t_{i1}, ..., t_{iC}]^T$, each corresponding to one labeled action vector x_i, are set to $t_{ij} = 1$ for vectors belonging to action class j, i.e., when $c_i = j$, and to $t_{ij} = -1$ otherwise.

In ELM, the network input weights $W_{in} \in \mathbb{R}^{D \times H}$ and the hidden layer bias values $b \in \mathbb{R}^H$ are randomly chosen, while the output weights $W_{out} \in \mathbb{R}^{H \times C}$ are analytically calculated. Let v_j denote the j-th column of W_{in}, u_k the k-th column of W_{out} and u_{kj} be the j-th element of u_k. For a given hidden layer activation function $\Phi(\cdot)$ and by using a linear activation function for the output neurons, the output $o_i = [o_{i1}, ..., o_{iC}]^T$ of the ELM network corresponding to training action vector s_i is given by:

$$o_{ik} = \sum_{j=1}^{H} u_{kj} \, \Phi(v_j, b_j, x_i), \quad k = 1, ..., C. \tag{1}$$

Many activation functions $\Phi(\cdot)$ can be employed for the calculation of the hidden layer output, such as sigmoid, sine, Gaussian, hard-limiting and Radial Basis (RBF) functions. The most popular choices are the sigmoid and the RBF functions, i.e.:

$$\Phi_{sigmoid}(v_j, b_j, x_i) = \frac{1}{1 + exp\left(-(v_j^T x_i + b_j)\right)}, \tag{2}$$

$$\Phi_{RBF}(\mathbf{v}_j, b_j, \mathbf{x}_i) = exp\left(-b_j \|\mathbf{x}_i - \mathbf{v}_j\|_2^2\right), \tag{3}$$

leading to MLP and RBF networks, respectively. However, since we are interested in BoF-based human action recognition, in this work we exploit the χ^2 activation function:

$$\Phi_{\chi^2}(\mathbf{v}_j, b, \mathbf{x}_i) = exp\left(-\frac{1}{2b_j}\sum_{d=1}^{D}\frac{(\mathbf{x}_{id} - \mathbf{v}_{jd})^2}{\mathbf{x}_{id} + \mathbf{v}_{jd}}\right), \tag{4}$$

which has been found to outperform both the above two alternative choices.

By storing the hidden layer neuron outputs in a matrix Φ:

$$\Phi = \begin{bmatrix} \Phi(\mathbf{v}_1, b_1, \mathbf{x}_1) & \cdots & \Phi(\mathbf{v}_1, b_1, \mathbf{x}_l) \\ \cdots & \ddots & \\ \Phi(\mathbf{v}_H, b_H, \mathbf{x}_1) & \cdots & \Phi(\mathbf{v}_{II}, b_{II}, \mathbf{x}_l) \end{bmatrix}, \tag{5}$$

equation (1) can be written in a matrix form as $\mathbf{O} = \mathbf{W}_{out}^T \Phi$. Finally, by assuming that the predicted network outputs $\mathbf{O}$ are equal to the desired ones, i.e., $\mathbf{o}_i = \mathbf{t}_i$, $i = 1, ..., l$, $\mathbf{W}_{out}$ can be analytically calculated by solving for:

$$\mathbf{W}_{out}^T \Phi = \mathbf{T}, \tag{6}$$

where $\mathbf{T} = [\mathbf{t}_1, ..., \mathbf{t}_l]$ is a matrix containing the network target vectors. Using (6), the network output weights minimizing $\|\mathbf{W}_{out}^T \Phi - \mathbf{T}\|_F$ are given by:

$$\mathbf{W}_{out} = \Phi^\dagger \mathbf{T}^T, \tag{7}$$

where $\|\mathbf{X}\|_F$ is the Frobenius norm of $\mathbf{X}$ and $\Phi^\dagger = \left(\Phi\Phi^T\right)^{-1}\Phi$ is the generalized pseudo-inverse of Φ^T. By observing (8), it can be seen that this equation can be used only in the cases where the matrix $\mathbf{B} = \Phi\Phi^T$ is invertible, i.e., when $N > D$. A regularized version of the ELM algorithm addressing this issue has been proposed in [12], where the network output weights are obtained, according to a regularization paramter $c > 0$, by:

$$\mathbf{W}_{out} = \left(\Phi\Phi^T + \frac{1}{c}\mathbf{I}\right)^{-1}\Phi\,\mathbf{T}^T. \tag{8}$$

After calculating the network output weights $\mathbf{W}_{out}$, a test action vector $\mathbf{x}_t$ can be introduced to the trained network and be classified to the action class corresponding to the maximal network output, i.e.:

$$c_t = arg \max_j o_{tj}, \; j = 1, ..., C. \tag{9}$$

3   Multi-view Regularized Extreme Learning Machine

The above described ELM algorithm can be employed for single-view (i.e., single-representation) action classification. In this section, we describe an optimization process that can be used for multi-view action classification, i.e., in the cases where each action video is represented by multiple action vectors $\mathbf{x}_i^v$, $v = 1, \ldots, V$.

Let us assume that the N training action videos are represented by the corresponding action vectors $\mathbf{x}_i^v \in \mathbb{R}^{D_v}$, $i = 1, \ldots, l, \ldots, N$, $v = 1, \ldots, V$. We would like to employ them, in order to train V SLFN networks, each operating on one view. To this end we map the action vectors of each view v to one ELM space $\mathbb{R}^{H_v}$, by using randomly chosen input weights $\mathbf{W}_{in}^v \in \mathbb{R}^{D_v \times H_v}$ and input layer bias values $\mathbf{b}^v \in \mathbb{R}^{H_v}$. H_v is the dimensionality of the ELM space related to view v.

In order to determine both the networks output weights $\mathbf{W}_{out}^v \in \mathbb{R}^{H_v \times C}$ and appropriate view combination weights $\gamma \in \mathbb{R}^V$ we can formulate the following optimization problem:

$$\text{Minimize:} \quad \mathcal{J} = \frac{1}{2} \sum_{v=1}^{V} \| \mathbf{W}_{out}^v \|_F^2 + \frac{c}{2} \sum_{i=1}^{N} \| \xi_i \|_2^2 \tag{10}$$

$$\text{Subject to:} \quad \left(\sum_{v=1}^{V} \gamma_v \mathbf{W}_{out}^{v\,T} \phi_i^v \right) - \mathbf{t}_i = \xi_i, \quad i = 1, \ldots, N, \tag{11}$$

$$\| \gamma \|_2^2 = 1, \tag{12}$$

where $\mathbf{t}_i \in \mathbb{R}^C$, $\phi_i^v \in \mathbb{R}^{H_v}$ are target vector of the i-th action video and the representation of $\mathbf{x}_i^v$ in the corresponding ELM space, respectively. $\xi_i \in \mathbb{R}^C$ is the error vector related to the i-th action video and c is a regularization parameter expressing the importance of the training error in the optimization process. Alternatively, we could employ the constraints $\gamma_v \geq 0$, $v = 1, \ldots, V$ and $\sum_{v=1}^{V} \gamma_v = 1$ [19].

By setting the representations of $\mathbf{x}_i^v$ in the corresponding ELM space in a matrix $\mathbf{\Phi}^v = [\phi_1^v, \ldots, \phi_N^v]$, the network responses corresponding to the entire training set are given by:

$$\mathbf{O} = \sum_{v=1}^{V} \gamma_v \mathbf{W}_{out}^{v\,T} \mathbf{\Phi}^v. \tag{13}$$

By substituting (11) in (10) and taking the equivalent dual problem, we obtain:

$$
\begin{aligned}
\mathcal{J}_D &= \frac{1}{2} \sum_{v=1}^{V} \| \mathbf{W}_{out}^v \|_F^2 + \frac{c}{2} \sum_{i=1}^{N} \| \left(\sum_{v=1}^{V} \gamma_v \mathbf{W}_{out}^{v\,T} \phi_i^v \right) - \mathbf{t}_i \|_2^2 + \frac{\lambda}{2} \| \gamma \|_2^2 \\
&= \frac{1}{2} \sum_{v=1}^{V} \| \mathbf{W}_{out}^v \|_F^2 + \frac{c}{2} \| \left(\sum_{v=1}^{V} \gamma_v \mathbf{W}_{out}^{v\,T} \mathbf{\Phi}^v \right) - \mathbf{T} \|_F^2 + \frac{\lambda}{2} \| \gamma \|_2^2 \\
&= \frac{1}{2} \sum_{v=1}^{V} \| \mathbf{W}_{out}^v \|_F^2 + \frac{c}{2} \gamma^T \mathbf{P} \gamma - c \mathbf{r}^T \gamma + \frac{c}{2} tr \left(\mathbf{T}^T \mathbf{T} \right) + \frac{\lambda}{2} \gamma^T \gamma, \tag{14}
\end{aligned}
$$

where $\mathbf{P} \in \mathbb{R}^{V \times V}$ is a matrix having its elements equal to $[\mathbf{P}]_{kl} = tr \left(\mathbf{W}_{out}^{k\,T} \mathbf{\Phi}^k \mathbf{\Phi}^{l\,T} \mathbf{W}_{out}^l \right)$ and $\mathbf{r} \in \mathbb{R}^V$ is a vector having its elements equal to $\mathbf{r}_v = tr \left(\mathbf{T}^T \mathbf{W}_{out}^{v\,T} \mathbf{\Phi}^v \right)$. By solving for $\frac{\partial \mathcal{J}_D(\gamma)}{\partial \gamma} = 0$, γ is given by:

$$\gamma = \left(\mathbf{P} + \frac{\lambda}{c} \mathbf{I} \right)^{-1} \mathbf{r}. \tag{15}$$

By substituting (11) in (10) and taking the equivalent dual problem, we can also obtain:

$$
\begin{aligned}
\mathcal{J}_D &= \frac{1}{2}\sum_{v=1}^{V}\|\mathbf{W}_{out}^v\|_F^2 + \frac{c}{2}\sum_{i=1}^{N}\|\left(\sum_{v=1}^{V}\gamma_v\mathbf{W}_{out}^{v\,T}\phi_i^v\right) - t_i\|_2^2 + \frac{\lambda}{2}\|\gamma\|_2^2 \\
&= \frac{1}{2}\sum_{v=1}^{V}\|\mathbf{W}_{out}^v\|_F^2 + \frac{c}{2}\|\left(\sum_{v=1}^{V}\gamma_v\mathbf{W}_{out}^{v\,T}\mathbf{\Phi}^v\right) - \mathbf{T}\|_F^2 + \frac{\lambda}{2}\|\gamma\|_2^2 \\
&= \frac{1}{2}\sum_{v=1}^{V}tr\left(\mathbf{W}_{out}^{v\,T}\mathbf{W}_{out}^v\right) + \frac{c}{2}tr\left(\sum_{v=1}^{V}\sum_{l=1}^{V}\gamma_v\gamma_l\mathbf{W}_{out}^{v\,T}\mathbf{\Phi}^v\mathbf{\Phi}^{l\,T}\mathbf{W}_{out}^l\right) \\
&\quad - c\sum_{v=1}^{V}tr\left(\gamma_v\mathbf{W}_{out}^{v\,T}\mathbf{\Phi}^v\mathbf{T}^T\right) + \frac{c}{2}tr\left(\mathbf{T}^T\mathbf{T}\right) + \frac{\lambda}{2}\gamma^T\gamma.
\end{aligned}
$$

By solving for $\frac{\partial \mathcal{J}_D(\mathbf{W}_{out}^v)}{\partial \mathbf{W}_{out}^v} = 0$, $\mathbf{W}_{out}^v$ is given by:

$$
\mathbf{W}_{out}^v = \left(\frac{2}{c\gamma_k}\mathbf{I} + \gamma_k\mathbf{\Phi}^v\mathbf{\Phi}^{v\,T}\right)^{-1}\mathbf{\Phi}^v(2\mathbf{T} - \mathbf{O})^T, \tag{16}
$$

As can be observed in (15), (16), γ is a function of $\mathbf{W}_{out}^v$, $v = 1, \ldots, V$ and $\mathbf{W}_{out}^v$ is a function of γ. Thus, a direct optimization of $\mathcal{J}_D$ with respect to both $\{\gamma_v, \mathbf{W}_{out}^v\}_{v=1}^{V}$ is intractable. Therefore, we propose an iterative optimization scheme formed by two optimization steps. In the following, we introduce a index t denoting the iteration of the proposed iterative optimization scheme.

Let us denote by $\mathbf{W}_{out,t}^v$, γ_t the network output and combination weights determined for the iteration t, respectively. We initialize $\mathbf{W}_{out,1}^v$ by using (8) and set $\gamma_{1,v} = 1/V$ for all the action video representations $v = 1, \ldots, V$. By using γ_t, the network output weights $\mathbf{W}_{out,t+1}^v$ are updated by using (16). After the calculation of $\mathbf{W}_{out,t+1}^v$, γ_{t+1} is obtained by using (15). The above described process is terminated when $(\mathcal{J}_D(t) - \mathcal{J}_D(t+1))/\mathcal{J}_D(t) < \epsilon$, where ϵ is a small positive value equal to $\epsilon = 10^{-10}$ in our experiments. Since each optimization step corresponds to a convex optimization problem, the above described process is guaranteed to converge in a local minimum of $\mathcal{J}$.

After the determination of the set $\{\gamma_v, \mathbf{W}_{out}^v\}_{v=1}^{V}$, the network response for a given set of action vectors $\mathbf{x}_l \in \mathbb{R}^D$ is given by:

$$
\mathbf{o}_l = \sum_{v=1}^{V}\gamma_v\mathbf{W}_{out}^{v\,T}\phi_l^v. \tag{17}
$$

4 Experiments

In this section, we present experiments conducted in order to evaluate the performance of the proposed MVELM algorithms. We have employed three publicly available databases, namely the Hollywood2, the Olympic Sports and the Hollywood 3D databases. In the following subsections, we describe the databases and evaluation measures used in our experiments. Experimental results are provided in subsection 4.4.

We employ the state-of-the-art action video representation proposed in [3], where each video is represented by five 4000-dimensional BoF-based vectors, each evaluated by employing a different descriptor type, i.e., HOG, HOF, MBHx, MBHy and Traj. We evaluate two commonly used unsupervised video representation combination schemes, i.e., the concatenation of all the available video representations before training a SLFN network by using the regularized ELM algorithm (eq. (8)) and the mean output of V SLFN networks, each trained by using one video representation using the regularized ELM algorithm (eq. (8)). The performance of these combination schemes is compared to that of the proposed MVRELM algorithm.

Regarding the parameters of the competing algorithms used in our experiments, the optimal value of parameter c used by both regularized ELM and MVRELM has been determined by linear search using values $c = 10^q$, $q = -5, \ldots, 5$. The optimal value of the parameter λ used by the proposed MVRELM algorithm has also be determined by applying linear search, using values $\lambda = 10^l$, $l = -5, \ldots, 5$. Finally, the parameters b_j used in the χ^2 activation function (4) have been set equal to the mean value of the χ^2 distances between the training action vectors and the network input weights. The number of network hidden neurons has been set equal to 500 in all the cases.

4.1 The Hollywood2 Database

The Hollywood2 database [13] consists of 1707 videos depicting 12 actions. The videos have been collected from 69 different Hollywood movies. The actions appearing in the database are: answering the phone, driving car, eating, ghting, getting out of car, hand shaking, hugging, kissing, running, sitting down, sitting up and standing up. Example video frames of the database are illustrated in Figure 1. We used the standard training-test split provided by the database (823 videos are used for training and performance is measured in the remaining 884 videos). Training and test videos come from different movies. The performance is evaluated by computing the average precision (AP) for each action class and reporting the mean AP over all classes (mAP), as suggested in [13]. This is due to the fact that some sequences of the database depict multiple actions.

4.2 The Olympic Sports Database

The Olympic Sports database [14] consists of 783 videos depicting athletes practicing 16 sports, which have been collected from YouTube and annotated using Amazon Mechanical Turk. The actions appearing in the database are: high-jump, long-jump, triple-jump, pole-vault, basketball lay-up, bowling, tennis-serve, platform, discus, hammer, javelin, shot-put, springboard, snatch, clean-jerk and vault. Example video frames of the database are illustrated in Figure 2. The database has rich scene context information, which is helpful for recognizing sport actions. We used the standard training-test split provided by the database (649 videos are used for training and performance is measured in the remaining 134 videos). The performance is evaluated by computing the mean Average Precision (mAP) over all classes, as suggested in [14]. In addition,

Fig. 1. Video frames of the Hollywood2 database depicting instances of all the twelve actions

since each video depicts only one action, we also measured the performance of each algorithm by computing the classification rate (CR).

Fig. 2. Video frames of the Olympic Sports database depicting instances of all the sixteen actions

4.3   The Hollywood 3D Database

The Hollywood 3D database [15] consists of 951 video pairs (left and right channel) depicting 13 actions collected from Hollywood movies. The actions appearing in the database are: dance, drive, eat, hug, kick, kiss, punch, run, shoot, sit down, stand up, swim and use phone. Another class referred to as 'no action' is also included in the

Fig. 3. Video frames of the Hollywood 3D database depicting instances of twelve actions

database. Example video frames of this database are illustrated in Figure 3. We used the standard (balanced) training-test split provided by the database (643 videos are used for training and performance is measured in the remaining 308 videos). Training and test videos come from different movies. The performance is evaluated by computing both the mean AP over all classes (mAP) and the classification rate (CR) measures, as suggested in [15].

4.4 Experimental Results

Tables 1, 2 illustrate the performance of the competing algorithms on the Hollywood2, the Olympic Sports and the Hollywood 3D databases. We denote by 'Conc. ELM' the classification scheme employing the concatenation of all the available video representations before training a SLFN network by using the regularized ELM algorithm (eq. (8)) and by 'ELM Mean' the classification scheme employing the mean output of V SLFN networks, each trained by using one video representation using the regularized ELM algorithm (eq. (8)).

As can be seen, use of the mean SLFN network outcome outperforms the use of an action video representation obtained by concatenating all the available action vectors before training in the Olympic Sports and the Hollywood 3D databases, while they achieve comparable performance on the Hollywood2 database. The proposed MVRELM algorithm outperforms both of them in all the three databases. When the performance is measured by using the mean average precision metric, it achieves performance equal to 56.26%, 80.53% and 29.86% on the Hollywood2, the Olympic Sports and the Hollywood 3D databases, respectively. In the case where the performance is measured by using the classification rate, it achieves performance equal to 74.63% and 33.44% on the Olympic Sports and the Hollywood 3D databases, respectively.

Table 1. Action Recognition Performance (mAP) on the Hollywood2, Olympic Sports and Hollywood 3D databases

	Conc. ELM	ELM Mean	MVRELM
Hollywood2	55.97 %	55.65 %	**56.26 %**
Olympic Sports	77.39 %	79.09 %	**80.53 %**
Hollywood 3D	28.26 %	28.73 %	**29.86 %**

Table 2. Action Recognition Performance (CR) on the Olympic Sports and Hollywood 3D databases

	Conc. ELM	ELM Mean	MVRELM
Olympic Sports	70.9 %	73.13 %	**74.63 %**
Hollywood 3D	29.22 %	32.47 %	**33.44 %**

5   Conclusions

In this paper, we proposed an extension of the ELM algorithm that is able to exploit multiple action representations. Proper regularization terms have been incorporated in the ELM optimization problem in order to extend the ELM algorithm to multi-view action classification. In order to determine both optimized network weights and action representation combination weights, we proposed an iterative optimization process. The proposed algorithm has been evaluated on three publicly available action recognition databases, where its performance has been compared with that of two commonly used video representation combination approaches, i.e., the vector concatenation before learning and the combination of classification outcomes based on learning on each view independently.

Acknowledgment. The research leading to these results has received funding from the European Union Seventh Framework Programme (FP7/2007-2013) under grant agreement number 316564 (IMPART). This publication reflects only the authors views. The European Union is not liable for any use that may be made of the information contained therein.

References

1. Turaga, P., Chellappa, R., Subrahmanian, V., Udrea, O.: Machine recognition of human activities: A survey. IEEE Transactions on Circuits and Systems for Video Technology 18(11), 1473–1488 (2008)
2. Ji, X., Liu, H.: Advances in View-Invariant Human Motion Analysis: Review. IEEE Transactions on Systems, Man and Cybernetics Part–C 40(1), 13–24 (2010)
3. Wang, H., Klaser, A., Schmid, C., Liu, C.L.: Dense Trajectories and Motion Boundary Descriptors for Action Recognition. International Journal of Computer Vision 103(60), 1–20 (2013)

4. Kittler, J., Hatef, M., Duin, R., Matas, J.: On combining classifiers. IEEE Transactions on Pattern Analysis and Machine Intelligence 20(3), 226–239 (1998)
5. Iosifidis, A., Tefas, A., Pitas, I.: View-invariant action recognition based on Artificial Neural Networks. IEEE Transactions on Neural Networks and Learning Systems 23(3), 412–424 (2012)
6. Huang, G., Zhu, Q., Siew, C.: Extreme Learning Machine: A new learning scheme for feedfowrard neural networks. In: IEEE International Joint Conference on Neural Networks (2004)
7. Bartlett, P.L.: The sample complexity of pattern classification with neural networks: The size of the weights is more important than the size of the network. IEEE Transactions on Information Theory 44(2), 525–536 (1998)
8. Minhas, R., Baradarani, A., Seifzadeh, S., Wu, Q.J.: Human action recognition using Extreme Learning Machine based on visual vocabularies. Neurocomputing 73(10), 1906–1917 (2010)
9. Iosifidis, A., Tefas, A., Pitas, I.: Multi-view Human Action Recognition under Occlusion based on Fuzzy Distances and Neural Networks. In: European Signal Processing Conference (2012)
10. Iosifidis, A., Tefas, A., Pitas, I.: Minimum Class Variance Extreme Learning Machine for Human Action Recognition. IEEE Transactions on Circuits and Systems for Video Technology 23(11), 1968–1979 (2013)
11. Iosifidis, A., Tefas, A., Pitas, I.: Dynamic action recognition based on Dynemes and Extreme Learning Machine. Pattern Recognition Letters 34, 1890–1898 (2013)
12. Huang, G., Zhou, H., Ding, Z., Zhang, R.: Extreme Learning Machine for Regression and Multiclass Classification. IEEE Transactions on Systems, Man and Cybernetics Part–B 42(2), 513–529 (2012)
13. Marszalek, M., Laptev, I., Schmid, C.: Actions in context. In: IEEE Conference on Computer Vision and Pattern Recognition (2009)
14. Niebles, J.C., Chen, C.-W., Fei-Fei, L.: Modeling Temporal Structure of Decomposable Motion Segments for Activity Classification. In: Daniilidis, K., Maragos, P., Paragios, N. (eds.) ECCV 2010, Part II. LNCS, vol. 6312, pp. 392–405. Springer, Heidelberg (2010)
15. Hadfield, S., Bowden, R.: Hollywood 3D: Recognizing Actions in 3D Natural Scenes. In: IEEE Conference on Computer Vision and Pattern Recognition (2013)
16. Lanckriet, G.R.G., Cristianini, N., Ghaoui, L.E., Bartlett, P., Jordan, M.I.: Learning the kernel matrix with semidefinite programming. Journal of Machine Learning Research 5, 27–72 (2013)
17. Bach, F.R., Lanckriet, G.R.G., Jordan, M.I.: Multiple kernel learning, conic duality, and the SMO algorithm. In: International Conference on Machine Learning (2004)
18. Damoulas, T., Girolami, M.A.: Combining feature spaces for classification. Pattern Recognition 42(11), 2671–2683 (2009)
19. Gonen, M., Alpaydin, E.: Multiple Kernel Learning Algorithms. Journal of Machine Learning Research 12, 2211–2268 (2011)

Classifying Behavioral Attributes
Using Conditional Random Fields

Michalis Vrigkas[1], Christophoros Nikou[1], and Ioannis A. Kakadiaris[2]

[1] Dept. of Computer Science & Engineering, University of Ioannina,
45110 Ioannina, Greece
[2] Computational Biomedicine Lab, Dept. of Computer Science,
University of Houston,
4800 Calhoun Rd, Houston, TX 77204, USA
{mvrigkas,cnikou}@cs.uoi.gr, ioannisk@uh.edu

Abstract. A human behavior recognition method with an application
to political speech videos is presented. We focus on modeling the behavior of a subject with a conditional random field (CRF). The unary
terms of the CRF employ spatiotemporal features (i.e., HOG3D, STIP
and LBP). The pairwise terms are based on kinematic features such as
the velocity and the acceleration of the subject. As an exact solution to
the maximization of the posterior probability of the labels is generally
intractable, loopy belief propagation was employed as an approximate
inference method. To evaluate the performance of the model, we also
introduce a novel behavior dataset, which includes low resolution video
sequences depicting different people speaking in the Greek parliament.
The subjects of the *Parliament* dataset are labeled as friendly, aggressive
or neutral depending on the intensity of their political speech. The discrimination between friendly and aggressive labels is not straightforward
in political speeches as the subjects perform similar movements in both
cases. Experimental results show that the model can reach high accuracy
in this relatively difficult dataset.

Keywords: Human Behavior Recognition, Conditional Random Field
(CRF), Loopy Belief Propagation (LPB).

1 Introduction

Recognizing human behaviors from video sequences is a challenging task for
the computer vision community [1,10,13]. A behavior recognition system may
provide information about the personality and psychological state of a person
and its applications vary from video surveillance to human-computer interaction.

The problem of human behavior recognition is challenging for several reasons.
First, constructing a visual model for learning and analyzing human movements
is difficult. Second, the fine differences between similar classes and the short
duration of human movements in time make the problem difficult to address.
In addition, annotating behavioral roles is time consuming and requires knowledge of the specific event. The variation of appearance, lighting conditions and

A. Likas, K. Blekas, and D. Kalles (Eds.): SETN 2014, LNAI 8445, pp. 95–104, 2014.
© Springer International Publishing Switzerland 2014

frame resolution makes the recognition problem amply challenging. Finally, the inadequate benchmark datasets are another obstacle that must be overcome.

In this paper, we are interested in characterizing human activities as behavioral roles in video sequences. The main contribution of this work is twofold. First, we introduce a method for recognizing behavioral roles (i.e., friendly, aggressive and neutral) (Figure 1). These behavioral classes are similar, as the involved people perform similar body movements. Our goal is to recognize these behavioral states by building a model, which allows us to discriminate and correctly classify human behaviors. To solve this problem, we propose an approach based on conditional random fields (CRF) [5]. Motivated by the work of Domke [2], which takes into account both model and inference approximation methods to fit the parameters for several imaging problems, we develop a structured model for representing scenes of human activity and utilize a marginalization fitting for parameter learning. Secondly, to evaluate the model performance, we introduce a novel behavior dataset, which we call the *Parliament* dataset [16], along with the ground truth behavioral labels for the individuals in the video sequences. More specifically, we have collected 228 low-resolution video sequences (320 × 240, 25fps), depicting 20 different individuals speaking in the Greek parliament. Each video sequence is associated with a behavioral label: friendly, aggressive and neutral, depending on the intensity of the political speech and the specific individual's movements.

(a)   (b)   (c)

Fig. 1. Sample frames from the proposed *Parliament* dataset. (a) Friendly, (b) Aggressive, and (c) Neutral.

The remainder of the paper is organized as follows: in Section 2, a brief review of the related work is presented. Section 3 presents the proposed approach including the model's specifications and the details of the method. In Section 4, the novel behavior recognition dataset is presented and experimental results are reported. Finally, conclusions are drawn in Section 5.

2   Related Work

The human activity categorization problem has remained a challenging task in computer vision for more than two decades. Many surveys [1,10] provide a good overview of human behavior recognition methods and analyze the properties of human behavior categorization. Previous work on characterizing human behavior has shown great potential in this area.

In this paper, the term "behavior" is used to describe both activities and events which are apparent in a video sequence. We categorize the human behavior recognition methods into two main categories: single- and multi-person interaction methods.

Single-Person Methods. Much research has focused on single person behavior recognition methods. A major family of methods relies on optical flow which has proven to be an important cue. Earlier approaches are based on describing behaviors by using dense trajectories. The work of Wang *et al.* [17] focused on tracking dense sample points from video sequences using optical flow. Yan and Luo [18] have also proposed an action descriptor based on spatio-temporal interest points (STIP) [7]. To avoid overfitting they have proposed a novel classification technique by combining the Adaboost and sparse representation algorithms. Our earlier work Vrigkas *et al.* [15] focused on recognizing single human behaviors by representing a human action with a set of clustered motion trajectories. A Gaussian mixture model was used to cluster the motion trajectories and the action labeling was performed by using a nearest neighbor classification scheme.

Multi-person Interaction Methods. Social interactions are an important part of human daily life. Fathi *et al.* [3] modeled social interactions by estimating the location and orientation of the faces of the persons taking part in a social event, computing a line of sight for each face. This information is used to infer the location an individual person attended. The type of interaction is recognized by assigning social roles to each person. The authors were able to recognize three types of social interactions: dialogue, discussion and monologue. Human behavior on sport datasets was introduced by Lan *et al.* [6]. The idea of social roles in conjunction with low-level actions and high-level events model the behavior of humans in a scene. The work of Ramanathan *et al.* [12] aimed at assigning social roles to people associated with an event. They formulated the problem by using a CRF model to describe the interactions between people. Tran *et al.* [14] presented a graph-based clustering algorithm to discover interactions between groups of people in a crowd scene. A bag-of-words approach was used to describe the group activity, while a SVM classifier was used to recognize the human activity.

3   Behavior Recognition Using CRF

In this paper, we present a supervised method for human behavior recognition. We assume that a set of training labels is provided and every video sequence is pre-processed to obtain a bounding box of the human in every frame and every person is associated with a behavioral label.

The model is general and can be applied to several behavior recognition datasets. Our method uses CRFs (Figure 2) as the probabilistic framework for modeling the behavior of a subject in a video. First, spatial local features are computed in every video frame capturing the roles associated with the bounding boxes. Then, a set of temporal context features are extracted capturing the relationship between the local features in time. Finally, the loopy belief propagation (LBP) [8] approximate method is applied to estimate the labels.

Let $r_j^t \in \mathcal{R}$ be the behavioral role label of the jth person in a bounding box at frame t, where $\mathcal{R}$ is the set of possible behavioral role labels and $t \in [0, T]$ is the current frame. Let x_j^t represent the feature vector of the observed j^{th} person at frame t. Our goal is to assign each person a behavioral role by maximizing the posterior probability:

$$\mathbf{r} = \arg\max_{\mathbf{r}} p(\mathbf{r}|\mathbf{x}; \mathbf{w}). \tag{1}$$

It is useful to note that our CRF model is a member of the exponential family defined as:

$$p(\mathbf{r}|\mathbf{x}; \mathbf{w}) = \exp\left(E(\mathbf{r}|\mathbf{x}; \mathbf{w}) - A(\mathbf{w})\right), \tag{2}$$

where $\mathbf{w}$ is a vector of parameters, $E(\mathbf{r}|\mathbf{x})$ is a vector of sufficient statistics and $A(\mathbf{w})$ is the log-partition function ensuring normalization:

$$A(\mathbf{w}) = \log \sum_{\mathbf{r}} \exp\left(E(\mathbf{r}|\mathbf{x}; \mathbf{w})\right). \tag{3}$$

Different sufficient statistics $E(\mathbf{r}|\mathbf{x}; \mathbf{w})$ in (2) define different distributions. In the general case, sufficient statistics consist of indicator functions for each possible configuration of unary and pairwise terms:

$$E(\mathbf{r}|\mathbf{x}; \mathbf{w}) = \sum_j \Psi_u(r_j^t, x_j^t; w_1) + \sum_j \sum_{k \in \mathcal{N}_j} \Psi_p(r_j^t, r_k^{t+1}, x_j^t, x_k^{t+1}; w_2), \tag{4}$$

where $\mathcal{N}_j$ is the neighborhood system of the jth person for every pixel in the bounding box. In our model temporal and spatial neighbors are considered. We use eight spatial and 18 temporal neighbors. The parameters w_1 and w_2 are the unary and the pairwise weights that need to be learned and $\Psi_u(r_j^t, x_j^t; w_1)$, $\Psi_p(r_j^t, r_k^{t+1}, x_j^t, x_k^{t+1}; w_2)$ are the unary and pairwise potentials, respectively.

Unary Potential: This potential predicts the behavior label r_j^t of the jth person in frame t indicating the dependence of the specific label on the location of the person. It may be expressed by:

$$\Psi_u(r_j^t, x_j^t; w_1) = \sum_{\ell \in \mathcal{R}} \sum_j w_1 \mathbb{1}(r_j^t = \ell)\psi_u(x_j^t), \tag{5}$$

where $\psi_u(x_j^t)$ are the unary features and $\mathbb{1}(\cdot)$ is the indicator function, which is equal to 1, if the jth person is associated with the ℓth label and 0 otherwise. The unary features are computed as a 36-dimensional vector of HoG3D values [4] for each bounding box. Then, a 64-dimensional spatio-temporal feature vector (STIP) [7] is computed, which captures the human motion between frames. The spatial relationship of each pixel in the bounding box and its 8×8 neighborhood is computed using a 16-dimensional Local Binary Pattern (LBP) feature vector [9]. The final unary features occur as a concatenation of the above features to a 116-dimensional vector.

Pairwise Potential: This potential represents the interaction of a pair of behavioral labels in consecutive frames. We define the following function as the pairwise potential:

$$\Psi_p(r_j^t, r_k^{t+1}, x_j^t, x_k^{t+1}; w_2) = \sum_{\substack{\ell \in \mathcal{R}, \\ m \in \mathcal{N}_\ell}} \sum_{\substack{j, \\ k \in \mathcal{N}_j}} w_2 \mathbb{1}(r_j^t = \ell)\mathbb{1}(r_k^{t+1} = m)\psi_p(x_j^t, x_k^{t+1}),$$

(6)

where $\psi_p(x_j^t, x_k^{t+1})$ are the pairwise features. We compute a 4-dimensional spatio-temporal feature vector, which is the concatenation of the 2D velocity and acceleration of the jth person along time. The acceleration features play a crucial role in the distinction between the behavioral classes, as different persons in different behavioral classes perform similar movements. In addition, the L_2 norm of the difference of the RGB values at frames t and $t+1$ is computed. We use eight spatial and 18 temporal neighbors creating an 18-dimensional feature vector. The final pairwise features are computed as the concatenation of the above features to a 22-dimensional vector.

To learn the model weights $\mathbf{w} = \{w_1, w_2\}$, we employ a labeled training set and seek to minimize:

$$\mathbf{w} = \arg\min_{\mathbf{w}} \sum_{\mathbf{r}} L(\mathbf{r}, \mathbf{x}; \mathbf{w}),$$

(7)

where $L(\cdot, \cdot)$ is a loss function, which quantifies how well the distribution (2) is defined by the parameter vector $\mathbf{w}$ matches the labels $\mathbf{r}$.

We select a clique loss function [2], which is defined as the log-likelihood of the posterior probability $p(\mathbf{r}|\mathbf{x}; \mathbf{w})$:

$$L(\mathbf{r}, \mathbf{x}; \mathbf{w}) = -\log p(\mathbf{r}|\mathbf{x}; \mathbf{w}).$$

(8)

The loss function is minimized using a gradient-descent optimization method. It can be seen as the empirical risk minimization of the Kullback-Leibler divergence between the true and predicted marginals.

Having set the parameters $\mathbf{w}$, an exact solution to Eq. (1) is generally intractable. For this reason, approximate inference is employed to solve this problem. In this paper, LBP [8] is used for computing the marginals using the full graphical model as depicted in Figure 2. For comparison purposes and for better insight of the proposed method, we have also tested a variant of the full graphical model by transforming it into a tree-like graph (Figure 3). This is accomplished by ignoring the spatial relationship between the observation nodes $\mathbf{x}$ and keeping only the temporal edges between the labels $\mathbf{r}$. In this case, tree-reweighted belief propagation [11] is considered for inference.

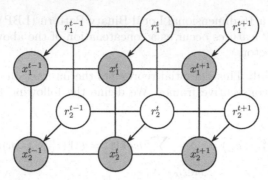

Fig. 2. Graphical representation of the model. The observed features are represented by **x** and the unknown labels are represented by **r**. Temporal edges exist also between the labels and the observed features across frames.

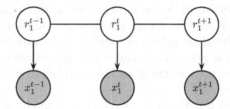

Fig. 3. Tree-like graphical representation of the model. The observed features are represented by **x** and the unknown labels are represented by **r**.

4   Experiments

The experiments are applied to the novel *Parliament* dataset [16]. The number of features are kept relatively small in order not to increase the model's complexity. Additionally, to show that the proposed method can perform well, different model variants are compared.

To evaluate our method, we collected a set of 228 video sequences, depicting political speeches in the Greek parliament, at a resolution of 320×240 pixels at 25 fps. The video sequences were manually labeled with one of three behavioral roles: friendly, aggressive, or neutral, according to specific body movements. These behaviors were recorded for 20 different subjects. The videos were acquired with a static camera and contain uncluttered backgrounds. Figure 1 delineates some representative frames of the *Parliament* dataset.

We used 5-fold cross validation to split the dataset into training and test sets. Accordingly, the model was learned from 183 videos, while the algorithm was tested on the remaining five videos and the recognition results were averaged over all the examined configurations of training and test sets. Within each class, there is a variation in the performance of an action. Each individual exhibits the same behavior in a different manner by using different body movements. This is an interesting characteristic of the dataset which makes it quite challenging.

Table 1. Behavior classification accuracies (%) using the graphical model with only temporal edges (3) and the full graphical model (2) presented in Figure 2

	Classification Accuracy(%)		
Method	Friendly	Aggressive	Neutral
Tree model (tree-reweighted BP)	100	49.23	84.48
Full model (loopy BP)	100	60.73	95.79

Table 2. Comparison between variants of the proposed method

Method	Accuracy(%)
CRF (unary only)	81.0
CRF (unary no spatio-temporal)	69.7
CRF (pairwise no spatio-temporal)	69.7
Full CRF model	**85.5**

We evaluated the proposed model with different variants of the method. First, we compared the full graphical model (Figure 2) with a variant of the method, which considers the graphical model as a tree-like graph (Figure 3). As it can be observed in Table 1, the full graphical model performs better than the tree-like graph, which uses only temporal edges between the labels. The second model ignores the spatial relationship between the features and the classification error is increased. Generally, the full graphical model provides strong improvement of more than 8% with respect to the tree model.

In the second set of experiments, we evaluated three variants of the proposed CRF model. First, we used the CRF model with only the unary potentials ignoring the pairwise potentials. The second variant uses only unary potential without the spatio-temporal features. Finally, the third configuration uses the full model without the spatio-temporal pairwise features. The classification results comparing the different models are shown in Table 2.

We may observe that the CRF model, which does not use spatio-temporal feature in either the unary potentials or the pairwise potentials, attains the worst performance between the different variants. It is worth mentioning that the first variant, which uses only unary features, performs better than the other two variants, which do not use spatio-temporal features. However, this is not a surprising fact, as in the case of the no spatio-temporal variants the classification is performed for each frame individually ignoring the temporal relationship between consecutive frames. The use of spatio-temporal features appears to lead to better performance than all the other approaches. We also observe that the full CRF model shows significant improvement over all of its variants. The full CRF model leads also to a significant increase in performance of 85.5%, with respect to the model with no spatio-temporal features. This confirms that temporal and spatial information combined together constitute an important cue for action recognition.

Figure 4 illustrates the overall behavior recognition accuracy, where the full CRF model exhibits the best performance in recognizing each of the three behaviors. The main conclusion we can draw from the confusion matrices is that adding temporal edges to the graphical model helps reduce the classification error between the different behavioral states. It is also worth noting that, due to missed and relatively close features in consecutive frames, the classes "friendly" and "aggressive" are often confused as the subject performs similar body movements. Feature selection may be employed to solve this problem.

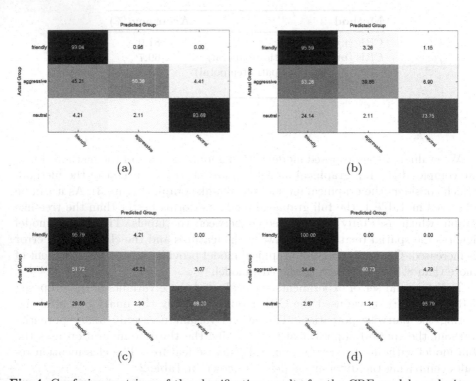

Fig. 4. Confusion matrices of the classification results for the CRF model employing (a) only unary potentials, (b) only unary potentials without spatio-temporal features, (c) the full model without spatio-temporal pairwise features, and (d) the full model

5   Conclusion

In this paper, we have presented a method for recognizing human behaviors in a supervised framework using a CRF model. We have also introduced a new challenging dataset (*Parliament*), which captures the behaviors of some politicians in the Greek parliament during their speeches. Several variants of the method were examined reaching an accuracy of 85.5%.

A direction of future research would be to study how the use of voice features and pose can help improve recognition accuracy. We are also interested in studying feature selection techniques to better separate the classes "friendly" and "aggressive". With these improvements, we plan to apply this method to several other datasets.

Acknowledgments. This work was supported in part by the University of Houston Hugh Roy and Lillie Cranz Cullen Endowment Fund.

References

1. Candamo, J., Shreve, M., Goldgof, D.B., Sapper, D.B., Kasturi, R.: Understanding transit scenes: A survey on human behavior-recognition algorithms. IEEE Transactions on Intelligent Transportation Sysstems 11(1), 206–224 (2010)
2. Domke, J.: Learning graphical model parameters with approximate marginal inference. IEEE Transactions on Pattern Analysis and Machine Intelligence 35(10), 2454–2467 (2013)
3. Fathi, A., Hodgins, J.K., Rehg, J.M.: Social interactions: A first-person perspective. In: Proc. IEEE Computer Society Conference on Computer Vision and Pattern Recognition, Providence, Rhode Island, USA, pp. 1226–1233 (2012)
4. Kläser, A., Marszałek, M., Schmid, C.: A spatio-temporal descriptor based on 3D-gradients. In: Proc. British Machine Vision Conference, University of Leeds, Leeds, UK, pp. 995–1004 (September 2008)
5. Lafferty, J.D., McCallum, A., Pereira, F.: Conditional random fields: Probabilistic models for segmenting and labeling sequence data. In: Proc. 18th International Conference on Machine Learning, Williams College, Williamstown, MA, USA, pp. 282–289 (2001)
6. Lan, T., Sigal, L., Mori, G.: Social roles in hierarchical models for human activity recognition. In: Proc. IEEE Computer Society Conference on Computer Vision and Pattern Recognition, Providence, Rhode Island, USA, pp. 1354–1361 (2012)
7. Laptev, I.: On space-time interest points. International Journal of Computer Vision 64(2-3), 107–123 (2005)
8. Murphy, K.P., Weiss, Y., Jordan, M.I.: Loopy belief propagation for approximate inference: An empirical study. In: Proc. Uncertainty in Artificial Intelligence, Stockholm, Sweden, pp. 467–475 (1999)
9. Ojala, T., Pietikäinen, M., Mäenpää, T.: Multiresolution gray-scale and rotation invariant texture classification with local binary patterns. IEEE Transactions on Pattern Analysis and Machine Intelligence 24(7), 971–987 (2002)
10. Poppe, R.: A survey on vision-based human action recognition. Image and Vision Computing 28(6), 976–990 (2010)
11. Prince, S.J.D.: Computer Vision: Models Learning and Inference. Cambridge University Press (2012)
12. Ramanathan, V., Yao, B., Fei-Fei, L.: Social role discovery in human events. In: Proc. IEEE Computer Society Conference on Computer Vision and Pattern Recognition, Portland, OR, USA (June 2013)
13. Smeulders, A.W.M., Chu, D.M., Cucchiara, R., Calderara, S., Dehghan, A., Shah, M.: Visual tracking: An experimental survey. IEEE Transactions on Pattern Analysis and Machine Intelligence 99(PrePrints), 1 (2013)

14. Tran, K.N., Bedagkar-Gala, A., Kakadiaris, I.A., Shah, S.K.: Social cues in group formation and local interactions for collective activity analysis. In: Proc. 8th International Conference on Computer Vision Theory and Applications, Barcelona, Spain, pp. 539–548 (February 2013)
15. Vrigkas, M., Karavasilis, V., Nikou, C., Kakadiaris, I.A.: Action recognition by matching clustered trajectories of motion vectors. In: Proc. 8th International Conference on Computer Vision Theory and Applications, Barcelona, Spain, pp. 112–117 (February 2013)
16. Vrigkas, M., Nikou, C., Kakadiaris, I.A.: The Parliament database (2014), http://www.cs.uoi.gr/~mvrigkas/Parliament.html
17. Wang, H., Kläser, A., Schmid, C., Cheng-Lin, L.: Action recognition by dense trajectories. In: Proc. IEEE Conference on Computer Vision and Pattern Recognition, Colorado Springs, United States, pp. 3169–3176 (2011)
18. Yan, X., Luo, Y.: Recognizing human actions using a new descriptor based on spatial-temporal interest points and weighted-output classifier. Neurocomputing 87, 51–61 (2012)

Rushes Video Segmentation Using Semantic Features

Athina Pappa, Vasileios Chasanis, and Antonis Ioannidis

Department of Computer Science and Engineering, University of Ioannina,
GR 45110, Ioannina, Greece
{apappa,vchasani,aioannid}@cs.uoi.gr

Abstract. In this paper we describe a method for efficient video rushes segmentation. Video rushes are unedited video footage and contain many repetitive information, since the same scene is taken many times until the desired result is produced. Color histograms have difficulty in capturing the scene changes in rushes videos. In the herein approach shot frames are represented by semantic feature vectors extracted from existing semantic concept detectors. Moreover, each shot keyframe is represented by the mean of the semantic feature vectors of its neighborhood, defined as the frames that fall inside a window centered at the keyframe. In this way, if a concept exists in most of the frames of a keyframe's neighborhood, then with high probability it exists on the corresponding keyframe. By comparing consecutive pairs of shots we seek to find changes in groups of similar shots. To improve the performance of our algorithm, we employ a face and body detection algorithm to eliminate false boundaries detected between similar shots. Numerical experiments on TRECVID rushes videos show that our method efficiently segments rushes videos by detecting groups of similar shots.

Keywords: Rushes summarization, semantic concept detectors, face detection.

1 Introduction

Video rushes segmentation and summarization is an important task in video processing. Rushes are unedited video used for movie and documentary editing. The duration of rushes videos is often ten times larger than the duration of the corresponding edited video. Thus, video rushes segmentation is necessary in order to provide fast access to video data to montage editors. The basic problems of rushes videos are three. First, the presence of useless frames such as colorbars, monochrome frames and frames containing clapboards. Second, the repetition of similar segments produced from multiple takes of the same scene and finally, the efficient representation of the original video in the video summary. In this paper, we focus on finding similar segments/shots that are captured under various circumstances, such as different camera positions or luminance conditions, changed background and even characters. Given the fact that similar shots are time ordered, grouping similar shots can be regarded as a video segmentation problem.

In [1], HSV color histograms and a sequence alignment algorithm are employed to cluster similar shots. In [2], histograms of dc-images are employed to compute similarity between extracted keyframes. In [3], hierarchical clustering on keyframes represented by Color layout and edge histograms is employed to group similar shots into

A. Likas, K. Blekas, and D. Kalles (Eds.): SETN 2014, LNAI 8445, pp. 105–114, 2014.

sets. In [4], spectral clustering on HSV color histograms is employed to cluster shots into groups, followed by a sequence alignment similarity metric.

In the method we propose herein, each video is segmented into shots, shots containing colorbars or monochrome frames are removed and for each shot we extract keyframes using the method described in [5]. Then, we define a neighborhood for each keyframe of a video shot. The neighborhood of a key-frame contains the frames that fall inside a window centered at the keyframe. For each frame of the neighborhood we compute semantic feature vectors based on semantic concept detectors available in bibliography ([6], [7]). Finally, each keyframe is represented by the mean of the semantic feature vectors of its neighborhood. A unique characteristic of rushes videos is that similar shots are time ordered, thus when a scene is recorded, a new group of similar shots is formed and ends when a new scene begins. With term "scene" we refer to similar shots produced from multiple takes of the same scenery. In our method, we seek to find when a new group of similar shots is formed, thus we compare successive shots to find scene boundaries. To improve the performance of our method, we employ a face and body detection algorithm.

The contribution of our method is three-fold. Firstly, each frame is represented with semantic feature vectors based on common semantic concept detectors. Color histograms have difficulty in capturing the scene changes in rushes videos, whereas the proposed feature vectors provide reliable segmentation. Secondly, to compute the semantic vector for each keyframe we also consider the semantic feature vectors of its neighboring frames. The neighborhood of a key-frame contains the frames that fall inside a window centered at the keyframe. The reason behind such a representation is that the extracted keyframe may not describe sufficiently the concepts of the video shot due to incorrect keypoints detection and description. In other words, by using the neighborhood of each keyframe, we aim to provide a more reliable representation with respect to the probability that certain concepts exist in a video shot. Finally, we employ a face and body detection algorithm to eliminate false detections of scene boundaries between successive shots that contain similar faces/bodies.

The rest of the paper is organized as follows. In Section 2 we describe the computation of semantic feature vectors and the representation of frames and shots. In Section 3 we present rushes segmentation and performance improvement using a face and body detection algorithm. In Section 4 we present numerical experiments. Finally, in Section 5 we conclude our work.

2 Semantic Features

Each video is segmented into shots manually to assess the performance of our method without having any errors introduced from the shot segmentation process. Moreover, for each shot, we extract keyframes using the method described in [5].

2.1 Frame Representation

Semantic concept detectors are employed in order to extract semantic features for each shot frame. Two different databases of semantic concept detectors are employed in the herein approach. The first one, named Vireo-374 detectors [6], is trained on TRECVID-2005 [8] development data using LSCOM annotation [9]. In order to train these detectors DoG detector and SIFT descriptor [10] are used for keypoint detection and description. The bag of visual words representation [11] is implemented for frame representation. More than 500k SIFT features are clustered into 500 visual words (visual vocabulary). For each frame, its corresponding set of descriptors is mapped into these 500 visual words resulting into a vector containing the normalized count of each visual word in the frame. The soft-weighting scheme [6] is used to weight the significance of each visual word in the frame, which has been demonstrated to be more effective than the traditional tf/tf-idf weighting schemes. LibSVM package [12] and Chi-square kernel are used for model training and prediction on test data.

The second database of semantic detectors, named Vireo-Web81 [7], is trained on approximately 160k images taken from social media such as Flickr. 81 concept detectors are trained with settings similar to Vireo-374.

The output of each SVM is a number in the continuous range [0,1], expressing the probability that each frame is related to the corresponding concept. Each shot frame is tested on 374 and 81 semantic detectors of video-374 and web81 databases, respectively. Thus, given K concepts, a frame f is represented from the following semantic vector:

$$v(f) = [c_1(f), c_2(f), \ldots, c_K(f)], \tag{1}$$

where $c_i(f)$ is the probability that frame f is related to concept c_i, $i = 1, \ldots, K$. Thus, vector v is a representation of frame f in the semantic space defined by K concepts. In the herein approach, for each frame f, two semantic feature vectors are computed, $v_{374}(f)$ and $v_{81}(f)$, corresponding to Vireo-374 [6] and Vireo-Web81 [7] detectors, respectively.

2.2 Shot Representation

Each shot is represented by a certain number of keyframes extracted using the method presented in [5] and their corresponding feature vectors. This is the most common approach for shot representation when further processing is required. However, in the herein approach to compute the feature vector of a key-frame we consider not only this frame itself, but also the feature vectors of its neighboring frames. The reason behind such a representation is that the extracted keyframe may not describe sufficiently the concepts of the video shot due to incorrect keypoints detection and description. In other words, by using the neighborhood of each keyframe, we aim to provide a more reliable representation with respect to the probability that certain concepts exist in a video shot. In this way, if a concept c_i exists in most of the frames of the neighborhood of a keyframe kf, then with high probability it exists on the corresponding keyframe, thus it is correctly represented in its semantic feature vectors $v_{374}(kf)$ and $v_{81}(kf)$.

More specifically, given a keyframe kf_i, we choose a set of frames in the neighborhood of kf_i as follows:

$$N_{kf_i} = \{\ldots, f_{i-3d}, f_{i-2d}, f_{i-d}, kf_i, f_{i+d}, f_{i+2d}, f_{i+3d}, \ldots\}, \tag{2}$$

where d is the distance between two frames.

Given the neighborhood of a shot's keyframe and their corresponding semantic features, we define the following shot representations:

- **Representation SR^1**: For each keyframe kf_i we compute a feature vector as the mean of the semantic features of its neighborhood.

$$SR^1_{kf_i} = \frac{\sum_{j \in N_{kf_i}} v_j}{N_{kf_i}}, \tag{3}$$

where $v_j, j = 1 \in N_{kf_i}$ is the semantic feature vector of j-th frame in neighborhood N_{kf_i} of keyframe kf_i.

- **Representation SR^2**: Each keyframe is represented by its corresponding semantic feature vector. This is the most common representation in video processing.

$$SR^2_{kf_i} = v_{kf_i}. \tag{4}$$

Summarizing, given a video shot $S = \{kf_1, \ldots, kf_N\}$, with N keyframes, the shot is finally represented by the following feature vectors:

$$SR^r_S = \{SR^r_{kf_i}, i = 1, \ldots, N\}, \tag{5}$$

where r=1, 2.

3   Rushes Segmentation

To find groups of repetitive and similar shots we compare successive pair of shots. If two shots are found different, then at the second shot starts a new group of similar shots. Thus, given a series of M videos shots $V = \{S_1, S_2, \ldots, S_M\}, i = 1, \ldots, M$, we seek to find groups of similar shots, or segment the video shot sequence in segments of similar shots.

Suppose we are given two shots i, j and the semantic feature vectors of their corresponding sets of keyframes (or their neighborhood) $S_i = \{SR^i_1, SR^i_2, \ldots, SR^i_{N_i}\}$ and $S_j = \{SR^j_1, SR^j_2, \ldots, SR^j_{N_j}\}$, respectively. N_i and N_j the number of frames that represent shots i, j, respectively. SR can be any of the two representations given from Eq. 3 and Eq. 4. The distance between these two shots is defined as the minimum distance among all possible pairs of their respective representative semantic feature vectors and is given from the following equation:

$$D(S_i, S_j) = \min_{SR^i_k \in S_i, SR^j_n \in S_j} (dist(SR^i_k, SR^j_n)), \tag{6}$$

where $k = 1, \ldots, N_i, n = 1, \ldots, N_j$ and $dist$ is the Euclidean distance:

$$dist(x, y) = \sqrt{\sum_h (x_h - y_h)^2}. \tag{7}$$

If distance D is over a predefined threshold t_d, a scene boundary is detected.

3.1   Face and Body Detection

In order to improve the performance of our method, we employ the well-known Viola & Jones algorithm [13] to detect faces and upper-body region, which is defined as the head and shoulders area. We detect faces and upper body regions on each keyframe of every video shot and its corresponding neighborhood. We expect to eliminate false detections, detected by our method, between shots that have similar faces or/and bodies. Face and body detection are performed only in case where scene boundary is detected from our method. Then, after extracting faces and bodies, we calculate the histograms of the detected regions in every frame containing the face/body. The distance between two shots with respect to face/ body histograms is defined as the minimum distance between all possible pairs of the face/body histograms of their respective representative frames. If this distance is below a predefined threshold, these shots are regarded as similar, thus scene boundary is removed and performance is expected to be improved.

4   Experiments

In this Section, we present the video dataset and the performance metrics that have been used in our experiments.

4.1   Datasets and Performance Metrics

We have tested our method on TRECVID 2008 Test Data which was available on the Rushes Summarization task of TRECVID 2008 [8]. The performance of our method was tested on 10 videos. To evaluate the performance of the proposed algorithm and the algorithms under comparison, we have used $F1$ metric provided from the following equation:

$$F1 = \frac{2 \times P \times R}{P + R}, \tag{8}$$

where P and R are Precision and Recall, respectively, and are computed form the following equations:

$$P = \frac{\#\text{correct detections}}{\#\text{correct detections} + \#\text{false detections}}, \tag{9}$$

$$R = \frac{\#\text{correct detections}}{\#\text{correct detections} + \#\text{missed detections}}. \tag{10}$$

4.2   Experimental Results

In Table 1, we present performance results of our method for both shot representations, R^1 and R^2. Four different experiments are presented. In the first two experiments presented as "VIREO - 374" and "VIREO - WEB81", semantic feature vectors $v_{374}(f)$

Table 1. Performance results of the proposed method

Method	Neighborhood (N)	Step (d) 0 0	1 3	1 5	1 7	3 7	5 7
VIREO - 374	SR^1	-	82.75	83.76	83.25	85.80	**87.43**
	SR^2	80.11	-	-	-	-	-
VIREO - WEB81	SR^1	-	84.38	84.11	**87.14**	86.21	86.81
	SR^2	79.92	-	-	-	-	-
CONCATENATION	SR^1	-	87.79	88.15	87.09	87.81	**85.59**
	SR^2	83.72	-	-	-	-	-
COMBINATION	SR^1	-	89.69	88.78	87.00	87.29	**92.99**
	SR^2	84.89	-	-	-	-	-

and $v_{81}(f)$ are employed to represent shot frames. In the third experiment, presented as "Concatenation", semantic feature vectors $v_{374}(f)$ and $v_{81}(f)$ are concatenated to form semantic feature vector $v_{con}(f)$ to represent shot frames. Finally, in the fourth experiment, presented as "Combination", the distance between two shots S_i, S_j is computed as the weighted average of the distances computed when semantic feature vectors $v_{374}(f)$ and $v_{81}(f)$ are employed to represent shot frames. The new weighted distance D_c is given from the following equation:

$$D_c(S_i, S_j) = \alpha D_{374}(S_i, S_j) + (1 - \alpha)D_{81}(S_i, S_j), \tag{11}$$

where $0 \leq \alpha \leq 1$, D_{374} and D_{81} are the distances computed from Eq. 6, when semantic feature vectors $v_{374}(f)$ and $v_{81}(f)$ are employed to represent shot frames, respectively. It is obvious that $\alpha = 0$ corresponds to experiment "VIREO - WEB81", whereas $\alpha = 1$ corresponds to experiment "VIREO - 374". When SR^1 representation is employed, the neighborhood of a keyframe N (Eq. 2), takes value 3, 5 or 7 when distance $d = 1$ and 7 when $d = 3, 5$. When SR^2 representation is employed only the keyframe is used, thus d, N are equal to zero. Threshold t_d is different for each experiment but same for all videos in the same experiment.

It is obvious that when a shot is represented by the neighborhoods of the keyframes the performance is better that using only keyframes. Moreover, better performance is achieved when the size of the neighborhood and distance from the keyframes increase. In Table 2, we present performance result after refining segmentation using face/body detection. We use thresholds $t_f = 0.01$ for face and $t_b = 0.02$ for body to define whether two shots are similar w.r.t to face/body detection. It is clear that the proposed refinement of scene boundaries increases the performance of the proposed method. In Table 3, we present performance results using only face and/or body detection to compare shots. Performance is poor due to absence of faces/bodies in many shots. Thus, face/body detection results can only serve as a refinement feature.

Table 2. Performance results of the proposed method after refinement with face/body detection

		$F1$ (in%)					
	Step (d)	0	1	1	1	3	5
Method	Neighborhood (N)	0	3	5	7	7	7
VIREO - 374	SR^1	-	83.41	83.76	83.25	85.80	**87.43**
	SR^2	80.68	-	-	-	-	-
VIREO - WEB81	SR^1	-	84.38	84.11	87.14	86.21	**87.77**
	SR^2	81.02	-	-	-	-	-
CONCATENATION	SR^1	-	87.79	88.15	87.09	87.81	**88.60**
	SR^2	84.49	-	-	-	-	-
COMBINATION	SR^1	-	89.69	88.78	90.18	87.29	**93.30**
	SR^2	85.60	-	-	-	-	-

Table 3. Performance results using only face and body detection

		$F1$ (in%)					
	Step (d)	0	1	1	1	3	5
Method	Neighborhood (N)	0	3	5	7	7	7
Face	SR^1	-	54.00	55.00	55.00	55.00	55.00
	SR^2	52.00	-	-	-	-	-
Body	SR^1	-	54.00	54.00	54.00	54.00	50.00
	SR^2	52.00	-	-	-	-	-
Face & Body	SR^1	-	54.00	53.00	54.00	54.00	50.00
	SR^2	53.00	-	-	-	-	-

4.3 Comparison

In this Section we present comparative results of our method using HSV color histograms instead of semantic feature vectors, in order to show the superiority of semantic features in rushes segmentation. In Table 4, we present performance results using HSV color histograms. We use 8 bins for hue and 4 bins for each of saturation and value, resulting into a 128 ($8 \times 4 \times 4$) dimension feature vector. The main disadvantage of these descriptors is that they only represent the color distribution of an object ignoring its shape and texture. Color histograms are also sensitive to noise, such as lighting changes. It is clear that HSV color histograms have difficulty in capturing the changes between groups of similar shots.

Moreover, since SIFT descriptors are employed to compute semantic features, we provide performance results using the number of matching descriptors between shots as a shot similarity metric. For each keyframe and its neighborhood (Eq. 2) we extract SIFT descriptors. The number of matching descriptors [10] between two shots serves as the shot similarity metric. More specifically, the maximum number of matching descriptors between all possible pairs of their respective representative frames is the final similarity value. Two shots belong to different groups, thus they are not similar, if their respective similarity value is below a threshold set to 0.04 in our experiments.

Table 4. Performance results using HSV color histograms and SIFT descriptors

Method	Step (d) Neighborhood (N)	$F1$ (in%) 0 0	1 3	1 5	1 7	3 7	5 7
HSV	SR^1	-	79.06	79.04	79.38	78.71	78.74
	SR^2	79.46	-	-	-	-	-
SIFT	SR^1	-	78.76	78.18	76.05	73.76	73.46
	SR^2	77.28	-	-	-	-	-
SIFT - IMPROVED	SR^1	-	82.84	83.54	83.40	83.13	81.53
	SR^2	80.14	-	-	-	-	-

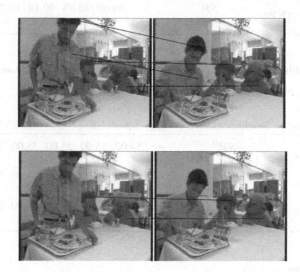

Fig. 1. Subset of the matching descriptors between two "similar" frames, before and after imposing spatial constraint

In Table 4, we present performance results using SIFT descriptors. It can be observed that matching SIFT descriptors does not provide good results. A main reason for this is that the same actors/object/setting may appear in two shots that belong to different groups/scenes. For this reason a spatial constraint on matching descriptors is employed. Given the coordinates (x, y) of a descriptor, we seek to find a matching descriptor with coordinates in area $(x \pm s, y \pm s)$, where s is set to 20 in our experiments. In Fig. 1 we present a subset of the matching descriptors between two "similar" frames, before and after imposing spatial constraint. Performance results are presented in Table 4. It is clear that performance is improved. However, semantic features vectors still provide the best performance.

In another experiment we carried out, we reduce the number of concepts employed to form semantic feature vectors. More specifically, for each concept we compute the mean probability of occurrence across all videos. If this mean value is below a predefined threshold t_c, the corresponding concept is not taken into consideration. In Fig. 2

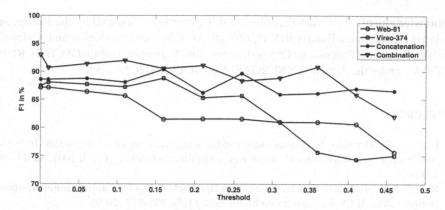

Fig. 2. Performance results of our method using $d=5$ and $N=7$ on a subset of concepts

and Fig. 3, we present performance results and the corresponding number of concepts with respect to threshold t_c, respectively. It can be observed that even with a subset of concepts, our method yields very good results.

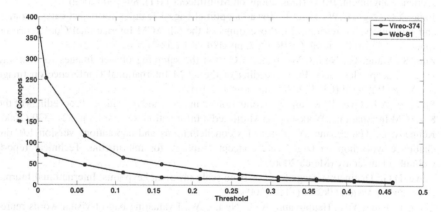

Fig. 3. Number of concepts w.r.t threshold t_c

5   Conclusions

In this paper a rushes video segmentation method is proposed. Contrary to existing approaches, shot frames are represented by semantic feature vectors extracted using common semantic concept detectors. Moreover, each keyframe is represented by the mean of the semantic features vectors of its neighborhood, defined as the frames that fall inside a window centered at the keyframe. Next, successive shots are compared to find boundaries between groups of similar shots. Face and body detection is employed to improve the performance of our method by eliminating false boundaries detected between shots with similar faces/bodies. Numerical experiments show that the proposed method can efficient segment rushes videos in groups of similar shots.

Acknowledgment. The work described in this paper is co-financed by the European Regional Development Fund (ERDF) (2007-2013) of the European Union and National Funds (Operational Programme Competitiveness and Entrepreneurship (OPCE II), ROP ATTICA), under the Action "SYNERGASIA (COOPERATION) 2009".

References

1. Dumont, E., Merialdo, B.: Rushes video parsing using video sequence alignment. In: Seventh International Workshop on Content-Based Multimedia Indexing, CBMI 2009, pp. 44–49 (2009)
2. Ren, J., Jiang, J.: Hierarchical modeling and adaptive clustering for real-time summarization of rush videos. IEEE Transactions on Multimedia 11(5), 906–917 (2009)
3. Rossi, E., Benini, S., Leonardi, R., Mansencal, B., Benois-Pineau, J.: Clustering of scene repeats for essential rushes preview. In: 10th Workshop on Image Analysis for Multimedia Interactive Services, WIAMIS 2009, pp. 234–237 (2009)
4. Chasanis, V., Likas, A., Galatsanos, N.: Video rushes summarization using spectral clustering and sequence alignment. In: TVS 2008: Proceedings of the 2nd ACM TRECVid Video Summarization Workshop, Vancouver, British Columbia, Canada, pp. 75–79 (2008)
5. Chasanis, V., Likas, A., Galatsanos, N.: Scene detection in videos using shot clustering and sequence alignment. IEEE Transactions on Multimedia 11(1), 89–100 (2009)
6. Jiang, Y.G., Ngo, C.W., Yang, J.: Towards optimal bag-of-features for object categorization and semantic video retrieval. In: Proceedings of the 6th ACM International Conference on Image and Video Retrieval, CIVR 2007, pp. 494–501 (2007)
7. Zhu, S., Wang, G., Ngo, C.W., Jiang, Y.G.: On the sampling of web images for learning visual concept classifiers. In: Proceeding of the ACM International Conference on Image and Video Retrieval (CIVR 2010), pp. 50–57 (2010)
8. Smeaton, A.F., Over, P., Kraaij, W.: Evaluation campaigns and trecvid. In: Proceedings of the 8th ACM International Workshop on Multimedia Information Retrieval, pp. 321–330 (2006)
9. Kennedy, L., Hauptmann, A.: Lscom lexicon definitions and annotations version 1.0, dto challenge workshop on large scale concept ontology for multimedia. Technical report, Columbia University (March 2006)
10. Lowe, D.G.: Distinctive image features from scale-invariant keypoints. International Journal of Computer Vision 60(2), 91–110 (2004)
11. Yang, J., Jiang, Y.G., Hauptmann, A.G., Ngo, C.W.: Evaluating bag-of-visual-words representations in scene classification. In: Proceedings of the International Workshop on Workshop on Multimedia Information Retrieval, MIR 2007, pp. 197–206 (2007)
12. Chang, C.C., Lin, C.J.: LIBSVM: A library for support vector machines. ACM Transactions on Intelligent Systems and Technology 2, 27:1–27:27 (2011), http://www.csie.ntu.edu.tw/~cjlin/libsvm
13. Viola, P., Jones, M.: Rapid object detection using a boosted cascade of simple features. In: Proceedings of the 2001 IEEE Computer Society Conference on Computer Vision and Pattern Recognition, CVPR 2001, vol. 1, pp. 511–518 (2001)

Activity Recognition for Traditional Dances Using Dimensionality Reduction

Vasileios Gavriilidis and Anastasios Tefas

Aristotle University of Thessaloniki, Department of Informatics,
Thessaloniki, Greece
vgavril@csd.auth.gr, tefas@aiia.csd.auth.gr

Abstract. Activity recognition is a complex problem mainly because of the nature of the data. Data usually are high dimensional, so applying a classifier directly to the data is not always a good practice. A common method is to find a meaningful representation of complex data through dimensionality reduction. In this paper we propose novel kernel matrices based on graph theory to be used for dimensionality reduction. The proposed kernel can be embedded in a general dimensionality reduction framework. Experiments on a traditional dance recognition dataset are conducted and the advantage of using dimensionality reduction before classification is highlighted.

Keywords: Random Walk Kernel, Activity Recognition, Dimensionality Reduction, Support Vector Machines.

1 Introduction

Activity recognition is an important and active area of computer vision research. Video surveillance and video annotation are two fields that use activity recognition of everyday actions such as walking, running and sitting. Surveys of activity recognition approaches can be found in [5,11,14]. The importance of generic activity recognition relies on the fact that it can be applied to many real-life problems, with most of them being human–centric [4]. An example of the activity recognition problem is dance recognition [6]. Dance recognition is a difficult problem, since it involves the movement of the body in a specific way that characterise a specific dance. Dances are performed in many cultures to express ideas or tell a story, which suggests their importance especially for countries with long history, such us Greece.

Dance recognition problems usually begin with video recordings and with labelling a video. In order for those videos to be used in a classifier, features need to be extracted. A commonly used framework for transferring the problem from video recording to a feature space, where all data have the same dimensions, is the bag–of–features approach [10]. Such methods for feature extraction from videos are *STIP*, *TRAJ* and *ISA* which have been proposed in [8,15,9], respectively.

A. Likas, K. Blekas, and D. Kalles (Eds.): SETN 2014, LNAI 8445, pp. 115–125, 2014.

Another example of feature extraction is dimensionality reduction used for transferring a feature space to a lower feature space. Dimensionality reduction is a commonly used preprocessing step in machine learning, especially when dealing with a high dimensional space of features which can enhance data separability [7]. Many methods for dimensionality reduction exist; the most common of them are embedded in the framework described in [16]. Using the aforementioned framework we can retain or avoid specific statistical or geometrical properties of our data. For this reason a graph is created, specifically a k–nearest neighbour graph.

Graph properties are described extensively in [2]. One of the properties of a graph, that will be used in this paper, is that if $\mathbf{W}$ represents the adjacency matrix between nodes, where $W(i, j) = 1$ if nodes i and j are connected and $W(i, j) = 0$ otherwise, then the ij–th element of the p-th power of adjacency matrix, $W^p(i, j)$, gives the number of paths of length p between nodes i and j. This notion can be applied to either directed or undirected graphs and can also be extended to weighted graphs, $W(i, j) \in [0, \inf)$. In this paper, we propose the use of the number of paths between two samples of the dataset as a similarity that can be embedded in a general dimensionality reduction framework as it will be explained in the following Sections.

The structure of the paper is as follows: In Section 2 we describe previous work and state the problem we solve. We then introduce our method for dimensionality reduction in Section 3, providing some theoretical background. In Section 4 we explain the way we conducted our experiments and present classification results on traditional dance recognition. We also show some interesting dimensionality reduction projections. Finally we give concluding remarks and discussion of future work in Section 5.

2   Prior Work and Problem Statement

Usually, activity recognition datasets consist of videos. Firstly, the bag–of–features approach [10] is typically performed and later a codeword is created by applying k–means to the extracted features. The last step is to map each recording video to a certain codebook and, thus, the original recording can be represented as a histogram of codewords. Depending on the number of centres of k–means a different codeword is produced and, hence, a different representation for each recording is created. Let the recordings represented as histograms of codewords be the data matrix $\mathbf{X}$.

Techniques for dimensionality reduction have always attracted interest in computer vision and pattern recognition. Graph embedding [16] provides a general framework for dimensionality reduction and many algorithms can be integrated into this framework. Let an undirected weighted graph $G\{X, W\}$ be defined as a vertex set X and similarity matrix $\mathbf{W}$ whose entries can be positive, negative or zero. Also let a diagonal matrix $\mathbf{D}$ be constructed as:

$$D_{ii} = \sum_{i \neq j} W_{ij}, \tag{1}$$

and Laplacian matrix as:

$$\mathbf{L} = \mathbf{D} - \mathbf{W}, \tag{2}$$

The aim of graph embedding is to find a procedure where desired characteristics between nodes of the graph are preserved and undesired properties of the data are suppressed after dimensionality reduction. Hence, a penalty graph is also defined as $G\{X, W^d\}$, where $\mathbf{W^d}$ is the same matrix as $\mathbf{W}$ but whose entries are to be suppressed in the new feature space. Graph embedding framework requires the solution to the generalized eigenvalue decomposition problem:

$$\tilde{\mathbf{L}}\mathbf{U} = l\tilde{\mathbf{B}}\mathbf{U}, \tag{3}$$

where $\tilde{\mathbf{L}} - \mathbf{L}, \mathbf{XLX}^T$ or $\mathbf{KLK}$ and $\tilde{\mathbf{B}} = \mathbf{I}, \mathbf{B}, \mathbf{K}, \mathbf{XBX}^T$ or $\mathbf{KBK}$, depending on the dimensionality reduction algorithm to be used with $\mathbf{B}$ typically being a diagonal matrix for scale normalization. After calculating the matrix $\mathbf{U}$, we choose those eigenvectors that correspond to the smallest eigenvalues of l.

3   Proposed Dimensionality Reduction Method

In the case of Locality Preserving Projections (LPP) a graph neighborhood of the data is incorporated [3]. It uses the notion of the Laplacian of the graph and then a transformation maps data to a subspace. The tranformation optimally preserves local neighborhood information and can be embedded to the general framework [16]. For the kernel version of LPP, the substitution in order to be embedded to the framework is $\tilde{\mathbf{L}} = \mathbf{KLK}$ and $\tilde{\mathbf{B}} = \mathbf{KBK}$. This suggests that the similarities in the new space will be comparable to the similarities of the original space after the transformation of the data through the kernel function $\Phi(.)$.

Even though kernel LPP typically uses the RBF kernel, this is not mandatory and any matrix can be chosen as long as it is a kernel. There are various kernel functions that can be used; linear, polynomial, RBF and sigmoid are some examples. Another kind of kernels, are random walk kernels which were first proposed in [13] and later were used as kernel matrices for semi–supervised learning using cluster kernels [1] .

Random walk kernel based on [1] is computed in two steps. First, RBF kernel matrix is computed and then, each value is normalised by the sum of its row. The resulted matrix can also be seen as a transition matrix of a random walk on a graph. This suggests probability of starting from one point and arriving at another. Using a diagonal matrix defined as in equation (1) the transition matrix has the form of:

$$\mathbf{P} = \mathbf{D}^{-1}\mathbf{K}. \tag{4}$$

thus the matrix $\mathbf{P}^p = (\mathbf{D}^{-1}\mathbf{K})^p$ can be interpreted as transition probability after p steps. Unfortunately, matrix $\mathbf{P}^p$ is not symmetric, hence it can not be used as a kernel.

Another example of random walk kernel is introduced in [12]. Assume that we have the adjacency matrix $\mathbf{W}$, with $W_{ij} = 1$ if samples i and j are neighbours and zero otherwise, and the Normalised Laplacian:

$$\tilde{\mathbf{L}} = \mathbf{D}^{-\frac{1}{2}}\mathbf{L}\mathbf{D}^{-\frac{1}{2}}. \tag{5}$$

the p–step random walk kernel is computed as:

$$\mathbf{K} = (a\mathbf{I} - \tilde{\mathbf{L}})^p, \text{ with } a \geqslant 2. \tag{6}$$

In general $\mathbf{W}$ has no restriction about the graphs it can be applied to. In addition, parameter a ensures positive definiteness of $\mathbf{K}$.

Starting from the simplest kernel, which is inner product, we propose a random walk kernel for dimensionality reduction. The inner product, expresses the similarity between i-th and j-th sample and is defined as:

$$W(i,j) = \mathbf{x}_i^T\mathbf{x}_j. \tag{7}$$

Let i–th and j–th samples be represented as nodes in an unweighted graph with $W(i,j) = 0$ meaning samples are not similar and $W(i,j) = 1$ meaning samples are similar.

We may now propose the similarity matrix:

$$\mathbf{W}^p = \underbrace{\mathbf{W}\mathbf{W}\dots\mathbf{W}}_{p \text{ times}}. \tag{8}$$

We can say that $W^p(i,j)$ expresses the similarity between i–th and j–th samples after visiting all possible paths passing from $p - 1$ in–between similar samples.

Extending the notion of the discrete values of similar and not similar (0 and 1) to continuous values, we define a relaxed definition of a weighted graph which can take values in $[0 - \inf)$, where 0 is the least similar and inf is the most similar. This way, when two samples' similarity is computed, more paths are approachable, since the only paths that are not viable are those that pass from an intermediate sample that has zero similarity. In reality, every single path is involved because even though the similarity of two samples can be small, it is rarely zero. For example, the similarity matrix passing from one intermediate sample can be computed as $\mathbf{W}^2 = \mathbf{X}^T\mathbf{X}\mathbf{X}^T\mathbf{X}$.

Without loss of generality, we assume that data matrix has zero mean, hence $\mathbf{X}\mathbf{X}^T = \mathbf{\Sigma}$, where $\mathbf{\Sigma}$ is the covariance matrix, thus $\mathbf{W}^2 = \mathbf{X}^T\mathbf{\Sigma}\mathbf{X}$ also holds. Moreover, it is straightforward to show that $\mathbf{W}^p = \mathbf{X}^T\mathbf{\Sigma}^{p-1}\mathbf{X}$, with $p \geqslant 1$.

So, $\mathbf{W}^p$ is a similarity matrix and $W^p(i,j)$ expresses the similarity of two samples beginning from the i-th sample and ending at the j-th sample after passing through $p-1$ intermediate samples. The goal is to connect similar nodes by several paths. Even if $\mathbf{W}^p$ is a similarity matrix, this does not necessarily mean that it can be used as a kernel matrix. We now prove that apart from $\mathbf{W}$, which is by definition a kernel matrix, $\mathbf{W}^p$ is also a kernel matrix.

It is safe to replace $\mathbf{W}$ by $\mathbf{K}$ since $\mathbf{W}$ is positive definite. $\mathbf{K}$ has an eigenvalue decomposition $\mathbf{K} = \mathbf{U}^T \mathbf{\Lambda} \mathbf{U}$, where $\mathbf{U}$ is an orthogonal matrix and $\mathbf{\Lambda}$ is a diagonal matrix of real and positive eigenvalues, that is, $\mathbf{\Lambda} = diag(\lambda_1, \lambda_2, \ldots, \lambda_D)$. So, now $\mathbf{W}^p$ can be written as:

$$\mathbf{W}^p = \underbrace{\mathbf{K}\mathbf{K}\ldots\mathbf{K}}_{p \text{ times}}$$

$$= \mathbf{U}^T \mathbf{\Lambda} \underbrace{\mathbf{U}\mathbf{U}^T}_{I} \mathbf{\Lambda} \underbrace{\mathbf{U}\mathbf{U}^T}_{I} \ldots \underbrace{\mathbf{U}\mathbf{U}^T}_{I} \mathbf{\Lambda} \mathbf{U}$$

$$= \mathbf{U}^T \underbrace{\mathbf{\Lambda}\ldots\mathbf{\Lambda}}_{p \text{ times}} \mathbf{U}$$

$$= \mathbf{U}^T \mathbf{\Lambda}^p \mathbf{U}. \tag{9}$$

Since eigenvalues $\lambda_i > 0, \forall i = 1, \ldots, N$ then $\lambda_i^p > 0, \forall i = 1, \ldots, N$, which leads to $\mathbf{x}\mathbf{W}^p\mathbf{x}^T \geq 0, \forall \mathbf{x}$ which is the definition of a positive definite matrix. Notice that no assumptions were made for the original kernel matrix. Thus, in general every kernel matrix elevated to any power is also a kernel matrix.

Now, $\mathbf{W}^p$ can safely be used as a Kernel. Moreover, when inner product is used as the initial kernel matrix, and assuming data have zero mean, we arrive at an interesting property. The covariance matrix, $\mathbf{\Sigma}$, is symmetric and has real values, so it has an eigenvalue decomposition that can be written as:

$$\mathbf{\Sigma} = \mathbf{U}\mathbf{D}\mathbf{U}^T. \tag{10}$$

Hence:

$$\mathbf{W}^p = \mathbf{X}^T \mathbf{\Sigma}^{p-1} \mathbf{X}$$

$$= \mathbf{X}^T \mathbf{U}\mathbf{D}^{p-1}\mathbf{U}^T \mathbf{X}$$

$$= (\mathbf{D}^{\frac{p-1}{2}}\mathbf{U}^T\mathbf{X})^T (\mathbf{D}^{\frac{p-1}{2}}\mathbf{U}^T\mathbf{X}). \tag{11}$$

So, kernel $\mathbf{W}^p$ can be calculated differently by multiplying data matrix $\mathbf{X}$ by $\mathbf{D}^{\frac{p-1}{2}}\mathbf{U}^T$. The calculation of inner product of the transformed data matrix with itself yields the same results as when using original data and $\mathbf{W}^p$.

RBF kernel is defined as:

$$K(\mathbf{x}_i, \mathbf{x}_j) = e^{-\frac{|\mathbf{x}_i - \mathbf{x}_j|^2}{2\sigma^2}}, \tag{12}$$

so $K^p(\mathbf{x}_i, \mathbf{x}_j), p \geqslant 1$ can be expressed as:

$$K^p(\mathbf{x}_i, \mathbf{x}_j) = \sum_{l_1}^{N} \cdots \sum_{l_{p-1}}^{N} e^{-\frac{|\mathbf{x}_i - \mathbf{x}_{l_1}|^2}{2\sigma^2}} \cdots e^{-\frac{|\mathbf{x}_{l_{p-1}} - \mathbf{x}_j|^2}{2\sigma^2}}$$

$$= \sum_{l_1}^{N} \cdots \sum_{l_{p-1}}^{N} e^{-\frac{|\mathbf{x}_i - \mathbf{x}_{l_1}|^2 + \cdots + |\mathbf{x}_{l_{p-1}} - \mathbf{x}_j|^2}{2\sigma^2}}. \tag{13}$$

By examining equation (13) we observe that the distance between two nodes is relative to the whole structure of the graph, since in order to compute the distance of two nodes, all the nodes of the graph are taken into account which resembles a graph based distance. The property we would like to retain is for the number of all possible paths after p steps to be the same after dimensionality reduction.

Finally, kernel LPP keeps the similarities between samples the same, after the dimensionality reduction by using $\mathbf{K}$. Using this notion, we similarly use $\mathbf{K}^p$ to keep the similarities after visiting all possible paths passing through $p - 1$ intermediate samples. In order to achieve this, equation (3) is used to embed our proposed method to the framework using $\tilde{\mathbf{L}} = \mathbf{K}^p \mathbf{L} \mathbf{K}^p$ and $\tilde{\mathbf{B}} = \mathbf{K}^p \mathbf{B} \mathbf{K}^p$. Notice that like kernel LPP our proposed method is unsupervised and the labels of the data are not required.

4   Experimental Results

We performed classification to a dataset of Greek traditional dances. The dataset consists of 10 videos of 5 Greek traditional dances, the *Lotzia*, the *Capetan Loukas*, the *Ramna*, the *Stankaina* and finally the *Zablitsaina*. In more detail, two professional dancing groups were recorded dancing. Each traditional dance was performed twice, once indoor by one group and once outdoor by another group. In Figure 1, two frames of two different videos are illustrated.

The 5 recordings of indoor were used for training and the outdoor recordings were used for testing. In order, to transform the video recordings to feature vectors we have extracted *ISA STIP* and *TRAJ*. Using overlapping clips of 80 to 100 frames we ended up with 78, 113, 110, 95 and 101 clips for each training video and for each testing video to 102, 107, 110, 106 and 91 clips, resulting to 497 and 516 short sequences overall, respectively. Also we have created a dataset consisting of only 8 videos out of 10, without the dance *Zablitsaina*. The different representations of the traditional dance dataset characteristics are depicted in Table 1.

All representations were scaled to the interval $[0, 1]$. We conducted experiments using SVM with the linear kernel and the RBF kernel. The evaluation of parameters was performed by using grid search of 5–fold cross validation. Using the best parameters found on training set, we trained once more using the entire training dataset in order to predict the classes of the test set. More specifically, we trained with exponentially growing sequences of $C \in \{2^{-5}, \ldots, 2^{15}\}$

Table 1. Representations of Traditional Dances Dataset

Extracted features	Train Samples	Test Samples	Clusters	Classes
isa.10	497	516	10	5
isa.100	497	516	100	5
stip.10	497	516	10	5
stip.100	497	516	100	5
stip.1000	497	516	1000	5
stip.2000	497	516	2000	5
traj.10	497	516	10	5
traj.100	497	516	100	5
traj.1000	497	516	1000	5
isa4.100	396	425	100	4
isa4.1000	396	425	1000	4

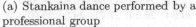

(a) Stankaina dance performed by a professional group

(b) Stankaina dance performed by another professional group with different costumes

Fig. 1. Sample Frame of Two Videos

and $\gamma \in \{2^{-15}, \ldots, 2^3\}$. Obviously, inner product uses only parameter C and the RBF kernel uses both parameters C and γ.

Apart from SVM, we also need to choose a kernel for the dimensionality reduction method that was proposed. We chose to evaluate dimensionality reduction using the kernels as described in equations (8) and (13). In addition, our proposed method requires the selection of the parameter p. Thus, we used a procedure for finding automatically the parameter p similarly to grid search. Assume, we want to find the parameter p when our data is projected onto a 2–dimensional space. We produce all different projections of original data using $p = \{1, \ldots, 11\}$, then for each projection we perform grid search, looking for parameters of the SVM, while we also keep the one of 11 projections that attained the best performance on the grid search.

As illustrated in Tables 2–5, the proposed dimensionality reduction method improves the performance of SVM. For the recognition of the 5 traditional dances, regardless of which features were extracted (*ISA STIP* and *TRAJ*), and also regardless of which kernel was used for classification the best SVM result attained was 51.74%. On the other hand, projecting data first to a lower

Table 2. Inner Product SVM + (Inner Product)^p

Dataset	SVM	Dimensions									
		1	2	3	4	5	6	7	8	9	10
isa.10	23.64	**33.53**	29.65	30.81	30.81	29.46	26.74	24.22	17.05	13.76	13.57
isa.100	40.12	**57.36**	33.53	40.31	33.33	49.61	39.53	23.45	34.30	32.95	34.30
stip.10	32.36	39.15	**40.12**	34.50	34.11	34.88	34.88	35.08	33.53	34.69	34.69
stip.100	33.72	36.43	36.24	32.75	**37.60**	35.66	35.27	31.40	32.17	22.48	23.06
stip.1000	36.05	34.30	33.72	**37.60**	30.04	30.23	29.65	29.65	29.65	29.07	35.66
stip.2000	30.43	35.66	33.14	28.68	28.29	28.29	32.56	34.11	37.79	38.18	**41.28**
traj.10	32.17	19.77	20.93	28.29	29.84	**32.36**	29.84	30.23	31.40	31.40	30.81
traj.100	32.75	20.16	27.71	34.50	30.81	33.72	34.50	34.50	35.47	36.63	**37.02**
traj.1000	**44.19**	27.52	25.19	41.47	43.22	43.41	43.80	35.85	38.57	40.89	39.92
isa4.100	54.59	30.12	37.65	48.94	56.47	68.71	71.29	76.47	31.06	31.06	**77.18**
isa4.1000	63.53	49.18	63.76	43.29	72.00	83.06	**89.18**	85.41	85.65	82.82	82.59

Table 3. RBF SVM + (Inner Product)^p

Dataset	SVM	Dimensions									
		1	2	3	4	5	6	7	8	9	10
isa.10	**40.70**	40.50	34.11	31.59	27.33	24.61	22.09	29.65	26.94	21.51	21.32
isa.100	51.74	50.58	54.26	50.97	**58.33**	43.22	38.18	27.91	27.52	27.52	18.60
stip.10	27.13	35.08	34.69	30.04	32.36	34.11	**37.21**	33.53	31.40	33.33	35.66
stip.100	21.32	**40.89**	37.21	31.59	29.46	27.91	27.33	32.56	29.65	28.88	32.56
stip.1000	22.09	26.94	**34.30**	32.17	28.68	29.84	28.29	27.71	29.26	29.07	23.26
stip.2000	22.67	21.71	28.29	29.65	29.46	31.01	31.78	29.26	25.19	31.01	**32.36**
traj.10	24.22	19.19	16.67	15.50	13.76	13.18	30.43	**36.82**	36.63	36.63	36.63
traj.100	20.74	21.51	15.12	22.09	20.54	20.74	21.71	21.12	23.06	25.97	**28.88**
traj.1000	22.67	23.26	33.33	31.59	36.63	35.27	37.40	**39.92**	**39.92**	35.08	34.69
isa4.100	54.82	21.88	24.00	49.88	**65.18**	24.24	50.59	52.94	50.59	50.12	49.18
isa4.1000	30.82	49.41	62.82	48.71	61.41	60.71	**82.82**	82.12	81.88	78.59	79.06

Table 4. Inner Product SVM + (RBF)^p

Dataset	SVM	Dimensions									
		1	2	3	4	5	6	7	8	9	10
isa.10	23.64	12.98	20.16	20.93	20.93	13.76	20.16	**27.71**	26.94	26.94	26.74
isa.100	40.12	43.99	35.47	49.81	48.26	54.46	37.98	38.37	44.77	43.99	**57.17**
stip.10	32.36	**39.73**	37.21	33.14	35.27	35.85	36.24	39.34	36.82	36.43	36.82
stip.100	33.72	37.21	35.47	36.43	35.27	36.82	35.66	42.44	**44.96**	42.25	32.36
stip.1000	36.05	34.30	36.24	**37.21**	36.63	36.43	36.43	36.63	28.68	24.81	20.54
stip.2000	30.43	36.05	**38.18**	29.84	31.01	29.46	30.04	29.65	26.16	29.65	30.23
traj.10	32.17	31.98	30.62	32.95	31.01	30.43	31.01	34.69	**34.88**	32.17	31.59
traj.100	32.75	31.78	36.24	34.69	**37.40**	36.82	34.69	34.11	33.14	30.62	28.88
traj.1000	**44.19**	20.93	35.85	23.84	29.46	34.11	26.94	27.91	26.16	26.94	25.19
isa4.100	54.59	73.88	70.59	68.00	**77.88**	54.35	56.47	56.47	57.18	57.41	57.88
isa4.1000	63.53	78.59	74.35	50.59	68.71	63.06	64.94	82.12	80.00	83.29	**88.71**

Table 5. RBF SVM + (RBF)^p

Dataset	SVM	Dimensions									
		1	2	3	4	5	6	7	8	9	10
isa.10	**40.70**	9.69	19.96	34.11	17.83	17.64	20.35	18.80	18.60	23.64	28.49
isa.100	51.74	29.65	31.01	**52.13**	45.35	49.42	24.42	48.26	25.00	27.71	35.85
stip.10	27.13	**35.47**	33.53	31.01	33.14	32.95	19.96	17.83	29.26	33.72	32.95
stip.100	21.32	33.33	**37.98**	33.91	34.88	34.69	30.04	30.43	31.78	31.78	30.81
stip.1000	22.09	36.43	36.05	33.91	**36.82**	32.95	29.07	22.09	29.65	25.97	19.96
stip.2000	22.67	24.22	23.84	36.43	**37.21**	30.62	27.13	26.74	22.87	30.23	29.26
traj.10	24.22	28.29	21.71	25.78	19.57	24.22	25.97	30.81	**31.40**	26.16	30.43
traj.100	20.74	34.30	34.30	**38.18**	36.43	37.40	32.56	35.66	35.27	32.75	29.26
traj.1000	22.67	33.72	25.58	28.10	**34.30**	32.95	34.11	33.53	34.11	32.56	31.01
isa4.100	54.82	**73.65**	61.00	64.94	72.71	34.82	32.24	29.18	29.65	24.47	30.35
isa4.1000	30.82	77.88	38.59	64.47	68.00	62.12	64.71	70.82	**78.82**	78.59	69.65

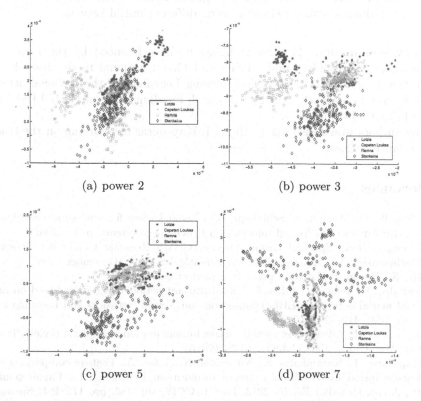

(a) power 2   (b) power 3

(c) power 5   (d) power 7

Fig. 2. isa4.100 projections using (Inner Product)^p with different values of p

space and then using SVM the best classification performance was 58.33%. Moreover, in the smaller dataset of 4 traditional dances, the best result, using SVM was 63.53% but using our proposed dimensionality reduction technique before classification improves classification accuracy to 89.18%. This means that the structure of the data can be represented in a lower dimensional space more effectively. For example, in Figure 2 some projections are illustrated, highlighting the structure of data with different values of p. It is obvious that different values of the parameter p of the proposed kernel result to significantly different representations with varying discriminality among the classes.

5   Conclusions

A novel kernel has been proposed which can be embedded to a dimensionality reduction framework. The proposed kernel produces representations that highlight the separability between classes. We performed classification using SVM as a classifier to a traditional dance recognition dataset and the advantage of using dimensionality reduction, before classifying, is highlighted. In addition, some interesting projections of the data were given. Future work can be focused on performing dimensionality reduction using different initial kernels.

Acknowledgements. This research has been co-financed by the European Union (European Social Fund - ESF) and Greek national funds through the Operation Program "Education and Lifelong Learning" of the National Strategic Reference Framework (NSRF) - Research Funding Program: THALIS-UOA-ERASITECHNIS MIS 375435.

The authors would also like to thank I. Kapsouras for working on the traditional dance dataset.

References

1. Chapelle, O., Weston, J., Scholkopf, B.: Cluster kernels for semi-supervised learning. In: Advances in Neural Information Processing Systems, p. 15 (2002)
2. Chung, F.R.K.: Spectral Graph Theory (CBMS Regional Conference Series in Mathematics, No. 92). American Mathematical Society (December 1996)
3. He, X., Niyogi, P.: Locality preserving projections (2002)
4. Iosifidis, A., Tefas, A., Pitas, I.: View-invariant action recognition based on artificial neural networks. IEEE Transactions on Neural Networks and Learning Systems 23(3), 412–424 (2012)
5. Ji, X., Liu, H.: Advances in view-invariant human motion analysis: A review. Trans. Sys. Man Cyber. Part C 40(1), 13–24 (2010)
6. Kapsouras, I., Karanikolos, S., Nikolaidis, N., Tefas, A.: Feature comparison and feature fusion for traditional dances recognition. In: Iliadis, L., Papadopoulos, H., Jayne, C. (eds.) EANN 2013, Part I. CCIS, vol. 383, pp. 172–181. Springer, Heidelberg (2013)
7. Kyperountas, M., Tefas, A., Pitas, I.: Salient feature and reliable classifier selection for facial expression classification. Pattern Recognition 43(3), 972–986 (2010)

8. Laptev, I., Marszalek, M., Schmid, C., Rozenfeld, B.: Learning realistic human actions from movies. In: IEEE Conference on Computer Vision and Pattern Recognition, CVPR 2008, pp. 1–8 (2008)
9. Le, Q.V., Zou, W.Y., Yeung, S.Y., Ng, A.Y.: Learning hierarchical invariant spatio-temporal features for action recognition with independent subspace analysis. In: Proceedings of the 2011 IEEE Conference on Computer Vision and Pattern Recognition, CVPR 2011, pp. 3361–3368. IEEE Computer Society, Washington, DC (2011)
10. Leung, T., Malik, J.: Representing and recognizing the visual appearance of materials using three-dimensional textons. International Journal of Computer Vision 43(1), 29–44 (2001)
11. Poppe, R.: A survey on vision-based human action recognition. Image Vision Comput. 28(6), 976–990 (2010)
12. Smola, A.J., Kondor, R.: Kernels and regularization on graphs (2003)
13. Szummer, M., Jaakkola, T.: Partially labeled classification with markov random walks. In: Advances in Neural Information Processing Systems 15. MIT Press, Cambridge (2001)
14. Turaga, P., Chellappa, R., Subrahmanian, V.S., Udrea, O.: Machine recognition of human activities: A survey. IEEE Transactions on Circuits and Systems for Video Technology 18(11), 1473–1488 (2008)
15. Wang, H., Kläser, A., Schmid, C., Liu, C.L.: Dense trajectories and motion boundary descriptors for action recognition. International Journal of Computer Vision 103(1), 60–79 (2013)
16. Yan, S., Xu, D., Zhang, B., Zhang, H.J., Yang, Q., Lin, S.: Graph embedding and extensions: A general framework for dimensionality reduction. IEEE Transactions on Pattern Analysis and Machine Intelligence 29(1), 40–51 (2007)

Motion Dynamic Analysis of the Basic Facial Expressions

Maja Kocoń

West Pomeranian University of Technology, Szczecin,
Faculty of Electrical Engineering,
Sikorskiego 37, 70-313 Szczecin, Poland
maja.kocon@zut.edu.pl

Abstract. In interaction systems, communication between user and the computer may be performed using a graphical display of human representation called avatar. This paper is focussed on the problem of facial motion analysis for human-like animation. Using similarities in motion data four criteria for characteristic points grouping (facial regions, movement directions, angles and distances) have been proposed. In order to estimate the number of clusters for selected facial expressions a dedicated algorithm has been applied. Based on the results of subjective assessment the most satisfying configuration of criteria, in terms of number of clusters and accuracy of emotions recognition, was a group of distance, region and angle between facial markers. In the result, the obtained groups may be used to simplify the number of control parameters necessary to synthesise facial expressions in virtual human systems. The final structure of the characteristic points can diminish overall computational resources usage by decreasing the number of points that need to be recalculated between animation phases. This is due to the fact, that the movement similarities were exploited to make the groups with the same properties be controlled by dominant markers.

Keywords: facial motion, grouping, characteristic points, expressions, motion classification, human-computer interaction (HCI).

1 Introduction

The popularity of the analysis and synthesis of the facial expressions is still growing. Because the face is playing a particularly important role in the communication, in many areas of science it is treated as a system that is able to transmit multiple messages at once. There are four basic classes of signals generated by the face: static signals that involve the construction of a face, slowly changing signals, where changes occur gradually over a specified period of time (such as growing up and aging), fast signals, such as facial expressions, and additional components, such as make-up, glasses and hair. In this paper the presented approach is focused on the analysis of the third type of the signals – facial expressions. The choice of facial expressions was motivated by he fact, that the face is one of the elements of non-verbal communication transmitting the most

A. Likas, K. Blekas, and D. Kalles (Eds.): SETN 2014, LNAI 8445, pp. 126–135, 2014.
© Springer International Publishing Switzerland 2014

information about the emotional state of a human [1]. It provides visual cues about the emotional state, and thus facial expression is a part of the natural language of communication [2].

The non-verbal message involves transmitting and receiving information at all words-free channels. It is expressed mainly by the facial expressions or gestures and indicates emotional states, expectations or intentions directed to the interlocutor. The importance of facial expressions in communication is described by the Mehrabian rule 7/38/55, where 7% of the information is transmitted by spoken words, 38% from tone of the voice and 55% by the facial expressions and body language. According to the experiments performed by Paul Ekman, six basic expressions are universal and easy to understand for most cultures: joy, sadness, fear, anger, surprise, disgust [3].

Nowadays, the main objective is to develop human-machine communication, that would be close to the natural communication between people. In HCI, facial motion synthesis is an active and significant topic in areas like low bit-rate communication or user-friendly interfaces [4], edutainment systems [5], portable personal guides, in autonomous robot platforms for domestic service applications, or social robots [6]. The researchers aim to extend traditional systems of the communication between the human and the machine, for systems oriented on solutions using the virtual reality. The basic requirement while creating avatars is a balance between computational cost and realism. Motion grouping approach proposed in this paper may be used for motion planning, facial expression recognition [7], clustering based search algorithm for motion estimation like in [8], or motion detection [9] without prior information about scene or object.

2   Related Works

In this section we only review approaches that use motion classification for facial motion synthesis, which are related to our approach. One closely related method is presented in [10], where an algorithm for creating a model of facial motion from a set of records of markers located on the face producing speech was proposed. In a presented approach 38 facial characteristic points are grouped into clusters, each cluster with one primary marker. In the first step all markers are defined as primary markers, then the displacement of each marker is formulated as a linear combination of the translation of its neighborhood and achieved by a least squares approach. Algorithm proposed by Lucerno seeks the weight values of points belonging to the group of the approximation of primary marker displacement, such that the error measure is minimal. The step is repeated for other markers and finally the marker with the smallest error is removed from the primary markers list. Markers removed from the list are added to the set of secondary markers. The algorithm is stopped when the expected number of primary markers is accomplished – for selected points 15 groups were adopted. Clustering has been also used in [8], where Zhang proposed a face clustering method based on the facial shapes. First, for the front image of the face the facial attributes are extracted using a modified Active Shape Models (ASM). Images are grouped into

7 classes and modified with ISODATA (Iterative Self-Organizing Data Analysis Technique) clustering method, that divides into several small classes.

3   Proposed Approach to Motion Analysis

First the data regarding the motion of facial expressions is captured and stored. Then we group the motion of characteristic points in accordance to the similarities between them and the proposed four criteria of motion grouping. Finally, we proposed a dedicated algorithm to define the control points and estimate the number of clusters for six basic facial expressions, as shown in Algorithm 1.

3.1   Data Collection

For movement analysis database of still images is used. The dataset contains images of 20 young people performing a series of facial displays - expressions of six basic emotions (joy, anger, sadness, surprise, fear and disgust) and a neutral state. To label and arrange the characteristic points on the captured faces basic information about the facial anatomy – muscle localisation and the face actions classification called FACS [11] is used. The 44 characteristic points are selected and placed on the volunteers' faces. Each face is captured in front and side view according to a method proposed in [12] for selected facial expressions. Most of the markers are concentrated in the areas of major importance for the expressions – around the mouth and eyes (see Figure 1(a) and (b)).

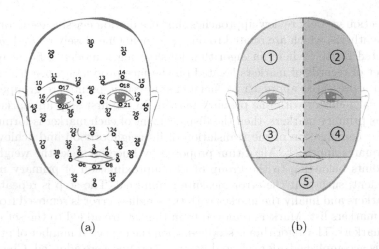

(a)   (b)

Fig. 1. Location of selected facial characteristic points (a) and facial regions (b)

3.2   Motion Grouping

The neutral state is selected as initial position of each expression. Control points' coordinates taken from the image in the neutral state is compared with the same points in other animation phase. The captured coordinates of points are normalised to the range $(-1, 1)$ accordingly to the image dimensions (Fig. 2).

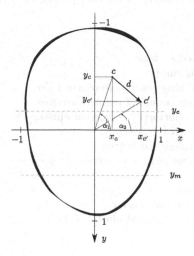

Fig. 2. An example of features used as constrains for clustering

As the cluster a group of characteristic points in a specified area is defined, where the points have the similar movement dependency. For grouping process the following criteria are proposed:

I) Facial regions – the properties of facial anatomy are used to select the regions of the face. As shown in Fig. 3(a) and Fig. 3(b) face has circular muscles, which on account of the structure and the opposite directions of movement cannot belong to the same group. Points located on the opposite sides of the face natural dimples created by the circular muscle, should be handled separately. For this reason, the eyes and mouth lines (at positions y_e, y_m (see Fig. 2) are introduced. The criterion uses the comparison of points coordinates with regions selected by the semi-symmetry of the face, mouth and eyes line (Fig. 1(b)). Thanks to such division lines across the mouth and eyes are avoided.

II) Movement directions – criterion based on comparison of signs obtained from coordinates differences of appropriate points.

III) Angles – checking condition of angle between line passing through the given point and the beginning of the coordinate system with horizontal axis (Fig. 2).

IV) Distances – criterion based on Euclidean distance d (Fig. 2) between the point in neutral state and the point in selected emotional state.

Algorithm 1. Clusters with master points calculation.

Input: point - set of points,
E - emotional state, $E \in \{joy, anger, sadness, surprise, fear, disgust\}$,
N - number of points, $n = 1, \ldots, N$.

Output: cluster - set of cluster numbers for each point n,
master - set of master points for each cluster m,
M - number of clusters and master points, $m = 1, \ldots, M$.

current_cluster ← 1
    For each point do
        cluster_assigned ← false
        If cluster(n) is empty
            For remaining points i from $n + 1$ do
                If constraints of point(i) are met
                    cluster(n) ← current_cluster
                    cluster_assigned ← true
            If cluster_assigned is true
                current_cluster ← current_cluster + 1
    For each point do
        If cluster(n) is empty
            cluster(n) ← current_cluster
            current_cluster ← current_cluster + 1
M ← current_cluster - 1
For each cluster do
    maximum_distance ← 0
    For each point do
        If point(i) belongs to cluster(m)
            δ ← distance of point(i) in neutral and E emotional state
            If $\delta >$ max_distance
                master(m) ← i
                max_distance ← δ

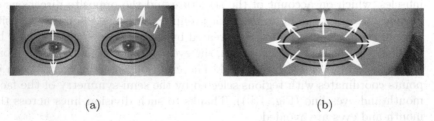

(a)   (b)

Fig. 3. Motion directions of muscles in upper (a) and lower (b) part of the face

Such criteria can provide different solutions from motion dependency point of view. Using presented properties an algorithm for face markers grouping is proposed, where the number of clusters are estimated for six different emotional states.

In the first stage points with the same fulfilled criteria are grouped into clusters. The unassigned single points become separate clusters. In each cluster a control point (called master) is selected based on a maximal distance between its position in neutral and specified emotional state.

The master point defines the motion properties of the rest of the points in the same group. Only one point in the cluster with the highest displacement is marked as a master. The range of motion is correlated with the weights that are associated with the masters. Points in clusters are dependent on a master point and are described by weight w in the interval $(0, 1)$. The value 1 is assigned to the master and for the associated points the weight changes its value proportionally to the Euclidean distance to the master point. For a selected point i weight is calculated as $w_i = \delta_i/\delta_{master}$, where δ_i denotes Euclidean distance between point i in two emotional states (neutral and a selected state).

Table 1. Number of clusters obtained for all criteria with angle tolerance equal to $3°$ and distance tolerance equal to 0.04

Constraint type	Surprise	Joy	Sadness	Anger	Disgust	Fear
facial regions	5	5	5	5	5	5
angle	21	19	17	7	31	15
facial regions/distance	10	8	8	9	7	6
facial regions/angle	27	32	26	17	37	22
angle/distance	29	21	18	10	32	16
facial regions/distance/angle	20	15	16	19	17	14
distance/regions/direction	12	11	12	9	14	9
angle/distance/regions/direction	31	32	27	19	37	22

4   Experimental Results

The results of grouping based on criterion III gives sizeable deviation (24 clusters) of the number of groups, i.e. it is evident in the case of disgust (31 clusters) and anger (7 clusters) states (see Fig.5(a)) for angle tolerance equal to $3°$. For the I and III criteria (Fig. 5(b)), and for the II and III criteria (see Fig. 5(c)) the greater deviations for the number of groups for all emotions is obtained, even for large angles tolerance than for distances. The neighbourhood of each marker is defined as a set of all markers that have the same direction, Euclidean distance and the points belong to the same face region. The examples of such motion clustering for expressions are presented in Fig. 4, where the black dots represent the master markers of each cluster. Additionally, the other markers in the cluster are linked to the master. Motion asymmetry in facial expressions results in asymmetry of the clusters between the two sides of the face.

As shown in Fig. 5(d) the clustering result is acceptable for a distance tolerance equal to 0.04 for each emotional state. In order to evaluate recognition of expressions (which were mapped on the three-dimensional model) a subjective

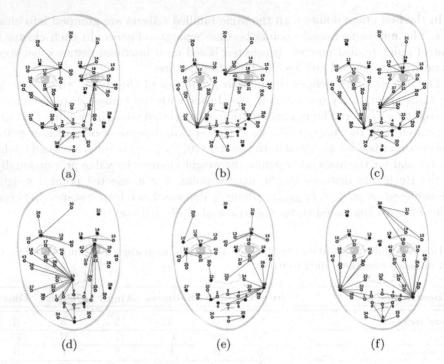

Fig. 4. The examples of clusters obtained for the expressions: surprise (a), joy (b), sadness (c), anger (d), disgust (e) and fear (f). The characteristic points were clustered based on a distance, facial regions and motion direction.

Table 2. Examples of the subjective recognition efficiency of the modeled emotional states using three-dimensional human head model

	Hit ratio for emotional states [%]					
Constraint type	**Surprise**	**Joy**	**Sadness**	**Anger**	**Disgust**	**Fear**
facial regions	0	0	0	0	0	0
angle	0	0	0	0	0	0
facial regions/distance	10	0	0	5	0	0
facial regions/angle	45	35	44	30	37	41
angle/distance	64	85	50	23	74	65
facial regions/distance/angle	95	100	97	100	85	98
distance/regions/direction	20	9	18	5	28	10
angle/distance/regions/direction	98	100	97	100	89	98

assessment on the group of 27 volunteers is performed. Each person evaluates how the synthesised facial expression resembles selected emotion. The results are shown in Tab. 2, where the most satisfying configurations of criteria are marked in grey. As can be seen, the recognition rate is similar in both cases.

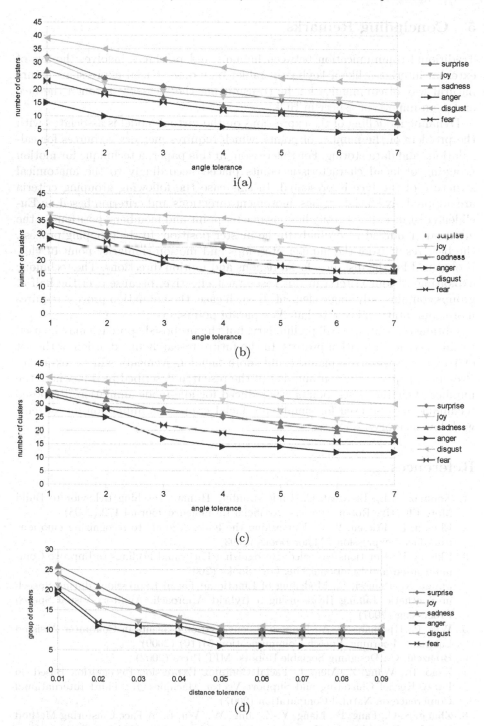

Fig. 5. Number of clusters for angles (a), angles/facial regions (b), angles/facial regions/ direction (c), and distance/facial regions/direction (d)

5   Concluding Remarks

Traditional communication between humans and machines involves the use of external interfaces like a keyboard, tablet or mouse. Facial expressions assure natural way of communication by transmitting the messages through the face and is an important aspect in HCI.

Dynamic modelling of the expressions on the virtual model is associated with the problem of the number of points, which requires memory resources for calculations and data storing. For this reason, in this paper, a technique for motion grouping of facial characteristic points placed accordingly to the anatomical structure of the face is presented. In this case the following grouping criteria are adopted: five facial regions, movement directions and criterion based on Euclidean distance. Each group has one master point and members' positions in the group are modified accordingly to the master position. In the grouping process, the best result from the number of groups and motion similarity point of view is obtained for the distance, facial regions and motion directions. The technique exploiting all four criteria in this case is not effective, because over the half of groups contains only single element. In such case, the animation process requires more computational cost to handle separate points.

Obtained results are still preliminary, but the proposed approach may be used to simplify the animation process. In the future research an extension of the set of facial expressions is planned and more facial movements will be explored. Presented paper is the continuation of the research described in [13], where the number of characteristic points was reduced for idle-mode animation. Proposed technique may be used for simplifying facial expression animation for systems with low memory resources.

References

1. Thomaz, A.L., Breazeal, C.: Understanding Human Teaching Behavior to Build More Effective Robot Learners. Artificial Intelligence Journal 172 (2008)
2. Ekman, P., Friesen, W.V.: Unmasking the Face. A guide to recognizing emotions from facial expressions. Malor Books (2003)
3. Ekman, P.: Emotions Revealed: Recognizing Faces and Feelings to Improve Communication and Emotional Life. Owl Books (2007)
4. Mana, N., Pianesi, F.: Modelling of Emotional Facial Expressions during Speech in Synthetic Talking Heads using a Hybrid Approach. Auditory-Visual Speech Processing (2007)
5. Wik, P., Hjalmarsson, A.: Embodied conversational agents in Computer Assisted Language Learning. Speech Communication 51(10) (2009)
6. Breazeal, C.: Designing Sociable Robots. MIT Press (2002)
7. Zhao, H., Wang, Z., Men, J.: Facial Complex Expression Recognition Based on Fuzzy Kernel Clustering and Support Vector Machines. In: Third International Conference on Natural Computation (2007)
8. Zhang, S.-C., Fang, B., Liang, Y.-Z., Jing, W., Wu, L.: A Face Clustering Method Based on Facial Shape Information. In: Proceedings of the 2011 International Conference on Wavelet Analysis and Pattern Recognition, pp. 44–49 (2011)

9. Yu, X., Chen, X., Gao, M.: Motion Detection in Dynamic Scenes Based on Fuzzy C-Means Clustering. In: International Conference on Communication Systems and Network Technologies, pp. 306–310 (2012)
10. Lucero, J.C., Maciel, S.T., Johns, D.A., Munhall, K.G.: Empirical modeling of human face kinematics during speech using motion clustering. Journal of the Acoustical Society of America 118(1), 405–409 (2005)
11. Ekman, P., Friesen, W.V., Hager, J.C.: Facial Action Coding System. The Manual. Research Nexus division of Network Information Research Corporation (2002)
12. Kocoń, M., Emirsajłow, Z.: Face Emotional States Mapping Based on the Rigid Bone Model. Journal of Applied Computer Science 19(2), 47–60 (2011)
13. Kocoń, M.: Idle Motion Synthesis of Human Head and Face in Virtual Reality Environment. In: Ma, M., Oliveira, M.F., Petersen, S., Hauge, J.B. (eds.) SGDA 2013. LNCS, vol. 8101, pp. 299–306. Springer, Heidelberg (2013)

An Intelligent Tool for the Automated Evaluation of Pedestrian Simulation

Evangelos Boukas[1], Luca Crociani[2], Sara Manzoni[2], Giuseppe Vizzari[2], Antonios Gasteratos[1], and Georgios Ch. Sirakoulis[1]

[1] Democritus University of Thrace, Xanthi, Greece
[2] University of Milano-Bicocca, Milan, Italy
evanbouk@pme.duth.gr,
{luca.crociani,manzoni,viz}@disco.unimib.it,
agaster@pme.duth.gr, gsirak@ee.duth.gr

Abstract. One of the most cumbersome tasks in the implementation of an accurate pedestrian model is the calibration and fine tuning based on real life experimental data. Traditionally, this procedure employs the manual extraction of information about the position and locomotion of pedestrians in multiple videos. The paper in hand proposes an automated tool for the evaluation of pedestrian models. It employees state of the art techniques for the automated 3D reconstruction, pedestrian detection and data analysis. The proposed method constitutes a complete system which, given a video stream, automatically determines both the workspace and the initial state of the simulation. Moreover, the system is able to track the evolution of the movement of pedestrians. The evaluation of the quality of the pedestrian model is performed via automatic extraction of critical information from both real and simulated data.

Keywords: pedestrian simulation, pedestrian detection, cellular automata, stereo vision, 3D reconstruction, agent based models.

1 Introduction

The pedestrian modeling has been studied the past decades extensively and different approaches have been followed, which can be classified mainly as *force*-based [1,2], *CA*-based [3,4] and *agent*-based models [5,6]. Yet, the research community has not reached the state of understanding or development that would allow the accurate modeling and simulation of the widest variety of pedestrian movement scenarios. The valorisation of pedestrian modeling and simulation techniques is mostly carried out by assessing their ability to assemble the evolution real life pedestrian movement circumstances.

The collection of crucial and meaningful data constitutes a challenge by itself. Usually the automated extraction of data from videos is employed on controlled groups of pedestrians, which are commonly equipped with wearable markers. However, during real life scenarios such markers do not exist and, therefore,

A. Likas, K. Blekas, and D. Kalles (Eds.): SETN 2014, LNAI 8445, pp. 136–149, 2014.
© Springer International Publishing Switzerland 2014

such approaches are unfeasible and manual extraction is required. For example, works in [7,8,9] employ manual extraction of experimental data from videos. The collection and process of this data is a dull, repetitive, tiring and error-prone task, thus making it a perfect candidate for automation. This proposed work aspires to fill this gap, while the approach followed is analyzed in the next sections. The approach of our method consists of three distinct modules, namely the "Computer Vision module", the "Pedestrian Simulation module" and the "Evaluation module" (Fig. 1). The "Computer Vision module" includes all the software and hardware required to capture and analyze the real world environment, including the 3D formation of the environment and the pedestrians position and specific attributes such as speed and direction. The "Pedestrian Simulation module" receives as input the information about the starting scenario including the pedestrian attributes and then simulates the evolution of the movement. Finally the output of the simulation is contrasted with the real evolution of the pedestrian movement to appraise the quality of the simulation.

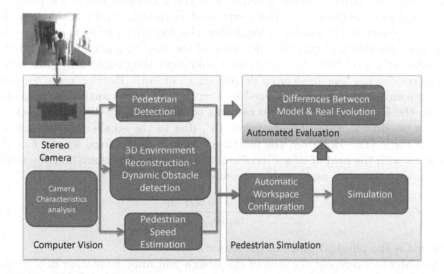

Fig. 1. The Approach Schematic includes the three major modules of the system: "Computer Vision", "Pedestrian Simulation" and "Evaluation"

2 Computer Vision Module

In this section the computer vision system is outlined. Firstly, we present the camera setup, then the 3D reconstruction process is analyzed, followed by the pedestrian position and attributes extraction, finally we provide the transition from the 3D world to the 2D simulation scenario.

2.1   Camera Setup

In order to accurately capture the formation and attributes of the surrounding environment, including depth information, we must firstly design our computer vision system in terms of hardware, i.e. the camera devices that are going to be employed [10]. In order to achieve the maximum accuracy, at the required range as depicted in Fig. 2, we need to consider a special stereo camera setup and to define the specific hardware attributes [11]. Firstly, the range resolution is the minimal change in range that the stereo vision system can differentiate. In general, resolution deteriorates with distance. The function that calculates the range l within which the resolution r is better than, or equal to a desired value is the following:

$$l = \sqrt{\frac{0.5 \cdot r \cdot b \cdot w}{c \cdot tan(0.5 \cdot F)}} \tag{1}$$

where l is the distance in which the desired resolution is achieved, r is the specified range resolution, b is the baseline, w is the horizontal image resolution, F is the cameras' field of view (FoV) expressed in radians, and c is the disparity precision expressed in pixels. In particular, the disparity precision concerns the sub-pixel resolution during the calculation of the disparity map, obtained by interpolation. Eq. 1 shows that given the resolution r the range l may grow either by increasing the baseline b or by decreasing F, or both. Besides, more accurate stereo results are typically obtained by keeping the stereo angle (the angle between the line-of-sight of the two cameras to the minimum-distance object) as low as possible and in all cases below 15°, due to the smaller correspondence search range [12]. Moreover, the function that relates the focal length f of the cameras with the field of view F is of important for the determination of a stereo system's parameters, and can be expressed as:

$$f = \frac{0.5 \cdot s \cdot 0.001 \cdot w}{tan(0.5 \cdot F)} \tag{2}$$

where s is the physical width of the sensor's pixels.

In order to overcome the step of the design and implementation of a special stereoscopic camera system, one could implement a vision system occupying a RGB-D sensor, such as the Microsoft Kinect or the Asus Xtion, that is able to capture both visual and depth information. The main disadvantage of fixed Commercial Off-The-Shelf (COTS) RGB-D solutions is that the accuracy drops

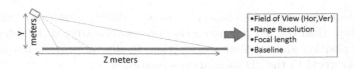

Fig. 2. The camera setup

significantly further than 5 *meters*. Specifically, the accuracy drops to less than 20 *centimeters* at a distance that is farther than 8 *meters*. An indicative example of the output of our vision system, which has been installed in a narrow corridor at the premisses of the Department of Informatics, Systems and Communication (DISCo) of the University of Milano-Bicocca, is presented in Fig. 3.

2.2   3D Scene Reconstruction

The next step comprises the 3D reconstruction of the scene. The latter is a straightforward procedure given the intrinsic and the extrinsic parameters of the utilized stereo rig. Making use of the depth information calculated in the disparity module, the position of each pixel onto the image plane are then expressed into 3D world coordinates. More specifically, pixels expressed in camera coordinates $(x_c, y_c, disp(x_c, y_c))$, with respect to the stereo geometry, are transformed in 3D points (x, y, z). The XY plane coincides with the image plane while the Z axis denotes the depth of the scene [13]. The relation between the world coordinates of a point $P(x, y, z)$ and the coordinates on the image plane $(x_c, y_c, disp(x, y))$ is expressed by the pin-hole model and the stereo setup as:

$$[x, y, z] = \left[\frac{x_c \cdot z}{f}, \frac{y_c \cdot z}{f}, \frac{b \cdot f}{disp(x_c, y_c)} \right] \qquad (3)$$

where, z is the depth value of a pixel depicted in (x_c, y_c), b is the stereo camera's baseline, f the focal length of the lenses expressed in pixels and $disp(x_c, y_c)$ the corresponding pixel's disparity value. In Eq. 3 x and y denote the abscissa and the ordinate in 3D world coordinates, respectively, which as a pair correspond to the (x_c, y_c) pixel on the image plane, respectively. In the case of the usage of an RGB-D sensor the disparity is obtained after a transformation of the depth image, since the disparity and the depth image are inversely proportional.

2.3   Traversable/Obstacle Free Area Extraction

In the next step, the area is partitioned into traversable and not-traversable one [14]. Using disparity map, a reliable v-disparity image is computed, as shown in Fig. 3. In a v-disparity image each pixel value corresponds to the number of pixels in the input image that lie on the same image line (ordinate) and posses disparity value equal to its abscissa. The terrain in the v-disparity image is modeled by a linear equation, the parameters of which can be found using Hough transform [15], condition to the fact that the a significant number of the input images' pixels belong to the terrain and not to obstacles. A tolerance region on both sides of the terrain's linear segment is considered and any point outside this region can be safely considered as originating from a barrier. The linear segments denoting the terrain and the tolerance region overlaid on the v-disparity image are shown in Fig. 3. Then pixels of the image that lie in the traversable area can be traced.

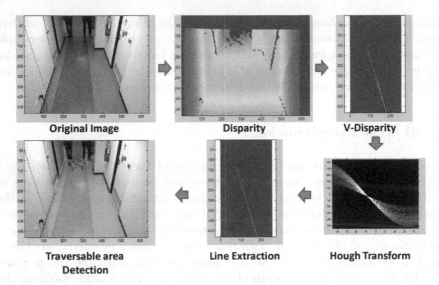

Fig. 3. The visual representation of the implemented algorithm for the computation of the floor

2.4   2D Simulation Scenario

The pedestrian simulation algorithm employees a cellular automaton (CA) that operates over a grid. Thus, the 3D reconstructed area should be transformed into a 2D grid. Based on the aforementioned procedure of the extraction of the obstacles in an area, each point of the point cloud that lays on an obstacle is projected on the floor plane, which has also been estimated by the v-disparity. Then, taking into consideration the the size of the CA cells, which may vary depending on the evaluated model (in our case it is $40cm \times 40cm$), the projected points are sampled on the cellular grid. Figure 4 depicts the steps required for this transformation. The resulting simulation scenario (workspace) is ready to be infused with virtual pedestrians. The following subsection describes the process of pedestrian position and attributes extraction.

2.5   Pedestrian Position and Velocity Extraction

Identifying moving objects in video sequence is a fundamental and critical task in video surveillance and, thus, it has been extensively studied in the past [16],[17],[18]. For the shake of executional acceleration and based on the fact that an indoors and almost "controlled" environment is assumed, a rather different approach is employed. The technique is based on the 3D perception of the environment which is already implemented in the previews parts of our system. The system can be partitioned to three major components:

- In-point-cloud analysis to extract pedestrian candidates
- Mean Shift clustering to count and locate pedestrians
- SIFT feature matching to track the pedestrians

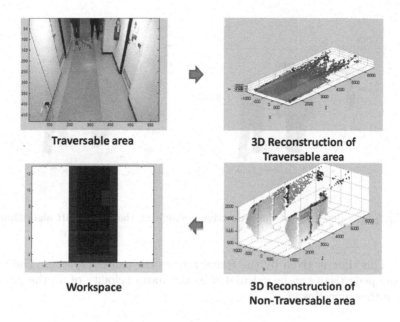

Fig. 4. Discrete steps of the algorithm for the automated formation of the workspace

Firstly, the extraction of those points, in the point cloud, that possibly correspond to pedestrians should be performed. This method is based on the fact that the empty observed environment has been classified to ground (traversable area) and to obstacles. A geometric analysis is performed directly on the point cloud, in order to extract those points that are above the floor and do not belong to an obstacle. This search is automatically windowed in an area that is defined from the 3D obstacles.

The number of pedestrians, which appear at each frame is unknown. Thus a clustering algorithm, namely the mean shift [19], is employed in order to segment the point cloud into pedestrians' sub-point clouds. The mean shift provides the ability to define the shape of the 3D clusters by adjusting the bandwidth. The bandwidth of our setup is set to 0.5 m. This selection is physically consistent with the size of pedestrians. An example of the extracted resulting clusters are presented in Fig.5. The next step comprises the tracking of the pedestrians, performed by employing the SIFT features. At each frame, SIFT features are extracted, detected and matched to the next frame's features. Next, they are tracked throughout the 3D reconstruction and pedestrian detection thusly leading to the tracking of the pedestrians. An example of pedestrian tracking through consecutive frames is presented in Fig.6.

The tracking of pedestrians provides the ability to extract an additional attribute, that is the personal velocity. The velocity of a point, that is matched in two consecutive frames, is calculated as the 3D Euclidean distance of its position in the respective reconstructed point clouds, divided by the time between these

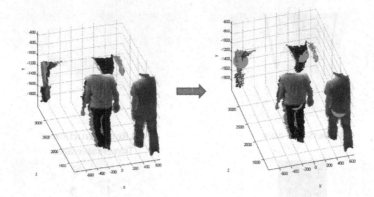

Fig. 5. The detection of the pedestrians exploiting the mean shift algorithm

frames. This time is given by the frame rate of the camera system. The velocity of the pedestrian can be calculated as the mean velocity of all the matched points of the same cluster.

3   Pedestrian Simulation Model

Having created the initial simulation scenario infused with the pedestrians we can simulate their movement and then validate the outputs of the simulator with the observed data. In this section the computational model used for pedestrian simulation will be briefly described[1], in order to understand the kinds of evaluation which can be performed.

3.1   Environment

The environment is modeled in a discrete way by representing it as a grid of squared cells with $40cm \times 40cm$ size (according to the average area occupied by a pedestrian [21]). Cells have a state indicating the fact that they are vacant or occupied by obstacles or pedestrians. The same cell can also be temporary occupied by two pedestrians, in order to allow simulation of overcrowded situations in which the density is higher than 6.25 ped/m^2 (i.e. the maximum density reachable by our discretisation).

The information related to the scenario[2] of the simulation are represented by means of *spatial markers*, special sets of cells that describe relevant elements in the environment. In particular, three kinds of spatial markers are defined: (i) *start* areas, that indicate the generation points of agents in the scenario.

---

[1] For a complete discussion of the model, see [20].

[2] It represents both the structure of the environment and all the information required for the realization of a specific simulation, such as crowd management demands (pedestrians generation profile, origin-destination matrices) and spatial constraints.

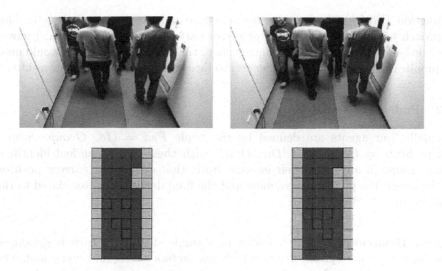

Fig. 6. An example of tracking through consecutive frames

Agent generation can occur in *block*, all at once, or according to a user defined *frequency*, along with information on type of agent to be generated and its destination and group membership; (ii) *destination* areas, which define the possible target locations of the pedestrians in the environment; (iii) *obstacles*, that identify all the non-walkable areas as walls and zones where pedestrians can not enter.

Space annotation allows the definition of virtual grids of the environment, as containers of information for agents and their movement. In our model, we adopt the *floor field* approach [3], that is based on the generation of a set of superimposed grids (similar to the grid of the environment) starting from the information derived from spatial markers. Floor field values are spread on the grid as a gradient and they are used to support pedestrians in the navigation of the environment, representing their interactions with static object (i.e., destination areas and obstacles) or with other pedestrians. Moreover, floor fields can be *static* (created at the beginning and not changed during the simulation) or *dynamic* (updated during the simulation). Three kinds of floor fields are defined in our model: (i) *path field*, that indicates for every cell the distance from one destination area, acting as a potential field that drives pedestrians towards it (static). One path field for each destination point is generated in each scenario; (ii) *obstacles field*, that indicates for every cell the distance from neighboring obstacles or walls (static); (iii) *density field*, that indicates for each cell the pedestrian density in the surroundings at the current time-step (dynamic).

Chessboard metric with $\sqrt{2}$ variation over corners [22] is used to produce the spreading of the information in the path and obstacle fields. Moreover, pedestrians cause a modification to the density field by adding a value $v = \frac{1}{d^2}$ to cells whose distance d from their current position is below a given threshold. Agents are able to perceive floor fields values in their neighborhood by means of a function $Val(f, c)$ (f represents the field type and c is the perceived cell). This approach to the definition of the objective part of the perception model moves the burden of its management from agents to the environment, which would need to monitor agents anyway in order to produce some of the simulation results.

3.2 Pedestrians and Movement

Formally, our agents are defined by the triple $Ped = \langle Id, \ Group, \ State \rangle$, where $State = \langle position, oldDir, \ Dest \rangle$, with their own numerical identifier, their group[3] (if any) and their internal state, that defines the current position of the agent, the previous movement and the final destination, associated to the relative path field.

Agent Behaviour. Agent behavior in a single simulation turn is organized into four steps: *perception, utility calculation, action choice* and *movement*. The *perception* step provides to the agent all the information needed for choosing its destination cell. In particular, if an agent does not belong to a group (from here called *individual*), in this phase it will only extract values from the floor fields, while in the other case it will perceive also the positions of the other group members within a configurable distance, for the calculation of the *cohesion* parameter. The choice of each action is based on an utility value assigned to every possible movement according to the function:

$$U(c) = \frac{\kappa_g G(c) + \kappa_{ob} Ob(c) + \kappa_s S(c) + \kappa_c C(c) + \kappa_d D(c) + \kappa_{ov} Ov(c)}{d} \quad (4)$$

$U(c)$ takes into account the behavioral components considered relevant for pedestrian movement, each one is modeled by means of a function that returns values in range $[-1; +1]$, if it represents an *attractive* element (i.e. its goal), or in range $[-1; 0]$, if it represents a *repulsive* one for the agent. For each function a κ coefficient has been introduced for its calibration: these coefficients, being also able to actually modulate tendencies based on objective information about agent's spatial context, complement the objective part of the perception model allowing agent heterogeneity. The purpose of the denominator d is to constrain the diagonal movements, in which the agents cover greater distances ($0.4 \times \sqrt{2}$ instead of 0.4) and assume higher speeds respect with the non-diagonal ones.

The first three functions exploit information derived by local floor fields: $G(c)$ is associated to goal attraction whereas $Ob(c)$ and $S(c)$ respectively to geometric and social repulsion. Functions $C(c)$ is a linear combination of the perceived positions of members of agent group in an extended neighborhood; they compute the level of attractiveness of each neighboring cell, relating to group cohesion phenomenon. Finally, $D(c)$ adds a bonus to the utility of the cell next to the agent according to his/her previous direction (a sort of *inertia* factor), while $Ov(c)$

---

[3] The model here described particularly considers social relationships between people. See [20] for a thorough discussion of this aspect.

describes the *overlapping* mechanism, a method used to allow two pedestrians to temporarily occupy the same cell at the same step, to manage high-density situations.

After the utility evaluation for all the cells in the neighborhood, the choice of action is stochastic, with the probability to move in each cell c as (N is the normalization factor): $P(c) = N \cdot e^{U(c)}$. On the basis of $P(c)$, agents move in the resulted cell according to their set of possible actions, defined as list of the eight possible movements in the Moore neighborhood, plus the action to keep the position (indicated as X): $A = \{NW, N, NE, W, X, E, SW, S, SE\}$.

3.3   Time and Update Mechanism

In the basic model definition time is also discrete; in an initial definition of the duration of a time step was set to 0.31 s. This choice, considering the size of the cell (a square with 40 cm sides), generates a linear pedestrian speed of about 1.3 m/s, which is in line with the data from the literature representing observations of crowd in normal conditions [21].

Regarding the update mechanism, three different strategies are usually considered in this context [23]: *ordered sequential, shuffled sequential* and *parallel* update. The first two strategies are based on a sequential update of agents, respectively managed according to a *static* list of priorities that reflects their order of generation or a *dynamic* one, shuffled at each time step. On the contrary, the parallel update calculates the choice of movement of all the pedestrians at the same time, actuating choices and managing conflicts in a latter stage. The two sequential strategies, instead, imply a simpler operational management, due to an a-priori resolution of conflicts between pedestrians. In the model, we adopted the parallel update strategy. This choice is in accordance with the current literature, where it is considered much more realistic due to consideration of conflicts between pedestrians, arisen for the movement in a shared space [4].

With this update strategy, the agents life-cycle must consider that before carrying out the *movement* execution potential conflicts, essentially related to the simultaneous choice of two (or more) pedestrians to occupy the same cell, must be solved. The overall simulation step therefore follows a three step procedure: (i) *update of choices* and *conflicts detection* for each agent of the simulation; (ii) *conflicts resolution*, that is the resolution of the detected conflicts between agent intentions; (iii) *agents movement*, that is the update of agent positions exploiting the previous conflicts resolution, and *field update*, that is the computation of the new density field according to the updated positions of the agents.

The resolution of conflicts employs an approach essentially based on the one introduced in [4], based on the notion of friction. Let us first consider that conflicts can involve two of more pedestrians: in case more than two pedestrians involved in a conflict for the same cell, the first step of the management strategy is to block all but two of them, chosen randomly, reducing the problem to the case of a simple conflict. To manage this latter, another random number $\in [0,1]$ is generated and compared to two thresholds, $frict_l$ and $frict_h$, with $0 < frict_l < frict_h \leq 1$: the outcome can be that all agents yield when the extracted number is lower than $frict_l$, only one agent moves (chosen randomly) when the extracted number is between $frict_l$ and $frict_h$ included, or even two agents move when the number is higher than $frict_h$ (in this case pedestrian overlapping occurs).

4   Automated Simulation Evaluation

Given the data which can be obtained with the methodology described in Sec. 2.5, a preliminary evaluation of the pedestrian model is based on metrics describing the space utilisation of pedestrians, that is, the way they walked in the analyzed/simulated scenario, facing the presence of obstacles or other people. Real world data for the simulation evaluation have been achieved with a small set of experiments in a corridor section, by performing 3 different scenarios. In the tests the corridor was crossed by respectively: (i) 1 person per side; (ii) 1 person from one side and 2 from the other; (iii) 2 persons per side. The simulation environment and some frame of the video is shown in Fig. 4 - 5.

The evaluation of the simulation model is automated by the tool in a simple way. In this phase, the *pedestrian simulation module* receives major inputs for the simulation configuration from the computer vision module (i.e., the scenario setting with the time schedule of pedestrian generation, obtained by analysing the boundaries of the observed environment). The calibration parameter set, for each simulation, is provided by the *automated evaluation module*. The main objective of this module is the investigation of the correct calibration for the simulator: starting from an initial configuration of the calibration weights, provided by the user, and a set of variable calibration parameters it issues, through the *simulation module*, a set of simulations with different configurations of weights. Once a single simulation is finished, results are compared with the observed data according to a user defined metric, that analyses one or more effects of the human behaviour. While the comparison is not acceptable (i.e., the difference between data is greater than a user defined threshold), the range of the calibration weights is explored with new simulations. Metrics used for the evaluation, with simulation results are discussed in the following susections.

4.1   Average Pedestrian Distances

A well-known effect of the human behaviour is the preservation of particular, physical distances among other people, differentiated by the situation and the relationship had with them in different situations. Studies in the field of anthropology [24] inform about average values of these *social* distances. On the other hand, the adaptivity of the human behaviour leads to high variability of distances regarding different situations: with the increasing of pedestrian densities as well as with incoming flows from other directions. Automatic calculation of the observed distances between pedestrians is therefore needed for better understanding if the simulation model is able to reproduce them properly.

Starting from the position of every pedestrian gathered in each frame of the video, distances D_{P_i,P_j}, less than a threshold r_{ped}[4], are collected for calculating

---

[4] We assumed $r_{ped} = 1.2m$, in order to represent the *personal space* of pedestrians.

the average. Then, the evaluation is performed by comparing this value with the one obtained by using the positions of the agents during the simulation. For this evaluation, only the parameter κ_s has been tuned by the automated tool.

Table 1 compares the data gathered with the three experiments, described at the beginning of this section, with the results achieved by simulating each respective scenario. After the calibration phase, it has been found an optimal value of κ_s close to 30. It is possible to see that, while with 3 and 4 persons in the scenario the simulated data are close to the real ones, in the case with 2 pedestrians simulations have an error near to 0.3 meters. This is probably due to the missing of a mechanism for managing the *anticipation*, or reservation of space between simulated pedestrians, as already explained in [25]. This mechanism would improve the cooperation between agents, letting them to avoid trajectories which lead to conflicts and to too short distances with other persons in low density situations.

Table 1. Comparison of average pedestrian lowest distances

Scenario	Real World [m]	Simulation [m]
(i)	1.05	0.76
(ii)	0.79	0.81
(iii)	0.82	0.81

4.2 Average Distances with Obstacles

In order to analyze the reproduction of trajectories by the simulator, another indicator must describe the distances maintained with obstacles and walls in the environment. With this aim, this analysis uses the positions of pedestrians and the configuration of the environment for calculating the average distance between pedestrian and obstacles. In particular, for each pedestrian and each frame, the minimum distance between its position and the nearby obstacles is calculated. If this is below a distance threshold r_{obs} (for the simulation we used $r_{obs} = 1.2$), it will be added to the set used for the average calculation.

Table 2 compares real world and simulation results. After the calibration phase, value of κ_{obs} has been rounded to 3.

Table 2. Evaluation of average distances with obstacles

Scenario	Real World [m]	Simulation [m]
(i)	0.53	0.64
(ii)	0.61	0.63
(iii)	0.56	0.63

5 Conclusions

In this paper an automated tool for the evaluation of pedestrian simulation models has been presented. The developed tool has been tested using real data versus simulated ones, produced by an existing pedestrian simulator [20] and the overall testing procedure has been analyzed. The tool performs adequately, highly improving the calibration and evaluation of the simulation model both in accuracy and in overall time. The automation of the procedure opens new areas of research. Future work is mainly focused on two directions. Firstly on the improvement of the tool itself and, secondly, on the fully automated calibration of a pedestrian simulator. In particular, the simulation evaluation procedure will be improved including data about local densities distribution in the space, which can be calculated based on the position of pedestrians. In addition, improving the output of the computer vision module with even more accurate tracking techniques, will enable the system to estimate sturdy instant velocities of people.

References

1. Helbing, D., Molnár, P.: Social force model for pedestrian dynamics. Phys. Rev. E 51(5), 4282–4286 (1995)
2. Moussad, M., Perozo, N., Garnier, S., Helbing, D., Theraulaz, G.: The walking behaviour of pedestrian social groups and its impact on crowd dynamics. PLoS ONE 5(4), e10047 (2010)
3. Burstedde, C., Klauck, K., Schadschneider, A., Zittartz, J.: Simulation of pedestrian dynamics using a two-dimensional cellular automaton. Physica A: Statistical Mechanics and its Applications 295(3-4), 507–525 (2001)
4. Kirchner, A., Nishinari, K., Schadschneider, A.: Friction effects and clogging in a cellular automaton model for pedestrian dynamics. Phys. Rev. E 67, 056122 (2003)
5. Henein, C.M., White, T.: Agent-based modelling of forces in crowds. In: Davidsson, P., Logan, B., Takadama, K. (eds.) MABS 2004. LNCS (LNAI), vol. 3415, pp. 173–184. Springer, Heidelberg (2005)
6. Shao, W., Terzopoulos, D.: Autonomous pedestrians. Graphical Models 69(5-6), 246–274 (2007)
7. Willis, A., Gjersoe, N., Havard, C., Kerridge, J., Kukla, R.: Human movement behaviour in urban spaces: Implications for the design and modelling of effective pedestrian environments. Environment and Planning B: Planning and Design 31(6), 805–828 (2004)
8. Schultz, M., Schulz, C., Fricke, H.: Passenger dynamics at airport terminal environment. In: Klingsch, W.W.F., Rogsch, C., Schadschneider, A., Schreckenberg, M. (eds.) Pedestrian and Evacuation Dynamics 2008, pp. 381–396. Springer, Heidelberg (2010)
9. Bandini, S., Gorrini, A., Vizzari, G.: Towards an integrated approach to crowd analysis and crowd synthesis: A case study and first results. arXiv preprint arXiv:1303.5029 (2013)
10. Kostavelis, I., Boukas, E., Nalpantidis, L., Gasteratos, A.: A mechatronic platform for robotic educational activities. Interdisciplinary Mechatronics, 543–568

11. Kostavelis, I., Boukas, E., Nalpantidis, L., Gasteratos, A., Rodrigalvarez, M.A.: Spartan system: Towards a low-cost and high-performance vision architecture for space exploratory rovers. In: 2011 IEEE International Conference on Computer Vision Workshops (ICCV Workshops), pp. 1994–2001. IEEE (2011)

12. Konolige, K.: Small vision systems: Hardware and implementation. In: International Symposium on Robotics Research, pp. 111–116 (1997)

13. Nalpantidis, L., Sirakoulis, G.C., Gasteratos, A.: Review of stereo vision algorithms: From software to hardware. International Journal of Optomechatronics 2(4), 435–462 (2008)

14. Kostavelis, I., Nalpantidis, L., Gasteratos, A.: Supervised traversability learning for robot navigation. In: Groß, R., Alboul, L., Melhuish, C., Witkowski, M., Prescott, T.J., Penders, J. (eds.) TAROS 2011. LNCS, vol. 6856, pp. 289–298. Springer, Heidelberg (2011)

15. De Cubber, G., Doroftei, D., Nalpantidis, L., Sirakoulis, G.C., Gasteratos, A.: Stereo-based terrain traversability analysis for robot navigation. In: IARP/EURON Workshop on Robotics for Risky Interventions and Environmental Surveillance, Brussels, Belgium (2009)

16. Vannoorenberghe, P., Motamed, C., Blosseville, J.M., Postaire, J.G.: Monitoring pedestrians in a uncontrolled urban environment by matching low-level features. In: IEEE International Conference on Systems, Man, and Cybernetics, vol. 3, pp. 2259–2264. IEEE (1996)

17. Viola, P., Jones, M.J., Snow, D.: Detecting pedestrians using patterns of motion and appearance. International Journal of Computer Vision 63(2), 153–161 (2005)

18. Dollar, P., Wojek, C., Schiele, B., Perona, P.: Pedestrian detection: An evaluation of the state of the art. IEEE Transactions on Pattern Analysis and Machine Intelligence 34(4), 743–761 (2012)

19. Cheng, Y.: Mean shift, mode seeking, and clustering. IEEE Transactions on Pattern Analysis and Machine Intelligence 17(8), 790–799 (1995)

20. Vizzari, G., Manenti, L., Crociani, L.: Adaptive pedestrian behaviour for the preservation of group cohesion. Complex Adaptive Systems Modeling 1(7) (2013)

21. Weidmann, U.: Transporttechnik der fussgänger - transporttechnische eigenschaftendes fussgängerverkehrs (literaturstudie). Literature Research 90, Institut füer Verkehrsplanung, Transporttechnik, Strassen- und Eisenbahnbau IVT an der ETH Zürich (1993)

22. Kretz, T., Bönisch, C., Vortisch, P.: Comparison of various methods for the calculation of the distance potential field. In: Klingsch, W.W.F., Rogsch, C., Schadschneider, A., Schreckenberg, M. (eds.) Pedestrian and Evacuation Dynamics 2008, pp. 335–346. Springer, Heidelberg (2010)

23. Klüpfel, H.: A Cellular Automaton Model for Crowd Movement and Egress Simulation. PhD thesis, University Duisburg-Essen (2003)

24. Hall, E.T.: The Hidden Dimension. Anchor Books (1966)

25. Suma, Y., Yanagisawa, D., Nishinari, K.: Anticipation effect in pedestrian dynamics: Modeling and experiments. Physica A: Statistical Mechanics and its Applications 391(1), 248–263 (2012)

Study the Effects of Camera Misalignment on 3D Measurements for Efficient Design of Vision-Based Inspection Systems

Deepak Dwarakanath[1,2,3], Carsten Griwodz[1,2],
Paal Halvorsen[1,2], and Jacob Lildballe[3]

[1] Simula Research Laboratory
Martin Linges vei 17/25, Lysaker 1325, Norway
deepakd@simula.no
[2] University of Oslo
Gaustadallen 23 B, N-0373 Oslo, Norway
{griff,paal}@ifi.uio.no
[3] Image House PantoInspect A/S
Carsten Niebuhrs Gade 10, 2, DK-1577 Copenhagen V, Denmark
jl@pantoinspect.com

Abstract. Vision based inspection systems for 3D measurements using single camera, are extensively used in several industries, today. Due to transportation and/or servicing of these systems, the camera in this system is prone to misalignment from its original position. In such situations, although a high quality calibration exists, the accuracy of 3D measurement is affected. In this paper, we propose a statistical tool or methodology which involves: a) Studying the significance of the effects of 3D measurements errors due to camera misalignment; b) Modelling the error data using regression models; and c) Deducing expressions to determine tolerances of camera misalignment for an acceptable inaccuracy of the system. This tool can be used by any 3D measuring system using a single camera. Resulting tolerances can be directly used for mechanical design of camera placement in the vision based inspection systems.

Keywords: Camera calibration, Vision based inspection systems, Camera misalignment and Regression models.

1 Introduction

With the advent of automation in all types of industries, manual intervention in the operations of machines is minimized. Nowadays, automatic inspection systems are used to inspect various types of faults or defects in several application areas such as sorting and quality improvements in food industry [11], [10], inspection of cracks in roads [4], crack detection of mechanical units in manufacturing industries [8], [9] and so on. Vision based inspection systems are increasingly growing with the advance in computer vision techniques and algorithms.

Typically, vision based inspection systems that inspect objects of interest and estimate measurements, are required to know a priori information about the

A. Likas, K. Blekas, and D. Kalles (Eds.): SETN 2014, LNAI 8445, pp. 150–163, 2014.

intrinsic (focal length, principal axes) and the extrinsic (position and orientation) parameters of the camera without any freedom of scale. These parameters are obtained by a camera calibration process [3],[5]. Usually, calibration is carried out offline, i.e., before the system is deployed and thereafter the calibrated parameters are used to recover 3D measurements from the 2D image of the camera [12], [13], [14]. The quality of the camera calibration is an important factor that determines the accuracy of the inspection system.

Although the quality of calibration might be very high, it is difficult to guarantee highly accurate measurements, if the camera is physically misaligned from the position assumed during calibration. However, the transportation or installation can cause misalignment, e.g., due to wrong mounting during installation, due to ways of handling the system during maintenance or service etc. Consequently, the performance of the inspection system degrades.

A possible correction to this problem would be to re-position the camera, physically, to its calibrated position or to run the calibration process after deployment. It is very difficult to physically re-position the camera with high precision. Alternatively, it might also be difficult to recalibrate in some situations based on the location and accessibility of the installed system.

Therefore, it becomes important to understand the effects of the offset in cameras' position and orientation on inaccuracies. The significance of the inaccuracies depends on design (acceptable inaccuracy level) and the application of the system. So, an important question is: what is the maximum tolerable camera misalignment for an acceptable inaccuracy of the system? By answering this question, we will be able to design and operate the system better. When the tolerance limits of the camera misalignment are known, the mechanical design of the camera housing and fixtures will need to adhere to these tolerances to maintain the inaccuracy below an acceptable level. Also, by using an empirical model, it is possible to estimate the camera misalignment and further re-calibrate the camera parameters to increase the robustness of the system.

This paper aims to enhance the design and operational aspects of vision-based inspection systems. The main contribution of this paper is to provide a simple statistical method or tool which can compute acceptable tolerance values for positions and orientations in all directions for a given accuracy requirements. This tool is useful in designing the mechanics and in increasing the robustness of the vision based inspection system. It is easily implementable and reproducible. The limitation of this tool is that the measurements are carried out on points that are assumed to be lying on a plane. However, the tool is easily extendable to measure 3D points as long as an appropriate calibration process is carried out based on known 3D points. Related work is described in section 2.

First, we identify a suitable use case for the study of effects of camera misalignment on 3D measurements. One such vision based inspection system that exhibits a similar purpose and problems mentioned so far, is the PantoInspect system [2]. This system is explained in detail in section 3. Details of our experimental design is explained in section 4. The simulation results and the empirically obtained

regression model is explained in section 5. Finally the paper is concluded by summarising the goal and evidence of the paper.

2   Related Work

The effects of misalignment of stereoscopic cameras are studied in [15], [16],
[19], however, in our case we study the effects due to misalignment of single
cameras. [15] focusses on the effects of calibration errors on depth errors, and
provides tolerances on calibration parameters. In [16], camera misalignment is
estimated and corrected. [19] studied misalignment effects in stereo cameras. In
the above papers, the approaches rely strongly on a second image and errors of
the cameras' orientation with respect to each other. Other papers only discuss
effects of camera misalignment on calibration parameters itself [15], [17], [18].
In our case, where we use a single camera, we assume that calibration is of
sufficiently high quality, but once calibrated, the effects of camera misalignment
due to certain factors requires more attention in practical systems and hence,
we study this in our paper. Our approach leads to an estimation of tolerances
for camera misalignment that aims directly at the mechanical design of single
camera vision systems. One major feature of our approach is that it is not specific
to one application, but can be used for any application of this type.

3   The PantoInspect System

PantoInspect is a fault inspection system, which inspects pantographs and measures the dimensions of the defects in their carbon strips. PantoInspect is installed, as shown in figure 1, over railway tracks to inspect trains running with
electric locomotives that are equipped with pantographs. Pantographs are mechanical components placed on one or more wagons of the train, which can be
raised in height so that they touch the contact wire for electricity. Pantographs
have one or more carbon strips that are actually in contact with the wire. Over
time, due to constant contact of carbon strips with the wire, and probably other
factors, various types of defects (cracks, edge chips etc.) are seen. Such defects
are detected by the PantoInspect system.

3.1   Principle

PantoInspect is mounted right above the train tracks on bridges or other fixtures.
The PantoInspect system receives a notification when the train is approaching
and prepares itself. When the train passes right below the system, three line
lasers are projected onto the carbon strips (depicted as green line in the figure),
and the camera captures the near infrared image of the laser. When defects are
present, the line deforms instead of remaining a straight line in the image. Hence,
the laser line defines the geometry of the defect. The system then analyses the
images, measures the dimension of the defects and notifies the user with alarms
on certain measurement thresholds.

Fig. 1. PantoInspect system: inspects defects on the pantographs mounted on the trains

The system measures various defects in the carbon strip based on the captured images. These defects are represented in figure 2, which are *(1)-thickness of carbon wear, (2)-vertical carbon cracks, (3)-carbon edge chips, (4)-missing carbon and (5)-abnormal carbon wear.* In general, all these defects are measured in terms of width and/or depth in real world metrics. Although the PantoInspect system measures various types of defects in pantographs, the common attribute in these measurements are width and depth. We therefore consider these attributes as the main 3D measurements in our scope of simulation and study of the effects of camera misalignment, in section 4.

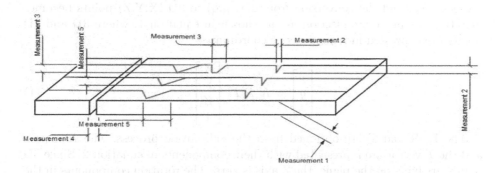

Fig. 2. Different carbon defects and the laser line deformations

3.2   Calibration

The system uses 2D pixel measurements in the image and estimates the real-world 3D scales. Camera calibration is an important step in obtaining such 3D measurements. For PantoInspect, this is carried out in the factory before installing the system, using Bouguet's method [1]. A number of checkerboard images are used to estimate the intrinsic parameter K of the camera that constitutes focal length and principle axes of the camera. Next, a single image of the

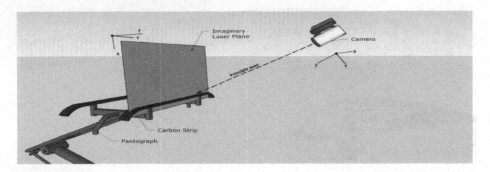

Fig. 3. Inspection scenario: world coordinates (Z=towards camera, Y=horizontal, X=vertical) and camera coordinates (Z=towards plane, Y=vertical, X=horizontal)

checkerboard that is placed exactly on the laser plane, is used to estimate the extrinsic parameter of the camera - position T and orientation R, with respect to the checkerboard coordinates.

3.3 Homography

In the scenario of PantoInspect system, we consider an imaginary plane passing vertically through the line laser as in figure 3. Then, the points representing defects are lying on a laser plane. These 2D points of the defects in the image are detected, and the conversion from 2D (p,q) to 3D (X,Y,Z) points becomes merely a ray-plane intersection [6], as shown in equation 1, where 3D and 2D points are expressed in homogeneous coordinates:

$$\begin{bmatrix} p \\ q \\ 1 \end{bmatrix} = K[R|T] \begin{bmatrix} X \\ Y \\ Z \\ 1 \end{bmatrix} \tag{1}$$

The K, R and T are obtained from the calibration process. The R matrix and the T vector are represented with their components in equation 2. Since 3D points are lying on the plane, the Z axis is zero. The rotation components in the 3rd column (r_{13}, r_{23}, r_{33}) are ignored because they are multiplied by zero:

$$\begin{bmatrix} p \\ q \\ 1 \end{bmatrix} = K * \begin{bmatrix} r_{11} & r_{12} & r_{13} & t_1 \\ r_{21} & r_{22} & r_{23} & t_2 \\ r_{31} & r_{32} & r_{33} & t_3 \end{bmatrix} * \begin{bmatrix} X \\ Y \\ 0 \\ 1 \end{bmatrix} = K * \underbrace{\begin{bmatrix} r_{11} & r_{12} & t_1 \\ r_{21} & r_{22} & t_2 \\ r_{31} & r_{32} & t_3 \end{bmatrix}}_{H} * \begin{bmatrix} X \\ Y \\ 1 \end{bmatrix} \tag{2}$$

Equation 2 describes a 2D-2D mapping between points on the image and points on the laser plane. This mapping is a homography (H). Using the homography, points on the plane can be recovered and measured for width and depth of defects that corresponds to defects detected in 2D pixel points.

4   Study Methodology

We have seen how the camera parameters play an important role in estimating the measurements in PantoInspect. However when the camera is misaligned from its original position, estimated 3D measurements incur inaccuracies in the performance of the system. To study the effects of camera misalignment on 3D measurements, we carry out a simulation of the PantoInspect image analysis for 3D measurements, under the conditions of camera misalignment.

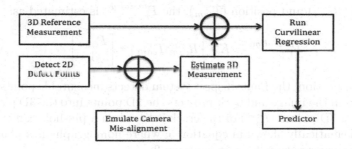

Fig. 4. Simulation procedure

For repeatability of this simulation in any application involving 3D measurements of points lying on a plane and a single camera, a general procedure is shown in figure 4, followed by a specific explanation of the procedure for our case study.

4.1   Error Computation

A set of points (P_w) that represents the crack edges on a plane are synthesized in the world coordinates. Note that the points are on the plane and hence their Z axis is 0. These 3D points are synthesised using a random number generator. From these points, the width (W_{known}) and depth (D_{known}) of cracks are computed and recorded. These known measurements in 3D space are our baseline and used as a reference to evaluate the accuracy of the inspection. A range of reference 3D measurements used are equal to real measurement of the defects (measured using an industrial caliper).

The projection of the known set of points, P_w are computed based on the known camera parameters $(K, R$ and $T)$. These points represent the 2D points (P_i) in image coordinates that are detected and further analysed by the PantoInspect system.

Typically, when the camera stays perfectly positioned and oriented, the width and depth of the cracks are measured with a reasonably good accuracy, due to high quality camera calibration process. To study the effects of camera misalignment on the accuracy of the measurements, the camera misalignment process needs to be emulated as if the camera had shifted position or orientation. Accordingly, points (P_i) are first represented in the camera coordinate system as P_{cam}, as depicted in equation 3.

$$P_{cam} = K^{-1} * \begin{bmatrix} P_i \\ 1 \end{bmatrix} \tag{3}$$

Next, the rotation or translation effects are introduced, as a result of which the detected points obtain new positions, represented as $P_i^{misalign}$ in the image coordinates. Due to this emulation process that is based on changed camera orientation (R_{cam}) and position (T_{cam}), the $P_i^{misalign}$ is estimated as:

$$P_i^{misalign} = K * \begin{bmatrix} R_{cam} & T_{cam} \end{bmatrix} * \begin{bmatrix} P_{cam} \\ 1 \end{bmatrix} \tag{4}$$

During inspection, the PantoInspect system detects measurable points (edges) of the cracks in the image and back-projects the 2D points into the 3D plane. The estimation of 3D points (P_w^{est}) of the crack is based on a pin-hole camera model and is mathematically shown in equation 5, where homography is a plane-plane projective transformation [6] as in equation 2:

$$P_w^{est} = H * P_i^{misalign} \tag{5}$$

Finally, the width (W^{est}) and depth (D^{est}) measurements are estimated and compared with the known values to compute the mean squared error, in equations 6 and 7. These errors $Error_{width}$ and $Error_{depth}$ represent the accuracy of the defect measurements:

$$Error_{width} = ||W - W^{est}||_2 \tag{6}$$

$$Error_{depth} = ||D - D^{est}||_2 \tag{7}$$

4.2   Prediction Model

The simulation produces data pertaining to error in the 3D measurements with respect to camera misalignment in terms of three positional $(T_{cam} = [t_x, t_y, t_z])$ and three rotational $(R_{cam} = [r_x, r_y, r_z])$ misalignments. Considering each of these camera misalignment components as a variable, and the error as the response to it, the error can be modelled using appropriate regression models. Once the data fits to a model, the parameters of that model can be used for prediction purposes [7].

This is helpful to make predictions of camera misalignment based on the error estimated in the system. Then, given the acceptable accuracy of the system, in terms of maximum allowable error in the measurements, one can deduce maximum limits or tolerances of camera misalignment to maintain an acceptable inaccuracy.

5   Simulation Results

5.1   Priori

The carbon strip on each pantograph measures about 1.2meters in length and between 30-50mm in width and 30mm in thickness. For simulation purposes, we assume that there are about five defects per pantograph, and the system inspects about 200 such pantograph, i.e., 1000 measurements.

The defect width of maximum 50mm and defect depth of maximum 30mm are assumed to be present across the length of the carbon strip. The camera used for inspection is calibrated offline, and hence, a priori calibration data is available for that camera. The K, R and T matrices are as follows:

$$K = \begin{bmatrix} 4100.8633085 & 0 & 947.0315701 \\ 0 & 4104.1593558 & 554.2504842 \\ 0 & 0 & 1 \end{bmatrix}$$

$$R = \begin{bmatrix} 0.0108693 & 0.9999407 & -0.0006319 \\ 0.7647318 & -0.0079055 & 0.6443002 \\ 0.6442570 & -0.0074863 & -0.7647724 \end{bmatrix}$$

$$T = \begin{bmatrix} -540.7246414 & -119.4815451 & 2787.2170789 \end{bmatrix}$$

5.2   Effect of Camera Misalignment

The simulation procedure explained in section 4 is for one camera-plane pair, where a single camera calibration parameter (K, R, T, as given above) is used to recover the 3D measurements. We have conducted experiments on 6 such pairs. We used two different cameras, and each camera calibration with three planes corresponding to three line lasers. Results from all the 6 configurations yields similar patterns and are explained as follows.

For every such configuration, the simulation was carried over a range of camera's positional misalignment between -100mm to +100mm and orientational misalignment between -40 and +40 degrees. For every new position and/or orientation of misalignment, the simulation was carried out for 1000 measurements each. As our goal was to determine tolerances of camera's positional and orientational misalignments independently, examining the effects due to both misalignments at the same time, was not required.

The results of the simulation as in figure 5 and figure 6, show the variation in mean squared error of both the width and depth measurements for every camera misaligned position and orientation. This error (measured in millimetres) represents the ability of the system to measure the inspected data accurately.

From figures 5(a) and 6(a), it can be seen that the camera translation t_x has the least effect on the errors compared to translations t_y and t_z. For insight into the camera axes for translation and rotation, please refer figure 3. The error for translations in t_y and t_z is higher, however, not significantly higher than 1mm, which might be an acceptable inaccuracy limit for certain applications.

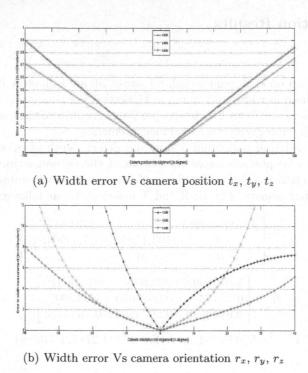

(a) Width error Vs camera position t_x, t_y, t_z

(b) Width error Vs camera orientation r_x, r_y, r_z

Fig. 5. Variation of error in 3D measurements (width) of the defects, due to changes in camera position and orientation about its camera centre

These effects are caused by the camera position misalignments, which shifts the back projected points, defining the width and depth measurements proportionally, so the relative width and depth measurements remain almost unchanged.

Interesting effects are seen due to camera rotation, which has slightly different effects on width and depth. From figures 5(b) and 6(b), it can be seen that the camera rotations r_y and r_z, has noticeable effects on the width and depth errors. When the camera is rotated around axes y and z, the resulting 2D image point moves symmetrically within the image. Furthermore, the rate of increase of width is higher than depth for r_y, because when camera is rotated around the y axis, the horizontal component of the 2D point is changed more than the y component and width is a function of the x component. Exactly the opposite is seen when depth increases at higher rate for r_z, because depth is a function of the y component.

Special cases are the errors due to r_x. Remember that the camera is placed in a position to look down at the laser lines. The rotation around x axis will have a drastic projective effects in the image plane. The projective properties result in a non-symmetric variation of the errors around zero. One more thing to notice is that the error increases very quickly on the negative r_x than positive side. This behaviour can be explained using projective geometric properties.

Consider an image capturing parallel lines and in perspective view, the parallel lines meet at vanishing (imaginary) point. It is possible to imagine that the width of parallel lines is shorter when the capturing device tilts downwards. Similarly, when our camera is tilted downwards, i.e., r_x in the positive (clockwise) direction, the defect points are moved upwards in the image plane, and the measurement becomes so small that the error seems to be constant. Contrarily, when the camera is tilted upwards, the detected points are moved downwards in the image plane, increasing the measurements and thereby the error.

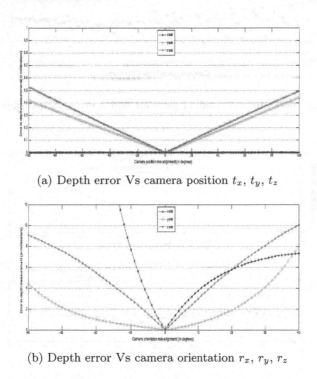

(a) Depth error Vs camera position t_x, t_y, t_z

(b) Depth error Vs camera orientation r_x, r_y, r_z

Fig. 6. Variation of error in 3D measurements (depth) of the defects, due to changes in camera position and orientation about its camera centre

5.3   Regression

By visual inspection of figures 5 and 6, we can say that errors are linearly varying with camera translations (t_x, t_y, t_z), and non-linear with camera rotations (r_x, r_y, r_z). We not only model the data for every rotation and translation but also their direction (positive(+) and negative(-)). This means we separate out the error data for variables r_x^+, r_x^-, r_y^+, r_y^-, r_z^+, r_z^-, t_x^+, t_x^-, t_y^+, t_y^-, t_z^+ and t_z^-.

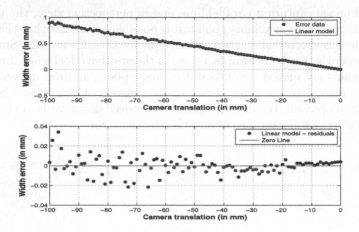

Fig. 7. Linear model fit and residual plots for width error data variation with t_z^-

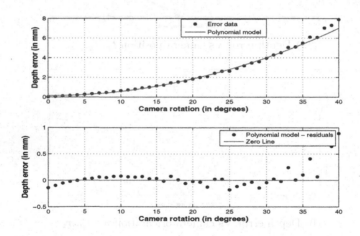

Fig. 8. Curvilinear (2 degree) model fit and residual plots for depth error data variation with r_y^+

We model the emphirical data related to translations as a simple linear regression model and the data related to rotations are modelled as a curvilinear regression of degree 2. This results in the estimation of model parameters and gives rise to expressions for prediction.

Figure 7 illustrates line fitting of variation in width due to t_z^- and figure 8 illustrates curve fitting of variation in depth due to r_y^+. Similarly, all the data are modelled suitably well and the model parameters are estimated. An exhaustive list of parameters is shown in the table 1 and table 2.

Table 1. Model parameters estimated for translation

Data	Linear		
f(x),x	p_0	p_1	RMSE
width, t_x^-	5.13e-07	-7.14e-06	6.36e-06
width, t_x^+	-1.73e-07	7.15e-06	5.47e-06
width, t_y^-	2.22e-03	-7.13e-03	6.47e-03
width, t_y^+	-1.28e-03	7.43e-03	6.41e-03
width, t_z^-	-4.04e-03	-8.93e-03	7.34e-03
width, t_z^+	3.84e-03	8.37e-03	7.20e-03
depth, t_x^-	5.09e-07	-4.23e-03	4.33e-06
depth, t_x^+	-6.48e-08	4.26e-06	3.51e-06
depth, t_y^-	1.54e-03	-4.23e-03	4.11e-03
depth, t_y^+	-2.7e-03	4.47e-03	4.118e-03
depth, t_z^-	-2.45e-03	-5.30e-03	5.62e-03
depth, t_z^+	1.77e-03	5.01e-03	3.83e-03

Table 2. Model parameters estimated for rotations

Data	Polynomial			
f(x),x	p_0	p_1	p_2	RMSE
width, r_x^-	0.926	-0.014	0.064	0.912
width, r_x^+	-0.212	0.356	-0.005	0.142
width, r_y^-	0.688	0.095	0.011	0.468
width, r_y^+	0.974	-0.177	0.020	0.563
width, r_z^-	0.085	-0.072	0.003	0.102
width, r_z^+	0.127	0.065	0.001	0.076
depth, r_x^-	0.386	-0.235	0.029	0.394
depth, r_x^+	0.426	0.370	-0.005	0.141
depth, r_y^-	0.158	0.005	0.002	0.096
depth, r_y^+	0.140	-0.001	0.004	0.106
depth, r_z^-	-0.032	-0.319	-0.002	0.150
depth, r_z^+	-0.099	0.338	-0.002	0.130

Now, we have the model fitted to our data with root mean squared error (RMSE) less than unity values that implies good confidence level for estimation. The estimated model parameters are now used to deduce equations for prediction. Examples are shown in equations 8 and 9:

$$width = p0 + p1 * (t_z^-) \tag{8}$$

$$depth = p0 + p1 * (r_y^+) + p2 * (r_y^+)^2 + p3 * (r_y^+)^3 \tag{9}$$

5.4 Tolerance

Let us consider, in case of PantoInspect, the acceptable inaccuracy is 0.5mm. For this acceptable level of inaccuracy we can find the camera misalignment (rotation and position) based on the estimated model parameters. By solving the equations defining the model for 0.5mm error, the maximum tolerance for the camera misalignments are estimated and are summarised as in table 3.

Table 3. Tolerances for camera misalignment, given the system inaccuracy limit as 0.5mm

Tolerances	X axis (deg/mm)	Y axis (deg/mm)	Z axis (deg/mm)
Rotation (width)	-0.46 to 0.82	-2.96 to 4.27	-4.73 to 5.12
Rotation (depth)	-0.11 to 0.19	-12.57 to 9.21	-1.68 to 1.79
Translation (width)	-6.97e04 to 6.98e04	-69.83 to 67.42	-56.41 to 59.20
Translation (depth)	-11.82e05 to 11.75e04	-117.93 to 112.35	-94.67 to 99.44

6   Conclusion

We identified the PantoInspect system as a suitable use case for measuring inspected data in 3D, using a single calibrated camera. To study the effects of camera misalignment on the accuracy of measurements, we emulated the camera misalignment in both position and orientation for several values, and obtained the width and depth error data. The resulting data was modelled using suitable regression models and we deduced expressions for prediction. Using the model parameter and expressions, we obtained tolerances for given acceptable inaccuracy limit.

Overall, our paper provided a statistical tool or study methodology, that is easily implementable and reproducible. Our approach can be directly used by single camera vision systems to estimate tolerances of camera misalignment for an acceptable (defined) accuracy.

The knowledge about tolerance is helpful for mechanical design considerations of the camera placement in vision based inspection system, to achieve a desired level of confidence in the accuracy of the system. However, our approach assumes that the measurements are carried out on points lying on a plane.

In the future, we would like to use the same model to estimate camera misalignment through bruteforce methods by which the physically re-alignment of the camera is possible. Alternatively, camera pose can be treated as estimating the homography between the camera plane and the plane containing laser lines. The PantoInspect system captures images of three laser lines. Using the knowledge of line distance ratios and line parallelism, it is possible to estimate the homography and hence the camera pose. Then, camera re-calibration on-the-fly, without the aid of the checkerboard, is possible.

Acknowledgement. We thank Lars Baunegaard With, Morten Langschwager and Claus Hoelgaard Olsen at Image House PantoInspect A/S, for discussions and encouragement.

References

1. Bouguet, J.Y.: Camera calibration toolbox for Matlab (2008), http://www.vision.caltech.edu/bouguetj/calib_doc/
2. Image House PantoInspect, Denmark, http://www.pantoinspect.dk/
3. Zhengyou, Z.: A Flexible New Technique for Camera Calibration. IEEE Transactions on Pattern Analysis and Machine Intelligence 22, 1330–1334 (1998)
4. Aurélien, C., et al.: Automatic Road Defect Detection by Textural Pattern Recognition Based on AdaBoost. Comp.-Aided Civil and Infrastruct. Engineering 27(4) (2012)
5. Roger, T.: A Versatile Camera Calibration Technique for High-accuracy 3D Machine Vision Metrology using Off-the-shelf TV Cameras and Lenses. IEEE Journal on Robotics and Automation, 323–344 (1987)
6. Hartley, R., Zisserman, A.: Multiple View Geometry in Computer Vision, 2nd edn. Cambridge University Press, New York (2003) ISBN: 0521540518
7. Raj, J.: The Art of Computer Systems Performance Analysis. John Wiley & Sons Inc. (1991)
8. Mar, N.S.S., et al.: Design of Automatic vision Based Inspection System for Solder Joint Segementation. Journal of AMME 34(2) (2009)
9. Dongming, Z., Songtao, L.: 3D Image Processing Method for Manufacturing Process Automation. Journal of Computing Industry 56(8) (2005)
10. Brosnan, T., et al.: Improving Quality Inspection of Food Products by Computer Vision - Review. Journal of Food Engineering 61, 3–16 (2004)
11. Narendra, V.G., Hareesh, K.S.: Quality Inspection and Grading of Agricultural and Food Products by Computer Vision - Review. IJCA (2010)
12. Heimonen, T., et al.: Experiments in 3D Measurements by Using Single Camera and Accurate Motion. In: Proceedings of the IEEE International Symposium, pp. 356–361 (2001)
13. Wei, S., et al.: 3D Displacement Measurement with a Single Camera based on Digital Image Correlation Technique. In: International Symposium on Advanced Optical Manufacturing and Testing Technologies, vol. 6723 (2007)
14. Araki, N., et al.: Vehicle's Orientation Method by Single Camera Image Using Known-Shaped Planar Object. IJICIC 7(7) (2009)
15. Zhao, W., Nandhakumar, N.: Effects of Camera Alignment Errors on Stereoscopic Depth Estimates. Pattern Recognition 29, 2115–2126 (1996)
16. Santoro, M., et al.: Misalignment Correction for Depth Estimation using Stereoscopic 3-D Cameras. In: IEEE 14th International Workshop, MMSP, pp. 19–24 (2012)
17. Godding, et al.: Geometric calibration and orientation of digital imaging systems. Aicon 3D Systems, Braunschweig (2002), http://www.falcon.de/falcon/eng/documentation
18. Eric, H., et al.: The Effects of Translational Misalignment when Self-Calibrating Rotating and Zooming Cameras. IEEE Transactions on Pattern Analysis and Machine Intelligence, 1015–1020 (2003)
19. Gasteratos, A., Sandini, G.: Factors Affecting the Accuracy of an Active Vision Head. In: Vlahavas, I.P., Spyropoulos, C.D. (eds.) SETN 2002. LNCS (LNAI), vol. 2308, pp. 413–422. Springer, Heidelberg (2002)

Design and Experimental Validation of a Hybrid Micro Tele-Manipulation System

Kostas Vlachos and Evangelos Papadopoulos

Department of Mechanical Engineering, National Technical University of Athens,
Heroon Polytechniou 9, 15780 Athens, Greece
{kostaswl,egpapado}@central.ntua.gr

Abstract. This paper presents analytical and experimental results on a new hybrid tele-manipulation environment for micro-robot control under non-holonomic constraints. This environment is comprised of a haptic tele-manipulation subsystem (macro-scale motion), and a visual servoing subsystem, (micro-scale motion) under the microscope. The first subsystem includes a 5-dof (degrees of freedom) force feedback mechanism, acting as the master, and a 2-dof micro-robot, acting as the slave. In the second subsystem, a motion controller based on visual feedback drives the micro-robot. The fact that the slave micro-robot is driven by two centrifugal force vibration micro-motors makes the presented tele-manipulation environment exceptional and challenging. The unique characteristics and challenges that arise during the micromanipulation of the specific device are described and analyzed. The developed solutions are presented and discussed. Experiments show that, regardless of the disparity between master and slave, the proposed environment facilitates functional and simple micro-robot control during micro-manipulation operations.

Keywords: micro-robotic mechanism, haptic mechanism, tele-manipulation, non-holonomic constraints.

1 Introduction

Recently, research in the area of robotic manipulation in the micro- and nano-worlds has gained a lot of interest and importance. The research activity focuses in areas such as microsurgery, direct medical procedures on cells, biomechatronics, micro-manufacturing, and micro-assembly, where tele-operated micro-robotic devices can be used. It is well known now that not only the visual but also the haptic feedback can be helpful for a successful tele-operated micromanipulation procedure, [1]. Therefore, some of the master manipulators are haptic devices, able to drive the micro-robots and at the same time to transmit torques and forces to the operator.

A haptic tele-operation system, for use in microsurgery, was presented by Salcudean and Yan, [2], and by Salcudean, et al., [3]. Their system consists of two magnetically levitated and kinematically identical wrists, acting as a macro-master and a micro-slave, and a conventional manipulator that transports them. A tele-nano-robotics system using an Atomic Force Microscope (AFM), as the nano-robot, has been proposed

A. Likas, K. Blekas, and D. Kalles (Eds.): SETN 2014, LNAI 8445, pp. 164–177, 2014.
© Springer International Publishing Switzerland 2014

by Sitti and Hashimoto, [4]. The system provides a 1-dof force feedback device for haptic sensing, using a linear scaling approach. A microsurgical tele-robot is presented, which consists of 6-dof parallel micromanipulator attached to a macro-motion industrial robot, and a 6-dof haptic master device, [5]. The system provides a disturbance observer to enhance the operator's perception.

A micro tele-operation system for tasks, such as micro-assembly or micro-manufacturing, was developed by Ando et al., [6]. The haptic master is a 6-dof serial link mechanism, and the slave is a parallel mechanism. Alternatively the Phantom, a commercial haptic interface, can be used as a master device, [7]. The Phantom was used as a haptic master by Menciassi et al., where a micro-instrument for microsurgery or minimally invasive surgery was tested, [8]. Sitti et al. used the same haptic interface to tele-operate a piezoresistive AFM probe used as a slave manipulator and force sensor, [9]. A bio-micromanipulation system for biological objects such as embryos, cells or oocytes was presented in [10]. The system uses a Phantom to provide an augmented virtual haptic feedback during cell injection. A similar system for microinjection of embryonic stem cells into blastocysts is described in [11], although the system has no haptic feedback. The mechanical design of a haptic device integrated into a mobile nano-handling station is presented in [12]. The Delta haptic device was proposed as a nano-manipulator in [13]. This device is also interfaced to an AFM.

The proposed tele-manipulation environment is designed by taking into account a micro-manipulation scenario. According to this, a micro-manipulation task consists of two phases. In the first phase, the micro-robot executes a macro-scale motion towards a target. In the second phase, the platform executes micro-scale motions, and the micro-assembly or micro-manipulation task is performed in the field-of-view of a microscope. While the first phase demands increased velocity, the second phase requires increased motion resolution. Consequently, the proposed environment consists of two subsystems. The first subsystem, which is first introduced in [14], is a haptic tele-manipulation master-slave system, responsible for the macro-scale motion of the micro-robot. The commanding master device is a 5-dof force feedback mechanism, while the executing slave is a non-holonomic 2-dof micro-robot with special behavior and driven by two centrifugal force actuators. This slave mechanism has a number of advantages relative to other micro-robotic devices; namely, it is characterized by low cost, complexity and power consumption. A detailed analysis of the micro-robot can be found in [15]. In this paper, the 3rd generation of the micro-robotic device is presented, and a brief description of the kinematics and dynamics are given. A novel methodology that compensates for the non-holonomic constraints is also presented. The second subsystem is responsible for the micro-scale motion of the micro-robot in the field-of-view of a microscope. It includes a video-microscope that records the motion of the micro-robot, the acquired images are transmitted to the visual servoing controller, and the calculated control values are transmitted wirelessly to the micro-robot. The use of the proposed hybrid tele-manipulation environment is illustrated by several experiments. These show that, regardless of the disparity between master and slave, the proposed environment facilitates functional and simple to the user micro-robot control during micromanipulation operations.

2   Haptic Subsystem of the Micro Tele-Manipulation Environment

The first subsystem of the tele-manipulation environment employs an existing 5-dof haptic mechanism as the master and a 2-dof micro-robotic platform driven by two centrifugal force actuators as the slave. A brief description of the master is given next.

2.1   Haptic Master Device

The master device is the haptic mechanism shown in Fig. 1. It consists of a 2-dof, 5-bar linkage and a 3-dof spherical joint. All dof are active. To reduce mechanism moving mass and inertia, all actuators are mounted on the base. The transmission system is implemented using tendon drives with capstans. Although this haptic device was not developed for micromanipulation, it is suitable for it, since it has been designed optimally to exhibit maximum transparency, as seen from the operator side, [16]. The mechanism handle can translate in the X- and Y-axes by 10 cm, rotate about the X axis by ±180°, and about the Y and Z axis by ±30°, maintaining an excellent functionality.

Fig. 1. The haptic master device

Employing a Lagrangian formulation yields the following mechanism equations of motion:

$$\mathbf{M}(\mathbf{q})\ddot{\mathbf{q}} + \mathbf{V}(\mathbf{q},\dot{\mathbf{q}}) + \mathbf{G}(\mathbf{q}) = \boldsymbol{\tau} + \mathbf{J}^T\mathbf{F}_T \tag{1}$$

where $\mathbf{q}$ is a vector containing the five joint angles, $\mathbf{J}$, and $\mathbf{M}$ are the mechanism 5×5 Jacobian, and mass matrix respectively, $\mathbf{V}$ contains the nonlinear velocity terms, and $\mathbf{G}$ is the gravity torques vector. The vector $\boldsymbol{\tau}$ contains joint input torques while the vector $\mathbf{J}^T\mathbf{F}_T$ resolves, to the five joints, the forces and torques applied to the mechanism endpoint. The device is thoroughly described, including kinematics and dynamics, in [17].

2.2   Micro Slave Device

The 3rd generation of a new mobile micro-robot originally introduced in [15], is employed in this paper. Therefore, a more detailed description is given next.

Motion Principle

A simplified 1-dof mobile platform of mass M is used, whose motion mechanism employs an eccentric mass m, rotated by a platform mounted motor O, as shown in Fig. 2. One cycle of operation is completed when the mass m has described an angle of 360°.

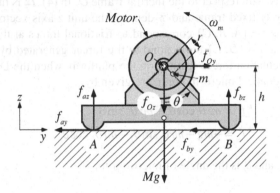

Fig. 2. Simplified 1-dof platform with rotating mass m

Gravitational and centrifugal forces exerted on the rotating mass are resolved along the y-, and z-axes to yield:

$$f_{Oy} = mr\omega_m^2 \sin\theta$$
$$f_{Oz} = -mg - mr\omega_m^2 \cos\theta \tag{2}$$

where ω_m is the actuation speed, θ is the rotation angle of the eccentric mass, g is the acceleration of gravity and r the length of the link between m and O. Above a critical value of actuation speed, $\omega_{critical}$, the actuation (centrifugal) forces overcome frictional forces and motion is induced. For counterclockwise rotation of the eccentric mass m, the platform exhibits a net displacement towards the positive y-axis. It has been shown analytically that the motion step the platform exhibits over a cycle of operation can be made arbitrarily small depending on the actuation speed ω, [15]. In practice, open-loop motion resolution is limited by the electronic driving modules and by the unknown non-uniform distribution of the coefficient of friction μ along the surface of the planar motion.

Platform Dynamics

The actuation principle mentioned above was employed to the design and implementation of a 2-dof micro-robot as shown in Fig. 3 (left).

The platform dynamics are presented in a compact matrix form by the Newton Euler equations:

$$M\dot{\mathbf{v}} = \mathbf{R}\sum_i {}^b\mathbf{f}_i, \quad i = \{A,B,C,D,E\} \tag{3}$$

$$I_{zz}\ddot{\psi} = \hat{\mathbf{z}}\sum_i ({}^b\mathbf{r}_i \times {}^b\mathbf{f}_i), \quad i = \{A,B,C,D,E\} \tag{4}$$

where b is the body-fixed frame, $\mathbf{R}$ is the rotation matrix between frame b and the inertial frame O, $\ddot{\psi}$ is the platform angular velocity, and $\mathbf{v} = [\dot{x}, \dot{y}, \dot{z}]^T$ is its center of mass (CM) velocity with respect to the inertial frame O. In (4), I_{zz} is the polar moment of inertia in the body fixed frame and $\hat{\mathbf{z}}$ denotes the unit z-axis vector. In both equations the subscripts $i = \{A, B, C\}$ correspond to frictional forces at the contact points of the platform, and $i = \{D, E\}$ correspond to the forces generated by the two vibrating motors. The actuation forces that act on the platform, when the DC micro-motors rotate (assuming identical micro-motors), are given by:

$$\begin{aligned} {}^b f_{ix} &= mr\ddot{\theta}_i \cos\theta_i - mr\dot{\theta}_i^2 \sin\theta_i \\ {}^b f_{iz} &= -mg - mr\ddot{\theta}_i \sin\theta_i - mr\dot{\theta}_i^2 \cos\theta_i \end{aligned} \tag{5}$$

where, $i = \{D, E\}$, and θ_i is the angle of micro-motor i.

Fig. 3. Schematic design of the base (left), and the 3rd generation micro-robot prototype (right)

Micro-robot Prototype

The 3rd generation of the micro-robot is presented in Fig. 3 (right). This includes two vibration DC motors fed by pic-controlled H-bridges, wireless communications to a PC commanding station, a needle with force sensing capabilities, and an on-board battery. It includes advanced features, such as optical flow displacement sensors, motor speed optical sensors, and battery recharging through a USB port.

Micro-robot Motion Capabilities

Simulation runs, and experiments on the basic motion capabilities of the micro-robot, indicated that the micro-robotic platform is capable of moving forward and backward, in a straight or curved line, while it can rotate both clockwise and anticlockwise, [18]. Moreover, due to non-holonomic constraints, it is impossible for the platform to move parallel to the Y-axis connecting the two motors. This would be a problem during a micromanipulation procedure because the motion of the platform towards the forward direction results in a small parasitic sideways deviation. More specifically, because of unmodeled dynamics, the platform deviates towards the sidewise direction from its straightforward motion by a small amount Δy. Since the platform is incapable of moving in the sidewise direction so as to correct this parasitic effect, a method of performing such a positioning correction is developed.

It is based on the execution of a V-shaped motion, divided into two symmetrical stages. The first part of the motion is achieved when the left motor rotates in the positive direction. In the second half of the motion only the right motor rotates with positive angular velocity, see Fig. 4 (left). This specific sequence of motions results in a net displacement towards the right of the platform, see Fig. 4 (right). Reversing the two angular velocities a displacement towards the left can be achieved.

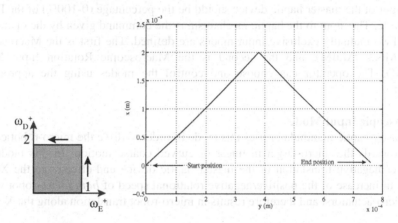

Fig. 4. Angular velocities graph for the sidewise displacement (left), and simulated motion of the platform (right)

2.3   Haptic Tele-Manipulation Environment Analysis

Slave Micro-robot Features
The design and special features of the slave micro-robot introduce a number of challenges that need to be tackled by the tele-manipulation environment design.

- The micro-robot is able for coarse and fine motion. Its translational sliding velocity is up to 1.5 mm/s.
- The slave micro-platform and the master haptic device are kinematical dissimilar.
- The inverse kinematics of the nonlinear micro-robot is not available in real time.
- The micro-robot exhibits complex nonholonomic characteristics.
- The vibration actuators must operate within a specific speed range (rpm). When this upper limit is exceeded, the micro-robot exhibits an additional undesirable vertical vibration. A low rpm limit also exists and is due to the need to overcome the support frictional forces, so that net motion may result.

Master Haptic Device Requirements

The above slave micro-robot features dictate the following requirements for the master haptic device.

- The master haptic device has to drive the micro-platform towards the target in coarse motion.
- To resolve the kinematical dissimilarity between the master and the slave, a mapping from the master haptic device Cartesian space to the micro-robot actuator space has to be developed.

Implementation

In the haptic tele-manipulation environment, the master haptic device transmits motion commands to the micro-robot. PWM circuits drive the micro-platform actuators, according to the percentage (0-100%) of their duty cycle. As a result, actuator angular velocities are set, and produce micro-robot translations and rotations. Consequently the output of the master haptic device should be the percentage (0-100%) of the PWM duty cycle. The input to the haptic mechanism is the command given by the operator's hand. Two mutually exclusive input modes are defined. The first is the Macroscopic Input Mode (MaIM), and the second is the Macroscopic Rotation Input Mode (MRIM). The operator can choose and control the modes using the appropriate software.

Macroscopic Input Mode

The master haptic manipulator uses this mode in order to drive the micro-robotic platform towards the micro-target in linear or curved coarse motion. In this mode the positive/ negative translation of the master haptic device end-effector in the X axis results in increase of the positive/negative rotational speed of *both* micro-robot vibration micro-actuators, and therefore results in micro-robot translation along the X axis.

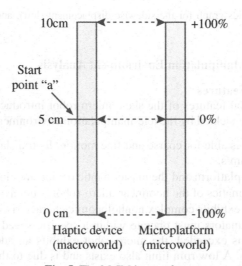

Fig. 5. The MaIM input scheme

To obtain a curved translation, a difference in the micro-actuator rotational velocities must exist. This is achieved by rotating the haptic device end-effector about the Y
axis. A positive/ negative rotation about this axis results in an increase of the rotational speed of the first/ second micro-actuator. As mentioned earlier, the haptic device
end-effector can translate in the X axis by 10 cm and rotate about the Y axis by about
±30°. Therefore, the start point of the end-effector is taken in the middle of its possible displacement, see Fig 5, point "a". A translation of the haptic device end-effector
from start point "a" results in a percentage command of the micro-actuator speeds q
according to,

$$q = 20(p-5) \quad [\%] \tag{6}$$

where p [cm] is the haptic device end-effector position. Additionally, for each degree
(°) of end-effector rotation about the Y axis, the corresponding micro-actuator speed
is increased by 1%.

Macroscopic Rotation Input Method

The master haptic device uses this mode to rotate the micro-robot without translation,
again in coarse motion. This mode is useful in changing fast the direction of micro-
platform motion, and can be achieved by rotating the micro-actuators in equal and
opposite speeds. To this end, the master operator translates the end-effector along the
X axis resulting in an increase of the rotational speed of both micro-actuators, but this
time with opposite speed direction.

Table 1 illustrates the presented input modes above. The "+"/ "−" symbols denote a
positive/negative rotational micro-actuator speed, the "↑" symbol denotes a micro-
actuator speed increase, while "0" denotes that the corresponding micro-actuator is
not influenced. During the MaIM phase, "1" denotes that the corresponding micro-
actuator is functioning, "0" denotes that the micro-actuator is not functioning.

Table 1. Haptic tele-manipulation environment input modes

	MaIM		MRIM	
In X positive	+	+	+	—
In X negative	—	—	—	+
About Y positive	↑	0	↑	0
About Y negative	0	↑	0	↑
	μMotor A	μMotor B	μMotor A	μMotor B

As discussed earlier, above a critical micro-actuator speed, the micro-robot vibrates
vertically and may even tip over. To indicate the limits of the permissible actuation
speed, a spring force proportional to haptic end-effector translation (and micro-
actuator speed) is applied to the operator. This force is given by,

$$f_{sp} = k(p-5) \tag{7}$$

where p is the haptic device end-effector translation, and k is a variable spring
constant. It was found by experimentation that tipping occurs at about 85% of the

maximum micro-actuator speed, depending on ground type or platform mass. To signal this limit, a spring constant three times harder than before is employed above the 85% of the maximum speed. To achieve a smooth transition, the spring constant is changing according to an exponential function. The maximum force applied to the operator is set at 5N. This value is slightly under the 15% of 35.5N, which is the average maximum controllable force a female can produce with her wrist according to Tan et al. in [19]. Measurements in [20] showed that humans exert forces up to 15% of their maximum ability, without fatigue for a long period of time. Consequently, the chosen spring constant, k, is defined as:

$$
k = \begin{cases} 0.33 & |p-5| \leq 4.25 \\ e^{0.68(|p-5|-4.25)} - 0.66 & 5.0 \geq |p-5| > 4.25 \\ 1 & |p-5| > 5.0 \end{cases} \tag{8}
$$

3   Visual Servoing Subsystem of the Micro Tele-Manipulation Environment

As mentioned earlier, the proposed tele-manipulation environment is designed by taking into account a micro-manipulation scenario, where a micro-manipulation task consists of two phases. In the first phase, the micro-robot executes a macroscale motion towards a target. In the second phase, the platform executes microscale motions, and a micro-manipulation task is performed in the field-of-view of a microscope. Assuming that the micro-robot, using the first subsystem described above, has positioned in the field-of-view of the microscope, the tele-manipulation environment switches to the second subsystem. In this subsystem, the motion of the micro-robot is not controlled from the haptic device anymore. A visual servoing controller undertakes this task, described by the following set of rules:

$$
\begin{bmatrix} \omega_{md} \\ \omega_{me} \end{bmatrix} = \begin{cases} [\omega_{md\downarrow} \ \omega_{me\downarrow}]^T & \text{if } y < y_{des} - \varepsilon \\ [\omega_{md\rightarrow} \ \omega_{me\rightarrow}]^T & \text{if } y_{des} - \varepsilon < y < y_{des} + \varepsilon \\ [\omega_{md\uparrow} \ \omega_{me\uparrow}]^T & \text{if } y > y_{des} + \varepsilon \end{cases} \tag{9}
$$

where $[\omega_{md\downarrow}, \omega_{me\downarrow}]^T$ and $[\omega_{md\uparrow}, \omega_{me\uparrow}]^T$ denote motor angular velocity pairs that result in a platform displacement with a positive or negative instantaneous curvature respectively. The vector $[\omega_{md\rightarrow}, \omega_{me\rightarrow}]^T$ denotes the pair of motor angular velocities that result in straight line translation, and 2ε designates the width of the acceptable path. The specific angular velocity pair values depend on system parameters and distance from the target, and are identified by experiments. The goal for the end-effector of the micro-robot is to follow a predefined horizontal corridor-like path of width 2ε, reach a desired target point, and then stop. The end-effector motion is recorded by a video-microscope, and the images are transmitted to the controller. The outcome of the image processing of each frame is the plane position of the end-effector. This information is fed back to the controller, and the control inputs are calculated, according to (9). The inputs, expressed as PWM commands, are transmitted wirelessly to the microrobot and the appropriate voltages are applied to its motors.

A graphical representation of the controller action is illustrated in Fig. 6. The colored strip represents part of the desired path. The platform is forced to translate inside the desired path strip. When the end-effector of the micro-robot reaches the target location, both motors are stopped.

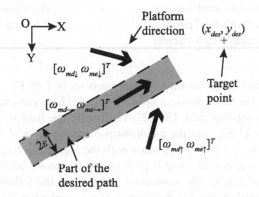

Fig. 6. Graphical representation of the controller action

4   Simulation of the Micro Tele-Manipulation Environment

Next, a model of the first subsystem of the micro tele-manipulation environment is defined. It consists of (a) the operator's hand, (b) the haptic mechanism, and (c) the micro-robotic system, see Fig. 7 (left). The operator's hand is modeled as a mass-spring-damper system, attached to the haptic mechanism modeled as a mass-damper system, see Fig. 7 (right). Note, that in the first subsystem, the haptic device is connected with a virtual spring defined by (8), with spring constant k.

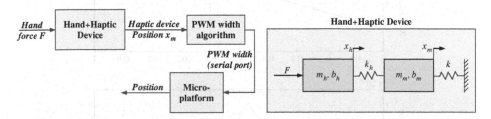

Fig. 7. The model of the haptic tele-manipulation system (left), including the user hand (right)

The transfer function of the "Hand+Haptic Device" block in Fig. 9 is described by (10), and the related symbols are defined in Table 2.

$$\frac{X_m(s)}{F(s)} = \frac{k_h}{m_h m_m s^4 + A s^3 + B s^2 + C s + k_h k} \qquad (10)$$

where $A = m_h b_m + b_h m_m$, $B = m_h (k + k_h) + b_h b_m + k_h m_m$, and $C = b_h (k + k_h) + k_h b_m$.

Table 2. Definition of the symbols in (10) and Fig. 9

Symbol	Definition	Symbol	Definition
F	Operator's hand force	m_m	Haptic mechanism mass
m_h	Operator's hand mass	b_m	Haptic mechanism damping
b_h	Operator's hand damping	x_m	Haptic mechanism position
x_h	Operator's hand position	k	Virtual spring constant
k_h	Operator's hand stiffness		

During the simulation, the operator's hand mass m_h is 1.46 Kg, the hand damping b_h is 3.6 Ns/m. and the hand stiffness k_h is 200 N/m. These represent average values taken from the relevant literature, [21-22]. The haptic mechanism apparent mass m_m in X axis is about 0.27 Kg, and the mechanism damping b_m is about 5 Ns/m. These values were found through experimentation with the haptic mechanism, see [17]. The input to the system is a step of about 0.18 N of the operator's hand force F. The virtual spring value k is 4 N/m. The simulation run realizes the following scenario. The motion of the micro-robot starts at point (0 m, 0 m) employing the haptic subsystem of the micro tele-manipulation environment. Here, the haptic device drives the micro-robot towards the field-of-view of the video-microscope. We assume that it begins at (0.0001 m, 0 m). When the micro-robot enters the field-of-view, the visual servoing subsystem takes control, and drives the micro-robot towards the desired target point at (0.001, 0), according to (9). As shown in Fig. 8, the proposed micro tele-manipulation environment successfully drives the micro-robot to the target point, and then stops.

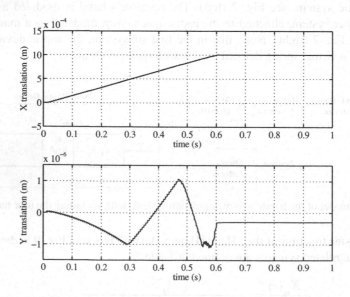

Fig. 8. The application of both subsystems of the micro tele-manipulation subsystem

5   Experimental Results

To validate the proposed environment, various experiments are conducted. The goal is to use the haptic device to drive the micro-robot towards the field-of-view of the video-microscope, and then let the visual servoing controller to drive the micro-robot to a target point using a predefined path. During the first phase of the experiment the operator moves the haptic device end-effector along the X axis and rotates it about the Y axis. The end-effector position and the angle are captured by encoders attached on the haptic device actuators (Maxon dc motors), and transmitted to a PC/104 tower. This tower is the control unit, running the algorithm that translates the operator input into the micro-robot input according to (6). At the same time the haptic device applies forces to the operator according to (7) and (8).

When the micro-robot reaches the field-of-view of the video-microscope, the second phase of the experiment begins, which is realized by the second subsystem of the micro tele-manipulation environment. The motion of the end-effector of the micro-robot is recorded by a video-microscope. The video camera pixel size was chosen so that the measurement resolution of the system is approximately 2 μm. The video camera selected was the Marlin F146B, from Allied Vision Technologies, GMBH. The acquired images are transmitted via a FireWire 400 port to a Core 2, 2 GHz PC laptop, and processed on-the-fly in Matlab. The outcome of the image processing of each frame is the plane position of the end-effector of the micro-robot. This information is fed back to the controller, and the control inputs are calculated, according to (9). The inputs, expressed as PWM commands, are transmitted wirelessly to the microrobot and the appropriate voltages are applied to its motors. The control loop duration is 80 ms. The path of the end-effector of the micro-robot under the microscope is shown in Fig. 9a. The desired target point is marked with the red "plus" symbol. We can see that when the end-effector enters the field-of-view of the microscope, the visual servoing controller force it to follow the predefined path towards the target.

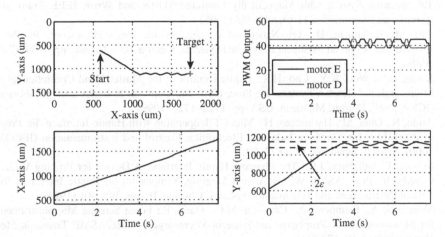

Fig. 9. (a) Path of the micro-robot end-effector, (b) PWM output from the controller, (c) x trajectory of the end-effector tip, (d) y trajectory of the end-effector tip

6   Conclusions

The analysis and several experimental results of a new hybrid micro-robot tele-manipulation environment are presented in this paper. The proposed environment combines two different subsystems. The first subsystem, employed during the coarse motion of the micro-robot, includes a 5-dof force feedback mechanism, acting as the master, and a 2-dof micro-robot, acting as the slave. Regardless of the disparity between master and slave and the fact that the slave micro-robot is driven by two centrifugal force vibration micro-motors, the environment gives to the operator the ability to drive and control the micro-platform in a functional and simple manner. In the second subsystem, a motion controller based on visual feedback drives the micro-robot in a predefined path under the field-of-view of a video-microscope.

The proposed environment manages to solve with success problems that arise during micromanipulation with the specific micro-robot, such as that the slave micro-platform and the master haptic device are kinematical dissimilar, that the vibration actuators must operate within a specific speed range (rpm), and that they must achieve high speed during the macroscopic motion and sub-micrometer positioning accuracy during the microscopic motion.

References

1. Salcudean, S.E., Ku, S., Bell, G.: Performance measurement in scaled teleoperation for microsurgery. In: Troccaz, J., Mösges, R., Grimson, E. (eds.) CVRMed-MRCAS 1997. LNCS, vol. 1205, pp. 789–798. Springer, Heidelberg (1997)
2. Salcudean, S.E., Yan, J.: Towards a Force-Reflecting Motion-Scaling System for Micro-surgery. In: Proc. IEEE Int. Conf. on Robotics and Automation (ICRA 1994), San Diego, CA, USA, pp. 2296–2301 (1994)
3. Salcudean, S.E., Wong, N.M., Hollis, R.L.: Design and Control of a Force-Reflecting Teleoperation System with Magnetically Levitated Master and Wrist. IEEE Trans. on Robotics and Automation 11(6), 844–858 (1995)
4. Sitti, M., Hashimoto, H.: Tele-Nanorobotics Using Atomic Force Microscope. In: Proc. IEEE/RSJ Int. Conf. on Intelligent Robots and Systems, Victoria, B.C., Canada, pp. 1739–1746 (1998)
5. Kwon, D.S., Woo, K.Y., Cho, H.S.: Haptic Control of the Master Hand Controller for a Microsurgical Telerobot System. In: Proc. IEEE Int. Conf. on Robotics and Automation (ICRA 1999), Detroit, Michigan, USA, pp. 1722–1727 (1999)
6. Ando, N., Ohta, M., Hashimoto, H.: Micro Teleoperation with Haptic Interface. In: Proc. of 2000 IEEE Int. Conf. on Industrial Electronics, Control and Instrumentation (IECON 2000), Nagoya, Japan, pp. 13–18 (2000)
7. Massie, T., Salisbury, J.K.: The Phantom Haptic Interface: A Device for Probing Virtual Objects. In: Proc. ASME Winter Annual Meeting, Symposium on Haptic Interfaces for Virtual Environment and Teleoperator Systems, Chicago, IL, pp. 295–301 (1994)
8. Menciassi, A., Eisinberg, A., Carrozza, M.C., Dario, P.: Force Sensing Microinstrument for Measuring Tissue Properties and Pulse in Microsurgery. IEEE/ASME Trans. on Mechatronics 8(1), 10–17 (2003)

9. Sitti, M., Aruk, B., Shintani, H., Hashimoto, H.: Scaled Teleoperation System for Nano-Scale Interaction and Manipulation. Advanced Robotics 17(3), 275–291 (2003)
10. Ammi, M., Ferreira, A.: Realistic Visual and Haptic Rendering for Biological-Cell Injection. In: Proc. IEEE Int. Conf. on Robotics and Automation (ICRA 2005), Barcelona, Spain, pp. 930–935 (2005)
11. Mattos, L., Grant, E., Thresher, R.: Semi-Automated Blastocyst Microinjection. In: Proc. IEEE Int. Conf. on Robotics and Automation (ICRA 2006), Orlando, Florida, USA, pp. 1780–1785 (2006)
12. Kortschack, A., Shirinov, A., Trueper, T., Fatikow, S.: Development of Mobile Versatile Nanohandling Micro-robots: Design, Driving Principles, Haptic Control. Robotica 23(4), 419–434 (2005)
13. Grange, S., Conti, F., Helmer, P., Rouiller, P., Baur, C.: The Delta Haptic Device as a Nanomanipulator. Proc. SPIE Micro-Robotics & Microassembly III 4568, 100–111 (2001)
14. Vlachos, K., Papadopoulos, E.: Analysis and Experiments of a Haptic Tele-Manipulation Environment for a Microrobot Driven by Centripetal Forces. ASME Journal of Computing Sciences and Information in Engineering - Special Issue on Haptics, Tactile and Multimodal Interfaces 8(4) (2008)
15. Vartholomeos, P., Papadopoulos, E.: Dynamics, Design and Simulation of a Novel Micro-robotic Platform Employing Vibration Microactuators. Journal of Dynamic Systems, Measurement and Control, ASME 128, 122–134 (2006)
16. Vlachos, K., Papadopoulos, E.: Transparency Maximization Methodology for Haptic Devices. IEEE/ASME Trans. on Mechatronics 11(3), 249–255 (2006)
17. Vlachos, K., Papadopoulos, E., Mitropoulos, D.: Design and Implementation of a Haptic Device for Urological Operations. IEEE Trans. on Robotics & Aut. 19(5), 801–809 (2003)
18. Vlachos, K., Vartholomeos, P., Papadopoulos, E.: A Haptic Tele- Manipulation Environment for a Vibration-Driven Micromechatronic Device. In: Proc. IEEE/ASME International Conference on Advanced Intelligent Mechatronics Systems (AIM 2007), ETH Zurich, Switzerland, September 4-7 (2007)
19. Tan, H.Z., Srinivasan, M.A., Ederman, B., Cheng, B.: Human Factors for the Design of Force-Reflecting Haptic Interfaces. ASME Dynamic Systems and Control 55(1), 353–359 (1994)
20. Wiker, S.F., Hershkowitz, E., Zilk, J.: Teleoperator Comfort and Psychometric Stability: Criteria for Limiting Master-Controller Forces of Operation and Feedback During Tele-manipulation. In: Proc. NASA Conference on Space Telerobotics, Pasadena, CA, USA, vol. I, pp. 99–107 (1989)
21. Gil, J.J., Avello, A., Rubio, A., Florez, J.: Stability Analysis of a 1 DOF Haptic Interface Using the Routh-Hurwitz Criterion. IEEE Trans. on Control System Technology 12(4), 583–588 (2004)
22. Salcudean, S.E., Zhu, M., Zhu, W.-H., Hashtrudi-Zaad, K.: Transparent Bilateral Teleoperation under Position and Rate Control. I. J. Robotic Research 19(12), 1185–1202 (2000)

Tackling Large Qualitative Spatial Networks
of Scale-Free-Like Structure

Michael Sioutis and Jean-François Condotta

Université Lille-Nord de France, Université d'Artois
CRIL-CNRS UMR 8188
Lens, France
{sioutis,condotta}@cril.fr

Abstract. We improve the state-of-the-art method for checking the consistency of large qualitative spatial networks that appear in the Web of Data by exploiting the scale-free-like structure observed in their underlying graphs. We propose an implementation scheme that triangulates the underlying graphs of the input networks and uses a hash table based adjacency list to efficiently represent and reason with them. We generate random scale-free-like qualitative spatial networks using the Barabási-Albert (BA) model with a preferential attachment mechanism. We test our approach on the already existing random datasets that have been extensively used in the literature for evaluating the performance of qualitative spatial reasoners, our own generated random scale-free-like spatial networks, and real spatial datasets that have been made available as Linked Data. The analysis and experimental evaluation of our method presents significant improvements over the state-of-the-art approach, and establishes our implementation as the only possible solution to date to reason with large scale-free-like qualitative spatial networks efficiently.

1 Introduction

Spatial reasoning is a major field of study in Artificial Intelligence; particularly in Knowledge Representation. This field has gained a lot of attention during the last few years as it extends to a plethora of areas and domains that include, but are not limited to, ambient intelligence, dynamic GIS, cognitive robotics, spatiotemporal design, and reasoning and querying with semantic geospatial query languages [15,18,22]. In this context, an emphasis has been made on qualitative spatial reasoning which relies on qualitative abstractions of spatial aspects of the common-sense background knowledge, on which our human perspective on the physical reality is based. The concise expressiveness of the qualitative approach provides a promising framework that further boosts research and applications in the aforementioned areas and domains.

The Region Connection Calculus (RCC) is the dominant Artificial Intelligence approach for representing and reasoning about topological relations [23]. RCC can be used to describe regions that are non-empty regular subsets of some topological space by stating their topological relations to each other. RCC-8 is the constraint language formed by the following 8 binary topological relations

A. Likas, K. Blekas, and D. Kalles (Eds.): SETN 2014, LNAI 8445, pp. 178–191, 2014.
© Springer International Publishing Switzerland 2014

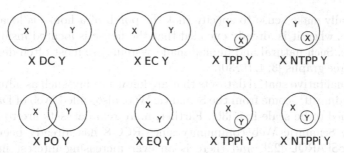

Fig. 1. Two dimensional examples for the eight base relations of RCC-8

of RCC: disconnected (*DC*), externally connected (*EC*), equal (*EQ*), partially overlapping (*PO*), tangential proper part (*TPP*), tangential proper part inverse (*TPPI*), non-tangential proper part (*NTPP*), and non-tangential proper part inverse (*NTPPI*). These eight relations are depicted in Figure 1 (2D case).

In the literature of qualitative spatial reasoning there has been a severe lack of datasets for experimental evaluation of the reasoners involved. In most cases, datasets consist of randomly generated regural networks that have a uniform node degree distribution [27] and scale up to a few hundred nodes in experimental evaluations [12,32]. These networks are often very hard to solve instances that do not correspond to real case scenarios [31] and are mainly used to test the efficiency of different algorithm and heuristic implementations. There has been hardly any investigation or exploitage of the stuctural properties of the networks' underlying graphs. In the case where the datasets are real, they are mainly small and for proof of concept purposes, such as the one used in [9], with the exception of a real large scale and *successfully* used dataset employed in [29], viz., the admingeo dataset [14]. In fact, we will make use of this dataset again in this paper, along with an even bigger one that scales up to nearly a million of topological relations.

It has come to our attention that the real case scenario datasets we are particularly interested in correspond to graphs with a scale-free-like structure, i.e., the degree distribution of the graphs follows a power law. Scale-free graphs seem to match real world applications well and are widely observed in natural and human-made systems, including the Internet, the World Wide Web, and the Semantic Web [3,4,16,30]. We argue that the case of scale-free graphs applies also to qualitative spatial networks and we stress on the importance of being able to efficiently reason with such scale-free-like networks for the following two main reasons:

- The natural approach for describing topological relations inevitably leads to the creation of graphs that exhibit hubs for particular objects which are cited more than others due to various reasons, such as size, significance, and importance. These hubs are in fact the most notable characteristic in scale-free graphs [4,16]. For example, if we were to describe the topological relations in Greece, Greece would be our major hub that would relate topologically to all of its regions and cities, followed by smaller hubs that would capture topological relations within the premises of a city or a neighborhood. It would not really make sense to specify that the porch of a house is located inside Greece, when it is already encoded that the house is located inside a city of Greece. Such natural and human-made systems are most often described by scale-free graphs [3, 4, 16, 30].

- Real qualitative spatial datasets that are known today, such as admingeo [14] and gadm-rdf[1], come from the Semantic Web, also called Web of Data, which is argued to be scale-free [30]. Further, more real datasets are to be offered by the Semantic Web community since RCC-8 has already been adopted by GeoSPARQL [22], and there is an ever increasing interest in coupling qualititave spatial reasoning techniques with linked geospatial data that are constantly being made available [19, 21]. Thus, there is a real need for scalable implementations of constraint network algorithms for qualitative and quantitative spatial constraints as RDF stores supporting linked geospatial data are expected to scale to billions of triples [19, 21].

In this paper, we concentrate on the consistency checking problem of large scale-free-like qualitative spatial networks and make the following contributions: (i) we explore and take advantage of the stuctural properties of the considered networks and propose an implementation scheme that triangulates their underlying graphs to retain their sparseness and uses a hash table based adjacency list to efficiently represent and reason with them, (ii) we make the case for a new series of random datasets, viz., *large* random scale-free-like RCC-8 networks, that can be of great use and value to the qualitative reasoning community, and (iii) we experimentally evaluate our approach against the state-of-the-art reasoners GQR [12], Renz's solver [27], and two of our own implementations which we briefly present here, viz., Phalanx and Phalanx$_\nabla$, and show that it significantly advances the state-of-the-art approach.

The organization of this paper is as follows. Section 2 formally introduces the RCC-8 constraint language, chordal graphs along with the triangulation procedure, and scale-free graphs and the model we follow to create them. In Section 3 we overview the state-of-the-art techniques and present our approach. In Section 4 we experimentally evaluate our approach against the state-of-the-art reasoners, and, finally, in Section 5 we conclude and give directions for future work.

We assume that the reader is familiar with the concepts of constraint networks and their corresponding constraint graphs that are not defined explicitly in this paper due to space constraints. Also, in what follows, we will refer to undirected graphs simply as graphs.

2   Preliminaries

In this section we formally introduce the RCC-8 constraint language, chordal graphs along with the triangulation procedure, and scale-free graphs together with the Barabási-Albert (BA) model.

---

[1] http://gadm.geovocab.org/

2.1   The RCC-8 Constraint Language

A (binary) qualitative temporal or spatial constraint language [25] is based on a finite set B of *jointly exhaustive and pairwise disjoint* (JEPD) relations defined on a domain D, called the set of base relations. The set of base relations B of a particular qualitative constraint language can be used to represent definite knowledge between any two entities with respect to the given level of granularity. B contains the identity relation Id, and is closed under the converse operation ($^{-1}$). Indefinite knowledge can be specified by unions of possible base relations, and is represented by the set containing them. Hence, 2^B represents the total set of relations. 2^B is equipped with the usual set-theoretic operations (union and intersection), the converse operation, and the weak composition operation. The converse of a relation is the union of the converses of its base relations. The weak composition $\diamond$ of two relations s and t for a set of base relations B is defined as the strongest relation $r \in 2^B$ which contains $s \circ t$, or formally, $s \diamond t = \{b \in B \mid b \cap (s \circ t) \neq \emptyset\}$, where $s \circ t = \{(x,y) \mid \exists z : (x,z) \in s \land (z,y) \in t\}$ is the relational composition [25,28]. In the case of the qualitative spatial constraint language RCC-8 [23], as already mentioned in Section 1, the set of base relations is the set $\{DC,EC,PO,TPP,NTPP,TPPI,NTPPI,EQ\}$, with EQ being the identity relation (Figure 1).

Definition 1. *An RCC-8 network comprises a pair (V, C) where V is a non empty finite set of variables and C is a mapping that associates a relation $C(v, v') \in 2^B$ to each pair (v, v') of $V \times V$. C is such that $C(v, v) \subseteq \{EQ\}$ and $C(v, v') = (C(v', v))^{-1}$.*

In what follows, $C(v_i, v_j)$ will be also denoted by C_{ij}. Checking the consistency of a RCC-8 network is $\mathcal{NP}$-hard in general [26]. However, there exist large maximal tractable subsets of RCC-8 which can be used to make reasoning much more efficient even in the general $\mathcal{NP}$-hard case. These maximal tractable subsets of RCC-8 are the sets $\hat{\mathcal{H}}_8, \mathcal{C}_8$, and $\mathcal{Q}_8$ [24]. Consistency checking is then realised by a path consistency algorithm that iteratively performs the following operation until a fixed point $\overline{C}$ is reached: $\forall i, j, k, C_{ij} \leftarrow C_{ij} \cap (C_{ik} \diamond C_{kj})$, where variables i, k, j form triangles that belong either to a completion [27] or a chordal completion [29] of the underlying graph of the input network. Within the operation, weak composition of relations is aided by the weak composition table for RCC-8 [20]. If $C_{ij} = \emptyset$ for a pair (i, j) then C is inconsistent, otherwise $\overline{C}$ is *path consistent*. If the relations of the input RCC-8 network belong to some tractable subset of relations, path consistency implies consistency, otherwise a backtracking algorithm decomposes the initial relations into subrelations belonging to some tractable subset of relations spawning a branching search tree [28].

2.2   Chordal Graphs and Triangulation

We begin by introducing the definition of a chordal graph. The interested reader may find more results regarding chordal graphs, and graph theory in general, in [13].

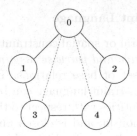

Fig. 2. Example of a chordal graph

Definition 2. *Let $G = (V, E)$ be an undirected graph. G is chordal or triangulated if every cycle of length greater than 3 has a chord, which is an edge connecting two non-adjacent nodes of the cycle.*

The graph shown in Figure 2 consists of a cycle which is formed by five solid edges and two dashed edges that correspond to its chords. As for this part, the graph is chordal. However, removing one dashed edge would result in a non-chordal graph. Indeed, the other dashed edge with three solid edges would form a cycle of length four with no chords. Chordality checking can be done in (linear) $O(|V|+|E|)$ time for a given graph $G = (V, E)$ with the maximum cardinality search algorithm which also constructs an elimination ordering α as a byproduct [5]. If a graph is not chordal, it can be made so by the addition of a set of new edges, called *fill edges*. This process is usually called *triangulation* of a given graph $G = (V, E)$ and can run as fast as in $O(|V| + (|E \bigcup F(\alpha)|))$ time, where $F(\alpha)$ is the set of fill edges that result by following the elimination ordering α, eliminating the nodes one by one, and connecting all nodes in the neighborhood of each eliminated node, thus, making it simplicial in the elimination graph. If the graph is already chordal, following the elimination ordering α means that no fill edges are added, i.e., α is actually a *perfect elimination ordering* [13]. For example, a perfect elimination ordering for the chordal graph shown in Figure 2 would be the ordering $1 \rightarrow 3 \rightarrow 4 \rightarrow 2 \rightarrow 0$ of its set of nodes. In general, it is desirable to achieve chordality with as few fill edges as possible. However, obtaining an optimum graph triangulation is known to be $\mathcal{NP}$-hard [5]. In a RCC-8 network fill edges correspond to universal relations, i.e., non-restrictive relations that contain all base relations.

Chordal graphs become relevant in the context of qualitative spatial reasoning due to the following result obtained in [29] that states that path consistency enforced on the underlying chordal graph of an input network can yield consistency of the input network:

Proposition 1. *For a given RCC-8 network $N = (V, C)$ with relations from the maximal tractable subsets $\hat{\mathcal{H}}_8, \mathcal{C}_8,$ and $\mathcal{Q}_8$ and for $G = (V, E)$ its underlying chordal graph, if $\forall (i, j), (i, k), (j, k) \in E$ we have that $C_{ij} \subseteq C_{ik} \diamond C_{kj}$, then N is consistent.*

Triangulations work particularly well on sparse graphs with clustering properties, such as scale-free graphs. We are about to experimentally verify this in Section 4.

2.3   Scale-Free Graphs

We provide the following simple definition of a scale-free graph and elaborate on the details:

Definition 3. *Graphs with a power law tail in their node degree distribution are called* scale-free graphs *[3].*

Scale-free graphs are graphs that have a power law node degree distribution. The degree of a node in a graph is the number of connections it has to other nodes (or the number of links adjacent to it) and the degree distribution $P(k)$ is the probability distribution of these degrees over the whole graph, i.e, $P(k)$ is defined to be the fraction of nodes in the network with degree k. Thus, if there are n number of nodes in total in a graph and n_k of them have degree k, we have that $P(k) = n_k/n$. For scale-free graphs the degree distribution $P(k)$ follows a power law which can be expressed mathematically as $P(k) \sim k^{-\gamma}$, where $2 < \gamma < 3$, although γ can lie marginally outside these bounds.

There are several models to create random scale-free graphs that rely on *growth* and *preferential attachment* [7]. Growth denotes the increase in the number of nodes in the graph over time. Preferential attachment refers to the fact that new nodes tend to connect to existing nodes of large degree and, thus, means that the more connected a node is, the more likely it is to receive new links. In real case scenarios, nodes with a higher degree have stronger ability to grab links added to the network. In a topological perspective, if we consider the example of Greece that we described in Section 1, Greece would be the higher degree node that would relate topologically to new regions (e.g., Imbros) in a deterministic and natural manner. In mathematical terms, preferential attachment means that the probability that a existing node i with degree k_i acquires a link with a new node is $p(k_i) = \frac{k_i}{\sum_i k_i}$.

Among the different models to create random scale-free graphs, the Barabási-Albert (BA) model is the most well-studied and widely known one [1,3]. The BA model considers growth and preferential attachment as follows. Regarding growth, it starts with an initial number m_0 of connected nodes and at each following step it adds a new node with $m \leq m_0$ edges that link the new node to m different existing nodes in the graph. When choosing the m different existing nodes to which the new node is linked, the BA model assumes that the probability p that the new node will be connected to node i depends on the degree k_i of node i with a value given by the expression $p \sim \frac{k_i}{\sum_i k_i}$, which is the preferential attachment that me mentioned earlier. The degree distribution resulting from the BA model is a power law of the form $P(k) \sim k^{-3}$, thus, it is able to create a subset of the total scale-free graphs that are characterised by a value γ such that $2 < \gamma < 3$. The scaling exponent is independent of m, the only parameter in the model (other than the total size of the graph one would like to obtain of course).

Scale-free graphs are particularly attractive for our approach because they have the following characteristics: (i) scale-free graphs are very sparse [10, 30], and (ii) scale-free graphs have a clustering coefficient distribution that also follows a power law, which implies that many low-degree nodes are clustered

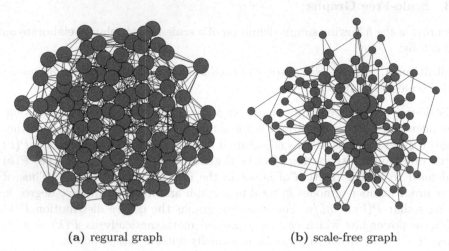

(a) regural graph   (b) scale-free graph

Fig. 3. Structures of a random regular graph with an average degree $k = 9$ and a scale-free graph with a preferential attachment $m = 2$, both having 100 nodes

together forming very dense subgraphs that are connected to each other through major hubs [11].

Due to the aforementioned characteristics, scale-free graphs present themselves as excellent candidates for triangulation, as sparseness keeps time complexity for triangulation low and chordal graphs also exhibit a clustering structure [13], thus, they are able to fit scale-free graphs quite effectively. As an illustration of scale-free graphs, Figure 3 depicts a random regural graph, such as the ones used for experimental evaluation in the field of qualitative spatial reasoning, and a random scale-free graph generated using the BA model. Notice that the bigger the node is, the higher its degree is (these nodes are the hubs).

3   Overview of Our Approach

In this section we describe our own implementations of generic qualitative reasoners that build on state-of-the-art techniques, and our practical approach of choice for tackling large scale-free-like RCC-8 networks.

State-of-the-art Techniques.   We have implemented Phalanx and Phalanx$_\triangledown$ in Python that are the generalised and code refactored versions of PyRCC8 and PyRCC8$_\triangledown$ respectively, originally presented in [29]. Phalanx$_\triangledown$ is essentially Phalanx with a different path consistency implementation that allows reasoning over chordal completions of the input qualitative networks, as described in [29]. In short, Phalanx and Phalanx$_\triangledown$ support small arbitrary binary constraint calculi developed for spatial and temporal reasoning, such as RCC-8 and Allen's interval algebra (IA) [2], in a way similar to GQR [12]. Further, Phalanx and Phalanx$_\triangledown$ present significant improvements over PyRCC8 and PyRCC8$_\triangledown$ regarding scalability and speed. In particular, the new reasoners handle the constraint matrix that

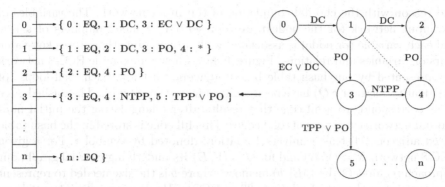

Fig. 4. Hash table based adjacency list for representing an RCC-8 network

reproponts a qualitative network more efficiently during backtracking search, i.e., they do not create a copy of the matrix at each forward step of the backtracking algorithm (as is the case with Renz's solver [27]), but they only keep track of the values that are altered at each forward step to be able to reconstruct the matrix in the case of backtracking. This mechanism is also used to keep track of unassigned variables (i.e., relations that do not belong to tractable subsets of relations and are decomposed to subrelations at each forward step of the backtracking algorithm) that may dynamically change in number due to the appliance of path consistency at each forward step of the backtracking algorithm. For example, the path consistency algorithm can prune a relation that belongs to a tractable subset of relations into an untractable relation, and vice versa. This allows us to apply the heuristics that deal with the selection of the next unassigned variable faster, as we keep our set of unassigned variables minimal. The path consistency algorithm implementation has been also modified to better handle the cases where weak composition of relations leads to the universal relation. In these cases we can continue the iterative operation of the path consistency algorithm since the intersection of the universal relation with any other relation leaves the latter relation intact. Finally, there is also a weight over learned weights dynamic heuristic for variable selection, but we still lack the functionality of restart and nogood recording that has been implemented in the latest version of GQR, release 1500[2], in the time of writing this paper [33]. In any case, and in defense of GQR which was found to perform poorly in [29] under release 1418, we state that the latest version of GQR has undergone massive scalability improvements and is currently the most complete and fastest reasoner for handling reasonably scaled random *regular* qualitative networks. However, in the experimens to follow, we greatly outperform GQR for large QCNs of scale-free-like structure. At this point, we can also claim that Renz's solver [27] has been fairly outdated, as it will become apparent in the experiments that we employ it for.

We improve the state-of-the-art techniques for tackling large scale-free-like RCC-8 networks by opting for a hash table based adjacency list to represent

---

[2] http://sfbtr8.informatik.uni-freiburg.de/R4LogoSpace/
     downloads/gqr-1500.tar.bz2

and reason with the chordal completion of the input network. The variables of
the input network (or the nodes) are represented by index numbers of a list,
and each variable (or node) is associated with a hash table that stores key-value
pairs of variables and relations. Figure 4 shows how an example RCC-8 network
is represented by our hash table based adjacency list approach. Self-loops (of
the identity relation EQ) have been omitted from the network. The dashed edge
$(1, 4)$ corresponds to a fill edge that results after triangulating the initial non-
chordal network consisting of solid edges. This fill edge is stored in the hash table
based adjacency list as a universal relation, denoted by symbol $*$. For a given
RCC-8 network $N = (V, C)$ and for $G = (V, E)$ its underlying chordal graph, our
approach requires $O(|V| + |E| \cdot b)$ memory, where b is the size needed to represent
a relation from the set of relations 2^B of RCC-8. Having a constraint matrix to
represent the input RCC-8 network (that is typically used by the state-of-the-art
reasoners), results in a $O(|V|^2 \cdot b)$ memory requirement, even if chordal graphs
are used leaving a big part of the matrix empty, as is the case with Phalanx$\triangledown$,
or Sparrow for IA [8]. Further, we still retain an $O(1)$ average access and update time complexity which becomes $O(\delta)$ in the amortized worst case, where
δ is the average degree of the chordal graph that corresponds to the input network. Given that we target large scale-free-like, and, thus, sparse networks, this
only incures a small penalty for the related experiments performed. The path
consistency implementation also benefits from this approach as the queue data
structure which is based on has to use only $O(|E|)$ of memory to store the rela-
tions compared to the $O(|V|^2)$ memory requirement of Phalanx, GQR, and Renz's
solver. Regarding triangulation, our hash table based adjacency list is coupled
with the implementation of the maximum cardinality search algorithm and a
fast fill in procedure (as discussed in Section 2.2), as opposed to the heuristic
based, but rather naive, triangulation procedure implemented in [29]. Though
the maximum cardinality search algorithm does not yield minimal triangulations
if the underlying graph of the input network is not chordal, it does guarantee
than no fill edges are inserted if the graph is indeed chordal. In addition, even
for the non-chordal cases we obtain much better results with this approach and
have a fine trade-off between time efficiency and good triangulations.

These techniques are implemented under the hood of our new reasoner which
is called Sarissa. Sarissa, as with our other tools presented here, is a generic and
open source qualitative reasoner written in Python.[3]

4   Experimental Evaluation

In this section we compare the performance of Sarissa with that of Renz's solver
[27], GQR (release 1500) [12], Phalanx, and Phalanx$\triangledown$, with their best performing
heuristics enabled.

We considered both random and real datasets. Random datasets consist of
RCC-8 networks generated by the usual A(n, d, l) model [27] and *large* RCC-8

---

[3] All tools and datasets used here can be acquired upon request from the authors or
found online in the following address: http://www.cril.fr/~sioutis/work.php.

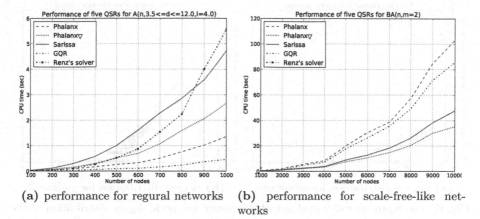

(a) performance for regural networks   (b) performance for scale-free-like networks

Fig. 5. Performance of five reasoners for randomly generated networks

networks generated by the $BA(n, m)$ model which we first introduce for benchmarking qualitative spatial reasoners in this paper. In short, model $A(n, d, l)$ creates random regural networks (like the one depicted in Figure 3a) of size n, degree d, and an average number l of RCC-8 relations per edge, whereas model $BA(n, m)$ creates random scale-free-like networks (like the one depicted in Figure 3b) of size n and a preferential attachment value m. For model $BA(n, m)$ the average number of RCC-8 relations per edge defaults to $|B|/2$, where B is the set of base relations of RCC-8. Real datasets consist of admingeo [14] and gadm-rdf[4] that comprise 11761/77907 nodes/edges and 276728/590865 nodes/edges respectively. In short, admingeo describes the administrative geography of Great Britain using RCC-8 relations, and gadm-rdf the world's administrative areas likewise. The experiments were carried out on a computer with an Intel Core 2 Quad Q9400 processor with a CPU frequency of 2.66 GHz, 8 GB RAM, and the Precise Pangolin x86_64 OS (Ubuntu Linux). Renz's solver and GQR were compiled with gcc/g++ 4.6.3. Sarissa, Phalanx, and Phalanx▽ were run with PyPy[5] 1.9, which implements Python 2. Only one of the CPU cores was used for the experiments.

Random Datasets. For model $A(n, d, l)$ we considered network sizes between 100 and 1000 with a 100 step and $l = 4$ ($= |B|/2$) relations per edge. For each size series we created 270 networks that span over a degree d between 3.5 and 12.0 with a 0.5 step, i.e., 15 network instances were generated for each degree. The results are shown in Figure 5a. GQR clearly outperforms all other reasoners with Phalanx coming close 2nd and Renz's solver last. In the particular case of Sarissa and Phalanx▽ that use chordal graphs we note that they pay an extra cost for calculating the triangles of relations for each appliance of path consistency as these are not precomputated and stored in advance for memory efficiency [29]. Sarissa also pays an additional cost for not being able to access or

---

[4] http://gadm.geovocab.org/
[5] http://pypy.org/

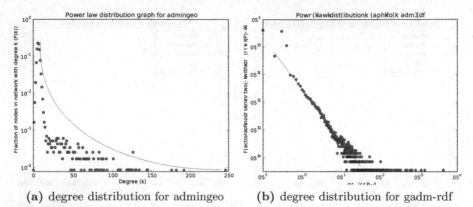

(a) degree distribution for admingeo   **(b)** degree distribution for gadm-rdf

Fig. 6. The figure provides evidence of the power law node degree distribution of the real datasets considered

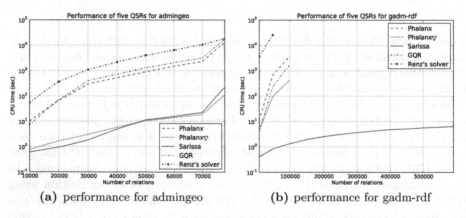

(a) performance for admingeo   **(b)** performance for gadm-rdf

Fig. 7. Performance of five reasoners for real datasets

update relational values in constant worst case time as it does not use a matrix. It is a fact that random regural networks are not triangulated very efficiently with our approach, which results in dense chordal graphs in most of the cases.

For model BA(n, m) we considered 30 networks for each size between 1000 and 10000 with a 1000 step and a preferential attachment value of $m = 2$. We found that for this specific value of m and for the network sizes considered, the networks lie within the *phase transition* region, where it is equally possible for networks to be consistent or inconsistent, thus, they are harder to solve. The results are shown in Figure 5b. Sarissa and Phalanx$\triangledown$ outperform all other reasoners by a large scale, and Renz's solver was able to solve only the networks of 1000 nodes (slower than all others) as it quickly hit the memory limit of our computer due to many recursive calls (leading to storing many copies of the matrix). We note that Sarissa is still burdened with the additional cost of not being able to access or update relational values in constant worst case time. To the best of our knowledge, the random datasets used in this paper are the biggest ones to date of all others that exist in literature.

Real Datasets. For experimenting with our real datasets, viz., admingeo and gadm-rdf, we created constraint networks of different size, by taking into account a small number of relations from the initial dataset and increasing it at every next step. Of course, for both datasets, the whole dataset was used as a final step. To backup our argument about the scale-free-like structure of real RCC-8 networks, we present Figure 6 that displays the power law degree distribution of our real networks. As gadm-rdf is a very large network, we display its degree distribution in log-log scale where the power law function is seen as a straight line [3]. The results for admingeo are shown in Figure 7a. Sarissa and Phalanx$_\nabla$ have approximately equal performance and significantly outperform all other reasoners. In the final step, both reasoners run in $\sim$ 150 sec, when the 3rd best reasoner for this experiment, viz., Phalanx, runs in $\sim$ 4 hours. Up to this point we have considered networks that fit the size of the matrix that accompanies all state-of-the-art reasoners. We proceed with gadm-rdf, a dataset almost 30 times bigger than admingeo. The results for gadm-rdf are shown in Figure 7b. Sarissa is the only implementation that was able to reason with the whole dataset. Sarissa completes the final step of the 590865 relations in under $\sim$ 7 sec, when the 2nd best reasoner for this experiment, viz., Phalanx$_\nabla$, can only reason up to 100000 relations in $\sim$ 7 min. GQR reasons up to 100000 relations in $\sim$ 28 min, Phalanx in double the time of GQR, and, finally, Renz's solver reasons up to 50000[6] relations in $\sim$ 7 hours. Gadm-rdf is the biggest real dataset to date to have been succesfully employed in an experimental evaluation of qualitative spatial reasoners. Surprisingly, Sarissa runs the gadm-rdf experiment faster than the admingeo one, but this is due to more relations being inferred in the latter case as a result of dataset particularities that affect the reasoning process.

At this point we conlude our experimental evaluations. Due to space constraints we omitted several graphs that would display the amount of edges considered by each implementation, the effect of the triangulations, and experiments with the $\mathcal{NP}_8$ class of RCC-8 relations [27].

5   Conclusion and Future Work

In this paper we have presented an approach that employs chordal graphs and a hash table based adjacency list implementation to tackle large scale-free-like qualitative spatial networks, and goes well beyond the state-of-the-art qualitative spatial reasoners which were found to come short of the task.

One could argue that even though being able to tackle a real dataset of nearly a million relations fairly easily, our approach is still far from the billion relations goal set in [19,21]. However, for the case of tractable RCC-8 networks and due to a particular patchwork property presented in [17], our approach allows for building a consistent RCC-8 enriched database incrementally. This can be achieved by initially reasoning with a small part of the dataset, and then for every new piece of data only considering relevant existing RCC-8 relations (if any), reasoning

---

[6] In practice, Renz's solver was able to fit the 100000 relations of the next step, but judging by its overall performance it would require several days to reason with them.

with the resulted fused piece of information, and continuing the process, while maintaining chordality [6]. In a likewise manner, for quering or updating data one would only have to consider relations relevant to his regural or update query. Future work consists of exploring this solution for datasets that scale up to billions of relations, and also further exploring and optimizing on the hierarchical structure that real datasets present, as argued in [21]. In particular, it would be interesting to explore which relations are used more than others in real datasets and whether this could be of some use or not. We would also like to investigate if stuctural or hierarchical properties are observed in real IA networks which we are currently in the process of obtaining from temporally enriched datasets. Another research direction would be to explore if SAT encodings are able to tackle large scale-free-like RCC-8 networks, although given that SAT encodings become too large when network sizes increase beyond a few hundred nodes this would be highly unlikely.

Finally, we feel that it is very important to motivate the qualitative reasoning community to get involved with the structure that real datasets present, and to this direction large random scale-free-like networks can be of great use and value to further improve existing reasoners and present (possibly mixed) solutions that can scale up to billions of relations.

Acknowledgments. This work was funded by a PhD grant from Université d'Artois and region Nord-Pas-de-Calais.

References

1. Albert, R., Barabási, A.L.: Statistical mechanics of complex networks. Rev. Mod. Phys. 74, 47–97 (2002)
2. Allen, J.F.: Maintaining knowledge about temporal intervals. CACM 26, 832–843 (1983)
3. Barabasi, A.L., Albert, R.: Emergence of scaling in random networks. Science 286, 509–512 (1999)
4. Barabasi, A.L., Bonabeau, E.: Scale-Free Networks. Scientific American, 50–59 (2003)
5. Berry, A., Blair, J.R.S., Heggernes, P.: Maximum Cardinality Search for Computing Minimal Triangulations. In: Goos, G., Hartmanis, J., van Leeuwen, J., Kučera, L. (eds.) WG 2002. LNCS, vol. 2573, pp. 1–12. Springer, Heidelberg (2002)
6. Berry, A., Heggernes, P., Villanger, Y.: A vertex incremental approach for maintaining chordality. Discrete Mathematics 306 (2006)
7. Bollobás, B.: Mathematical results on scale-free random graphs. In: Handbook of Graphs and Networks, pp. 1–37. Wiley (2003)
8. Chmeiss, A., Condotta, J.F.: Consistency of Triangulated Temporal Qualitative Constraint Networks. In: ICTAI (2011)
9. Christodoulou, G., Petrakis, E.G.M., Batsakis, S.: Qualitative Spatial Reasoning Using Topological and Directional Information in OWL. In: ICTAI (2012)
10. Del Genio, C.I., Gross, T., Bassler, K.E.: All Scale-Free Networks Are Sparse. Phys. Rev. Lett. 107, 178701 (2011)
11. Dorogovtsev, S.N., Goltsev, A.V., Mendes, J.F.F.: Pseudofractal scale-free web. Physical Review E 65, 066122+ (2002)
12. Gantner, Z., Westphal, M., Wölfl, S.: GQR-A Fast Reasoner for Binary Qualitative Constraint Calculi. In: AAAI Workshop on Spatial and Temporal Reasoning (2008)

13. Golumbic, M.C.: Algorithmic Graph Theory and Perfect Graphs, 2nd edn. Elsevier Science (2004)
14. Goodwin, J., Dolbear, C., Hart, G.: Geographical Linked Data: The Administrative Geography of Great Britain on the Semantic Web. TGIS 12, 19–30 (2008)
15. Hazarika, S.: Qualitative Spatio-Temporal Representation and Reasoning: Trends and Future Directions. IGI Global (2012)
16. Hein, O., Schwind, M., Knig, W.: Scale-Free Networks - The Impact of Fat Tailed Degree Distribution on Diffusion and Communication Processes. Wirtschaftsinformatik 47, 21–28 (2006)
17. Huang, J.: Compactness and its implications for qualitative spatial and temporal reasoning. In: KR (2012)
18. Koubarakis, M., Kyzirakos, K.: Modeling and Querying Metadata in the Semantic Sensor Web: The Model stRDF and the Query Language stSPARQL. In: Aroyo, L., Antoniou, G., Hyvönen, E., ten Teije, A., Stuckenschmidt, H., Cabral, L., Tudorache, T. (eds.) ESWC 2010, Part I. LNCS, vol. 6088, pp. 425–439. Springer, Heidelberg (2010)
19. Koubarakis, M., Kyzirakos, K., Karpathiotakis, M., Nikolaou, C., Sioutis, M., Vassos, S., Michail, D., Herekakis, T., Kontoes, C., Papoutsis, I.: Challenges for Qualitative Spatial Reasoning in Linked Geospatial Data. In: BASR (2011)
20. Li, S., Ying, M.: Region connection calculus: Its models and composition table. Artif. Intell. 145, 121–146 (2003)
21. Nikolaou, C., Koubarakis, M.: Querying Incomplete Geospatial Information in RDF. In: Nascimento, M.A., Sellis, T., Cheng, R., Sander, J., Zheng, Y., Kriegel, H.-P., Renz, M., Sengstock, C. (eds.) SSTD 2013. LNCS, vol. 8098, pp. 447–450. Springer, Heidelberg (2013)
22. Open Geospatial Consortium: OGC GeoSPARQL - A geographic query language for RDF data. OGC® Implementation Standard (2012)
23. Randell, D.A., Cui, Z., Cohn, A.: A Spatial Logic Based on Regions and Connection. In: KR (1992)
24. Renz, J.: Maximal Tractable Fragments of the Region Connection Calculus: A Complete Analysis. In: IJCAI (1999)
25. Renz, J., Ligozat, G.: Weak Composition for Qualitative Spatial and Temporal Reasoning. In: van Beek, P. (ed.) CP 2005. LNCS, vol. 3709, pp. 534–548. Springer, Heidelberg (2005)
26. Renz, J., Nebel, B.: Spatial Reasoning with Topological Information. In: Freksa, C., Habel, C., Wender, K.F. (eds.) Spatial Cognition 1998. LNCS (LNAI), vol. 1404, pp. 351–371. Springer, Heidelberg (1998)
27. Renz, J., Nebel, B.: Efficient Methods for Qualitative Spatial Reasoning. JAIR 15, 289–318 (2001)
28. Renz, J., Nebel, B.: Qualitative Spatial Reasoning Using Constraint Calculi. In: Handbook of Spatial Logics, pp. 161–215 (2007)
29. Sioutis, M., Koubarakis, M.: Consistency of Chordal RCC-8 Networks. In: ICTAI (2012)
30. Steyvers, M., Tenenbaum, J.B.: The Large-Scale Structure of Semantic Networks: Statistical Analyses and a Model of Semantic Growth. Cognitive Science 29, 41–78 (2005)
31. Walsh, T.: Search on High Degree Graphs. In: IJCAI (2001)
32. Westphal, M., Wölfl, S.: Qualitative CSP, Finite CSP, and SAT: Comparing Methods for Qualitative Constraint-based Reasoning. In: IJCAI (2009)
33. Westphal, M., Wölfl, S., Li, J.J.: Restarts and Nogood Recording in Qualitative Constraint-based Reasoning. In: ECAI (2010)

Modularizing Ontologies for the Construction of $E - \mathcal{SHIQ}$ Distributed Knowledge Bases

Georgios Santipantakis[1] and George A. Vouros[2]

[1] Department of Information and Communications Systems Eng.,
University of the Aegean, Karlovassi, Samos, Greece
`gsant@aegean.gr`
[2] Department of Digital Systems, University of Piraeus,
Karaoli & Dimitriou 80, Piraeus Greece
`georgev@unipi.gr`

Abstract. Ontology modularization methods aim either to extract modules, or partition ontologies into sets of modules. Each module covers a specific part of the whole that should "make sense", while it preserves additional properties. Ontology modularization may aim at reusability of knowledge, reduction of complexity, efficient reasoning, and tooling support, e.g. for efficient ontology maintenance and evolution. This paper presents a generic framework for the modularization of $\mathcal{SHIQ}$ ontologies, towards the construction of distributed $E-\mathcal{SHIQ}$ knowledge bases. The aim is to compute decompositions for correct, complete and efficient distributed reasoning. The proposed framework combines locality-based rules with graph-based modularization techniques using a generic constraint problem solving framework. The paper presents experimental results concerning the modularization task.

Keywords: Ontology modularization, Description Logics, Distributed reasoning.

1 Introduction

Modularity of ontologies is a critical issue for purposes such as reusability, maintenance, evolution, efficiency on reasoning. The proliferation of web ontologies, many of which include a large body of knowledge, makes modularity a necessity rather than a nice feature that ontologies must have. Towards the modularization of large ontologies, there are many and significant efforts in the recent past [1], but there are challenges ahead.

Modularization denotes either the extraction of modules from large ontologies (e.g. for reusability purposes) or the partitioning of ontologies into modules (e.g. for facilitating evolution and maintenance or reasoning tasks). In both cases, modules should not be arbitrary chunks of knowledge. Modules must "make sense", covering, as much as possible, well-defined subject matters, while they must preserve the meaning of terms that they include. However, modules may bear a definite association to other modules, or to the original ontology: The degree that this may

A. Likas, K. Blekas, and D. Kalles (Eds.): SETN 2014, LNAI 8445, pp. 192–206, 2014.

happen depends on the purposes that modularization aims to serve. For instance, aiming at reusability, modules should preserve a kind of context-independency (i.e. they have to be reusable in different contexts as independent chunks of knowledge); while aiming at efficient engineering or reasoning, modules may be associated among themselves so as to preserve the coherency of the whole and ensure the *correctness* [2] of the decomposition.

Considering individual modules rather than the whole decomposition, *local correctness* requires that modular fragments of a theory entail only what the original theory entails [2]. *Local completeness* requires that entailments of the original theory concerning only the signature of a specific module, should be entailed by that module. For a specific module to be *self-contained* it should entail all and only the entailments involving its own terms.

Considering the whole *decomposition* of an ontology, rather than individual modules, specific desiderata include the following: (a) *Correct and complete reasoning*: The entailments of the original ontology and only these must be entailed by reasoning over *the collection of modules* extracted. While this may be implied by the correctness and completeness of the individual modules, in cases where modules are not complete, this must be implied by the combination of modules. (b) *Decidability*: The modular ontology must be in a decidable fragment of a representation language. Other desired properties include the *size of modules* (in terms of the elements, or the axioms included), the *expressiveness of the specifications* in each module (e.g. some modules may need to maintain a low level of expressiveness of their specifications), the *type of network* formed by the associated modules, etc.

In this paper we aim at solving the following problem: Given an ontology within the $\mathcal{SHIQ}$ fragment of Description Logics, partition this ontology into an arbitrary number of modules that (a) form a distributed $E-\mathcal{SHIQ}$ knowledge base, such that (b) it can be used for correct and complete reasoning, (c) each module preserves to a great extent the meaning of the terms in its signature, so as modules to make sense: This means that we aim at decompositions which preserve the meaning of most terms within modules. Nevertheless, all terms must preserve their meaning by considering the coupling of modules.

The aim is to perform efficient reasoning with the distributed $E-\mathcal{SHIQ}$ knowledge base. Towards this purpose, as shown by the experiments performed using the $E-\mathcal{SHIQ}$ reasoner [3], additional properties that must be preserved by the networks of associated modules, include: (a) Axioms must be distributed between modules in an as much as possible even way, without having, extremely large modules that may be distant, (b) networks must have a small diameter, and (c) associated modules must not form large cycles[1].

---

[1] Showing results concerning the efficiency of the distributed $E-\mathcal{SHIQ}$ reasoner when applied to the distributed knowledge bases produced, is beyond the scope of this paper. Rather, this paper proposes the modularization method for the partitioning of large ontologies for correct and complete reasoning, while preserving the meaning of ontology terms to a great extent.

Existing modularization methods can be distinguished to those that are based on logical foundations, and to those that apply heuristics for manipulating graphs. While Grau et al. [4], [5] propose methods for extracting local-based module(s) from any ontology, graph-based approaches apply heuristics to partition [6], [7], [8], [9], [10] an ontology into modules. These methods usually utilize network metrics and empirical "distance measures" to define the module boundaries.

This paper revises the notion of locality-based modules to also include associations between modules in $E - \mathcal{SHIQ}$ distributed knowledge bases. It also presents a modularization method which combines rules for constructing well-formed $E - \mathcal{SHIQ}$ knowledge bases with rules for preserving locality of modules in a constraints satisfaction problem. The method uses a constraint problem solving framework together with graph-based modularization methods for producing the decomposition. The modularization method is generic in several aspects: (a) The set of constraints may be reduced or enhanced, (b) constraints may be considered being soft rather than hard, (c) the constraint problem solver used may be replaced by state of the art solvers. The work in this paper also includes experimental results on a random corpus of ontologies, showing the potential of the method proposed.

The paper is structured as follows: Section 2 present preliminaries on $E - \mathcal{SHIQ}$ and locality-based modularization and discusses their interaction. Section 3 presents locality in the context of $E - \mathcal{SHIQ}$ and section 4 describe the modularization method. Section 5 presents experimental results on applying the method on a corpus of ontologies. Section 6 concludes the paper.

2 $E - \mathcal{SHIQ}$ and Locality-Based Modularization

This section presents background knowledge on the $E - \mathcal{SHIQ}$ representation framework [3] and on locality-based modularization [4]. It concludes with discussing the flexibility that $E - \mathcal{SHIQ}$ offers for ontology modularization, extending the notion of locality-based modules by taking also into account associations of modules with other modules.

To provide concrete examples of what is discussed, throughout the paper, we consider the ontology $\mathcal{O}$ with the following axioms:

$$Conference \equiv MedicalConference \sqcup OtherConference \qquad (1)$$
$$Conference \sqsubseteq Event \qquad (2)$$
$$Event \sqsubseteq HumanActivity \qquad (3)$$
$$PediatricConference \sqsubseteq MedicalConference \qquad (4)$$
$$Article \sqsubseteq PublishedMaterial \sqcap \exists PresentedAt.Event \qquad (5)$$
$$MedicalArticle \sqsubseteq Article \sqcap \forall PresentedAt.MedicalConference \qquad (6)$$

The E-$\mathcal{SHIQ}$ representation framework [3] belongs to the family of modular representation frameworks for Description Logics [11]. It provides constructors for associating ontologies (modules) that are within the $\mathcal{SHIQ}$ fragment of Description Logics. Specifically:

- $E - \mathcal{SHIQ}$ supports subjective concept-to-concept correspondences between concepts in different modules.
- $E - \mathcal{SHIQ}$ provides constructors for relating individuals in different modules via link relations (representing domain-specific relations), as well as via subjective individual correspondences (representing subjective equalities between individuals in different modules). Link relations may be further restricted via value and cardinality restrictions, and they can be hierarchically related with other link relations from the same module.
- $E - \mathcal{SHIQ}$ supports "punning" by allowing roles and link relations to have the same name within the same module. This allows peers to reason with roles and link relations locally. To take further advantage of punning, $E - \mathcal{SHIQ}$ allows a restricted form of transitive axioms, aiming to support the computation of the transitivity closure of a role in any module by local means.

Formally: Given a non-empty set of indices I and a collection of modules indexed by I, let N_{C_i}, N_{R_i} and N_{U_i} be the sets of concept, role and individual names, respectively. For some $R \in N_{R_i}$, $Inv(R)$ denotes the inverse role of R and $(N_{R_i} \cup \{Inv(R)|R \in N_{R_i}\})$ is the set of $\mathcal{SHIQ}$ i-roles, i.e. the roles of the i-th ontology. An i-role axiom is either a role inclusion axiom or a transitivity axiom. Let $\mathcal{R}_i$ be the set of i-role axioms.

Let $\mathcal{E}_{ij}$ be the set of ij-link relations relating individuals in i and j, $i \neq j \in I$. Link relations are not pairwise disjoint, but are disjoint with respect to the set of concept names. An $ij - relation\ box$ $\mathcal{R}_{ij}$ includes a finite number set of $ij - link\ relation$ inclusion axioms in case $i \neq j$, and transitivity axioms of the form $Trans(E, (i,j))$, where E is in $(\mathcal{E}_{ij} \cap N_{R_i})$, i.e. it is an ij-link relation and an i-role. The restricted form of transitivity axioms preserve the locality of specifications for the module i. In case $i = j$, then $\mathcal{R}_{ij} - \mathcal{R}_i$ (with an abuse of notation) includes a finite number set of $i - role$ inclusion axioms. Subsequently we use the term *property* to denote both roles and link-relations.

The sets of $i - concepts$ are inductively defined by the constructors within the $\mathcal{SHIQ}$ fragment of Description Logics.

Let $i : C$ and $i : D$ possibly complex concepts and $i : C \sqsubseteq i : D$ (or $i : C \sqsubseteq D$) a *general concept inclusion* (GCI) axiom. A finite set of GCI's is a TBox for i and it is denoted by $\mathcal{T}_i$.

Concept correspondences may be concept *onto* concept, or concept *into* concept: Let $C \in N_{C_i}$, $D \in N_{C_j}$ with $i \neq j \in I$. A concept *onto* (*into*) concept correspondence from i to j that holds for j, is of the form $i : C \overset{\sqsupseteq}{\Rightarrow} j : D$ (corresp. $i : C \overset{\sqsubseteq}{\Rightarrow} j : D$).

Definition (Distributed Knowledge Base). A *distributed knowledge base* $\Sigma = \langle \mathbf{T}, \mathbf{R}, \mathbf{C} \rangle$ is composed by the distributed TBox $\mathbf{T}$, the distributed RBox $\mathbf{R}$, and a tuple of sets of correspondences $\mathbf{C} = (\mathbf{C}_{ij})_{i \neq j \in I}$ between modules. A *distributed TBox* is a tuple of TBoxes $\mathbf{T} = (\mathcal{T}_i)_{i \in I}$, where each $\mathcal{T}_i$ is a finite set of i-concept inclusion axioms. A *distributed RBox* is a tuple of ij-property boxes $\mathbf{R} = (\mathcal{R}_{ij})_{i,j \in I}$, where each $\mathcal{R}_{ij}$ is a finite set of property inclusion axioms and transitivity axioms.

A *distributed ABox* (DAB) includes a tuple of local ABox'es $\mathcal{A}_i$ for each ontology i, and sets $\mathcal{A}_{ij}, i \neq j$ with individual correspondences of the form $j{:}a \stackrel{\equiv}{\mapsto} i{:}b$, and property assertions of the form $(a, b) : E_{ij}$, where E_{ij} is an ij-link relation in $\mathcal{E}_{ij}, i \neq j$. Thus, individual correspondences are specified from the subjective point of view of i and, together with assertions concerning linked individuals, these are made locally available to i.

Example: Let us for instance consider two (i.e. $I = \{1, 2\}$) "parts" of the example ontology $\mathcal{O}$: M_1 and M_2. Then, the $E - \mathcal{SHIQ}$ distributed knowledge base is $\Sigma = \langle \mathbf{T}, \mathbf{R}, \mathbf{C} \rangle$, and is composed by the distributed TBox $\mathbf{T}$, the distributed RBox $\mathbf{R}$, and a tuple of sets of correspondences $\mathbf{C} = (\mathbf{C}_{ij})_{i \neq j \in I}$ between ontology units. Specifically,

- $\mathbf{T} = (\mathcal{T}_i)_{i \in I}$, where
  $\mathcal{T}_1 = \{1, 2, 3, 4\}$, (indicating the axioms included) and
  $\mathcal{T}_2 = \{5, 6\}$.
- $\mathcal{R} = ((R_i)_{i \in I}, (R_{ij})_{i \neq j \in I})$, where $R_i = R_{ij} = \emptyset$, $i, j \in I$,
- $\mathbf{C} = (\mathbf{C}_{ij})_{i \neq j \in I}$, where
  $\mathbf{C}_{21} = \{2 : MedicalConference \stackrel{\equiv}{\rightarrow} 1 : MedicalConference, 2 : Event \stackrel{\equiv}{\rightarrow} 1 : Event\}$
  $\mathbf{C}_{12} = \{1 : MedicalConference \stackrel{\equiv}{\rightarrow} 2 : MedicalConference, 1 : Event \stackrel{\equiv}{\rightarrow} 2 : Event\}$
- $DAB = ((\mathcal{A}_i)_{i \in I}, (\mathcal{A}_{ij})_{i \neq j \in I})$, where $\mathcal{A}_i = \emptyset$ and $\mathcal{A}_{ij} = \emptyset$, for any $i, j \in I$

For the sake of brevity, we use equivalence subjective correspondences: These are actually specified by means of onto and into subjective correspondences. Please notice that both modules hold subjective knowledge on concepts correspondences, and these are symmetric. Finally, it must be noticed that the property *PresentedAt* is a 2-role, only: $E - \mathcal{SHIQ}$ does not support correspondences between roles.

A distributed knowledge base forms a network of associated (via correspondences and link relations) modules. Associations have specific direction and may form cycles (as also shown in the example above).

Definition (Domain relations). Domain relations $r_{ij}, i \neq j \in I$ represent equalities between individuals, from the subjective point of view of j. A *domain relation* $r_{ij}, i \neq j$ from Δ_i to Δ_j is a subset of $\Delta_i \times \Delta_j$, s.t. in case $d' \in r_{ij}(d_1)$ and $d' \in r_{ij}(d_2)$, then according to the subjective view of j, $d_1 = d_2$ (denoted by $d_1 =_j d_2$). Also, given a subset D of $\Delta^{\mathcal{I}_i}$, $r_{ij}(D)$ denotes $\cup_{d \in D} r_{ij}(d)$.

Given that domain relations represent equalities, in case $d_1 \in r_{ij}(d)$ and $d_2 \in r_{ij}(d)$, then $d_1 =_j d_2$ (it must be noticed that d_1 and d_2 are individuals in j). Therefore, $E - \mathcal{SHIQ}$ domain relations are globally one-to-one relations.

Definition (Distributed Interpretation). Given the index I and $i, j \in I$, a *distributed interpretation* $\mathfrak{I}$ of a distributed knowledge base Σ is the tuple formed by the interpretations $\mathcal{I}_{ij} = \langle \Delta_i, \Delta_j, \cdot^{\mathcal{I}_{ij}} \rangle$, $i, j \in I$, and a set of domain relations r_{ij}, in case $i \neq j \in I$. Formally, $\mathfrak{I} = \langle (\mathcal{I}_{ij})_{i,j \in I}, (r_{ij})_{i \neq j \in I} \rangle$.

A local interpretation $\mathcal{I}_i$ satisfies an i-concept C w.r.t. a distributed knowledge base Σ, i.e. $\mathcal{I}_i \models i : C$ iff $C^{\mathcal{I}_i} \neq \emptyset$. $\mathcal{I}_i$ satisfies an axiom $C \sqsubseteq D$ between i-concepts (i.e. $\mathcal{I}_i \models i : C \sqsubseteq D$) if $C^{\mathcal{I}_i} \subseteq D^{\mathcal{I}_i}$. Also, $\mathcal{I}_{ij}$ satisfies an *ij-property inclusion axiom* $R \sqsubseteq S$ ($\mathcal{I}_{ij} \models R \sqsubseteq S$) if $R^{\mathcal{I}_{ij}} \subseteq S^{\mathcal{I}_{ij}}$. A transitivity axiom $Trans(E; (i, j))$ is satisfied by $\mathfrak{I}$ iff $E^{\mathcal{I}_i} \cup E^{\mathcal{I}_{ij}}$ is transitive.

Definition (Distributed entailment and satisfiability). $\Sigma \models_d X \sqsubseteq Y$ if for every $\mathfrak{I}$, $\mathfrak{I} \models_d \Sigma$ implies $\mathfrak{I} \models_d X \sqsubseteq Y$, where X and Y are either i-concepts or ij-properties, $i, j \in I$. Σ is satisfiable if there exists a $\mathfrak{I}$ s.t. $\mathfrak{I} \models_d \Sigma$. A concept $i{:}C$ is satisfiable with respect to Σ if there is a $\mathfrak{I}$ s.t. $\mathfrak{I} \models_d \Sigma$ and $C^{\mathcal{I}_i} \neq \emptyset$.

The $E-\mathcal{SHIQ}$ distributed reasoner implements a complete and sound tableau algorithm [3] for combining local reasoning chunks corresponding to the individual modules in a peer-to-peer fashion, inherently supporting the propagation of subsumptions between them.

Locality-Based Modularization. The motivation behind locality-based modularization is to ensure that the modules constructed are self-contained, as defined in the introduction. The aim is to enforce a separation between a module and its context, and thus to ensure that this model can be combined with any other module. Formally, a module $\mathcal{M}$ for an ontology $\mathcal{O}$ in the language L, w.r.t a signature $\mathcal{S}$ is an ontology $\mathcal{M} \subseteq \mathcal{O}$ s.t. $\mathcal{M}$ and $\mathcal{O}$ entail the same axioms over $\mathcal{S}$ in L.

As it is mentioned in [4], this notion can be formalized using the notion of *model based conservative extensions*. In this case, every model of a module $\mathcal{M}$ of $\mathcal{O}$ can be extended to a model of $\mathcal{O}$ without changing the interpretation domain or the interpretation of symbols in $\mathcal{S}$. Thus, given an $\mathcal{O}$ and $\mathcal{S} \subseteq Sig(\mathcal{O})$, a module $\mathcal{M} \subseteq \mathcal{O}$ is defined to be a *locality based module* of $\mathcal{O}$ for $\mathcal{S}$ if $\mathcal{O}$ is a model conservative extension of $\mathcal{M}$ for $\mathcal{S}$.

Example. Considering our example, any model $\mathcal{I}$ of the ontology $\mathcal{M}_1 = \{1, 2, 3, 4\}$ (abusing the notation for the brevity of presentation) can be extended to an interpretation $\mathcal{J}$ such that any symbol in the signature of $\mathcal{M}_1$ is interpreted by $\mathcal{J}$ in the same way as in $\mathcal{I}$, and all symbols that are not in this signature as the empty set. According to the above definitions $\mathcal{O}$ is a conservative extension of $\mathcal{M}_1$ and $\mathcal{M}_1$ is a module of $\mathcal{O}$ for $Sig(\mathcal{M}_1)$. As a result, each axiom constructed by symbols in $Sig(\mathcal{M}_1)$ is entailed by $\mathcal{M}_1$ iff it is entailed by $\mathcal{O}$.

Since the problem of checking whether any module $\mathcal{M}$ is a locality based module of $\mathcal{O}$ for a signature $\mathcal{S}$ is undecidable for fairly lightweight fragments of OWL, we need to compute approximations. According to [4], a sufficient condition for a conservative model is locality:

Definition ($\emptyset$-locality). Let $\mathcal{S}$ be a signature. An interpretation is $\emptyset$-local for $\mathcal{S}$ if for every class A and property R not in $\mathcal{S}$, we have $A^{\mathcal{I}} = R^{\mathcal{I}} = \emptyset$. An axiom α is $\emptyset$-local for $\mathcal{S}$ if $\mathcal{I} \models \alpha$ for each $\mathcal{I}$ that is $\emptyset$-local for $\mathcal{S}$. An ontology $\mathcal{O}$ is $\emptyset$-local for $\mathcal{S}$ if every axiom in $\mathcal{O}$ is $\emptyset$-local for $\mathcal{S}$.

Example. We can easily check that axioms (5) and (6) in $\mathcal{O}\backslash\mathcal{M}_1$ are $\emptyset$-local for $\mathrm{Sig}(\mathcal{M}_1)$: Any interpretation $\mathcal{I}$ that interprets all symbols in $\mathrm{Sig}(\mathcal{O}) \setminus \mathrm{Sig}(\mathcal{M}_1)$ as the empty set, is $\emptyset$-local for $\mathcal{S}=\mathrm{Sig}(\mathcal{M}_1)$.

However, $\mathcal{M}_1$ is not $\emptyset$-local for $\mathrm{Sig}(\mathcal{M}_2)$ if we consider that $\mathrm{Sig}(\mathcal{M}_2)$ includes the terms $Event$ and/or $MedicalConference$: Axiom (3) for instance can not be made $\emptyset$-local for any interpretation that interprets $HumanActivity$ as the empty set, since $Event \in \mathrm{Sig}(\mathcal{M}_2)$. This is the case for the axiom (1), as well, due to the concept $MedicalConference$. Since checking $\emptyset$-locality may be proved costly as well, one may use the following syntactic conditions for checking $\bot$-locality for a specific signature $\mathcal{S}$. $\bot$-locality implies $\emptyset$-locality [4].

Given a signature $\mathcal{S} \subseteq Sig(\mathcal{O})$ for a $\mathcal{SHIQ}$ ontology $\mathcal{O}$, the following grammar defines the positive $\bot$-concepts $C_{\mathcal{S}}^+$ for $\mathcal{S}$:

$$C_{\mathcal{S}}^+ ::= A^+ \mid (\neg C^-) \mid (C \sqcap C^+) \mid (\exists R^+.C) \mid (\exists R.C^+) \mid (\geq nR^+.C) \mid (\geq nR.C^+) \quad (7)$$

where A^+ is a concept name not in $\mathcal{S}$ and R^+ a role not in $\mathcal{S}$, $C \in Sig(\mathcal{O})$ and $R \in Sig(\mathcal{O})$. It must be noticed that given that $\mathcal{S} \subseteq Sig(\mathcal{O})$, a concept or role in $Sig(\mathcal{O})$ may not be in $C_{\mathcal{S}}^+$ or in $C_{\mathcal{S}}^-$. The negative $\bot$-concepts $C_{\mathcal{S}}^-$ for $\mathcal{S}$ are as follows:

$$C_{\mathcal{S}}^- ::= (\neg C^+) \mid (C_1^- \sqcap C_2^-) \mid C^- \sqcup C \mid \forall R^+.C \mid \forall R.C^- \quad (8)$$

The other constructs of $\mathcal{SHIQ}$ can be expressed using the above constructors, so they can be used in local concepts as well. A local axiom a for $\mathcal{S}$ should be either $C^+ \sqsubseteq C$ or $C \sqsubseteq C^-$. A module is $\bot$-local for $\mathcal{S}$ if all its axioms are local for $\mathcal{S}$.

Definition ($\bot$-module). Let $\mathcal{O}$ be an ontology and let $\mathcal{S}$ be a signature, $\mathcal{S} \subseteq Sig(\mathcal{O})$. $\mathcal{M} \subseteq \mathcal{O}$ is a $\bot$-module for $\mathcal{O}$ for $\mathcal{S}$, if $\mathcal{O}\backslash\mathcal{M}$ is $\bot$-local for $\mathcal{S} \cup Sig(\mathcal{M})$.

3 $E - \mathcal{SHIQ}$ Locality-Based Modules

Given a distributed $E - \mathcal{SHIQ}$ knowledge base, we have to determine when the individual $E - \mathcal{SHIQ}$ modules are local. First, we need to point out that given the rules for $\bot$-locality in (7), R in $E - \mathcal{SHIQ}$ may be either a role or a link relation. Denoting a link relation with E, then for an $E - \mathcal{SHIQ}$ module $\mathcal{M}$ the rules for positive and negative $\bot-$concept are as follows for $\mathcal{S} = Sig(\mathcal{M})$:

$$C_{\mathcal{S}}^+ ::= A^+ \mid (\neg C^-) \mid (C \sqcap C^+) \mid (\exists R^+.C^+) \mid (\exists E^+.C^-) \mid (\geq nR^+.C^+) \mid (\geq nE^+.C^-)$$

$$C_{\mathcal{S}}^- ::= (\neg C^+) \mid (C_1^- \sqcap C_2^-) \mid C^- \sqcup C \mid \forall R^-.C^- \mid \forall E.C^- \quad (9)$$

Given these rules, $E - \mathcal{SHIQ}$ offers flexibility towards constructing well-formed distributed knowledge bases. To show this, together with the effect of modules' associations to locality, let us consider the two parts, $\mathcal{M}_1$ and $\mathcal{M}_2$ of the example ontology $\mathcal{O}$. Then, we may consider the following options to associate the two modules:

1. In case *Event* and/or *MedicalConference* belong in $Sig(\mathcal{M}_1)$, then the property *PresentedAt* can be formed as an 2-role and a 21-link relation.

2. In case *Event* (and/or *MedicalConference*) belongs in $Sig(\mathcal{M}_2)$, then we may either

(a) Replace the axiom (2) (and/or (4)) in $\mathcal{M}_1$ by subjective correspondences for the module $\mathcal{M}_1$, or

(b) Retain the axioms (2) (and/or (4)) in $\mathcal{M}_1$ and associate the two modules with equivalence correspondences for *Event* (and/or *MedicalConference*).

3. In case *Event* (and/or *MedicalConference*) belong in $Sig(\mathcal{M}_1) \cap Sig(\mathcal{M}_2)$, then there should exist equivalence correspondences between corresponding concepts in both modules.

4. Another option is as follows: In case *Event* and *MedicalConference* belong in $Sig(\mathcal{M}_1)$, we can name the concepts $\exists PresentedAt.Event$ and $\forall PresentedAt.Medical-Conference$, let these names be A and MA respectively, replace these complex concepts in axioms (5) and (6) with their names, enhance the signature of $Sig(\mathcal{M}_1)$ with *PresentedAt*, A, MA, and include the new equivalence axioms in $\mathcal{M}_1$. The new axioms will be as follows:

$$A \equiv \exists PresentedAt.Event \tag{10}$$

$$MA \equiv \forall PresentedAt.MedicalConference \tag{11}$$

$$Article \sqsubseteq PublishedMaterial \sqcap A \text{ (replacing axiom (5))} \tag{12}$$

$$MedicalArticle \sqsubseteq Article \sqcap MA \text{ (replacing axiom (6))} \tag{13}$$

with $\mathcal{M}_1$ including axioms (1),(2),(3),(4),(10),(11) and $\mathcal{M}_2$ axioms (12),(13). The two modules should be associated with equivalence correspondences for A and MA[2].

Options 1 and 2(a) result to $\mathcal{M}_1$ being a $\bot$-module for $Sig(\mathcal{O}\backslash\mathcal{M}_2)$. $\mathcal{M}_2$ may not be a $\bot$-module for $Sig(\mathcal{O}\backslash\mathcal{M}_1)$ due to the concept $\exists PresentedAt.Event$. 2(b) is not considered as an option by the modularization method. Option 4 is being considered in cases where the other options can not be applied (e.g. in case *PresentedAt* should be formed as a role, and concepts in axioms (2) and (4) should be 1-concepts due to other constraints). In this case $\mathcal{M}_2$ is a $\bot$-module for $Sig(\mathcal{O}\backslash\mathcal{M}_1)$, but $\mathcal{M}_1$ is not a $\bot$-module for $Sig(\mathcal{O}\backslash\mathcal{M}_2)$ due to the complex concept $\exists PresentedAt.Event$. Also, option 3 is considered by the proposed modularization method only when optimizations are performed (this is shown below). However, in these cases, due to the equivalence correspondences, partitions may not be $\bot$-modules. If we do *not* consider the terms associated via equivalence correspondences to belong in the signature of any module, then all parts are $\bot$-local. The reason for this is the occurrence of correspondences specifying subjective relations of the form $i : X \sqsupseteq j : C$, where C is a term in the signature of module $\mathcal{M}_j$, while the term X is not. These specifications may not preserve the meaning of the term $j : C$, given that its meaning is restricted by an external concept, and $\mathcal{M}_j$ is not a $\bot-$module.

---

[2] It must be noticed that in all cases we choose to specify correspondences only from the module to which a term belongs. For instance, for the case 2(a), the correspondence for *Event* is form $\mathcal{M}_1$. We can have correspondences from the other modules, but this is not necessary for the correctness and completeness of the reasoning for the distributed knowledge base.

Other options exist as combinations of the above, although some of them may not be valid for $E - \mathcal{SHIQ}$: Specifically, a role can not be shared between two or more modules, given that $E - \mathcal{SHIQ}$ does not support correspondences between roles. To maintain the notion of locality in the presence of concept correspondences we revisit the definition of $\perp$-module for $E - \mathcal{SHIQ}$:

Definition ($\perp - E$-module). Let $\mathcal{O}$ be an ontology and let $\mathcal{S}$ be a signature, $\mathcal{S} \subseteq Sig(\mathcal{O})$. $\mathcal{M} \subseteq \mathcal{O}$ is a $\perp - E$-module for $\mathcal{O}$ for $\mathcal{S}$, if $\mathcal{O} \backslash \mathcal{M}$ is $\perp$-local for $\mathcal{S}^{restr} = \mathcal{S} \cup Sig(\mathcal{M}) - \{C | C$ *is a concept name and there exists a correspondence of the form* $X \stackrel{\exists}{\Rightarrow} C$ *from the subjective point of view of* $\mathcal{M}\}$.

For our purposes, since we aim at performing reasoning tasks with *all* associated modules (in contrast to [4] where modules should be context-independent chunks of knowledge), the existence of these terms do not have unintended effects to the reasoning tasks. Nevertheless, partitioning an ontology into modules that are as much as possible context-independent, is desirable.

The modularization method takes advantage of the flexibility offered by $E - \mathcal{SHIQ}$ so as to compute $\perp - E$-modules, and applies locality-based constraints with graph-based modularization rules, using a constraint problem solving framework.

4   The Modularization Framework

The intuition behind the proposed modularization method is to keep highly-dependent ontology elements in the same module, subject to satisfying the constraints for $\perp$−locality. The major steps of the method are (a) the construction of a dependency graph for specifying the dependencies between ontology concepts and roles, (b) the clustering of ontology concepts and roles into groups so as to satisfy the locality constraints, and (c) the construction of modules. Finally, further processing may optimize the network of associated modules.

Groups constructed during the clustering step *are not* modules: Having two elements in the same group (or different groups), point out the preference to keep them in the same module (or different modules respectively).

The Dependency Graph: Given an ontology $\mathcal{O}$, the *dependency graph* for that ontology is a directed graph $G = \langle \mathbf{E}, \mathbf{V} \rangle$, where $\mathbf{V}$ is a set of nodes corresponding to (terms or complex) concepts and roles, and a set of unidirectional *dependency edges* $\mathbf{E}$ connecting the nodes. Each node for a concept C in the graph is associated with a state variable S_C. The state S_R of a node corresponding to an ontology role R, comprises two variables $S_{R_{from}}$ and $S_{R_{to}}$. These variables range to a finite set $\mathbf{D} \subset \{1, 2, 3, ...\}$, specifying the maximum number of available groups.

The set of edge types in the dependency graph are defined according to the ontology specifications and the constructors available in the $\mathcal{SHIQ}$ fragment of Description Logics:

E1: Two nodes N_C and N_D representing concepts C and D can be connected:
   (a) With an edge of type $subc - dep$ if $C \sqsubseteq D^3$,
   (b) with an edge of type $cap - dep$, if C is of the form $\sqcap_i D_i$, $i = 1, 2...$ and there
       is a D_k, such that $D = D_k$ (the equality specifies equality between the terms
       lexicalizing the concepts),
   (c) with an edge of type $cup - dep$, if C is of the form $\sqcup_i D_i$, $i = 1, 2...$ and there
       is a D_k, such that $D = D_k$,
   (d) with an edge of type $compl$, in case C and D are concept names and C is of
       the form $(\neg D)$, or
E2: A concept C is related to a role R via an edge of type Restr$-dep$, if C is of the
    form Restr $R.D$, where Restr $\in \{\forall, \exists, \leq n, \geq n\}$.
E3: A role R is related to a concept C via an edge $values - dep$, if there is a restriction
    of the form Restr$R.C$, where Restr $\in \{\forall, \exists, \leq n, \geq n\}$.
E4: A node N_R corresponding to a role R can be related to a node N_S corresponding
    to a role S as follows:
   (a) with a $subr$ $dependency$ in case $R \sqsubseteq S$, or
   (b) with an $inv - dependency$ in case R is the inverse of S.
   (c) Transitivity of roles do not impose further dependencies.

Dependencies and Constraints: Edges in the dependency graph specify how
nodes (i.e. ontology concepts and roles) are related. These are related to constraints between associated nodes' states. Constraints between the states of
nodes can be distinguished into generic constraints (GC) for E-$\mathcal{SHIQ}$ and locality preserving constraints (LC). While the former suffice for the construction of
a valid $E - \mathcal{SHIQ}$ distributed knowledge base, the later are necessary for computing $\bot$−local partitions for the signature of remaining part of the ontology,
according to formula (9). Specifically, the constraints are the following:

GC1: If there is a $Restr - dep$ between a node A_C and a node A_R, then it must hold
     that $S_C = S_{R_{from}}$.
GC2: If there is a $values - dep$ between a node A_R and a node A_C, then it must hold
     that $S_C = S_{R_{to}}$.
GC3: If there is a $subc - dep$ between nodes N_C and N_D, then $S_C = S_D{}^4$.
GC4: If there is a $subr - dep$ or $inv - dep$ between nodes N_R and N_S, then it must
     hold that $S_{S_{from}} = S_{R_{from}}$ and $S_{S_{to}} = S_{R_{to}}$

LC1: If there is a $cap - dep$ between nodes N_C and N_D, and D is a concept name,
     then $S_C = S_D$. If D is a complex concept, then $S_C \neq S_D$.
LC2: If there is a $cup - dep$ between nodes N_C and N_D, then $S_C = S_D$.
LC3: If there is an edge $Restr\text{-}dep$ between C and R, where $Restr \in \{\exists, \geq n\}$ and there
     is no $Restr\text{-}dep$ between C' and R where $Restr \in \{\forall, \leq n\}$, then $S_{R_{from}} = S_{R_{to}}$.
LC4: If there is an edge $Restr - dep$ between C and R, where $Restr \in \{\forall, \leq n, \}$, then
     $S_{R_{from}} \neq S_{R_{to}}$.

---

[3] Please notice that any $C \equiv D$ and $disjoint(C, D)$ axiom can be expressed using
  subsumption relations
[4] In this case the constraint may be soft. In $E - \mathcal{SHIQ}$ the concepts C and D may result to different modules with correspondences between them. This holds for complex
  concepts as well as mentioned for option (4) in section 3

LC5: If there is a *Restr-dep* between C and R, where $Restr \in \{\forall, \leq n\}$, and there is a *Restr-dep* between C' and R, where $Restr \in \{\exists, \geq n\}$, then $S_{R_{from}} \neq S_{R_{to}}$.

It must be noticed that not any combination of constraints can be solved if they are considered to be hard.

Constraints Problem Solving: Constraints can be distinguished into hard and soft constraints. The only requirement is that, if there is a hierarchy of roles in the ontology, the constraint GC4 should be a hard constraint. Initially, each state variable is assigned a value from **D** so as to satisfy all the constraints associated to it. If a subset of **D** satisfies the constraints (or if no value satisfies all the constraints), a random value is chosen. This task ends with (probably many) violated hard constraints which are resolved using a branch-and-bound solver with initial values those already assigned to state variables. The solver consults only the part of the graph that contains the conflicts, aiming to minimize the conflicts by examining remaining variable values via a backtrack search[5]. Given the solution computed by the CSP solver, a hill-climbing algorithm minimizes the remaining conflicts introduced by soft constraints. Constraints that are not satisfied, are resolved by applying any of the options mentioned in section 3, during the formation of modules. The options apply to any type of constraints.

Once the state values of the nodes are decided, dependency graph nodes are clustered into groups. The signature of each module contains those concept names and roles that are connected with a path of nodes s.t. all the nodes in the path belong in the same group. Forming modules in this way, it is ensured that concepts and roles within modules are semantically dependent, satisfy the constraints, and thus modules "make sense".

Formation of Modules: At this point we can estimate the maximum number of axioms of each module, as well as the number of cycles and the diameter of the network. Then, we can apply further optimization techniques to satisfy specific properties for the network of associated $E - \mathcal{SHIQ}$ modules. An optimization method applied, aims to minimize the coefficient of variation of the distribution of axioms (CV) in the network of associated modules. The optimization will merge modules that have a common neighbor, if this action reduces CV. This is repeated on the network, until there is no merging that can further reduce CV. This optimization reduces the number of modules in the network, and increases the even distribution of axioms in the modules. Also, it does not violate locality constraints, since the merging of two $\perp-$local modules $\mathcal{M}_i$, $\mathcal{M}_j$, w.r.t. $Sig(\mathcal{O})\backslash Sig(\mathcal{M}_i)$ and $Sig(\mathcal{O})\backslash Sig(\mathcal{M}_j)$ respectively, is also a $\perp-$local module w.r.t. $Sig(\mathcal{O})\backslash Sig(\mathcal{M}_i \cup \mathcal{M}_j)$.

Finally, the distribution of axioms to the modules is done as follows: For each axiom α in the ontology, the module $\mathcal{M}$ that will host the axiom α, is the one that maximizes the function:

$$U(\mathcal{M}, \alpha) = \frac{|Sig(\mathcal{M})| + |Sig(\mathcal{M}) \cap Sig(\alpha)|}{|tbox(\mathcal{M})| + 1 + |Sig(\alpha)| - |Sig(\mathcal{M}) \cap Sig(\alpha)|} \quad (14)$$

---

[5] The CSP solver can be found at http://bach.istc.kobe-u.ac.jp/cream/

where $Sig(\mathcal{M})$ is the signature of $\mathcal{M}$, $tbox(\mathcal{M})$ is the set of axioms in $\mathcal{M}$, and $Sig(\alpha)$ is the set of terms in the axiom α. Once the module that will host the axiom is decided, the process will construct any correspondences and link-relations specified by the axiom. The intuition for formula (14) is to find the module $\mathcal{M}$ that includes most of the terms in $Sig(\alpha)$, subject to that the number of axioms and correspondences in $\mathcal{M}$ (counted in the denominator) will be kept low. The unintended effect of this rule is to change the signature of modules and use the option (3) mentioned in section 3 for establishing correspondences between modules.

By considering all the cases for building and associating $E - \mathcal{SHIQ}$ modules, as these are mentioned in section 3, the following theorem can be proved:

Theorem 1. *The modularization method produces a network of associated* $\perp - E$*-modules that form a distributed* $E - \mathcal{SHIQ}$ *knowledge base satisfying correctness and completeness of reasoning.*

The time complexity for the dependency graph and module construction tasks, is linear to the number of axioms of the ontology, thus the complexity of the method depends on the CSP solver. The worst-case complexity is the exhaustive search for the entire dependency graph, i.e. $O(s^n)$, where s is the number of states and n the number of nodes in the dependency graph. However, given that the CSP solver applies to a small part of the dependency graph with the initial values, the complexity of the process is significantly reduced.

5   Experimental Results

We have gathered many, mostly large ontologies by crawling web ontology repositories[6]. We created a corpus of 12 ontologies, chosen by their size and categorized to small (between 100-499 axioms), medium (between 500-4999 axioms) and large (5000 and more axioms). Table 1 presents the corpus used in our experiments showing the id of each ontology, the number of concept and role names, the number of axioms and their expressiveness.

Table 1. Ontologies used in the experiments

ID	69ade	7106b	cabro	biopax	76dda	00016	00380	7d540	fly	9ed40	f6cd1	8bd89
#Concept Names	147	15	59	41	75	96	4244	144	6599	8223	7596	12909
#Role Names	20	34	13	33	103	229	28	23	0	3	604	2114
#Axioms	127	145	100	338	513	1055	3046	613	6587	8715	8716	28263
Expressivity	$\mathcal{ALC}$	$\mathcal{SHIN}(D)$	$\mathcal{ALCHIQ}$	$\mathcal{ALCHN}(D)$	$\mathcal{SHIN}(D)$	$\mathcal{SHIN}$	$\mathcal{ALE}$	$\mathcal{ALC}$	$\mathcal{AL}$	$\mathcal{ALCUIN}(D)$	$\mathcal{ALCHI}$	$\mathcal{AL}$

We apply the proposed modularization method (referred to as *E-SHIQ Md* in the following tables) on each ontology and compare the results to the output

---

[6] Crawled as of June 25th, 2013 from http://bioportal.bioontology.org/, http://www.cs.ox.ac.uk/isg/ontologies/ and http://owl.cs.manchester.ac.uk/owlcorpus

Table 2. Modularization results for (a) small, (b) medium, (c) large ontologies

(a)

ontology	algorithm	0-9	10-19	20-29	30-49	50-79	80-99	100-199	200-299
69ade	localityExtr	5	6	3	18	33	35	47	0
	E-SHIQ Md	5	0	0	0	0	0	1	1
7106b	localityExtr	1	0	1	5	8	0	0	0
	E-SHIQ Md	11	2	0	0	1	0	0	0
biopax	localityExtr	4	2	1	2	8	6	18	0
	E-SHIQ Md	4	0	0	0	0	1	1	0
cabro	localityExtr	1	0	0	2	37	19	0	0
	E-SHIQ Md	7	0	0	2	0	0	0	0

(b)

ontology	algorithm	0-9	10-19	20-29	30-49	50-99	100-499	500-999	1000-1999	2000-2999	3000-4000
00016	localityExtr	0	0	0	0	0	96	0	0	0	0
	E-SHIQ Md	2	1	0	2	3	0	1	0	0	0
00380	localityExtr	13	19	17	25	65	504	690	1378	1465	68
	E-SHIQ Md	1	1	0	3	2	2	2	0	0	1
76dda	localityExtr	0	0	0	0	0	75	0	0	0	0
	E-SHIQ Md	3	1	2	1	2	1	0	0	0	0
7d540	localityExtr	5	7	10	20	55	47	0	0	0	0
	E-SHIQ Md	1	2	5	3	1	2	0	0	0	0

(c)

ontology	algorithm	0-49	50-99	100-199	200-499	500-799	800-999	1000-1499	1500-2999	3000-4999	5000-9999	10000-15000
8bd89	localityExtr	62	99	0	0	96	22	353	1244	1261	2257	7515
	E-SHIQ Md	366	31	63	25	6	0	1	1	0	0	0
9ed40	localityExtr	0	0	0	0	0	0	469	1412	2279	4063	0
	E-SHIQ Md	26	19	27	4	1	0	0	1	0	0	0
f6cd1	localityExtr	9	15	25	115	146	119	349	1295	2083	3440	0
	E-SHIQ Md	58	53	1	5	1	1	0	0	0	0	0
fly	localityExtr	15	20	61	251	203	91	369	1390	2323	1876	0
	E-SHIQ Md	108	31	4	2	1	0	0	0	0	0	0

of the locality module extractor (*localityExtr*) reported in [5]. In all cases we consider all the GC constraints hard, and the LC constraints soft. The results are presented in tables 2(a)-(c), corresponding to the size categories. Each table presents per ontology and algorithm, the number of extracted modules of size (number of axioms) within the range shown in the header of the column. For example, in table 2(a), both algorithms constructed 5 modules that contain at most 9 axioms for the ontology *69ade*.

Table 3. Network statistics

Ontology	69ade	7106b	cabro	biopa	76dda	00016	00380	7d540	fly	9ed40	f6cd1	8bd89
Modules	7	13	9	5	9	8	12	14	146	77	119	483
Diameter	2	3	4	3	4	2	2	4	20	8	8	7
BackEdges	6	1	0	1	2	10	21	2	1	3	37	23
Total Correspondences	285	79	45	100	204	317	4071	312	2928	4327	3536	13713
Total Link Restrictions	0	0	0	3	0	0	0	0	0	0	0	0

The method *localityExtr* is being used as a baseline, although its objectives are quite different from those of *E-SHIQ Md*. Actually, *localityExtr* extracts a module for each concept name in the ontology, thus replicates many axioms in different modules. *E-SHIQ Md* constructs $\perp - E-$local modules, with no replication of axioms but with associations between modules. As the results show, *E-SHIQ Md* constructs a significantly smaller set of modules than *localityExtr*, and the modules contain less axioms (especially for large ontologies) than in the case of *localityExtr*. Furthermore, *E-SHIQ Md* constructs small numbers of large modules, while the largest modules are still significantly smaller (and less) than those produced by the *localityExtr*.

Finally, for each network, we estimate the number of existing cycles by the number of "back-edges", i.e. the edges that appear in the network but not in the minimum spanning tree. The results in table 3 show that the networks have a small diameter and a low number of "back-edges" compared to the number of terms and axioms in each ontology. Also, the high number of correspondences, show the strong association of modules. In these experiments, the number of link restrictions is negligible, as a result of (a) the fact that LC4 and LC5 are soft constraints, and (b) GC4 is a hard constraint, which in the presence of role hierarchy it restricts the values for the state variables involved in LC4, LC5.

6   Concluding Remarks

In this paper we have presented a modularization framework that, given an ontology, constructs a network of associated modules forming an E-$\mathcal{SHIQ}$ distributed knowledge base. The proposed framework computes ontology decompositions that satisfy properties towards efficient reasoning with E-$\mathcal{SHIQ}$. We have conducted experiments on a set of randomly selected ontologies of different size and expressivity, showing the construction of small networks (low number of modules, even distribution of axioms and short network diameter).

Further work aims at showing that the distributed knowledge constructed result to indeed very efficient reasoning, even for very large ontologies, by running the distributed E-$\mathcal{SHIQ}$ reasoner on the constructed knowledge bases. Towards making reasoning more efficient we also aim to test alternative optimizations, while also thoroughly studying different configurations towards achieving better modularization results according to the level of difficulty each ontology presents.

Acknowledgements. This research project is being supported by the project "IRAK-LITOS II" of the O.P.E.L.L. 2007 - 2013 of the NSRF (2007 - 2013), co-funded by the European Union and National Resources of Greece.

References

1. Pathak, J., Johnson, T.M., Chute, C.G.: Survey of modular ontology techniques and their applications in the biomedical domain. Integr. Comput.-Aided Eng. 16(3), 225–242 (2009)
2. Grau, B.C., Parsia, B., Sirin, E., Kalyanpur, A.: Modularity and web ontologies. In: Proc. KR 2006, pp. 198–209. AAAI Press (2006)
3. Vouros, G.A., Santipantakis, G.M.: Combining ontologies with correspondences and link relations: The e-shiq representation framework. arXiv:1310.2493 (2013)
4. Cuenca Grau, B., Horrocks, I., Kazakov, Y., Sattler, U.: A logical framework for modularity of ontologies. In: 20th Int. Joint Conference on A.I., pp. 298–303 (2007)
5. Grau, B.C., Horrocks, I., Kazakov, Y., Sattler, U.: Modular reuse of ontologies: Theory and practice. J. Artif. Int. Res. 31(1), 273–318 (2008)
6. Konev, B., Lutz, C.: Logical difference and module extraction with CEX and MEX. In: Description Logics. CEUR W. (2008)

7. Seidenberg, J., Rector, A.: Web ontology segmentation: Analysis, classification and use. In: Proc. of the 15th Int. Conf. on World Wide Web, pp. 13–22. ACM Press (2006)
8. Doran, P., Tamma, V., Iannone, L.: Ontology module extraction for ontology reuse: an ontology engineering perspective. In: 16th ACM Conf. on Information and Knowledge Management, pp. 61–70 (2007)
9. Stuckenschmidt, H., Schlicht, A.: Structure-based partitioning of large ontologies. In: Stuckenschmidt, H., Parent, C., Spaccapietra, S. (eds.) Modular Ontologies. LNCS, vol. 5445, pp. 187–210. Springer, Heidelberg (2009)
10. Noy, N.F., Musen, M.A.: Specifying ontology views by traversal. In: McIlraith, S.A., Plexousakis, D., van Harmelen, F. (eds.) ISWC 2004. LNCS, vol. 3298, pp. 713–725. Springer, Heidelberg (2004)
11. Zimmermann, A.: Logical Formalisms for Agreement Technologies. In: Agreement Technologies. Law, Governance and Technology Series, pp. 69–82. Springer (2013)

On the 'in many cases' Modality: Tableaux, Decidability, Complexity, Variants

Costas D. Koutras[1], Christos Moyzes[2], Christos Nomikos[3], and Yorgos Zikos[2]

[1] Department of Computer Science and Technology
University of Peloponnese
End of Karaiskaki Street, 22 100 Tripolis, Greece
ckoutras@uop.gr
[2] Graduate Programme in Logic, Algorithms and Computation (MPLA)
Department of Mathematics, University of Athens
Panepistimioupolis, 157 84 Ilissia, Greece
cmoyzes@yahoo.gr, zikos@sch.gr
[3] Department of Computer Science and Engineering
University of Ioannina
P.O. Box 1186, 45110 Ioannina, Greece
cnomikos@cs.uoi.gr

Abstract. The modality *'true in many cases'* is used to handle non-classical patterns of reasoning, like *'probably φ is the case'* or *'normally φ holds'*. It is of interest in Knowledge Representation as it has found interesting applications in *Epistemic Logic*, *'Typicality'* logics, and it also provides a foundation for defining *'normality'* conditionals in Non-Monotonic Reasoning. In this paper we contribute to the study of this modality, providing results on the *'majority logic'* Θ of V. Jauregui. The logic Θ captures a simple notion of *'a large number of cases'*, which has been independently introduced by K. Schlechta and appeared implicitly in earlier attempts to axiomatize the modality *'probably φ'*. We provide a tableaux proof procedure for the logic Θ and prove its soundness and completeness with respect to the class of neighborhood semantics modelling 'large' sets of alternative situations. The tableaux-based decision procedure allows us to prove that the satisfiability problem for Θ is NP-complete. We discuss a more natural notion of 'large' sets which accurately captures *'clear majority'* and we prove that it can be also used, at the high cost however of destroying the finite model property for the resulting logic. Then, we show how to extend our results in the logic of complete majority spaces, suited for applications where either a proposition or its negation (but not both) are to be considered *'true in many cases'*, a notion useful in epistemic logic.

Keywords: default modality, majority modal logic, tableaux proof procedure.

1 Introduction

Commonsense Reasoning deals very often with patterns of reasoning corresponding to sentences like *'in most days, Jim will have a coffee after work'*, *'normally my favourite basketball team should win tomorrow - after all, we are in terrible shape this period'*,

A. Likas, K. Blekas, and D. Kalles (Eds.): SETN 2014, LNAI 8445, pp. 207–220, 2014.

'*it will probably rain tomorrow*' (meaning that the speaking person considers more probable that it will rain tomorrow, than it will not), '*Stella estimates that she had a successful exam today*' (in the sense that she would bet that her grading will be beyond a certain threshold, rather than below it), etc. These are typical examples of inference patterns which can be considered to fall within a certain scheme: a fact is considered to be true in '*most*' of the *states of affairs* (*cases*, *scenarios*) the agent can think of. It is a pattern of inference that can be handled with the machinery of Modal Logic.

Modal Logic traditionally **studies logics of qualified truth**: '*necessarily true*', '*known or believed to be true*', '*henceforth true*', are some of the most important and well-known interpretations of the modal operator, in areas such as *epistemic, doxastic* and *temporal logic*. In Knowledge Representation and Commonsense Reasoning, it seems obvious that a modality intended to be read as '*true in a large number of cases*' (described in related approaches as '*true in most cases*', '*majority true*' [14], '*probably true*' ([11,4], in a qualitative sense), '*normally true*', '*true by default*' [13], etc.) is of interest to AI applications. Modalities of this type have been employed in Epistemic Logic in order to capture weak notions of belief [11,1,15]. Commonsense Reasoning studies logics of '*normality*': inferring that an entity has '*normally*' or '*typically*' a property P is at the heart of Knowledge Representation and the central question in Non-Monotonic Reasoning. In that respect, the study of a '*normality*' modality seems essential for the field.

In this paper we work on the logic Θ of V. Jauregui from [13,14], which axiomatizes the modality we call '*true in many cases*'. In Jauregui's papers it is called the '*majority*' modality, or '*mostly true*' modality, as it is supposed to capture '*truth in a majority of the possible states of affairs*'. It is intuitively nontrivial to define an acceptable interpretation of the generalized quantifiers '*many*', '*most*', '*in a large number of*' (see the discussion in Section 3) and the notion employed by Jauregui is simple and natural, yet it is not strict. Thus, we prefer to call it '*true in many cases*' modality, and perhaps, it would be more fair to call it '*true in a collection of significant cases*' modality. Leaving the details apart, it is obvious that such a modality is a serious candidate for capturing the reading of modality '*normally φ*' and '*typically φ*' which are of central interest in KR.

In this paper, we provide a sound and complete tableaux-based proof procedure for Θ in Section 5. The decision procedure allows us to pin down the complexity of Θ which is shown to be at the lower level expected for a modal logic (Section 6.2). Then, in Section 7 we proceed to define collections of '*large sets*' by '*clear majority*' as one would have normally expected for a majority modality. This is certainly interesting, both for the finite and the infinite case, and it can serve as the basis of '*majority*' semantics ([24]); yet, it comes at the cost of destroying the finite model property, as we prove with a combinatorial argument. Further on, in Section 8 we discuss a variant of Θ, which focuses on negation-complete 'normality' theories. This is of interest in epistemic reasoning, in treatments of *weak belief* or *qualitative probability*: assume scenarios where probability has to be assigned to exactly one of φ and $\neg\varphi$, as the '*estimation*' operator in [15]. We show that our results carry through in this case with a reasonable number of adjustments to the machinery we provide.

In Section 2 we provide the necessary background material in order to establish notation and terminology. In Section 3 we define the 'large' sets notion underlying the model theory of the 'majority' modality we work on and review other relevant definitions of 'largeness'. In Section 4 we briefly go through the Hilbert-style axiomatization of Θ and its semantics from [14]. Finally, in Section 9 we discuss related work and future research questions. Due to space limitations, some proofs are omitted or sketched in this version and are left for the full report.

2 Background Material

Modal Logic. The language of propositional modal logic, extends classical logic with a modal operator $\Box\varphi$, traditionally read as '*necessarily φ*'. In this paper, it will be read as '*in most cases φ*'. *Modal logics* are sets of modal formulas containing classical propositional logic (i.e. containing all tautologies in the augmented language $\mathcal{L}_\Box$) and closed under rule **MP**. $\frac{\varphi,\varphi\supset\psi}{\psi}$. The smallest modal logic is denoted as **PC** (propositional calculus in the augmented language). **Normal** are called those **modal logics**, which contain all instances of axiom **K**. $\Box\varphi\wedge\Box(\varphi\supset\psi)\supset\Box\psi$ and are closed under rule **RN**. $\frac{\varphi}{\Box\varphi}$. By $\mathbf{KA_1\ldots A_n}$ we denote the normal modal logic axiomatized by axioms $\mathbf{A_1}$ to $\mathbf{A_n}$.

Relational Possible-Worlds Models. Normal modal logics are interpreted over **Kripke** (or relational) possible-worlds models: a *Kripke model* $\mathfrak{M} = \langle W, \mathcal{R}, V\rangle$ consists of a set W of *possible worlds* (*states, situations*) and a *binary accessibility relation* between them: $\mathcal{R} \subseteq W \times W$.

Scott-Montague Possible-Worlds Models. The so-called *Scott-Montague semantics*, also called **neighborhood semantics**, were introduced independently by D. Scott and R. Montague; the reader is referred to [5] and [21,17] for more details. In *Scott-Montague models*, each state is associated to '*neighborhoods*' (subsets) of states (or possible worlds). A **neighborhood model** is a triple $\mathfrak{N} = \langle W, \mathcal{N}, V\rangle$, where W is a set of possible worlds (states), $\mathcal{N} : W \to \mathcal{P}(\mathcal{P}(W))$ is a **neighborhood function** assigning to a state the set of its '*neighborhoods*' and V is again a valuation. Inside a state, formulas of the form $\Box\varphi$ become true at w iff the set of states $\overline{V}(\varphi)$ where φ holds (called the *truth set* of φ, $\overline{V}(\varphi) = \{v \in W \mid \mathfrak{N}, v \models \varphi\}$), belongs to the set of neighborhoods of w: $\overline{V}(\varphi) \in \mathcal{N}(w)$. The pair $\mathfrak{F} = \langle W, \mathcal{N}\rangle$ is called a **Scott-Montague** (neighborhood) **frame**.

For a complete treatment of modal logic, the reader is referred to [12,10,2]. For a readable and thorough treatment of modal tableaux, we refer the reader to the books of M. Fitting [9,8], whose methods, notation and terminology we use in this paper.

3 Large Sets and Majorities

We assume a set W of '*states*' or '*possible worlds*'. *Which subsets of W would we accept to consider as large? Which subsets of W correspond to the phrase: 'many' states?* For a finite W, the answer could be an '*overwhelming majority*' or a '*simple majority*' (any subset with cardinality strictly more than $|W|/2$). For an infinite W, things are more difficult. In Mathematical Logic and Model Theory, '*large subsets*' are captured by the notion of filters over W: a **filter over** (a nonempty set) W is a collection F of subsets of W, such that: (i) $W \in F$ and $\emptyset \notin F$, (ii) $X \in F$ and

$X \subseteq Y \subseteq W$ implies $Y \in F$ (*filters are upwards closed*), (iii) $X \in F$ and $Y \in F$ implies $(X \cap Y) \in F$ (*filters are closed under intersection*). This definition disallows the *improper filter* over W (which is just the whole powerset algebra). **Ultrafilters** over W are the *maximal* (proper) *filters*, or equivalently, the filters satisfying the following completeness requirement: for every $X \subseteq W$, either $X \in F$ or $(W \setminus X) \in F$.

The following definition from [14] introduces a notion of **weak filter**.

Definition 1. *Let W be a non-empty set and $\mathcal{K} \subseteq 2^W$ be a non-empty collection of W. $\mathcal{K}$ represents a **collection of large subsets** of W if it satisfies the following conditions:*

 (i) *For every $S \in \mathcal{K}$ and $T \supseteq S$, it holds that $T \in \mathcal{K}$: $\mathcal{K}$ is closed under supersets.*
(ii) *For every $S \in \mathcal{K}$ it holds that $W \setminus S \notin \mathcal{K}$: $\mathcal{K}$ cannot contain a set and its complement (with respect to W).*

In [20] a different, but provably equivalent, notion of large sets had been given: it is essentially the same with the previous one, replacing the second condition for the following one:

(iii) If $S, T \in \mathcal{K}$, then $S \cap T \neq \varnothing$.

Throughout this paper we will be freely switching between the two definitions.

Other notions of collections of 'large sets' exist. A fine-grained definition of a collection F of 'majorities' has been given by E. Pacuit and S. Salame [18,19]: (i) either $X \in F$ or $(W \setminus X) \in F$, (ii) $X \in F$, $Y \in F$ and $X \cap Y = \emptyset$ imply that $X = (W \setminus Y)$, (iii) if X is a large set, and a finite subset of it is replaced by a set of greater cardinality that the one removed, a large set is obtained. The motivation of this definition has to do with applications of graded modal logic [22].

4   The Logic Θ of the '*in many cases*' Modality

In the previous Section, we have given the notion of 'weak filter' which represents a collection of 'large subsets' of the possible worlds at hand. Given our intended interpretation of the modality as '*true in many cases*' ('*true in a large number of cases*'), we proceed to axiomatize the logic of the following class of neighborhood structures:

Definition 2 ([14]). *A Scott-Montague model $\mathcal{M} = \langle W, \mathcal{N}, V \rangle$ is a Θ-model if for every $w \in W$, $\mathcal{N}(w)$ is collection of large subsets of W.*

In [14] it is argued convincingly that this is not a normal modal logic, as **K** is not validated by the 'majority' interpretation of the modality. It is proved that the logic Θ which corresponds to the 'majority frames' above is axiomatized as follows:

Definition 3 ([14]). Θ *is the smallest modal logic containing axioms*

$$\mathbf{N.}\ \Box\top$$

$$\mathbf{D.}\ \Box\varphi \supset \Diamond\varphi$$

and is closed under the rule

$$\mathbf{RM.}\ \frac{\varphi \supset \psi}{\Box\varphi \supset \Box\psi}$$

The proofs of soundness and completeness of Θ with respect to the class of 'majority' frames (Θ-frames) can be found in [14, Chapter 3]. They are typical canonical model arguments.

5 Tableaux for Θ

In this section we present a tableau system for Θ. We assume the reader has a working knowledge of tableaux proof procedures; we follow [9] to which we refer for details. This logic, not involving axiom **B**, or a notion of symmetry in terms of Scott-Montague frames [5], suggests that a tableau system like the one used in [9] for the logics **K**, **T**, **D** etc., can be adopted. Such a system indeed works; however, in order to develop a systematic procedure for finding (or not finding) a proof, we opt for a *prefixed tableau* system. Although we will not be using the prefixes to ultimately represent a notion of accessibility (there is none), the prefixes still provide notation for naming worlds. Having a systematic procedure not only do we use it to prove completeness, but we can easily also deduce decidability and the finite model property.

Some terminology is in order: The version of *prefix* used is simply a positive integer (the prefixes used for universal Kripke frames). A *prefixed formula* is an expression of the form $n\ \varphi$, where n is a prefix and φ is a formula. A tableau branch is *closed* if it contains both $n\ \varphi$ and $n\ \neg\varphi$ for some prefix n and formula φ. A tableau is *closed* if all of its branches are closed. A tableau or branch is *open* if it is not closed. The terminology and the techniques we use draw from [8,9].

5.1 Tableaux Rules

For the alphabet of our tableaux, we assume $\Diamond\varphi$, $\varphi \supset \psi$, $\varphi \equiv \psi$ are abbreviations for $\neg\Box\neg\varphi$, $\neg\varphi \vee \psi$, $(\varphi \supset \psi) \wedge (\psi \supset \varphi)$ respectively, thus no corresponding rules have to be specified.

Definition 4. *A Θ-tableau for a formula φ is a tableau that starts with the prefixed formula $1\ \neg\varphi$ and is extended using any of the rules below.*

[Double negation rule] $\dfrac{n\ \neg\neg\varphi}{n\ \varphi}$

[Conjunctive rules] $\dfrac{n\ \varphi \wedge \psi}{\begin{array}{c} n\ \varphi \\ n\ \psi \end{array}} \quad \dfrac{n\ \neg(\varphi \vee \psi)}{\begin{array}{c} n\ \neg\varphi \\ n\ \neg\psi \end{array}}$

[Disjunctive rules] $\dfrac{n\ \varphi \vee \psi}{n\ \varphi \mid n\ \psi} \quad \dfrac{n\ \neg(\varphi \wedge \psi)}{n\ \neg\varphi \mid n\ \neg\psi}$

[D-rule] $\dfrac{n\ \Box\varphi}{n\ \neg\Box\neg\varphi}$

[π_1-rule] $\dfrac{n\ \neg\Box\psi}{m\ \neg\psi}$ for any prefix m new to the branch.

$$n \ \Box\varphi$$
$$[\pi_2\text{-rule}] \ \frac{n \ \neg\Box\psi}{m \ \varphi} \ \text{for any prefix } m \text{ new to the branch.}$$
$$m \ \neg\psi$$

The double negation, conjunctive and disjunctive rules, are standard for the propositional part of any modal logic. Regarding [D-rule], as its names suggests, it exists to tend to axiom **D**. Next, Θ is a monotonic modal logic. The appropriate rule, is that for any pair $\Box\varphi, \Diamond\psi$ there is a world such that φ, ψ hold ([π_2-rule], see [9] regarding the Logic **U**, and specifically Chapter 6.13 for a tableau for **U**). Finally, the effect of axiom **N** is reflected by [π_1-rule], since introducing a new prefix due to a single $\Diamond$-formula implies that it is true for a reason, and not by default. Note that φ can be the same as ψ.

Definition 5. *A closed Θ-tableau for a formula φ is a Θ-tableau proof for φ.*

We give a tableau proof for axiom **K.** $\Box(p \wedge q) \supset (\Box p \wedge \Box q)$ as an example.

$$
\begin{array}{llr}
1 \ \neg(\neg\Box(p \wedge q) \vee (\Box p \wedge \Box q)) & & (1) \\
1 \ \neg\neg\Box(p \wedge q) & & (2) \\
1 \ \neg(\Box p \wedge \Box q) & & (3) \\
1 \ \Box(p \wedge q) & & (4) \\
1 \ \neg\Box p & 1 \ \neg\Box q & (5) \\
2 \ p \wedge q & 2 \ p \wedge q & (6) \\
2 \ \neg p & 2 \ \neg q & (7) \\
2 \ p & 2 \ p & (8) \\
2 \ q & 2 \ q & (9)
\end{array}
$$

Lines (2) and (3) are by a conjunctive rule. Line (4) is from (2) by double negation rule. Line (5) is from (3) by a disjunctive rule. Lines (6) and (7) are from (4) and (5) by [π_2-rule]. Lines (8) and (9) are from (6) by conjunction. Then the tableau is closed.

5.2 Soundness

Definition 6. *[Satisfiable] Suppose S is a set of prefixed formulas. We say S is Θ-satisfiable if there is a Θ-model $\langle W, \mathcal{N}, V \rangle$ and a function $\theta : prefixes \rightarrow W$ such that for any $n \ \phi \in S$, it holds that $\theta(n) \models \phi$.*
We say a tableau is Θ-satisfiable if some branch of it is Θ-satisfiable. A branch is Θ-satisfiable if the set of prefixed formulas on it is Θ-satisfiable.

Proposition 1. *A closed tableau is not Θ-satisfiable.*

PROOF. Suppose a tableau was closed and satisfiable. This means that for some formula φ and prefix n, both $n \ \varphi$ and $n \ \neg\varphi$ occur on a tableau's branch, and there is a model $\langle W, \mathcal{N}, V \rangle$ and function θ such that (Def. 6) $\theta(n) \models \varphi$ and $\theta(n) \models \neg\varphi$. We derive a contradiction. ∎

Proposition 2. *Applying any of the rules to a Θ-satisfiable tableau, gives another Θ-satisfiable tableau.*

Theorem 1. *[Soundness] If φ is not Θ-valid, there is no Θ-tableau proof for φ.*

5.3 Completeness

To achieve completeness, we will provide a *systematic procedure* of applying the tableaux rules, making sure everything that can be derived actually is. If the *systematic procedure* fails to produce a proof, then it will actually construct a Θ-*model* satisfying $\neg\varphi$, a *counter-model* witnessing non-validity.

Systematic Procedure

Notation. $\Diamond n$ and $\Box n$ for some prefix n are sets (intended to serve as registries so as to remember $\Diamond$-formulas and $\Box$-formulas that were found on a branch).

Stage 1: Write down $1 \; \neg\varphi$. Also $\Diamond 1 = \Box 1 = \varnothing$.

After stage k we stop when tableau is closed or all **occurrences** of formulas are *finished* (see below). Otherwise we proceed with stage $k + 1$.

Stage $k + 1$: Reading the formulas starting with the leftmost branch and from top to bottom, we encounter the first *unfinished* occurrence of a prefixed formula F.

1. If F is $n \; \neg\neg\varphi, n \; \varphi\wedge\psi, n \; \neg(\varphi\vee\psi), n \; \varphi\vee\psi, n \; \neg(\varphi\wedge\psi), n \; \Box\varphi$ use the appropriate rule, for each open branch including F. That is, for the disjunctive case we split the end of each branch and for the rest of the cases we just add the appropriate formulas at the end of the branch provided they do not already occur.
2. If F is $n \; \Box\varphi$, we add φ to $\Box n$. For each open branch $\mathcal{B}$ that includes F and for each formula $\psi \in \Diamond n$, if there is no prefix m such that $\mathcal{B}$ includes $m \; \varphi$ and $m \; \psi$, we add $m \; \varphi$ and $m \; \psi$, where m is now the smallest positive integer new to $\mathcal{B}$.
3. If F is $n \; \neg\Box\varphi$, we add $\neg\varphi$ to $\Diamond n$. For each open branch $\mathcal{B}$ that includes F and for each formula $\psi \in \Box n$, if there is no prefix m such that $\mathcal{B}$ includes $m \; \neg\varphi$ and $m \; \psi$, we add $m \; \neg\varphi$ and $m \; \psi$, where m is the smallest positive integer new to $\mathcal{B}$. If $\Box n = \varnothing$ (we repeat the same without the use of $\Box$-formulas) if there is no prefix m such that $\mathcal{B}$ includes $m \; \neg\varphi$ for some prefix m, we add $m \; \neg\varphi$, where m is the smallest positive integer new to $\mathcal{B}$.

F might not fall into one of the above cases (e.g. $n \; P$, P atomic) but then we just skip it. After the above we declare that occurrence of F **finished**.

Construction of Counter-Model

Notation. Given a branch of a tableau we define $[\varphi] = \{n \mid n \; \varphi \text{ is on the branch}\}$. Given a model, $|\varphi| = \overline{V}(\varphi)$ is the truth set of φ.

Definition 7. *Let $\mathcal{T}$ be an open tableau generated by the systematic procedure, $\mathcal{B}$ an open branch of $\mathcal{T}$. We define a model $\mathfrak{M} = \langle W, \mathcal{N}, V \rangle$ as follows:*

- *W is the set of prefixes on $\mathcal{B}$.*
- *If $n \; P$, P atomic, occurs on the branch then $n \models P$. Otherwise $n \models \neg P$.*
- *$\mathcal{N}(n) = \{S \subseteq W \mid \exists\varphi \in \mathcal{L}_\Box \text{ such that } S \supseteq [\varphi] \; \& \; n \; \Box\varphi \text{ occurs on } \mathcal{B}\} \cup \{W\}$.*

Proposition 3. *$\mathfrak{M}$ is a Θ-model.*

Proposition 4. [Key fact] *Let $\mathfrak{M}$ be a model as in Def. 7. For any prefix n and formula φ:*

(i) if n φ occurs on $\mathcal{B}$ then $\mathfrak{M}, n \models \varphi$.
(ii) if n $\neg\varphi$ occurs on $\mathcal{B}$ then $\mathfrak{M}, n \models \neg\varphi$.

Theorem 2. *[Completeness] If φ has no Θ-tableau proof, φ is not Θ-valid.*

PROOF. Since φ has no Θ-*tableau* proof, the tableau generated by following the systematic procedure has an open branch from which we construct a counter model. $1 \neg\varphi$ occurs on the branch, and by the Key Fact (Prop. 4) $1 \models \neg\varphi$. So $\neg\varphi$ is Θ-satisfiable i.e. φ is not Θ-valid. ∎

We show that the axiom **C.** $(\Box p \wedge \Box q) \supset \Box(p \wedge q) \notin \Theta$. The resulting tree is quite large, for illustration purposes we only follow one of the branches that will stay open.

$$1 \neg(\neg(\Box p \wedge \Box q) \vee \Box(p \wedge q)) \quad (1)$$
$$1 \neg\neg(\Box p \wedge \Box q) \quad (2)$$
$$1 \neg\Box(p \wedge q) \quad (3)$$
$$1 \Box p \wedge \Box q \quad (4)$$
$$2 \neg(p \wedge q) \quad (5)$$
$$1 \Box p \quad (6)$$
$$1 \Box q \quad (7)$$
$$2 \neg p \quad (8)$$
$$1 \neg\Box\neg p \quad (9)$$
$$3 \neg(p \wedge q) \quad (10)$$
$$3 p \quad (11)$$
$$1 \neg\Box\neg q \quad (12)$$
$$4 \neg(p \wedge q) \quad (13)$$
$$4 q \quad (14)$$
$$5 \neg\neg p \quad (15)$$
$$5 p \quad (16)$$
$$6 \neg\neg p \quad (17)$$
$$6 q \quad (18)$$
$$3 \neg q \quad (19)$$
$$7 \neg\neg q \quad (20)$$
$$7 p \quad (21)$$
$$8 \neg\neg q \quad (22)$$
$$8 q \quad (23)$$
$$4 \neg p \quad (24)$$

After (3)		After (7)	
$\Diamond 1$	$\Box 1$	$\Diamond 1$	$\Box 1$
$\neg(p \wedge q)$		$\neg(p \wedge q)$	p
			q

After (9)		After (12)	
$\Diamond 1$	$\Box 1$	$\Diamond 1$	$\Box 1$
$\neg(p \wedge q)$	p	$\neg(p \wedge q)$	p
$\neg\neg p$	q	$\neg\neg p$	q
		$\neg\neg q$	

The counter-model $\mathcal{M} = \langle W, \mathcal{N}, V \rangle$ derived from this branch has $W = \{1, \ldots, 8\}$, $V(p) = \{3, 5, 6, 7\}$, $V(q) = \{4, 6, 7, 8\}$. The only prefix with $\Box$-formulas is 1 so for $w \neq 1$ we have $\mathcal{N}(w) = W$ and $\mathcal{N}(1)$ contains all supersets of $|p|$ and $|q|$. We refrain from writing them down explicitly.

6 Decidability and Complexity

6.1 Finite Model Property

Notation. $S(\varphi) = \{\chi \in \mathcal{L}_\Box \mid \chi \text{ is } \psi, \neg\psi, \neg\neg\psi \text{ or } \neg\Box\neg\psi, \text{ where } \psi \text{ a subformula of } \varphi\}$.

Remark 1. All formulas occurring on a Θ-tableau for a formula φ belong to $S(\varphi)$. An easy proof is by induction on the number of rules applied.

Remark 2. $S(\varphi)$ is finite, in fact of size $O(m)$.

Remark 3. A Θ-tableau branch has a finite amount of prefixes, in fact $O(m^2)$. For a prefix to be introduced, a $\neg\square$-formula or a combination of one $\neg\square$-formula with a $\square$-formula (with the same prefix) is needed on the branch.

Let φ be a Θ-satisfiable formula. Then an attempt to prove $\neg\varphi$ using the systematic procedure will fail. So there exists an open branch from which we can construct a model (Def. 7) that satisfies φ. The number of prefixes on the branch is finite (Remark 3), and so the model derived will also be finite.

6.2 Complexity

It has been shown that the satisfiability problem for a multi-agent extension of the smallest (epistemic) monotonic modal logic is in **NP** ([23], the logic $\mathcal{E}_{\{3\}}$). Logic Θ deals with the reasoning of a single agent, and occurs from the smallest monotonic modal logic by adding axioms **N** and **D**. Assuming tableaux can provide the basis of an **NP** algorithm for the satisfiability in $\mathcal{E}_{\{3\}}$, one may guess that also Θ-SAT is in **NP**; [D-rule] and [π_1-rule] reflect the effect of these two axioms on Θ-models and do not seem they would burden the complexity. We prove this is indeed the case; the systematic procedure in section 5.3 will be used in the **NP** algorithm mentioned.

Let a formula φ be the 'input' for the satisfiability problem, and $size(\varphi) = m$. Our algorithm is:

- Run the systematic procedure for the tableau starting with $1\ \varphi$ with the exception that when you read a disjunction formula, non-deterministically choose which subformula to keep.
- When the procedure stops, if it was because the branch closed, answer NO. Otherwise, answer YES.

Remark 4. The resulting tableau has only one branch; using non-determinism we chose a single (computation) path.

The *correctness* of the algorithm, based on our soundness and completeness results, is evident. However, we must show it is indeed an algorithm.

Proposition 5. *The algorithm described terminates in a finite number of steps.*

PROOF. Assume not. Then the single resulting branch is infinite. Due to Remark 2 and the fact that existing formulas do not get added again, only a finite number of formulas can occur with the same prefix. So it must be the case that there are infinite prefixes. Due to Remark 3 we derive a contradiction. ∎

Proposition 6. Θ-*SAT is in* **NP**.

PROOF. Reading or writing any formula takes time $O(m)$. The algorithm described is non-deterministic, and for any choice made, it holds that each prefix has $O(m)$ formulas and there are $O(m^2)$ prefixes. So checking if a formula already exists, checking if the tableau is closed, adding prefixes for each pair of $\square$ and $\neg\square$ formulas, are all polynomial procedures.   ∎

Proposition 7. Θ-*SAT is* **NP**-*hard*.

PROOF. Satisfiability in propositional logic is a special case of Θ-SAT.   ∎

Theorem 3. Θ-*SAT is* **NP**-*complete*.

7   On the Notion of 'large sets': Finite vs Infinite

When it comes to infinite sets, the definition of large subsets by V. Jauregui seems reasonable enough. In the case of finite sets however, intuition suggests that a large subset must be more than half of the whole. To this end, one might be tempted to alter the definition of large sets, only for the case of finite cardinalities. We argue that Θ-tableaux are still sound and complete with respect to Θ. However, the finite model property ceases to hold.

Notation. Given a model and a formula φ, $|\varphi| = \overline{V}(\varphi)$ is the truth set of φ. Given a set B, $|B|$ is its cardinality. On the same note, $||\varphi||$ is the cardinality of $|\varphi|$.

Definition 8. *Let W be a non-empty set. A non-empty collection F of subsets of W is a collection of* large sets *if*

- *F is closed under supersets.*
- *F does not contain a set and its complement.*
- *If $|W| = n$, $n \in \omega$ (W is finite), $B \in F \Rightarrow |B| > n/2$.*

Regarding soundness: If F is a collection of large sets by Def. 8 it is also by Def. 1.

Regarding completeness: Having constructed a counter-model as in Def. 7, we add infinite copies of existing worlds. This way the counter-model becomes infinite and the condition we just added for the neighborhoods is no longer required.

To disprove the finite model property, since we had it with the classic definition, we must take advantage of the new found power of $\square$. We want to come up with formulas $\varphi_1, \ldots, \varphi_m$ that impose different valuations such that n worlds are not enough. Each pair of these formulas must have at least one common satisfying valuation, so that their truth sets can qualify as large subsets with the classic definition. We make it so that they have exactly one common satisfying valuation, unique for each pair. Given this we can close under supersets.

Which is the smallest number formulas that can serve for this purpose? On one hand, we want $\sum ||\varphi_i|| > mn/2$. On the other hand each world satisfies at most two formulas so $\sum ||\varphi_i|| \leq 2n$. For these two to lead to a contradiction we want $mn/2 > 2n \Rightarrow m > 4$. We therefore provide 5 formulas, with 4 atom variables involved, which is the least amount so that there are at least $\begin{pmatrix} 5 \\ 2 \end{pmatrix} = 10$ valuations available.

The 10 out of 16 valuations:

Atoms \ Valuation	1	2	3	4	5	6	7	8	9	10
p	T	T	T	T	T	T	T	T	F	F
q	T	T	T	T	F	F	F	F	T	T
r	T	T	F	F	T	T	F	F	T	T
s	T	F	T	F	T	F	T	F	T	F

$\varphi_1 \equiv (p \wedge q \wedge r \wedge s) \vee (p \wedge q \wedge r \wedge \neg s) \vee (p \wedge q \wedge \neg r \wedge s) \vee (p \wedge q \wedge \neg r \wedge \neg s)$

$\varphi_2 \equiv (p \wedge q \wedge r \wedge s) \vee (p \wedge \neg q \wedge r \wedge s) \vee (p \wedge \neg q \wedge r \wedge \neg s) \vee (p \wedge \neg q \wedge \neg r \wedge s)$

$\varphi_3 \equiv (p \wedge q \wedge r \wedge \neg s) \vee (p \wedge \neg q \wedge r \wedge s) \vee (p \wedge \neg q \wedge \neg r \wedge \neg s) \vee (\neg p \wedge q \wedge r \wedge s)$

$\varphi_4 \equiv (p \wedge q \wedge \neg r \wedge s) \vee (p \wedge \neg q \wedge r \wedge \neg s) \vee (p \wedge \neg q \wedge \neg r \wedge \neg s) \vee (\neg p \wedge q \wedge r \wedge \neg s)$

$\varphi_5 = (p \wedge q \wedge \neg r \wedge \neg s) \vee (p \wedge \neg q \wedge \neg r \wedge s) \vee (\neg p \wedge q \wedge r \wedge s) \vee (\neg p \wedge q \wedge r \wedge \neg s)$

	Satisfied by
φ_1	valuations 1,2,3,4
φ_2	valuations 1,5,6,7
φ_3	valuations 2,5,8,9
φ_4	valuations 3,6,8,10
φ_5	valuations 4,7,9,10

Proposition 8. *The formula* $\psi = \Box\varphi_1 \wedge \Box\varphi_2 \wedge \Box\varphi_3 \wedge \Box\varphi_4 \wedge \Box\varphi_5$ *is*

(i) satisfied in an infinite model.

(ii) not satisfied in a finite model.

PROOF. (i) We define the set $W = \{valuation\ i \mid i = 1, \ldots 10\}$ and the valuation function $V(w) = w$. We then add infinite copies of any existing world to W. Finally we define $\mathcal{N}(w) = \{S \subseteq W \mid S \supseteq |\varphi_i|\ i = 1, \ldots 5\}$. It is easy to check that $w \models \psi$.

(ii) The proof is the idea described above. Suppose it was satisfied in a model of size n, at some world $w \in W$.

- the formula ψ is a conjunction, so each $\Box\varphi_i$ is true in w. By construction, each φ_i is satisfied by a different 'large' set.
- Each φ_i is true in more than half of the worlds so $\sum \|\varphi_i\| > 5n/2$.
- A single valuation satisfies at most two of the given formulas. As such, a world can belong to at most two truth sets. Consequently $\sum \|\varphi_i\| \leq 2n$.

Then $5n/2 < 2n$ and we derive a contradiction. ∎

8 Θ_c: The Logic of Complete Majority Spaces

In the case someone is interested in complete majority spaces, a variant of the logic Θ, appropriate for the new models, is the one including axiom $\mathbf{D_c}$. $\Diamond\varphi \supset \Box\varphi$. We do not prove soundness & completeness in terms of Hilbert style axiomatization, we do however sketch proofs in accordance with the work in Section 5.

Weak Ultrafilters. The definition of a weak ultrafilter, is the same as in Def. 1 except:

(ii) $S \in \mathcal{K} \Leftrightarrow W \backslash S \notin \mathcal{K}$: $\mathcal{K}$ is complete with respect to the subsets of W

The following result is proved in [15].

Proposition 9. *Consider a $W \neq \varnothing$ and a weak filter F over W. Then, assuming the axiom of choice, there exists a weak ultrafilter U over W extending F.*

Semantics. Same as in Def. 2, but now a collection of large subsets is a weak ultrafilter.

Tableaux rules

- propositional rules

$$[\textbf{CD-rule}] \quad \frac{n \; \neg \Box \varphi}{n \; \Box \neg \varphi}$$

$$[\pi\text{-rule}] \quad \frac{n \; \Box \varphi}{m \; \varphi} \quad \text{for any prefix } m \text{ new to the branch.}$$
$$\frac{n \; \Box \psi}{m \; \psi}$$

We still have axiom **D** in the axiomatization, however, by choosing to turn $\Diamond$ into $\Box$ we have no need for [**D**-rule]. For the same reason [π_1-rule] and [π_2-rule] also become obsolete; we use the new [π-rule] instead. We do need a rule for a single $\Box$-formula; it is a matter of notation, φ can be the same as ψ.

Soundness [**CD**-rule]: We cannot of course rely on existing axiomatization and must use the definition of our (new) models. We have $\theta(n) \models \neg \Box \varphi \Rightarrow |\varphi| \notin \mathcal{N}(\theta(n)) \Rightarrow |\neg \varphi| \in \mathcal{N}(\theta(n)) \Rightarrow \theta(n) \models \Box \neg \varphi$.
[π-rule]: We have $\theta(n) \models \Box \psi \Rightarrow |\psi| \in \mathcal{N}(\theta(n)) \Rightarrow |\neg \psi| \notin \mathcal{N}(\theta(n)) \Rightarrow \theta(n) \models \neg \Box \neg \psi$. Now the proof follows as in Prop. 2.

Completeness Systematic procedure:
Everything is the same as in Section 5.3, except that there is no use for $\Diamond n$ sets and:

1. If F is $n \; \neg \neg \varphi, n \; \varphi \wedge \psi, n \; \neg(\varphi \vee \psi), n \; \varphi \vee \psi, n \; \neg(\varphi \wedge \psi), n \; \neg \Box \neg \varphi$ use the appropriate rule, for each open branch including F. That is, for the disjunctive case we split the end of each branch and for the rest cases we just add the appropriate formulas at the end of the branch provided they do not already occur.
2. If F is $n \; \Box \varphi$, we add φ to $\Box n$. For each open branch $\mathcal{B}$ that includes F and for each formula $\psi \in \Box n$, if there is no prefix m such that $\mathcal{B}$ includes $m \; \varphi$ and $m \; \psi$, we add $m \; \varphi$ and $m \; \psi$, where m is the smallest positive integer new to $\mathcal{B}$.

Existence of Counter-model:
As in Def. 7. However we have to make sure the counter-model is in accordance with the new definition:

- $\mathcal{N}^-(n) = \{S \subseteq W \mid \exists \varphi \in \mathcal{L}_\Box \text{ such that } S \supseteq [\varphi] \ \& \ n \ \Box\varphi \text{ occurs on } \mathcal{B}\} \cup \{W\}$.
Then we take $\mathcal{N}(n)$ to be any complete extension.

We temporarily use the term 'existence' and not 'construction' of a counter-model. The reason is the existence of a counter-model is now based on Prop. 9. After discussing decidability for Θ_c one should be convinced that also in this case, the number of prefixes, and therefore, the number of the worlds in the counter-model, is finite. And so a counter-model can be constructed algorithmically.

The proofs for the respective needed propositions, that the counter-model is indeed a Θ_c-model and the [Key fact] follow in the same lines.

Decidability and Complexity. It is easy to see that all relevant remarks regarding Θ still hold for Θ_c, perhaps with some changes in $S(\varphi)$. That is, each prefix has at most finite $O(m)$ formulas and there are at most $O(m^2)$ prefixes. We can readily deduce the presence of the finite model property and that Θ_c-SAT is **NP-complete**.

9   Related Work and Future Research

The modality we have studied in this paper, was introduced in [13]. Yet, similar ideas have appeared earlier in the Modal Logic and the Commonsense Reasoning literature.

In [11], a *'probably true'* modality is axiomatized, in combination with a *belief operator*; it is interesting that the axiomatization of *'probably'* is essentially the logic Θ of V. Jauregui. The *belief & probability possible-words models* employed are similar to the majority frames of [13], however, the work emphasizes in applications of this framework in more complex logics of action. Andreas Herzig attributes the essential ideas of his *'probably true'* operator to the earlier work of J. Burgess [4], although the latter work has been written in the late sixties and uses algebraic techniques for examining a logic that adjoins a *'probably true'* operator to the well-known **S5** modal logic. The idea of 'large' subsets has been independently introduced in [20].

We should note at this point that the *'in many cases true'* modality studied here, is readily suited for modelling weak notions of belief or notions of (qualitative) probability in the setting of Epistemic Logic; recent work is reported in [15,1]. For applications in *default reasoning* however, it has been argued that a *'normality'* modality does not suffice and the focus should be (and really is) on *'normality'* conditionals . The archetypical example in Non-Monotonic Reasoning is to infer that Tweety, a penguin, does not fly, although it is a bird. Assuming $\Box\varphi$ is a normality modality, representing the assertion *'birds typically fly'* as $\Box(bird \supset fly)$ or $bird \supset \Box fly$ is subject to criticism; the former falls prey to the *'paradoxes of strict implications'* [12] and the latter has been criticised within the KR community for carrying the same limitations as circumscriptive or autoepistemic defaults [3]. Still, it remains interesting to study the *'normality'* modality, as it provides a foundations for proceeding to *'normality by majority'* conditionals for defeasible reasoning; see Chapter 4 of [14].

As for future work, the most interesting question is to find more accurate (and probably more complex) definitions of 'largeness', investigate the emerging logics and compare the results to Θ, both in terms of expressivity and their computational properties.

References

1. Askounis, D., Koutras, C.D., Zikos, Y.: Knowledge means 'All', belief means 'Most'. In: del Cerro, et al. (eds.) [6], pp. 41–53
2. Blackburn, P., de Rijke, M., Venema, Y.: Modal Logic. Cambridge Tracts in Theoretical Computer Science, vol. 53. Cambridge University Press (2001)
3. Boutilier, C.: Conditional logics of normality: A modal approach. Artificial Intelligence 68(1), 87–154 (1994)
4. Burgess, J.P.: Probability logic. J. Symb. Log. 34(2), 264–274 (1969)
5. Chellas, B.F.: Modal Logic, An Introduction. Cambridge University Press (1980)
6. del Cerro, L.F., Herzig, A., Mengin, J. (eds.): JELIA 2012. LNCS, vol. 7519. Springer, Heidelberg (2012)
7. Dubois, D., Welty, C.A., Williams, M.-A.(eds.): Principles of Knowledge Representation and Reasoning: Proceedings of the Ninth International Conference (KR 2004), Whistler, Canada, June 2-5. AAAI Press (2004)
8. Fitting, M., Mendelsohn, R.L.: First-Order Modal Logic. Synthése Library, vol. 277. Kluwer Academic Publishers (1998)
9. Fitting, M.C.: Proof Methods for Modal and Intuitionistic Logics. D. Reidel Publishing Co., Dordrecht (1983)
10. Goldblatt, R.: Logics of Time and Computation, 2nd edn. CSLI Lecture Notes, vol. 7. Center for the Study of Language and Information. Stanford University (1992)
11. Herzig, A.: Modal probability, belief, and actions. Fundam. Inform. 57(2-4), 323–344 (2003)
12. Hughes, G.E., Cresswell, M.J.: A New Introduction to Modal Logic. Routledge (1996)
13. Jauregui, V.: The 'Majority' and 'by Default' Modalities. In: Orgun, Thornton (eds.) [16], pp. 263–272
14. Jauregui, V.: Modalities, Conditionals and Nonmonotonic Reasoning. PhD thesis, Department of Computer Science and Engineering, University of New South Wales (2008)
15. Koutras, C.D., Moyzes, C., Zikos, Y.: A modal logic of Knowledge, Belief and Estimation. Technical Report (2013),
   http://users.uop.gr/~ckoutras/KMZ-KBE-Full.pdf
16. Orgun, M.A., Thornton, J. (eds.): AI 2007. LNCS (LNAI), vol. 4830. Springer, Heidelberg (2007)
17. Pacuit, E.: Neighborhood semantics for modal logic: An introduction. Course Notes for ESSLLI 2007 (2007)
18. Pacuit, E., Salame, S.: Majority logic. In: Dubois, et al. (eds.) [7], pp. 598–605
19. Salame, S.: Majority Logic and Majority Spaces in contrast with Ultrafilters. PhD thesis, Graduate Center, City University of New York (2006)
20. Schlechta, K.: Filters and partial orders. Logic Journal of the IGPL 5(5), 753–772 (1997)
21. Segerberg, K.: An essay in Clasical Modal Logic. Filosofiska Studies, Uppsala (1971)
22. van der Hoek, W.: On the semantics of graded modalities. Journal of Applied Non-Classical Logics 2(1) (1992)
23. Vardi, M.: On the complexity of epistemic reasoning. In: Proceedings of the Fourth Annual Symposium on Logic in Computer Science, pp. 243–252. IEEE Press, Piscataway (1989)
24. Zikos, Y.: Modal Epistemic Logics without Negative Introspection: Epistemic structures and extensions with estimation and information. PhD thesis, Graduate Programme in Logic, Algorithms & Computation (MPLA), Dept. of Mathematics, University of Athens. In: Greek (2012)

Reasoning in Singly-Connected Directed Evidential Networks with Conditional Beliefs

Wafa Laâmari and Boutheina Ben Yaghlane

LARODEC Laboratory - Institut Supérieur de Gestion de Tunis, Tunisia

Abstract. Directed evidential networks are powerful tools for knowledge representation and uncertain reasoning in a belief function framework. In this paper, we propose an algorithm for the propagation of belief functions in the singly-connected directed evidential networks, when each node is associated with one conditional belief function distribution specified given all its parents.

1 Introduction

The development of techniques for representing and reasoning with uncertain knowledge has received considerable attention in the last few decades. Several different frameworks have been proposed for handling uncertainty, including probability theory [4], fuzzy set theory [10], and evidence theory [5].

Due to the power of the evidence theory in dealing with uncertain information, so far, a panoply of graphical models based on belief functions has been proposed to easily model the uncertainty in the problems and to perform inferences under the belief function framework [1,6,9]. These graphical models, called belief function networks or evidential networks, provide an adequate tool for coping with situations of incomplete knowledge and total ignorance.

Xu et al. have proposed Evidential Networks with Conditional belief functions (ENCs) as a belief function network with conditional dependencies [9]. ENCs encode conditional dependence relations between random variables using conditional belief functions. These conditional belief functions are specified per edge[1] and not per child node like conditional probabilities in Bayesian networks (BNs). Computations in an ENC are efficient thanks to its knowledge representation using conditional beliefs [9]. Nevertheless, the representation and the propagation algorithm in this network both proposed by Xu are not quite efficient since they are restricted to graphs with only binary relations among variables.

In order to address this limitation, Ben Yaghlane et al. have presented Directed EVidential Networks with conditional belief functions (DEVNs) [1].

DEVNs generalize ENCs by allowing to represent n-ary relations between variables (i.e. relations for any number of nodes). Furthermore, DEVNs provide more

---

[1] In ENCs, each conditional belief function is defined per edge i.e. for a node given one of its parent nodes separately. For instance, if a node A has two parents B and C in an ENC, then we have to specify two conditional belief functions for A: the belief of A conditionally to B and the belief of A conditionally to C.

A. Likas, K. Blekas, and D. Kalles (Eds.): SETN 2014, LNAI 8445, pp. 221–236, 2014.

flexibility for the representation of conditional relations than ENCs. Indeed, conditional belief functions in these networks can be specified either per one parent (i.e. per edge like in ENCs) or for all parents (i.e. per child node like in BNs).

Despite the flexibility of knowledge representation in DEVNs, the proposed algorithms for the case of singly-connected DEVNs have been limited to conditionals specified per edge [2], and no algorithms have been presented in the literature for the belief propagation in singly-connected DEVNs with conditional distributions specified given all the parents.

In this paper, we propose a novel algorithm for reasoning in singly-connected directed evidential networks weighted by conditional beliefs specified for each node given all its parents.

The remainder of the paper is organized as follows. Section 2 recalls necessary material on belief functions. In section 3, we present a brief survey of directed evidential networks with conditional beliefs. Section 4 introduces our algorithm for the belief propagation in singly-connected DEVNs with conditional distributions specified given all the parents, while section 5 gives an illustrative example of the proposed algorithm.

2   Belief Function Theory and Related Concepts

The theory of belief functions [5,8], also referred to as evidence theory, has become one of the most popular tool in artificial intelligence for the representation of incomplete knowledge and uncertain reasoning. In this section, we recall basic concepts and necessary operations on belief functions that we will use in the sequel. For details, the reader is referred to [5,3,8].

2.1   Some Basic Concepts about Belief Function Theory

Let $\Theta_{N_k} = \{\theta_{k1}, \ldots, \theta_{kp}\}$ be a finite space of all possible elementary values of a variable N_k. Θ_{N_k} is named the *frame of discernment* or the *universe of discourse*. The elementary values θ_{ki}, for each $i = 1, \ldots, p$, relative to the variable N_k, called also hypotheses, are assumed to be mutually exclusive and exhaustive.

All possible subsets S of Θ_{N_k} are elements of the *power set* of Θ_{N_k}. The latter set is denoted by $2^{\Theta_{N_k}}$ and is formally defined as $2^{\Theta_{N_k}} = \{S : S \subseteq \Theta_{N_k}\}$. Every element of the power set $2^{\Theta_{N_k}}$ is called a proposition, an event or an assumption.

A function $m^{N_k}: 2^{\Theta_{N_k}} \to [0,1]$ is said to be a *basic belief mass* (bbm) or a *mass function* if it satisfies the following axiom:

$$\sum_{S \in 2^{\Theta_{N_k}}} m^{N_k}(S) = 1 \tag{1}$$

where $m^{N_k}(S)$ expresses the degree of belief given by a source of information to support exactly the proposition S. The mass assigned to the whole frame of discernment Θ_{N_k}, denoted by $m^{N_k}(\Theta_{N_k})$, is the part of belief we are unable to allocate to any particular subset of Θ_{N_k}. A mass function m^{N_k} is called a *vacuous belief* when $m^{N_k}(\Theta_{N_k}) = 1$. It allows to characterize a state of total ignorance.

The *belief* in a subset S of Θ_{N_k}, denoted by $\text{bel}^{N_k}(S)$, is the sum of the bbm's of the subsets Q of S. The *plausibility* of a subset S of Θ_{N_k}, denoted by $\text{pl}^{N_k}(S)$, is the sum of the bbm's of the subsets Q of Θ_{N_k} that are compatible with S. Given a bbm m^{N_k}, $\text{bel}^{N_k}(S)$ and $\text{pl}^{N_k}(S)$ are derived, for $S \subseteq \Theta_{N_k}$, as follows:

$$\text{bel}^{N_k}(S) = \sum_{Q \subseteq S, Q \neq \emptyset} m^{N_k}(Q) \tag{2}$$

$$\text{pl}^{N_k}(S) = \sum_{Q \cap S \neq \emptyset} m^{N_k}(Q) \tag{3}$$

2.2 Basic Operations on Belief Functions

Let $N = \{N_1, \ldots, N_n\}$ be a finite set of random variables, where each variable $N_j \in N$ $(j = 1, \ldots, n)$ is associated with its frame of discernment Θ_{N_j}. Let A and B be two disjoint subsets of N. Their frames, denoted by Θ_A and Θ_B, are the Cartesian product of the frames of the variables they include, respectively.

Let m^{AB} be a bbm defined on the product space $\Theta_{AB} = \Theta_A \times \Theta_B$. The *marginalization* of m^{AB} to Θ_A produces a new bbm m^A as follows:

$$m^A(S') = m^{AB \downarrow A}(S') = \sum_{S \subseteq (\Theta_{AB}), S^{\downarrow A} = S'} m^{AB}(S) \tag{4}$$

where $S^{\downarrow A}$ is the projection of $S \subseteq \Theta_{AB}$ to Θ_A by dropping extra coordinates in each element of S.

Let m^A be a bbm defined on Θ_A. The *vacuous extension* of m^A to Θ_{AB} produces a bbm m^{AB} which is defined as follows:

$$m^{AB}(S') = m^{A \uparrow AB}(S') = \begin{cases} m^A(S) & \text{if } S' = S \times \Theta_B, S \subseteq \Theta_A \\ 0 & \text{otherwise} \end{cases} \tag{5}$$

Suppose m^A and m^B are two bbm's defined on the spaces Θ_A and Θ_B, respectively. The *combination* of m^A and m^B into a single mass function m^{AB}, can be done, $\forall S \subseteq \Theta_{AB}$, as follows:

$$m^{AB}(S) = (m^A \otimes m^B)(S) = \sum_{S_1 \cap S_2 = S} m^{A \uparrow AB}(S_1) * m^{B \uparrow AB}(S_2) \tag{6}$$

where both $m^{A \uparrow AB}$ and $m^{B \uparrow AB}$ are computed using the equation (5).

3 Directed Evidential Network with Conditional Belief Functions Basics

Directed evidential networks with conditional belief functions (DEVNs) [1] are an encoding of uncertain information expressed under the belief function framework.

3.1 Directed Evidential Network with Conditional Belief Functions

A DEVN is a model based on directed acyclic graph (DAG) G=(N,E), where N={$N_1, \ldots, N_n$} is a finite set of nodes representing different random variables and E={$E_1, \ldots, E_y$} is a set of edges representing conditional dependencies between them. Each node N_k in the DEVN takes its values on a frame of discernment Θ_{N_k}. The set of the parent nodes of N_k is denoted by $Pa(N_k)$. The set of its child nodes is denoted by $Ch(N_k)$. Each root node N_k in G is associated with an a priori bbm m^{N_k}[2] satisfying the axiom given by the equation (1). Unlike in BNs, each child node N_j in the DEVN is associated with an a priori vacuous belief characterizing the state of total ignorance in this node, and also with a conditional belief function. There are two different ways to specify conditional belief functions distributions in DEVNs. In fact, conditional beliefs in these networks can be defined:

(i) Per edge like conditionals in ENCs: Each edge between a parent node N_j and a child node N_k is weighted by a conditional belief function $m[N_j](N_k)$[3] over N_k given N_j (simply denoted by $m^{N_k}[N_j]$).

(ii) Per child node similar to conditional probabilities considered by Pearl in BNs: Each child node N_k is associated with a conditional belief function $m[Pa(N_k)](N_k)$ over N_k given all its parent nodes $Pa(N_k)$ (this belief function is simply denoted by $m^{N_k}[Pa(N_k)]$). This case will be considered throughout the rest of this paper.

To illustrate, a DEVN with conditional parameters defined per edge and another one with conditionals specified per child node are given in Figures 1 and 2, respectively. Each variable N_k (k=1,...,3) takes its values on the frame $\Theta_{N_k}=\{\theta_{k1},\theta_{k2}\}$.

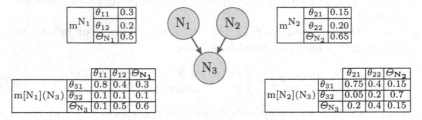

m^{N_1}		
θ_{11}	0.3
θ_{12}	0.2
Θ_{N_1}	0.5

m^{N_2}		
θ_{21}	0.15
θ_{22}	0.20
Θ_{N_2}	0.65

$m[N_1](N_3)$	θ_{11}	θ_{12}	Θ_{N_1}
θ_{31}	0.8	0.4	0.3
θ_{32}	0.1	0.1	0.1
Θ_{N_3}	0.1	0.5	0.6

$m[N_2](N_3)$	θ_{21}	θ_{22}	Θ_{N_2}
θ_{31}	0.75	0.4	0.15
θ_{32}	0.05	0.2	0.7
Θ_{N_3}	0.2	0.4	0.15

Fig. 1. A DEVN with conditionals per edge

3.2 Foundations of Reasoning in Directed Evidential Network with Conditional Belief Functions Defined per Edge

Let Θ_Y and Θ_X be the frames associated with two variables Y and X, respectively. Let us consider a set of conditional plausibility functions $\{pl^X[y'](x) : y' \in \Theta_Y, x \subseteq \Theta_X\}$ which quantifies the plausibility of a subset x of Θ_X when we know which element y' of Θ_Y holds. In [7], Smets has derived the *Disjunctive Rule of Combination* (DRC) to build the plausibility function $pl^X[y](x)$ for any $x \subseteq \Theta_X$ conditionally to any subset $y \subseteq \Theta_Y$ as follows:

$$pl^X[y](x) = 1 - \prod_{y' \in y}(1 - pl^X[y'](x)) \tag{7}$$

---

[2] m, bel and pl are equivalent representations of a same piece of information. In this paper, we use bbm's and plausibilities for representing the quantitative level in DEVNs.

[3] The notations $m[N_j](N_k)$ and $m^{N_k}[N_j]$ used throughout this paper can be read as the mass of N_k given N_j. They correspond to the classical notation $m(N_k| N_j)$.

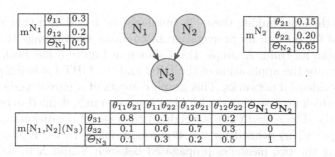

Fig. 2. A DEVN with conditionals per child node

Simultaneously with the DRC, Smets has derived the *Generalized Bayesian Theorem* (GBT) to build the conditional plausibility function $pl^Y[x](y)$ for any subset y of Θ_Y given any subset $x \subseteq \Theta_X$. Thanks to the duality GBT-DRC [7], the following equality relation is satisfied $\forall y \subseteq \Theta_Y$ and $\forall x \subseteq \Theta_X$:

$$pl^Y[x](y) = pl^X[y](x) \qquad (8)$$

Once $pl^X[y](x)$ is built using equation (7), the relation in (8) allows to derive the GBT which builds the conditional plausibility function $pl^Y[x](y)$ from the conditional plausibility functions $pl^X[y'](x)$ as follows:

$$pl^Y[x](y) = pl^X[y](x) = 1 - \prod_{y' \in y}(1 - pl^X[y'](x)) \qquad (9)$$

Now, suppose there exists some a priori information over Θ_Y, given by a bbm m_0^Y, then knowing the conditional plausibility functions $pl^X[y'](x)$, one can compute the plausibility pl^X induced on X for any $x \subseteq \Theta_X$ as follows:

$$pl^X(x) = \sum_{y \subseteq \Theta_Y} m_0^Y(y) \times pl^X[y](x) \qquad (10)$$

where $pl^X[y](x)$ is given by equation (7).

Similarly, given some basic belief masses over Θ_X, denoted by m_0^X, and the conditional plausibility functions $pl^X[y'](x)$, then one can compute the plausibility pl^Y induced on Y for any $y \subseteq \Theta_Y$ as follows:

$$pl^Y(y) = \sum_{x \subseteq \Theta_X} m_0^X(x) \times pl^Y[x](y) \qquad (11)$$

where $pl^Y[x](y)$ is given by equation (9).

The inference mechanism in singly-connected evidential networks with conditionals specified per edge is based on reasoning with conditionals defined given one variable. The DRC and the GBT, proposed for reasoning with conditionals specified for a variable conditionally to another one, provide the tools necessary to reason in these networks. Smets has shown that the DRC can be used for top down propagation to compute the message that a parent should send to its child through the edge linking them [7]. Similarly, he has shown that the GBT can be applied for bottom up propagation to compute the message that a parent receives from its child. A simple DAG shown in Figure 3 has been used by Smets to illustrate the application of the DRC and the GBT for belief propagation in these evidential networks. This graph consists of a parent node Y and a child node X which are associated with bbm's m_0^Y and m_0^X, defined over Θ_Y and Θ_X, respectively. The edge (Y,X) is weighted by a set of conditional plausibility functions $pl^X[y'](x)$ defined for $x \subseteq \Theta_X$ conditionally to $y' \in \Theta_Y$. $\alpha_{Y \to X}$ and $\alpha_{X \to Y}$, denoting the two messages propagated between Y and X in both directions through the edge (Y,X), correspond to the plausibility functions pl^X and pl^Y computed respectively by the equations (10) and (11). In what follows, we refer to these equations used in evidential networks as the *top down propagation rule* and the *bottom up propagation rule*, respectively.

Once the node X has received the message $\alpha_{Y \to X}$ coming from its parent Y, it combines it with its prior plausibility function[4] pl_0^X and reports the result as its marginal plausibility pl^X, and so does the node Y.

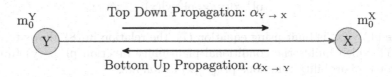

Fig. 3. Propagation Principle in belief networks with conditionals for X given Y

The algorithm for reasoning in larger and more complicated singly-connected directed evidential networks with conditionals specified per edge was proposed in [2]. This algorithm is based on a local propagation up and down the DEVN. It generalizes the propagation principle encountered in Smets' message passing schema [7] in the sens that all messages between neighboring nodes in the DEVN are computed by the top down propagation and the bottom up propagation rules.

4   Belief Propagation in Singly-Connected DEVNs with Conditionals per Child Node for All the Parents

In this section, we propose a new algorithm for belief function propagation in singly-connected DEVNs weighted by conditionals specified per child node given all the parents. Before proceeding, we start by showing how reasoning with a conditional defined for a variable X conditionally to a set of variables can be done using the top down propagation and the bottom up propagation rules. Then, we show that although the initial network is singly-connected, the evidential reasoning can not be done by a local propagation of beliefs using these two propagation rules in this network, unless some required modifications are done.

---

[4] The plausibility pl_0^X relative to X is derived from its bbm m_0^X using equation (3).

4.1   Reasoning with a Conditional Defined for a Variable Conditionally to a Set of Variables

Let X be a variable having the frame of discernment Θ_X, and Y={$P_1,\ldots,P_n$} be a set of random variables, where each variable $P_i \in Y$ is associated with its frame of discernment Θ_{P_i}. $\Theta_Y = \Theta_{P_1} \times \ldots \times \Theta_{P_n}$ is the frame of discernment of Y.

Let {$pl^X[y'](x) : y' = (p'_1,\ldots,p'_n) \in \Theta_Y$} denote a set of conditional plausibility functions quantifying the plausibility of a subset x of Θ_X given an element $y' = (p'_1,\ldots,p'_n) \in \Theta_Y$, where $p'_i \in \Theta_{P_i}$ for each $i = 1,\ldots,n$.

For any $y \subseteq \Theta_Y$ and represented by $p_1 \times \ldots \times p_n$, where $p_i \subseteq \Theta_{P_i}$ for each $i = 1,\ldots,n$, the plausibility function $pl^X[y](x)$ of any subset $x \subseteq \Theta_X$ given y, and the plausibility function $pl^Y[x](y)$ for y given any subset $x \subseteq \Theta_X$, can be computed by applying the DRC and the GBT given in equations (7) and (9), respectively. When applying these two equations for this case, Y is considered as a joint or a composed variable (Figure 4) and not as a single one like for the case of conditionals defined per edge that we presented in Section 3.2.

Now, given the conditional plausibility functions $pl^X[y'](x)$, a prior bbm m_0^X over Θ_X, and also a prior bbm m_0^Y over Θ_Y, one can compute the plausibility functions pl^Y and pl^X induced, respectively, on the joint variable Y and on the variable X using the top down propagation and the bottom up propagation rules given by equations (10) and (11), respectively.

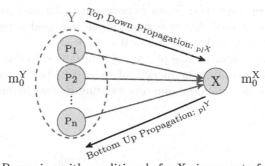

Fig. 4. Reasoning with conditionals for X given a set of variables Y

4.2   New Solution for Reasoning in DEVNs with Conditionals Specified per Child Node Given All the Parents

In what follows, we start by considering the belief reasoning in a simple example of singly-connected DEVN weighted by conditionals defined per child node, then we generalize this reasoning to singly-connected DEVNs that are more complex.

Let D be the singly-connected DEVN given in figure 5.a, in which the child node N_i, having two parents P_1 and P_2, is associated with the conditional plausibility function $pl^{N_i}[P_1,P_2]$. Adapting the reasoning for a variable conditionally to a set of variables, presented in Section 4.1, to the belief propagation in D whose conditionals are defined per child node given all the parents, is not possible, unless some modifications are considered. This is due to the fact that:

(i) Reasoning with the conditional plausibility function $pl^{N_i}[P_1,P_2]$ using equations (10) and (11) requires a prior bbm $m_0^{N_i}$ associated to the variable N_i and a prior bbm $m_0^{P_1,P_2}$ associated to the composed or the joint variable $\{P_1,P_2\}$. However, in D, we have not a prior bbm $m_0^{P_1,P_2}$, but we have two prior bbm's $m_0^{P_1}$ and $m_0^{P_2}$ relative to the single parents P_1 and P_2, respectively.

(ii) Given the conditional $pl^{N_i}[P_1,P_2]$ which is specified for the variable N_i given the two variables P_1 and P_2, the top down propagation and the bottom up propagation rules can be applied to compute the messages propagated between the node N_i and the joint node $\{P_1,P_2\}$ representing its parents. However, in D, we have not a single node representing the joint variable $\{P_1,P_2\}$, but we have two nodes representing each parent P_j of N_i separately.

One way to elaborate in this issue would be to merge the two nodes representing the parents of N_i in order to have a single one representing the joint variable $\{P_1,P_2\}$. This new composed node, would be associated with the bbm $m_0^{P_1,P_2}$ obtained by the combination of the two mass functions $m_0^{P_1}$ and $m_0^{P_2}$ of the two merged parent nodes P_1 and P_2 on the product space $\Theta_{P_1} \times \Theta_{P_2}$. The resulting graph is given in figure 5.b. It is a tree D' in which the direction of the edge $(\{P_1,P_2\},N_i)$ linking the child node N_i to the composed one $\{P_1,P_2\}$ representing its parents in D, is dropped. By dropping the direction of this edge in D', the conditional dependence relation among the variable represented by the child node and those represented by the composed one is lost. Thus, a third node is introduced between these two nodes in order to maintain this relation. This node is referred to as a *mediator* or a *conditional node* and is represented by a rectangle labeled by the conditional relation $N_i|P_1, P_2$.

The conditional plausibility table $pl^{N_i}[P_1,P_2]$, initially stored at the child node N_i in D, would be stored after the merger of P_1 and P_2 in the mediator linking the child node N_i to the composed one representing its two parents in D'.

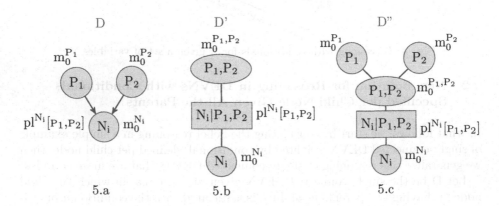

Fig. 5. A singly-connected DEVN with conditionals specified per child node D and the representations of the transformed network D' and D"

Intuitively, by merging the parents of the child node into a single node, the initial singly-connected DEVN D whose conditionals are specified per child node turns into a new graph D' in which we can use a principle of belief propagation based on reasoning with conditionals specified given a set of variables. The messages sent in D' between the composed node and the child node N_i in the two directions pass through the mediator or the conditional node between them. In fact, this node, storing the conditional plausibility $pl^{N_i}[P_1, P_2]$, serves as a bridge between the composed node and N_i by playing the same role as the one of an edge between them. The conditional relation with which this node is labeled allows to know whether the sender is the composed parent node or the child node and to decide if the top down propagation is the rule to be used or the bottom up propagation. Unlike the other nodes, this conditional node neither sends messages to its two neighbors nor receives messages from them.

The representation of the transformed graph D' presents a weakness since the a priori bbms of the merged parent nodes are lost due to the fusion process which leads to the disappearance of the single parent nodes in the tree D' after their merger into a single one. To tackle this problem, we propose to construct a new graph from D by grouping all the parent nodes of a child node in a new composed node, but without vanishing them. In other word, when merging the parent nodes of a child node into one composed node, the single merged parent nodes must persist in the resulting graph (assumption A). Now, if we consider the new assumption A when merging the parent nodes in the DEVN of figure 5.a, we will obtain the tree D" shown in figure 5.c. D" is constructed from D by first grouping the parents P_1 and P_2 of N_i in a new composed node Π_i labeled $\{P_1, P_2\}$ without the deletion of nodes P_1 and P_2, then by adding edges from each single parent node P_j ($j = 1,2$) to the composed node Π_i, and finally by introducing the conditional node $N_i|P_1, P_2$ between Π_i and N_i.

The representation of the transformed graph D" given above for a simple evidential network D containing one child node having only two parents could be easily generalized to the case where the DEVN has many child nodes having any number p of parent nodes. The generalization is presented in Section 4.3.

4.3   From a General Singly-Connected DEVN with Conditionals Specified Given All the Parents to a Tree D"

Let D=(N,E) denote a singly-connected DEVN with conditionals defined per child node and let $F \subseteq N$ be the set of child nodes in D. Recall that $Pa(N_i)$ denotes the set of the parents of a node N_i in D. The tree structure D" is structured so that at a time a child node in the network D is considered, and a subtree of D" is constructed for the part of D composed of this child node and its parent nodes. The construction process of D" from D is formally described by Algorithm 1.

Algorithm 1. Construct a Tree Structure D" from D

Require: D=(N,E)
Ensure: D"=(N",E")
  Initialization
  $\zeta \leftarrow$ F; /∗ ζ denotes the set of child nodes in D∗/
  $\vartheta \leftarrow \emptyset$; /∗ ϑ denotes the set of non conditional nodes in D"∗/
  $\beta \leftarrow \emptyset$; /∗ β denotes the set of conditional nodes in D"∗/
  E" $\leftarrow \emptyset$; /∗ E" denotes the set of undirected edges in D"∗/
  N" $\leftarrow \emptyset$;/∗ N" denotes the set of nodes in D"∗/
  while $|\zeta| \geq 1$ **do**
    Pick a candidate variable c $\in \zeta$
    if $|$Pa(c)$| = 1$ **then**
      n1 $\leftarrow$ Pa(c)
      n2 $\leftarrow$ {c|Pa(c)}
      n3 $\leftarrow$ {c}
      $\vartheta \leftarrow \vartheta \cup$ {n1,n3}
      $\beta \leftarrow \beta \cup$ {n2}
      E" $\leftarrow$ E" $\cup$ {(n1,n2),(n2,n3)}
    else {$|$Pa(c)$| > 1$}
      P $\leftarrow$ Pa(c)
      n1 $\leftarrow$ P
      $\vartheta \leftarrow \vartheta \cup$ {n1}
      while $|$P$| \geq 1$ **do**
        n2 $\leftarrow$ p where p $\in$ P
        $\vartheta \leftarrow \vartheta \cup$ {n2}
        E" $\leftarrow$ E" $\cup$ {(n2,n1)}
        P $\leftarrow$ P-{n2}
      end while
      n3 $\leftarrow$ {c|Pa(c)}
      n4 $\leftarrow$ {c}
      $\vartheta \leftarrow \vartheta \cup$ {n4}
      $\beta \leftarrow \beta \cup$ {n3}
      E" $\leftarrow$ E" $\cup$ {(n1,n3),(n3,n4)}
    end if
    $\zeta \leftarrow \zeta$-{c}
  end while
  N" $\leftarrow \vartheta \cup \beta$

4.4 Rules for Making Inference in D"

We give now the different rules which will be used later for belief propagation in D".

Rules for Computing Messages: Let ϑ and β denote the sets of non-conditional and conditional nodes in D", respectively, and let $\text{Nei}_{\vartheta}^{N_i^"} = \left\{N_s^" \in \vartheta | (N_i^", N_s^") \in E"\right\}$ and $\text{Nei}_{\beta}^{N_i^"} = \left\{N_s^" \in \beta | (N_i^", N_s^") \in E"\right\}$ be the non-conditional and the conditional neighbors of a non-conditional node $N_i^"$ in D", respectively. Suppose also $\text{Nei}^{N_j^"}$ denotes the two neighboring nodes of a conditional node $N_j^"$. Recall that the two neighbors of each conditional node are non-conditional nodes.

Recall also that each conditional node in D" is introduced between two non-conditional nodes to show, as we have already explained, the conditional dependence relation among the variables that the two nodes represent and to play in the tree the same role as a directed edge in a DAG. So considered as a mediator between these two nodes, a conditional node $N_j^" \in \beta$ can neither send nor receive any messages. Each non-conditional node $N_i^" \in \vartheta$ sends messages to other nodes in D" according to the following rules:

(1) If the neighboring node N_j'' of N_i'' is a conditional node (i.e. $N_j'' \in \mathrm{Nei}_\beta^{N_i''}$), then N_i'' sends a message to the node N_k'', which is the second neighbor of N_j''. Let $\alpha_{N_i'' \to N_k''}$ denote the message from N_i'' to N_k''. This latter depends on N_k'':

(i) If N_k'' is the child node of N_i'', then: $\alpha_{N_i'' \to N_k''}$ is a plausibility function on N_k'', computed for any $n_k'' \subseteq \Theta_{N_k''}$ by the top down propagation rule as follows:

$$\alpha_{N_i'' \to N_k''} = pl_{N_i'' \to N_k''}(n_k'') = \sum_{n_i'' \subseteq \Theta_{N_i''}} m^{N_i''}(n_i'') \times pl^{N_k''}[n_i''](n_k'') \qquad (12)$$

where $pl^{N_k''}[n_i''](n_k'')$ is the plausibility of any $n_k'' \subseteq \Theta_{N_k''}$ conditionally to any $n_i'' \subseteq \Theta_{N_i''}$ obtained by the equation (7), and $m^{N_i''}$ is a bbm on $\Theta_{N_i''}$, so it can be represented by $m^{N_i''}$, $bel^{N_i''}$ or $pl^{N_i''}$ and is computed for any $n_i'' \subseteq \Theta_{N_i''}$ by:

$$pl^{N_i''} = pl_0^{N_i''} \otimes \left(\otimes \{ \alpha_{N_s'' \to N_i''} | N_s'' \in \mathrm{Nei}_\vartheta^{N_i''} \} \right)$$
$$\otimes \left(\otimes \left\{ \alpha_{N_u'' \to N_i''} | N_u'' \in \mathrm{Nei}^{N_t''}, N_t'' \in (\mathrm{Nei}_\beta^{N_i''} - \{N_j''\}) \text{ and } N_u'' \neq N_i'' \right\} \right) \qquad (13)$$

In words, the plausibility function $pl^{N_i''}$ defined on N_i'' is the combination of its a priori plausibility distribution $pl_0^{N_i''}$ with all messages that N_i'' receives from its other non-conditional neighbors together and with all messages that N_i'' receives from the neighbors of its conditional neighbors except the conditional node N_j''.

(ii) If N_k'' represents the parents of N_i'', then: $\alpha_{N_i'' \to N_k''}$ is the plausibility function computed for any $n_k'' \subseteq \Theta_{N_k''}$ by the bottom up propagation rule as follows:

$$\lambda_{N_i'' \to N_k''} = pl_{N_i'' \to N_k''}(n_k'') = \sum_{n_i'' \subseteq \Theta_{N_i''}} m^{N_i''}(n_i'') \times pl^{N_k''}[n_i''](n_k'') \qquad (14)$$

where $pl^{N_k''}[n_i''](n_k'')$ is the plausibility function for any $n_k'' \subseteq \Theta_{N_k''}$ conditionally to any $n_i'' \subseteq \Theta_{N_i''}$ obtained by the equation (9), and $m^{N_i''}$ is a bbm on $\Theta_{N_i''}$ whose corresponding plausibility function is computed for any $n_i'' \subseteq \Theta_{N_i''}$ by (13).

(2) If the neighboring node N_j'' of N_i'' is a non-conditional node (i.e $N_j'' \in \mathrm{Nei}_\vartheta^{N_i''}$), N_i'' sends a message $\alpha_{N_i'' \to N_j''}$ to the node N_j'', where $\alpha_{N_i'' \to N_j''}$ is computed by:

$$\alpha_{N_i'' \to N_j''} = [pl_0^{N_i''} \otimes \left(\otimes \{ \alpha_{N_k'' \to N_i''} | N_k'' \in (\mathrm{Nei}_\vartheta^{N_i''} - \{N_j''\}) \} \right)$$
$$\otimes \left(\otimes \left\{ \alpha_{N_u'' \to N_i'} | N_u'' \in \mathrm{Nei}^{N_j''}, N_j'' \in \mathrm{Nei}_\beta^{N_i''} \text{ and } N_u'' \neq N_i'' \right\} \right)]^{\downarrow(N_i'' \cap N_j'')} \qquad (15)$$

In words, the message that N_i'' sends to its non-conditional neighbor N_j'' is the combination of its a priori plausibility with all messages that N_i'' receives from its other non-conditional neighbors and also with all messages that it receives from the neighbors of its conditional neighbors which are suitably marginalized.

Rule for Computing Marginals: When a non-conditional node N_i'' in D" has received a message from each of its non-conditional neighbors and also from the neighbors of its conditional neighbors, it combines all messages together with its own a priori plausibility function $pl_0^{N_i''}$ and reports the result as its marginal plausibility $pl^{N_i''}$ as follows:

$$pl^{N_i''} = \left[pl_0^{N_i''} \otimes \left(\otimes \left\{ \alpha_{N_k'' \to N_i''} \middle| N_k'' \in Nei_{\vartheta}^{N_i''} \right\} \right) \right.$$

$$\left. \otimes \left(\otimes \left\{ \alpha_{N_u'' \to N_i''} \middle| N_u'' \in Nei^{N_j''}, N_j'' \in Nei_{\beta}^{N_i''} \text{ and } N_u'' \neq N_i'' \right\} \right) \right] \quad (16)$$

4.5 Reasoning in DEVNs with Conditionals Specified per Child Node

Before running the message passing algorithm (MPA), an initialization phase is applied during which each conditional distribution in D is associated with the corresponding conditional node in D" and each a priori one is associated with the corresponding non-conditional node. The MPA works in three steps by:

(1) picking a non-conditional node in D" and designating it as a root node R.

(2) applying an inward phase by collecting messages from the leaves towards the root. Each node N_i'' waits for messages from nodes which are not in the root direction, and upon receiving all of them, it passes a message immediately to the unique node from which it did not receive a message, using equation (12), (14) or (15). This phase ends when R collects messages from all its non-conditional neighboring nodes and also from the second neighbors of its conditional neighbors, and updates its marginal using equation (16).

(3) applying an outward phase by distributing messages away from R, beginning with R itself until reaching the leaves. The computation of messages is done, using equation (12), (14) or (15), depending on the type of the neighbor. When the leaves receive messages, we can readily therefore calculate the marginal distribution for every variable in the graph using the equation (16).

5 Illustration

As an illustration, let us consider the DEVN D of the example below with the following a priori and conditional plausibility functions. For the sake of the simplicity, all the variables are binary. The conditional plausibility functions $pl_0^{N_2}$, $pl_0^{N_4}$ and $pl_0^{N_5}$ are those corresponding to the vacuous beliefs defined in Section 2.1 .

$$pl_0^{N_1} = \begin{matrix} n_{11} \\ n_{12} \\ \Theta_{N_1} \end{matrix} \begin{pmatrix} 1.0 \\ 0.3 \\ 1.0 \end{pmatrix} \qquad pl^{N_2}[N_1] = \begin{matrix} n_{21} \\ n_{22} \\ \Theta_{N_2} \end{matrix} \begin{matrix} n_{11} & n_{12} \\ \begin{pmatrix} 0.5 & 0.5 \\ 0.8 & 0.9 \\ 1.0 & 1.0 \end{pmatrix} \end{matrix} \qquad pl_0^{N_3} = \begin{matrix} n_{31} \\ n_{32} \\ \Theta_{N_3} \end{matrix} \begin{pmatrix} 0.6 \\ 1.0 \\ 1.0 \end{pmatrix}$$

$$pl^{N_5}[N_3] = \begin{matrix} n_{51} \\ n_{52} \\ \Theta_{N_5} \end{matrix} \begin{matrix} n_{31} & n_{32} \\ \begin{pmatrix} 0,5 & 0,55 \\ 0,8 & 0,85 \\ 1 & 1 \end{pmatrix} \end{matrix} \qquad pl^{N_4}[N_2, N_3] = \begin{matrix} n_{41} \\ n_{42} \\ \Theta_{N_4} \end{matrix} \begin{matrix} n_{21}n_{31} & n_{21}n_{32} & n_{22}n_{31} & n_{22}n_{32} \\ \begin{pmatrix} 0,9 & 0,5 & 0,8 & 0.85 \\ 0,2 & 0,9 & 0,9 & 0.5 \\ 1.0 & 1.0 & 1.0 & 1.0 \end{pmatrix} \end{matrix}$$

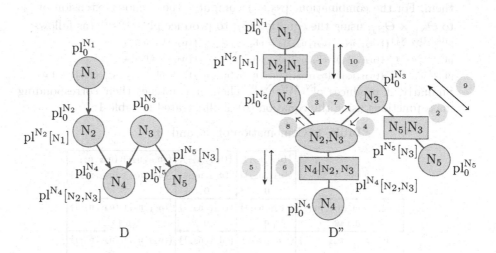

Fig. 6. A DEVN D with conditionals per child node and its corresponding tree D"

Let us suppose that we pick N_4 as a root node in the tree D" built from D using Algorithm 1, then the messages of the inward pass and the outward pass performed on D" are generated in the order shown in figure 6. These messages are computed as follows:

- The message ① that N_1 sends to N_2 through the mediator node $N_2|N_1$ corresponds to $\alpha_{N_1 \rightarrow N_2}$ which is computed using equation (12). This message is given, for each $n_2 \subseteq \Theta_{N_2}$, by the plausibility function $pl_{N_1 \rightarrow N_2}$ as follows:

  $pl_{N_1 \rightarrow N_2}(\{n_{21}\}) = 0.7 * 0.5 + 0 * 0.5 + 0.3 * [1 - (1 - 0.5) * (1 - 0.5)] = 0.575$

  $pl_{N_1 \rightarrow N_2}(\{n_{22}\}) = 0.7 * 0.8 + 0 * 0.9 + 0.3 * [1 - (1 - 0.8) * (1 - 0.9)] = 0.854$

  $pl_{N_1 \rightarrow N_2}(\{\Theta_{N_2}\}) = 0.7 * 1 + 0 * 1 + 0.3 * [1 - (1 - 1) * (1 - 1)] = 1$

- The message ② that N_5 sends to N_3 through the mediator node $N_5|N_3$ corresponds to $\alpha_{N_5 \rightarrow N_3}$ which is computed using equation (14). This message is given, for each $n_3 \subseteq \Theta_{N_3}$, by the plausibility function $pl_{N_5 \rightarrow N_3}$ as follows:

  $pl_{N_5 \rightarrow N_3}(\{n_{31}\}) = 0 * 0.5 + 0 * 0.8 + 1 * 1 = 1$

  $pl_{N_5 \rightarrow N_3}(\{n_{32}\}) = 0 * 0.55 + 0 * 0.85 + 1 * 1 = 1$

  $pl_{N_5 \rightarrow N_3}(\{\Theta_{N_3}\}) = 0*[1-(1-0.5)*(1-0.55)]+0*[1-(1-0.8)*(1-0.85)]+1*[1-(1-1)*(1-1)] =$
  $0 * 0.775 + 0 * 0.97 + 1 * 1 = 1$

- When receiving the message ①, the non-conditional node N_2, computes the message ③ that it should send to its non-conditional neighbor $\{N_2,N_3\}$ using equation (15). This message, corresponding to $(pl_0^{N_2} \otimes ①)^{\downarrow N_2}$, is as follows:

  $pl_{N_2 \rightarrow \{N_2,N_3\}}(\{n_{21}\}) = 0.575$ $pl_{N_2 \rightarrow \{N_2,N_3\}}(\{n_{22}\}) = 0.854$ $pl_{N_2 \rightarrow \{N_2,N_3\}}(\Theta_{N_2}) = 1.0$

- Similarly, using equation (15), N_3 computes the message ④ that it should send to its non-conditional neighbor $\{N_2,N_3\}$. This latter is as follows:

  $pl_{N_3 \rightarrow \{N_2,N_3\}}(\{n_{31}\}) = 1.0$ $pl_{N_3 \rightarrow \{N_2,N_3\}}(\{n_{32}\}) = 1.0$ $pl_{N_3 \rightarrow \{N_2,N_3\}}(\Theta_{N_3}) = 1.0$

- When $\{N_2,N_3\}$ receives the two messages ③ and ④ from its neighbors N_2 and N_3, respectively, it computes its new plausibility function by combining them. For the combination, $\{N_2, N_3\}$ computes the vacuous extension of ③ to $\Theta_{N_1} \times \Theta_{N_2}$, using the equation (5), to produce $pl^{N_2\uparrow\{N_2,N_3\}}$ as follows:

$$pl^{N_2\uparrow\{N_2,N_3\}}(\{(n_{21},n_{31}),(n_{21},n_{32})\}) = pl_{N_2\rightarrow\{N_2,N_3\}}(\{n_{21}\}) = 0.575$$

$$pl^{N_2\uparrow\{N_2,N_3\}}(\{(n_{22},n_{31}),(n_{22},n_{32})\}) = pl_{N_2\rightarrow\{N_2,N_3\}}(\{n_{22}\}) = 0.854$$

$$pl^{N_2\uparrow\{N_2,N_3\}}(\{(n_{21},n_{31}),(n_{22},n_{31}),(n_{21},n_{32}),(n_{21},n_{32})\}) = pl_{N_2\rightarrow\{N_2,N_3\}}(\Theta_{N_2}) = 1.0$$

Similarly, it produces $pl^{N_3\uparrow\{N_2,N_3\}}$. Then, it combines their corresponding mass functions using the equation (6) as illustrated in table 1:

Table 1. Combination of ③ and ④

	$\{(n_{31}, n_{21}), (n_{31}, n_{22})\}$ **0**	$\{(n_{32}, n_{21}), (n_{32}, n_{22})\}$ **0**	$\{(n_{31}, n_{21}), (n_{32}, n_{21}), (n_{31}, n_{22}), (n_{32}, n_{22})\}$ **1**
$\{(n_{21}, n_{31}), (n_{21}, n_{32})\}$ **0.146**	$\{(n_{21}, n_{31})\}$ **0**	$\{(n_{21}, n_{32})\}$ **0**	$\{(n_{21}, n_{31}), (n_{21}, n_{32})\}$ **0.146**
$\{(n_{22}, n_{31}), (n_{22}, n_{32})\}$ **0.425**	$\{(n_{22}, n_{31})\}$ **0**	$\{(n_{22}, n_{32})\}$ **0**	$\{(n_{22}, n_{31}), (n_{22}, n_{32})\}$ **0.425**
$\{(n_{21}, n_{31}), (n_{22}, n_{31}), (n_{21}, n_{32}), (n_{22}, n_{32})\}$ **0.429**	$\{(n_{21}, n_{31}), (n_{22}, n_{31})\}$ **0**	$\{(n_{21}, n_{32}), (n_{22}, n_{32})\}$ **0**	$\{(n_{21}, n_{31}), (n_{22}, n_{31}), (n_{21}, n_{32}), (n_{22}, n_{32})\}$ **0.429**

The node $\{N_1, N_2\}$ is now ready to compute, using equation (12), the message ⑤ it should send to the node N_4 through the conditional node $N_4|\{N_2, N_3\}$. This message is given, for each $n_4 \subseteq \Theta_{N_4}$, as follows:

$$pl_{\{N_1,N_2\}\rightarrow N_4}(\{n_{41}\}) = 0.9631; \ pl_{\{N_1,N_2\}\rightarrow N_4}(\{n_{42}\}) = 0.96535; \ pl_{\{N_1,N_2\}\rightarrow N_4}(\{\Theta_{N_4}\}) = 1$$

- Upon receiving ⑤, the root node N_4, computes its marginal plausibility function pl_{N_5} using equation (16). Then it sends the message ⑥ to the node $\{N_2, N_3\}$ through the conditional node $N_4|\{N_2, N_3\}$. ⑥ is computed using equation (14) and is given as follows:

$$pl_{N_4\rightarrow\{N_2,N_3\}}(\{(n_{31}, n_{21})\}) = 1.0; \ pl_{N_4\rightarrow\{N_2,N_3\}}(\{(n_{31}, n_{22})\}) = 1.0$$

$$pl_{N_4\rightarrow\{N_2,N_3\}}(\{(n_{31}, n_{21}),(n_{31}, n_{22})\}) = 1.0; \ pl_{N_4\rightarrow\{N_2,N_3\}}(\{(n_{32}, n_{21})\}) = 1.0$$

$$pl_{N_4\rightarrow\{N_2,N_3\}}(\{(n_{32}, n_{22})\}) = 1.0; \ pl_{N_4\rightarrow\{N_2,N_3\}}(\{(n_{32}, n_{21}),(n_{32}, n_{22})\}) = 1.0$$

$$pl_{N_4\rightarrow\{N_2,N_3\}}(\{(n_{31}, n_{21}),(n_{32}, n_{21})\}) = 1.0; \ pl_{N_4\rightarrow\{N_2,N_3\}}(\{(n_{31}, n_{22}),(n_{32}, n_{21})\}) = 1.0$$

$$pl_{N_4\rightarrow\{N_2,N_3\}}(\{(n_{31}, n_{21}),(n_{31}, n_{22}),(n_{32}, n_{21}),(n_{32}, n_{22})\}) = 1.0$$

- $\{N_3, N_4\}$ is ready now to send the message ⑦ to N_3. This message is computed using equation (15) and it corresponds to $(③ \otimes ⑥)^{\downarrow N_3}$. So, for each $n_3 \subseteq \Theta_{N_3}$, this message is given by the plausibility function $pl_{\{N_2,N_3\}\rightarrow N_3}$ as follows:

$$pl_{\{N_2,N_3\}\rightarrow N_3}(\{n_{31}\}) = 1 \qquad pl_{\{N_2,N_3\}\rightarrow N_3}(\{n_{32}\}) = 1 \qquad pl_{\{N_2,N_3\}\rightarrow N_3}(\{\Theta_{N_3}\}) = 1$$

- Similarly, $\{N_3, N_4\}$ computes the message ⑧ it should send to N_2 using equation (15). This message corresponds to $(④ \otimes ⑥)^{\downarrow N_2}$. So, for each $n_2 \subseteq \Theta_{N_2}$, this message is given by the plausibility function $pl_{\{N_2,N_3\}\rightarrow N_2}$ as follows:

$$pl_{\{N_2,N_3\}\rightarrow N_2}(\{n_{21}\}) = 1 \qquad pl_{\{N_2,N_3\}\rightarrow N_2}(\{n_{22}\}) = 1 \qquad pl_{\{N_2,N_3\}\rightarrow N_2}(\{\Theta_{N_2}\}) = 1$$

- When receiving the message ⑦, N_3 can compute its marginal plausibility function by combining $pl_0^{N_3}$ with ⑦ and ② using equation (16). For each $n_3 \subseteq \Theta_{N_3}$, its marginal plausibility function pl^{N_3} is as follows:

$$\text{pl}^{N_3}(\{n_{31}\}) = 0.6 \qquad \text{pl}^{N_3}(\{n_{32}\}) = 1.0 \qquad \text{pl}^{N_3}(\{\Theta_{N_3}\}) = 1$$

Then, it sends the message ⑨ to N_5 which is computed using equation (12). This message is given, for each $n_5 \subseteq \Theta_{N_5}$, by the plausibility function $\text{pl}_{N_3 \to N_5}$ as follows:

$$\text{pl}_{N_3 \to N_5}(\{n_{51}\}) = 0.685 \qquad \text{pl}_{N_3 \to N_5}(\{n_{52}\}) = 0.922 \qquad \text{pl}_{N_3 \to N_5}(\{\Theta_{N_5}\}) = 1$$

When receiving the message ⑨, N_5 combines it with $\text{pl}_0^{N_5}$, using equation (16), to compute its marginal plausibility function which is as follows:

$$\text{pl}^{N_5}(\{n_{51}\}) = 0.685 \qquad \text{pl}^{N_5}(\{n_{52}\}) = 0.922 \qquad \text{pl}^{N_5}(\{\Theta_{N_5}\}) = 1$$

- When receiving the message ⑧, N_2 computes its marginal plausibility function by combining $\text{pl}_0^{N_2}$ with the two messages ⑧ and ① using equation (16). For each $n_2 \subseteq \Theta_{N_2}$, its marginal plausibility function pl^{N_2} is as follows:

$$\text{pl}^{N_2}(\{n_{21}\}) = 0.575 \qquad \text{pl}^{N_2}(\{n_{22}\}) = 0.854 \qquad \text{pl}^{N_2}(\{\Theta_{N_2}\}) = 1$$

Then, it computes the message ⑩ it should send to N_1, using equation (14). This message is given, for each $n_1 \subseteq \Theta_{N_1}$, by the plausibility function $\text{pl}_{N_2 \to N_1}$ as follows:

$$\text{pl}_{N_2 \to N_1}(\{n_{11}\}) = 1 \qquad \text{pl}_{N_2 \to N_1}(\{n_{12}\}) = 1 \qquad \text{pl}_{N_2 \to N_1}(\{\Theta_{N_1}\}) = 1$$

When receiving the message ⑩, N_1 combines $\text{pl}_0^{N_1}$ with ⑩, using equation (16), to compute its marginal plausibility function which is as follows:

$$\text{pl}^{N_1}(\{n_{11}\}) = 1 \qquad \text{pl}^{N_1}(\{n_{12}\}) = 0.3 \qquad \text{pl}^{N_1}(\{\Theta_{N_1}\}) = 1$$

6 Conclusion and Future Work

A new algorithm for belief function reasoning in singly-connected evidential networks weighted by conditionals specified per child node has been proposed in this paper. Our propagation algorithm first transforms the initial evidential network with conditionals defined per child node given all the parents into a tree structure. The algorithm then exploits the GBT and the DRC to perform the evidential inference step by step through this tree using the conditional belief functions. The work can be extended by including a linkage between our algorithm for reasoning in singly-connected DEVNs with conditionals specified per child node and the one for reasoning in singly-connected DEVNs with conditionals specified per edge proposed in [2]. We plan to propose a new method that could be used in an hybrid singly-connected DEVNs in which some conditionals are specified per edge and some others are specified per child node. This will offer more flexibility to the experts when specifying the conditional parameters.

References

1. Ben Yaghlane, B., Mellouli, K.: Inference in Directed Evidential Networks Based on the Transferable Belief Model. IJAR 48(2), 399–418 (2008)
2. Yaghlane, B.B., Mellouli, K.: Updating directed belief networks. In: Hunter, A., Parsons, S. (eds.) ECSQARU 1999. LNCS (LNAI), vol. 1638, pp. 43–54. Springer, Heidelberg (1999)
3. Dempster, A.P.: Upper and lower probabilities induced by a multivalued mapping. Annals of Mathematical Statistics 38, 325–339 (1967)

4. Pearl, J.: Probabilistic Reasoning in Intelligent Systems: Networks of Plausible Inference. Morgan Kaufmann (1988)
5. Shafer, G.: A Mathematical Theory of Evidence. Princeton University Press, Princeton (1976)
6. Shenoy, P.P.: Valuation networks and conditional independence. Uncertainty in Artificial Intelligence, 191–199 (1993)
7. Smets, P.: Belief Function: The Disjunctive Rule of Combination and the Generalized Bayesian Theorem. Int. J. Approx. Reasoning 9, 1–35 (1993)
8. Smets, P., Kennes, R.: The transferable belief model. Artificial Intelligence 66, 191–234 (1994)
9. Xu, H., Smets, P.: Evidential Reasoning with Conditional Belief Functions. In: Heckerman, D., et al. (eds.) Proceedings of Uncertainty in Artificial Intelligence (UAI 1994), pp. 598–606. Morgan Kaufmann, San Mateo (1994)
10. Zadeh, L.A.: Fuzzy Sets. Information and Control 8, 338–353 (1965)

A Formal Approach to Model Emotional Agents Behaviour in Disaster Management Situations

Petros Kefalas[1], Ilias Sakellariou[2],
Dionysios Basakos[3], and Ioanna Stamatopoulou[1]

[1] The University of Sheffield International Faculty, City College, 3 L. Sofou, 54624, Thessaloniki, Greece
[2] University of Macedonia, 156 Egnatia Str., 54636, Thessaloniki, Greece
[3] South-East European Research Center, 24 P. Koromila, 54622, Thessaloniki, Greece
{kefalas,istamatopoulou}@city.academic.gr,iliass@uom.edu.gr,
dbasakos@seerc.org

Abstract. Emotions in Agent and Multi-Agent Systems change their behaviour to a more 'natural' way of performing tasks thus increasing believability. This has various implications on the overall performance of a system. In particular in situations where emotions play an important role, such as disaster management, it is a challenge to infuse artificial emotions into agents, especially when a plethora of emotion theories are yet to be fully accepted. In this work, we develop a formal model for agents demonstrating emotional behaviour in emergency evacuation. We use state-based formal methods to define agent behaviour in two layers; one that deals with non-emotional and one dealing with emotional behaviour. The emotional level takes into account emotions structures, personality traits and emotion contagion models. A complete formal definition of the evacuee agent is given followed by a short discussion on visual simulation and results to demonstrate the refinement of the formal model into code.

Keywords: Agent State-Based Modelling, Formal Methods, Emotional Agents, Emergency Evacuation.

1 Introduction

Human emotions significantly change behaviour in complex environments where resources are a primary concern [8,29]. This fact has brought new ideas and solutions to the Multi-Agent System (MAS) paradigm. For example, the use of emotions in a context-aware decision support system resulted to lesser communication time between agents [17] where in other cases emotions as well as personality and mood led to faster compromises among agents engaging in a negotiation [28]. Furthermore, an attempt was made to model the social function of emotions and their interconnection with socials norms to improve controllability in MAS [9]. Finally, emotions can be seen as a leverage to teamwork and cooperation between agents [20].

A. Likas, K. Blekas, and D. Kalles (Eds.): SETN 2014, LNAI 8445, pp. 237–250, 2014.

In the current case, we investigate modelling of emotional agents in disaster management situations and in particular emergency evacuation. It is known that emotions affect the way crowd behaves in such cases. According to a non-emotional behaviour, all agents in danger follow a specific exit plan and the building is evacuated in a timely fashion. However, in reality, people's emotions drive their behaviour; certain people can start experiencing fear or panic under certain circumstances such as lose of direction, detachment from family members, delay in finding and following an exit plan. It is therefore a challenge to devise a formal model that would be able to describe emotions, personality traits and emotion contagion in a way suitable to lead towards simulation of emergency evacuation scenarios.

The aim of this paper is to introduce a formal model for emotional agents. The model is based on a type of finite state machines, namely X-Machines, which have demonstrated a number of advantages in formal modelling of agents. The main contribution is the addition of an emotional meta-level machine to the basic model, thus clearly and elegantly separating modelling of the rational (non-emotional) and that of emotional agent behaviour in cases such as emergency evacuation. We briefly demonstrate how the model can lead to simulation, thus visualising the overall behaviour of the crowd in disaster management scenarios.

The current paper is structured as follows: Section 2 deals with formal modelling of agents using a state-based method, namely X-Machines. The main contribution is in section 3, where we define an meta-level extension that deals explicitly with emotional behaviour of agents. Such behaviour is prominent in emergency evacuation and section 4 presents such a case study together with the formal agent models. In section 5, we briefly discuss how the models lead to simulation and present some results. Before we conclude, related work is presented in section 6.

2   A Formal Model for Agents

There exist numerous formal methods, either general or specialised to agent modelling [11,4,26]. Agents and MAS, as software artifacts can benefit from formal modelling in terms of unambiguous specification, verification of the model towards given properties and finally formal testing of the implementation.

2.1   X-machines

We have worked with *X-machines* for a long period of time. X-machines are state-based machines extended with a memory structure. That makes modeling more intuitive and leads towards implementation. The memory structure also makes the machine more compact compared to memory-less state machines. Another important difference is that the transitions between states are not triggered by inputs alone, but by functions that accept an input and the memory values and produce an output and new memory values. Again, this leads nicely towards the final implementation through refinement.

It has been demonstrated that X-Machines and its extensions are particularly useful for modelling biological and biology-inspired MAS [14]. The great advantage over other methods is their strong legacy of theory and practice in:

- modelling potential for dynamically structured MAS [30],
- refinement, animation and simulation [25],
- testing methods that prove correctness [12] with tools for automatic test generation [5],
- model checking for verification of properties [7]

Definition 1. *An X-machine ($\mathcal{X}$) is defined as:* $\mathcal{X} = (\Sigma, \Gamma, Q, M, \Phi, F, q_0, m_0)$ *[12], where:*

- Σ *and* Γ *are the input and output alphabets.*
- Q *is a finite set of states.*
- M *is a (possibly) infinite set called memory.*
- Φ *is a set of partial functions* φ; *each such function maps an input, a memory value and an emotional states to an output and a possibly different memory value,* $\varphi : \Sigma \times M \to \Gamma \times M$.
- F *is the next state partial function,* $F : Q \times \Phi \to Q$, *which given a state and a function from the type* Φ *determines the next state.* F *is often referred to as a state transition diagram.*
- q_0 *and* m_0 *are the initial state and initial memory.*

2.2   Example: An Agent Evacuating on Emergency

The $\mathcal{X}$ model of an agent that evacuates a building on emergency is shown in Fig. 1. The figure depicts the state diagram F, where transitions are labeled through functions in Φ. The agent starts at *no emergency* state until it *perceives a danger* of some sort. Then it *wanders around* in order to find an evacuation plan. While *evacuating* by following the plan, it may *get disorientated* or *loose family* members. In such cases, it keeps *wandering around* until it *finds the family* member or *finds a plan* respectively. The computation ends when the *exit is found*.

The memory of $\mathcal{X}$ agent model holds the evacuation plan (sequence of coordinates), the current position of the agent, the status of the family member and the walking speed towards the exit.

The input alphabet Σ contains sets of percepts, such as the other agents positions, the empty space positions, the emergency alarm etc. The output alphabet Γ is a set of abstract messages that at simulation could be translated to visual output on the status and position of the agent.

An example function in Φ is:

$\varphi_{found-exit} : (Percept, (Plan, Pos, S, Ch)) \mapsto ("Exited", (Plan, Pos', S, Ch))$
$if\ (Pos', empty) \in Percept \wedge canMove(Pos, Pos', S) \wedge door(DoorPos) \in Percept$
$\wedge\ distance(Pos', DoorPos) < distance(Pos, DoorPos)$

The actual model is simplified here for exposition purposes and includes a number of additional functions that deal with the agent behaviour.

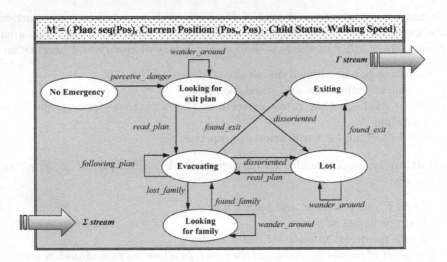

Fig. 1. An abstract $\mathcal{X}$ model of an agent that evacuates a building on emergency

2.3   Computation of $\mathcal{X}$

Definition 2. *An computation state in $\mathcal{X}$ is defined as the tuple (q, m), with $q \in Q$ and $m \in M$. A computation step, which consumes an input $\sigma \in \Sigma$ and changes the computation state $(q, m) \vdash (q', m')$ with $q, q' \in Q$, $m, m' \in M$, such that $\varphi(\sigma, m) = (\gamma, m')$ and $F(q, \varphi) = q'$.*

A *computation defined* as the series of computation steps that take place when all inputs are applied to the initial computation state (q_0, m_0), which for the case above could be, for instance, $(no\_emercency, (\epsilon, (15, 42), child\_close, 1m/sec)$.

3 $^{em}\mathcal{X}$-Machines

Emotions influence agent perception, learning, behaving, communication, etc. An agent acting under emotions exhibits a different behaviour than the same agent acting in a rational (emotion-less) way. This is clear in situations where disaster management is required, such as emergency evacuation. In such events, agents, depending on their personality, appear to have increased chances to experience *fear* that may eventually turn into *panic*. Such emotions could alter what they perceive and what they communicate to other agents. It is also important to note that agents behaviour is altered when they operate as a family group, for instance if there are parents accompanying children.

So far, there is not yet a widely accepted definition of emotions supported by a complete theory that can describe how emotional processes affects reasoning in general [15]. Most commonly used psychological theories in agent design today refer to appraisal process of stimulus [16] and the reactions to three types of stimuli (OCC model) [21].

There exist two basic options to achieve emotional behaviour of artificial agents: (a) to hard-wire emotions into the agent, (b) to model emotions at a different level than the rational behaviour. In this work, we chose the latter as a more elegant approach to emotions modelling.

Definition 3. *An Emotional X-machine is defined as a tuple* $^{em}\mathcal{X} = (\mathcal{X}, \mathcal{E})$ *where* $\mathcal{X}$ *is an* X-machine *and* $\mathcal{E}$ *is a meta-machine defined as* $\mathcal{E} = (^e\Sigma, \ ^e\Gamma, \ \rho_\sigma, \ \rho_\gamma, \rho_\varphi, \ E, \ P, \ C, \ ^e\Phi)$, *where:*

- $^e\Sigma$ *and* $^e\Gamma$ *are the input and output alphabet.*
- ρ_σ *and* ρ_γ *are the input and output revision functions.*
- ρ_φ *is the behaviour revision function.*
- E *is a representation of an emotional theory.*
- e_0 *is the representation of the initial emotional state.*
- P *is a personality trait type.*
- C *is a contagion model type.*
- $^e\Phi : E \times P \times C \times M \times \Sigma \rightarrow E$ *is the set of emotions revision functions* $^e\varphi$, *that given an emotions structure* $e \in E$, *a contagion model* $c \in C$, *a personality trait* $p \in P$ *and a memory tuple* $m \in M$ *returns a new emotion structure* $e' \in E$.

Fig. 2 shows an abstract $^{em}\mathcal{X}$ model. The upper meta-layer represents $\mathcal{E}$ and the lower layer the $^{em}\mathcal{X}$ machine.

It is important to note that agent models in this context do not have an affective behaviour towards humans, and thus factors like body language, speech etc. are not taken into account.

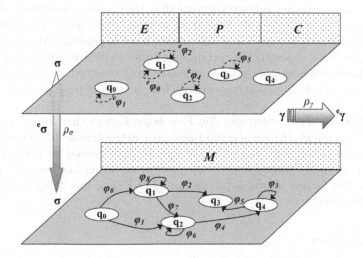

Fig. 2. An abstract $^{em}\mathcal{X}$ model with non-emotional behaviour as $\mathcal{X}$. at the lower layer and emotional behaviour as $\mathcal{E}$ at meta-level.

3.1   Input and Output Revision

Input and output revision refer to the way the environment is perceived and what the agent communicates to its environment (and other agents) under emotions. This may significantly differ from a situation where the agent behaves rationally. Especially in disaster scenarios, the personality trait and the dominant emotions would greatly affect perception and outward communication. In principle, the two revision functions may be defined as:

$$\rho_\sigma : {}^e\Sigma \times E \times P \times C \to \Sigma \text{ and } \rho_\gamma : \Gamma \times E \times P \times C \to {}^e\Gamma$$

3.2   Behaviour Revision

The behaviour revision function ρ_φ determines which functions of $\mathcal{X}$ are applicable in a given emotional state E. It is defined as: $\rho_\varphi : E \times \mathcal{X} \to \Phi$

3.3   Emotions

Artificial emotions are plugged-in to the $\mathcal{E}$ meta-level definition in order to facilitate modelling of emotional agents. By extracting E at a meta-level, various opportunities are open to experiment with different theories. In fact, E serves as a formal structured representation of artificial emotions or an emotional theory, for instance the OCC model [21].

3.4   Personality Trait

Individual emotion strength updates depend on the rate of change of E, different for each evacuee, since evidence suggests that there exist individual differences in affective response to emotion eliciting stimuli. *Personality trait*, for example, is one relevant factor. Some individuals have a predisposition (sensitivity response) towards experiencing certain emotions, so different personality traits are responsible for how quickly an emotional state is reached, maintained and recovered from, resulting to some agents reaching a state of panic or hysteria more easily [2].

Psychologists argue about the *Big Five* basic factors that affect personality traits: (a) openness, (b) conscientiousness, (c) extroversion, (d) agreeableness, and (e) neuroticism [18]. So, either P can be represented as crisp values of different personality traits (some count more than a hundred) or a vector with any of the five factors above, expressed as NEO-FFI or any other psychological personality inventory.

3.5   Contagion

Emotional contagion is a result of interaction between agents which could affect each others emotions. It is the case that in emergency situations, emotions (especially calmness, fear and panic) may propagate when agents of various personalities interact. For example, security personnel is assumed to have a calming effect to evacuees, and on the contrary, detachment of a family member during evacuation may result into increased level of fear.

There are various contagion models depending on the situation, most of them based on perception, message exchange and proximity of agents [10], [6]. The above definition allows flexibility to define one that suits the situation as well as change it, if necessary, without affecting the basic rational $\mathcal{X}$ model.

3.6 Computation of $^{em}\mathcal{X}$

The computation of $^{em}\mathcal{X}$ is similar to this in $\mathcal{X}$ but it includes an additional number of steps which deal with emotions.

Definition 4. *An $^{em}\mathcal{X}$ computation state is defined as the tuple (q, m, e), with $q \in Q$ and $m \in M$ and $e \in E$. A computation step, which consumes an input $\sigma \in \Sigma$ and changes the computation state $(q, m, e) \vdash (q', m', e')$ is essentially composed of the following substeps:*

- *firstly, the input revision function $\rho_\sigma(^e\sigma, e, p, c) \vdash \sigma$, where $^e\sigma \in {}^e\Sigma, e \in E, p \in P, c \in C$ and $\sigma \in \Sigma$.*
- *the behaviour revision function ρ_φ produces a set of functions φ^a of $\mathcal{X}$ that are applicable in the current emotional state.*
- *a transition in $\mathcal{X}$ takes place by triggering a function $\varphi \in \varphi^a$ at the lower layer: $(q, m, e) \vdash (q_1, m', e)$ with $q, q_1 \in Q$, $m, m' \in M$ and $e \in E$, such that $\varphi(\sigma, m) = (\gamma, m')$ and $F(q, \varphi) = q_1$.*
- *an emotions revision in $^{em}\mathcal{X}$ takes place by triggering an emotional function at meta-level (changes emotions structure E): $(q_1, m', e) \vdash (q', m', e')$ with $q_1, q' \in Q, e, e' \in E$ and $m' \in M$ such that $^e\varphi(e, p, c, m', \sigma) = (e')$.*
- *finally, the output revision function produces the final output γ of $^{em}\mathcal{X}$, thus $\rho_\gamma(\gamma, e, p, c) \vdash^e \gamma$, where $\gamma \in \Gamma, e \in E, p \in P, c \in C$ and $^e\gamma \in {}^e\Gamma$.*

In the above, a transition in $\mathcal{X}$ takes place first. Then a function in $^{em}\mathcal{X}$ revises the emotions but not the states. A *computation* is defined as the series of computation steps that take place when all inputs are applied to the initial computation state (q_0, m_0, e_0).

4 Case Study: Emergency Evacuation

The above described agent for evacuation can be modelled as a $^{em}\mathcal{X}$ by adding the meta layer $\mathcal{E}$ for emotional behaviour. One needs to define the elements for the $^{em}\mathcal{X}$ tuple. In this paper, we will assume for the sake of simplicity that $^e\Sigma = \Sigma, {}^e\Gamma = \Gamma, \rho_\sigma = \rho_\gamma = \epsilon$, which means we consider agents whose incoming perception and outgoing messages are not affected by emotions.

As emotional structure E, we will use a simplified approach with a vector $E = ((e_1, v_1), (e_2, v_2), ..., (e_n, v_n))$ where e_i are basic emotions and v_i its *strength*, i.e. $v_i = 0..100$. One of the basic emotions is *Horror* [23] which can be assigned with different crisp *emotion descriptors*, such as {*calm, alarmed, fear, terror, panic, hysteria*}. Thus, the initial value of *Horror* in E_0 is $(calm, 0)$. In the following $SV_H(E)$ stands for the strength value v_H of *Horror* given the emotion vector E.

As personality trait P, we could define different types in a set such as $\{confident, helpful, coward, self - centered\}$. Alternatively, we choose a sample of factors that determine a personality type, i.e. $(openness, extraversion)$. These factors would represent the rate with which the *emotion strength* changes.

A contagion model C for the evacuee, such as ASCRIBE [1], can be adopted. It introduces *contagion strength* s_{iQj} that determines the strength by which agent j influences on some state Q agent i:

$$s_{ij} = expressiveness_j * (1 - \frac{dis(Pos_i, Pos_j)}{dis_{infl}}) * openness_i \qquad (1)$$

where the middle factor determines the *channel strength*, in our case the euclidean distance between the agents $dis(Pos_i, Pos_j)$, in the area of influence dis_{infl} (the radius of the area containing agents). The overall contagion strength is determined by:

$$s_i = \sum_{i \in Agents} s_{ij} \qquad (2)$$

where *Agents* is the set of agents currently located in the area of influence of agent i. Contagion is used in the emotion revision functions to update the *strength* of the basic emotions in E, in this case the *emotional descriptors* of horror.

The emotion revision function is similar to that reported in [27], i.e. the emotion level is determined by an *individual emotion update* (f_{ind}) and a *social emotion update* (f_{social}), the latter being determined by emotion contagion. Thus, emotion revision function is given by the following equations:

$$f_{ind}(M, P, E) = c_{inc} * P - f_{dec}(\Sigma, E, P) \qquad (3)$$

where P is the personality trait and c_{inc} a constant defined as a model/experiment parameter. In equation 3, f_{dec} determines the set of inputs that decrease the emotion level of the agents, such as the perception of a plan in Σ:

$$f_{dec}(\Sigma, E, P) = \begin{cases} c_{dec} * P * SV_H(E), & if\ (seq(Pos_i), plan) \in \Sigma \\ 0, & otherwise \end{cases} \qquad (4)$$

where c_{dec} is a constant that determines the decrease in emotional strength, given the perception of the agent (plan). The social part of the revision function is determined by:

$$f_{social}(\Sigma, E) = \sum_{j \in Agents} \frac{(s_{ij}/s) * (SV_H(E) - SV_{H_j}(E_j))}{|Agents|} \qquad (5)$$

where s is the overall contagion strength of the agent as given in equation 2, and $|Agents|$ is the number of agents in the area of influence. Thus, the overall emotion function ${}^eF$ of Definition 3 is given in equation 7.

$$v'_H = SV_H(E) + f_{ind}(M, P, E) + f_{social}(\Sigma, E) \tag{6}$$
$$^e\Phi = (F_H(v'_H), v'_H) \tag{7}$$

where F_H is a mapping function between the emotion strength value v'_H and the crisp values of *Horror*. In the specific example the behaviour revision function ρ_φ, is simply given by equations 8 and 9.

$$\rho_\varphi(E, X) = \begin{cases} \Phi_{panic} & if\ SV_H(E) > 80 \\ \Phi - \{dissoriented\} & otherwise \end{cases} \tag{8}$$

$$\Phi_{panic} = \{wander\_around, dissoriented, found\_exit, read\_plan\} \tag{9}$$

5   From Formal Modelling to Simulation and Results

One the most important benefits in specifying a model using $^{em}\mathcal{X}$, is that due to the state based orientation of the latter, an executable model can be derived with relative ease. Such an executable model can be implemented in an agent simulation platform, for initial testing and evaluation of the agent specification. Refinements of $^e\mathcal{X}$ models to executable simulations in NetLogo [34] are reported in [31,27]. In this work we follow the same approach, by reusing parts of a domain specific language (DSL) for $^{em}\mathcal{X}$, augmenting the work described in the aforementioned papers appropriately to support the new meta model for emotions.

The evacuation area the agent model was tested against, was a shopping mall as the latter is depicted in Fig 3. In the figure, white areas represent shops were people (evacuees) are initially located. Exits are depicted a darker areas (red) on the top left and bottom center of the shopping mall. The figure presents the state of evacuation several time points after the alarm event occurs.

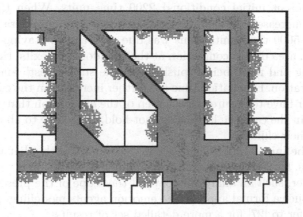

Fig. 3. The Shopping Mall Simulation Area

In the simulation environment, each individual is considered to occupy a 0.4 × 0.4 m space, as usual in evacuation simulations that follow the discrete space approach. The total area is about 3000 square meters. Evacuees located initially inside shops, upon perceiving the alarm, proceed to the exits, following evacuation plans (paths) that can be found in the form of instructions at shop doors. During the evacuation, increased emotional levels lead to the agent getting "lost", i.e. the agent is randomly exploring the shopping mall space, until it perceives new instructions from a door location and resumes evacuation. Such agents are depicted by a yellow (light) color in Figure 4.

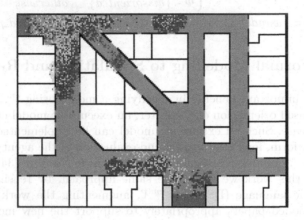

Fig. 4. The Shopping Mall Simulation Area a while after an alarm was issued

A set of experiments was conducted to demonstrate the feasibility of the model refinement and to obtain an initial insight on how emotions and emotion contagion can affect evacuation times. An initial set of experiments concerned 2000 evacuees on the office floor and the evacuation time was on average (10 runs with different initial conditions) 2200 time units. When the number of evacuees was increased to 4000, evacuation times were considerably longer, at an average of 5000 time units. This was due to evacuees staying longer inside the evacuation area due to congestion at the corridors and exits, their emotional level increasing and more being "pushed" to the state "Lost" and engage in a random exploration. Evacuation time are further increased in the case of parents, since the latter have to ensure at each step of the evacuation that their children are near, and in the case the latter does not hold, they have to abort evacuation and look for their children.

Although the initial experiments are in accordance with what is expected in such situations, further experimentation and model validation is required for the model. However, such an analysis is beyond the scope of the present work, that aims to introduce a formal approach to emotion agents modelling. An interested reader may refer to [27] for a more detailed set of results.

6   Related Work: Emotions in Artificial Agents

In previous work [31,27], we have attempted to plug-in emotions within the agent model. In fact, the definition of emotions $\mathcal{X}$-Machine contained E as a separate memory element with personality trait as part of the memory and with contagion only implied and hard-wired in emotion revision functions. That initial model was created to facilitate refinement to simulation and build confidence on validity of the models. The proposed revision of $^{em}\mathcal{X}$ with a meta-level machine is more elegant with respect to theory of state-based machines and leads to a more natural development of agent models; rational and emotional behaviour are modelled as two separate entities and thus susceptible to change without affecting one another.

There also exist a number of computational models of emotions, most of them logically formalised through the BDI framework. One of the first attempt was dMars, a BDI descendant, that comprised four modules, one of them being an emotional module [22]. The system was also provided with a personality component inside the emotional module which is comprised by three traits (a) the motivational concerns, i.e. tendency to specific goals, (b) an emotion threshold which represents the point at which an emotion is asserted and (c) the rate of decay for an emotion.

Another attempt is reported for the BDIE architecture, a modular model with embedded emotional capabilities and four segregated modules/systems: (a) *Perceptual* (belief), (b) *Emotional*, (c) *Behaviour* (Intentions), and (d) *Motivational* (Desires) [3]. The Emotional system takes into account primary (fear and surprise) and secondary emotions (happiness, sadness and anger) for the purpose of affective and cognitive appraisal respectively through the use of first and second level evaluators associated with the Perceptual system (Belief). Connected to all three other components, the Emotional system can affect the perceptual process, provide reactive capabilities and finally modifies behaviour.

Similar to the above is a conceptual BDI architecture with internal representations of *Affective Capabilities* and *Resources* for an Emotional Agent [24]. Capabilities were abstract plans available to the agent and Resources were the means that turn Capabilities into plans. Two new modules were introduced: (a) a *Sensing and Perception Module*, and (b) an *Emotional State Manager*. The first is responsible for capturing information from external stimuli. The latter comprised a set of artificial emotions with a decay rate function, and also controls capabilities and resources.

The DETT architecture for situated agents in combat simulation was presented in [33]. The emotional aspect of the DETT design lay on the OCC model [21] and is supported by two reasoning processes: an appraisal and an analysis process. Agents within the system sense their surroundings and other agents through a digital pheromone that they emit in the environment and decays over time. DETT introduces four new concepts: (a) *Disposition*, (b) *Emotion*, (c) *Trigger* and (d) *Tendency*. Dispositions are closely related to emotions in one-on-one relationship, e.g. irritability and anger or cowardice and fear, and can be thought as personality traits associated with an affective state. The appraisal process takes in to account the agents disposition and the current trigger belief (pheromone) and elicits an emotion that affects the analysis process by imposing a tendency on the resulting intention.

Finally, the PEP-BDI architecture [13] considers physiology, emotions and personality in the decision-making process. Emotions are based on OCC model [21]. A simplified personality model is used mapping specific personality traits as emotional tendencies. Later, the PEP-BDI was updated to model (a) *empathy* (the ability to understand and share the feeling of other), (b) *placebo* (a simulated and ineffectual treatment that has psychological benefits) and (c) *nocebo* (the opposite effect of placebo). The agent's emotions are a combination of three mechanisms: (a) *internal dynamics*, (b) *event dynamics* and (c) *external dynamics*.

In terms of emergency evacuation simulation, the role of emotions as well as the type of agents in emergency evacuation was widely explored. Since the focus of this work is on the theoretical model, an interested reader may refer to [32,35,19].

7   Conclusions

We have presented a formal method for emotional agent development. The basic characteristic of $^{em}\mathcal{X}$ is that formalising non-emotional and emotional behaviour can be regarded as two separate modelling activities, since there are two state-based machine, one for the former and a meta-machine for the latter. This also has a number of significant advantages on software development process, such as incremental refinement, testing and verification. We briefly showed how the models can turn to simulation by using the NetLogo framework and some results to demonstrate the visual behaviour of the model were presented.

It would be interesting to develop other models using different emotional structures, personality traits and emotional contagion approaches. Although $^{em}\mathcal{X}$ seem to be generic enough, it is a challenge to acquire valuable experience when dealing with a variety of theories, especially appraisal and communication. The next step towards this would be further experimentation with modelling and of course simulation of case studies on emergency evacuation and comparison of simulation results with real scenarios.

References

1. Bosse, T., Hoogendoorn, M., Klein, M.C.A., Treur, J., van der Wal, C.N.: Agent-based analysis of patterns in crowd behaviour involving contagion of mental states. In: Mehrotra, K.G., Mohan, C.K., Oh, J.C., Varshney, P.K., Ali, M. (eds.) IEA/AIE 2011, Part II. LNCS, vol. 6704, pp. 566–577. Springer, Heidelberg (2011)
2. Dalgleish, T., Power, M.: Handbook of Cognition and Emotion. John Wiley and Sons, Chichester (1999)
3. Hernandez, D.J., Oscar Deniz, J.L., Hernandez, M.: BDIE: A BDI like architecture with emotional capabilities. In: American Association for Artificial Intelligence Spring Symposium (2004)

4. dInverno, M., Luck, M., Georgeff, M., Kinny, D., Wooldridge, M.: The dMARS architechure: A specification of the distributed multi-agent reasoning system. Autonomous Agents and Multi-Agent Systems 9(1-2), 5–53 (2004)
5. Dranidis, D., Bratanis, K., Ipate, F.: JSXM: A tool for automated test generation. In: Eleftherakis, G., Hinchey, M., Holcombe, M. (eds.) SEFM 2012. LNCS, vol. 7504, pp. 352–366. Springer, Heidelberg (2012)
6. Durupinar, F.: From Audiences to Mobs: Crowd Simulation with Psychological Factors. Ph.D. thesis, Bilkent University, Department of Computer Engineering (July 2010)
7. Eleftherakis, G., Kefalas, P.: Model checking safety critical systems specified as X-machines. Analele Universitatii Bucharest Matematica-Informatica 49(1), 59–70 (2000)
8. Elster, J.: Rationality and the emotions. The Economic Journal 106(438), 1386–1397 (1996)
9. Fix, J., von Scheve, C., Moldt, D.: Emotion-based norm enforcement and maintenance in multi-agent systems: Foundations and petri net modeling. In: Proceedings of the 5th International Joint Conference on Autonomous Agents and Multiagent Systems, pp. 105–107. ACM (2006)
10. Hoogendoorn, M., Treur, J., van der Wal, C.N., van Wissen, A.: Modelling the interplay of emotions, beliefs and intentions within collective decision making based on insights from social neuroscience. In: Wong, K.W., Mendis, B.S.U., Bouzerdoum, A. (eds.) ICONIP 2010, Part I. LNCS, vol. 6443, pp. 196–206. Springer, Heidelberg (2010)
11. Ingrand, F.F., Georgeff, M.P., Rao, A.S.: An architecture for real-time reasoning and system control. IEEE Expert: Intelligent Systems and Their Applications 7(6), 34–44 (1992)
12. Ipate, F., Holcombe, M.: An integration testing method that is proved to find all faults. International Journal of Computer Mathematics 63(3), 159–178 (1997)
13. Jiang, H., Vidal, J.M., Huhns, M.N.: Ebdi: An architecture for emotional agents. In: AAMAS 2007: Proceedings of the 6th International Joint Conference on Autonomous Agents and Multiagent Systems, pp. 1–3. ACM, New York (2007)
14. Kefalas, P., Stamatopoulou, I., Sakellariou, I., Eleftherakis, G.: Transforming Communicating X-machines into P Systems. Natural Computing 8(4), 817–832 (2009)
15. Kleinginna, P., Kleinginna, A.: A categorized list of emotion definitions, with suggestions for a consensual definition. Motivation and Emotion 5, 345–379 (1981)
16. Lazarus, R.: Emotion and Adaptation. Oxford University Press (1991)
17. Marreiros, G., Santos, R., Ramos, C., Neves, J.: Context-aware emotion-based model for group decision making. IEEE Intelligent Systems 25(2), 31–39 (2010)
18. McCrae, R.R., Costa, P.T.: Validation of the five-factor model of personality across instruments and observers. Journal of Personality and Social Psychology 52(1), 81 (1987)
19. Miyoshi, T., Nakayasu, H., Ueno, Y., Patterson, P.: An emergency aircraft evacuation simulation considering passenger emotions. Computers & Industrial Engineering 62(3), 746–754 (2012)
20. Nair, R., Tambe, M., Marsella, S.: The role of emotions in multiagent teamwork. Who Needs Emotions (2005)
21. Ortony, A., Clore, G., Collins, A.: The cognitive structure of emotions. Cambridge University Press, Cambridge (1988)
22. Padgham, L., Taylor, G.: A system for modelling agents having emotion and personality. In: Cavedon, L., Wobcke, W., Rao, A. (eds.) PRICAI-WS 1996. LNCS, vol. 1209, pp. 59–71. Springer, Heidelberg (1997)

23. Parrott, W.: Emotions in Social Psychology. Psychology Press, Philadelphia (2001)
24. Pereira, D., Oliveira, E., Moreira, N., Sarmento, L.: Towards an architecture for emotional BDI agents. In: EPIA 2005: Proceedings of 12th Portuguese Conference on Artificial Intelligence, pp. 40–46. Springer (2005)
25. Petreska, I., Kefalas, P., Gheorghe, M.: A framework towards the verification of emergent properties in spatial multi-agent systems. In: Proceedings of the Workshop on Applications of Software Agents, pp. 37–44 (2011)
26. Rosenschein, S.J., Kaelbling, L.P.: A situated view of representation and control. Artificial Intelligence 73, 149–173 (1995)
27. Sakellariou, I., Kefalas, P., Stamatopoulou, I.: Evacuation simulation through formal emotional agent based modelling. In: 6th International Conference on Agents and Artificial Intelligence, ICART 2014, vol. 2- Agents, pp. 193–200. SciTePress (2014)
28. Santos, R., Marreiros, G., Ramos, C., Neves, J., Bulas-Cruz, J.: Personality, emotion, and mood in agent-based group decision making. IEEE Intelligent Systems 26(6), 58–66 (2011)
29. Sloman, A.: Beyond shallow models of emotion. Cognitive Processing: International Quarterly of Cognitive Science 2(1), 177–198 (2001)
30. Stamatopoulou, I., Kefalas, P., Gheorghe, M.: OPERAS: A formal framework for multi-agent systems and its application to swarm-based systems. In: Artikis, A., O'Hare, G.M.P., Stathis, K., Vouros, G. (eds.) ESAW 2007. LNCS (LNAI), vol. 4995, pp. 158–174. Springer, Heidelberg (2008)
31. Stamatopoulou, I., Sakellariou, I., Kefalas, P.: Formal agent-based modelling and simulation of crowd behaviour in emergency evacuation plans. In: 24th International Conference on Tools with Artificial Intelligence, ICTAI 2012, pp. 1133–1138. IEEE (2012)
32. Tsai, J., Fridman, N., Bowring, E., Brown, M., Epstein, S., Kaminka, G., Marsella, S.C., Ogden, A., Rika, I., Sheel, A., Taylor, M., Wang, X., Zilka, A., Tambe, M.: ESCAPES: Evacuation simulation with children, authorities, parents, emotions, and social comparison. In: Innovative Applications Track of the 10th Int. Joint Conf. on Autonomous Agents and Multiagent Systems (2011)
33. Van Dyke Parunak, H., Bisson, R., Brueckner, S., Matthews, R., Sauter, J.: A model of emotions for situated agents. In: AAMAS 2006: Proceedings of the Fifth International Joint Conference on Autonomous Agents and Multiagent Systems, pp. 993–995. ACM, New York (2006)
34. Wilensky, U.: NetLogo. Center for Connected Learning and Computer-Based Modeling, Northwestern Univ., Evanston, IL (1999), http://ccl.northwestern.edu/netlogo/
35. Zoumpoulaki, A., Avradinis, N., Vosinakis, S.: A multi-agent simulation framework for emergency evacuations incorporating personality and emotions. In: Konstantopoulos, S., Perantonis, S., Karkaletsis, V., Spyropoulos, C.D., Vouros, G. (eds.) SETN 2010. LNCS, vol. 6040, pp. 423–428. Springer, Heidelberg (2010)

Policies Production System for Ambient Intelligence Environments

Nikos P. Kotsiopoulos and Dimitris Vrakas

Department of Informatics, Aristotle University of Thessaloniki, Greece
{kpnikola,dvrakas}@csd.auth.gr

Abstract. This paper presents a tool for designing Policies that govern the operation of an Ambient Intelligence (AmI) environment in order to minimize energy consumption and automate every-day tasks in smart settlements. This tool works on top of a semantic web services middleware and interacts with the middleware's ontology in order to facilitate the designing, monitoring and execution of user defined rules that control the operation of a network of heterogeneous sensors and actuators. Furthermore, it gives the user the capability to organize these rules in tasks, in order to aggregate and discern relative rules. The main objective of this system is to provide a better monitoring and management of the resources, so as to achieve energy efficiency and reduce power consumption. The work presented in this paper is part of the Smart IHU project, which is developed at International Hellenic University.

Keywords: Policies, Sensor Networks, Ambient Intelligence, Smart Building, Energy Efficiency.

1   Introduction

Buildings are responsible for 40% of energy consumption and 36% of EU CO_2 emissions. Energy performance of buildings is key to achieve the EU Climate & Energy objectives, namely the reduction of a 20% of the Greenhouse gases emissions by 2020 and a 20% energy savings by 2020 [1]. Improving the energy performance of buildings is a cost-effective way of fighting against climate change and improving energy security, while also creating job opportunities, particularly in the building sector. In this context, efforts are currently focused on supplying energy efficient buildings with the appropriate energy resources, by assuring the operational needs with the minimum possible energy cost and environmental protection. To achieve this, a variety of smart management systems and architectures have been developed. All these systems are based on several technologies and concepts emerged the last few years, such as The Internet of Things, Wireless Sensor Networks, distributed computing, Semantic Data, etc.

The Internet of Things refers to uniquely identifiable objects (things) and their virtual representations in an Internet-like structure. The term Internet of Things was first used by Kevin Ashton in 1999 [2]. The concept of the Internet of Things first became popular through the Auto-ID Center and related market analysts publications [3].

A. Likas, K. Blekas, and D. Kalles (Eds.): SETN 2014, LNAI 8445, pp. 251–263, 2014.
© Springer International Publishing Switzerland 2014

Radio-frequency identification (RFID) is often seen as a prerequisite for the Internet of Things. RFID and sensor technology enable computers to observe, to identify and understand the world, without the limitations of human-entered data. Internet of Things frameworks might help support the interaction between "things" and allow for more complex structures like Distributed computing and the development of Distributed applications. Currently, they seem to focus on real time data logging solutions like Pachube [4]. Pachube is an on-line database service allowing developers to connect sensor-derived data (e.g. energy and environment data from objects, devices & buildings) to the Web and to build their own applications based on that data.

One of the main architectures that deployed under this concept is the Wireless Sensor Network (WSN). A WSN consists of spatially distributed autonomous sensors in order to monitor physical or environmental conditions, such as temperature, sound, vibration, pressure, motion or pollutants and cooperatively pass their data through the network to a specified location. Recently implemented networks are bi-directional, also enabling control of sensor activity. Nowadays such networks are used in many industrial and consumer applications, such as industrial process monitoring and control, energy management of a building, machine health monitoring, and so on.

The main characteristics of a WSN include: Power consumption constrains for nodes using batteries or energy harvesting, Ability to cope with node failures, Mobility of nodes, Dynamic network topology, Communication failures, Heterogeneity of nodes, Scalability to large scale of deployment, Ability to withstand harsh environmental conditions, Unattended operation and Power consumption. A recent article on agent-based simulation published in the IEEE Communications magazine gives examples and tutorials on how to develop custom agent-based simulation models for wireless sensors, mobile robots and P2P networks in a short period of time [5].

At this point, a very important framework needs to be considered. Semantic Web is a collaborative movement led by the World Wide Web Consortium (W3C) [6] that promotes common formats for data on the World Wide Web. By encouraging the inclusion of semantic content in web pages, the Semantic Web aims at converting the current web of unstructured documents into a "web of data". It builds on the W3C's Resource Description Framework (RDF). According to the W3C, "The Semantic Web provides a common framework that allows data to be shared and reused across application, enterprise, and community boundaries." [6] The main contribution of this framework is that data could be exchanged between machines, regardless the platform they are using, in a global, unified way.

The merging of the technologies mentioned above, allows the emergence of a new vision: the Ambient Intelligence (AmI) [8]. Ambient Intelligence implies a seamless environment of computing, advanced networking technology and specific interfaces. It is aware of the specific characteristics of human presence and personalities, takes care of needs and is capable of responding intelligently to spoken or gestured indications of desire, and even can engage in intelligent dialogue. Ambient Intelligence should also be unobtrusive, often invisible: everywhere and yet in our consciousness, nowhere unless we need it. Interaction should be relaxing and enjoyable for the citizen, and not involve a steep learning curve.

The concept of Ambient Intelligence (AmI) provides a vision of the Information Society where the emphasis is on greater user-friendliness, more efficient services support, user-empowerment, and support for human interactions. People are surrounded by intelligent intuitive interfaces that are embedded in all kinds of objects and an environment that is capable of recognizing and responding to the presence of different individuals in a seamless, unobtrusive and often invisible way.

As part of this research a tool is developed, which facilitates the monitoring and management of an ambient intelligence environment that keeps the above specifications. The user is provided with capabilities for synthesizing upper level rules that connect sensor data and actuators commands in a semantic way. In this way, the user can program the devices that are part of the network of the environment depending on his own preferences. Apart from the graphical definition of rules, the tool also embodies an execution module that collects real time sensor data, forms sets of triggered rules, resolves any upcoming conflicts based on information from the ontology and executes the selected rules by actually operating on the establishments devices.

The rest of the paper is organized as follows: The next section reviews related work in the areas of agent and rule based systems in the context of ambient intelligence environments. Section 3 presents the smart IHU infrastructure, focusing on the developed middleware based on SOA and its ontology. Section 4 presents in detail the policies designing tool and outlines its main capabilities, while section 5 concludes the paper and poses future directions.

2   Related Work

An energy management system (EMS) is a system of computer-aided tools used by operators of electric utility grids to monitor, control, and optimize the performance of the generation and power supply system. Under the concept of Smart Energy Management, two main categories of systems can be distinguished:

- **Agent-Based Systems:** Software agents are inherently distributed systems that offer a convenient way of modeling processes that are distributed over space and time. The combination of distributed and coordinated autonomy makes agent-based systems well-suited for a wide variety of problems in energy management. Areas of interest for the special issue, cover the full spectrum of agent-related topics applied to energy management. A Multi-Agent Approach to Electrical Distribution Networks Control and a heterogeneous agent-based monitoring and control system are presented in [14], [15].
- **Rule-Based Systems:** As far as Building Energy Management is concerned, in [12], an intelligent decision support model using rule sets based on a typical building energy management system is presented. This model can control how the building operational data deviates from the settings as well as carry out diagnosis of internal conditions and optimize building's energy operation. The system integrates a decision support model that contributes to the management of the daily energy operations of a typical building. Another field in which such systems can be integrated is hybrid vehicles. In [13], an overview of different control methods

is given and a new rule-based EMS is introduced, based on the combination of Rule-Based and Equivalent Consumption Minimization Strategies (RB-ECMS).

Usually the goals of an agent with an overall aim of energy efficiency and agents taking into consideration user preferences in a room are conflicting. One agent tries to maximize energy savings while other agents try to maximize user value. In terms of the Intelligent Building, this is the main trade-off. Another type of conflicting goal situation can be exemplified by the adjustment of temperature in a meeting room in which people with different preferences regarding temperature will meet. In addition to that, agent based systems sometimes need to reason under uncertainty which may lead to undesirable effects. The main characteristic of agent-based systems is that they are autonomous and they don't require human intervention. These systems are suitable when the aim is general power consumption reduction and efficiency and human monitoring is not required.

On the other hand Rule-Based systems are more suitable in the case that user wants certain operations to be performed under certain circumstances. These systems' main objective as well, is to provide power efficiency and better usage of resources. One benefit towards agent-based systems is that the computation time in rule-based systems is considerably smaller, as they don't take into consideration all the environmental parameters but just those who were selected by the user. Rule-based systems operate in an autonomous way defined by the user.

The system developed for this research belongs to the second category. It is a Rule-Based system that provides the user the capability to create and set policies under which an AmI environment will operate and manage its resources. In essence, user defines the behavior of the environment depending on its state. In that way, the system gives him the capability to act instantly towards the changes that occur in the environment without monitoring the devices himself. Furthermore, it provides him the option to form sequences of conditions that concern various changes in the state of the environment, which they could not be evaluated directly before, and lots of occurrences would have slipped through. In order to support portability, the system is platform-independent integrating a Web Services middleware.

One of the most important characteristic of the system is that it was designed to focus on the operations which the smart devices perform. By this way, the user does not need to know much information about the devices themselves but he can make his selections regarding the operations he wants to do.

On the following sections the architecture and the application that implemented the policies system, are analyzed.

3   System Overview

The Smart International Hellenic University (Smart IHU) project [9] is a research project in the field of Information Communication Technologies (ICT) for sustainable growth, energy efficiency and better quality of life. It follows the Green ICT guidelines and the prototype of the Smartbuilding/Smartgrid. The aim of the project is to design, develop and evaluate a platform consisting of sensor networks of smart devices, create a middleware for the integration of heterogeneous networks and provide a variety of functionalities.

3.1   Smart Building Overview

The Smart Building concept enables remote monitoring and management of processes while providing energy efficiency. The objective of this platform is to design, develop and evaluate a smart building in the International Hellenic University (IHU) and deliver the following services to the end users: Power Consumption Monitoring, Energy Efficiency savings and, Building Automation.

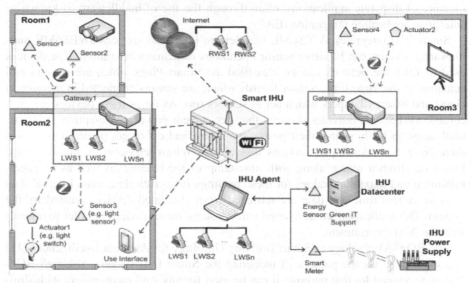

Fig. 1.   Architecture of the Smart University System

In the smart building environment, whose architecture is presented in Figure 1, a number of different sensors and gateways are placed throughout the building. The deployed networks involve different communication protocols, such as WiFi and Zigbee, and industry standards for the building automation. However, the proposed architecture introduces integration of different software architectures based on web services. More particularly, the system is designed for remote Internet-based operation: all building-wide monitoring and controlling capabilities are published in the form of modular web services, while automation design involves one centralized system to control the lights, electrical devices and room temperature in a room.

3.2   Information Integration

Smart IHU, as most ambient intelligence approaches, is based on the Service Oriented Architecture (SOA). SOA is a set of principles and methodologies for designing and developing software in the form of interoperable services. Smart IHU architecture, as presented in Figure 1, facilitates the integration of heterogeneous data by associating each sensor and actuator with Semantic Web Services, described in OWL-S and based on an ontology manager hosted in the IHU Agent.

3.3   Middleware and Ontology

In the computer industry, middleware is a general term for any programming that serves to "glue together" or mediate between two separate and often already existing programs. Typically, middleware programs provide messaging services, so that different applications on different platforms can communicate. The systematic tying together of disparate applications, often through the use of middleware, is known as enterprise application integration (EAI).

Smart IHU integrates aWESoME middleware [10]. The services aWESoME middleware provides, can be either sensor operations or actuator operations. The devices used to form the network can be classified as: Smart Plugs which are sensors and actuators at the same time, Sensor Boards which are sensors connected in a common board and Smart Clampers which act as sensors too. As far as these devices are concerned, aWESoME provides services that get current power consumption in Watts, total usage in kWh, switch their power supply on and off or get power status. Also there have been developed services that always return temperature, humidity and luminance from a sensor along with timestamp of the reading, as well as averages, minimum and maximum values for these readings in a given time span. Internal data such as system time and date are retrieved from simulated services created by the system. The application we developed will consume these services in order to interact with the AmI environment.

The BOnSAI ontology (a Smart Building Ontology for Ambient Intelligence) [11] is implemented for the purpose of modeling the Smart IHU system. Although BOnSAI is developed for that purpose, it can be used for any AmI environment with similar characteristics. It is designed to maintain all the relevant information about the devices, the services and the operations they provide, the attributes of the environment or even characteristics of the user. Operations of the services provided, are classified into sensor operations and actuator operations. This discrimination is substantial for segregating the operations in relevance to their function. As far as actuator operations are concerned, the user can define which operations are conflicting with each other, in order to prevent concurrent activation of them.

4   Prestige

The Smart IHU architecture which complies with the principles defined in an AmI environment requires high-level applications that will facilitate and manage its operation. PRESTIGE (a Policies Production System for AmI Environments) is a desktop application developed under this framework, Figure 2. It implements a rule-based system for energy management of an AmI environment. Its main objective is to provide better monitoring and management of the resources, so as to achieve energy efficiency and reduce power consumption.

4.1   Technical Specifications

The tool is implemented in Java programming language. JDK 7 and its relevant API are used for the design of the system's data structures and functions. The GUI (Graphical User Interface) is developed with java swing, the primary java GUI widget toolkit. Swing was preferred against AWT because it provides more powerful and flexible components.

PRESTIGE is based on the BOnSAI ontology [11] and aWESoME middleware which we mentioned above. The system derives from BOnSAI all the relevant information for the attributes and characteristics of the Smart IHU environment. This information includes data about the devices and the functions they perform, the services and their operations, the parameters of the environment and their domain, the location of every component in the environment and finally, data about the actions and the effects they have. For that purpose, Apache Jena framework [15] is used. Jena is a Java framework for building Semantic Web applications. PRESTIGE makes use of the ontology API for handling OWL and RDFS ontologies, which is provided, in order to retrieve all the relevant data from a specific BOnSAI ontology file which is an instantiation of an AmI environment. All the data retrieved, are stored in static data structures designed to maintain all the needed information.

In order to use the services that manage and monitor the devices, aWESoME middleware is integrated in the system. The services are classified according to the operation they perform into two main categories: to those who perform sensor operations and to those who perform actuator operations. This discrimination is made at BOnSAI ontology instantiation. Sensor Operations are used to form policies under which specific Actuator Operations will be performed. Any service that makes use of a device(Sensor, Actuator), takes device's ID as input, unlike to those who are used for monitoring which have no input. The connection with aWESoME middleware is established with the deployment of Web Service Clients which consume the WSDL descriptions of the services provided by the middleware. For that purpose, Java API for XML Web Services (JAX-WS) is used [17].

4.2   Operation

The tool's main operation is to provide the user the capability to form policies under which, specified actions will be performed in an AmI environment. The system retrieves all the data regarding the service operations from the ontology file of instances when application is initiated. After the tool is started, four main functions are provided:

(i) *Rules Synthesis:*
The system gives the user the capability to organize rules in tasks, in order to aggregate and discern relative rules. Thus, the first thing to do is to create a new task or load an

already saved one. Then he can add new rules or edit them. All these operations can be initiated either from menus or from the relevant toolbar buttons, as shown in Figure 2. A rule consists of conditions (at least one) and actions (at least one). A condition is a comparison expression in which the left part is the parameter (luminance level, power consumption, temperature, etc) that the user wants to check and the right part is the value for the comparison. The real-time value of this parameter is obtained by a web-service which interacts with the relevant sensor device. The domain of the value is defined by the parameter, in the ontology. At that point, where the user chooses to create a condition, the tool gives him a list of sensor operations, a list of devices that support the selected operation, a list of comparison symbols depending on the operation and a corresponding value field to fill in. After the user makes his choices he can add the condition. Since a condition is created, the user can edit the conditions list adding new ones or deleting them.

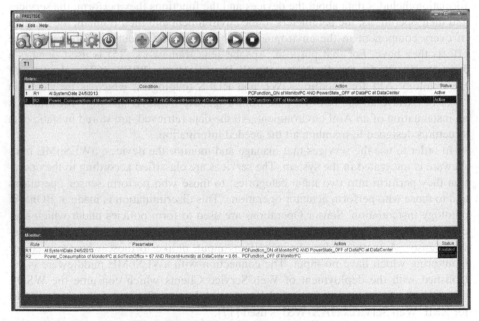

Fig. 2. PRESTIGE application main interface

In correspondence to that, the same procedure must be done for inserting actions (turn on or off devices, set luminance level, etc), which are assignment expressions. When user chooses to insert an action, the tool gives him a list of actuator operations to choose, a list of devices that support the selected operation and a relevant value field depending on the operation. The actions which are created by the user for a specific rule are bind together with logic "AND" as well as the conditions. This means that the actions of a rule will be ready for execution only if all the conditions which are set for that rule, are verified. In addition to the above, the user has to assign a number to the rule he wants to add. This number has a range from 1 to 100 and is used to represent the priority of a rule towards another. The smaller the number, the higher priority is set for this rule. The priority factor will be used in order to avoid simultaneous execution of conflicting rules. Finally, since the user has inserted all the conditions and actions needed, he can choose to add the rule. The rule is then created by the tool from the condition and action lists and is inserted in the rule table of the selected task. Every rule is assigned to a specific ID that defines it. Since a rule is created, subsequently the user can edit it, remove it or add new rules (each rule is independent of another).

(ii) Monitoring:

Every task integrates two lists: the list of all the rules that are composed by the user, upper table in Figure 2 and the monitoring list, bottom table in Figure 2, which includes all the activated rules. The activated rules are the ones that the user selected from the rules list, in order to be monitored and evaluated. A rule is idle by default. In case the user activates a rule (a capability provided by the tool) then the rule is automatically inserted in the monitoring list. The monitoring list is managed by a thread which runs in parallel to the application. This thread scans the list consecutively at a predefined period of time and checks the rules included in it. If all the conditions of an active rule are verified then the conflict resolution mechanism (described below) is triggered, in order to determine whether the actions of the rule will be performed or not. All the rules that are verified and executed, constitute the execution set. At anytime, user can disable an already active rule, which means that rule is removed from monitoring list and becomes idle.

(iii) Conflict Resolution:

The rules that contain actions which can be performed at the same time and affect the same device, changing its state, are conflicting. To ensure that conflicting rules cannot be executed simultaneously, a control mechanism is introduced. Whenever all the conditions of a rule are verified and the relevant actions are about to be performed, this mechanism is applied in order to conclude whether the rule will be executed or not, based on a priority factor selected by the user and the execution set. The rule is compared with the others that are included in the execution set. If the rule's action conflicts with another that has lower priority according to the factor selected, then the action is performed and the rule enters the execution set. The other rule with the lower priority is excluded from the set. PRESTIGE provides to the user a list of four factors to choose. At anytime, the user can select from the menu which one of the factors below will be used. These factors are:

- **Priority Number:** A number with a range from 1 to 100. This number is inserted when user creates a rule, as described above. The lower the number the bigger priority for the rule.
- **Earliest Time of Activation (ETOA):** The rule that was activated first, will have bigger priority against a conflicting rule that was activated later.
- **Latest Time of Activation (LTOA):** The rule that was activated last, will have bigger priority against a conflicting rule that was activated earlier.

- **Rule Length:** The more conditions a rule consists of, the lower priority it has. This factor can be used for rules that are created for a specific device and consist of one or two conditions.

Looking into recent conflict resolution literature, a lot of interesting approaches can be found. In [18] a representation model, called contextual defeasible logic is presented along with a proposed algorithm for distributed query evaluation that implements the proof theory of contextual defeasible logic. In addition, a rule-based recognition system for hierarchically-organized activities is proposed in [19]. This system returns only logically consistent scenarios. In our implementation we used the control mechanism, described above, in order to make the conflict resolution function easier to be configured and more transparent towards the user.

(iv) Execution:
The execution of a rule regards the application of the actions that includes. Every action concerns an operation that will be performed by a web-service that controls a specific actuator device. The web-service that is assigned for this operation is triggered and the relevant action is performed. An executed rule is indicated with the label "Enabled" in the monitoring list, first rule in Figure 2. In case the rule is not verified or rejected by the conflict resolution mechanism, it is not executed and it is indicated with the label "Disabled", second rule in Fig. 2. In the following section, a real-life scenario of using PRESTIGE in a Smart Building is presented.

4.3   Real-Life Scenario

In order to evaluate the operation of the tool, a real-life scenario created which includes various rules and multiple tasks. The tool was set to run on a smart Building that complies with the specifications of the Smart IHU architecture. The scenario consists of five tasks, Table 1. The first task (Environment) is about monitoring environmental parameters, the second (Power) is about reducing power consumption reduction and the third (Time) is about performing actions at predefined date and time. These tasks are generic and concern the management of the building. The last two tasks (Lab, Office) are more specific and handle the operation of the devices in two rooms. The rules for each task are implemented according to the procedure that is indicated in section 4.2. For instance, regarding the first rule of the environmental task, we selected to monitor the external temperature and humidity and to turn off all the PCs in the building in case that the conditions we set for these attributes are verified. This rule's priority number is set to 1. Before this rule is activated, the monitoring time was set to 40 seconds, the priority number is selected as priority factor and the office and lab task's rules with priority number equal to 4, were already executed. When this rule is activated and enters the monitoring list, the web-services which retrieve the data from temperature and humidity sensors respectively, are triggered every 40 seconds. If the values retrieved verify both the conditions, then the conflict resolution mechanism is applied on every action that is going to be performed. The execution set consists of the two rules mentioned above. The mechanism detects the conflict regarding the state of the Monitor PC. Based on the priority factor, the action of the first rule of the environment task which has higher priority is executed and the office task's rule is excluded from the execution set. Whenever any other rule of either task is activated, the same procedure is followed. The table of all the tasks and rules created for this scenario is shown below:

Table 1.   Table of policies divided into three tasks

Task	Condition(s)	Action(s)
Environmental	Temperature at Data Center > 47 AND Humidity > 80%	Turn OFF Data PC at Data Center AND Turn OFF Monitor PC AND Turn OFF Mainframe
	Temperature at Office < 17 Light > 70%	Turn ON Radiator at Office Set Luminance Level to 40%
Power	Power Consumption at Lab > 800	Turn OFF Data PC AND Turn OFF Mainframe
	Calibration of Data PC > 2	Turn OFF Data PC
Time	At 13:00 pm	Turn ON Mainframe
	After 25/4/12 AND at 11:00 pm	Turn OFF Radiator at Lab
Lab	At 8:30 pm	Turn ON Data PC
Office	At 9:00 pm	Turn ON Monitor PC

5   Conclusions

Research activity in Ambient Intelligence field is growing rapidly nowadays. Nevertheless, there are still many matters and issues to be considered. The huge number of capabilities and functionalities that an AmI Environment can provide makes management even more difficult and complex. The main objective for an Ami Environment is to be able to adapt its operation in proportion to interaction with human or elements incorporated in it.

In terms of AmI technology there have been proposed and developed many applications and architectures under which an AmI system will be constructed and operate. IHU (International Hellenic University) deployed such an architecture, Smart IHU. This specific project regards the implementation of a 'Smart' Building according to the standards of an AmI System. The main target of Smart IHU, is the efficient management of the devices of the settlement in correspondence to the state of the environment they belong, so as to achieve power efficiency and much better usage of the available resources. So far, several tools have been developed to support its operation, which aim to provide remote management and administration of the system for a certified user.

One functionality that was not provided by any other system, was the ability towards the user to program the devices to adapt their operation in an autonomous way, any time they sense a sequence of events/changes that occur in the environment.

This conception, led to the implementation of a policies writing system by which a user will be able to create rules that define the operation of the devices of the AmI environment.

PRESTIGE (a Policies Writing System for AmI Environments) which is presented in this paper, is a tool that we developed for this purpose. It provides the user the capability to program the operation of the devices, defining conditions upon which relevant actions will be performed. PRESTIGE was set to operate in Smart IHU environment for almost a year and proved to be very effective. By using this system, the user has a much more effective supervision of the AmI Environment. Certainly, there are many improvements to be done, in order to make the system more independent and efficient.

References

1. Directive 2010/31/EU of 19 May 2010 on the energy performance of buildings
2. Ashton, K.: That 'Internet of Things' Thing. In: RFID Journal (July 22, 2009). Abgerufen am (April 8, 2011)
3. Analyst Geoff Johnson interviewed by Sue Bushell in Computerworld (July 24, 2000) (M-commerce key to ubiquitous internet)
4. Panchube Project, http://community.pachube.com/about
5. Niazi, M., Hussain, A.: Agent based Tools for Modeling and Simulation of Self-Organization in Peer-to-Peer, Ad-Hoc and other Complex Networks, Feature Issue. IEEE Communications Magazine 47(3), 163–173 (2009)
6. XML and Semantic Web W3C Standards Timeline (February 4, 2012)
7. W3C Semantic Web Activity. World Wide Web Consortium (W3C) (November 7, 2011)
8. Zelkha, E., Epstein, B., Birrell, S., Dodsworth, C.: From Devices to "Ambient Intelligence". In: Digital Living Room Conference (June 1998)
9. Stavropoulos, T.G., Tsioliaridou, A., Koutitas, G., Vrakas, D., Vlahavas, I.P.: System Architecture for a Smart University Building. ICANN (3), 477–482 (2010)
10. Stavropoulos, T.G., Vrakas, D., Arvanitidis, A., Vlahavas, I.: A System for Energy Savings in an Ambient Intelligence Environment. In: Kranzlmüller, D., Toja, A.M. (eds.) ICT-GLOW 2011. LNCS, vol. 6868, pp. 102–109. Springer, Heidelberg (2011)
11. BOnSAI Ontology, http://lpis.csd.auth.gr/ontologies/ontolist.html
12. Doukas, H., Patlitzianas, K.D., Iatropoulos, K., Psarras, J.: Intelligent building energy management system using rule sets. Building and Environment 42(10), 3562–3569 (2007)
13. Hofman, T., Steinbuch, M., van Druten, R.M., Serrarens, A.F.A.: Rule-based energy management strategies for hybrid vehicle drivetrains: A fundamental approach in reducing computation time. In: 4th IFAC Symposium on Mechatronic Systems 2006 (2006)
14. Prymek, M., Horak, A.: Multi-agent approach to power distribution network modelling. Integr. Comput.-Aided Eng. 17(4), 291–303 (2010)
15. Ponci, F., Cristaldi, L., Faifer, M., Riva, M.: Multi agent systems: An example of power system dynamic reconfiguration. Integr. Comput.-Aided Eng. 17(4), 359–372 (2010)
16. Jena Project, http://incubator.apache.org/jena/
17. JAX-WS Reference Implementation (RI) Project, http://jax-ws.java.net/

18. Bikakis, A., Antoniou, G.: Contextual Defeasible Logic and Its Application to Ambient Intelligence. IEEE Transactions on Systems, Man and Cybernetics, Part A: Systems and Humans 41(4), 705–716 (2011)
19. Filippaki, C., Antoniou, G., Tsamardinos, I.: Using Constraint Optimization for Conflict Resolution and Detail Control in Activity Recognition. In: Keyson, D.V., et al. (eds.) AmI 2011. LNCS, vol. 7040, pp. 51–60. Springer, Heidelberg (2011)

Nature-Inspired Intelligent Techniques for Automated Trading: A Distributional Analysis

Vassilios Vassiliadis and Georgios Dounias

Management and Decision Engineering Laboratory, Department of Financial and Management Engineering, University of the Aegean, 41 Kountouriotou Str. GR-82100, Greece
v.vassiliadis@fme.aegean.gr, g.dounias@aegean.gr

Abstract. Nowadays, the increased level of uncertainty in various sectors has posed great burdens in the decision-making process. In the financial domain, a crucial issue is how to properly allocate the available amount of capital, in a number of provided assets, in order to maximize wealth. Automated trading systems assist the aforementioned process to a great extent. In this paper, a basic type of such a system is presented. The aim of the study focuses on the behavior of this system in changes to its parameter settings. A number of independent simulations have been conducted, for the various parameter settings, and distributions of profits/losses have been acquired, leading to interesting concluding remarks.

Keywords: automated trading system, ant colony optimization, technical indicators, distributional analysis.

1   Introduction

In the financial sector, there are a number of crucial issues, which affect the decision-making process. Market news, corporate developments and a vast network of individual investors' choices, all of them play a vital role in the formation of the global financial picture. If any technological advances are added in the above factors, it can be easily understood that the decision-making process is not an easy task, by no means. In the financial domain, interesting tasks to be tackled could be the following: forecast/predict the future price of an asset, optimally allocate the available amount of capital in a number of assets, produce buy/sell signals based on a set of technical rules, whose main purpose is to identify market trends, patterns or other characteristics. In this paper, the problems of optimal asset allocation and finding proper buy/sell signals are tackled with the application of an automated trading system.

An automated trading system refers to the implementation of a specific trading strategy, which comprises a set of rules and technical indicators [1]. Automation assists the trading process to a great extent, especially if someone considers merits such as the elimination of emotional trading (by the individual investor), more consistent behavior etc. What is more, efficient algorithms are able to handle the vast amount of available information leading to quick decisions. In this paper, in particular, the work focuses on the application of a hybrid nature-inspired intelligent system as the first

A. Likas, K. Blekas, and D. Kalles (Eds.): SETN 2014, LNAI 8445, pp. 264–272, 2014.

component of the trading process, and afterwards a set of technical rules based on statistical properties.

Nature-inspired intelligence consists of algorithms, whose strategy stems from the way real-life systems and networks work and evolve. They are stochastic problem-solving approaches, aiming at approximating the optimal solutions, most of the time leading to a near-optimum point. However, due to their effective searching strategies, this solution is acceptable both in terms of execution time and quality. Two of the most widely applied algorithms of this category are the Ant Colony Optimization (ACO) and the Particle Swarm Optimization (PSO) algorithms [2].

The aim of this paper is to present the applicability of such a trading system, and study its behavior through a parameter tuning process. Results are based on independent simulation leading to distribution of outcomes, which partially eliminates the issue of stochasticity, in a way. This kind of analysis leads to interesting remarks, as it will be shown. The current paper is organized as follows. In section 2, a brief presentation of automated trading systems is shown. In section 3, the proposed trading system is presented. In section 4, the statistical properties of the simulations' results are discussed and analyzed. Finally, in the last section, some interesting concluding remarks are outlined.

2   Literature Review

Automated trading is not necessary related to the application of artificial intelligent schemes. In this section, the focus is going to be to automated trading facilitated by the use of intelligent algorithms. In [1], the design and optimization of an automated trading system is discussed. The optimization process refers to the parameter tuning of the technical indicator used, i.e. MACD, and the aim of the paper is to enhance the performance of the system itself. Results indicate that the optimized settings of the technical indicator work generally better than default ones. In [6], an emulation of a trading system consisting of rules based on combinations of different indicators at different frequencies and lags is presented. At first, a genetic algorithm is applied in order to produce an initial portfolio (set) of trading rules. Afterwards, a Genetic Programming type algorithm is used in order to produce these new rules, using this initial population of rules. Data consist of US Dollar/British Pound spot prices from 1994 to 1997. The best produced rule found by the developed system is found to be modestly, but significantly, profitable. In [7], authors introduce adaptive reinforcement learning as the basis for a fully automated trading system, designed to trade on foreign exchange markets. The specific intelligent algorithm applied was recurrent reinforcement learning (RRL). The trading system comprises three stages: the basic trading system (layer 1), the risk and performance layer (layer 2) and the parameter optimization layer (layer 3). Layer 1 refers to the application of RRL, whereas layer 2 evaluates trade recommendations by considering additional risk factors related to the real world conditions, before taking the final decision. A quite interesting approach is presented in [8], where a genetic algorithm based fuzzy neural network is applied in order to formulate the knowledge base of fuzzy inference rules which can measure the qualitative effect on the stock market. As a next step, these effects are integrated with technical indicators through the artificial neural network. Data from the Taiwan stock market were used to assess the utilization of the proposed hybrid scheme. Results indicate that the NN considering both the quantitative and qualitative factors performs better than simpler cases. In another study [9], an adaptive computational intelligence system for learning and evolving trading rules is proposed. The rules are represented using a fuzzy logic rule base, whereas an evolution process similar to the genetic algorithm is applied in order to enhance their ability. Data consist of stocks for the period 1999-2005. Simulation results indicate that the proposed intelligent scheme can beat both individual trading rules and market indices. Finally, an important and quite recent study [10] deals with the parameter optimization process of technical indicators, with the use of a nature-inspired intelligent algorithm, namely the particle swarm optimization (PSO). PSO optimizes the weights of the technical indicators. The proposed system is compared to individual technical indicators, the market itself, and another trading system optimized by a genetic algorithm-based MOO method. Results indicated that the system performed well in both training and testing data sets.

As it can be seen by the previous analysis, trading systems are standardized processes. They might refer to the management of technical indicators or even more complex systems. The important thing to note is that computational intelligence may provide suitable algorithms which can enhance the performance of the system at hand, thus leading to better decision-making for investors.

3   Automated Trading-System

Within the framework of this study, the proposed automated trading system comprises of two individual processes. More specifically, the first one deals with the formation of an optimal asset portfolio, whereas the latter one aims at producing buy/sell signals based on the price fluctuations of the constructed portfolio (which can be referred as a 'synthetic asset'). In the current section, a brief description of these components is going to be made.

Optimal portfolio construction is a challenging task for decision makers. In essence, the goal is to find a combination of assets, and the corresponding percentage of capital to be invested in each one of them, in order to optimize a given objective and satisfy some realistic constraints. The first person who provided a complete framework for this kind of problems was Harry M. Markowitz, with his seminal paper [11]. In this study, the optimization problem is decomposed into two sub-problems. The first one refers to the optimal asset selection, whereas the second one deals with optimal weight (percentage of capital invested in each asset) calculation. For the construction of the synthetic asset, Ant colony optimization algorithm (ACO) [12] was applied. In the process of constructing the synthetic asset, a mathematical programming methodology, namely the Levenberg-Marqardt algorithm (LMA) [13], is applied for weight calculation. The synthetic asset is constructed in the training interval.

A set of technical indicators are, then, applied to the constructed asset in the investing interval (out-of-sample data). These indicators are applied separately, so each one of them provides a different profit/loss profile. The first one is based on the concept of moving averages and is called the Moving Average Convergence Divergence (MACD) [14]. The second one is a typical investors' benchmark, which is based on buying the underlying asset in the beginning of the investing interval and selling it at the end of it.

At this point, it is crucial to highlight specific aspects of the proposed trading scheme, which refer to the time period of analysis:

- The investing interval succeeds the training interval, and can be considered as unknown data to the system.
- The two intervals do not overlap.
- The system is not static, but it moves through time (rolling window concept), and can be explained as follows. Let us consider that the first estimation time interval contains the first $1:n$ observations. In this sample, the fund is optimally constructed. Thereafter, in time interval $n+1:n+1+m$, technical indicators are applied to the fund. The next estimation interval is defined at the time period $1+rw:n+rw$, where rw is the length of the rolling window. The corresponding forecasting interval as $n+rw+1:n+rw+1+m$. This is repeated until the full time period under investigation is covered.

In order to make this point clearer, an example from the first time period is provided. Based on the parameters shown below, the first estimation interval is 1:100, in which the hybrid algorithm (ACO with LMA component) is applied with the aim of finding a near-optimum, if not the optimal, portfolio. The optimization problem is shown below. Then, the optimized fund is traded in the forecasting interval, 101:150, in which two commonly used technical rules are applied separately. In essence, buy and sell signals are traced in this time period. As it is aforementioned, the system is dynamic. The next fund is constructed in the following time interval 26:125, and it is traded in the interval 126:175. So, estimation and forecasting interval of different, but not the same, funds do overlap.

Finally, we outline the optimization problem:

Objective: $\qquad\qquad Maximi(\mathrm{w}): U_0$

$$\text{s.t.}$$

$$D_0 < H$$

$$\sum_{i=1}^{k} w_i = 1$$

$$w_l \leq w_i \leq w_u, i = 1, \dots, k$$

$$k = N$$

where,

U_0, is the upside deviation defined as $U_0 = \sqrt{\int_0^\infty (r)^2 * p_r(r)dr}$ for a specific distribution of portfolio's returns. The measure of upside deviation refers to the part of positive returns, in the distribution. Investors aim at maximizing this objective.

D_0, is the downside deviation defined as $D_0 = \sqrt{\int_{-\infty}^0 (r)^2 * p_r(r)dr}$ for a specific distribution of portfolio's returns. In other words, it measures the deviation of negative returns from zero. This is an unwanted attribute from the investors. In our case, this metric is considered as a restriction and it must not exceed a certain threshold [15].

$[w_l\ w_u]$, are the upper and lower acceptable percentages for capital invested in each asset.

k, is the cardinality constraint, referring to the maximum allowable number of assets included in the portfolio.

In the following figure, the overall trading mechanism is depicted.

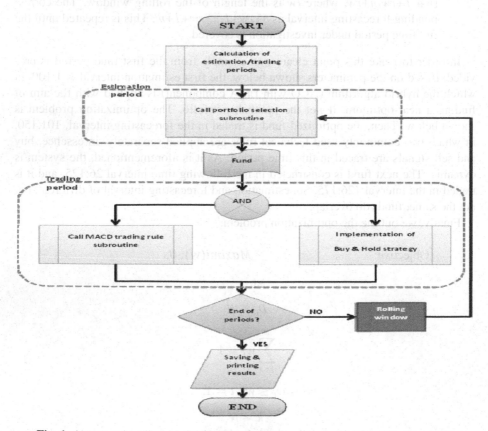

Fig. 1. Automated trading mechanism based on nature-inspired intelligent components

4   Simulation Results

As it was aforementioned, in order to get a better understanding of the algorithmic system's behavior, a set of 100 independent simulations were executed, for various combinations of settings. In the following table, the parameter settings both for the algorithms and the optimization problem are presented.

Table 1. Parameter settings

Ant Colony Optimization Algorithm	
Population	100/200
Generation	20/30
Evaporation rate	70%
Percentage of best ants (applied in the solution update process)	10%
Portfolio Optimization problem	
Cardinality	10
[wl wu]	[-0.5 0.5]
H (downside deviation of DJIA[1])	0.0106
System's parameters	
Estimation time interval	100
Forecasting time interval	50
Rolling window	25

Dataset comprises daily closing prices of 30 stocks from the Dow Jones Industrial Average (DJIA) for the time period 03/Jan/2005 - 11/Nov/2011. This time period was characterized by instability and many uptrend and downtrend cases.

In Table 2, the main statistical measures describing a distribution are presented. Numbers in the table's cell refer to profit/loss achieved by the system, in each case.

For each one set of parameters, 100 independent runs of the trading system were executed. The main reason for doing that was the stochastic behavior of the nature-inspired component (i.e. ant colony optimization algorithm). In each single run, the 'optimal' portfolio (synthetic asset) found by the ACO algorithm was different, thus leading a number of profit/loss profiles. So, the distribution produced by the set of independent executions could shed some light as far as the behavior of the NII technique is concerned, and how this affects the profit/loss of the overall strategy.

The main statistical measures used to describe the distribution were: average profit/loss, standard deviation, skewness, kurtosis, and maximum and minimum value. As the table indicates, increasing the number of generations by 50%, slightly affects the

---

[1] DJIA stands for Dow Jones Industrial Average. This financial index is considered by many experts as the market representative – benchmark.

Table 2. Basic statistical measures for the simulations' results

	Population 100 /generation 20	Population 100/ generation 30	Population 200/generatio n 20	Benchmark
Average value	1014,1	1018,2	1079	592,6
Standard deviation	531,1	489,9	504,5	749,3
Skewness	0,0783	-0,097	0,1956	0,2633
Kurtosis	2,428	2,5449	2,9134	2,2574
Maximum	2311,5	2038,4	2617	2236,1
Minimum	-19,9	-289,1	-58,4	-809,6

mean value, in a positive way. However, it sure yields a more narrow distribution (values around the mean) as the standard deviation decreases. Values of skewness indicate that in both cases the majority of profits/losses are centered on the mean value. Kurtosis in both cases approximates the value of 3, which is characteristic of the normal distribution. An odd outcome is that both the maximum and minimum profit/loss is smaller in the case where the number of generations increased. This should make us skeptical and cautious before leading to a safe conclusion. However, it was expected that the increase of the number of generations could yield better results. On the other hand, increasing the size of population by 100%, induce a clearer effect on the mean value (and the overall distribution, as well). The average profit has been increased at about 6,5%, and in the same time the standard deviation of profits/losses has been decreased at about -5%. Skewness and kurtosis lead to the same remark, i.e. the distribution of results approaches the case of normal distribution. The maximum value has increased 13,22%, whereas the minimum value has decreased at about 190%. Ignoring the effect on the minimum value, the overall picture of the distribution has shown that by increasing the size of population, the trading system is guided to better solutions, from an investor's point of view.

Moreover, in order to highlight some aspects of the proposed system's efficiency, results from a standard benchmark technique are presented in the last column of table 2. The benchmark's specific characteristic is that it incorporates a random searching algorithm, rather than an intelligent technique, in order to form the synthetic asset. As it can be seen from the basic statistical analysis, the distribution yielded from the independent simulations of the random benchmark averages low, in comparison to the intelligent technique. Also, the standard deviation of profits is very large, partly explained by the large difference between the minimum and maximum value. Skewness and kurtosis are almost comparable to the other cases. However, as it is mentioned above, the difference is obvious in the measures of average value and standard deviation.

5   Conclusions

In the scope of this study, a type of automated trading system has been presented. The system consists of two basic components: a NII algorithm for constructing the synthetic asset, and a set of technical indicators for producing buy/sell signals based on the behavior of this asset. The NII applied, was ACO algorithm, which is based on the way a real-life ant colony works and evolves. This trading scheme may act as a decision support tool for individuals, who are interested in investing in financial markets and in the same time taking into consideration much of the economy's information.

Due to the stochasticity of the system, mainly the NII component, a number of independent simulations were executed, for various values of the parameter settings. Therefore, the authors wanted to check the behavior of the profit/loss profile in each case. Based on the outcomes, a preliminary assumption might be that the size of population positively affects the system's performance. However, this cannot be said for the number of generations, as it would be expected. What is more, the proposed trading system yields better result than a standard financial benchmark, namely the random portfolio selection method.

A main future goal is to provide results from additional simulation experiments, so as to lead to safer conclusions regarding the system's performance. More parameters should be checked, as well. What is more, a set of simulations using other NII algorithms, such as genetic algorithms, particle swarm optimization (PSO) algorithm etc., are underway.

References

1. Tucnik, P.: Optimization of Automated Trading System's Interaction with Market Environment. In: Forbrig, P., Günther, H. (eds.) BIR 2010. LNBIP, vol. 64, pp. 55–61. Springer, Heidelberg (2010)
2. Brabazon, A., O'Neill, M.: Biologically Inspired Algorithms for Financial Modeling. Natural Computing Series. Springer, Heidelberg (2006)
3. Carter, J.F.: Mastering the Trade-Proven Techniques from Intraday and Swing Trading Setups. McGraw-Hill, New York (2006)
4. Kaufman, P.J.: New Trading Systems and Methods, 4th edn. John Wiley & Sons, New Jersey (2005)
5. Tucnik, P.: Automated Trading System Design. In: Godara, V. (ed.) Pervasive Computing for Business: Trends and Applications. IGI Global, Sydney (2010)
6. Dempster, M.A.H., Jones, C.M.: A real-time adaptive trading system using genetic programming. Quantitative Finance 1, 397–413 (2001)
7. Dempster, M.A.H., Leemans, V.: An automated FX trading system using adaptive reinforcement learning. Expert Systems with Applications 30, 543–552 (2006)
8. Kuo, R.J., Chen, C.H., Hwang, Y.C.: An intelligent stock trading decision support system through integration of genetic algorithm based fuzzy neural network and artificial neural network. Fuzzy Sets and Systems 118, 21–45 (2001)
9. Ghandar, A., Michalewicz, Z., Schmidt, M., To, T.D., Zurbrugg, R.: Computational Intelligence for Evolving Trading Rules. IEEE Transactions on Evolutionary Computation 13(1), 71–85 (2009)

10. Briza, A.C., Naval, P.C.: Stock trading system based on the multi-objective particle swarm optimization of technical indicators on end-of-day market data. Applied Soft Computing 11, 1191–1201 (2011)
11. Markowitz, H.: Portfolio Selection. The Journal of Finance 7(1), 77–91 (1952)
12. Dorigo, M., Stultze, M.: Ant Colony Optimization. MIT Press (2004)
13. More, J.J.: The Levenberg-Marquardt algorithm: Implementation and Theory. Lecture Notes in Mathematics, vol. 630, pp. 103–116 (1978)
14. Appel, G.: Technical Analysis Power Tools for Active Investors. Financial Times Prentice Hall (1999)
15. Kuhn, J.: Optimal risk-return tradeoffs of commercial banks and the suitability of probability measures for loan portfolios. Springer, Heidelberg (2006)

Combining Clustering and Classification for Software Quality Evaluation

Diomidis Papas[1] and Christos Tjortjis[2]

[1] Department of Computer Science & Engineering, University of Ioannina
P.O. Box 1186, GR 45110 - Ioannina, Greece
[2] School of Science & Technology, International Hellenic University
14th km Thessaloniki – Moudania, 57001 Thermi, Greece
c.tjortjis@ihu.edu.gr

Abstract. Source code and metric mining have been used to successfully assist with software quality evaluation. This paper presents a data mining approach which incorporates clustering Java classes, as well as classifying extracted clusters, in order to assess internal software quality. We use Java classes as entities and static metrics as attributes for data mining. We identify outliers and apply K-means clustering in order to establish clusters of classes. Outliers indicate potentially fault prone classes, whilst clusters are examined so that we can establish common characteristics. Subsequently, we apply C4.5 to build classification trees for identifying metrics which determine cluster membership. We evaluate the proposed approach with two well known open source software systems, Jedit and Apache Geronimo. Results have consolidated key findings from previous work and indicated that combining clustering with classification produces better results than stand alone clustering.

1 Introduction

Quality evaluation is an important software engineering issue, addressed by various methods, in many cases involving metrics [1][2]. As the volumes of code produced increase so does the need for automating the process. Experience shows that collecting and analyzing fine grained test defects from large, complex software systems is difficult [1]. Data mining has been shown to facilitate quality evaluation when applied directly to source code as well as metrics extracted from code [3][4][5].

Static analysis using software quality metrics means that the code is analyzed without having to execute the program [2]. Static analysis tools for finding low-level programming errors are especially useful for evaluating maintainability, understandability, testability and expandability of the software [6]. Static analysis can also be applied early in the development process, to provide early fault detection, at a point where the code does not have to be fully functional, or even executable. Several tools of this nature already exist [7]. However size scaling challenges obstruct the evaluation of large data sets. Static analysis is unlikely to be adopted for improving software quality in the real world if it does not scale beyond small benchmarks.

In order to deal with this issue, we propose static analysis, using object oriented metrics combined with data mining techniques for analyzing large and real-world

A. Likas, K. Blekas, and D. Kalles (Eds.): SETN 2014, LNAI 8445, pp. 273–286, 2014.

software systems. Using these metrics reflects a software system's source code attributes, such as volume, size, complexity, cohesion and coupling. Our approach is suitable for Java systems, which can easily be extended to cater for other object oriented languages. Data mining in static analysis allows for managing large volumes of data and is capable of producing unexpected results. This work does not only focus on software quality assessment, but also assesses the suitability of metrics for the evaluation, which is a useful and novel part of the evaluation process.

In order to do so, we identify outliers and employ K-means for clustering Java classes together according to their metric related similarity. Outliers are candidates for manual inspection, as they may be fault prone. Subsequently we use clusters as class labels and employ C4.5 decision tree classification algorithm for evaluating the selected metrics, in order to reflect their importance on defining clusters and evaluate software quality. Using C4.5 allows for establishing which metrics play an important role in the evaluation process and highlights metrics which do not affect tree building. We used source code from various large open source java systems in order to validate this approach. Experiments indicated that combining clustering with classification produces better results than stand alone clustering.

The rest of this paper is organized as follows: background and related work are discussed in section 2. Section 3 details the approach. Experimental results for validating the approach are described in section 4. Section 5 briefly discusses evaluation issues and threats to validity. The paper concludes with directions for future work in section 6.

2   Background and Related Work

Different quality metrics can be used to evaluate source code [8]. Chidamber and Kemerer in their seminal work [9] proposed the following metrics, now known as CK Suite: Weighted Methods per Class (WMC), Response For a Class (RFC), Depth of Inheritance Tree (DIT), Number Of Children (NOC), Coupling Between Object classes (CBO), Lack of Cohesion in Methods (LCOM). Several additions to the CK Suite have been made to cater for complexity [10]. Other metrics often used in quality assessment include Halstead's Maintainability Index (MI) [11], McCabe's Cyclomatic Complexity (CC) [12] and Lines Of Code (LOC). Various techniques have been proposed for analyzing source code and improving software development and maintenance.

Metrics help efficiently assessing software quality; however, they can be hard to manually calculate for vast amounts of code. Several approaches employ data mining to extract useful information from metrics for large software systems [3][13][14][15]. Details on object oriented metrics and rational for their selection can be found in [16]. Related work on object oriented source code can also be found in [17] where a subset of the CK object oriented metrics was used.

Mining large data volumes poses challenges, starting off with data preprocessing, metric and algorithm selection [18]. Clustering, and in particular K-means, has been used for mining source code and metrics, due to its simplicity and low-time complexity. It requires pre-defining the number of clusters K, but selecting a suitable value for

K can be done by running a number of experiments, depicting the Sum of Squared Error (SSE) over K and identifying a "knee" in the diagram [19]. Identifying outliers can be also very useful, given that these represent "unusual" instances.

Classification, on the other hand, has not been extensively used for source code metrics, despite its simplicity and ability to extract rules that can be easily understood and interpreted by users. Decision trees classifiers produce descriptive models suitable for source code assessment.

Tribus et al. [5] focused on using classifiers for knowledge discovery and troubleshooting software written in C. Menzies et al. used data mining to predict errors and assist large project management [4]. They used metrics such as McCabe's CC, Halstead's MI as well as LOC for C code, and classifiers such as C4.5. Prasad et al. proposed an approach for source code evaluation by knowledge engineering [23]. It discovers weaknesses and errors in code using text mining, specifically using the frequency of words or symbols in C++ code.

Alternative approaches were formulated previously by Antonellis, et al. [17], where the criteria for code quality evaluation were associated with the ISO/ICE-9126 standard for software maintainability, which also includes functionality, efficiency and portability. Object-oriented metrics were used to measure class similarity, assess software maintainability and manage large systems [21][22]. We use this work that showed the correlation between source code analysis and classes' similarity as a foundation for this paper, particularly for selecting object-oriented metrics and clustering algorithms, for analyzing, understanding, and controlling software.

3   Approach

This section presents the proposed approach which: (i) extracts metrics from Java code, (ii) finds outliers and potentially fault prone Java classes, and clusters classes based on their similarity according to selected metrics, and (iii) categorizes clusters using classification, in order to get insights into the clustering results and to produce a description model capable of assessing metric values in each cluster, with regards to their ability to evaluate software quality.

3.1   Preprocessing and Outlier Detection

Initially, the source code is parsed to extract data, such as variable names, functions, dependencies and calculate metrics for every class, such as cohesion, coherence, complexity and size. Data and metrics are stored in a database [20]. Each class is treated as a vector with as many dimensions as the number of attributes (metrics) used, that is seven.

At this point we can look for extreme points (outliers) in the 7-dimensional space. The existence of outliers can indicate individuals or groups that display behavior very different from most of the individuals of the dataset. Outlier detection has many applications, including data cleaning. In order to do so, we use the Inter-Quartile Range (IQR) technique, used for describing the spread of a distribution.

It is based on the graphical technique of constructing a box plot, which represents the median of all the observations and two hinges, or medians of each half of the data set. Most values are expected in the interquartile range (H) to be located between the two hinges. Values lying outside the ±1.5H range are termed as "mild outliers" and values outside the boundaries of ±3H as "extreme outliers". This method represents a practical alternative for manual outlier detection, in the case of examining each variable class individually, and proves to be very efficient in handling multidimensional values.

Frequently, outliers are removed to improve the accuracy of the estimators, but sometimes, deleting an outlier that has a certain meaning, means also deleting its certain explanation. In our case, despite of the fact that we find outliers, that does not block out the continuation of the process, because they are part of the software source code considered.

3.2   Clustering Methodology

The next step involves clustering Java classes and corresponding metrics using k-Means to establish similarity, without outlier removal. Keeping outlier classes is advisable as they are not an effect of noise or faulty information, but part of the software. For determining the most appropriate number of clusters K, we took into account that a small number of clusters is desirable in this domain, as it provides better software overview and essentially easier error or weakness prediction. A grouping into a large number of clusters would not facilitate error discovery; k-Means is fast for small values for K.

k-means is repeatedly executed providing information on data smoothness. The measure used here is the Sum of Squared Error (SSE). Selection of the right SSE requires several iterations of the algorithm, which increases considerably the duration of the process, but produces alternative sets of clusters and, in several cases, a "knee" in the diagram indicates an appropriate value for K.

It should be noted that, although the values for K we are interested in is small enough to facilitate software analysis and comprehension, there is no 'right' or 'wrong' cluster number. The "ideal" K is defined either using the SSE or by analyzing each set of clusters and the classes they contain. Collected results are stored in tables and clusters are analyzed for controlling the characteristic values for each cluster, as well as, the uniformity using the mean and variance.

3.3   Classification into Clusters Methodology

In the final step of the process, a decision tree is built, using C4.5 in order to get insights into any source code vulnerabilities. Internal nodes of the tree correspond to some metric and leaves represent clusters. C4.5's use of information gain serves not only for categorizing data, but also for highlighting which metric is higher in the tree hierarchy. Metrics that play more important role in node splitting are the most effective on clustering.

C4.5's post-pruning evaluates the estimated misclassification error at each node and propagates this error up the tree. At each node, C4.5 compares the weighted error of each child node with the misclassification error, if the children nodes were pruned assigned as the class label of the majority class. So, metrics that had no part in cluster separation are not present in the tree hierarchy and their ability to evaluate software quality is deemed low.

Metrics that are present in the tree hierarchy characterize the clusters. In other words, we can test the utility of every metric on a specific data set. Adding up to previous results, we conclude that it would take more clusters to be able to separate into groups, according to the different characteristics evaluated. When these metrics are missing, the software presents universality and regularity. However, as the clustering process divides the source code into clusters with related classes, there is no need for extended division of the existing clusters. Thus, through the descriptive model is created a subway map for software evaluation leading to clusters.

It is a handy and informative way to identify weaknesses in the software source code, and certainly a way to know which metric values need improvement, to migrate any class to a different cluster. It is also a useful guide, for the developers, when extending the software, since they know that the desired characteristics need to have classes created with the objective of smoothness and good software design. Certainly, it is not an illustrative tool that can operate standalone.

4   Experimental Results

This section describes experiments conducted to analyze and find weaknesses in source code of Java open source systems. We detail here two case studies: a code editor and an application server. First we describe the experimental setup.

1. Extract and store software metrics in a database using Java Analyzer [20]. For the remaining steps we used Weka [19].
2. Apply Outlier detection with IQR in order to detect classes with special or exceptional characteristics. This process identifies fault-prone areas of code that require further testing. A maintenance engineer is able to access these classes directly, as they are shown separated from the rest of the source code. We do not remove these classes for the rest of the process.
3. Apply k-Means Clustering to classes based on their metric values. We select a low SSE value, in order to ensure that the classes in the same cluster are similar as opposed to classes in different clusters.
4. As soon as the clustering process is finished, the maintenance engineer can look into each cluster separately, in order to judge for every cluster, but he/she can get an overview of the system without having to examine each class separately.
5. Finally we classify the clusters that are formed in step 3, in order to assess the ability of metrics to evaluate software quality. Building the decision tree enables analyzing the ability of each metric to support software quality assessment.

4.1   Case Study 1: JEdit

JEdit is an open source code editor for 211 programming languages, written in Java and well-known to java developers [24]. Its large size and public availability make it suitable for data mining and for result replication if needed. We used 4 recent versions of JEdit (4.3, 4.4.1, 4.5 and 5.0), in order to be able to compare results and track evolution traits. We applied preprocessing and looked for outliers in versions 4.3, 4.4.1, and 4.5; outlier classes are available in all editions. High complexity, outlier classes and corresponding WMC values are shown in Table 1.

Table 1. *JEdit* outlier classes

Class Name	WMC
Parser	351
GUI Utilities	71
ActionHandler	41

Table 2. Clustering 4 versions of *JEdit*

Version	Classes	Outliers	Clusters	SSE
4.3	808	172	14	6.1
4.4.1	935	182	4	7.7
4.5	953	-	5	9.7
5.0	1077	155	5	10.5

We conducted outlier qualitative analysis and observed classes which have sufficiently high RFC, i.e. classes with many local methods, thereby reducing code extensibility, and in many cases associated with high complexity and large LOC. As a result, controlling these classes is quite difficult, whilst scalability is limited. Regarding inheritance, we observed low values for DIT and NOC, which limit code reuse. Finally, there are outliers with very little consistency, resulting in reduced encapsulation and data encryption. Greater method consistency means better class implementation.

Next we applied clustering. Table 2 displays comparative experimental data from analyzing each of the 4 versions of JEdit. SSE shows how close to each other are the classes in clusters, as points in the 7- dimensional space. Avoiding outlier removal resulted in outliers getting grouped together into clusters with extreme values for some metrics. Such clusters are observed in all of JEdit's versions.

A typical example is the 2nd cluster in JEdit 4.4.1, which contains only four classes. Typical outlier class here is *Parser* with 366 LOC and 44 CBO. Also, a cluster found in JEdit 5.0 consisting of 42 classes, contains the same classes as the corresponding cluster of JEdit 4.4.1. An important observation is that in each version of JEdit there was one cluster containing the largest part of the code, except from classes that have high or low values on some metrics, such as outliers, classes associated with the Graphical User Interface (GUI) or interface classes.

The final step of the process involves cluster classification, and produced similar results for all the JEdit versions. This step attempts to assess the metrics' ability to evaluate software quality and determine how easy it is for each metric to partition the code. This provides useful information related to code disadvantages and aspects the design team has to focus on. Fig. 1 shows part of the pruned tree with 99.48 % accuracy created by C4.5 for JEdit 4.5.

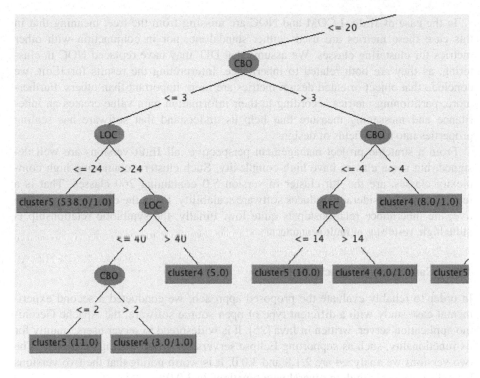

Fig. 1. Classification results for *JEdit*

All cases of classifying clusters in JEdit with pruning had a confidence factor of 0.25. However, increasing confidence factor did not improve accuracy. For instance, when confidence factor set to 1 and the tree is not pruned, results were the same. So, we found that omitting pruning did not improve accuracy, and, given that pruned trees are easier to understand one could opt for skipping pruning.

<table>
<tr><th colspan="3">Table 3. JEdit: metric hierarchy</th></tr>
<tr><th>#</th><th>Metric</th><th>Metric Type</th></tr>
<tr><td>1st</td><td>DIT</td><td>Inheritance</td></tr>
<tr><td>2nd</td><td>RFC</td><td>Messaging</td></tr>
<tr><td>3rd</td><td>CBO</td><td>Coupling</td></tr>
<tr><td>4th</td><td>LOC</td><td>Volume</td></tr>
<tr><td>5th</td><td>WMC</td><td>Complexity</td></tr>
</table>

Table 3. *JEdit*: metric hierarchy

Table 4. Clustering *Geronimo*

Version	Classes	Clusters	SSE
2.1.8	2.523	5	51.1
3.0.0	3.100	7	3128

In the case of JEdit, LCOM and NOC are missing from the tree, meaning that in this case these metrics are used neither standalone, nor in conjunction with other metrics for clustering classes. We assume that DIT may have replaced NOC in clustering, as they are both related to inheritance. Interpreting the results for JEdit, we conclude that object oriented design metrics are more important than others. Furthermore, partitioning metrics according to their information gain value creates an inheritance and messaging measure that help us understand that software has scaling properties into these fields of design.

From a strategic project management perspective, all JEdit versions are well designed, but some classes have high complexity. Such clusters, containing high complexity classes, are the 4th cluster in version 5.0 containing 260 classes. That is a feature which considerably reduces software scalability. From the code reuse perspective, the inheritance relationship is quite low. Finally, the symbiotic relationship is quite high, resulting in fault proneness.

4.2   Case Study 2: Apache Geronimo

In order to reliably evaluate the proposed approach, we conducted a second experimental case study with a different type of open source software, the Apache Geronimo application server, written in Java [25]. It is widespread to server users, mainly for its functionality, such as supporting Eclipse servers for group writing Java code. The two versions we analyzed are 2.1.8 and 3.0.0. It is worth noting that the two versions have differences, including several new functions in 3.0.0.

This time we did not preprocess for finding outliers and extreme values. It is a large software system, and we wanted to analyze all the code and evaluate the characteristics of clustering in grouping outliers. Thus, groups of outliers were expected to be displayed after clustering [18]. First we clustered version 2.1.8. The iterative process did not result in finding a 'knee' in the curve of SSE, a fact that complicated the selection of K. The uniformity of the SSE and the number of clusters show that the code is consistently written. Nevertheless, 5 is a number of clusters where the slope of the SSE curve starts stagnating. So it is preferred to choose k=5 as this is also a convenient number of groups of classes, as explained earlier.

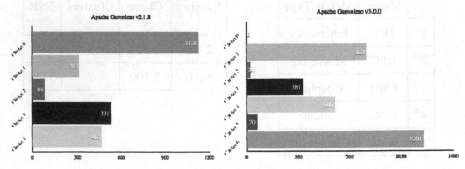

Fig. 2. Clustering results for *Apache Geronimo* v.2.1.8 & 3.0.0

As far as version 3.0.0 is concerned, in a similar fashion we chose K=7. The figure below shows how the SSE decreases in relation to the number of clusters. As we see, the curve displays a knee between 3 and 4, but the slope of the SSE is large also between 3 and 10. This shows that a good K, is between 3 and 10 and will be chosen according to our needs. R should not be too large, because of the difficulty of further analysis results e.g. K = 50. For the continuity of the selected number of clusters, the SSE varies linearly with the number of clusters.

Observing the distribution of clusters in the two versions, we see that it has changed enough, nevertheless, in both cases there are clusters with small numbers of classes, outliers, mainly due to complexity and coherence. Their percentage in the case of version 2.1.8 is 3% of the total code (Cluster 3) while in case of 3.0.0 constitutes 2.3% (Cluster 5). Whilst in the same direction as the previous version, the clusters of the next version contain the same classes. From a strategic perspective, the versions of Geronimo are well written and the most crowded classes have good metric values and require no special changes. The fact that some classes have larger size than others should not be of concern, as it is expected that some classes of the system to handle more data and functions than others.

Generally, the system is not badly designed; nevertheless one could reduce the consistency of complex classes breaking them into smaller, thus distributing functionality. Considering classes with many correlations, that are directly related, one could try reducing the connections. Cluster 0 of version 3.0.0 appears to have large children with several abstract classes, which could help future software expansion. Increasing the heredity in relation to the earlier version, indicates that the designers were concerned about future extensions, while moving in the same direction and reducing the complexity in relation to the number of classes.

In the next part of the experiment, we classify classes according to the previously resulted clusters, aiming at understanding important each metric is in affecting the clustering process. In other words, we try to explain and evaluate the ability of every metric used for clustering in the evaluation, to partition the software. In the case of Apache Geronimo, the classification process produced more complex results, as its size was bigger than JEdit. The size of the generated tree for 5 clusters in version 2.1.8 was 59 and the total number of leaves was 30. Again, as with JEdit, the highest information gain metric was DIT, followed by RFC. It is interesting that both versions of Geronimo produced the same metric hierarchy in the classification tree, as well as identical results with JEdit at the top and bottom of the tree. Table 5 displays the metric hierarchy produced by classification for Apache Geronimo.

In the case of classification accuracy, C4.5 misclassified seven instances (0.28% classification error) with confidence factor 0.25. We also examined other options in the classification process in order to find better results. The results without pruning were not better results in terms of accuracy but changed the metric hierarchy. More specifically, WMC was found second in the hierarchy along with RFC, in order to classify instances from clusters with outliers with big complexity.

Table 5. Apache *Geronimo* 2.1.8: metric hierarchy

#	Metric	Metric Type
1st	DIT	Inheritance
2nd	RFC	Messaging
3rd	LOC	Volume
4th	CBO	Coupling
5th	LCOM	Cohesion
6th	WMC	Complexity

We did not use the unpruned tree to evaluate the ability of the metrics because of the complexity of the tree consisting of 92 nodes, which appeared to merge metrics in order to find a good classification result. Using all of the metrics reduced accuracy from 99.72% to 99.33%. We continued trying out our options with 0.1 confidence factor, where accuracy was only reduced to 99.25% whilst reducing the tree size to 55 with 28 leaves.

5   Evaluation and Threats to Validity

The proposed evaluation was based on two criteria: firstly, it should be flexible, suitable and easy for analyzing systems and for assessing the ability of metrics to evaluate quality of systems with different functionality and nature. Secondly, it should be valid, reflecting the views and intuitions of the experts. Based on these criteria, we conducted two case studies on JEdit and Apache Geronimo, open source Java applications.

The aim of these case studies was to evaluate the selection of metrics, as well as the approach for assessing software quality. Starting with the evaluation and the selection of the metrics, we used a very popular suite, the CK metric suite [10] and a metric extraction application, which was made in order to extract and save the metric information from java source code [20]. The metric extraction rules we follow are described in section 2.

The proposed approach aims at finding weaknesses in source code, by identifying outliers and discovers classes that require attention by the software engineers. In section 4, we suggested several classes that need the attention of a supervisor software engineer. Search classes in modern software are oversized so their management becomes quite difficult; controlling such classes is quite laborious. The previous subprocess produces good results as the clustering of classes. In this part of the process we used a statistical overview. The IQR is a famous and useful path to find outliers in an unknown allocation. In our case, they were different across systems we tested, so validating the process was an important decision.

Thereafter, according to the proposed approach, we group similar classes through clustering. We display groups of classes with similar characteristics, which are not necessarily related to the class that implements them. Ranking the classes in clusters is determined by their distances, according to the values of their variables. This is suitable for their evaluation, regardless of their function, particularly in cases where the assessment has to be extended in the software. It is possible that someone outside the software development team can control the operation of the group.

The clustering process also has supervisory scope by the supervisor of the development team, and who can recognize the parts of code (clusters) which need better design. With regards to the validity of this process, we used SSE to guarantee that classes in the same cluster are correlated and classes in different clusters are not. With the continuous examination of the number of clusters, we tried to achieve the best possible result for their selection, so that a small number of them characterize the entire cluster population.

After the clustering process, we continue to the final and the most crucial part of the approach, where we use classification to access the ability of the metrics to evaluate the software. The aim of this process is to assess the ability of each metric to evaluate software quality depending on their ability of partitioning classes into clusters. We used the well known classification algorithm C4.5, which uses information gain as a splitting criterion. Also, by using pruning, we aim to display only the important metrics. Metrics that are not displayed in the tree do not play a crucial role in software evaluation.

Aiming to facilitate managerial decision making development, a decision tree is used as a classifier, with the objective knowledge about the behavior of groups that were created by clustering. Assistance is provided through understanding clusters, and the manager's decision to lead their team to draw lines using set point measures that lead to clusters with desired characteristics. Also, the decision tree can be used to understand the weaknesses of the source, as observed in the experimental procedure and the case of Apache Geronimo, where many classes were not reusing code without using data abstraction.

6   Conclusions and Further Work

We propose a source code quality evaluation approach, based on static analysis, using object oriented metrics. The use of these metrics reflects attributes, such as volume, size, complexity, cohesion and coupling. This work also focuses on assessing metric suitability for evaluation, which is to the best of our knowledge is novel. In order to do so, we employ C4.5 to evaluate the selected metrics and source code attributes in order to reflect their importance on evaluating software quality. By using this decision tree algorithm, we can separate the metrics which had a premium role in the process of evaluation and also make a decision related to the metrics participation in the process of quality evaluation.

Despite the positive results of this approach, there are certain limitations. The most important limitation is the lack of full automation, as decisions have to be made during the data mining process. This limitation may be overcome with further work on the availability of open source big projects and the ability to track to big companies' projects.

The proposed approach produces good results in the field of fault behavior detection with data preprocessing, grouping/organizing the classes with clustering techniques and finally categorizing the clusters using a description model with classification, so project managers have the ability to understand better the advantages and disadvantages of code. This approach facilitates maintenance engineers to identify classes which are fault prone and more difficult to understand and maintain, as well as, to assess the capability of expanding the system.

Data preprocessing and mining object oriented metrics extracted from source code, has the desirable result of testing driven by the metric characteristics instead of conducting directly changes on the source code. That reflects the most important aspects of a system concerning its quality and maintainability. The selected metric suite is the CK-suite [9], a well-known metric suite used for measuring the design of object oriented programs.

Starting with data preprocessing we chose the IQR statistical method because of its capability to respond to unknown data distributions, where the spread of the values is unknown, and differs across systems. In other words, with this type of preprocessing we can propose a small volume of likely fault prone classes, in a large class collection, so that the maintenance team, instead of checking all of the source code can immediately check the potentially fault prone proposed classes.

Secondly, we employ k-Means in order to manage large volumes of classes. k-Means offers a popular solution for clustering data, depending on their distance in space. Clustering utilizes the selected metrics for measuring distance. Every class is represented by a 7-dimension vector in space, so the algorithm works iteratively in order to group the classes. Classes with similar characteristics tend to be on the same cluster and non-associated classes are placed in other clusters. Then, we characterize each cluster as a single version of a category. Instead of just statistically analyzing the clustering results for evaluating metrics, we propose a classification process, using C4.5 in order to categorize clusters according to the features (metrics) used for node splits. This analysis facilitates decision making and assists categorization of clusters of similar classes using a decision tree.

In addition, we have experimented with several open source systems. Arguably, more can be done to expand the data sets to be used, both in terms of identifying systems of different kinds, and identifying important and relevant flaws and other software problematic behavior.

The results of our experiment show, that using clustering and classification algorithms on software metrics can facilitate fault prone classes detection and create system overviews, so further analysis can easily take place. In addition, maintainability and extendibility can be assessed by the "clustering followed by classification" technique we propose.

We plan to use other clustering techniques such as density based or hierarchical clustering in the future, given that the number of clusters is not known in advance. Using human experts will also consolidate validating the approach.

To sum up, the proposed approach provides a data mining model that can be used to discover useful information about software internal quality according to selected metrics. Different metric suites may assess software quality from another point of view. Data mining is a dynamic field and providing potential adjustments to software engineering offers notable results, especially as there is a growing need for discovering new methods to address contemporary software systems.

Acknowledgements. We would like to thank F. Vartziotis for providing his Java Source Code Analyzer.

References

[1] Tian, J.: Quality-Evaluation Models and Measurements. IEEE Software 21, 84–91 (2004)

[2] Li, H.F., Cheung, W.K.: An Experimental investigation of software metric and their relationship to software development effort. IEEE Transaction on Software Engineering 15(5), 649–653 (1989)

[3] Kanellopoulos, Y., Makris, C., Tjortjis, C.: An Improved Methodology on Information Distillation by Mining Program Source Code. Data & Knowledge Engineering, Elsevier 61(2), 359–383 (2007)

[4] Menzies, T., Greenwald, J., Frank, A.: Data Mining Static Code Attributes to Learn Defect Predictors. IEEE Transactions on Software Engineering 32(11), 2–13 (2007)

[5] Tribus, H., Morrigl, I., Axelsson, S.: Using Data Mining for Static Code Analysis of C. In: Zhou, S., Zhang, S., Karypis, G. (eds.) ADMA 2012. LNCS (LNAI), vol. 7713, pp. 603–614. Springer, Heidelberg (2012)

[6] Bush, W.R., Pincus, J.D., Sielaff, D.J.: A Static Analyzer for Finding Dynamic Programming Errors. Software-Practice and Experience 20, 775–802 (2000)

[7] Spinnelis, D.: Code Quality the Open Source Perspective. Addison Wesley (2006)

[8] Fenton, N.E.: Software Metrics: A Rigorous Approach. Cengage Learning EMEA (1991)

[9] Chidamber, S.R., Kemerer, C.F.: Towards a Metrics Suite for Object Oriented Design. In: Proc. Conf. Object Oriented Programming Systems, Languages, and Applications (OOPSLA 1991), vol. 26(11), pp. 197–211 (1991)

[10] Chidamber, S.R., Kemerer, C.F.: A metrics suite for object oriented design. IEEE Transactions on Software Engineering 20(6), 476–493 (1994)

[11] Halstead, M.: Elements of Software Science. Elsevier (1977)

[12] McCabe, T.J.: A Complexity Measure. IEEE Transactions on Software Engineering SE-2(4), 308–320 (1976)

[13] Dick, S., Meeks, A., Last, M., Bunke, H., Kandel, A.: Data mining in software metrics databases. Fuzzy Sets and Systems 145(1), 81–100 (2004)

[14] Zhong, S., Khoshgoftaar, T.M., Seliya, N.: Expert-Based Software Measurement Data Analysis with Clustering Techniques. IEEE Intelligent Systems, Special Issue on Data and Information Cleaning and Preprocessing, 22–30 (2004)

[15] Nagappan, N., Ball, T., Zeller, A.: Mining Metrics to Predict Component Failures. In: Proc. 28th Int'l Conf. Software Engineering (ICSE 2006), pp. 452–461 (2006)

[16] Kanellopoulos, Y., Antonellis, P., Antoniou, D., Makris, C., Theodoridis, E., Tjortjis, C., Tsirakis, N.: Code Quality Evaluation methodology using the ISO/IEC 9126 Standard. Int'l Journal of Software Engineering & Applications 1(3), 17–36 (2010)

[17] Antonellis, P., Antoniou, D., Kanellopoulos, Y., Makris, C., Theodoridis, E., Tjortjis, C., Tsirakis, N.: Employing Clustering for Assisting Source Code Maintainability Evaluation according to ISO/IEC-9126. In: Proc. Artificial Intelligence Techniques in Software Engineering Workshop (AISEW 2008) in ECAI 2008 (2008)

[18] Dunham, M.H.: Data Mining: Introductory and Advanced Topics. Pearson Education (2006)

[19] Witten, I.H., Frank, E.: Data Mining: Practical machine learning tools and techniques, 2nd edn. Morgan Kaufmann (2005)

[20] Vartziotis, F.: Java Source Code Analyzer for Software Assessment, BSc Dissertation, Department of Computer Science & Engineering University of Ioannina (2012)

[21] Kanellopoulos, Y., Heitlager, I., Tjortjis, C., Visser, J.: Interpretation of Source Code Clusters in Terms of the ISO/IEC-9126 Maintainability Characteristics. In: Proc. 12th European Conf. Software Maintenance and Reengineering (CSMR 2008), pp. 63–72. IEEE Comp. Soc. Press (2008)

[22] Antonellis, P., Antoniou, D., Kanellopoulos, Y., Makris, C., Theodoridis, E., Tjortjis, C., Tsirakis, N.: Clustering for Monitoring Software Systems Maintainability Evolution. Electronic Notes in Theoretical Computer Science, Elsevier 233, 43–57 (2009)

[23] Prasad, A.V.K., Krishna, S.R.: Data Mining for Secure Software Engineering-Source Code Management Tool Case Study. Int'l Journal of Engineering Science and Technology 2(7), 2667–2677 (2010)

[24] JEdit website, http://www.jedit.org (last accessed: January 15, 2014)

[25] Apache Geronimo website, http://geronimo.apache.org (last accessed: January 15, 2014)

Argument Extraction from News, Blogs, and Social Media

Theodosis Goudas[1], Christos Louizos[2],
Georgios Petasis[3], and Vangelis Karkaletsis[3]

[1] Department of Digital Systems
University of Piraeus
Athens, Greece
theodosis.fox@gmail.com
[2] Department of Informatics & Telecommunications
University of Athens
Athens, Greece
chr.louizos@gmail.com
[3] Software and Knowledge Engineering Laboratory,
Institute of Informatics and Telecommunications,
National Centre for Scientific Research (N.C.S.R.) "Demokritos",
GR-153 10, P.O. BOX 60228, Aghia Paraskevi, Athens, Greece
petasis,vangelis@iit.demokritos.gr

Abstract. Argument extraction is the task of identifying arguments, along with their components in text. Arguments can be usually decomposed into a claim and one or more premises justifying it. Among the novel aspects of this work is the thematic domain itself which relates to Social Media, in contrast to traditional research in the area, which concentrates mainly on law documents and scientific publications. The huge increase of social media communities, along with their user tendency to debate, makes the identification of arguments in these texts a necessity. Argument extraction from Social Media is more challenging because texts may not always contain arguments, as is the case of legal documents or scientific publications usually studied. In addition, being less formal in nature, texts in Social Media may not even have proper syntax or spelling. This paper presents a two-step approach for argument extraction from social media texts. During the first step, the proposed approach tries to classify the sentences into "sentences that contain arguments" and "sentences that don't contain arguments". In the second step, it tries to identify the exact fragments that contain the premises from the sentences that contain arguments, by utilizing conditional random fields. The results exceed significantly the base line approach, and according to literature, are quite promising.

1 Introduction

Argumentation is a branch of philosophy that studies the act or process of forming reasons and of drawing conclusions in the context of a discussion, dialogue,

A. Likas, K. Blekas, and D. Kalles (Eds.): SETN 2014, LNAI 8445, pp. 287–299, 2014.

or conversation. Being an important element of human communication, its use is very frequent in texts, as a means to convey meaning to the reader. As a result, argumentation has attracted significant research focus from many disciplines, ranging from philosophy to artificial intelligence. Central to argumentation is the notion of *argument*, which according to [1] is "a set of assumptions (i.e. information from which conclusions can be drawn), together with a conclusion that can be obtained by one or more reasoning steps (i.e. steps of deduction)". The conclusion of the argument is often called the claim, or equivalently the consequent or the conclusion of the argument, while the assumptions are called the support, or equivalently the premises of the argument, which provide the reason (or equivalently the justification) for the claim of the argument. The process of extracting conclusions/claims along with their supporting premises, both of which compose an argument, is known as argument extraction and constitutes an emerging research field.

Arguments are used in the context of a live or textual dialogue. An argument is the part of the sentence which contains one or more premises, that serve as a support to a claim, which is the conclusion [1,2,3]. According to the state of the art, there are relationships between claims and premises that existing approaches exploit in order to perform the identification of arguments in a sentence. Being an emerging research field, the existing research is rather limited and focused on specific domains such as law texts[4] and scientific publications. Social Media is a much less explored domain with only one publication related to product reviews on Amazon [5].

The difficulty of processing social media texts lies in the fact that they are expressed in an informal form, and they do not follow any formal guidelines or specific rules. Therefore, if we consider the variety of different users that publish a message and the fact that most messages are simple and informal, the probability of an argumentative sentence is rather low. Furthermore, some messages may even lack proper syntax or spelling.

Although there are a number of issues and difficulties in performing argument extraction on social media, the processing of such corpora is of great importance. Nowadays, the way that we communicate has changed. If someone wants to discuss something, or just seeks advice on a specific subject of interest, he/she just "posts" or replies to "posts" in social media, possibly providing arguments about a specific subject. It is also quite possible to post something entirely irrelevant or without any support for a possible claim. Therefore, the automated argument extraction on such corpora is extremely useful in order to acquire all the informative posts/comments (containing arguments) and discard the non-informative ones (the messages without an argument). Such a process can be extremely desirable for a wide range of applications, from supporting the decision making of a potential product buyer, who needs to decide based on product reviews from owners, to summarising discussions.

Argument extraction can also help in politics. Within the political domain it could help politicians identify the peoples' view about their political plans, laws, etc. in order to design more efficiently their policies. Additionally, it could help the voters in deciding which policies and political parties suit them better. Social media is a domain that contains a massive volume of information on every possible subject, from religion to health and products, and it is a prosperous place for exchanging opinions. Its nature is based on debating, so there already is plenty of useful information that waits to be identified and extracted.

However, argument extraction is not an easy task, as in many cases it is difficult even for humans to distinguish whether a part of a sentence contains an argument element or not. It may require some thought to recognize the premises and the claim, and how related they are to each other in the context of a correctly composed argument. Automatic argument extraction is a quite complex procedure, but there are a number of approaches that try to tackle this problem. Following the state of the art, our approach studies the applicability of existing approaches on the domain of social media. Following a two-step approach, we classify sentences as argumentative (containing arguments) or not, through the use of machine learning techniques, such as Logistic Regression, Random Forest, Support Vector Machines, etc. As a second step, Conditional Random Fields are employed in order to extract segments that correspond to premises in argumentative sentences.

The rest of the paper is organized as follows; Section 2 refers to the related work on argument extraction, section 3 describes the proposed methodology and the corresponding features used for our approach. Section 4 presents the experimental results and the tools we utilized and finally, section 5 concludes the paper and proposes some future directions.

2   Related Work

The area of automatic argument extraction is a relative new research field, as it has already been mentioned. One implication of this, is the absence of widely used corpora in order to comparably evaluate approaches for argument extraction. A recent and extensive survey of theories of argumentation, argumentation representations and applications targeting the social semantic web can be found in [6]. However, despite the plethora of applications targeting argumentation, almost all of them rely on manual entry of arguments by the users, and the do not attempt to automatically identify and extract them from documents. Since our work is focused on automatic argument extraction, we are going to present the most influential approaches that relate to the automatic identification and extraction of argument elements from texts.

Understanding discourse relations between statements is a key factor for identifying arguments and their components in a textual document. For this reason argumentation models, as well as cue words, are employed in order to find these possible discourse relations. Most recent approaches employ machine learning and statistical approaches, usually dividing the problem as a multiple step approach. Palau et al. [4,7] methodology for extracting arguments from legal documents use this type of approach: as a first step they work at the sentence level by trying to identify possible argumentative sentences. Seeing it as a classification task, they employ feature vectors of fixed length as a representation, containing suitable features for the selected domain. Employing different classifiers, such as maximum entropy [8], naive Bayes [9], and support vector machines [10], they comparatively evaluate their approach on the Araucaria corpus[1] and on the ECHR corpus [11], achieving an accuracy of 73% and 80% respectively. As a second step they try to identify groups of sentences that refer to the same argument, using semantic distance based on the relatedness of words contained in sentences. As a third step they detect clauses of sentences through a parsing tool, which are classified as argumentative or not with a maximum entropy classifier. Then argumentative clauses are classified into premises and claims through support vector machines. The structure of the argument is identified by employing a context-free grammar that was manually created, obtaining 60% accuracy on the ECHR corpus. Another machine learning based approach, presented in Angrosh et al.[12], employs supervised learning (conditional random fields [13]) for context identification and sentence classification of sentences in the "related work" section of research articles, based on rhetorical features extracted.

There are also approaches that employ rules in order to perform the same task. Schneider and Wyner [5,14] propose a methodology on the camera-buying domain, where the actual argument extraction is performed through the usage of a rule-based system. The system is given as input an argumentation scheme and an ontology concerning the camera and its characteristic features. These are used to define the relevant parts of the document, concerning the description of the parts of the camera. After this step is performed, the argumentation schemes are populated and along with discourse indicators and other domain specific features, the rules are constructed. An interesting aspect of this work is the fact that they applied argument extraction on product reviews in an electronic shop which is related to social media, in contrast to the majority of the work presented in the area of argument extraction which focuses on legal documents and scientific publications.

3   Proposed Approach

In order to perform argument extraction in the context of social media we followed a two-step approach. The first step includes the identification of sentences containing arguments or not. This step is necessary in order to select only the sentences that contain arguments, which constitute the input for the second step. The second step involves the usage of Conditional Random Fields (CRFs) [13] in order to identify the textual fragments that correspond to claims and premises.

3.1   Step A: Identification of Argumentative Sentences

Seeing the identification of argumentative sentences as a supervised classification task, we explored a small set of machine learning classifiers, such as Logistic

---

[1] http://araucaria.computing.dundee.ac.uk/
doku.php#araucaria_argumentation_corpus

Regression [15], Random Forest [16], Support Vector Machines [10], Naive Bayes [9] etc. Our main research axis is not to identify the best performing machine learning algorithm for the task, but rather to study the applicability of features from the state of the art to the domain of social media. The suitability of the existing features in this domain will be evaluated and existing features will be complemented with new features that are more suitable for our domain.

The features that we have examined can be classified in two categories: features selected from the state of the art approaches, and new features that look promising for the domain of our application, which involves texts from social media. The features taken from the state of the art approaches are:

1. *Position*: this feature indicates the position of the sentence inside the text. The possible values are nominals from this set {top, top-mid, middle, middle-bot, bottom} which indicate one of the five possible positions of the sentence in the document. The motivation for this feature is to check whether the position of the sentence in the document is decisive for argument existence.

2. *Comma token number*, is the number of commas inside a sentence. This feature represents the number subordinate clauses inside a sentence, based on the idea that sentences containing argument elements may have a large number of clauses.

3. *Connective number*: is the number of connectives in the sentence, as connectives usually connect subordinate clauses. This feature is also selected based on the hypothesis that sentences containing argument elements may have a large number of clauses.

4. *Verb number*: is the number of the verbs inside a sentence, which indicates the number of periods inside a sentence.

5. *Number of verbs in passive voice*: this feature is a different version of the previous feature which takes into account the voice of the verbs, counting only the one found in passive voice.

6. *Cue words*: this feature indicates the existence and the number of cue words (also known as discourse indicators). Cue words are identified through a predefined, manually constructed, lexicon. The cue words in the lexicon are structural words which indicate the connection between periods or subordinate clauses.

7. *Domain entities number*: this feature indicates the existence and the number of entity mentions of named-entities relevant to our domain, in the context of a sentence.

8. *Adverb number*: this feature indicates the number of adverbs in the context of a sentence.

9. *Word number*: the number of words in the context of a sentence. This feature is based in the hypothesis that when we have an argument, usually, we deal with a larger sentence.

10. *Word mean length*: this is a metric of the average length (in characters) of the words in the context of a sentence.

In addition to the features found in the literature, we have examined the following set of additional/complementary features:

1. *Adjective number*: the number of adjectives in a sentence may characterize a sentence as argumentative or not. We considered the fact that usually in argumentation opinions are expressed towards an entity/claim, which are usually expressed through adjectives.

2. *Entities in previous sentences*: this feature represents the number of entities in the nth previous sentence. Considering a history of $n = 5$ sentences, we obtain five features, with each one containing the number of entities in the respective sentence. These features correlate to the probability that the current sentence contains an argument element.

3. *Cumulative number of entities in previous sentences*: This feature contains the total number of entities from the previous n sentences. Considering a history of $n = 5$ we obtain four features, with each one containing the cumulative number of entities from all the previous sentences.

4. *Ratio of distributions*: we created a language model from sentences that contain argument elements and one from sentences that do not contain an argument element. The ratio between these two distributions was used used as a feature. We have created three ratios of language models based on unigrams, bigrams and trigrams of words. The ratio can be described as
$$\frac{P(X|\text{sentence contains an argument element})}{P(X|\text{sentence does not contain an argument element})},$$
where $X \in \{unigrams, bigrams, trigrams\}$.

5. *Distributions over unigrams, bigrams, trigrams of part of speech tags (POS tags)*: this feature is identical to the previous one with the exception that unigrams, bigrams and trigrams are extracted from the part of speech tags instead of words.

3.2   Step B: Extraction of Claims and Premises

Once we have identified the argumentative sentences, our approach proceeds with the extraction of the segments that represent the premises and the claims. In order to perform this task Conditional Random Fields (CRFs) [13] were employed, because it is a structured prediction algorithm, required for the task of the identification of claims and premises segments. In addition, CRFs can also take local context into consideration, which is important for the nature of this problem, as it can help maintain linguistic aspects such as the word ordering in the sentence. The features utilized in this step are: *a*) the words in these sentences, *b*) gazetteer lists of known entities for the thematic domain related to the arguments we want to extract, *c*) gazetteer lists of cue words and indicator phrases, *d*) lexica of verbs and adjectives automatically acquired using Term Frequency - Inverse Document Frequency (TF-IDF) [17] between two "documents": The first document contained all the verbs/adjectives in an argumentative sentence whereas the second one contained the verbs/adjectives from the non-argumentative ones. The reason for restricting lexica to verbs and adjectives was the fact that premises usually contain a lot of adjectives and attribute claims through verbs.

4   Empirical Evaluation

In this section the performance of the proposed approach will be examined. The performance metrics that will be used in order to evaluate our approach is accuracy, precision, recall and F1-measure. The accuracy denotes the correctness of the prediction for the instances of both classes that are to be classified. In our case where arguments are sparse compared to the sentences that do not contain arguments, accuracy is not enough as we are mainly interested in the detection of sentences that contain arguments. Precision, recall and F1-measure can complement this task. Precision denotes how well the classifier can classify instances correctly within the performed classifications, whereas recall measures the fraction of relevant instances that are correctly retrieved from all the possible instances. F1-measure combines precision and recall as the harmonic mean.

4.1   Corpus and Preparation

All the experiments were conducted on a corpus of 204 documents collected from the social media, concerning the thematic domain of renewable energy sources. All documents are written in Greek, and originate from various sources, such as news, blogs, sites, etc. The corpus was constructed by manually filtering a larger corpus, automatically collected by performing queries on popular search engines (such as Bing[2]), Google Plus [3], Twitter [4], and by crawling sites from a list of sources relevant to the domain of renewable energy. The selected documents were manually annotated with domain entities and text segments that correspond to argument premises. It must be noted that claims are not expressed literally in this thematic domain, but instead they are *implied*: in this specific domain claims are not represented into documents as segments, but they are implied by the author as positive or negative views of a specific renewable energy entity or technology. Thus, in our evaluation corpus, domain entities play the role of claims, as authors argument in favor or again technologies by presenting and commenting on their various advantages or disadvantages.

The corpus has a total of 16000 sentences, where only 760 of them were annotated as containing argument elements. Related corpora that were used in the evaluation of similar approaches are the Araucaria corpus [18], which is a general corpus that has a structured set of documents in English, and the ECHR corpus [19] which is a corpus that contains annotated documents from the domain of law and legal texts, which is also in English. Unfortunately, we weren't able to gain access to any of them, limiting our ability to compare the proposed approach to the current state of the art for the English language. To our knowledge, no corpus annotated with arguments exists for the Greek language.

Our approach has been implemented within the Ellogon language engineering platform [20], as well as the Weka [21] framework. Ellogon was utilized for

---

[2] http://www.bing.com/
[3] https://plus.google.com/
[4] https://twitter.com/

the linguistic processing of the Greek language (tokenisation, sentence splitting, part-of-speech tagging, cue word lookup, etc.) and the creation of the feature vectors. The first step of our approach, concerning the classification of sentences as argumentative or not, was performed with the help of Weka. The second step of our approach, which is the identification of the segments of premises, was performed with the help of the CRF implementation contained in Ellogon.

4.2 Base Case

Since this specific corpus is used for the first time for argument extraction it is useful to calculate a base case that can be used to measure the performance of our approach. For this reason we have constructed a simple base case classifier: All manually annotated segments (argument components) are used in order to form a gazetteer, which is then applied on the corpus in order to detect all exact matches of all these segments. All segments identified by this gazetteer are marked as argumentative segments, while all sentences that contain at least one argumentative segment identified by the gazetteer, are characterised as an argumentative sentence. Then argumentative segments/sentences are compared to their "gold" counterparts, manually annotated by humans. Sentences that contain these recognized fragments are marked as argumentative for the first step base case, while segments marked as argumentative are evaluated for the second step base case. The results are taken through 10-fold cross validation on the whole corpus (all 16.000 sentences) and are shown in Table 1.

Table 1. Evaluation results of the base-case classifiers

	Precision	Recall	F1-Measure
Step A	14.84%	35.52%	20.50%
Step B	23.10%	21.15%	21.24%

4.3 Evaluation of the Argumentative Sentences Identification

In order to characterize and classify a sentence as a sentence which contains arguments or not, we utilized a number of well-known classifiers. Each sentence is represented by a fixed-size feature vector, using the features described in section 3, including a class representing whether it is argumentative or not. The labelled instances were used as input in order to test a variety of classifiers including Support Vector Machines, Naive Bayes, Random Forest and Logistic Regression.

The training and the evaluation of the classifiers was achieved by using the corpus already described in subsection 4.1. As already mentioned there are too many instances that correspond to sentences without arguments. So in order to create a more balanced dataset we applied a sampling which randomly ignores negative examples so as the resulting set contains an equal number of instances

from both classes. We performed two evaluations: one using 10-fold cross validation on the sampled dataset, and one splitting the initial dataset in two parts.
The first part contained 70% of the instances, was sampled and used as a training set. The obtained model was evaluated on the remaining 30% of (unsampled)
instances which was used as a test set. The performance of the second approach
achieved 49% accuracy. The overall performance of the first approach (10-fold
cross validation on sampled dataset) is shown in tables 2, 3 and 4.

Table 2. Results of various classifiers for the first step, evaluated with 10-fold cross
validation (both classes)

Step A: State of the art + new features				
	Precision	Recall	F1-Measure	Accuracy
Naive Bayes	74.10%	74.00%	74.00%	73.99%
Random Forest	74.60%	74.40%	74.30%	74.38%
Logistic Regression	**77.10%**	**77.10%**	**77.10%**	**77.12%**
Support Vector Machines	76.00%	76.00%	76.00%	76.01%
Step A: State of the art features				
	Precision	Recall	F1-Measure	Accuracy
Naive Bayes	67.40%	65.40%	64.60%	65.44%
Random Forest	64.50%	64.50%	64.50%	64.47%
Logistic Regression	68.30%	**68.30%**	**68.20%**	**68.25%**
Support Vector Machines	**68.40%**	68.10%	68.00%	68.12%

Table 3. Results of various classifiers for the first step, evaluated with 10-fold cross
validation (only positive class)

Step A: State of the art + new features			
	Precision	Recall	F1-Measure
Naive Bayes	72.50%	76.10%	74.30%
Random Forest	72.70%	72.50%	72.60%
Logistic Regression	**76.80%**	76.90%	**76.80%**
Support Vector Machines	74.70%	**77.70%**	76.20%
Step A: State of the art features			
	Precision	Recall	F1-Measure
Naive Bayes	61.30%	**81.40%**	**69.90%**
Random Forest	64.50%	62.40%	63.40%
Logistic Regression	68.60%	65.70%	67.10%
Support Vector Machines	**70.30%**	61.30%	65.50%

4.4   Evaluation of the Claim and Premise Segments Extraction

In order to utilize conditional random fields for the identification of premise
fragments in a sentence we used the BIO representation. Each token is tagged

Table 4. Results of various classifiers for the first step, evaluated with 10-fold cross validation (only negative class)

Step A: State of the art + new features			
	Precision	Recall	F1-Measure
Naive Bayes	75.50%	71.90%	73.70%
Random Forest	73.30%	73.50%	73.40%
Logistic Regression	**77.40%**	**77.30%**	**77.40%**
Support Vector Machines	**77.40%**	74.40%	75.90%
Step A: State of the art features			
	Precision	Recall	F1-Measure
Naive Bayes	**73.30%**	49.90%	59.40%
Random Forest	64.50%	66.50%	65.50%
Logistic Regression	67.90%	70.80%	69.30%
Support Vector Machines	66.50%	**74.80%**	**70.40%**

Table 5. Example of the BIO representation of a sentence

BIO tag	word	prev. word	next word	...
B-premise	Wind	-	turbines	...
I-premise	turbines	Wind	generate	...
I-premise	generate	turbines	noise	...
I-premise	noise	generate	in	...
O	in	noise	the	...
O	the	in	summer	...
O	summer	the	-	...

with one of three special tags, B for starting a text segment (premise), I for a token in a premise other than the first, and O for all other tokens (outside of the premise segment). For example the BIO representation of the sentence "Wind turbines generate noise in the summer" is presented in Table 5.

The overall performance of the second step is shown in the table 6. The dataset was composed from all the sentences that contained argumentative fragments from the manual annotation.

It is clear that in both steps the results of the proposed approach are above the base case. In the first step, where we identify sentences that contain arguments, there is an increase in performance from 20% to 77%, by using the logistic regression classifier. Continuing to the second step also our results are above the base case. We have measured an increase from 22% to 43% in F1-measure, regarding the identification of the argumentative fragments, through the use of conditional random fields. Additionally, our corpus had very sparse argumentative sentences in many domains. Following the state of the art, approaches are evaluated on datasets containing an equal number of instances for argumentative and non argumentative segments. Thus, we also performed a similar evaluation through the use of subsampling where negative examples were randomly rejected.

Table 6. Evaluation results of CRFs for the second step, evaluated with 10-fold cross validation

Step B: Identifying claim/premise segments		
	Precision	Recall	F1-Measure
CRF	62.23%	32.43%	42.37%

5 Conclusion

In this research paper we proposed a two step approach for argument extraction on a corpus obtained from social media, concerning renewable energy sources in the Greek language. In the first step we employed a statistical approach through the use of machine learning and more specifically, the logistic regression classifier. The results concerning this first phase are quite promising, since they exceeded significantly the accuracy of our base case classifier in the identification of argumentative sentences. The addition of complementary features was also justified, since they increased the performance further, thus providing a more accurate extraction of argumentative sentences. As far as the second step is concerned, CRFs are quite promising due to the fact that they are a structure prediction algorithm, required for the identification of segments, and due to their performance on the task that outperformed the base classifier.

Regarding future work, it would be interesting to explore additional new features for the first step in order to boost the accuracy even further, but considering features like verbal tense and mood, which according to [22] are good indicators of arguments. In addition, we could possibly explore more sophisticated machine learning algorithms that better suit the task of identifying sentences that contain arguments. For the argumentative segment extraction we would try other structure prediction algorithms such as Markov models and explore complementary features as well. Additionally, it would be nice to have a more comparable evaluation with the rest of the state of the art, if the Araucaria and the ECHR corpora are made publicly available again. Finally since we would prefer to work on real-world data, it would also be interesting to explore techniques that can counter the unbalanced data that are present in our dataset, without sampling.

Acknowledgments. The research leading to these results has received funding from the European Union's Seventh Framework Programme (FP7/2007-2013) under grant agreement no 288513. For more details, please see the NOMAD project's website, http://www.nomad-project.eu.

References

1. Besnard, P., Hunter, A.: Elements of Argumentation. MIT Press (2008)
2. Blair, J., Anthony Tindale, C.W.: Groundwork in the Theory of Argumentation. Argumentation library, vol. 21. Springer (2012)
3. Cohen, C., Copi, I.M.: Introduction to Logic, 11th edn. Pearson Education (2001)
4. Palau, R.M., Moens, M.F.: Argumentation mining: the detection, classification and structure of arguments in text. In: ICAIL, pp. 98–107. ACM (2009)
5. Wyner, A., Schneider, J., Atkinson, K., Bench-Capon, T.: Semi-automated argumentative analysis of online product reviews. In: Proceedings of the 4th International Conference on Computational Models of Argument, COMMA 2012 (2012)
6. Schneider, J., Groza, T., Passant, A.: A review of argumentation for the social semantic web. Semantic Web 4(2), 159–218 (2013)
7. Moens, M.F., Boiy, E., Palau, R.M., Reed, C.: Automatic detection of arguments in legal texts. In: ICAIL, pp. 225–230. ACM (2007)
8. Berger, A.L., Pietra, V.J.D., Pietra, S.A.D.: A maximum entropy approach to natural language processing. Comput. Linguist. 22(1), 39–71 (1996)
9. Nir Friedman, D.G., Goldszmidt, M.: Bayesian network classifiers. Machine Learning 29, 131–163 (1997)
10. Cortes, C., Vapnik, V.: Support-vector networks. Machine Learning 20(3), 273–297 (1995)
11. Mochales, R., Ieven, A.: Creating an argumentation corpus: Do theories apply to real arguments?: A case study on the legal argumentation of the echr. In: Proceedings of the 12th International Conference on Artificial Intelligence and Law, ICAIL 2009, pp. 21–30. ACM, New York (2009)
12. Angrosh, M.A., Cranefield, S., Stanger, N.: Ontology-based modelling of related work sections in research articles: Using crfs for developing semantic data based information retrieval systems. In: Proceedings of the 6th International Conference on Semantic Systems, I-SEMANTICS 2010, pp. 14:1–14:10. ACM, New York (2010)
13. Lafferty, J., McCallum, A., Pereira, F.: Conditional random fields: Probabilistic models for segmenting and labeling sequence data. In: Proc. 18th International Conf. on Machine Learning, pp. 282–289. Morgan Kauffmann (2001)
14. Schneider, J., Wyner, A.: Identifying consumers' arguments in text. In: Maynard, D., van Erp, M., Davis, B. (eds.) SWAIE. CEUR Workshop Proceedings, vol. 925, pp. 31–42. CEUR-WS.org (2012)
15. Colosimo, M.S.B.: Logistic regression analysis for experimental determination of forming limit diagrams. International Journal of Machine Tools and Manufacture 46(6), 673–682 (2006)
16. Leo, B.: Random forests. Machine Learning 45(1), 5–32 (2001)
17. Manning, C.D.: Prabhakar Raghavan, H.S.: Introduction to Information Retrieval. Cambridge University Press (2008)
18. Reed, C., Rowe, G.: Araucaria: Software for argument analysis, diagramming and representation. International Journal of AI Tools 14, 961–980 (2004)
19. Palau, R.M., Moens, M.F.: Argumentation mining. Artif. Intell. Law 19(1), 1–22 (2011)
20. Petasis, G., Karkaletsis, V., Paliouras, G., Androutsopoulos, I., Spyropoulos, C.: Ellogon: A new text engineering platform. In: Third International Conference on Language Resources and Evaluation (2002)

21. Hall, M., Frank, E., Holmes, G., Pfahringer, B., Reutemann, P., Witten, I.H.: The weka data mining software: An update. SIGKDD Explorations 11(1) (2009)
22. Florou, E., Konstantopoulos, S., Koukourikos, A., Karampiperis, P.: Argument extraction for supporting public policy formulation. In: Proceedings of the 7th Workshop on Language Technology for Cultural Heritage, Social Sciences, and Humanities, pp. 49–54. Association for Computational Linguistics, Sofia (August 2013)

A Learning Analytics Methodology for Student Profiling

Elvira Lotsari[1], Vassilios S. Verykios[2], Chris Panagiotakopoulos[3],
and Dimitris Kalles[2]

[1] Faculty of Pure and Applied Sciences, Open University of Cyprus, Cyprus
[2] School of Science and Technology, Hellenic Open University, Greece
[3] Department of Education, University of Patras, Greece

Abstract. On a daily basis, a large amount of data is gathered through the participation of students in e-learning environments. This wealth of data is an invaluable asset to researchers as they can utilize it in order to generate conclusions and identify hidden patterns and trends by using big data analytics techniques. The purpose of this study is a threefold analysis of the data that are related to the participation of students in the online forums of their University. In one hand the content of the messages posted in these fora can be efficiently analyzed by text mining techniques. On the other hand, the network of students interacting through a forum can be adequately processed through social network analysis techniques. Still, the combined knowledge attained from both of the aforementioned techniques, can provide educators with practical and valuable information for the evaluation of the learning process, especially in a distance learning environment. The study was conducted by using real data originating from the online forums of the Hellenic Open University (HOU). The analysis of the data has been accomplished by using the R and the Weka tools, in order to analyze the structure and the content of the exchanged messages in these fora as well as to model the interaction of the students in the discussion threads.

Keywords: Data Analytics, Social Network Analysis, Text Mining, Educational Data Mining, Learning Analytics.

1   Introduction

Nowadays, the online fora have become one of the most popular communication tools in e-learning environments. That communication, especially in distance education, is among the key factors to benefit learning. For example, an online discussion forum provides motivation for collaboration and group-work for achieving a common goal with personal contribution from every participant. Moreover, an online forum is a significant source of information for educators, and this is why Learning Analytics has become an attractive field among researchers. The online asynchronous discussions, which take place in these environments, play an important role in the collaborative learning of students. According to Brindley et al. [3], collaborative learning appears to increase the sense of community, which is related to learner satisfaction

A. Likas, K. Blekas, and D. Kalles (Eds.): SETN 2014, LNAI 8445, pp. 300–312, 2014.

and retention. These factors are important for the students off campus in distance education, not only for their cognitive improvement but also to avoid drop out. The students are actively engaged in sharing information and perspectives through the process of interaction with other students [5]. In this paper, by using a Learning Analytics methodology we discover information by linking patterns that are hidden in the educational contexts of students, and we evaluate them in order to improve the quality of the online student learning at large. From the text messages exchanged among students, we can also extract useful information and figure out certain points for providing personalized help [1]. In order to take full advantage of all this information derived from the participation of the students, we need to understand their patterns of interactions and answer questions like "who is involved in each discussion?", or "who is the active/peripheral participant in a discussion thread?" [9].

In this study, by using social network analysis techniques, we try to focus on the analysis of the interaction of students in online discussions. Text mining was conducted to explore patterns and trends through the content of the exchanged messages. We used the well-known statistical software environment R as well as the data mining toolkit WEKA, for the data analysis since they both provide a broad range of statistical, data mining and visualization techniques.

The rest of the paper is structured as follows. In Section 2 we outline the related work on social network analysis and mining on online forums with the main emphasis to distinguish the contributions of this paper. In Section 3, we describe the learning analytics methodology that we follow for student performance profiling. In Section 4 we present our analysis and we justify its practicality by evaluating the experimental results produced. Finally, we conclude and summarize our findings in Section 5.

2   Related Work

Lopez et al. [8] describe the potential of the classification via a clustering approach in an educational context. The idea of using this kind of approach is to predict the final marks of the students by examining their participation in the forums. In this work, three experiments were carried out. Through these experiments the authors compared the accuracy of several clustering algorithms with that of traditional classification algorithms. The comparison was conducted in the base of predicting whether a student passes or not a course based on his participation in forums.

An interesting broad overview of recent studies on social network analysis techniques was presented in Rabbany et al. [10]. In their study, the authors described existing works and approaches on applying social network techniques for assessing the participation of the students in the online courses. They presented their specific social network analysis toolbox, for visualizing, monitoring and evaluating the participation of the students in a discussion forum. Following this line of research, in our study, we use both text mining and social network analysis techniques to assess the learning process of students' participation in the online discussion.

3   Student Profiling via Text Mining and Social Network Analysis Techniques

The methodology of learning analytics includes the gathering of the data, which are derived from the students and the learning environment they participate, and the intelligent analysis of this data for drawing conclusions regarding the degree of the participation of students in the forums and how this affects learning. The main goal of this methodology is to understand and optimize the learning processes and also to improve the environments in which these processes occur [6].

In this section, we demonstrate the methodology that we followed for student profiling. We employed text mining and social network analysis techniques in order to uncover hidden and important patterns from the participation of the students in the online forum.

3.1   Description of the Data

As we have already mentioned, the study was conducted using real data in Greek language from the Hellenic Open University. We draw data from the Information Systems postgraduate program of study and, specifically, from a module named "Specialization in Software Technology". The data is anonymized by replacing the names of the students with the registration number (ID). The data set consists of 64 students.

3.2   Text Mining of Forum Data

Our analysis starts by extracting the text of messages from the discussion forum. Thereafter, the text is converted to a corpus from which we removed punctuations, numbers and hyperlinks. After that, the corpus is transformed in order to build a document-term matrix. In this matrix, each row represents a term, each column represents a document and an entry in this matrix is the number of the occurrences of the term in the document. In order to reduce the dimension of the matrix, we created a dictionary with specific terms pertaining to the learning materials of the module we studied. Thus, the matrix only contains words from the dictionary.

In order to find links between words and groups of words, from the document-term matrix, we apply different graph mining techniques. First, we find frequent terms with frequency greater or equal than ten. A plot of words along with their frequencies is presented in Figure 1. Then we find an association between a pair of words by using function "findAssocs" from *tm* package from R. For instance, the terms that associated with the word "correlation" with a value of greater or equal than 0,25 are the following ones: "entity" (0.62), "type" (0.47), "ternary" (0.34), and "attribute" (0.29), which indicates a high correlation among terms related to one of the main subjects of the module, which is the Conceptual Database Modeling. Another example is the word "class" that is highly correlated with the terms "method" (0.63) and "superclass" (0.46), all of them referring to the Java language.

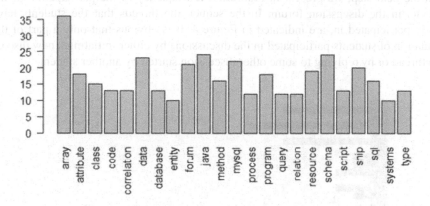

Fig. 1. A plot of terms along with their frequency of occurrence for terms that appear at least ten times in the forum discussions

Then, we applied hierarchical clustering, a method of cluster analysis which attempts to build a hierarchy of clusters, following an agglomerative method (bottom-up). This method starts with each term in its own cluster, and eventually all terms belong to the same cluster. As we can see in Figure 2, the dendrogram is shaped into nine clusters. In each cluster, we can discern the discussion topic. For instance, the 3rd cluster, from the right, includes words such as "data", "database", "systems", "sql", "query" and "relation", which are all referring to the Relational Database Model.

Cluster Dendrogram

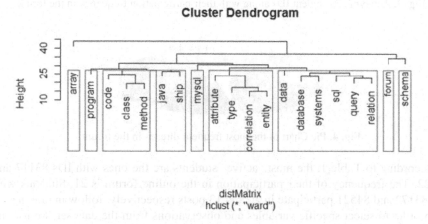

distMatrix
hclust (*, "ward")

Fig. 2. Clusters of terms indicating frequently co-occurring terms in the discussion forum

In the next step, we present in Figure 3, the frequency of the participation of the students in the discussion forum. In the sequel, the threads that the students have mostly participated in, are indicated in Figure 4. It is obvious that only a part of the population of students participated in the discussions by either initiating a new discussion thread or by replying to some other discussion started by another student.

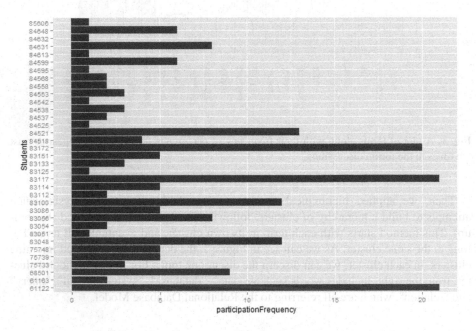

Fig. 3. Anonymized student IDs along with their participation frequency in the forum

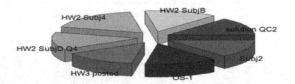

Fig. 4. Pie Chart of the most frequent threads in the forum

According to Table 1, the most "active" students are the ones with IDs 83117 and 61122. The frequency of their participation in the online forum is 21. Students with IDs 83172 and 84521 participate in 20 and 13 posts respectively, follow in ranking.

In order to select specific variables and observations from the data set, we use the *subset()* function. Thus, we select rows that have a value of participation no greater than 21. Then, we maintain the variables "student id", "start posting" and "final mark". The results are summarized in Table 1. The variable "start posting" represents the number of posts that each student has started, while "final mark" is the total score for each student.

Table 1. Indicators related to the participation of students in the forum along with final grade information for analyzing the effect of student participation

STUDENT ID	PARTICIPATION	START POSTING	FINAL MARK
85606	1	-	7.0
84632	1	1	8.7
84613	1	-	8.5
84595	1	1	6.2
84542	1	-	5.6
84525	1	-	7.2
83125	1	-	9.0
83051	1	-	6.1
84568	2	1	7.2
84558	2	1	6.8
84537	2	-	6.6
83112	2	-	-
83054	2	-	7.2
61163	2	1	-
84538	3	-	5.3
83133	3	2	5.4
75733	3	2	6.9
84553	3	-	7.7
84518	4	-	7.1
83151	5	2	-
83114	5	-	8.4
83086	5	-	7.4
75748	5	1	7.1
75739	5	1	6.6
84599	6	2	6.7
84648	6	3	7.2
84631	8	3	6.3
83056	8	4	8.0
68501	9	1	-
83100	12	5	6.8
83048	12	4	6.4
84521	13	2	5.6
83172	20	7	9.0
83117	21	2	6.9
61122	21	9	7.3

3.3 Social Network Analysis of Forum Data

In this section, we analyze the interaction of the students in the online forum as well as the correlation between the terms that are spotted in their discussions. Our analysis is conducted by using social network analysis techniques provided through various libraries in R. For that purpose, we built a network of students based on their co-occurrence in the same thread and a two-mode network that relies on both terms and posts.

First we built a network of students to illustrate the interactions among students in the same class. Each node represents a student and each edge represents a correlation between two students. The label size of vertices in the graph is based on their degree of participation and the width of edges is based on their weights. Thicker edges represent higher degree of correlation. The network of students is depicted in Figure 5. From the graph, we can understand how influential a student is within this social network. The students with higher levels of participation in the discussion forum are at the center of the network. For instance, students with IDs 83117, 61122 and 83172 are located close to the center as, according to Table 1, they have the highest frequency of participation in the forum. In other words, they are the most active students in the class.

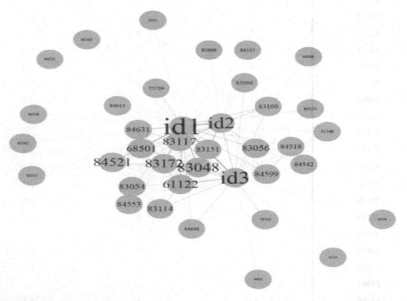

Fig. 5. Network of students: The size of nodes indicates the degree of student's participation in the online forum as well as the centrality/leadership in the discussion. The labels id1, id2 and id3 are referring to course/module instructors.

Subsequently, we built a two-mode network, which is composed of two types of nodes: students and threads. With the turquoise color, we illustrate the nodes of threads and with purple color the nodes of students. The graph in Figure 6 represents the threads each student participates in, as well as how many different students are involved in each thread. For example, the student with ID 84525 participates in the 3rd thread. However, in the 3rd thread two more students are involved: 61163 and 84631.

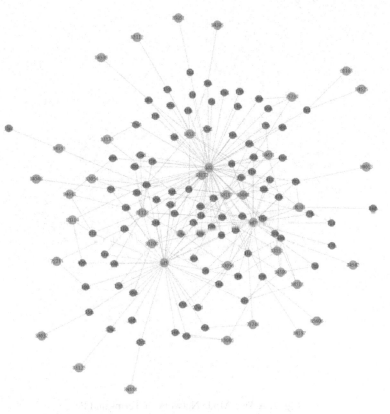

Fig. 6. A Two-Mode Network of Students and Threads

Finally, we built a two-mode network which consists of both terms and posts. With green color we demonstrate the vertices of terms and with pink color the vertices of posts.

Figure 7 presents a group of posts and their associated keywords, such as "operating systems", "mysql database management system", "page table", "virtual machine", "sql query", "programming method", "key constraint", "BlueJ Java IDE", "linux shell script", "awk-sed-grep", and "ternary correlation".

Through the R statistical package, we can select the discussions that contain a specific group of terms we are interested in. Thus, we can distinguish the topics in which the majority of students are involved, and as result, we can identify either any weaknesses a group of students possibly has with respect to the understanding of the study materials or areas where certain study materials are not adequately explained for the whole class.

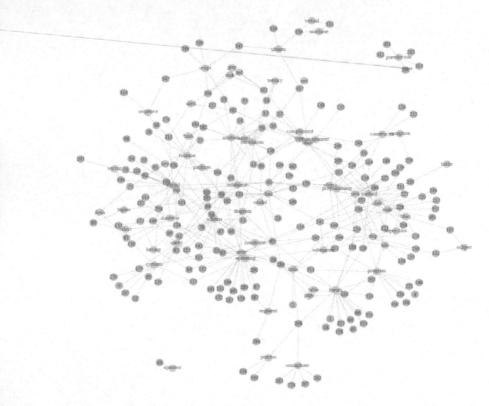

Fig. 7. A Two-Mode Network of Terms and Posts

3.4   From Data in Learning Management Systems to Student Performance

A forum mechanism helps capture the vibes of an online community and allows a community moderator (that's the role of the tutor in a student community) to appreciate how individual members demonstrate unique personality traits when contributing to group discussion activities. But a forum mechanism, nowadays, rarely exists in a vacuum. More often than not, it is part of a learning management system which serves as the focal point for most educational activities, including grading. It is, thus, straightforward to reflect on how one might be able to associate forum activity indices with student performance.

As a matter of fact, this particular strand of questioning has influenced the preliminary results reported in this section. We have built a dataset out of the students in the module, which consists of project (homework) performance, forum activity and final exam performance. Homework in the course of a HOU module, consists of six (6) projects, distributed throughout a 10-month period (spanning a full academic year). Forum activity is as reported in Table 1. We have used the WEKA data mining tool for all of our experiments below.

A casual first observation arose after we clustered the data (using a k-means variant), focusing on the six homework grades and the forum participation metric, where the result was a clear emergence of two clusters, with one of the clusters consisting of students with higher homework grades and lower forum participation and the other cluster consisting of students with lower homework grades and higher forum participation (Table 2). This is a most striking observation and allows one to conjecture that forum higher-caliber students do not feel like they have enough to gain from participating in a forum discussion.

Table 2. Mean values for the pair of emerging clusters

Attribute	More Active (42)	Less Active (22)
Homework #1	9.15	8.36
Homework #2	8.56	5.74
Homework #3	9.59	6.64
Homework #4	8.43	3.34
Homework #5	8.26	6.20
Homework #6	7.72	5.27
Participation	2.05	5.05
Start	0.57	1.41

The above results cannot capture how a student progresses through a module. They treat homework grades and forum participation as quantities that may be interesting to mine for associations but, from another point of view, may also be treated as constant (i.e., they do not capture how a student may progress from low performance to higher performance throughout a module). Now, as most experienced tutors/instructors will likely testify, it is rather unusual for a student to demonstrate a huge shift in performance within the time limits of a module. As a result, we deem the above results to be fairly accurate.

However, this also gives rise to a more compelling question. Given that one has access to forum participation and homework grades, is it straightforward to attempt to forecast the final exam grade based on this data [2, 4]. Table 3 shows the results obtained through two simple regression techniques, a linear one and a tree [7] one (note that results may be interpreted in terms of forecasting though, in reality, they refer to cross-validated testing of data spanning one academic year). Therein, both techniques confirm that the 3rd homework is important in determining whether a student will do well or not; subsequently, the tree technique focuses on the 2nd homework whereas the linear technique elevates the importance of how many threads a student initiates (allowing the observer to conjecture that interested students who tend to initiate discussions may eventually surpass their difficulties).

Table 3. Forecasting the final student grade

Model		RMSE
Linear	0.3083 * START + 0.407 * PROJ1 + 0.8547 * PROJ3 + -0.2115 * PROJ4 + 0.1942 * PROJ5 + 0.1168 * PROJ6 + -6.6887	1.744
Tree	if PROJ3 < 5.85 then forecast 1.36 elseif PROJ3 >= 5.85 then if PROJ2 < 7.4 then forecast 5.4 elseif PROJ2 >= 7.4 then forecast 6.8	1.845

We note that the mean exam grade is about 6. As a result the RMSE reported captures fairly well the extent to which we may offer feedback to the student with some confidence as regards the predicted exam performance. It goes without saying that this cannot be used as an advice. This is counter-productive. It may trigger a self-fulfilling prophecy if failure is forecasted and could trigger complacency if success is forecasted. Rather, it should be interpreted as a warning bell. Furthermore, it is completely different to forecast failure in a module where students customarily pass in excess of 90% (as is the case in the module we report on) as opposed to a module where students pass at a rate of about 30% (as is the case in many first year modules).

4   Evaluation and Results

In this work we used traditional data mining, along with text mining and social network analysis techniques in order to analyze data originating from the participation of students in discussion forums along with data related to the performance of students in the module. We managed, through graphs, to outline the profile of the students who participate in a discussion online forum. Specifically, Figure 3 and Figure 5 give us the frequency of participation of students and they demonstrate the active as well as the peripheral students. From Figure 6, an instructor can derive information about which students participate in which threads and also how many different students are involved in each thread. Thereby, s/he has an overall view of the difficulties that the students in the module may face. This enables the instructor to focus his attention on some specific concepts in his course. By doing so, he will try to enrich his educational material and he will ameliorate the learning process. The topics that are mostly discussed on the discussion forum stand out in Figure 4.

At the end, and by looking at the characteristics of each student demonstrated in Table 1, we can deduce that their final mark is not strongly related to their participation in the discussion forum. We could say that the performance of the mediocre students, regarding their courses is improved by expressing their queries and by exchanging messages and aspects with their fellow students and also their instructors. A coincidence with the experimental results presented above, is presented with the results in Section 3.4, which indicates that a trend may have been identified as opposed to something of temporary nature.

5   Conclusions and Future Work

In this study, we present a learning analytics methodology that we followed for student profiling. We used text mining and social network analysis techniques along with classification and clustering techniques, in order to draw conclusions and unearth important patterns from raw data related to the participation of postgraduate students in the online forum of the module they have registered in.

We use both R and Weka software environments for the data analysis and mining in order to illustrate who is involved in each discussion and who is the active/peripheral participant in a discussion thread. In addition, we manage to visualize the groups of terms that were mostly discussed in the online forum. Moreover, we summarize the characteristics of each student in a table, from which we can conclude that students' final mark is not based on their participation on the discussion forum. Other complementary results generated with classification and clustering techniques are also enlightening about the complicated process of the student learning in a group of peers and from a distance.

In the future, we plan to analyze a dataset of bigger volume and variability that it will consist of data about postgraduate students that have a temporal dimension, observing the progress students make as they move along the thematic modules of the entire program of study.

References

1. Abel, F., Bittencourt, I., Costa, E., Henze, N., Krause, D., Vassilev, J.: Recommendations in Online Discussion Forums for E-Learning Systems. IEEE Transactions on Learning Technologies 3(2), 165–176 (2010)
2. Kalles, D., Pierrakeas, C.: Analyzing Student Performance in Distance Learning with Genetic Algorithms and Decision Trees. Applied Artificial Intelligence 20(8), 655–674 (2006)
3. Brindley, J.E., Walti, C., Blaschke, L.M.: Creating Effective Collaborative Learning Groups in an Online Environment. IRRODL 10(3) (2009),
   http://www.irrodl.org/index.php/irrod/article/view/675/1271
   (retrieved January 10, 2014)
4. Kalles, D., Pierrakeas, C., Xenos, M.: Intelligently Raising Academic Performance Alerts. In: 1st International Workshop on Combinations of Intelligent Methods and Applications (CIMA), 18th European Conference on Artificial Intelligence, Patras, Greece, pp. 37–42 (July 2008)
5. Yusof, E.N., Rahman, A.A.: Students' interactions in online asynchronous discussion forum: A social network analysis. In: International Conference on Education Technology and Computer, pp. 25–29 (2009)
6. Siemens, G., Baker, R.S.J.: Learning Analytics and Educational Data Mining: Towards Communication and Collaboration. In: LAK 2012 (2012)

7. Breiman, L., Friedman, J.H., Olshen, R.A., Stone, C.J.: Classification and regression trees. Wadsworth, Monterey (1984)
8. Lopez, M.I., et al.: Classification via clustering for predicting final marks based on student participation in forums. In: Educational Data Mining Proceedings (2012)
9. de Laat, M., Lally, V., Lipponen, L., Simons, R.-J.: Investigating patterns of interaction in networked learning and computer-supported collaborative learning: A role for social network analysis. International Journal of Computer-Supported Collaborative Learning 2(1), 87–103 (2007)
10. Reihaneh Rabbany, K., Takaffoli, M., Zaïane, O.R.: Social network analysis and mining to support the assessment of on-line student participation. ACM SIGKDD Explorations Newsletter 13(2), 20–29 (2012)

A Profile-Based Method for Authorship Verification

Nektaria Potha and Efstathios Stamatatos

Dept. of Information and Communication Systems Eng.
University of the Aegean
83200 – Karlovassi, Greece
pothanektaria@hotmail.com, stamatatos@aegean.gr

Abstract. Authorship verification is one of the most challenging tasks in style-based text categorization. Given a set of documents, all by the same author, and another document of unknown authorship the question is whether or not the latter is also by that author. Recently, in the framework of the PAN-2013 evaluation lab, a competition in authorship verification was organized and the vast majority of submitted approaches, including the best performing models, followed the instance-based paradigm where each text sample by one author is treated separately. In this paper, we show that the profile-based paradigm (where all samples by one author are treated cumulatively) can be very effective surpassing the performance of PAN-2013 winners without using any information from external sources. The proposed approach is fully-trainable and we demonstrate an appropriate tuning of parameter settings for PAN-2013 corpora achieving accurate answers especially when the cost of false negatives is high.

1   Introduction

Nowadays, text categorization provides effective solutions for handling the huge volumes of electronic text produced in Internet media [1]. The three main directions of distinguishing between texts are their topic, sentiment, and style. The latter is a useful factor to identify document genre and reveal information about the author(s). Authorship analysis attracts constantly increasing attention due to the large potential of important applications in intelligence (e.g., linking terrorist proclamations), security (e.g., verifying the identity of a person using a system), civil law (e.g., solving copyright disputes) etc.

Authorship attribution is the identification of the true author of a document given samples of undisputed documents from a set of candidate authors and has a long research history [6, 8, 20]. There are three main forms of this task usually examined in the relevant literature:

- *Closed-set attribution*: The set of candidate authors surely includes the true author of the questioned documents. This is the easiest version of the problem and most studies have focused on this, providing encouraging results. It should be noted that it is not an unrealistic scenario since in many forensic applications the investigators are able to filter out most of the persons involved in a case and produce a closed-set of suspects.

A. Likas, K. Blekas, and D. Kalles (Eds.): SETN 2014, LNAI 8445, pp. 313–326, 2014.

- *Open-set attribution*: The set of candidate authors may not contain the true author of some of the questioned documents. This is a much more difficult task especially when the size of the candidate set is small [12]. This setting fits all kind of applications including cases where anyone can be the true author of a questioned document (e.g., identifying the person behind a post in a blog).
- *Authorship verification*: This may be seen as a special case of open-set attribution where the set of candidate authors is singleton. As mentioned earlier, small candidate sets in open-set attribution are hard to be solved. All authorship attribution cases can be transformed to a set of separate authorship verification problems. So, the ability of a method to deal effectively with this fundamental task is crucial.

Very recently, there have been attempts to focus on fundamental problems of authorship attribution. Koppel et al. discuss the problem of determining if two documents are by the same author [13, 14]. This is a special case of the authorship verification task where the set of documents by the candidate author is singleton. In the PAN-2013 evaluation lab [9], a competition in authorship verification was organized where each verification problem consisted of a set of (up to 10) documents of known authorship by the same author and exactly one questioned document. The study of various attribution methods in such fundamental problems enables us to extract more general conclusions about their abilities and properties.

All authorship attribution methods fall under one of the following basic paradigms:

- *Instance-based paradigm*: All available samples by one author are treated separately. Each text sample has its own representation. Since these approaches are usually combined with discriminative machine learning algorithms, like support vector machines, they require multiple instances per class. Hence, when only one document is available for a candidate author, this document has to be split into multiple samples.
- *Profile-based paradigm*: All available text samples by one candidate author are treated cumulatively, that is they are concatenated in one big document and then a single representation is extracted to become the profile of the author.

In general, the former is more effective when multiple documents per author are available or when long documents (that can be split into multiple samples) are available. On the other hand, the profile-based paradigm is more effective when only short and limited samples of documents are available. Despite these advantages that are crucial when only one or two documents of known authorship are available, in PAN-2013 evaluation campaign 17 out of 18 participants followed the instance-based paradigm [9]. The only profile-based submission was ranked at the 11th position [2]. Therefore, it seems that instance-based approaches are more appropriate for authorship verification.

In this paper we claim the opposite. We present an authorship verification method following the profile-based paradigm and apply this method to the corpora produced in the framework of PAN-2013 using exactly the same evaluation setting. We provide evidence that profile-based authorship verification can be very effective surpassing the best performing submissions of that competition. The proposed approach is fully-trainable.

We show how the parameters of our method can be tuned given a training corpus so that the proposed method to be effectively applied to different natural languages and genres.

The rest of this paper is organized as follows: Section 2 presents previous work in authorship verification while Section 3 describes the proposed profile-based method. In Section 4 the experiments performed using the PAN-2013 corpora are presented and Section 5 includes the main conclusions drawn from this study and discusses future work directions.

2   Previous Work

The authorship verification task was first discussed by Stamatatos et al. [18]. They proposed an attribution model based on stylometric features extracted from an NLP tool and used multiple regression to produce the response function for a given author. Then, a threshold value (defined as a function of the multiple correlation coefficient) determines whether or not a questioned document was written by the examined author. This model was applied to a corpus of newspaper articles in (Modern) Greek providing good false acceptance rates and moderate false rejection rates.

A seminal authorship verification approach was proposed in [11]. The so-called *unmasking* method builds an SVM classifier to distinguish an unknown text from the set of known documents (all by a single author). Then, it removes a predefined amount of the most important features and iterates this procedure. If the drop in classification accuracy is not high, then the unknown document was written by the examined author. The logic behind this method is that at the beginning it will always be possible for the classifier to distinguish between the texts. When the the texts are by the same author, the differences will be focused on very specific features while when the texts are not by the same author the differences will be manifold. After the removal of some important features, texts by the same author will be difficult to be distinguished while in the opposite case, it will continue to be relatively easy to find other differences among them. The unmasking method is very effective when long documents are available since the unknown document has to be segmented into multiple pieces to train the SVM classifier. Its application to books was exceptional [11]. However, if only short documents are available, this method fails [16].

More recently, Koppel and Winter proposed the *impostors* method to determine whether two documents were by the same author [14]. This method first finds documents of similar genre and topic in the Web (the so-called impostors) and then it builds an ensemble model to verify whether one of the given documents is more similar to the other given document (same author) or one of the impostors (different author). Essentially, this method attempts to transform authorship verification from a one-class classification problem (i.e., the class of documents by a certain author) to a multi-class classification problem by introducing additional classes using documents found in external sources (i.e., the Web) and achieves very good results. However, since this process is automated, there is always the danger of retrieving a document that accidentally is by the same author with the documents of questioned authorship.

In the PAN-2013 evaluation lab, an authorship verification competition was organized [9]. The produced corpora covered three natural languages (i.e., English, Greek, and Spanish) and consist of a set of verification problems. Each problem provides a set of up to 10 documents by a single author and exactly one questioned document. In total, 18 teams participated in this competition. In general, the participant verification models can be distinguished into two main categories [9]:

- *Intrinsic verification models*: They are based exclusively on the set of documents of known documents by the same author and the questioned documents. They face the verification task as a one-class classification problem. Typical approaches of this category are described in [5, 7, 15].
- *Extrinsic verification models*: In addition to the given set of documents of known and unknown authorship, they use additional documents from external sources. They face the verification task as a multi-class classification problem. The winner participant, a modification of the impostors method, followed this approach [17]. Other similar approaches are described in [22-23].

The organizers of the evaluation campaign also reported the performance of a simple meta-model combining all the submitted outputs [9]. That heterogeneous ensemble had the best overall performance in both binary answers and real scores.

As concerns text representation, all kinds of features already studied in authorship attribution can also be used in authorship verification. At PAN-2013, the participants mainly used character features (i.e., letter frequencies, punctuation mark frequencies, character n-grams, etc.) and lexical features (i.e., word frequencies, word n-grams, function word frequencies, etc.) that are also language-independent. The use of more sophisticated syntactic and semantic features doesn't seem to offer a significant advantage in this task possibly due to the low accuracy of the tools used to extract such features [9].

An important aspect is the appropriate parameter tuning of a verification model. Especially when the corpus comprises texts coming from different genres and natural languages, the verification model could be fine-tuned for each language/genre separately to improve its performance [7, 17]. According to each particular verification method, the parameters can be the type of used features, the number of used features, the threshold value used to produce the final decision, etc.

3   The Proposed Method

The method examined in this paper is a modification of the *Common N-Grams* (CNG) approach originally proposed by Keselj et al. [10] for closed-set attribution and later modified by Stamatatos [19]. Following, the profile-based paradigm, this method first concatenates all samples of known authorship into a single document and then extracts a character *n*-gram representation vector from this big document to serve as the author profile. Another vector is produced from the questioned document and the two vectors are compared using a dissimilarity function. If the resulting score is above

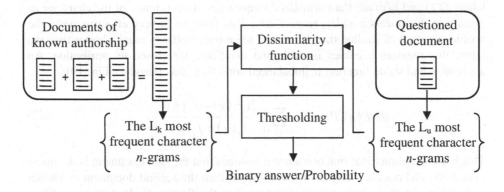

Fig. 1. The proposed profile-based approach for authorship verification

a certain threshold the questioned document is assigned to the author of known documents. This process is depicted in Figure 1. The original CNG approach uses profiles of the same length [10]. The modification of Stamatatos [19] uses assymetric profiles where the profile of the unknown text has the maximum possible length while the profile of the known texts by one candidate author is pre-defined. In our approach, the profile lengths of known and unknown documents are parameters to be set.

In total, the proposed approach has 4 parameters to be tuned. The first is the order of character n-grams (n). The second is the profile size of the questioned document (L_u), while the third refers to the corresponding profile size of the documents of known authorship (L_k). The last one is the dissimilarity function (d) discussed in Section 3.1.

Three PAN-2013 participants were also based on modifications of CNG. Jankowska, et al. [7] and Layton, et al. [15] modified this method to follow the instance-based paradigm, that is they produce separate representation vectors for each document of known authorship. The method of Jankowska, et al. requires at least two documents of known authorship [7]. Therefore in problems with just one document of known authorship they split it into two segments. The method described in [2] is more similar to ours since it also follows the profile-based paradigm. However, in our method we extract appropriately-tuned profile lengths for the questioned and known documents. Moreover, we examine a wider range of parameter values and select appropriate language-specific parameter settings.

3.1 Dissimilarity Function

Given two documents x and y and their profiles $P(x)$ and $P(y)$ (i.e., the sets of the most frequent character n-grams), the original CNG method [10] used a symmetrical dissimilarity function described as follows:

$$d_0(P(x),P(y)) = \sum_{g \in P(x) \cup P(y)} \left(\frac{2(f_x(g) - f_y(g))}{f_x(g) + f_y(g)} \right)^2 \qquad (1)$$

where $f_x(g)$ and $f_y(g)$ are the normalized frequencies of occurrence of the character n-gram g in documents x and y, respectively. This function is very effective when the profile sizes are of similar size. However, when one profile is much shorter than the other, this measure becomes unstable and unreliable for closed-set attribution. An alternative and stable function in imbalanced conditions was introduced in [19]:

$$d_1(P(x), P(y)) = \sum_{g \in P(x)} \left(\frac{2(f_x(g) - f_y(g))}{f_x(g) + f_y(g)} \right)^2 \tag{2}$$

This is not a symmetrical function since it assumes that the first document is the questioned one and possibly shorter or much shorter than the second document of known authorship. Another alternative measure used in the Source Code Author Profiling (SCAP) method with very good results is the simplified profile intersection (SPI):

$$SPI(P(x), P(y)) = |P(x) \cap P(y)| \tag{3}$$

That is the mere counting of common character n-grams in both profiles. Note that SPI is a similarity function while d_0 and d_1 are dissimilarity functions. To have comparable dissimilarity measures one can use $1 - SPI(P(x),P(y))$. In this study we used normalized versions of d_0, d_1, and SPI measures, as the one described in [21].

3.2   Production of Binary Answers and Probability Estimates

Having a dissimilarity score is not enough in authorship verification. We need a binary answer: a positive one in case the questioned document is estimated to be by the same author or a negative one in case it is estimated the opposite. In addition, we need a probability score for a positive answer to show the degree of certainty of that estimation. To produce binary answers, the most common approach is the definition of a threshold value. Any problem with score more than that threshold is considered to be a positive case. Usually, the definition of such threshold values depends on the training corpus [7, 17].

In this study, we use a simple thresholding procedure. Based on the dissimilarity scores produced for the problems of the training corpus that belong to the same genre/language we scale these values to the set [0,1] inclusive. Then, we use the same scaling function for every given evaluation problem belonging to the same genre/language. That way, the resulting score can be seen as a probability estimation of a negative answer (since we originally have dissimilarity rather than similarity scores). Its complementary value corresponds to the probability estimate of a positive answer. Let x be a verification problem, $score(x,dissimFunction)$ be the dissimilarity score for this problem based on $dissimFunction$, and Y be a set of training verification problems of similar genre/language. Then, the probability estimate of a positive answer is expressed as:

$$p_+(x) = 1 - scale(score(x, dissimFunction), Y) \tag{4}$$

Table 1. Statistics of the PAN-2013 authorship verification corpus

	#problems	#documents	#characters (thousands)
Training	**35**	**189**	**1,535**
- English	10	42	265
- Greek	20	130	1,204
- Spanish	5	17	65
Test	**85**	**435**	**3,211**
- English	30	157	977
- Greek	30	178	1,714
- Spanish	25	100	520

Then, according to the percentage of positive/negative problems in the training corpus, we estimate the threshold value. For example, in a balanced corpus with 50% positive and 50% negative verification problems (as the one used in PAN-2013 competition), a "positive" binary answer (same author) is assigned to any verification problem x with $p_+(x)>0.5$. All problems with probability score lower than 0.5 will get the binary value "negative" (different author). Finally, all problems with score equal to 0.5 will remain unanswered, given that this option is allowed (as happened in the PAN-2013 competition).

4 Experimental Study

4.1 The PAN-2013 Evaluation Setting

In the framework of PAN-2013, an authorship verification corpus was built and released in early 2013 [9]. It includes a set of separate verification problems, each problem provides a set of up to 10 documents of known authorship, all by the same author, and exactly one questioned document. The corpus is segmented into a training part and an evaluation part. The latter was used for the final ranking of the participants and was released after the end of the submission deadline.

Three natural languages are represented in the corpus: English, Greek, and Spanish. The English part includes extracts from published textbooks on computer science and related disciplines. The Greek part contains opinion articles from a weekly newspaper while the Spanish part includes excerpts from newspaper editorials and short fiction. The PAN-2013 organizers report that the Greek part of the corpus is more challenging since they used stylometric techniques to match documents by different authors and find stylistically different documents by the same author. The language of each problem is encoded in its code name.

Table 1 shows some statistics of this corpus. As can be seen, the Greek part has more and longer documents while the Spanish part is under-represented especially in

Table 2. Global and local parameter settings of our approach extracted from the PAN-2013 training corpus

	L_u	L_k	n	d
Global	10,000	2,000	5	d_1
Local				
- English	1,000	1,000	5	d_1
- Greek	10,000	2,000	5	d_1
- Spanish	10,000	2,000	5	d_1

the training corpus. The latter makes the estimation of appropriate parameter settings for the Spanish part very difficult.

The PAN-2013 participants were asked to produce a binary YES/NO answer for each problem (corresponding to same author or different author) and, optionally, a probability estimate of a positive answer. Submissions were ranked based on recall and precision of correct answers combined by the (micro-average) F_1 measure. In addition, the participants that also produced probability estimates were ranked according to the area under the receiver operating characteristic curve (ROC-AUC) [9]. In this paper, we follow exactly the same evaluation settings to achieve compatibility of comparison with previously reported results.

4.2   Experiments

To find the most appropriate values for the 4 parameters of our method we examined a range of possible values and extracted the best models based on their performance on the PAN-2013 training set. We used ROC-AUC as the evaluation criterion. The following range of values were examined: $L_k \in \{1,000, 2,000, ..., 20,000\}$, $L_u \in \{1,000, 2,000, 10,000\}$, $n \in \{3,4,5\}$, and $d \in \{d_0, d_1, SPI\}$ as defined in formulas (1), (2), and (3). We first examined the entire training set and extracted global parameter settings. Then, the language information was considered and local parameter settings were produced for each one of the three languages.

Global Settings. The extracted global parameter settings, where the whole training corpus was considered, can be seen in Table 2. Figure 2 shows the AUC of authorship verification models based on different dissimilarity functions and the range of values of L_k when L_u=10,000 and n=5 for the full PAN-2013 training and test corpora. In both training and test corpora the basic patterns are the same. The best and more stable dissimilarity function is d_1. In addition, d_0 is competitive only for small values of L_k while its performance is negatively affected by increasing L_k. On the other hand, SPI achieves its best performance in around L_k=8,000. After that point its performance is similar with that of d_1. The best performing model for the training corpus ($d=d_1$, L_k=2,000) may not be the best performing model for the test corpus but it is very close to that.

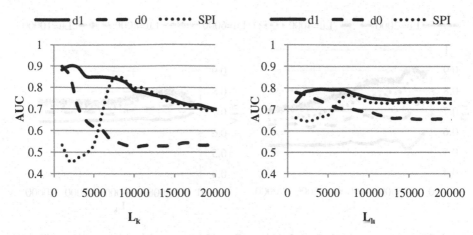

Fig. 2. The performance (AUC) of the proposed verification models on the training (left) and test (right) corpora with L_u=10,000 and n=5 and different dissimilarity functions

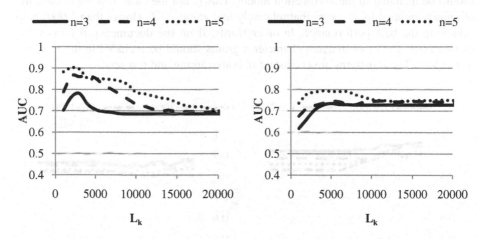

Fig. 3. The performance (AUC) of the proposed verification models on the training (left) and test (right) corpora with L_u=10,000 and d=d_1 and different orders of character n-grams

Figure 3 depicts the AUC scores of the verification models on the training and test sets based on L_u=10,000, d=d_1 and different values of n and L_k. Long character n-grams (n=5) seem to be the best and more stable option. On the other hand short n-grams (n=3) perform poorly. The same pattern applies to both training and test corpora.

Figure 4 shows the AUC scores of the verification models on the training and test sets based on d=d_1 and n=5 for different values of L_k and L_u. Apparently, increasing L_u helps to improve performance. For L_u>7,000 the performance is stabilized. This means that from the document of unknown authorship, all possible character n-grams

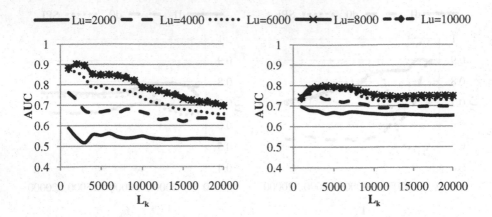

Fig. 4. The performance (AUC) of the proposed verification models on the training (left) and test (right) corpora with $d=d_1$, $n=5$, and different sizes of L_u

should be included in the verification model. This is not the case with the documents of known authorship. It seems that relatively low values of L_k (lower than 5,000) help achieving the best performance. In other words, from the documents of known authorship only the most frequent character n-grams should be included in the verification model. These patterns are consistent in both training and test sets.

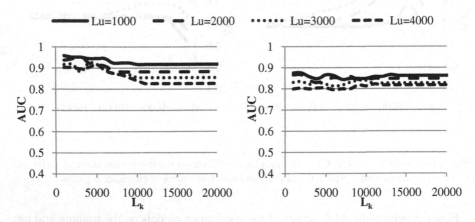

Fig. 5. The performance (AUC) of the proposed verification models on the English part of the training (left) and test (right) corpora with $d=d_1$, $n=5$, and different sizes of L_u

Local Settings. To extract local settings, we examine each subset of problems of the training set belonging to a certain language separately. As can be seen in Table 1, the Spanish part of the PAN-2013 training is very limited and it does not enable the

Table 3. F1 scores of the proposed models, the participants and meta-model of PAN-2013

	Overall	English	Greek	Spanish	PAN-2013 rank
Seidman [17]	0.753	0.800	**0.833**	0.600	1st
Halvani [5]	0.718	0.700	0.633	0.840	2nd
Layton et al. [15]	0.671	0.767	0.500	0.760	3rd
Jankowska et al. [7]	0.659	0.733	0.600	0.640	5th
Van Dam [2]	0.600	0.600	0.467	0.760	11th
Meta-model [9]	**0.814**	**0.867**	0.690	**0.898**	-
Our method (global settings)	0.729	0.633	0.767	0.800	-
Our method (local settings)	0.788	0.800	0.767	0.800	-

Table 4. AUC scores of the proposed models, the participants, and meta-model of PAN-2013

	Overall	English	Greek	Spanish	PAN-2013 rank
Jankowska et al. [7]	0.777	0.842	0.711	0.804	1st
Seidman [17]	0.735	0.800	**0.830**	0.600	2nd
Ghaeini [4]	0.729	0.837	0.527	**0.926**	3rd
Meta-model [9]	0.841	0.821	0.756	**0.926**	-
Our method (global settings)	0.789	0.795	0.787	0.917	-
Our method (local settings)	**0.845**	**0.877**	0.787	0.917	-

estimation of appropriate parameter values (i.e., most of the parameter value combinations give perfect results). Therefore, for the Spanish language we used the global parameter settings. Moreover, to enrich the English part of the training corpus, we augmented it by adding more problems based on variations of the initial problems in English. For instance, from a problem with three documents of known authorship we can produce five more problems taking all available subsets of the three known documents as separate verification problems. That way, we formed an augmented version of the English part of the training corpus consisting of 24 problems, all of them variations of the initial 10 problems.

The extracted local parameter settings can be seen in Table 2. The global parameter values coincide with those of the Greek part of the corpus. As already mentioned the global parameter settings were selected for the Spanish part. As concerns English, for parameters n and d, the selected values remain the same with the global settings but L_u and L_k are different (smaller).

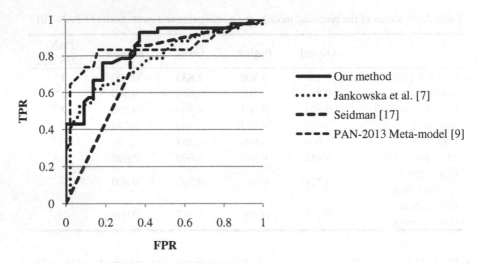

Fig. 6. The ROC curves of the proposed approach (local settings) on the test corpus (all 3 languages) and the corresponding curves of the PAN-2013 winners and the PAN-2013 meta-model

The performance of the verification models on the English part of the training and test corpora for $d=d_1$, $n=5$ and different values of L_u and L_k is shown in Figure 5. Apparently, low values of L_u seem to be the most effective ones. This is consistent in both training and test corpora. When compared with the results depicted in Figure 4, we see that the pattern obtained from the entire training corpus (also valid for the Greek part of the corpus) does not apply to the English part of the corpus. For the latter, the most effective option is to extract profiles of equal and small size (1,000 character n-grams) from both the unknown document and the documents of known authorship, that is only the most frequent character n-grams are necessary to achieve good performance.

Comparison with PAN-2013 Participants. As already mentioned, the evaluation procedure we followed is directly comparable with the one performed in the framework of the PAN-2013 competition on authorship verification [9]. Therefore, we can directly compare our results with those of the PAN-2013 participants.

Table 3 shows the performance in terms of F_1 of the binary answers of our method on the test corpus with global and local settings. Overall results as well as language-specific results are presented. Moreover, the corresponding results of the top performing PAN-2013 participants together with the only profile-based participant method [2] and the meta-model combining all submitted methods are reported. The proposed approach based on local settings outperforms every single PAN-2013 participant when the overall performance (F_1) is considered. However, the meta-model continues to be the overall best performing model. On the other hand, our approach achieves more balanced performance in all three languages in comparison to the meta-model. The version of our method based on global settings is also very effective with the exception of the English part and would be ranked 2nd at PAN-2013.

The evaluation of our approach based on the AUC scores of the probability estimates for the entire test corpus and its every language-specific part, is shown in Table 4. Again, the corresponding results for the best performing methods from PAN-2013 and the meta-model combining all submitted models are reported. The proposed approach based on local settings outperforms all others in overall AUC including the PAN-2013 meta-model. Our method achieves the best results in the English part and it is very close to the best results in the Spanish part of the test corpus.

Finally, Figure 6 depicts the ROC curves for the whole test corpus (including 3 languages) of our method (using local settings) and the corresponding curves of the two best performing models at PAN-2013 as well as the meta-model combining all submitted methods. As can be seen, our approach clearly outperforms the methods of [7] and [17]. It also outperforms the meta-model for large FPR values. On the other hand, the meta-model is more effective for low FPR values. This means that when the cost of false positive errors (i.e., incorrect assignment of a document to an author) is considered high, the meta-model wins. In contrast, when the cost of the false negative errors (i.e., miss of a real assignment) is considered high, our approach is better.

5   Conclusions

In this paper, we examined a profile-based method for authorship verification. In contrast to prior evidence, we demonstrated that a profile-based method can be very effective in this task. Our approach is better than any single PAN-2013 participant achieving higher overall F_1 and AUC scores. Moreover, it is very competitive to the heterogeneous meta-model [9], especially when false negatives have high cost.

The fact that the proposed method is less effective in the Greek part of the corpus is partially explained by the difficulty of this corpus since PAN-2013 organizers took special care so that the texts by different authors to be stylistically similar and the texts by the same author to be stylistically dissimilar. This difficulty is reflected in the average performance of PAN-2013 participants on this part of the corpus that was significantly lower with respect to the rest of the corpus. However, a better explanation is that PAN-2013 organizers used a variation of CNG to find stylistically similar or dissimilar texts [9]. It can be claimed, therefore, that the Greek part of the PAN-2013 corpus is negatively biased for approaches based on modifications of CNG.

The proposed approach is fully-trainable. Although the training corpus used in this study is not large, we managed to extract language-specific parameter settings improving the performance in comparison with the case when global settings are used. The performance patterns are consistent in both training and test corpora demonstrating the robustness of our method.

The proposed approach belongs to the family of intrinsic verification methods where no external resources are used by the verification model. Given that extrinsic models seem to be very effective in authorship verification, it could be interesting to investigate how our method can be modified to also use external resources and transform the verification task from a one-class problem to a multi-class problem. Another important future work dimension is to apply the discussed method to verification problems with short documents (e.g., tweets) where the profile-based paradigm has an inherent advantage over instance-based methods.

References

1. Aggarwal, C.C., Zhai, C.X.: A Survey of Text Classification Algorithms. In: Aggarwal, C.C., Zhai, C.X. (eds.) Mining Text Data, pp. 163–222. Springer (2012)
2. van Dam, M.: A Basic Character n-gram Approach to Authorship Verification – Notebook for PAN at CLEF 2013. In: Forner et al (eds.) [3] (2013)
3. Forner, P., Navigli, R., Tufis, D. (eds.): CLEF 2013 Evaluation Labs and Workshop – Working Notes Papers (2013)
4. Ghaeini, M.R.: Intrinsic Author Identification Using Modified Weighted KNN – Notebook for PAN at CLEF 2013. In: Forner et al (eds.) [3] (2013)
5. Halvani, O., Steinebach, M., Zimmermann, R.: Authorship Verification via k-Nearest Neighbor Estimation – Notebook for PAN at CLEF 2013. In: Forner et al (eds.) [3] (2013)
6. Holmes, D.I.: Authorship attribution. Computers and the Humanities 28, 87–106 (1994)
7. Jankowska, M., Kešelj, V., Milios, E.: Proximity based One-class Classification with Common n-Gram Dissimilarity for Authorship Verification Task – Notebook for PAN at CLEF 2013. In: Forner et al (eds.) [3] (2013)
8. Juola, P.: Authorship Attribution. Foundations and Trends in IR 1, 234–334 (2008)
9. Juola, P., Stamatatos, E.: Overview of the Author Identification Taskat PAN 2013. In Forner et al (eds.) [3] (2013)
10. Keselj, V., Peng, F., Cercone, N., Thomas, C.: N-gram-based Author Profiles for Authorship Attribution. In: Proc. of the Pacific Association for Computational Linguistics, pp. 255–264 (2003)
11. Koppel, M., Schler, J., Bonchek-Dokow, E.: Measuring Differentiability: Unmasking Pseudonymous Authors. Journal of Machine Learning Research 8, 1261–1276 (2007)
12. Koppel, M., Schler, J., Argamon, S.: Authorship Attribution in the Wild. Language Resources and Evaluation 45, 83–94 (2011)
13. Koppel, M., Schler, J., Argamon, S., Winter, Y.: The "Fundamental Problem" of Authorship Attribution. English Studies 93(3), 284–291 (2012)
14. Koppel, M., Winter, Y.: Determining if Two Documents are by the Same Author. Journal of the American Society for Information Science and Technology 65(1), 178–187 (2014)
15. Layton, R., Watters, P., Dazeley, R.: Local n-grams for Author Identification – Notebook for PAN at CLEF 2013. In: Forner et al (eds.) [3] (2013)
16. Sanderson, C., Guenter, S.: Short Text Authorship Attribution via Sequence Kernels, Markov Chains and Author Unmasking: An Investigation. In: Proc. of the International Conference on Empirical Methods in Natural Language Engineering, pp. 482–491 (2006)
17. Seidman, S.: Authorship Verification Using the Impostors Method – Notebook for PAN at CLEF 2013. In: Forner et al (ed.) [3] (2013)
18. Stamatatos, E., Fakotakis, N., Kokkinakis, G.: Automatic Text Categorization in Terms of Genre and Author. Computational Linguistics 26(4), 471–495 (2000)
19. Stamatatos. E.: Author Identification Using Imbalanced and Limited Training Texts. In: Proc. of the 4th International Workshop on Text-based Information Retrieval (2007)
20. Stamatatos, E.: A Survey of Modern Authorship Attribution Methods. Journal of the American Society for Information Science and Technology 60, 538–556 (2009)
21. Stamatatos, E.: Intrinsic Plagiarism Detection Using Character n-gram Profiles. In: Proc. of the 3rd Int. Workshop on Uncovering Plagiarism, Authorship, and Social Software Misuse (2009)
22. Veenman, C.J., Li, Z.: Authorship Verification with Compression Features – Notebook for PAN at CLEF 2013. In: Forner et al (eds.) [3] (2013)
23. Vilariño, D., Pinto, D., Gómez, H., León, S., Castillo, E.: Lexical-Syntactic and Graph-Based Features for Authorship Verification – Notebook for PAN at CLEF 2013. In: Forner et al (eds.) [3] (2013)

Sentiment Analysis for Reputation Management: Mining the Greek Web

Georgios Petasis[1,2], Dimitrios Spiliotopoulos[1,3],
Nikos Tsirakis[4], and Panayiotis Tsantilas[4]

[1] Intellitech Digital Technologies PC
petasisg@yahoo.gr, dimitris@intellitech.gr
[2] Software and Knowledge Engineering Laboratory,
Institute of Informatics and Telecommunications,
National Centre for Scientific Research (N.C.S.R.) "Demokritos",
GR-153 10, P.O. BOX 60228, Aghia Paraskevi, Athens, Greece
petasis@iit.demokritos.gr
[3] Athens Technology Centre
Rizariou 10, Chalandri, GR-15233, Athens, Greece
d.spiliotopoulos@atc.gr
[4] Palo Ltd.
{nt,pt}@palo.gr

Abstract. Harvesting the web and social web data is a meticulous and complex task. Applying the results to a successful business case such as brand monitoring requires high precision and recall for the opinion mining and entity recognition tasks. This work reports on the integrated platform of a state of the art Named-entity Recognition and Classification (NERC) system and opinion mining methods for a Software-as-a-Service (SaaS) approach on a fully automatic service for brand monitoring for the Greek language. The service has been successfully deployed to the biggest search engine in Greece powering the large-scale linguistic and sentiment analysis of about 80.000 resources per hour.

1 Introduction

Sentiment analysis and opinion mining are relatively new areas of natural language processing that seek to capture an aspect of text beyond the purely factual. Contrary to facts, which are objective expressions about entities, events and their attributes, opinions are subjective expressions of emotions, feelings, attitudes or sentiments towards entities, events and their properties. One important aspect of opinions is the fact that they have targets: opinions are expressed for objects (i.e. entities or events) and their attributes. There are several levels of granularity regarding the detailing of the target identification in sentiment analysis. The vast majority of approaches that have been presented in the literature can be classified in the following three categories: a) Document level: determine whether a document expresses opinion and identify the sentiment of the document as a whole. b) Sentence level: identify is the sentence contains opinions and determine

A. Likas, K. Blekas, and D. Kalles (Eds.): SETN 2014, LNAI 8445, pp. 327–340, 2014.
© Springer International Publishing Switzerland 2014

the sentiment of the whole sentence. *c*) Attribute level: identify object attributes and determine the sentiment towards these attributes.

Reputation management on the other hand, relates to monitoring the reputation or the public opinion of an individual, a brand or a product. Social Web is of course a valuable resource for detecting and monitoring customer feedback, in order to detect early warning signals to reputation problems and content which damages the reputation of an entity. However, the detection of this information is not an easy task, not only because of the technological challenges the identification and extraction technologies face with natural language processing, but also due to size of the social web and the amount of resources that need to be processed. As a result, the employed technologies must be both accurate in the results that they produce, and computationally efficient in order to be exploited in a commercial environment.

In this paper we present a real world application which applies natural language processing on the large scale, aiming to detect opinion polarity about a vast collection of individuals, companies and products in the Greek Web, as harvested by the larger search engine in Greece. Commercialised under the brand name "PaloPro", this application is the first commercial automated platform for reputation management in Greece, driven by the co-operation of two companies: Intellitech[1], responsible for the linguistic analysis, and Palo[2] which harvests the Greek Web and commercialises the final product. We will try to present an overview of the "PaloPro" application and the challenges we are facing regarding the linguistic technologies employed for detecting named-entities and opinions about these entities in the context of a large-scale, real-world application for the less linguistically resourced Greek language.

The rest of the paper is organised as follows: In section 2 the application "PaloPro" is presented, while section 3 presents "OpinionBuster", which is responsible for recognising named-entities (section 3.1) and detecting polarity for each recognised entity mention (section 3.2). An empirical evaluation with the help of two manually annotated "gold" corpora is presented in section 4, along with an evaluation on two specific entities, while section 5 concludes this paper.

2 A Real-World Application for Large-Scale Reputation Management: "PaloPro"

PaloPro is a subscription service which aggregates all news, blog posts, discussions and videos in Greek through a simple, friendly and useful tool for monitoring and analysis, in effect a Reputation Management System. The user has the opportunity to view in real-time, the source of the buzz, the parameters that affect the positive, negative or neutral reputation towards an organization and, ultimately, the overall polarity sentiment and trend on the Web. This is achieved by gathering and processing all references through natural language technologies that extract entities and opinions about these entities. Being a commercial

---

[1] Intellitech Digital Technologies PC: http://www.intellitech.gr
[2] Palo Digital Technologies Ltd: http://www.palo.gr

subscription service, the requirements for accurate results are high for the underlying linguistic processing infrastructure, aiming at achieving accuracy over 85% for both the named-entity recognition and the polarity detection tasks.

The data are collected and cleaned by a plethora of real-time crawlers, which aggregate data from different sources, including traditional news, forums and social media such as blogs, Twitter and Facebook posts. The crawling and storage procedure is fully controlled in such a way that the system may provide a near real-time analysis to the end user. Based on the update frequency of each source, the crawling mechanism is adjusted and prioritizes consecutively all the sources. Multiple layers of spam filtering are deployed to ensure that clean data are provided to the analysis modules. The amount of documents crawled in a typical day usually exceeds 2.5 million documents. The main content is collected from about 1.500 different websites which are categorised based on their importance (rank) and the news domain of expertise. Most of them are news portals spanning broad domains of news articles

A complementary source of content of journalistic orientation are the 10.000 blogs that the mechanism is parsing. The text is usually informal, sometimes with relaxed syntax. In blog posts, there is, also, a larger number of idiomatic expressions compared to traditional journalistic sources. A very large portion of the data comes from social networks such as Facebook, Twitter and Youtube. The system collects and analyses the all the posts, tweets and video comments from all Greek open profiles and in parallel leverages the potential sources and multimedia within these posts. Forum posts is another source of content with informal text, like Blogs, but also contains continuity and related text snippets that represent the forum conversations. From this type of source more detailed insights about user interactions are collected.

PaloPro is organised around the notion of the "workspace" or "dashboard", via which the reputation of sets of user-selectable entities or user-specified keywords are monitored. The user may create a new workspace and is expected to select one or more persons, companies, locations, brands, or product names from a large database of monitored entities (figure 2), and/or define a set of keywords, in case an entity is not contained into the database of monitored objects. The user may define any number of workspaces, all of which are visible when the user logs on to system, as shown in figure 1.

Custom dashboards specific to business of journalistic needs may be created and edited. The auto-generated dashboard information may be accessed at any time and updated instantly with real-time data. Each dashboard, once selected, is initially presented through an overall summary, which presents activity over time (figure 4). This summary is followed by a more detailed report over the various sources, the top influencers, and the "sentiment radar", which present various aspects of the analytics. Various levels of abstraction may be accessed, offering schemas that range from an overview report to the detailed information extracted (as represented by the text segments that are analysed in the actual documents) about an entity. For example, figure 5 lists all the postings found in Facebook about an entity, in a specific day.

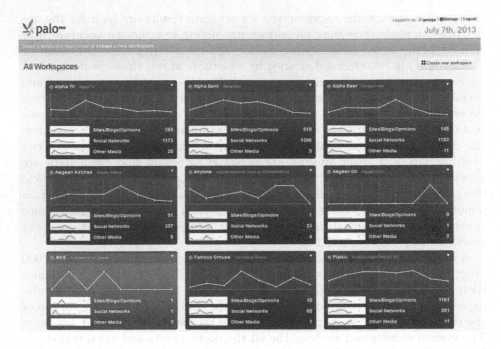

Fig. 1. The initial view of PaloPro, presenting the set of user-defined workspaces

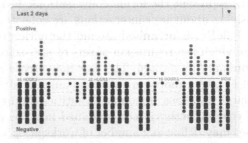

Fig. 2. Selecting entities from the system's database, during workspace creation

Fig. 3. The "Sentiment Radar", providing an overview of the overall opinion polarity for an entity over time

Through the system, a user has access to information related to different entities or keywords such as persons, organisations, companies, brands, products, events etc. that are monitored by the system in the crawled corpora, along with sentiment (currently limited to polarity) about them. Automated alerts can be set up so that the service may deliver instant notifications whenever the data matches some predefined, user-specified criteria, as new information is extracted or when the extracted information exceeds certain user-configurable thresholds.

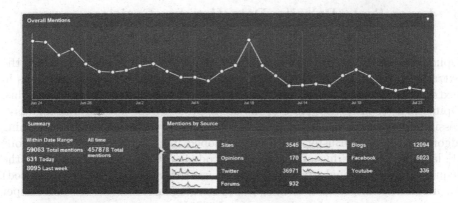

Fig. 4. Overall summary of a dashboard, summarising activity over time

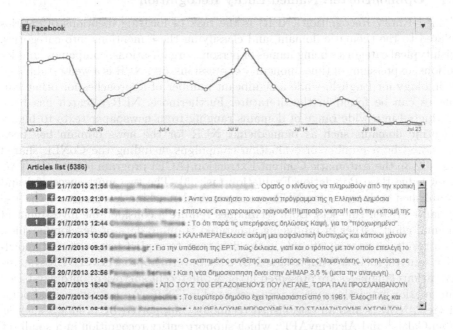

Fig. 5. Facebook insights about the closing of the Greek national television organisation on June 11, 2013

In addition, within PaloPro, a competitive reputation analysis involves identifying competitive results that rank for content and other parameters, to empower the end user to identify instances where existing content could potentially be promoted and where gaps occur in content that may be enhanced further.

3   Large-Scale Polarity Detection for Entities: "OpinionBuster"

OpinionBuster is the product that powers PaloPro, as it is responsible for the extraction of named-entities and the polarity associated with their mentions in texts. Able to locate entities and polarity to a wide range of thematic domains, OpinionBuster integrates state of the art approaches for natural language processing, ranging from ontologies and rule-based systems to machine learning algorithms. OpinionBuster has been developed in the context of the Ellogon[3] [1] language engineering platform: being coded in C/C++, Ellogon offers the required computational efficiency (both in used memory and processing speed) for a commercial product, achieving a processing speed of 100 documents per second, per processing thread, on an Intel 3930K processor.

3.1   OpinionBuster: Named-Entity Recognition

Named Entity Recognition (NER) is the task of locating mentions of entities related to the thematic domain, and classifying these mentions into categories, with typical categories being names of persons, organisations, companies, and locations, expressions of time, monetary expressions, etc. NER is a well-established technology for English, while a significant number of approaches for other languages can be found in the literature. Furthermore, NER research has been conducted in a wide range of domains ranging from newspaper texts to highly scientific domains such as biomedicine. NER for the news domain has been promoted by a number of evaluation campaigns including the CoNLL shared tasks [2,3], the Automatic Content Extraction (ACE) program [4] and the TAC Knowledge Base Population Evaluation task [5]. The two most successful and established techniques for NER are supervised machine learning and the use of hand-written rule-sets. Both techniques require a considerable investment of manual effort, either in producing annotated training data or developing rules. As a result, more recent trends in the field tend to exploit large external knowledge sources, such as Wikipedia or DBPedia. Several approaches of NER systems for various languages are presented in [6], while recent surveys of ontology-based information extraction systems are presented in [7,8,9]. From a commercial point of view, NER is also an established technology supported by products such as OpenCalais[4] and AlchemyAPI[5], which support entity recognition in a small set of languages, including English, French, German, Italian, Portuguese, Russian, Spanish, and Swedish. To our knowledge, OpinionBuster is the first product that offers NER for the Greek language.

However, using any approach for reputation management requires a high level of accuracy, and usually requires entities that are not commonly found, such as political parties, or products of a specific company and its competitors. Achieving high accuracy levels without the use of domain knowledge is very difficult,

---

[3] http://www.ellogon.org
[4] http://www.opencalais.com/
[5] http://www.alchemyapi.com/

if not impossible. As a result, OpinionBuster exploits a large set of knowledge sources, as well as state-of-the-art approaches for its NER component, including: *a*) Open (and linked) data based on various sources, such as the various languages of Wikipedia (as entities can appear either in Greek or in other languages, depending on their place of origin), various governmental sites that provide lists of parliament representatives and government members, the registry of companies that participate to the Greek stock market, etc. *b*) An ontology of entities maintained internally by Intellitech, which contains entities that are mainly found in the Greek market (such as products and companies), usually associated with a thematic domain which can aid in entity disambiguation. *c*) A NER extraction grammar, specifically designed for the extraction of named-entities. This grammar is a probabilistic context-free grammar and has been automatically extracted from (manually selected) positive examples only, with the help of the eg-GRIDS+ grammatical inference algorithm [10,11]. *d*) A thematic domain identifier, which classifies a document into one or more predefined thematic domains, aiming at providing a disambiguation context for named entity disambiguation. *e*) A machine learning based NER component based on Conditional Random Fields [12,13,14]. *f*) A rule-based co-reference resolution component. *g*) A rule-based named entity disambiguation component, which disambiguates mentions of entities that share the same surface forms according to the thematic domain(s) of the document and the context the forms appear within. *h*) A set of filtering rules, that combine the information generated by all the aforementioned components and decide upon the final classification of word forms detected as possible mentions of entities.

The motivation behind the use of so many knowledge sources and processing approaches, is of course the requirement for high accuracy. Detecting unambiguous entity names in Greek such as "Obama" may be trivial, but identifying that "Alpha" refers to "Alpha TV" station, "Alpha" beer or "Alpha Bank" requires contextual and domain information. Similarly, the word form "Aegean" may refer to even more entities, including the Aegean sea, the Aegean Airlines, 2-3 hotels named "Aegean", to "Aegean Oil", to the shipping companies "Aegean Ferries" and "Aegean Flying Dolphins", to "Aegean College", to "Aegean Power", to the newspapers "Aegean Press" and "Aegean Times", to the "Rethimno Aegean" basketball team, to the helicopter model "Aegean Hawk", etc. It is not uncommon for companies to use popular words in their names, such as the company "Πλαίσιο" ("Plaisio"), which has several meanings in Greek, including "frame" and "in the context of". Distinguishing among "στο πλαίσιο της περιοχής" (at the local "Plaisio" store) from the "στο πλαίσιο της έρευνας" (in the context of research) and the rest of the more than 6.000 expressions we have already identified the word "πλαίσιο" is used, is not an easy task.

3.2 OpinionBuster: Sentiment Analysis

Sentiment analysis and opinion mining are research areas of natural language processing that seek to capture an aspect of text beyond the purely factual. Contrary to facts, which are objective statements about entities, events and their attributes, opinions are subjective expressions of emotions, feelings, attitudes or sentiments towards entities, events and their properties. Sentiment analysis is an active and popular research field, where many new approaches are presented each year. Almost all approaches exploit a knowledge source (i.e. a lexicon) of sentiment bearing words, and try to detect sentiment or polarity of a word in its context. Sentiment Analysis within a multilingual context has to meet several challenges, especially since the majority of research on sentiment analysis has concentrated only on monolingually and mostly for English. There are mainly two approaches in multilingual sentiment analysis: statistical and lexical. Statistical approaches need training data from different languages that are usually sparse, while lexical approaches demand lexical resources in different languages that are not always available.

In order to alleviate the problem of resources scarcity, several approaches have been presented that aim in acquisition of lexica or grammars for sentiment analysis. In [15] an approach is presented that tries to project resources for English into Romanian. Having as a starting point a lexicon of English sentiment bearing words and annotated corpora for subjectivity (subjective/objective), both the lexicon and the annotated corpora are translated into Romanian, and subsequently used for training a statistical classifier for performing sentence level subjectivity classification. The automatic extraction of subjectivity lexica for languages with scarce resources is also studied in [16], where bootstrapping is applied on a small raw corpus initialized with a basic lexicon of a small set of seed words. The focus of this method is also on Romanian but it is applicable to any other language. Moreover, in [17], domain specific keywords are selected by comparing the distribution of words in a domain-specific document with the distribution of words in a general domain corpus. The context of each keyword helps to produce collocation patterns. By these local grammar patterns, sentiment bearing phrases are extracted and classified. This approach applied the proposed local grammar approach for performing sentiment classification of financial news streams within a multilingual framework (English, Arabic, and Chinese).

Machine learning approaches have been broadly exploited in sentiment analysis. The cornerstone on sentiment analysis is [18] where the authors compare the effectiveness of Naive Bayes, Maximum Entropy and Support Vector Machines in order to classify opinion in movie review documents. In [19] the authors combine two machine-learning classifiers through precision-based vote weighting, in order to explore the challenges of portability across domains and text genres. Their sentiment analysis system integrates a corpus-based classifier with a lexicon-based system trained on WordNet glosses and synsets, aiming at developing a system that relies on both general and domain-specific knowledge.

Besides research on sentiment classification of documents, there is also significant work on sentiment classification of sentences, mainly through supervised statistical learning. Sentiment level classification of newspaper headlines exploiting a variety of machine learning techniques has been the goal of the Affective Text Task of SemEval '07 [20]. A similar task, concerning the sentiment classification of newspaper headlines is addressed in [21]. Moreover in [21], structured models such as Hidden Markov Models (HMMs) are exploited in sentiment classification of headlines. The advantage of HMMs against other machine learning approaches employed until now in sentiment analysis is that the majority of them are based on flat bag-of-features representations of sentences, without capturing the structural nature of sub-sentential interactions. In contrast, HMMs, being sequential models, encode this structural information, since sentence elements are represented as sequential features.

OpinionBuster employs a rule-based approach for performing polarity detection, based on compositional polarity classification [22]. OpinionBuster is currently restricted to detecting the positive, negative or neutral polarity for entity mentions in texts. It analyses the input texts with the aid of a polarity lexicon that specifies the prior polarity of words, which contains more than 6.000 Greek words (and more than 12.000 unique word forms, as Greek is an inflectional language). As a second step, a chunker is used to determine phrases that are the basis for a compositional treatment of phrase-level polarity assignment. Once polarity has been detected, it is distributed over the involved entity mentions with the help of subcategorization frames for verbs, which in our case are manually constructed patterns aiming at detecting the basic syntactic structures around the verbs, in order to distinguish whether the entity mentions receive or generate the polarity detected in the phrases. In case, however, a verb is encountered that cannot be handled by a rule then a simple heuristic is applied, which assigns the detected polarity to all entity mentions within the phrase.

4   Empirical Evaluation

In order to evaluate our system, we have manually annotated a corpus with all mentions of entities, along with the polarity these mentions can be associated with. The corpus has been collected from two popular Greek news papers, "Real News"[6] and "Kathimerini"[7] by monitoring the RSS feeds provided by the news papers. Despite the fact that our system covers a large number of domains, we have opted to monitor only the section related to politics, from both news papers. The two newspapers were monitored for a period of about two months, from December 1st, 2012 to January 31st, 2013. From the collected corpus, 2,300 texts were selected and manually annotated by two annotators. Inter-annotator agreement was measured above 97% for the task of annotating mentions of entities, and above 89% for the task of polarity detection for these entity mentions.

The annotated corpus that has been used as a gold standard, contains 49,511 entity mentions. Regarding named entity recognition, OpinionBuster was able to identify 48,827 entity mentions, out of which 45,789 mentions were identical to manually annotated ones, leading to a precision of 93.78%, with a recall equal to 92.48% and an F1-Measure equal to 93.12%. Regarding polarity detection, OpinionBuster was able to identify a polarity for all entity mentions recognised

---

[6] http://www.real.gr/
[7] http://www.kathimerini.gr/

(48,827), 31,754 of which were correct, leading to a precision of 65.03%, with a recall equal to 64.13% and an F1-Measure equal to 64.58%. Most of the failures related to opinion mining have to do with the absence of subcategorization frames for the involved verbs, without which our system is not able to attribute polarity to the correct entity mentions, resulting in the use of a simple heuristic that distributes the average polarity of a phrase to all entity mentions within the phrase. It should be noted that all the documents of the gold corpus used in this empirical evaluation are news items, and that the corpus does not contain any comments done by users or other kind of social data, such as tweets or Facebook postings.

4.1 Evaluation on the NOMAD Corpus

NOMAD[8] (Policy Formulation and Validation through non Moderated Crowd-sourcing) is an EU-funded project that aims to aid modern politicians in testing, detecting and understanding how citizens perceive their own political agendas, and also in stimulating the emergence of discussions and contributions on the informal web (e.g. forums, social networks, blogs, newsgroups and wikis), so as to gather useful feedback for immediate (re)action. In this way, politicians can create a stable feedback loop between information gathered on the Web and the definition of their political agendas based on this contribution. The ability to leverage the vast amount of user-generated content for supporting governments in their political decisions requires new ICT tools that will be able to analyze and classify the opinions expressed on the informal Web, or stimulate responses, as well as to put data from sources as diverse as blogs, online opinion polls and government reports to an effective use. NOMAD aims to introduce these different new dimensions into the experience of policy making by providing decision-makers with fully automated solutions for content search, selection, acquisition, categorization and visualization that work in a collaborative form in the policy-making arena.

One of the central elements within the NOMAD project is the identification of *arguments* in favour or against a topic, and the opinion polarity expressed on the informal Web towards these arguments. For the purposes of evaluation of the NOMAD system, a "gold" annotated corpus has been created, from 500 articles gathered from the Greek Web, relevant to the thematic domain of renewable energy sources. These 500 articles have been collected by performing queries on popular search engines using suitable terms, without restring their origin. As a result the corpus contains articles from news, sites, blogs, etc. The articles have been manually annotated with entities relevant to renewable energy sources, and arguments towards these entities, related to the advantages and disadvantages of the various energy sources (represented by the entities). In addition, each argument has been labelled with the opinion polarity of the author of each article towards the argument, using three labels "positive", "neutral" and "negative". The corpus has been annotated by two annotators, where conflicts have been

---

[8] http://www.nomad-project.eu/

resolved by a third annotator in order to create an annotated corpus of high-quality.

OpinionBuster has been applied on this corpus, with the aim to label the manually annotated arguments with opinion polarity information, exploiting both internal (the words of the arguments) and contextual information (the words of the sentence containing the argument). OpinionBuster has been applied on 120 articles (out of the 500 annotated articles), which contained 940 annotated arguments. OpinionBuster assigned a polarity label on 814 arguments, out of which 604 were correct, exhibiting a precision of 74.20%, with a recall equal to 64.25% and an F1-Measure equal to 68.87%. Most of the errors of OpinionBuster on this thematic domain can be attributed to various energy-related terminology that was absent from the polarity lexicon, but also on the absence of domain knowledge about specific objects, such as the negative impact nuclear power has on the public opinion, leading to negativity of arguments related to nu clear power, without this negativity being expressed linguistically in the articles. Finally, OpinionBuster failed to detect correctly situations where comparisons were made, and an energy source that pollutes the environment may be thought positively, if it is polluting less than an alternative energy source.

4.2 Case Study: Empirical Evaluation on Two Specific Entities

In the previous two empirical evaluations, OpinionBuster has been evaluated with the help of manually annotated corpora, containing a wide range of entities and polarities associated to them. In this third evaluation we are going to evaluate OpinionBuster's output on real system data, as processed by PaloPro. In order to perform this evaluation, we concentrated on only two entities, the mobile telephone company "Vodafone", and the Greek bank "Τράπεζα Άλφα" ("Alpha Bank"). All documents (news articles, blogs, tweets and Facebook postings) referring to both entities, have been collected and evaluated by two annotators: For each document, the annotators have measured whether each entity has received the correct opinion polarity considering all the mentions of the entity in the document. The evaluation results are shown in tables 1 and 2, where the number of documents are displayed (both the total number of documents containing the entity, and the number of documents in which the entity has been labelled with the correct opinion polarity), along with accuracy. As we can see

Table 1. Evaluation results for the entity "Vodafone"

	Correct	Total	Accuracy
Sites	7	9	77.78 %
Blogs	18	18	100.00 %
Facebook	166	183	90.71 %
Twitter	122	158	77.22 %
Overall	313	371	84.37 %

Table 2. Evaluation results for the entity "Alpha Bank"

	Correct	Total	Accuracy
Sites	62	78	79.49 %
Blogs	55	69	79.49 %
Facebook	7	8	87.50 %
Twitter	100	129	77.52 %
Overall	223	282	79.08 %

from the results shown in these two tables, OpinionBuster performs quite well on this task, achieving an accuracy around 80%.

5   Conclusions

In this paper the first large-scale real-world application for reputation management for the Greek Web has been presented. Online Reputation Management is a novel and active application area for the natural language processing research community. Sentiment analysis plays a central role in this area, as it provides the main mechanism for keeping track of polarity, opinion, attitude, feelings on the web, etc. People use the social media to write news, blog posts, comments, reviews and tweets about all sort of different topics. Even simplistic sentiment analysis, such as polarity detection, can provide valuable insight to reputation management specialists, when tracking products, brands and individual persons, as the specialist can easily determine whether the monitored entities are viewed positively or negatively on the Web. PaloPro provides polarity analysis across the different data inputs and strives for precise and accurate results not only at the document level, but also on the attribute level by extracting opinion polarity for specific mentions of an entity in texts. Mining opinion polarity at the attribute level eliminates false results and makes the analysis more precise for the tracked entities, in comparison to polarity mining at the document or sentence level.

In PaloPro users seek to monitor their company, organization, services or products. The data related to these categories often contains valuable insights about the thoughts, needs and wants of consumers/clients. Most users do online research but most of the time it's impossible to monitor their reputation across all the data channels. PaloPro and its sentiment analysis feature ascertains how news, blogs and social media users affect reputation by applying robust sentiment analysis methods to classify polarity for this reputation. Prior to public release of this feature, potential customer survey results suggested that even opinion polarity mining can became a good starting point for creating an automated management platform for reputation.

Regarding the natural language processing infrastructure, responsible for the recognition of entity mentions and their polarity, the performance has been measured to be above 93% for the detection of entity mentions, which is an excellent result for the Greek language, on the thematic domain of news about politics.

On the other hand, polarity detection did not exhibit the same performance levels, measuring a performance of about 64%, lower than the desired performance of 85%.

Acknowledgements. The authors would like to acknowledge partial support of this work from the European Union's Seventh Framework Programme (FP7/2007-2013) under grant agreement no 288513. For more details, please see the NOMAD project's website, http://www.nomad-project.eu.

References

1. Petasis, G., Karkaletsis, V., Paliouras, G., Androutsopoulos, I., Spyropoulos, C.D.: Ellogon: A New Text Engineering Platform. In: Proceedings of the 3rd International Conference on Language Resources and Evaluation (LREC 2002), May 20 31, pp. 72–78. European Language Resources Association, Las Palmas (2002)
2. Tjong Kim Sang, E.F.: Introduction to the conll-2002 shared task: Language-independent named entity recognition. In: Proceedings of the 6th Conference on Natural Language Learning, COLING 2002, vol. 20, pp. 1–4. Association for Computational Linguistics, Stroudsburg (2002)
3. Tjong Kim Sang, E.F., De Meulder, F.: Introduction to the conll-2003 shared task: Language-independent named entity recognition. In: Proceedings of the Seventh Conference on Natural Language Learning at HLT-NAACL 2003, CONLL 2003, vol. 4, pp. 142–147. Association for Computational Linguistics, Stroudsburg (2003)
4. Doddington, G.R., Mitchell, A., Przybocki, M.A., Ramshaw, L.A., Strassel, S., Weischedel, R.M.: The automatic content extraction (ace) program - tasks, data, and evaluation. In: LREC. European Language Resources Association (2004)
5. Ji, H., Grishman, R., Dang, H.: Overview of the TAC 2011 Knowledge Base Population Track. In: TAC 2011 Proceedings Papers (2011)
6. Nadeau, D., Sekine, S.: A survey of named entity recognition and classification. Lingvisticae Investigationes 30, 3–26 (2007)
7. Karkaletsis, V., Fragkou, P., Petasis, G., Iosif, E.: Ontology Based Information Extraction from Text. In: Paliouras, G., Spyropoulos, C.D., Tsatsaronis, G. (eds.) Multimedia Information Extraction. LNCS (LNAI), vol. 6050, pp. 89–109. Springer, Heidelberg (2011)
8. Petasis, G., Karkaletsis, V., Paliouras, G., Krithara, A., Zavitsanos, E.: Ontology Population and Enrichment: State of the Art. In: Paliouras, G., Spyropoulos, C.D., Tsatsaronis, G. (eds.) Multimedia Information Extraction. LNCS (LNAI), vol. 6050, pp. 134–166. Springer, Heidelberg (2011)
9. Iosif, E., Petasis, G., Karkaletsis, V.: Ontology-Based Information Extraction under a Bootstrapping Approach, ch. 1, pp. 1–21. IGI Global, Hershey (2012)
10. Petasis, G., Paliouras, G., Spyropoulos, C.D., Halatsis, C.: Eg-GRIDS: Context-Free Grammatical Inference from Positive Examples Using Genetic Search. In: Paliouras, G., Sakakibara, Y. (eds.) ICGI 2004. LNCS (LNAI), vol. 3264, pp. 223–234. Springer, Heidelberg (2004)
11. Petasis, G., Paliouras, G., Karkaletsis, V., Halatsis, C., Spyropoulos, C.D.: E-GRIDS: Computationally Efficient Grammatical Inference from Positive Examples. GRAMMARS 7, 69–110 (2004); Technical Report referenced in the paper: http://www.ellogon.org/petasis/bibliography/GRAMMARS/GRAMMARS2004-SpecialIssue-Petasis-TechnicalReport.pdf

12. Lafferty, J.D., McCallum, A., Pereira, F.C.N.: Conditional random fields: Probabilistic models for segmenting and labeling sequence data. In: Proceedings of the Eighteenth International Conference on Machine Learning, ICML 2001, pp. 282–289. Morgan Kaufmann Publishers Inc., San Francisco (2001)
13. Sha, F., Pereira, F.: Shallow parsing with conditional random fields. In: Proceedings of the 2003 Conference of the North American Chapter of the Association for Computational Linguistics on Human Language Technology, NAACL 2003, vol. 1, pp. 134–141. Association for Computational Linguistics, Stroudsburg (2003)
14. Sutton, C., McCallum, A.: An introduction to conditional random fields. Foundations and Trends in Machine Learning 4(4), 267–373 (2012)
15. Mihalcea, R.: Using wikipedia for automatic word sense disambiguation. In: Sidner, C.L., Schultz, T., Stone, M., Zhai, C. (eds.) HLT-NAACL, pp. 196–203. The Association for Computational Linguistics (2007)
16. Carmen Banea, R.M., Wiebe, J.: A bootstrapping method for building subjectivity lexicons for languages with scarce resources. In: Proceedings of the Sixth International Conference on Language Resources and Evaluation (LREC 2008), European Language Resources Association (ELRA), Marrakech, Morocco (2008), http://www.lrec-conf.org/proceedings/lrec2008/
17. Devitt, A., Ahmad, K.: Sentiment polarity identification in financial news: A cohesion-based approach. In: Carroll, J.A., van den Bosch, A., Zaenen, A. (eds.) ACL. The Association for Computational Linguistics (2007)
18. Pang, B., Lee, L., Vaithyanathan, S.: Thumbs up? sentiment classification using machine learning techniques. In: Proceedings of EMNLP, pp. 79–86 (2002)
19. Andreevskaia, A., Bergler, S.: When specialists and generalists work together: Overcoming domain dependence in sentiment tagging. In: Proceedings of ACL 2008: HLT, pp. 290–298. Association for Computational Linguistics, Columbus (2008)
20. Strapparava, C., Mihalcea, R.: Semeval-2007 task 14: Affective text. In: Proceedings of the 4th International Workshop on Semantic Evaluations, SemEval 2007, pp. 70–74. Association for Computational Linguistics, Stroudsburg (2007)
21. Rentoumi, V., Giannakopoulos, G., Karkaletsis, V., Vouros, G.A.: Sentiment analysis of figurative language using a word sense disambiguation approach. In: Proceedings of the International Conference RANLP 2009, pp. 370–375. Association for Computational Linguistics, Borovets (2009)
22. Klenner, M., Petrakis, S., Fahrni, A.: Robust compositional polarity classification. In: Proceedings of the International Conference RANLP 2009, pp. 180–184. Association for Computational Linguistics, Borovets (2009)

Splice Site Recognition Using Transfer Learning

Georgios Giannoulis[1], Anastasia Krithara[2],
Christos Karatsalos[3], and Georgios Paliouras[2]

[1] University of Houston, Texas, USA
[2] National Center for Scientific Research (NCSR) 'Demokritos', Athens, Greece
[3] University of Athens, Athens, Greece

Abstract. In this work, we consider a transfer learning approach based on K-means for splice site recognition. We use different representations for the sequences, based on n-gram graphs. In addition, a novel representation based on the secondary structure of the sequences is proposed. We evaluate our approach on genomic sequence data from model organisms of varying evolutionary distance. The first obtained results indicate that the proposed representations are promising for the problem of splice site recognition.

1 Introduction

Computational biology provides a wide range of applications for machine learning methods. These methods are often used to model biological mechanisms to describe them and ultimately understand them. For building such models it is important to have a reasonably sized training set, which is often not available for many applications. In the biomedical domain obtaining additional labeled training examples can be very costly in both money and time. Thus, it may be useful to combine information from other related tasks as a way of obtaining more accurate models and reducing labeling cost. However, many machine learning methods work well only under the common assumption that the training and test data are drawn from the same domain. When the domain changes most statistical models need to be rebuilt from scratch using newly collected and labeled training data. Knowledge transfer would greatly improve the performance of learning by avoiding expensive data labeling efforts. In recent years, *transfer learning* has emerged as a new learning framework to address this problem. It tries to extract knowledge from previous experience and apply it to new learning domains or tasks.

Existing transfer learning approaches can be categorized into three main types [9], based on the characteristics of the source and target domains and tasks:

1. *Inductive transfer:* The target task is different from the source task and some labeled data in the target domain are required. For document classification, two tasks are considered different if either the label sets are different in the two domains, or the source and target documents are very imbalanced in terms of user-defined classes. Depending on the availability of labeled data in the source domain, we distinguish two subcategories:

A. Likas, K. Blekas, and D. Kalles (Eds.): SETN 2014, LNAI 8445, pp. 341–353, 2014.
© Springer International Publishing Switzerland 2014

- Labeled data in the source domain are available. This setting is similar to multitask learning.
- No labeled data in the source domain are available. This setting is similar to self-taught learning.

Most existing approaches of this type focus on the former subcategory.

2. *Transductive transfer learning setting:* The source and target tasks are the same, while the source and target domains differ. For document classification, two domains are considered different if either the term features are different, or their marginal distributions are different. No labeled data for the target domain are available, while labeled data are available for the source domain.

3. *Unsupervised transfer learning:* Similar to inductive transfer learning, the target task is different from but related to the source task. However, the unsupervised transfer learning focuses on solving unsupervised learning tasks in the target domain, such as clustering. There are no labeled data available in either the source or the target domains.

In our work, we are focusing on transductive transfer learning. In particular, we are taking a closer look at a common special case of splice site recognition, where different tasks correspond to different organisms. Splice site recognition is a sub-problem of the most general topic of gene prediction problem.

In figure 1 the major steps in protein synthesis are presented: transcription, post-processing and translation. In the post-processing step, the pre-mRNA is transformed into mRNA. One necessary step in the process of obtaining mature mRNA is called splicing. The mRNA sequence of a eukaryotic gene is "interrupted" by noncoding regions called introns. A gene starts with an exon and may then be interrupted by an intron, followed by another exon, intron and so on until it ends in an exon. In the splicing process, the introns are removed. There are two different splice sites: the exon-intron boundary, referred to as the donor site and the intron-exon boundary, that is the acceptor. Splice sites have quite strong consensus sequences, i.e. almost each position in a small window around the splice site is representative of the most frequently occurring nucleotide when many existing sequences are compared in an alignment [11]. The vast majority of all splice-sites are so called canonical splice-sites, which are characterized by the presence of the dimers GT and AG for donor and acceptor sites, respectively [15]. These dimers occur very frequently at non splice-sites positions, which makes this specific classification problem extremely unbalanced. For splice site recognition, one must solve two classification problems: discriminating true from decoy splice sites for both acceptor and donor sites. Because all these basic mechanisms tend to be relatively well conserved throughout evolution, we can benefit from transferring knowledge from a different organism to another, taking into account the commonalities and the differences between the two domains.

We are applying a transfer learning method to face the problem of poorly annotated genomes, for predicting splice sites. We are using a modified version of clustering algorithm of K-means, in which the commonalities between the two domains are taken into account. In this work, we are focusing more on the different representations of the sequence, and how the latter can influence the results.

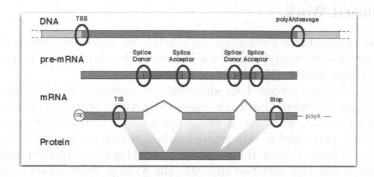

Fig. 1. Splice sites in the DNA sequences [12]

The rest of the paper is organized as follows. In the next section, the state-of-the-art in splice site recognition is presented. Then, the representations that we propose are described. In the fourth section, we explain the proposed transfer learning approach. Then, the experimental evaluation of our methods is presented, as well as the obtained results. In the last section, the main conclusion and the future directions of this work are presented.

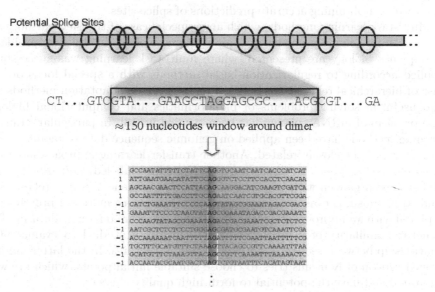

Fig. 2. Example of splice sites and non splice site sequences [12]

2   Related Work

In the literature, there are several approaches for splice-site detection. Most of them are based on Support Vector Machines (SVMs), neural networks and Hidden Markov Models (HMM).

In [14] SVMs are proposed for splice-site recognition: the SVM classifier is trained, using as labeled data, a subsequence consisting of only local information around the potential splice site. A new support vector kernel is also proposed. A comparison is performed in [11], where Markov models are proposed, as well as SVMs with different kernels: the locality improved kernel, originally proposed for recognition translation initiation sites [21], the SVM-pairwise kernel using alignment scores [14], the Tangent vectors Of Posterior log-odds (TOP) kernel making use of a probabilistic model [16], the standard polynomial kernel [17] and the weighted degree kernel [14]. A predictor based on the latter kernel has been successfully used in combination with other information for predicting the splice-site form of a gene, while outperforming other HMM based approaches [12]. [19] proposed the usage of linear SVMs on binary features computed from di-nucleotides, an approach which also outperformed previous Markov models. In [10], a different approach has been proposed, based on a multilayer neural network method with Markovian probabilities as inputs. A comparison between different approaches is performed in [15]. The latter comparison has shown that the engineering of the kernel, the careful choice of features and a sound model selection procedure are important for obtaining accurate predictions of splice-sites.

Multi-task learning methods, which are a special case of transfer learning, are often used for solving problems of computational biology. In [18], two problems of sequence biology are presented, where multi-task learning was successfully applied according to regularization-based methods with a special focus on the case of hierarchical relationship between tasks. Domain adaptation methods are also useful in solving problems of bioinformatics and computational biology. The problem of mRNA splicing has been studied in [13]. In particular, transfer learning methods have been applied on genomic sequence data of model organisms that are not closely related. Another transfer learning approach has been proposed in [6], where an algorithm that combines labeled sequences from a well studied organism with labeled and unlabeled sequences from a related less studied organism is evaluated. In [20] recurring sequence motifs of proteins are explored with an improved K-means clustering algorithm on a new dataset. The structural similarity of recurring sequence clusters is studied to evaluate the relationship between sequence motifs and their structures. In the latter, an improved version of K-means tries to choose suitable initial points, which are well separated and have the potential to form high-quality clusters.

3   Data Representation

As in the majority of the above methods, we consider the task of identifying the so-called acceptor splice sites within a large set of potential splice sites based on a sequence window around a site. In this study, we choose to experiment with different representations based on these sequence windows. In particular, we propose the application of the n-gram graph (NGG) representation methodology [4], which manages to capture both local and global characteristics of the analysed sequences.

The main idea behind the n-gram graphs is that the neighborhood between sub-sequences in a sequence contains a crucial part of the sequence information. The n-gram graph (Figure 3), as derived from a single sequence, is essentially a histogram of the co-occurrences of symbols. The symbols are considered to co-occur when found within a maximum distance (window) of each other. The size of the window, which is a parameter of the n-gram graph, allows for fuzziness in the representation of co-occurrences within a sequence. The fact that n-gram graphs take into account co-occurrences offers the local descriptiveness. We also achieve robustness, since we do not consider only one neighbour but as many as the window dictates. The fact that they act as a histogram of such co-occurrences provides their global representation potential.

As opposed to probabilistic models, the n-gram graphs are deterministic. As opposed to n-gram models, n-gram graphs offer more information, based on the representation of co-occurrences. Overall, they provide a trade-off between expressiveness and generalization.

The n-gram graph framework, also offers a set of important operators. These operators allow combining individual graphs into a model graph (the update operator), and comparing pairs of graphs providing graded similarity measurements (similarity operators). In the sequence composition setting, the representation and set of operators provide one more means of analysis and comparison, one that is lacking from widely-implemented probabilistic models such as HMMs.

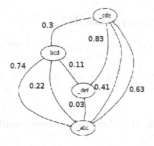

Fig. 3. n-gram graph representation [4]

The n-gram graph is a graph $G = < V^G, E^G, L, W >$, where V^G is the set of vertices, E^G is the set of edges, L is a function assigning a label to each vertex *and to each edge* and W is a function assigning a weight to every edge. The graph has n-grams labeling its vertices $v^G \in V^G$. The edges $e^G \in E^G$ connecting the n-grams indicate proximity of the corresponding vertex n-grams. The weight of the edges can indicate a variety of traits. In our implementation we apply as weight the number of times the two connected n-grams were found to co-occur.

It is important to note that in n-gram graphs *each vertex is unique*. To create the n-gram graph from a given sequence, a fixed-width window D_{win} of characters around a given n-gram N_0 is used. All character n-grams within the window are considered to be neighbors of N_0. These neighbors are represented as connected vertices in the text graph. Each edge $e = < a, b >$ is weighted based on the number of co-occurrences of the neighbors within a window in the sequence.

Based on the above representation of n-gram graphs, we experiment with three variations: we consider the whole sequence window around the acceptor, only the sequence part before the acceptor and finally the sequence part after the acceptor. In other words, we divide each sequence in two parts according to the dimer AG (the acceptor), so we have one n-gram graph for representing the left part of the sequence, one for the right and one for the whole sequence. The idea is to see if the subsequence after the splice site is more important than the subsequence of the splice site for the task of recognition, or if the whole subsequence is needed. We experiment with combinations of all three of them (Figure 5).

The second representation we propose is based on the idea of representing the structure of the sequence, i.e. the so called *secondary structure* of the sequence [1], using n-gram graphs. The intuition behind the use of the structure is that splice site positions, compared to genome windows that are in coding or non coding genome, also differ in their structure compositions, as suggested in [3,8]. That occurs since splice site positions are "loosely" connected compared to genome regions, in order for the spliceosome to attach. To capture this information, we obtain the most probable m-RNA structure which has the least energy.

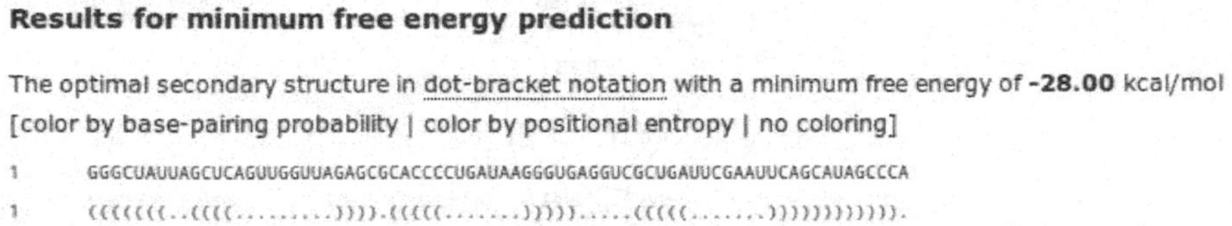

Results for minimum free energy prediction

The optimal secondary structure in dot-bracket notation with a minimum free energy of **-28.00** kcal/mol
[color by base-pairing probability | color by positional entropy | no coloring]

```
1     GGGCUAUUAGCUCAGUUGGUUAGAGCGCACCCCUGAUAAGGGUGAGGUCGCUGAUUCGAAUUCAGCAUAGCCCA

1     ((((((((..((((.........)))).(((((.......))))).....(((((.......))))))))))))).
```

Fig. 4. RNAfold web server result [5]

For the calculation of the structure feature, we used the RNAfold web server[1], which predicts minimum free energy structures and base pair probabilities from single RNA or DNA sequences [5]. The result can be represented in a *dot-bracket notation*, i.e. using the three symbols alphabet " ( ) . ": The set of matching parenthesis denotes a match, while the dots represent the non matching elements, as shown in Figure 4. Based on this alphabet we create the n-gram graph as before, by consedering as sequence the given representation.

---

[1] http://rna.tbi.univie.ac.at/cgi-bin/RNAfold.cgi

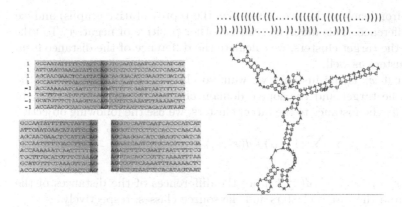

Fig. 5. The four different representations used

4   Proposed Approach

We propose a modified version of the K-means clustering algorithm, for transferring knowledge from an organism with well annotated genome (source domain) to another organism with poorly annotated genome (target domain). We use the data representations that we analyzed in the previous section and the N-gram graph distance function as a distance measure. We assume that we have two classes, the positive one (if a sequence is a splice site) and a negative one. For each of the two classes, we create two representative N-gram graphs, based on the sequences from the source domain which belong to each of the classes. The representative graph for a set of sequences, can be seen as an analogy to the centroid of a set of vectors.

In the n-gram graph framework there are different ways to measure similarity. We choose the Value Similarity (VS) function [4]. This measure quantifies the ratio of common edges between two graphs, taking into account the ratio of weights of common edges. In this measure each matching edge e having weight w_e^i in graph G^i contributes to VS, while not matching edges do not contribute. As we want to measure distance instead of similarity, we use the $distance = 1 - VS$.

In our method, we want to take into account the domain difference. In particular, we first initialize the target centroids of the clusters to be the same as the source domain centroids. Then, in each iteration, we take into account both the distance from the target clusters (which change over the iterations, as instances of the target domain are assigned to them) and the source classes (which remain stable). The intuition behind this approach is that in each iteration, the target centroids will be "moved" closer to the target domain data. As we are considering different organisms, we suppose that the distribution of the data are a bit different.

The distance on its own does not provide enough information, but the difference of the distances between the two classes has been proven much more informative. As a result, for every sequence of the target domain we calculate the distance from each of the two classes (i.e. the representative graphs) and we keep their difference. This difference can be either positive of negative. To take into account the target clusters, we calculate the difference of the distance from the target clusters as well.

Suppose that x_i^j is the instance we want to classify, and c_j and k_j are the centroids of the target and the source domain clusters, respectively. Then, in order to classify the instance to the target clusters, we use the following objective function:

$$J = \sum_j \sum_i (1 - \alpha) * d(x_i^j, c_j) + \alpha * d(x_i^j, k_j) \tag{1}$$

where $\sum_j d(x_i^j, c_j)$ and $\sum_j d(x_i^j, k_j)$ are the differences of the distances of the instance x_i from the target clusters and the source classes, respectively.

The parameter α takes values from zero to one, depending on how much we want the source domain to impact the classification. For α zero, then only the source domain instances are taken into account, while for α one, the source sequences are taken into account only for the initialization.

The steps of the proposed approach are given in algorithm (1).

Algorithm 1. Proposed Approach

- Represent all sequences as n-gram graphs
- Compute the source domain centroids, by calculating the mean graph
- Initialize the centroids for the target domain, using the source domain centroids

repeat

- Assign each instance of the target domain to cluster according to the objective function (1)
- When all instances are assigned to the clusters, recalculate the new centroids

until *convergence or a number of iterations* ;

To measure the distance between the instances and the centroids we use the distance function of n-gram graphs, which is a graph similarity measure [GK10].

As we mentioned in the previous section, we want to study the different representations we propose. For this reason, we used different strategies:

- Each of the four representations alone (the whole sequence, sequence before the acceptor, sequence after the acceptor, structure representation).
- All Features Majority Strategy (AFMS). The idea is to use majority voting between the 4 representations of each sequence. In case of a tie the sum of absolute values which is higher is selected.
- All Features Ensemble Strategy (AFES). AFES computes the sum of the distances from each representation of the sequence. The sequence is classified according to the sign of the output (negative class if the sum is negative, positive if the sum is positive).

5   Experiments

5.1   Dataset

To evaluate the proposed approaches, we used the dataset on splice sites, provided by [15]. We consider the task of identifying the so-called acceptor splice sites within a large set of potential splice sites based on a sequence window around a site. The idea is to consider the recognition of splice sites in different organisms (Figure 6): in all cases, we used the very well studied model organism C.elegans as the source domain. As target organisms we chose two additional nematodes, namely, the close relative C.remanei, which is diverged from C.elegans by 100 million years, and the more distantly related P.pacificus, a lineage which diverges from C.elegans by more than 200 million years. The third target organism is D.melanogaster, which is separated from C.elegans by 990 million years. Finally, A.thaliana diverges from the other organisms by more than 1,600 million years. It is assumed that a larger evolutionary distance will likely also have led to an accumulation of functional differences in the molecular splicing machinery. We therefore expect that the differences of classification functions for recognizing splice sites in these organisms will increase with increasing evolutionary distance.

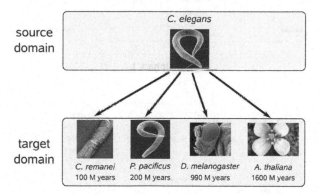

Fig. 6. The distance in years between C.elegans and the other organisms

The dataset contain C.elegans as source with 25000 examples with ratio positive/negative=0.01. The target organisms contain 2500 examples due to limitations in computational resources. For the target organism the ratio positive/negative ratio was also kept to 0.01.

Evaluation Measures. To evaluate the performance of the models, we measure our prediction accuracy in terms of area under the Receiver Operator Characteristic Curve (auROC) [7,2]. The reason we chose this measure is that the dataset is very unbalanced and accuracy would be misleading. In addition, this is the standard measure used in various works in the literature.

5.2   Results

Our intention was to measure the impact of using the source domain knowledge on the final result. This is why we introduced the parameter α, which controls how much weight we give to the centroids of the source domain. The α parameter can vary from zero to one. Zero means that we only take into account the source data and not the target clusters. If α is one, it means that in the first iteration we use the source centroids, but from the second iteration, we only use the centroids found from the target domain data. For all other values of α in between, the linear combination of the aforementioned is used. We tested all the representations and the proposed strategies for different values of α. Below, we present the results obtained for α 0.2, 0.6 and 1.

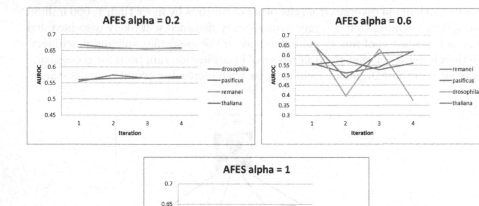

Fig. 7. Results for all organisms, using AFES

From the Figures 7 and 8 it can be seen that in the case of $\alpha = 0.2$ the results are stable across the different iterations, because the centroids from the target domain do not contribute much. Thus, this can be considered as the base case for the experiments. In case of $\alpha = 0.6$, the contribution of the current centroids increases, but the initial centroid still contribute. It is observed in that case that most of the algorithms perform worse than in 0.2. Also it can be seen that drosophila oscillates and needs many more iterations to converge. That could indicate that the more "knowledge" is pumped from the target organism the worse the results are. If that was verified for $\alpha = 1.0$ then the method would be inapplicable. But instead it can be seen that when we use $\alpha = 1.0$,

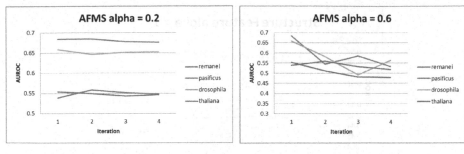

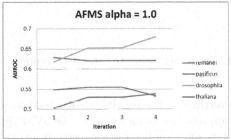

Fig. 8. Results for all organisms, using AFMS

thus initializing with the centroids of the source organism, and then we iterate only using knowledge from the target domain, the results are much better for AFMS and AMES methods. We see that in these cases we reach auROC about 0.65 or more, with the algorithm converging quite fast.

That indicates that the knowledge obtained from the source domain is better to be used only for the initialization of the centroids and not during the iterations. In addition, comparing AFMS and AFES, it can be seen that AFMS is more stable than AFES in most of the cases, without extreme oscillations. Also, the classification potential of AFMS strategy seems to be greater in most organisms, which clearly indicates that the majority vote is the better strategy.

As mentioned before, we experiment also with each representation alone. The first three representations (the whole sequence, sequence before the acceptor and sequence after the acceptor) are doing worse than the ensemble and the majority strategies (AFES and AFMS, respectively). Nevertheless, the structure feature alone, seems to give some important information, at least for the closely related organisms. For the evolutionarily furthest organisms, it is more difficult to achieve good results, most probably because the secondary structure of the DNA sequence has changed more over time. In Figure 9, we can see the obtained results for $\alpha = 1.0$. That indicates that the novel proposed feature of constructing n-gram graphs from the representation of the structure can give us some important information, and it could be used as an independent additional feature for splice sites algorithms.

It is worth mentioning that we used only a subset of the whole dataset, due to computational limitations, thus we cannot present an exact comparison with

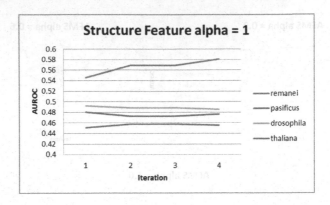

Fig. 9. The results using the structure representation

other approaches. Nevertheless, the results we obtained seems to be comparable with state-of-the-art approaches, as for example the SVM approaches in the work of [13], where the results on a similar dataset vary from 40% to 75%.

6   Conclusions

In this paper, we studied the problem of splice site recognition. We proposed different representations for the sequences, as well as a transfer learning approach based on K-means. The proposed representations are based on n-gram graphs. We experimented with the different parts of the sequences around the splice sites acceptor and the preliminary results are promising. We proposed a novel representation based on the secondary structure of the sequences. To our knowledge, such a feature has not been mentioned in the literature for the splice site recognition problem. Our results indicate that the secondary structure contains important information and should be studied more thoroughly.

As future steps, more experiments should take place to better understand the importance of the different representations, as well as the differences between the organisms. Also, a detailed comparison with state-of-the-art approaches should be done.

Acknownledgement.   The authors want to thank Sotiris Konstantinidis for the interesting discussions on the secondary structure of the gene sequences.

References

1. Buratti, E., Baralle, F.E.: Influence of rna secondary structure on the pre-mrna splicing process. Mol. Cell. Biol. 24(24), 10505–10514 (2004)
2. Fawcett, T.: ROC Graphs: Notes and Practical Considerations for Data Mining Researchers. In: Technical report hpl-2003-4 HP Laboratories (2003)

3. Gelfman, S., Burstein, D., Penn, O., Savchenko, A., Amit, M., Schwartz, S., Pupko, T., Ast, G.: Changes in exon–intron structure during vertebrate evolution affect the splicing pattern of exons. Genome Research 22(1), 35–50 (2012)
4. Giannakopoulos, G., Karkaletsis, V.: Summarization system evaluation variations based on n-gram graphs. In: Text Analysis Conference, NIST (2010)
5. Gruber, A.R., Lorenz, R., Bernhart, S.H., Neuböck, R., Hofacker, I.L.:
6. Herndon, N., Caragea, D.: Naïve bayes domain adaptation for biological sequences. In: BIOINFORMATICS 2013, pp. 62–70 (2013)
7. Metz, C.E.: Basic principles of ROC analysis. Seminars in Nuclear Medicine 8(4), 283–298 (1978)
8. Michael, D., Manyuan, L.: Intronexon structures of eukaryotic model organisms. Nucleic Acids Research 27(15), 3219–3228 (1999)
9. Pan, S.J., Yang, Q.: A survey on transfer learning. IEEE Transactions on Knowledge and Data Engineering 22(10), 1345–1359 (2010)
10. Rajapakse, J.C., Ho, L.S.: Markov encoding for detecting signals in genomic sequences. IEEE/ACM Transactions on Computational Biology and Bioinformatics ?(?), 131 142 (2005)
11. Rätsch, G., Sonnenburg, S.: Accurate splice site prediction for caenorhabditis elegans. In: Kernel Methods in Computational Biology. MIT Press series on Computational Molecular Biology, pp. 277–298. MIT Press (2004)
12. Rätsch, G., Sonnenburg, S., Srinivasan, J., Witte, H., Müller, K.-R., Sommer, R., Schölkopf, B.: Improving the c. elegans genome annotation using machine learning. PLoS Computational Biology 3, e20 (2007)
13. Schweikert, G., Widmer, C., Schölkopf, B., Rätsch, G.: An empirical analysis of domain adaptation algorithms for genomic sequence analysis. In: Koller, D., Schuurmans, D., Bengio, Y., Bottou, L. (eds.) NIPS, pp. 1433–1440. Curran Associates, Inc. (2008)
14. Sonnenburg, S., Rätsch, G., Jagota, A., Müller, K.-R.: New methods for splice-site recognition. In: Dorronsoro, J.R. (ed.) ICANN 2002. LNCS, vol. 2415, pp. 329–336. Springer, Heidelberg (2002)
15. Sonnenburg, S., Schweikert, G., Philips, P., Behr, J., Rätsch, G.: Accurate Splice Site Prediction. BMC Bioinformatics, Special Issue from NIPS Workshop on New Problems and Methods in Computational Biology Whistler, Canada 8(suppl. 10), S7 (2007)
16. Tsuda, K., Kawanabe, M., Rätsch, G., Sonnenburg, S., Müller, K.-R.: A new discriminative kernel from probabilistic models. Neural Computation 14, 2397–2414 (2002)
17. Vapnik, V.N.: The Nature of Statistical Learning Theory. Springer-Verlag New York, Inc., New York (1995)
18. Widmer, C., Rätsch, G.: Multitask learning in computational biology. In: ICML Unsupervised and Transfer Learning. JMLR Proceedings, vol. 27, pp. 207–216. JMLR.org (2012)
19. Yamamura, M., Gotoh, O., Dunker, A., Konagaya, A., Miyano, S., Takagi, T.: Detection of the splicing sites with kernel method approaches dealing with nucleotide doublets. Genome Informatics Online 14, 426–427 (2003)
20. Zhong, W., Altun, G., Harrison, R., Tai, P.C., Pan, Y.: Improved K-means clustering algorithm for exploring local protein sequence motifs representing common structural property. IEEE Trans. Nanobioscience 4(3), 255–265 (2005)
21. Zien, A., Rätsch, G., Mika, S., Schölkopf, B., Lengauer, T., Müller, K.-R.: Engineering support vector machine kernels that recognize translation initiation sites. Bioinformatics 16(9), 799–807 (2000)

An Intelligent Platform for Hosting Medical Collaborative Services

Christos Andrikos[1], Ilias Maglogiannis[2], Efthymios Bilalis[3], George Spyroglou[1],
and Panayiotis Tsanakas[1,4]

[1] School of Electrical and Computer Engineering, National technical University of Athens
[2] Dept. of Digital Systems, University of Piraeus, Greece
[3] Division of Information Technology, Biomedicine, Greece
[4] Greek Research and Education Network (GR-NET), Greece
{candrikos,panag}@cslab.ntua.com, imaglo@unipi.gr,
tbilalis@enternet.gr, gspyro@gmail.com

Abstract. Recent developments in cloud computing technologies, the wide-spread use of mobile smart devices and the expansion of electronic health record system, raise the need of on-line collaboration among geographically distributed medical personnel. In this context, the paper presents a web based intelligent platform, capable of hosting medical collaborative services and featuring intelligent medical data management and exchange. Our work emphasizes on client-side medical data processing over an intelligent online workflow library. We introduce a Remote Process Calling scheme based on WebRTC (peer-to-peer) communication paradigm, eliminating the typical bandwidth bottleneck of centralized data sharing and allowing the execution of intelligent workflows.

Keywords: Electronic health record, telemedicine, collaborative diagnosis, peer to peer networks, intelligent workflows, DICOM format.

1   Introduction and Related Work

Team-based treatment has become common practice, mostly in complex medical cases where difficult decisions are required. For example, when determining the disease stage in a cancer patient, or when planning a treatment strategy that involves concurrent or sequential treatments of different modalities (chemotherapy or radiation), several disciplines are involved and synchronous interaction among them in a multidisciplinary team (MDT) is preferred. This change in healthcare practice, from a single clinician to a group of clinicians managing a patient, resulted in the development of multidisciplinary team meetings (MDTMs), also being recommended world-wide, particularly for publically funded healthcare. Furthermore, as healthcare continues to become more centralized and specialized, communication technology is being deployed to enable multidisciplinary team (MDT) services to be provided over large geographical areas. One of the most vital procedures requested by clinicians during an MDTM, is medical image and report sharing. We propose an intelligent

A. Likas, K. Blekas, and D. Kalles (Eds.): SETN 2014, LNAI 8445, pp. 354–359, 2014.

web based software collaboration platform, leveraging robust Internet technologies such as WebRTC, NoSQL and AI on Big Data, while hiding all interoperability issues from the users. The development of similar distributed collaborative systems has received the attention of several research groups during the last years. INTERMED [1] is designed to enhance the communication among patients and multidisciplinary health providers. TeleMed [2] is a visualized, action-oriented decision-support tool, providing to the physicians collaborative sessions and access to basic patient data. HTML5 Zero Footprint DICOM viewer is the latest medical imaging development product by LEADTOOLS, offering image processing on the browser. Typical implementations are bandwidth and device dependent, while they do not support collaborative creation of workflows. In medical image processing, the exchanged data between servers and clients are bandwidth intensive. In this work we introduce an intelligent collaboration platform fusing the principles of heterogeneous Workflow Management Systems and AI. The innovation of the proposed system resulted by the adoption of client-side computing enabled with WebRTC and Web 2 web stacks (HTML 5, Java-Script, CSS 3) [3]. The paper introduces a PRPC (Peer Remote Process Calling) scheme that enables clinicians to collaborate over a web application. Collaborating clinicians can follow intelligent pathways with medical image processing support.

2   System Architecture

According to Figure 1, the proposed system consists of User Access Control (UAC), Real Time Communication (RTC) signaling and Participant server (PAS) subsystems. UAC is responsible for user authentication and authorization. RTC coordinates initial communication stages, while PAS enumerates securely the user profiles to all potential callers-participants. It also hosts a database with dynamically adopted workflows associated with specific work scenarios. PAS provides clinicians with the required URIs and methods for transparent (HL7 messaging) interoperability with third party clinical systems (e.g. PACS, LIS, EMR). AI algorithms analyze clinician interactions through Big Data analytics in EMRs, offering partial differential diagnosis or new tests.

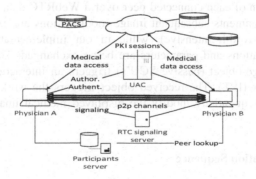

Fig. 1. System Interconnection

2.1   User Application Module Block Diagram

The collaborative web based software platform features multi-channel video conferencing, workspace screen and file sharing, chat rooms and annotations. Figure 2 presents the modular architecture of the client collaborative environment, as well as the corresponding protocols used for data exchange.

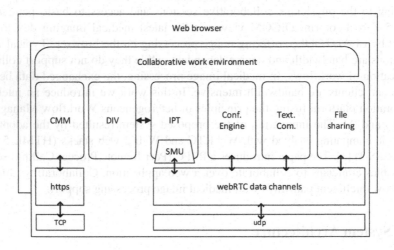

Fig. 2. Client module structure

The proposed software encapsulates three autonomous modules: Image Processing Toolbox (IPT), DICOM image viewer (DIV) and Smart Communication Unit (SCU). The IPT is based on our own developed JS image processing library that reads images from the DIV, a web whiteboard that renders medical images (format agnostic). Images are fetched from the participant's PACS channel or local data storage. Symmetric SCUs exchange asynchronous JSON messages describing the shared image processing commands. During the initialization of a collaborative session, the MDTM moderator shares (publish) an image on the common whiteboard, while it gets displayed on the screen of each connected peer over a WebRTC data channel. In typical collaborative environments subsequent image modifications are exchanged as image data sets [4] (bandwidth intensive), while in our implementation only pairs of workflow identifications and parameters are being exchanged. The reception of the broadcasted message-object (passive SCU's) triggers an interaction with the Image Processing Toolbox (IPT). The received object triggers the workflow that is correlated with, which sequentially modify the displayed medical image in the DICOM image viewer.

2.2   Communication Sequence

The described collaborative work environment has strict security requirements, due to the exchange of highly sensitive data and leverages https protocol and PKI authorization. UAC requests a private key from a third trusted acquiring a digital signature (Figure 3). WebRTC provides secure channels based on encryption policies. During registration user A acquires a private signature. PAS (user directory) is informed for the new registration and returns to user A the manifest of all online participants matching to his contact list. After user B logins, PAS updates asynchronously the contact list of physician A. After initial negotiations, the data channels are set up and the call between A and B commences.

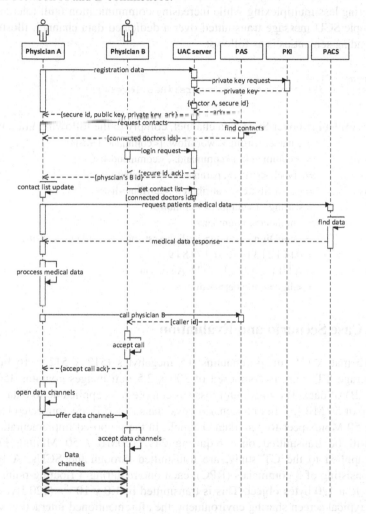

Fig. 3. Communicational sequence diagram for a collaborative session

Client server-connection is based on https protocol. Authorization, authentication, accessibility is provided by the User Access Control unit. UAC request a private key from a third trusted party acquiring a digital signature. WebRTC provides secure channels based on encryption policies. Moreover there is no need to encrypt all data transferred through channels as they have not the same sensitivity. The sequence of the exchanged messages is illustrated in Figure 3. During registration user A receives his secure identification and acquires a private signature. PAS is informed for the new registration and returns user A the list of his online contacts. After user B login, PAS update asynchronously the contact list of physician A. A calls B and after negotiating the communication parameters the data channels are set up to support the collaborative services. Last but not least, every client's module is assigned to a dedicated data channel offering less multiplexing while increasing communication fault tolerance. A typical example SCU message transmitted over a dedicated data channel, illustrating the corresponding semantics is as follows:

```
{
  name: "myWorkflow",
  workflow:[{label: "im2bw", parameters:[RGB,level]}]
}
```

All messages exchanged over SCU data channel, comply to the following grammar:

<S>	::= { name: <string>, workflow: [<command-list>]}
<command-list>	::= <command> | <command>, <command-list>
<command>	::= {label: <string>, parameters: [<attribute-list>] }
<attribute-list>	::= ε | <attribute> | <attribute> ,<attribute-list>
<attribute>	::= <string> | <number> | <fpnum>
<fpnum>	::= <number>, <number>
<string>	::= <nonDigit> | <digit> | <digit><string> | <nonDigit><string> | ε
<digit>	::= 0 | 1 | 2 | 3 | 4 | 5 | 6 | 7 | 8 | 9
<nonDigit>	::= A | B | ... | z | _ | ... | ! | A | ... | ω
<number>	::= <digit><number> | <digit>

3   Use Case Scenario and Evaluation

A single 512 matrix CT[1] image contains 0.5 megabytes (512 x 512 x 16 bits) of data. An average CT study is composed of 300 x 2.5 mm images contains 150 MB (300 x 0.5 MB) of data. The maximum lossless compression applicable to data is 3:1, giving a total of 50 MB [5]. In our scenario physicians A and B are connected through a symmetric 50 Mbit/s peer-to-peer data channel. In the proposed implementation the CT study will be transmitted once requiring 24s (150MB / 50 Mbit/s). Further workflows, applied to the CT study, are transmitted through the SCUs. A typical workflow consisting of 3 commands (RPC), each one requiring 3 floating-point arguments, leads to a 120 bytes object. This is transmitted in $1.8 \, x \, 10^{-5}$s (120 Bytes / 50 Mbit/s. In a typical screen sharing environment, the aforementioned interaction should last 0.08s. (0.5 MB / 50Mbit/s) plus the latency due to image processing. This does not apply with our approach, as processing takes place almost simultaneously on both client devices.

---

[1] Computer Tomography.

4   Conclusion

The proposed collaborative work environment promotes physician collaboration and easy data exchange using almost any smart device, leveraging access to intelligent workflow libraries. The consumer demand and bring-your-own-device trend, lead us to implement the client framework on the web browser, instead as a standalone application. Our implementation does not require any plug-ins or external software. It resembles a typical web application, while the main image processing takes place in the client side. The meaning and practical use of facts or evidence is subjective upon different situations and participants [6]. Our proposed collaboration paradigm unleashes medical scientific evidence as the most essential process for better diagnosis, elevating it from grounded moral and situational considerations.

Acknowledgment. Part of this work has been funded by Project: "PINCLOUD - Providing Integrated eHealth Services for Personalized Medicine utilizing Cloud Infrastructure", Operational Programme «Competitiveness and Entrepreneurship» (OPCE II).

References

[1] Stiefel, S.C., Huyse, F.J., Söllner, W., Slaets, J., Lyons, J., Latour, C., van der Wal, N., De Jonge, P.: Operationalizing integrated care on a clinical level: The INTERMED project. Medical Clinics of North America 90(4), 713–758 (2006)

[2] Kilman, D., Forslund, D.: An international collaboratory based on virtual patient records. Communications of the ACM 40(8), 111–117 (1997)

[3] Catayama, S., Goda, T., Shiramatsu, S., Ozono, T., Shintani, T.: A fast synchronization mechanism for collaborative web applications based on HTML5. In: SNPD 2013 - 14th ACIS International Conference on Software Engineering, Artificial Intelligence, Networking and Parallel/Distributed Computing (2013)

[4] Maglogiannis, I., Delakouridis, C., Kazatzopoulos, L.: Enabling collaborative medical diagnosis over the Internet via peer to peer distribution of electronic health records. Journal of Medical Systems 30(2), 107–116 (2006)

[5] Strickland, N.H.: Multidetector CT: What do we do with all the images generated? British Journal of Radiology 77(SPEC ISS), S14–S19 (2004)

[6] Måseide, P.: The deep play of medicine: Discursive and collaborative processing of evidence in medical problem solving. Communication and Medicine 3(1), 43–54 (2006)

Knowledge-Poor Context-Sensitive Spelling Correction for Modern Greek

Spyridon Sagiadinos, Petros Gasteratos, Vasileios Dragonas, Athanasia Kalamara, Antonia Spyridonidou, and Katia Kermanidis

Ionian University, Department of Informatics, Corfu, Greece
{p10gast,p10drag,p10kala1,p10sagi,p10spyr,kerman}@ionio.gr

Abstract. In the present work a methodology for automatic spelling correction is proposed for common errors on Modern Greek homophones. The proposed methodology corrects the error by taking into account morphosyntactic information regarding the context of the orthographically ambiguous word. Our methodology is knowledge-poor because the information used is only the endings of the words in the context of the ambiguous word; as such it can be adapted even by simple editors for real-time spelling correction. We tested our method using Id3, C4.5, Nearest Neighbor, Naive Bayes and Random Forest as machine learning algorithms for correct spelling prediction. Experimental results show that the success rate of the above method is usually between 90% and 95% and sometimes approaching 97%. Synthetic Minority Oversampling was used to cope with the problem of class imbalance in our datasets.

Keywords: Context-sensitive spelling correction, Random Forest, Modern Greek, SMOTE, knowledge-poor spelling prediction, supervised learning, imbalanced dataset, minority class over-sampling.

1   Introduction

Nowadays, we are all accustomed to using a modern word processor which includes automatic spelling correction. However, these spelling correction tools usually rely on dictionaries to detect misspellings.

More difficult to detect are errors on valid words, according to the accompanying dictionary, but they are not the words that were intended for in the particular sentence. Instead they are words that look or sound similar to the correct word. For example, the words "peace" and "piece" of the English language are pronounced the same, both are valid and any English dictionary should contain them; however if the user uses by mistake the one in place of the other, an error would occur because their meaning is totally different and a common spell checker would not detect it.

These errors account for anywhere from 25% to over 50% of observed spelling errors [1,2] in the English language. In many other languages, and the Greek language is a good example of this, there is more than one way to pronounce a vowel. For example in the Greek language there are two distinct vowels that sound as an "o", namely "o" and "ω", six different ways someone could write the sound "e" (as in "be"),

A. Likas, K. Blekas, and D. Kalles (Eds.): SETN 2014, LNAI 8445, pp. 360–369, 2014.

"ι", "η", "υ", "ει", "οι" and "υι", and two ways to form in writing the sound "e" (as in "best"), "ε" and "αι".

The above reasons create lots of ambiguities, that, unless we have enough information about the context of the word in the sentence or the whole text, are difficult to solve. Some common types of orthographic ambiguity of homophones in the Greek language are presented in Table 1 between Word1 and Word2.

Table 1. Greek language common ambiguities

Word 1	Meaning	Word 2	Meaning	Pronounced as
λύπη	sorrow (noun)	λείπει	is missing (verb)	`lipi
καλή	good (adjective, feminine, singular)	καλοί	good (adjective, masculine, plural)	ka`li
πίνετε	drink (verb, active, plural, 2nd person)	πίνεται	drink (verb, passive, singular, 3rd person)	`pinete

Those kinds of errors are quite frequent. A big part of the adjectives, numerals and pronouns end in "η" in their feminine form and in "οι" in the plural form, forming homophones. A big part of Greek verbs end in "αι" in the 3rd personal singular passive form and in "ε" in the 2nd person plural active form. The remaining word is the same, forming thus another set of homophones that often get misspelled.

Since the above problem focuses on valid words, the error correction method must be based on information obtained from the surrounding words in the sentence and the meaning they hold, thus any spelling correction methodology has to adopt a context-based approach. Various context-based approaches have been suggested that use either statistical techniques [3,4,5] or machine learning techniques based on the words appearing before or after the critical, orthographically ambiguous, word [6,7,8,9]. The machine learning techniques mentioned above use predefined confusion sets of ambiguous words, features based on the presence of particular words, and part-of-speech (PoS) tags in the context of the critical word. These features are used by methods like Bayes [8] to predict the correct spelling.

The work presented here is the first, to the authors' knowledge, regarding context sensitive spelling correction for Modern Greek. Our method tries to resolve the ambiguity by using the endings of the surrounding words; as such it doesn't depend on any 'high' level linguistic information, i.e. PoS tags, morphological processing, syntactic analysis. This feature makes our method easily adaptable to any word processor for real-time spelling correction in contrast to related work. Also this is the first time that a work in the field of spelling correction copes with the problem of class imbalance (SMOTE)[10].

As the Greek language can have numerous categories and types of ambiguities, we chose to experiment with two of the most common types. The first ambiguity set is the one occurring from verbs that can be written in two different forms, one in the active voice and one in the passive voice, both forms sounding the same, and the only difference in writing is the ending of the verb. For example:

- Εσείς <u>πίνετε</u> κρασί.   (Translation: "You (plural) drink wine".)
- Αυτό το νερό δεν <u>πίνεται</u>.   (Translation: "This water cannot be drunk".)

The words underlined are the same verb (drink) in a different voice value, but is pronounced exactly the same in both sentences. The only way to find out which is the correct way to spell it is by understanding the meaning of the whole sentence. The second ambiguity set is similar:

- Αυτή η καρέκλα είναι πολύ <u>καλή</u>.   (This chair is very good. The word "chair" is feminine in the Greek language)
- Αυτοί οι μαθητές είναι <u>καλοί</u>.   (These pupils are good.)

The same adjective (good) appears in both sentences but in the first it is singular /feminine and in the second it is plural/masculine. Again the word is pronounced exactly the same, although written with a different ending, and the only way to discover the difference is by reading the whole sentence and understanding the meaning of it.

2   Related Work

As far as we know there is no work addressing this kind of errors for Modern Greek automatically. Nevertheless there is work on other languages (mostly English), that addresses the same problem using a variety of methods and algorithms.

Golding and Roth [6] present a Winnow-based algorithm (WinSpell). They use two types of features: context words and collocations. Context-word features test for the presence of a particular word within ±k words of the target word; collocations test for a pattern of up to ℓ contiguous words and/or PoS tags around the target word.

Schaback and Li [11] present a method that corrects non-word and real word errors simultaneously. To achieve this they include features from the character level, phonetic level, word level, syntax level, and semantic level. For the syntactic level features they use a fixed length of three PoS tags and no explicit words. They train their system using the above features for the 14.000 most frequent lemmata in their lexicon.

Carslon and Fete [7] use predefined confusion sets together with a database of n-gram statistics for sizes 1 to m, and context words less than m words to the left and right of the target word. The algorithm then selects the word from the confusion set with the highest probability. If no candidate is found m is reduced until m = 1, where the result is the most frequent word.

Golding and Schabes [8] use a combination of two methods. The first method is the use of PoS tags trigrams (not of words, as in previous works). This method gives good results when the words in the confusion set have different PoS tags. The second method is Bayes, a Bayesian hybrid method [12], for the case where the words have the same PoS tag.

Mays, Damerau and Mercer [5] study the effectiveness of applying a statistical model of language that has demonstrated success in the task of speech recognition in the field of spelling correction. In this model, syntactic, semantic, and pragmatic knowledge is conflated into word trigram conditional probabilities. These conditional probabilities are derived from statistics gathered from large bodies of text.

3   Spelling Correction of Modern Greek Homophones

3.1   Overview

As already stated earlier, the method presented here tries to resolve the ambiguity by obtaining information from the endings of the words before and after the critical word.

The first step is to create a feature-value vector which will contain those endings. We chose to experiment with a maximum of five words before and after the critical word, and with a maximum of three letters for each ending, thus creating a vector which will hold a maximum of 30 features (five words before, five words after and for each word the last one, two and three letters).

The next step was to create two datasets to experiment with, one for each ambiguity set. This was done with the help of a corpus large enough to provide us with enough sentences that fall into one of our ambiguity sets. For each sentence a vector was created containing the values of the characteristics discussed above.

The Modern Greek text corpus used for the experimental process comes from the Greek daily newspaper "Eleftherotypia" (http://www.elda.fr/catalogue/en/text/ W0022.html). A subset of the corpus (250K words) is used for the experiments described herein.

After the creation of the two datasets we experimented on various combinations of the above features, using various machine learning algorithms, in an effort to find the combination that produces the highest performance in correctly resolving the ambiguity.

3.2   Creating the Datasets

We chose to experiment with two of the most frequent types of ambiguity in the Greek language. The first one is whether a verb should be written with the ending "-αι" or "-ε". The second one is whether a word should be written with the ending "-οι" or "-η". Of course, for such an ambiguity to exist, the critical word should be orthographically correct with both endings, so the first step towards the creation of the datasets was to extract the corpus' sentences that contain such words, and then check them with traditional dictionary spell-checking software if they are valid with both endings. We discarded the sentences that contained no words matching our criteria.

The next step towards creating the dataset was to choose the set of features the vector would contain. As stated earlier, we had to be able to experiment with combinations of words and their endings as features and the words should be as close to the critical word as possible. Only the words of the current sentence would be taken into account so, if, for example, the critical word was the first word of the sentence, then the features corresponding to the words positioned before that word would receive a dash ("-") value. The same applies if we seek the final three letters in a word that contains only one or two letters.

For example, let's suppose that the word "καλοί" is our critical word in the sentence "αυτοί οι μαθητές είναι καλοί", of page 3. Let's also suppose that we want to take into account 2 words before and 2 words after the word "καλοί" for the creation of our vector and our goal is to find out whether the word "καλοί" is correct or whether it should be replaced with the word "καλή" which is pronounced exactly the same. Table 2 contains the vector for this example.

Table 2. Sample vector for example of page 4

1w-2	2w-2	3w-2	1w-1	2w-1	3w-1	1w+1	2w+1	3w+1	1w+2	2w+2	3w+3	c
ς	ές	τές	ι	αι	ναι	-	-	-	-	-	-	οι

In the column labels of Table 2, the first character is the number of word ending characters and the last two characters form the position of the word relative to the critical word. For example, 3w-1 stands for the last three characters of the word right before (-1) "καλοί", i.e. the word "είναι" in our example. We observe that since our critical word is the final word of the sentence, we put dashes to the values corresponding to the words following the critical word. The last column is the class label of the word, pointing out that the word in this sentence should be written with a "οί" instead of "η". In both our ambiguity sets the class takes one of two values, i.e. the spelling form of the critical word.

We chose to include one more feature in the verbs' (-ε/-αι) ambiguity set: whether the sentence is a question or not. We chose to do so because, after a careful examination of the corpus, we noticed that when a question mark was present at the end of the sentence, one of the two classes was heavily favored.

Our vectors consisted of 31 features (plus one only for the verbs vector) because we used 5 words before and 5 after the word instead of the 2 before and 2 after of our previous example. One vector was created for every corpus' word that matched our type of ambiguity.

After the completion of the previous procedure we noticed that both of our datasets were imbalanced as shown on Table 3.

Table 3. Original class distribution

	Dataset 1 (ε/αι)	Dataset 2 (η/οι)
Class 1(αι/οι)	727	376
Class 2 (ε/η)	60	1669
Total	787	2045

Table 4. Class distribution after SMOTE

	Dataset 1 (ε/αι)	Dataset 2 (η/οι)
Class 1(αι/οι)	727	1669
Class 2 (ε/η)	724	1669
Total	1451	3338

To balance the classes of the datasets we applied the SMOTE filter of WEKA 3.6.10 software http://www.cs.waikato.ac.nz/ml/weka. With SMOTE [10] - the minority class is over-sampled by taking each minority class sample and introducing synthetic examples along the line segments joining any/all of the k minority class nearest neighbors. Even though our features are all nominal values, the implementation of SMOTE in WEKA can handle this type of value as described in [10]. The result is shown in Table 4.

The above are the final datasets that were used in our experiments.

3.3 Experimental Setup

We used WEKA 3.6.10 to conduct our classification experiments. For each dataset the same procedure was followed. We chose to experiment with the following classification algorithms:

- Id3
- C4.5
- Nearest Neighbor (k-NN)
- NaiveBayes
- RandomForest

We used 10-fold cross validation for testing. Also C4.5 was in prune mode with a confidence factor set to 0.25 and 2 as the minimum number of objects in a leaf. Nearest Neighbor used no distance weighting, LinearNNSearch as the nearest neighbor search algorithm and the window size was set to 0. Random Forest was using unlimited maximum depth and the number of features used for each run was calculated by the formula: $log_2(n)+1$ where n is the total number of features.

For every experiment, a number of features and an algorithm had to be chosen. Initially we started with all features available, running an experiment for every algorithm. After that, we continued by removing features of the words that were further from the critical word, concluding the experiments with only 1 feature selected. We experimented with all possible combinations that exist, starting with 5 words before and 5 words after the critical word (we will refer to it as [-5,5] window) and reducing features one by one, thus shrinking the window towards the critical word: [-5,4] , [-5,3] , ... , [-5,0] and then [-4,5] , [-4,4] , ... , [-4,0], concluding with [0,1]. This is a total of 35 combinations (6*6 excluding the [0,0] window) and for each combination all 5 algorithms were tested for a total of 13*35=455 experiments (Nearest Neighbor for k=1,3,5 and Random Forest for the number of created trees=10,20,...,70) .

3.4 Results

After running the experiments we analyzed the results to find the best combination of feature set and algorithm for each of the two ambiguity sets. These are presented in Tables 5 and 6.

We observe that for both ambiguity sets Id3 and Random Forest scored the highest results. However the results of Id3 (based on the classified instances) are misleading since he gave a lot of unclassified examples (sometimes they were about 21% of all the examples) so we expect that if those examples were classified randomly (as the more daring C4.5 algorithm does) its score would dramatically decrease. That leaves us with our second best choice which is the Random Forest algorithm.

Table 5. Results for verbs ending in   "-αι" or "-ε"

Algorithm	Window	Classes	Precision	Recall	F-measure
Id3	[0 , 3]	-αι	0.954	0.966	0.960
		-ε	0.978	0.970	0.974
Random Forest (50 trees)	[-2 , 4]	-αι	0.952	0.950	0.951
		-ε	0.950	0.952	0.951
Nearest Neighbor (k=1)	[0, 3]	-αι	0.953	0.949	0.951
		-ε	0.949	0.953	0.951
Naive Bayes	[-2, 5]	-αι	0.957	0.923	0.940
		-ε	0.925	0.959	0.942
C4.5	[-2, 1]	-αι	0.926	0.911	0.918
		-ε	0.912	0.927	0.919

Table 6. Results for words ending in   "-οι" or "-η"

Algorithm	Window	Classes	Precision	Recall	F-measure
Id3	[-5 , 5]	-οι	0.953	0.956	0.954
		-η	0.953	0.956	0.954
Random Forest (60 trees)	[-2 , 5]	-οι	0.912	0.958	0.935
		-η	0.956	0.908	0.931
Naive Bayes	[-2, 3]	-οι	0.910	0.940	0.925
		-η	0.938	0.907	0.922
Nearest Neighbor (k=1)	[-2, 1]	-οι	0.899	0.944	0.921
		-η	0.941	0.894	0.917
C4.5	[-3, 0]	-οι	0.875	0.889	0.882
		-η	0.887	0.873	0.880

Other sensible choices that gave us not much lower scores could be the Naive Bayes algorithm (about 94%) and the Nearest Neighbor algorithm for k=1 (about 93%), while C4.5 and Nearest Neighbor for k=3 and k=5 usually failed to achieve scores higher than 90%.

Golding and Roth [6] with their Winspell algorithm achieve an average result of 96.4%. Golding and Schabes [8] with their hybrid Trigram – Bayes method achieve an average result of around 93.6%. Our method achieves an average result of 94.2% for the two ambiguity sets. But as we have already mentioned we use only low level information (word endings) in contrast to the others methods which use high level information (PoS tags).

As we can see, almost all of the algorithms give their best results for window sizes that favor the words following the critical word. This is an indication that in Modern Greek, for these ambiguity sets, the syntactic information of the words after the critical word are more important in resolving the ambiguity. Also the slightly lower results that our method achieved for words ending in "-οι, -η" is an indication that most likely more features need to be included (bigger window size).

In Table 7 we can see the effect of different window sizes on the results of one of the algorithms (Random Forest with 10 trees). By varying the one of the two size parameters the difference is not so large (around 0.020) and that holds for almost all of the algorithms.

Table 7. Window size effect on Random Forest (10 trees)

Window	Classes	Precision	Recall	F-measure
[-5, 5]	-οι	0.909	0.944	0.926
	-η	0.942	0.905	0.923
[-4 , 5]	-οι	0.896	0.944	0.919
	-η	0.941	0.891	0.915
[-3, 5]	-οι	0.901	0.946	0.923
	-η	0.943	0.896	0.919
[-2, 5]	-οι	0.897	0.951	0.923
	-η	0.948	0.891	0.918
[-1, 5]	-οι	0.901	0.949	0.925
	-η	0.946	0.897	0.921
[0, 5]	-οι	0.877	0.941	0.908
	-η	0.936	0.868	0.901

In Table 8 we can see the results of the Random Forest algorithm for the verbs ambiguity set. The results show that the maximum difference between the results is small (around 0.01). So we do not believe that the number of trees is a decisive factor of our experiments.

Table 8. Different number of trees for Random Forest [-2, 4]

Trees	Classes	Precision	Recall	F-measure
10	-αι	0.958	0.935	0.946
	-ε	0.937	0.959	0.947
20	-αι	0.958	0.946	0.952
	-ε	0.947	0.959	0.953
30	-αι	0.958	0.948	0.953
	-ε	0.948	0.959	0.953
40	-αι	0.958	0.950	0.954
	-ε	0.951	0.959	0.955
50	-αι	0.960	0.956	0.958
	-ε	0.956	0.960	0.958
60	-αι	0.960	0.955	0.957
	-ε	0.955	0.960	0.957
70	-αι	0.959	0.956	0.957
	-ε	0.956	0.959	0.957

In Table 9 we can see the effect of using SMOTE. The results for two of the algorithms (Naive Bayes and Random Forest) for the minority class before its application are very low. The use of SMOTE dramatically changes that.

Table 9. Results before and after using SMOTE (window size [-5, 5])

Algorithm	SMOTE	Classes	Precision	Recall	F-measure
Naive Bayes	No	-αι	0.929	0.974	0.951
		-ε	0.240	0.100	0.141
Naive Bayes	Yes	-αι	0.962	0.900	0.930
		-ε	0.905	0.964	0.934
Random Forest (10 trees)	No	-αι	0.928	1.000	0.963
		-ε	1.000	0.067	0.125
Random Forest (10 trees)	Yes	-αι	0.953	0.939	0.946
		-ε	0.946	0.953	0.947

4   Suggestions for Further Experimenting

In the method presented herein we experimented with various machine learning algorithms and various combinations of features for the automatic spelling correction of Modern Greek homophones. Our method was limited to two types of ambiguity, so should someone wish to extend our research, this could be done by applying the methodology to more spelling ambiguities.

Furthermore, there still are numerous combinations of features that could be tested; someone for example could create vectors with just one, two or three letters for word endings. Finally, other supervised learning algorithms (e.g. Support Vector Machines) could be experimented with.

5   Conclusion

Words that are pronounced the same but have a different meaning constitute a serious orthographic ambiguity problem. Context-sensitive spelling correction is the solution but at what cost in resources. In Modern Greek, as this work shows, we can use low level information, such as the endings of words around the target word, to correct this type of errors. Such information is easily available to any word processor, so this method can be easily adapted to a spell checker to address this type of errors.

References

1. Kukich, K.: Techniques for automatically correcting words in text. ACM Computing Surveys 24(4), 377–439 (1992)
2. Damerau, F.J., Mays, E.: An Examination of Undetected Typing Errors. Information Processing and Management 25(6), 659–664 (1989)

3. Angell, R.C., Freund, G.E., Willett, P.: Automatic Spelling Correction Using A Trigram Similarity Measure. Information Processing and Management 19(4), 255–261 (1983)
4. Kashyap, R.L., Oommen, B.J.: Spelling correction using probabilistic methods. Pattern Recognition Letters 2, 147–154 (1984)
5. Mays, E., Damerau, F.J., Mercer, R.L.: Context Based Spelling Correction. Information Processing and Management 27(5), 517–522 (1991)
6. Golding, A.R., Roth, D.: A Winnow-Based Approach to Context-Sensitive Spelling Correction. Machine Learning 34, 107–130 (1999)
7. Carlson, A., Fette, I.: Memory-Based Context-Sensitive Spelling Correction at Web Scale. In: Proceedings of the IEEE International Conference on Machine Learning and Applications, ICMLA (2007)
8. Golding, A.R., Schabes, Y.: Combining Trigram-based and Feature-based Methods for Context-Sensitive Spelling Correction. In: Proceedings of the 34th Annual Meeting of the Association for Computational Linguistics, Santa Cruz, CA (1996)
9. Ingason, A.K., Jóhannsson, S.B., Rögnvaldsson, E., Loftsson, H., Helgadóttir, S.: Context-Sensitive Spelling Correction and Rich Morphology. In: Proceedings of the 17th Nordic Conference of Computational Linguistics NODALIDA, pp. 231–234. Northern European Association for Language Technology (NEALT), Tartu (2009)
10. Chawla, N.V., Bowyer, K.W., Hall, L.O., Kegelmeyer, W.P.: SMOTE: Synthetic Minority Over-sampling Technique. Journal of Artificial Intelligence Research 16(1), 321–357 (2002)
11. Schaback, J., Li, F.: Multi-Level Feature Extraction for Spelling Correction. In: IJCAI 2007 (2007)
12. Golding, A.R.: A Bayesian hybrid method for context-sensitive spelling correction. In: Proceedings of the Third Workshop on Very Large Corpora, Boston, MA, pp. 39–53 (1995)

An Overview of the ILSP Unit Selection Text-to-Speech Synthesis System

Pirros Tsiakoulis, Sotiris Karabetsos, Aimilios Chalamandaris,
and Spyros Raptis

Institute for Language and Speech Processing – Research Centre ATHENA,
Artemidos 6 & Epidavrou, GR 15125, Athens, Greece
{ptsiak,sotoskar,achalam,spy}@ilsp.gr

Abstract. This paper presents an overview of the Text-to-Speech synthesis system developed at the Institute for Language and Speech Processing (ILSP). It focuses on the key issues regarding the design of the system components. The system currently fully supports three languages (Greek, English, Bulgarian) and is designed in such a way to be as language and speaker independent as possible. Also, experimental results are presented which show that the system produces high quality synthetic speech in terms of naturalness and intelligibility. The system was recently ranked among the first three systems worldwide in terms of achieved quality for the English language, at the international Blizzard Challenge 2013 workshop.

Keywords: Text to speech, unit selection, TTS, concatenative speech synthesis.

1 Introduction

Text-to-Speech (TTS) synthesis is a major domain of research and development in digital signal processing and language technologies. The scope of TTS systems is to dynamically convert textual input into synthetic voice. In recent years, TTS systems have shown a significant improvement as far as the quality of the synthetic speech is concerned and have become an essential component in human computer interaction and artificial intelligence applications [1], [2], [3].

Nowadays, modern TTS systems employ a corpus-based technology and are categorized as either Unit Selection systems or Statistical Parametric systems usually based on Hidden Markov Models (HMM) [1]. Among them, although HMM synthesis may offer some advantages in terms of computational resources and voice manipulation and adaptation, Unit Selection is still the predominant approach for achieving high quality, near-natural speech synthesis. In principle, this method makes no explicit assumptions regarding the underlying speech model and relies on runtime selection and concatenation of speech units from a recorded large speech database based on explicit matching criteria, so as to capture the characteristics of a targeted voice and at the same time deliver context-specific prosodic behavior [4]. Although the framework of unit selection systems is common, early design methodologies and decisions, adoption of language or speaker specific underlying models and techniques

A. Likas, K. Blekas, and D. Kalles (Eds.): SETN 2014, LNAI 8445, pp. 370–383, 2014.

(e.g., rule-based), are critical factors that influence the flexibility to easily adapt to other languages as well as to produce sufficient speech output quality.

This paper presents an overview of the ILSP TTS System, a core engine for corpus-based unit selection speech synthesis systems, developed at the Institute for Language and Speech Processing (ILSP)/ R.C. "ATHENA" and initially designed based on the Greek language. However, following and relying basically on a data driven approach, most of its modules are designed to be language-independent, with already successful migrations and small customizations to other languages such as English, Bulgarian as well as Hindi, offering equally high-quality results. This is confirmed from the results of the Blizzard Challenge 2013 workshop [5], an international challenge of the speech synthesis community, where the ILSP TTS system ranked among the first three systems worldwide for the English language and first for the Hindi language. A description of the underlying system and techniques used are provided, as well as information about obtained evaluation results. The rest of this paper is organized as follows. First, a description of the system is given with some detail on significant modules. Next, experimental evaluation results are presented for all languages. The paper concludes with discussion and issues for further work.

2   The ILSP Unit Selection TTS System

A general block diagram of a corpus based unit selection TTS system is shown in Fig. 1a. Based on that, the general architecture of the ILSP Corpus-based Unit Selection TTS system is depicted in Fig. 1b. There are two main components, namely the Frontend Natural Language Processing unit (NLP) and the Backend Digital Signal Processing unit (DSP). The NLP component accounts for every aspect of the linguistic processing of the input text, whereas the DSP component accounts for the speech signal manipulation and the output generation.

The speech database usually consists of a sufficient corpus of appropriately selected naturally spoken utterances, carefully annotated at the unit level. The speech units are diphones that is, speech chunks formed as an adjacent pair of phones including the transition phase between them. Each utterance comes from a text corpus designed to cover as many units as possible in different phonetic and prosodic contexts. The resulting repository of speech units may have little or great redundancy that also significantly affects both speech variability and overall quality. Also, the speech database contains all the necessary (meta-) data and functional parameters for the unit selection stage of the synthesis.

2.1   The NLP Frontend Module

The NLP component is mainly responsible for the tokenization and sentence splitting, the analysis and the transformation of the input text into an intermediate symbolic format, appropriate to feed the DSP component. Furthermore, it provides all the essential information regarding prosody, that is, pitch contour, phoneme durations and intensity. It is usually composed of a word- and sentence- tokenization module, a text normalizer, a letter-to-sound module and a prosody generator. All these components are essential for disambiguating and expanding abbreviations, numerals and acronyms, for producing correct pronunciation, and also for identifying prosody related anchor points. More specifically, regardless the language, the steps that are followed at the NLP module are as follows. The input text is fed into a parsing module, where sentence boundaries are identified and extracted. This step is important since all remaining modules perform only sentence-level processing. The identified sentences are then fully expanded by a text normalization module, taking care of numbers, abbreviations and acronyms.

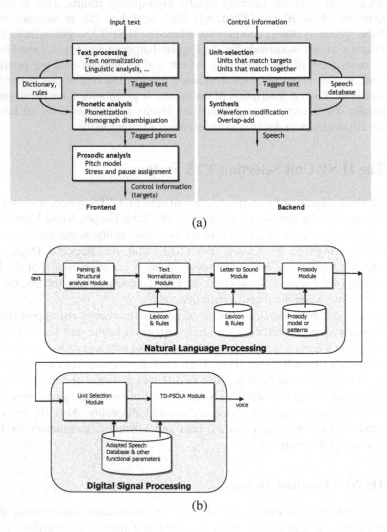

Fig. 1. General architectural diagram of (a) corpus based unit selection TTS and, (b) the ILSP TTS system

Then, the letter-to-sound module transforms the expanded text in an intermediate symbolic form related to phonetic description (i.e., grapheme to phoneme conversion). For each supported language, a method similar to the one described in [6] was followed that is the extraction of a set of automatically-derived rules together with a lexicon-based approach and an exception dictionary, produced from the analysis of a large text corpus of each language. A custom phoneme set was adopted for each language.

Regarding prosodic analysis, a distinct characteristic of the ILSP TTS system is that no explicit prosodic modeling is performed. Neither by assuming explicit prosody model nor in terms of target pitch values and duration models. The overall approach used for handling prosody is by taking into account the distance of a diphone from prosodically salient units in its vicinity, such as stressed syllables, pauses, and sentence boundaries, and the type of these units discriminating between declarative, interrogative and exclamatory sentences. This information is fed to the target cost component of the overall cost function in the unit selection module explained later. The main motivation behind such a rather plain but data-driven approach, is that naturalistic prosody patterns can be expected to emerge from the corpus through the unit selection process, assuming that the corpus is large enough and that the major factors affecting prosody have been taken into account into recordings. It is assumed that, in corpus based TTS systems, intonation and the units in the speech database cannot be treated separately. This fact leads to data-driven intonation models which resort to the speech database not only to retrieve speech units but also to acquire actual pitch patterns of the specific speaker. In terms of language dependency, only minor adaptations and customizations are necessary as, for example, the secondary stress encountered in other languages (e.g., English).

2.2   The DSP Backend Module

The DSP component includes all the essential modules for the proper manipulation of the speech signal, that is, selection of units to be synthesized, prosodic analysis and modification, speech signal processing and generation.

The unit selection module performs the selection of the speech units from the speech database using explicit matching criteria [4]. Using a spoken corpus (i.e., the speech database) as the acoustic inventory this module provides a mechanism to automatically select the optimal sequence of database units that produce the final speech output, the quality of which depends on its efficiency. The optimization criterion is the minimization of a total cost function which is defined by two partial cost functions, namely the target cost and the concatenation or join cost functions.

The target cost function measures the similarity of a candidate unit with its predicted specifications (as derived from NLP) and is defined as,

$$C^t(t_i, u_i) = \sum_{j=1}^{p} w_j^t \cdot C_j^t(t_i, u_i) \tag{1}$$

where, $u_1^n = \{u_1, u_2, \ldots, u_n\}$ are the candidate (sequence) units, $t_1^n = \{t_1, t_2, \ldots, t_n\}$ are the target (sequence) units, $C_j^t(t_i, u_i)$ is a partial target cost, p is the dimension of the target feature vector and w_j^t is a weighting factor for every partial target cost. The target feature vector typically employs target values for prosody and contextual features. The concatenation (join) cost function accounts for the acoustic matching between pairs of candidate units and is defined as,

$$C^c(u_{i-1}, u_i) = \sum_{j=1}^{q} w_j^c \cdot C_j^c(u_{i-1}, u_i) \tag{2}$$

where, $C_j^c(u_{i-1}, u_i)$ is a partial join cost , q is the dimension of the join feature vector and w_j^c is a weighting factor for every partial join cost.

The target and join feature vectors typically includes similarity measurements for the spectral, prosodic and contextual dimensions. The total cost function is defined as,

$$C(t_1^n, u_1^n) = \sum_{i=1}^{n} W^t \cdot C^t(t_i, u_i) + \sum_{i=2}^{n} W^c \cdot C^c(u_{i-1}, u_i) \tag{3}$$

where, W^t and W^c are the scalar weights that denote the significance of the target and the join costs, respectively.

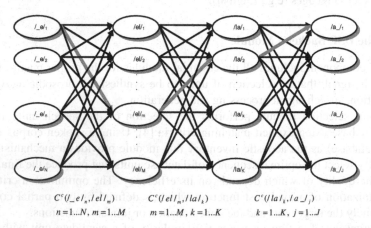

Fig. 2. An example illustrating the unit selection process for the diphone sequence {/_e/,/el/,/la/,/a_/}: The best path is depicted with the solid grey line and the best sequence path is based on the cumulative total score

The goal of the unit selection module is to search and find the speech unit sequence which minimizes the total cost, hence to specify,

$$\hat{u}_1^n = \min_{u_1 \ldots u_n} C(t_1^n, u_1^n) \qquad (4)$$

The selection of the optimal speech unit sequence incorporates a thorough search (usually a Viterbi search) which involves comparisons and calculations of similarity measures between all available units, often employing heuristics to guide and/or limit the search for higher efficiency. An example of the unit selection search is shown in Fig. 2 for the utterance /ela/ comprising the diphones $\{/\_e/,/el/,/la/,/a\_/\}$ having N, M, K and J number of instances in the speech database respectively.

For the target cost, the ILSP TTS system employs two cost components namely, one that accounts for the similarity of the phonetic context, which spans two phones on each side of the diphone and one that accounts for the similarity of the prosodic context i.e., pattern. For the concatenation cost, also two components are utilized, one that accounts for pitch continuity (pitch difference) and one that accounts for spectral similarity. For the latter, the system currently employs Euclidean distance on Mel Frequency Cepstral Coefficients (MFCCs). The weights W^t, W^c, w_1^t, w_2^t w_1^c, w_2^c, for each component of the cost functions are manually tuned and are phoneme dependent.

Since not only the spectral cost but also the total join cost in general, are important factors for achieving high quality speech synthesis [7], [8], [9], a data-driven approach can be sought for here as well, which will exploit the natural similarity of consecutive speech frames in the speech database. To this end, there is an ongoing research in the group towards establishing a framework for the computation of the total concatenation jointly with the spectral cost based on one-class classification approaches while at the same time alleviating the need for weight tuning [10].

After unit selection, the next step is to produce the synthetic speech signal by concatenation the selected diphones. Only minor modification is performed to the resulting pitch contour in order to remove any significant discontinuities at the boundaries of consecutive voiced units and to smooth the overall pitch curve. A polynomial interpolating function (similar to low-pass filtering) is used on the pitch contour to perform the smoothing. Finally, a custom Time Domain Overlap Add (TD-OLA) method is used to concatenate the selected units and apply the smooth pitch contour, in a pitch synchronous method, that is by extracting the pitch periods of the speech signal, windowing each segment with a Hanning window centered on every glottal closure point and then moving the segments closer or further apart to achieve pitch lifting or lowering. The manipulated segments of the consecutive units are overlapped and added to perform their concatenation [11].

3   TTS System Software Platform

The architectural design of the underlying software platform of the TTS system follows a pipelined modular paradigm developed in C++. Every component of the system, as depicted in Fig. 1b, is a separate module that implements a common high level module interface. The communication between the components is performed via a component independent data structure. This universal data structure is an XML based schema which is an extension to the Speech Synthesis Markup Language (SSML). Each component enriches the incoming XML structure by updating the nodes and attributes that are relevant to its designed purpose, e.g., convert text to phonemes and add the phoneme related elements to the XML document. This modular middleware highly facilitates the seamless integration of new components, such as text normalization modules, letter-to-sound converters, etc. This enables rapid development of new languages and/or voices, as only the language and/or voice dependent modules need to be developed.

The data components of the system also follow this modular approach. Every data module is exposed via an interface to every module that needs to use it. The data packaging is transparent to the modules, and data modules are independently developed. The system can be configured to run with any combination of processing and data modules depending on the desired outcome, e.g. a specific language/voice combination or a text-only processor.

4   Experimental Evaluation

TTS system evaluation has to do mainly with assessing the produced synthetic voice in terms of achieved quality, the latter being projected in several dimensions covering the notion of naturalness and intelligibility. Until now, the ILSP speech synthesis system has been evaluated against a number of either formal or informal acoustic experiments for all supported languages. These experiments and their outcome are described as follows.

4.1   Greek

The system has been evaluated against a set of acoustic experiments with the participation of 10 native Greek-speaking people comprised of both speech experts as well as non-experts. The speech database was 4-hour long with a female speaker. The experiments aimed to evaluate different dimensions of the synthetic speech quality via a sentence-level and a paragraph-level acoustic test. The stimuli consisted of 30 randomly selected sentences with an average of 15 words per sentence, as well as medium-sized paragraphs which were synthesized using the TTS system, and the listeners were asked to rate three quality dimensions for each sentence as well as five quality dimensions for each paragraph by grading on a scale of 1 to 5 for each dimension where 1 means low quality and 5 means natural quality as shown in table 1. For sentence-based evaluation the dimension of articulation is considered whereas for paragraph-based evaluation the more general dimension of pronunciation is used. Tables 2 and 3 summarize the mean scores (MOS) and the standard deviations of the responses.

Table 1. Scale labels for MOS evaluation

	Naturalness	Ease of listening	Articulation	Pleasantness	Intelligibility	Pronuncia-tion
1	Unnatural	No meaning understood	Bad	Very unpleasant	Unclear all the time	Bad
2	Inadequately natural	Effort required	Not very clear	Unpleasant	Not very clear	Not very clear
3	Adequately natural	Moderate effort	Fairly clear	Fair	Fairly clear	Fairly clear
4	Near natural	No appreciable effort required	Clear enough	Pleasant	Clear enough	Clear enough
5	Natural	No effort required	Very clear	Very Pleasant	Very clear	Very clear

Table 2. MOS evaluation results for the Greek language on a sentence level

	Naturalness	Ease of listening	Articulation
MOS	3.68	4.35	4.05
STD	0.61	0.62	0.67

Table 3. MOS evaluation results for the Greek language on a paragraph level

	Natural-ness	Ease of listening	Pleasantness	Intelligibility	Pronunciation
MOS	3.58	3.73	3.74	3.79	3.50
STD	0.68	0.55	0.80	0.71	0.73

From the results it is observed that the TTS system achieve high performance as far as its output quality is concerned given that scales of 4 and 5 correspond to near natural or natural speech.

4.2   English

For the English language, the ILSP TTS system was formally assessed in the context of the international speech synthesis scientific challenge namely, the Blizzard Challenge 2013 [5]. The aim of this challenge is to evaluate TTS systems over the same speech data that is to build TTS systems using the same speech database, differing only on the tools and techniques that each participant employs for its own system. The 2013 challenge was to build a TTS system from a large amount of audiobook speech data that is to give a notion of expressive speech synthesis [12], [13].

As well as for all other systems, for the tasks of the Blizzard challenge the ILSP TTS system was built in two ways: 1) by using all available audio data, after having discarded 8 out of the 30 available audiobooks (Task 1) and 2) by using only two audiobooks (Task 2). More details can be found in [12]. For the assessment of the TTS systems in coping with books, seven different aspects were tested in total: overall impression, pleasantness, speech pauses, stress, intonation, emotion and listening.

Table 4. The overall results for Task 1 on paragraphs for all systems and all listeners

	Overall Impression	Pleasantness	Speech pauses	Stress	Intonation	Emotion	Listening Effort
A	4,7	4,6	4,6	4,7	4,6	4,6	4,7
B	1,7	1,7	1,9	1,9	1,8	2	1,5
C	2,7	2,5	3	2,9	2,6	2,4	2,7
F	1,7	1,7	2,2	2	1,9	1,7	1,8
H	1,8	1,7	2,4	2,1	1,7	1,3	1,9
I	2,7	2,5	3,1	3	2,7	2,4	2,7
K	3	3	3,2	3	3	2,8	3
L	2,8	2,9	2,8	2,7	2,6	2,8	2,6
M	3,6	3,5	3,4	3,3	3,2	3,3	3,3
N	2,2	2,3	2,1	2,1	2,1	2,1	2,1
P	1,1	1,1	1,5	1,2	1,1	1,1	1

Table 5. The overall results for Task 2 on paragraphs for all systems and all listeners

	Overall Impression	Pleasantness	Speech pauses	Stress	Intonation	Emotion	Listening Effort
A	5,0	4,7	4,9	4,9	4,8	4,8	4,9
B	1,9	2,0	2,1	2,0	2,0	2,4	1,8
C	2,7	2,7	3,3	3,0	2,9	2,6	2,9
D	2,0	1,9	1,9	2,0	2,0	2,1	1,8
E	2,0	2,0	2,2	2,2	2,1	2,4	1,8
F	2,4	2,1	2,7	2,6	2,4	2,2	2,3
G	1,5	1,4	2,8	2,4	2,3	1,9	1,7
H	2,1	2,2	3,0	2,8	2,3	1,8	2,5
I	2,6	2,5	3,2	3,0	2,8	2,5	2,7
J	2,2	2,2	2,4	2,4	2,4	2,4	2,2
K	2,9	3,3	3,3	3,2	3,3	3,2	3,3
L	3,1	3,0	3,2	3,0	2,9	3,1	2,9
M	3,0	3,4	3,4	3,3	3,2	3,2	3,2
N	2,8	3,0	2,9	2,8	2,8	2,8	2,8
O	1,0	1,0	1,9	1,6	1,4	1,2	1,1

In the next tables the results of the MOS evaluation are given. It is important to notice that a large body of evaluators was participated to assess the TTS systems. In the results our system is identified with the letter "L", while "A" and "B" are the natural speech and the "Festival" system accordingly, and act as a benchmark system.

The ILSP TTS system performed exceedingly well, especially in Task 2 of limited data compared to Task 1, where it was rated first in the overall impression criterion among all listeners. In addition, the ILSP TTS system ranked among the first three systems.

4.3   Indian

The ILSP TTS system has also been formally assessed in the context of the Blizzard Challenge 2013 on building a TTS system for 4 Indian languages, namely Hindi, Bengali, Kannada, and Tamil. The assessment of the stimuli focuses on the natural-ness and the similarity to the original speaker, as well as on the word error rate. In both metrics for similarity to the original speaker and naturalness, our system was rated first in all subtasks, with significant difference from the rest, in most cases. The results are given in the following table. Although the training data was very limited the results were exceedingly good except for the subtask of Kannada, where the data set included very poor recordings This is a substantial result giving a clear evidence that not only the TTS system but also the tools and the techniques it utilizes is to a large extent language and speaker independent.

Table 6. The overall results for the Indian language tasks for our system. All data and all listeners are included.

	Naturalness	Similarity
Hindi	3,6	3,0
Bengali	3,8	3,4
Kannada	3,7	2,5
Tamil	3,8	3,3

4.4   Bulgarian

To assess the Bulgarian speech synthesis system, a set of acoustic experiments was performed similarly to the ones regarding the Greek language targeting different dimensions of the quality, covering naturalness, intelligibility and speech flow. A final set of questions was used to capture the participants' opinion regarding the appropriateness of the synthesis system for different application areas. A group of 30 native Bulgarian speakers participated in the evaluation. Among them, 10 had a background in linguistics or previous experience related to the subject and, for the purposes of these experiments, where considered as a distinct group. The experiments were performed in an unsupervised setting, after the necessary guidelines and instructions have been provided to the participants. They were able listen to each stimulus more than once.

The aim of the first experiment was to evaluate the performance of the TtS system in terms of naturalness. The MOS was again used as the subjective scoring method. The stimuli consisted of 35 randomly selected, medium-sized sentences with an average of 13 words per sentence. The listeners were asked to rate three quality dimensions for each sentence by scoring on a scale of 1 to 5 for each dimension according to the label scales of table 2 and table 1. Table 7, summarizes the MOS and the standard deviations of the responses, discriminating between "expert" and "non-expert" listeners. Interestingly enough, the opinions of the two groups where highly consistent. It is worth noting that the "ease of listening" and the "articulation" received remarkably high grades, which were consistent among both experts and non-experts. Furthermore, the overall score for "naturalness" which lies near 4 is particularly high, considering that 4 corresponded to "near natural".

Table 7. MOS evaluation results for the Bulgarian language on a sentence level

		Naturalness	Ease of listening	Articulation
Non-Experts	MOS	3,53	4,41	4,13
	STD	0,96	0,66	0,77
Experts	MOS	3,46	4,39	4,08
	STD	1,00	0,68	0,81
Overall	MOS	3,67	4,44	4,24
	STD	0,87	0,56	0,63

Table 8. MOS evaluation results for the Bulgarian language on a paragraph level

		Quality	Ease of listening	Pleasantness	Understandability	Pronunciation
Non-Experts	MOS	3,57	3,69	3,67	3,75	3,47
	STD	0,76	0,83	0,86	0,70	0,78
Experts	MOS	3,54	3,64	3,53	3,72	3,48
	STD	0,84	0,87	0,84	0,75	0,83
Overall	MOS	3,62	3,78	3,96	3,80	3,46
	STD	0,55	0,75	0,83	0,59	0,68

Table 8, illustrates the MOS results obtained for the assessment on a paragraph level. Once again, the TTS system performed very well and no appreciable deviation was observed between the responses of the expert and non-expert groups. This gives a clear evidence of the high quality synthetic speech that the system delivers.

A final set of questions was used to capture the participants' opinion regarding how appropriate it would be for the synthesis system to be used in different application areas. A rating scale of 1 to 5 with 1 corresponding to "inappropriate" and 5 to "completely appropriate" was used. The results obtained for the different application areas are summarized in the figure below ("Bad/Poor" corresponds to rates 1-2, "Fair" corresponds to rate 3, and "Good/Excellent" corresponds to rates 4-5). The results offer a clear indication that the synthesis system is highly regarded as a very appropriate tool in almost all the application areas. It is worth noting that the lowest score was received for "Audio books". This was expected (as shown in section 4.2) since book reading not only represents one of the most demanding areas for TTS technology, but also because the formal speaking style, as the one used for this system, usually employed in synthetic voices is often less appropriate. It is important to notice that the TTS system for the Bulgarian language was based on a speech database of about 2h of duration using a female speaker narrating in a neutral reading style.

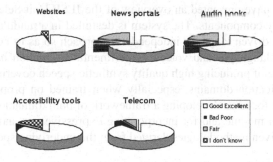

Fig. 3. Responses regarding the suitability of the TTS system in different application areas

5   Discussion - Towards High Quality Expressive Speech Synthesis

One of the most important scientific and development challenges in next generation TTS, is Emotional or Expressive Speech Synthesis as it can enhance future natural speech interfaces and dialog systems [13]. Currently, as most approaches in generating expressive speech synthesis employ either simplified modifications of prosodic quantities or try to identify and model universalities in how expressiveness is manifested across speakers in general, the obtained results are rather poor. Employing a hardwired set of emotions leaves a large set of interesting issues and applications unaddressed as such models are unable to capture the rich variability and subtle nuances of expression in human speech. Fully-blown emotions cannot be expected in most domains and applications where it is impossible to cast rich expressive styles in terms of such a plain (and archetypical) set of emotions. Many speech applications involve other expressive speaking styles in addition to, or instead of, the expression of emotions.

To this end, a trainable data-driven framework capable of looking and extracting measurable regularities, patterns and latent structure in the acoustic and prosodic features of expressive human speech would be beneficial compared to conventional approaches of model-based categorical analysis [14]. Also, such an approach is more consistent with the perceptual attributes of expressive speech, the underlying recorded corpus as well as the specific speaker and would address the whole chain of analyzing, modeling and synthesizing expressive speech by a proper integration to the unit selection process. In other words, this approach aims to reveal underlying structure and expressive speaking styles directly linked to the given speaker and speech corpus in an efficient trainable and integrable manner. This is an ongoing work of the group towards the enhancement of the TTS system, where some preliminary indicators has shown a very promising potential [12].

6   Conclusions and Further Work

In this paper we have presented an overview of the ILSP Unit Selection TTS system describing its key components. The system is designed in a modular architecture and it follows a data driven language independent approach so as to be as transparent as possible to new languages and voices. Experimental evaluation has shown that the system is capable of producing high quality synthetic speech covering many and often demanding application domains, especially when trained on proper speech stimuli. Future work will focus on developing a framework of both trainable cost functions for the unit selection module and for incorporating expressiveness and emotional notion based on data driven methodologies derived from the underlying speech corpus.

Acknowledgements. The work presented in this paper relating to emotion analysis, modeling and expressive speech synthesis has received co-funding from the POLYTROPON project (KRIPIS-GSRT, MIS: 448306). The authors' contribution in this work is of equal importance.

References

1. Benesty, J., Sondhi, M., Huang, Y. (eds.): Springer Handbook of Speech Processing. Springer (2008)
2. Li, D., Wang, K., Wu, C.: Speech Technology and Systems in Human-Machine Communication. IEEE Signal Processing Magazine 22(5), 12–14 (2005)
3. Gilbert, M., Feng, J.: Speech and Language Processing over the Web: Changing the way people communicate and access information. IEEE Signal Processing Magazine 25(3), 18–28 (2008)
4. Dutoit, T.: Corpus-based Speech Synthesis. In: Benesty, J., Sondhi, M.M., Huang, Y. (eds.) Springer Handbook of Speech Processing, Part D, ch. 21, pp. 437–455. Springer (2008)
5. The Blizzard Challenge 2013 Workshop (2013), http://www.synsig.org/index.php/Blizzard_Challenge
6. Chalamandaris, A., Raptis, S., Tsiakoulis, P.: Rule-based grapheme-to-phoneme me-thod for the Greek. In: Proc. Interspeech 2005: 9th European Conference on Speech Communication and Technology, Lisbon, Portugal, September 4-8 (2005)

7. Klabbers, E., van Santen, J.P.H., Kain, A.: The Contribution of Various Sources of Spectral Mismatch to Audible Discontinuities in a Diphone Database. IEEE Transactions on Audio Speech, and Language Processing 15(3), 949–956 (2007)

8. Vepa, J., King, S.: Subjective Evaluation of Join Cost and Smoothing Methods for Unit Selection Speech Synthesis. IEEE Trans. Audio, Speech and Language Processing 14(5), 1763–1771 (2006)

9. Toda, T., Kawai, H., Tsuzaki, M., Shikano, K.: An evaluation of cost functions sensitively capturing local degradation of naturalness for segment selection in concatenative speech synthesis. Speech Communication 48(1), 45–56 (2006)

10. Karabetsos, S., Tsiakoulis, P., Chalamandaris, A., Raptis, S.: One-Class Classification for Spectral Join Cost Calculation in Unit Selection Speech Synthesis. IEEE Signal Processing Letters 17(8), 746–749 (2010)

11. Chalamandaris, A., Tsiakoulis, P., Karabetsos, S., Raptis, S.: An Efficient and Robust Pitchmarking Algorithm on the Speech Waveform for TD-PSOLA. In: Proc. of the IEEE ICSIPA 2009 (IEEE International Conference on Signal and Image Processing Applications 2009), paper 190, Malaysia (November 2009)

12. Chalamandaris, A., Tsiakoulis, P., Karabetsos, S., Raptis, S.: The ILSP Text-to-Speech System for the Blizzard Challenge 2013. In: Proc. Blizzard Challenge 2013 Workshop, Barcelona, Spain (2013)

13. Marc, S.: Expressive Speech Synthesis: Past, Present, and Possible Futures. In: Tao, J.H., Tan, T.N. (eds.) Affective Information Processing. Springer Science+Business Media LLC (2009)

14. Raptis, S.: Exploring Latent Structure in Expressive Speech. In: Proc. IEEE CogInfoCom 2013, 4th IEEE International Conference on Cognitive Infocommunications, Budapest, Hungary, December 2-5, pp. 741–745 (2013)

An Artificial Neural Network Approach
for Underwater Warp Prediction

Kalyan Kumar Halder, Murat Tahtali, and Sreenatha G. Anavatti

School of Engineering and Information Technology
The University of New South Wales
Canberra, ACT 2600, Australia
k.halder@student.unsw.edu.au,
{m.tahtali,a.sreenatha}@adfa.edu.au

Abstract. This paper presents an underwater warp estimation approach based on generalized regression neural network (GRNN). The GRNN, with its function approximation feature, is employed for a-priori estimation of the upcoming warped frames using history of the previous frames. An optical flow technique is employed for determining the dense motion fields of the captured frames with respect to the first frame. The proposed method is independent of the pixel-oscillatory model. It also considers the interdependence of the pixels with their neighborhood. Simulation experiments demonstrate that the proposed method is capable of estimating the upcoming frames with small errors.

Keywords: Artificial neural network, optical flow, prediction, and underwater imaging.

1 Introduction

When imaging through the water, light rays from objects go through several reflection and refraction before being captured by the camera, resulting in non-uniform blurring and random geometric distortions of the acquired short-exposure images. These degradation effects are aggravated by light attenuation, path radiance, and particle scattering [1–5]. Therefore, underwater imaging poses significant challenges at extended ranges when compared with similar problems in the air. Fig. 1 illustrates a common example of underwater imaging problem where the camera observes an underwater object through the water surface. When the water surface is still, the camera observes the object p at its original location, that is, there is no distortion in the captured image. However, when the water is wavy, the normal to the water surface N is tilted by an angle. The apparent position of p changes to p', resulting in a geometrically distorted image.

Prediction of the turbulence induced warping ahead of time is of interest, as the estimation of the next warped frames can provide two types of advantages [6]; firstly, it may reduce the computational burden of the image registration algorithm by starting with a better estimation of warp in post-processing applications. Secondly, it can provide a better approximation of the corrective surface

A. Likas, K. Blekas, and D. Kalles (Eds.): SETN 2014, LNAI 8445, pp. 384–394, 2014.
© Springer International Publishing Switzerland 2014

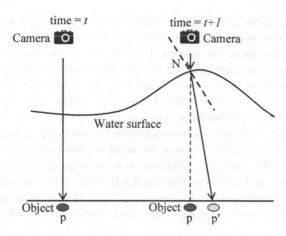

Fig. 1. A simple illustration of underwater imaging and the consequence of refraction

curvature needed to be assumed by the deformable mirrors in real-time adaptive optics (AO) applications. A few shift maps prediction methods have been proposed for imaging through the air. In [7], a linear Kalman filter approach on a pixel-by-pixel basis is introduced for predicting the warping or shift maps, where the average wander of each pixel of a static scenery over a certain period of time is assumed to be zero. Based on this, each pixel wander is modeled using a simple oscillator system and characterized by time-dependent differential equations, which is not always a practical assumption [8]. In a subsequent paper [9], a statistical approach is presented for estimating the covariance matrices required for Kalman filter based shift maps restoration. In [10], the authors propose a hybrid extended Kalman filter (HEKF) for fine tuning the oscillator parameters and improving the performance of warp estimation. A robust extended Kalman filter (REKF) is proposed in [11] to handle the time-varying model uncertainties. One of the limitations of these implementations of Kalman filter approaches is that each pixel is assumed to oscillate independently of its neighbors, and also independently in the horizontal and vertical directions. But in reality, there exists a substantial correlation between the wander of each pixel and the wander of its neighbors. Another limitation is that inappropriate selection of Kalman filter parameters may cause inaccurate prediction and sometimes divergence. Therefore, in order to predict the warping of underwater images, we considered a neural network estimator as a possible replacement for the existing Kalman filter. This will not only eliminate several limitations of Kalman filter approaches but also incorporate intelligence into the system.

Artificial neural networks (ANNs) are computational tools modeled on the interconnection of the neurons in the animal central nervous systems. Over the last few decades, ANNs have been widely used in image processing applications because of their adaptive and learning capabilities. They are applied for a variety of imaging application, e.g., image preprocessing, reconstruction, restoration, enhancement, compression, segmentation, feature extraction and optimization

[12]. Radial basis networks (RBNs), with their function approximation feature, can be utilized for warping function estimation of upcoming frames in underwater imaging. This eliminates the model dependency of the prediction techniques and assists the measurement of each pixel's shifts considering its neighborhood. In comparison with standard feed-forward neural network (FFNN) and back-propagation neural network (BPNN), RBNs may require more neurons, but they can be designed to be quicker than others [13]. The training data of the RBN are obtained from the previously captured frames by applying an image registration technique. There are several image registration techniques in the literature, such as, differential elastic image registration, non-rigid image registration, gradient based optical flow, and cross-correlation. Each registration technique has its own advantages and disadvantages. Among them, optical flow techniques are capable of providing better measurements of the pixel warping within shorter processing time [14–16].

In this paper, we present a simple and efficient algorithm for predicting the warping of upcoming frames of the underwater object or scene. We employ a GRNN, a variant of RBN for its fast learning feature and highly parallel structure [13]. A high accuracy optical flow technique based on coarse-to-fine strategy is utilized for determining the flow vectors. The performance of the algorithm is analyzed by applying it to synthetically warped and real-world video sequences.

The rest of the paper is organized as follows: section 2 presents an insight into the image registration technique based on optical flow. Section 3 describes the structure of the GRNN designed for experiments. Section 4 presents the details of the proposed warp estimation algorithm. Simulation experiments are included in section 5. Finally, section 6 concludes the paper and provides our future research directions.

2   Image Registration

Image registration is used for determining the motion fields between two image frames which are taken at different times t and $t + \Delta t$. The optical flow constraint states that the gray value of a moving pixel should be consistent along the flow vector and the flow field should be piecewise smooth [14], i.e.,

$$I(x, y, t) = I(x + x_s, y + y_s, t + 1) \tag{1}$$

where $\mathbf{u} = (x_s, y_s)$ is the optical flow vector of a pixel at $\mathbf{x} = (x, y)$ from time t to time $t + 1$. The objective function in the continuous spatial domain can be written as:

$$E(x_s, y_s) = \int \psi(|I(\mathbf{x} + \mathbf{u}) - I(\mathbf{x})|^2) + \alpha\phi(|\nabla x_s|^2 + |\nabla y_s|^2)d\mathbf{x} \tag{2}$$

where $\psi(\cdot)$ and $\phi(\cdot)$ are robust functions [17], ∇ is the gradient operator and α weights the regularization. A discrete version of (2) is considered here for simplicity in implementation. After modifying the objective function in (2), it becomes:

$$E(dx_s, dy_s) = \int \psi \left(|I(\mathbf{x} + \mathbf{u} + d\mathbf{u}) - I(\mathbf{x})|^2 \right) +$$

$$\alpha\phi \left(|\nabla(x_s + dx_s)|^2 + |\nabla(y_s + dy_s)|^2 \right) d\mathbf{x} \quad (3)$$

Using first-order Taylor series, the term $I(\mathbf{x} + \mathbf{u} + d\mathbf{u}) - I(\mathbf{x})$ can be expanded as:

$$I(\mathbf{x} + \mathbf{u} + d\mathbf{u}) - I(\mathbf{x}) \approx I_z(\mathbf{x}) + I_x(\mathbf{x})dx_s + I_y(\mathbf{x})dy_s \quad (4)$$

where $I_z(\mathbf{x}) = I(\mathbf{x} + \mathbf{u}) - I(\mathbf{x})$, $I_x(\mathbf{x}) = \frac{\partial}{\partial x}I(\mathbf{x} + \mathbf{u})$, $I_y(\mathbf{x}) = \frac{\partial}{\partial y}I(\mathbf{x} + \mathbf{u})$. The continuous function in (3) can be discretized as:

$$E(dX_S, dY_S) = \sum_{\mathbf{x}} \psi \left(\left(\delta_{\mathbf{x}}^T(I_z + I_x dX_S \mid I_y dY_S) \right)^2 \right) + \alpha\phi \left((\delta_{\mathbf{x}}^T D_x(X_S + dX_S))^2 \right.$$

$$\left. + (\delta_{\mathbf{x}}^T D_y(X_S + dX_S))^2 + (\delta_{\mathbf{x}}^T D_x(Y_S + dY_S))^2 + (\delta_{\mathbf{x}}^T D_y(Y_S + dY_S))^2 \right) \quad (5)$$

where X_S, Y_S are the vectorized form of x_s, y_s; $I_x = \text{diag}(I_x)$ and $I_y = \text{diag}(I_y)$ be diagonal matrices where the diagonals are the frames I_x and I_y; D_x and D_y represent the matrix corresponding to $x-$ and $y-$ derivative filters; $\delta_{\mathbf{x}}$ is the column vector that has only one nonzero (one) value at location $\mathbf{x}$, e.g., $\delta_{\mathbf{x}} I_x = I_x(\mathbf{x})$. Assuming

$$f_{\mathbf{x}} = \left(\delta_{\mathbf{x}}^T(I_z + I_x dX_S + I_y dY_S) \right)^2, \text{ and } g_{\mathbf{x}} = \left(\delta_{\mathbf{x}}^T D_x(X_S + dX_S) \right)^2 +$$

$$\left(\delta_{\mathbf{x}}^T D_y(X_S + dX_S) \right)^2 + \left(\delta_{\mathbf{x}}^T D_x(Y_S + dY_S) \right)^2 + \left(\delta_{\mathbf{x}}^T D_y(Y_S + dY_S) \right)^2 \quad (6)$$

(5) can be rewritten as:

$$E(dX_S, dY_S) = \sum_{\mathbf{x}} \psi(f_{\mathbf{x}}) + \alpha\phi(g_{\mathbf{x}}) \quad (7)$$

In this approach, the iterative reweighted least square (IRLS) method is used to find dX_S, dY_S so that the gradient $\left[\frac{\partial E}{\partial dX_S}; \frac{\partial E}{\partial dY_S} \right] = 0$. Deriving $\frac{\partial E}{\partial dX_S}$ and $\frac{\partial E}{\partial dY_S}$ using (7) and setting those equal to zero, the obtained equations are as follows:

$$\begin{bmatrix} \Psi' I_x^2 + \alpha L & \Psi' I_x I_y \\ \Psi' I_x I_y & \Psi' I_y^2 + \alpha L \end{bmatrix} \begin{bmatrix} dX_S \\ dY_S \end{bmatrix} = - \begin{bmatrix} \Psi' I_x I_z + \alpha L X_S \\ \Psi' I_y I_z + \alpha L Y_S \end{bmatrix} \quad (8)$$

where L is a generalized Laplacian filter defined as $L = D_x^T \Phi' D_x + D_y^T \Phi' D_y$, $\Psi' = \text{diag}(\psi'(f_{\mathbf{x}}))$, $\Phi' = \text{diag}(\phi'(g_{\mathbf{x}}))$. The equations in (8) contain nonlinear functions and are solved by the fixed-point iterations [15,16]. Using few outer and inner fixed-point iterations, the shift map is computed through a coarse-to-fine refining scheme on a dense Gaussian pyramid.

3   Generalized Regression Neural Network

GRNN, as proposed by D.F. Specht in [13] is a special case of RBNs with a one pass learning algorithm and is capable of approximating any arbitrary linear or non-linear function from historical data. The structure of a GRNN is comparatively simple and is capable to converge to the underlying function of the data with only a few samples [13]. Fig. 2 shows the general architecture of GRNN. It consists of four layers: input, pattern, summation, and output layers. In Fig. 2, u and v represent the input and output vectors, respectively, and m is the total number of vectors. In this paper, the GRNN is trained for an image window of 4×4 pixels at a time which means the value of m is 16. The basic output equation of the GRNN with m inputs and one output is given by [18]:

$$v(u) = \frac{\sum_i W_i \theta_i(u)}{\sum_i \theta_i(u)} \tag{9}$$

where W_i is the weight connection between the ith neuron in the pattern units and the corresponding neuron in the summation units; θ_i is the Gaussian radial basis function such that

$$\theta_i(u) = \exp\left[-\frac{(u - u_i)^T(u - u_i)}{2\sigma^2}\right] \tag{10}$$

where u_i is a single training vector in the input space, and σ is the smoothing factor. In GRNN, the smoothing factor is a constant between 0 and 1, which is the

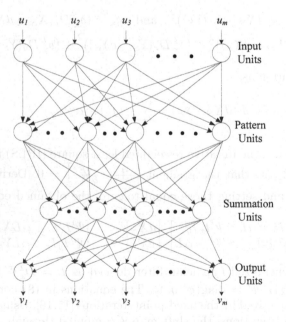

Fig. 2. General GRNN architecture

only parameter needed to be chosen. When σ is large, the function approximation is forced to be smooth, whereas a smaller value of σ allows the data to fit very closely. Therefore, appropriate smoothing factor can smooth out noise and provide better estimation of warping functions.

4 Warp Estimation Algorithm

The warp estimation algorithm is developed for predicting the next distorted frame of the underwater object given only a few short-exposure frames of the object as input. No previous knowledge of the waves or the underwater object is assumed. In this algorithm, GRNN is applied for determining the underlying input-output relationship or mapping from a set of input-output data [19]. The shifts of pixels are considered as training data for the network. Estimation is limited to one directional shift (either $x-$ or $y-$ direction) at a time. The first warped frame is assumed as the reference frame. To start with the algorithm at least one input-output data is required. Therefore, the estimation may start for the 3rd upcoming frame. The procedures are described in steps below:

1. Initialization: Apply the image registration technique to determine the shifts of each pixel of the first two frames, say z_1 and z_2. Where z represents the measured pixel shifts in the $x-$ or $y-$ direction. z_1 is by default zero and is considered as input data while z_2 is considered as output or target data for training with the neural network.
2. For frame k ($k > 2$),
   2.1. Training: Train the GRNN with the input-output data set.
   2.2. Prediction: Simulate the network for predicting the pixel's next shift $\hat{z}_k$ with the present input value z_{k-1}.
   2.3. Filtering: Pass the estimated shifts through a median filter to soften the outliers.
   2.4. Registration: Capture the kth frame and apply the image registration for calculating its pixel shifts, z_k. The number of training data is increased by one.
3. $k = k + 1$, go to step 2 until stop.

The accuracy of the estimation depends on the number of training data. For estimating the kth frame, the number of training data available is $(k-2)$. When the GRNN is trained with multiple input predictor variables, z will be a matrix instead of a vector.

5 Simulation Experiments

The proposed underwater warp estimation method was implemented in MATLAB and tested on an Intel Core i7-2600 CPU 3.40GHz machine with 8GB RAM. The performance of the method is measured by using a synthetically warped underwater sequence [20]. Fig. 3 shows a sampling of the test sequence.

The sequence consists of 61 frames, each of 268×292 pixels. The method was also applied on a real underwater sequence [5]. The real sequence contains 120 frames, each of 192×288 pixels, a sampling is shown in Fig. 4. The estimation capability of the proposed method is verified by determining various quality metrics, e.g., mean squared error (MSE) and variance map.

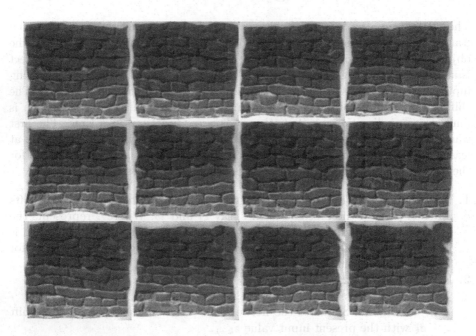

Fig. 3. A sampling of synthetically distorted Brick images

Fig. 4. A sampling of naturally distorted Water-Colgate images

5.1 A Single Pixel's Shift

The GRNN was trained considering a neighborhood of 4×4 pixels to predict the next warp of each pixel using the trained network. The estimated shifts were compared with the measured shifts obtained through the optical flow technique. Fig. 5 (a) and (b) show the comparison for the synthetic Brick sequence for the pixel at image coordinate ($x = 230$, $y = 230$) in the $x-$ and $y-$ directions, respectively. It is noted that, even though the pixel's wander is not periodic, the neural network estimator copes up with the changes, proving a good estimation closer to the measured values. The MSEs between the estimated and measured shifts are obtained as 0.47 and 0.38 for the $x-$ and $y-$ directional shifts, respectively. Similarly, Fig. 6 shows the results for the Water-Colgate sequence for the pixel at image coordinate ($x = 170$, $y = 170$); MSE of 0.61 and 1.04 are calculated for the $x-$ and $y-$ directional shifts, respectively

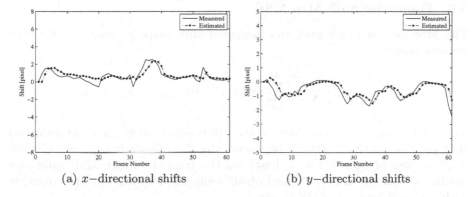

(a) $x-$directional shifts (b) $y-$directional shifts

Fig. 5. Estimated and measured shifts of the pixel at image coordinate ($x = 230$, $y = 230$) for the Brick sequence

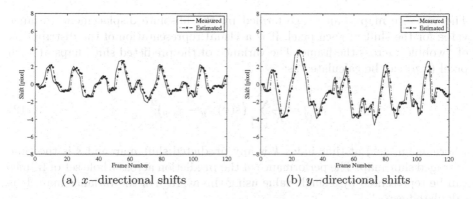

(a) $x-$directional shifts (b) $y-$directional shifts

Fig. 6. Estimated and measured shifts of the pixel at image coordinate ($x = 170$, $y = 170$) for the Water-Colgate sequence

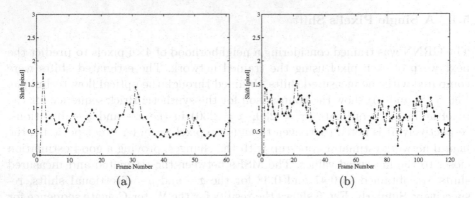

Fig. 7. Frame by frame shift map MSE for (a) Brick sequence, and (b) Water-Colgate sequence

5.2   Framewise Shift Map MSE

The MSE between estimated and measured shift maps is calculated for each frame k using:

$$MSE_k = \frac{1}{M \times N} \sum_{x=1}^{N} \sum_{y=1}^{M} \left(\hat{s}(k)_{x,y} - s(k)_{x,y} \right)^2, \quad k = 1, ..., K \qquad (11)$$

where $\hat{s}(k)$ and $s(k)$ at time index k are any predicted shift map and measured shift map, respectively. $M \times N$ represents the size of each frame, and K is the total number of frames. Fig. 7 illustrates the frame by frame MSE values for the Brick sequence and the Water-Colgate sequence, respectively. The errors are within 1 pixel for most of the frames.

5.3   Variance Map

The variance map is an image formed by the absolute displacement variance value for the shift at each pixel. It is a visual representation of the distribution of "wobble" across the frame. The variance of the predicted shift maps at each pixel (x,y) can be calculated as:

$$\sigma_{x,y}^2 = \frac{1}{K} \sum_{k=1}^{K} \left(\hat{s}(k)_{x,y} - \bar{\hat{s}}_{x,y} \right)^2 \qquad (12)$$

where again, $\hat{s}(k)$ at time index k is any predicted shift map and $\bar{\hat{s}}$ is the time averaged shift map. The performance of the prediction across whole set of frames can be represented by a single value using the average of the variance map. It is calculated as:

$$\langle \sigma^2 \rangle = \frac{1}{M \times N} \sum_{x} \sum_{y} \sigma_{x,y}^2 \qquad (13)$$

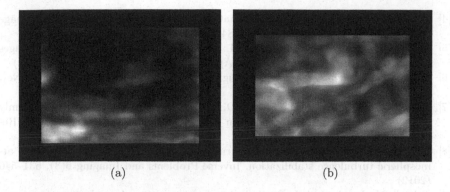

(a)   (b)

Fig. 8. ROI variance maps: (a) Brick sequence, and (b) Water-Colgate sequence

where $\langle \rangle$ is the average operator. Fig. 8 (a) and (b) present the region of interest (ROI) variance maps for the Brick and Water-Colgate sequences, respectively. A central ROI was chosen to discard edge artifacts. The darker areas indicate lower variance. For the Brick sequence, the low variance areas dominate with some lighter regions; mean variance of 0.46 is calculated. Whereas for the Water-Colgate sequence, as expected, the variance is comparatively higher because of the higher distortions, which is also reflected by the higher mean variance value of 1.33.

6 Conclusion

In this paper, a GRNN based approach has been implemented for predicting the warping of upcoming geometrically distorted frames in underwater imaging. The proposed approach is independent of pixel oscillatory model and considers the interdependence of each pixel with its neighborhood as it is the case in reality. The simulation tests have been carried out on synthetic and real-world video sequences. It has been demonstrated that the method has good warp prediction capabilities. The real-time parallel implementation of this method using GPUs (graphical processing units) or FPGAs (field programmable gate arrays) will allow its application to real-time surveillance.

References

[1] Hou, W.: A simple underwater imaging model. Optics Letters 34(17), 2688–2690 (2009)
[2] Kanaev, A.V., Hou, W., Woods, S., Smith, L.N.: Restoration of turbulence degraded underwater images. Optical Engineering 51(5) (2012)
[3] Boffety, M., Galland, F., Allais, A.-G.: Influence of polarization filtering on image registration precision in underwater conditions. Optics Letters 37(15), 3273–3275 (2012)

[4] Wang, G., Zheng, B., Sun, F.F.: Estimation-based approach for underwater image restoration. Optics Letters 36(13), 2384–2386 (2011)

[5] Wen, Z., Lambert, A., Fraser, D., Li, H.: Bispectral analysis and recovery of images distorted by a moving water surface. Applied Optics 49(33), 6376–6384 (2010)

[6] Tahtali, M.: Imaging techniques through the atmosphere. The University of New South Wales (2007)

[7] Tahtali, M., Lambert, A.J., Fraser, D.: Progressive restoration of nonuniformly warped images by shiftmap prediction using Kalman filter. In: Proc. Signal Recovery and Synthesis (2007)

[8] Mao, Y., Gilles, J.: Non rigid geometric distortions correction-application to atmospheric turbulence stabilization. Inverse Problems and Imaging 6(3), 531–546 (2012)

[9] Tahtali, M., Lambert, A.J.: Statistical turbulence approach to the covariance matrices in the shiftmap prediction using Kalman filter. In: Proc. OSA Optics and Photonics Technical Digest (2009)

[10] Tahtali, M., Lambert, A., Fraser, D.: Self-tuning Kalman filter estimation of atmospheric warp. In: Proc. SPIE, vol. 7076 (2008)

[11] Kallapur, A., Tahtali, M., Petersen, I.: A pixel-wise robust extended Kalman filter for restoration of geometrically warped anisoplanatic images. In: Proc. IEEE International Conference on Control Applications, pp. 280–285 (2010)

[12] Egmont-Petersen, M., de Ridder, D., Handels, H.: Image processing with neural networks-a review. Pattern Recognition 35, 2279–2301 (2002)

[13] Specht, D.F.: A general regression neural network. IEEE Transactions on Neural Networks 2(6), 568–576 (1991)

[14] Brox, T., Bruhn, A., Papenberg, N., Weickert, J.: High accuracy optical flow estimation based on a theory for warping. In: Pajdla, T., Matas, J(G.) (eds.) ECCV 2004. LNCS, vol. 3024, pp. 25–36. Springer, Heidelberg (2004)

[15] Liu, C.: Beyond pixels: Exploring new representations and applications for motion analysis. Massachusetts Institute of Technology (2009)

[16] Halder, K.K., Tahtali, M., Anavatti, S.G.: An improved restoration method for non-uniformly warped images using optical flow technique. In: Proc. DICTA (2013)

[17] Black, M.J., Anandan, P.: The robust estimation of multiple motions: Parametric and piecewise-smooth flow fields. Computer Vision and Image Understanding 63(1), 75–104 (1996)

[18] Jwo, D.-J., Lai, C.-C.: Neural network-based GPS GDOP approximation and classification. GPS Solutions 11(1), 51–60 (2007)

[19] Halder, K.K., Tahtali, M., Anavatti, S.G.: A new pixel shiftmap prediction method based on generalized regression neural network. In: Proc. IEEE ISSPIT (2013)

[20] Tian, Y., Narasimhan, S.G.: Seeing through water: image restoration using model-based tracking. In: Proc. ICCV, pp. 2303–2310 (2009)

Audio Feature Selection for Recognition of Non-linguistic Vocalization Sounds

Theodoros Theodorou[1], Iosif Mporas[1,2], and Nikos Fakotakis[1]

[1] Artificial Intelligence Group, Wire Communications Laboratory
Dept. of Electrical and Computer Engineering, University of Patras
26500 Rion-Patras, Greece
{theodorou,imporas,fakotaki}@upatras.gr
[2] Dept. of Mechanical Engineering
Technological Educational Institute of Western Greece
26334 Koukouli-Patras, Greece

Abstract. Aiming at automatic detection of non-linguistic sounds from vocalizations, we investigate the applicability of various subsets of audio features, which were formed on the basis of ranking the relevance and the individual quality of several audio features. Specifically, based on the ranking of the large set of audio descriptors, we performed selection of subsets and evaluated them on the non-linguistic sound recognition task. During the audio parameterization process, every input utterance is converted to a single feature vector, which consists of 207 parameters. Next, a subset of this feature vector is fed to a classification model, which aims at straight estimation of the unknown sound class. The experimental evaluation showed that the feature vector composed of the 50-best ranked parameters provides a good trade-off between computational demands and accuracy, and that the best accuracy, in terms of recognition accuracy, is observed for the 150-best subset.

Keywords: Non-linguistic vocalizations, sound recognition, audio features, classification algorithms.

1 Introduction

Over the last decade, there is an increase in the scientific community's interest about processes that involve automatic signal processing. Audio is a corner stone on the types of signals of interest due to the fact that there is a big amount of applications in which the audio data are available and accessible and there are also numerous applications in which audio data manage to express the information that should be under processing.

Since speech plays a significant role in our life, automatic speech processing toolkits have been investigating several underline characteristics that subsist within the speech intervals. As a typical example, an automatic speech recognizer exports from a voice signal the transcription in a series of letters, in contrast of a human ear that can perceive underline characteristics about the speaker (e.g. identification, emotional and

A. Likas, K. Blekas, and D. Kalles (Eds.): SETN 2014, LNAI 8445, pp. 395–405, 2014.

linguistic details). One major phenomenon that subsists within the speech intervals is the non linguistic sounds. This type of audio event includes vocalizations that can't be transcript (in contrast with humans talking that can be transcript into a series of letters). Nevertheless, non linguistic sounds can offer details about underline characteristics, for instance speaker's health, emotional status and sleepiness/boredom could be revealed from cough, laugh or yawing.

Owing to this observation, several studies have investigating the effect on adding into the set of events of interest the non linguistic sounds. Characteristics examples could be found in articles [1,2] in which the authors utilize the non linguistic sound in interesting types of experiments and more particularly they visualized laughing, crying, sneezing and yawning and they create a real time cough detection and processing system correspondingly. The basic areas of applications in which non linguistic sounds take place among the events of interest are the medical decisions [2, 3, 4, 5, 6], the animation [1], the paralinguistic recognition for post processing emotion recognition [7] and the surveillance [8].

The nature of the audio problem (e.g. the goals of the processing) defines the set of the events of interest. Non linguistic sounds occur in several speech intervals (especially in those where the speaker doesn't dictate an a priori text) but their discrimination (as long as the post processing recognition and discrimination among them or among their subcategories) should start from the labeling while the a priori close set of events of interest is defined. While some of the non linguistic sounds could be subcategorized, the main sound events are (i) laugh [9, 10, 11, 12, 13, 14, 15, 7], (ii) cough [16, 2, 3, 5, 6], (iii) snoring [17, 18], (iv) cry [9, 4], (v) scream [9, 19, 20, 8], (vi) breathing and other noises [10, 11, 18], (vii) sighing [11] and (viii) raised voice [19].

Non linguistic sounds are commonly handled with typical audio processing architectures. A decomposing of the audio signals into a frame sequence and subsequently into a feature vector sequence following by a classification algorithm is a typical method of processing.

Starting with the pre-processing and the parameterization, typical type of analysis is the short-time analysis of the audio signal in both time and frequency domain. The audio signal is divided into a series of frames and thereafter a series of feature extraction algorithms are applied in each frame. Several well known and commonly used, in the audio processing literature, feature have been explored, such us (i) the Mel frequency cepstral coefficients MFCC [9, 16, 12, 2, 3, 4, 20, 18], (ii) Spectral Features [16, 13, 19, 20, 17] (iii) the pitch [12, 14, 7, 19, 13, 17], (iv) the zero crossing rate (ZCR) [16, 12, 20], (v) the Perceptual Linear Prediction PLP [10, 14, 7], (vi) the Linear Prediction Coefficients LPC [4, 8], (vii) the energy [12, 14, 7] and (viii) the Harmonic to Noise Ratio [16].

During the classification, the feature vector sequence is driven into a powerful machine learning algorithm. Each vector is assigned as one of the classes that a priori has been defined as class of the close set of events of interest. Either as events of interest in an audio processing algorithm or as discrimination target in an audio discrimination problem, non linguistic sounds have been driven into several types of machine learning algorithms (e.g. probabilistic or discriminative). Some of the commonly used are (i) the Support Vector Machine SVM [9, 7, 16], (ii) the hidden markov models HMM / the hidden markov models HMM with automatic speech recognizer ASR / the Gaussian mixture models GMM [18, 10, 11, 7, 16, 2, 3, 8, 20], (iii) the Neural Networks [10, 12, 16, 4], (iv) the Boosting Technology [13], (v) the k-Nearest Neighbor [17] and (vi) the fuzzy logic [19].

Expanding the architecture block diagram with techniques commonly found within architecture schematics of audio recognition problems, studies have shown that the discrimination ability of the feature set could be explored. There are techniques that evaluate the discrimination ability of a feature into the specific set of audio events of interest and techniques that are applied onto the feature vector sequence to change the feature space into a less dimensional component space. Commonly found, among the non linguistic recognition problems, techniques are (i) the Non-Negative Matrix Factorization [10], (ii) the Mutual Information [16] and (iii) the Principal Component Analysis [15].

In the present work, we aim to apply architecture of sequential discrete steps into a database for discriminate non linguistic vocalization. After the initial pre-processing and the parameterization of the audio recordings, we investigate the effect of evaluation of the features based on their relevance in the discrimination problem. Moreover we created subspaces that hold only the most relevant features (each subspace is defined from different minimum level of relevance) and we explore their corresponding models we powerful machine learning algorithms. The rest of the article is organized as followed: Session 2 holds information about the system description, in session 3 we analyze the details about the experimental setup concerning the audio events of interest in the database, the selection of features and the evaluation and classification algorithms, in session 4 there are the results and finally session 5 holds the conclusions.

2   System Description

The discrimination of non linguistic events of interest from speech events is based on a two phase classification method. Initially the training phase produces suitable training models for the upcoming testing signals using the information of a close set of training recording, while the testing phase fed by the training phase seeks to categorize the incoming data. A short-time analysis of the audio signals in both time and frequency domains is the base in which the recognition results are compared with the labels of the events in frame level. A technique of initial evaluation of the significance of the feature regardless of their relevance during the training phase and the forwarding of the outcome in the testing phase is acting upon the models. The details about the current architecture appeared in Figure 1.

With more detailed analysis, the training phase starts by defining an audio recording set $X = \{X^r\}$ that consists of labeled audio files, each of which within there are

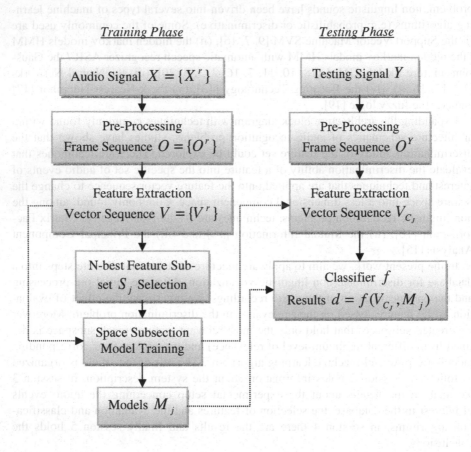

Fig. 1. Block diagram of general architecture

labeled the audio events of interest. The process of discrete steps, that construct the training phase, starts with a short time analysis by decomposing the audio signal into a sequence of parameters forward from a technique that selects features with high discrimination ability and ends with the construction of sound models. The short time analysis divides each audio recording into frames. The frames of all files are extracted from the same analysis in terms of equal and constant size and time shift step. Thereafter the set of files that include the frame sequences $O = \{O^r\}$ are driven into the feature extraction block. Within, a number of parameterization algorithms extract feature in each frame. With each frame decomposed as a set of parameters, these frame sequences can be projected into a feature space. As a result, the frame sequences are replaced from feature vector sequences. Afterwards, the files of feature vectors sequences $V = \{V^r\}$ are driven into a feature ranking algorithm.

Each feature is ranked about its relevance to the discrimination, namely its discrimination ability. This process measures the degree of necessity of the feature, since in the upcoming step, a feature subset S_j of the N features with ranking score above a priori target level is computed. At the end of the training phase, the subsets along with the initial feature vector sequence create the training models M_j.

Before the incoming audio file Y enters the testing phase, information about the training phase fed the testing procedure. Apart from the fact that the pre-processing stage should be the same with the one of the training phase, the subsets selection about the features, and of course the corresponding models, should inform the corresponding testing steps. Afterwards the incoming audio recording is sequentially transformed into a frame sequence O^Y and into a feature vector sequence V_{C_J}. The classification results are produces when the feature vector sequence is driven into the classifier f with the corresponding training models.

Further fine tuning of this architecture and more specific during the feature extraction or the feature ranking/selection is the key element on the processes of restructuring the multidimensional feature space into a less dimensional component space. The selection of subsets is based on experimental conditions.

3   Experimental Setup

The experimental setup for the evaluation of the architecture described in Section 2 is presented in the current Section. The following subparagraphs referring to the collection of data, the description of the feature set and the evaluation and classification algorithms.

3.1   Audio Data Description

For the training and the evaluation of our architecture we relied on existing audio data collection, due to the lack of one database appropriate and widely accepted for experimenting on non linguistic recognition and discrimination. In particular, our data were collected from (i) the BBC broadcast news database [21], (ii) the BBC SFX Library [22], (iii) the Partners In Rhyme database [23] (iv) and the SoundBible database [24]. The events gathered from non broadcast sources have been convolved with silence intervals of broadcast transmissions. All audio data were stored in single-channel audio files with sampling frequency 8 kHz and resolution analysis 8 bits per sample. The audio dataset is manually annotated by an expert audio engineer. The selected audio data collection of audio recordings, total duration of approximately 354 seconds, consists of speech events and eleven different non linguistic vocalizations. The time distribution of each sound event appears in the following Table.

Table 1. Duration distrubution of sound events of interest

Sound Type	Duration (in seconds)
Breathing	31.01
Burp	22.30
Cough	26.35
Cry	9.82
Hiccup	1.06
Kiss	15.11
Laugh	71.71
Scream	42.41
Sneeze	2.63
Speech	103.28
Whistle	10.08
Yawning	17.85

3.2   Feature Extraction

Considering the type of our problem, a typical pre-processing algorithm based on short time analysis and frame blocking is quite appropriate. In our experiments we rely on dividing the audio strings into overlapping frames of constant length of 25msec with constant time shift of 10mesc. Additional pre-processing is based on applying a 1st order FIR pre-emphasis filter followed by a Hamming windowing.

In the literature there is a big amount of well known feature extraction algorithms that have commonly used in audio recognition problems in which events such us speech or music have a big share in the time distribution. Our experiments were carried out using the OpenSmile [25] framework. Our feature extraction processed was based on extracting an big amount of feature and potentially features that cover different categories of characteristics. The feature vector is initially constructed using the time domain feature of (i) zero crossing rate (ZCR). Thereafter we added the (ii) energy. From the domain of features that are extracted from filter banks, we use the standard algorithmic procedures to extract the (iii) Mel Spectrum, the (iv) MFCC [26] and the (v) CHROMA coefficients [27, 28]. With the usage of statistical function on the FFT Magnitude we compute the (vi) energy of bands, the (vii) roll off, the (viii) flux, the (ix) centroid, the (x) maximum position and the (xi) minimum position are computing. Additionally with the usage of a combine technique of autocorrelation/cepstrum/pitch we compute the (xii) pitch, the (xiii) pitch envelope and the (xiv) voicing probability. The feature vector was completed by adding the (xv) first and second derivatives (delta and double delta coefficients) of all the previously mentioned features.

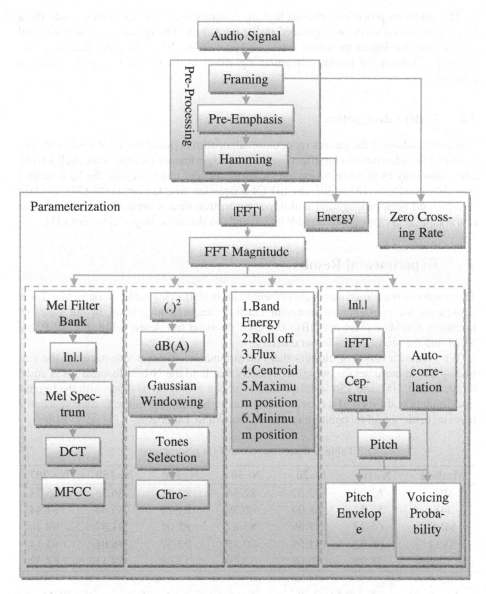

Fig. 2. The Pre-Processing and Parameterization Procedure

3.3   Feature Evaluation and Selection

After the extraction of the features, the evaluation ranks the significance of each feature, namely its discriminative ability in the specific audio dataset. The evaluation was carried out using the ReliefF algorithm [29]. This mathematical algorithm calculates the quality of each feature and with that it indicates the degree of importance.

The selection procedure ensures that the features with ranking scores inside the a priori determined levels will grouped inside the subset. The resulting subsets are used for the construction of the sound type classification models during the training phase as well as reform the feature extraction algorithm in the test phase, as described in Section 2.

3.4   Pattern Recognition

The construction of the pattern recognition algorithm is based on the WEKA software toolkit. The selection of classifiers used in our experiments include some well known and commonly used machine learning algorithms, and more specific the (i) k-nearest neighbor classifier (IBk) [30], the (ii) C4.5 decision tree learner (J48) [31], the (iii) two-layered back-propagation multilayer perceptron neural network (MLP) [32], the (iv) a support vector classifier (SMO) [33] and (v) the naïve Bayes classifier [34].

4   Experimental Results

The results of our experiments are presented in the following table. In particular Table 2 presents the appliance of powerful machine learning algorithm, in our case the k-nearest neighbor classifier (IBk) the C4.5 decision tree learner J48, the MLP, the SVM and the Naive Bayes in our database.

We created a series of clusters that corresponds to different subspaces of the feature space. In more details, we create clusters that hold the N-best features for N equal to 10, 20, 50, 100, and 150 features that have been evaluated as those with the biggest discrimination ability and we create a last cluster holding the entire feature space. the non-linguistic sound recognition results are shown in Table 2.

Table 2. Detection accuracy (in percentages)

Method	N=10	N=20	N=50	N=100	N=150	N= 207
IBk	62.22	72.02	82.56	83.12	86.35	85.73
J48	58.21	68.09	80.39	81.22	85.45	84.44
MLP	65.23	77.66	83.87	85.01	91.87	89.46
SVM	66.32	81.55	90.75	92.37	**96.01**	95.14
N. Bayes	48.98	50.08	52.76	53.08	59.11	57.32

As can be seen in Table 2, the two discriminative classifeirs, i.e. the SVM and MLP achieved the highest non-liguistic sound recognition scores. Specifically, the support vector machine method outperformed all other classification algorithms achieving performance equal to 96%, when using the N=150 best audio features. The second best perfoming classifier, i.e. the MLP neural network achieved significantly lower performance in all N-best cases. The superiority of the SVM algorithm is probably owed to the high dimensionality of the feature space, since SVMs do not suffer from teh curse of dimentionality phenomenon.

It is worth mentioning that for all evaluated classification methods the best performance was achieved for the N=150 best audio features, which indicated the importance of feature ranikng and selection of feature subspace. Moreover, the N=50 best fearures offer a good trade-off between computational demands and accuracy, since the non-linguistic sound recognition performance for the N=50 best audio features is comparable to the one achieved for the N=150 best features.

5   Conclusion

In this article we presented an architecture for non-linguistic sound recognition from audio signals. Specifically, we investigate the applicability of various subsets of audio features, which were formed on the basis of ranking the relevance and the individual quality of several audio features. Based on the ranking of the large set of audio descriptors, we performed selection of subsets and evaluated them on the non-linguistic sound recognition task. During the audio parameterization process, every input utterance is converted to a single feature vector, which consists of 207 parameters. Next, a subset of this feature vector is fed to a classification model, which aims at straight estimation of the unknown sound class. The experimental evaluation showed that the best performing algorithm was the support vector machines achieving recognition accuracy equal to 96.01% for the 150 best audio features. Finally, the feature vector composed of the 50-best ranked parameters was found to provide a good trade-off between computational demands and accuracy.

Acknowledgement. This paper was partially supported by the DRYMOS Project (2012-1-LEO05-10056), co-funded by the Leonardo Da Vinci Programme.

References

1. Cosker, D., Edge, J.: Laughing, Crying, Sneezing and Yawning: Automatic Voice Driven Animation of Non-Speech Articulation. In: Proceedings of Computer Animation and Social Agents, CASA 2009 (2009)
2. Sun, Z., Purohit, A., Yang, K., Pattan, N., Siewiorek, D., Smailagic, A., Lane, I., Zhang, P.: CoughLoc: Location-Aware Indoor Acoustic Sensing for Non-Intrusive Cough Detection. In: International Workshop on Emerging Mobile Sensing Technologies, Systems, and Applications (2011)
3. Matos, S., Birring, S.S., Pavord, I.D., Evans, D.H.: Detection of Cough Signals in Continuous Audio Recordings Using Hidden Markov Models. IEEE Transactions on Biomedical Engineering 53(6), 1078–1083 (2006)
4. Reyes-Galaviz, O.F., Reyes-Garcia, C.A.: A System for the Processing of Infant Cry to Recognize Pathologies in Recently Born Babies with Neural Networks. In: SPIIRAS, ISCA (eds.) The 9th International Conference "Speech and Computer" SPECOM 2004, St. Petersburg, Russia, pp. 552–557 (September 2004)
5. Abaza, A.A., Day, J.B., Reynolds, J.S., Mahmoud, A.M., Goldsmith, W.T., McKinney, W.G., Petsonk, E.L., Frazer, D.G.: Classification of voluntary cough sound and airflow patterns for detecting abnormal pulmonary function. Cough 2009 5(1):8 (November 20, 2009)

6. Drugman, T., Urbain, J., Bauwens, N.: Audio and Contact Microphones for Cough Detection. In: Interspeech 2012, Portland, Oregon (2012)
7. Truong, K.P., van Leeuwen, D.A.: Automatic discrimination between laughter and speech. Speech Communication 49(2), 144–158 (2007)
8. Chan, C.-F., Yu, E.W.M.: An Abnormal Sound Detection and Classification System for Surveillance Applications. In: 18th European Signal Processing Conference EUSIPCO 2010, August 23-27 (2010)
9. Dat Tran, H., Li, H.: Sound Event Recognition with Probabilistic Distance SVMs. IEEE Transactions on Audio, Speech, and Language Processing 19(6), 1556–1568 (2011)
10. Weninger, F., Schuller, B., Wollmer, M., Rigoll, G.: Localization of Non-Linguistic Events in Spontaneous Speech by Non-Negative Matrix Factorization and Long Short-Term Memory. In: 2011 IEEE International Conference on Acoustics, Speech and Signal Processing (ICASSP 2011), May 22-27, pp. 5840–5843 (2011)
11. Wöllmer, M., Marchi, E., Squartini, S., Schuller, B.: Robust Multi-stream Keyword and Non-linguistic Vocalization Detection for Computationally Intelligent Virtual Agents. In: Liu, D., Zhang, H., Polycarpou, M., Alippi, C., He, H. (eds.) ISNN 2011, Part II. LNCS, vol. 6676, pp. 496–505. Springer, Heidelberg (2011); Special Session "Computational Intelligence Algorithms for Advanced Human-Machine Interaction". IEEE Computational Intelligence Society
12. Petridis, S., Pantic, M.: Audiovisual Discrimination Between Speech and Laughter: Why and When Visual Information Might Help. IEEE Transactions on Multimedia 13(2), 216–234 (2011)
13. Escalera, S., Puertas, E., Radeva, P., Pujol, O.: Multi-modal Laughter Recognition in Video Conversations. In: IEEE Computer Society Conference on Computer Vision and Pattern Recognition Workshops, June 20-25, pp. 110–115. CVPR Workshops (2009)
14. Petridis, S., Pantic, M.: Fusion of Audio and Visual Cues for Laughter Detection. In: Proceedings of the 2008 International Conference on Content-Based Image and Video Retrieval, CIVR 2008, pp. 329–338 (July 2008)
15. Petridis, S., Pantic, M.: Audiovisual Laughter Detection Based on Temporal Features. In: 2008 International Conference on Multimodal Interfaces ICMI 2008, Chania, Crete, Greece, October 20-22 (2008)
16. Drugman, T., Urbain, J., Dutoit, T.: Assessment of Audio Features for Automatic Cough Detection. In: 19th European Signal Processing Conference (Eusipco 2011), Barcelona, Spain (2011)
17. Mikami, T., Kojima, Y., Yamamoto, M., Furukawa, M.: Automatic Classification of Oral/Nasal Snoring Sounds based on the Acoustic Properties. In: 2012 IEEE International Conference on Acoustics, Speech and Signal Processing, ICASSP 2012, March 25-30, pp. 609–612 (2012)
18. Duckitt, W.D., Tuomi, S.K., Niesler, T.R.: Automatic Detection, Segmentation and Assessment of Snoring from Ambient Acoustic Data. Physiological Measurement 27(10), 1047–1056 (2006)
19. Lopatka, K., Czyzewski, A.: Automatic regular voice, raised voice and scream recognition employing fuzzy logic. AES 132nd Convention, Budapest, Hungary, April 26-29 (2012)
20. Gerosa, L., Valenzise, G., Tagliasacchi, M., Antonacci, F., Sarti, A.: Scream and Gunshot Detection in Noisy Environments. In: Proceedings of the 2007 IEEE Conference on Advanced Video and Signal Based Surveillance AVSS 2007, pp. 21–26 (2007)
21. BBC Postcasts & Downloads, online data collections,
   http://www.bbc.co.uk/podcasts/series/globalnews

22. The BBC Sound Effects Library Original Series (May 2006),
    http://www.sound-ideas.com
23. http://www.partnersinrhyme.com/soundfx/human.shtml
24. http://soundbible.com/tags-laugh.html
25. Eyben, F., Wöllmer, M., Schuller, B.: openSMILE - The Munich Versatile and Fast Open-Source Audio Feature Extractor. In: Proc. ACM Multimedia (MM), pp. 1459–1462. ACM, Florence, Italy, October 25-29, 2010 (2009) ISBN 978-1-60558-933-6
26. Slaney, M.: Auditory Toolbox. Version 2. Technical Report #1998-010. Interval Research Corporation (1998)
27. Lee, K., Slaney, M.: Automatic Chord Recognition from Audio Using an HMM with Supervised Learning. In: Proceedings of the 1st ACM Workshop on Audio and Music Computing Multimedia, AMCMM 2006, pp. 11–20 (2006)
28. Bartsch, M.A., Wakefield, G.H.: Audio Thumbnailing of Popular Music Using Chroma-Based Representations. IEEE Transactions on Multimedia 7(1), 96–104 (2005)
29. Robnik-Sikonja, M., Kononenko, I.: An adaptation of Relief for attribute estimation in regression. In: 4th International Conference on Machine Learning, pp. 296–304 (1997)
30. Aha, D., Kibler, D.: Instance-based learning algorithms. Machine Learning 6, 37–66 (1991)
31. Quinlan, R.: C4.5: Programs for Machine Learning. Morgan Kaufmann Publishers, San Mateo (1993)
32. Mitchell, T.M.: Machine Learning. McGraw-Hill International Editions (1997)
33. Keerthi, S.S., Shevade, S.K., Bhattacharyya, C., Murthy, K.R.K.: Improvements to Platt's SMO Algorithm for SVM Classifier Design. Neural Computation 13(3), 637–649 (2001)
34. Bishop, C.M.: Pattern Recognition and Machine Learning. Springer (2006)

Plant Leaf Recognition Using Zernike Moments and Histogram of Oriented Gradients

Dimitris G. Tsolakidis, Dimitrios I. Kosmopoulos, and George Papadourakis

Department of Informatics Engineering,
Technological Educational Institute of Crete,
GR-71004, Heraklion, Greece
dimitri_ts0@hotmail.com,
dkosmo@ie.teicrete.gr, papadour@cs.teicrete.gr

Abstract. A method using Zernike Moments and Histogram of Oriented Gradients for classification of plant leaf images is proposed in this paper. After preprocessing, we compute the shape features of a leaf using Zernike Moments and texture features using Histogram of Oriented Gradients and then the Support Vector Machine classifier is used for plant leaf image classification and recognition. Experimental results show that using both Zernike Moments and Histogram of Oriented Gradients to classify and recognize plant leaf image yields accuracy that is comparable or better than the state of the art. The method has been validated on the *Flavia* and the *Swedish Leaves* datasets as well as on a combined dataset.

Keywords: Leaf recognition, Zernike moments, Histogram of oriented gradients, support vector machine.

1 Introduction

Plants play a vital role in the environment. There is huge volume of plant species worldwide and their classification has become an active area of research [1]. A plant database is of obvious importance for archiving, protection and education purposes. Moreover, recognition of plants has also become essential for exploiting their medicinal properties and for using them as sources of alternative energy sources like bio-fuel. The classification of plant leaves is a useful mechanism in botany and agriculture [3]. Additionally, the morphological features of leaves can be employed in the early diagnosis of certain plant diseases [5].

Plant recognition is a challenging task due to the huge variety of plants and due to the many different features that need to be considered. There are various ways to recognize a plant, like flower, root, leaf, fruit etc. Recently, computer vision and pattern recognition techniques have been applied towards automated process of plant recognition [2]. Leaf recognition plays an important role in plant classification and its key issue lies in whether the chosen features have good capability to discriminate various kinds of leaves. Computer aided plant recognition is still challenging due to improper models and inefficient representation approaches.

A. Likas, K. Blekas, and D. Kalles (Eds.): SETN 2014, LNAI 8445, pp. 406–417, 2014.
© Springer International Publishing Switzerland 2014

A lot of work has been focused on the shape description of the leaves. In the past decade, research on contour-based shape recognition [18-19] was more active than that on region-based [17]. In [15] they introduced a multiscale shape-based approach for leaf image retrieval. The leaf represented by local descriptors associated with margin sample points. Within this local description, they studied four multiscale triangle representations: the well-known triangle area representation (TAR), the triangle side lengths representation (TSL) and two other representations, triangle oriented angles (TOA) and triangle side lengths and angle representation (TSLA). In this research they used 1-NN as classifier. In [16] they proposed a contour-based shape descriptor, named Multiscale Distance Matrix (MDM), to capture shape geometry while being invariant to translation, rotation, scaling, and bilateral symmetry and to classify the plants they used 1-NN as classifier. The color information was incorporated in the plant identification in [11] and [12] and RBPNN was used as classifier. However most researchers avoid using color, mainly due to its dependency on the illumination.

Some other researchers focused on green leaves and ignored color information on the leaf. In [10] they used PNN to classify 32 species of plants. All the plants they used in their research had green leaves. Also in [24] Zulkifli used General Regression Neural Networks (GRNN) and invariant moment to classify 10 kinds of plants. They did not include color features to the classifier. Furthermore, in [14] they used K-SVM to classify 32 species of plants and they also did not use any color features.

This paper differs from the previous approaches due to the fact that we propose a method for recognizing leafs using as shape descriptor the Zernike Moments (ZM) and as a descriptor for the interior of the leaf the Histogram of Oriented Gradients (HOG). Support Vector Machine (SVM) has been used as a classifier, which is among the best methods for discriminative models.

Experimental results on *Flavia* dataset [21] indicates that the proposed method yields an accuracy rate of 97.18%, on *Swedish Leaves* dataset [22] 98.13%. When we combine both *Flavia* and *Swedish Leaves* the obtained accuracy is 97.65%. To our knowledge these results are similar or better than the state of the art, and it is the first time someone combines these two popular databases.

An overview of the method is given in Fig. 1. More specifically we perform a preprocessing step, then we extract a feature vector per image and finally we do the classification of the image.

The rest of the paper is organized as follows. In the next section we describe the preprocessing steps. In section 3 we outline the feature extraction method and in section 4 we outline the classification method. In section 5 we give the experimental results of our method and section 6 concludes this paper.

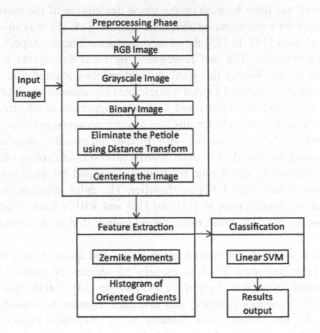

Fig. 1. Proposed method for leaf classification

2   Image Pre-processing

2.1   Convert RGB Image to Binary Image

Each RGB image is firstly converted into grayscale. We do not employ color due to its dependency on the illumination, so after that we calculate a threshold using Otsu's method and using this threshold level we convert the grayscale image to binary, so that we can have the leaf image in white and background in black. All images are scaled in 512x512 resolution.

2.2   Eliminating the Petiole

Some leaves have petioles so we have to eliminate them, because they can distort the overall shape. For that we use the Distance Transform operator which applies only to binary images. It computes the Euclidean distance transform of the binary image. For each pixel in binary image, the distance transform assigns a number that is the distance between that pixel and the nearest nonzero pixel of binary image.

2.3   Center the Image

After converting the image to binary we find the connected components of image and use the centroid property to find the center of mass of the region, so we can move the image to the center. This is necessary for the Zernike Moments calculation.

Fig. 2. a) RGB image, b) Grayscale image, c) Binary image and petiole elimination, d) Centered binary image, e) Cropped Grayscale image

3   Feature Extraction

In this paper we use Zernike Moments (ZM) on centered binary images and Histogram of Oriented Gradients (HOG) on cropped grayscale images to extract and calculate features of leaf image.

3.1   Zernike Moments (ZM)

We use Zernike Moments (ZM) to extract features using the shape of leaf. The computation of Zernike moments from an input image consists of three steps: computation of radial polynomials, computation of Zernike basis functions, and computation of Zernike moments by projecting the image on to the basis functions.

The procedure for obtaining Zernike moments from an input image begins with the computation of Zernike radial polynomials. The real-valued 1-D radial polynomial R_{nm} is defined as

$$R_{nm} = \sum_{s=0}^{(n-|m|)/2} c(n,m,s)\, \rho^{n-2s}, \tag{1}$$

where,

$$c(n,m,s) = (-1)^s \frac{(n-s)!}{s! \left(\dfrac{n+|m|}{2} - s \right)! \left(\dfrac{n-|m|}{2} - s \right)!} \tag{2}$$

In (1), n and m are generally called order and repetition, respectively. The order n is a non-negative integer, and the repetition m is an integer satisfying n $/m/ =$ (even) and $/m/\leq n$.

The radial polynomials satisfy the orthogonal properties for the same repetition,

$$\int_0^{2\pi} \int_0^1 R_{nm}(\rho,\theta)R_{n'm}(\rho,\theta)\rho\, d\rho\, d\theta$$

$$= \left\{ \begin{array}{l} \frac{1}{2(n+1)}, \ n = n' \\ 0, \text{otherwise} \end{array} \right.$$

Zernike polynomials $V(\rho,\theta)$ in polar coordinates are formed by

$$V_{nm} = R_{nm}(\rho)e^{jm\theta}, |\rho| \leq 1 \tag{3}$$

where (ρ,θ) are defined over the unit disk, $j = \sqrt{-1}$ and R_{nm} is the orthogonal radial polynomial defined in equation (1).

Finally, the two dimensional Complex Zernike Moments for a NxN image are defined as,

$$Z_{nm} = \frac{n+1}{\pi} \int_0^{2\pi} \int_0^1 f(\rho,\theta)V_{nm}^*(\rho,\theta)\rho\, d\rho\, d\theta \tag{4}$$

where $f(x,y)$ is the image function being described and * denotes the complex conjugate [6].

3.2   Image Reconstruction Using Zernike Moments (ZM)

Let $f(x,y)$ be an image function with dimension NxN, their moments of order n with repetition m are given by,

$$\hat{f}(\rho,\theta) = \sum_{n=0}^{N_{max}} \sum_{m=0}^{N_{max}} Z_{nm} V_{nm}(\rho,\theta) \tag{5}$$

Expanding this using real-values functions, produces:

$$\hat{f}(\rho,\theta) = \sum_{n=0}^{N_{max}} \sum_{m>0} C_{nm} \cos(n\theta) + S_{nm} \sin(n\theta)R_{nm}(\rho) + \frac{C_{n0}}{2} R_{n0}(\rho) \tag{6}$$

composed of their real (Re) and imaginary (Im) parts:

$$C_{nm} = 2\text{Re}[\mathbf{Z}_{nm}] = \frac{2n+2}{\pi} = \sum_x \sum_y f(\rho,\theta)R_{nm}(\rho)\cos(m\theta) \qquad (7)$$

$$S_{nm} = -2\text{Im}[\mathbf{Z}_{nm}] = \frac{-2n-2}{\pi} = \sum_x \sum_y f(\rho,\theta)R_{nm}(\rho)\sin(m\theta) \qquad (8)$$

bounded by $x^2 + y^2 \leq 1$.

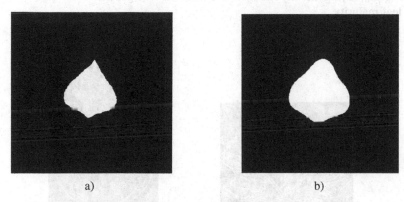

a)   b)

Fig. 3. a) Original image, b) Reconstructed image from Zernike Moments

Based on [23] the Zernike Moments have the following advantages:

- Rotation Invariance: The magnitudes of Zernike Moments are invariant to rotation.
- Robustness: They are robust to noise and minor variations in shape.
- Expressiveness: Since the basis is orthogonal, they have minimum information redundancy.

3.3   Histogram of Oriented Gradients (HOG)

The Histograms of Oriented Gradients (HOGs) are feature descriptors used in computer vision and image processing for the purpose of object detection (e.g., [20]). The technique counts occurrences of gradient orientation in localized portions of an image. This method is similar to that of edge orientation histograms, scale-invariant feature transform descriptors, and shape contexts, but differs in that it is computed on a dense grid of uniformly spaced cells and uses overlapping local contrast normalization for improved accuracy.

The essential concept behind the Histogram of Oriented Gradient descriptors is that local object appearance and shape within an image can be described by the distribution of intensity gradients or edge directions. The implementation of these descriptors can be achieved by dividing the image into small connected regions, called cells, and for each cell compiling a histogram of gradient directions or edge orientations for the pixels within the cell. The combination of these histograms then represents the descriptor. For improved accuracy, the local histograms can be contrast-normalized by calculating a measure of the intensity across a larger region of the image, called a block, and then using this value to normalize all cells within the block. This normalization results in better invariance to illumination changes or shadowing [8]. Since the HOG descriptor operates on localized cells, the method upholds invariance to geometric and photometric transformations, except for object orientation.

The concept of HOG is particularly appealing for the classification of leaves due to the nature of their region, which contains many visible veins (see Fig. 4). Those veins are very informative about the specific class the leaf belongs to. Furthermore, the gradients that HOG capitalizes upon, are unlike the color features that some researchers use (e.g., [12]), generally robust to illumination changes and color differences due to the leaf maturity.

Fig. 4. Veins of leaf

4   Classification

For the classification we have employed the Support Vector Machine (SVM), which is appropriate for the task of discriminative classification between different classes [9]. SVM can simultaneously minimize the empirical classification error and maximize the geometric margin. SVM can map the input vectors to a higher dimensional space where a maximal separating hyperplane is constructed. Two parallel hyperplanes are constructed on each side of the hyperplane that separate the data. An assumption is made that the larger the margin or distance between these parallel hyperplanes the better the generalization of the classifier will be. We consider a set of n data points of the form $\{(\mathbf{x}_1, y_1), (\mathbf{x}_2, y_2), (\mathbf{x}_3, y_3), \ldots\ldots\ldots (\mathbf{x}_n, y_n)\}$, where y_n is either 1 or -1 indicating the class to which $\mathbf{x}_n$ the point belongs. Each $\mathbf{x}_n$ is a p-dimensional real vector. We want to find the maximum-margin hyperplane that divides the points having $y_n = 1$ from those having $y_n = -1$. Any hyperplane can be written as the set of points x satisfying

$$\mathbf{w}.\mathbf{x} - b = 0, \tag{9}$$

where "." denotes the inner product and $\mathbf{w}$ the normal vector to the hyperplane. The parameter $\frac{b}{\|\mathbf{w}\|}$ determines the offset of the hyperplane from the origin along the normal vector $\mathbf{w}$. If the training data are linearly separable, we can select two hyperplanes in a way that they separate the data and there are no points between them, and then try to maximize their distance. The region bounded by them is called "the margin". Slack variables allow a tradeoff between misclassification of samples and overall performance. More details can be found in [9].

5   Experimental Results

To test the proposed method we first used *Flavia* dataset, then we used the *Swedish Leaves* dataset and at last we combined both the *Flavia* and *Swedish Leaves* dataset. We have 47 species from both datasets, 32 species from *Flavia* dataset and 15 species from *Swedish Leaves* dataset.

In *Flavia* dataset we used 50 samples per species. For each species we used 40 samples for training and 10 for testing.

In *Swedish Leaves* dataset first we used 50 samples per species for training and 25 samples for testing and second we used 25 samples for training and 50 for testing to compare results with other methods.

After the calculation of Zernike Moments and Histogram of Oriented Gradients on both datasets, we concatenated the features from both datasets, but this time we used 50 samples per species from Swedish dataset. After that, we used 40 samples per species for training and 10 samples for testing. The feature extraction from both datasets is the same.

To compare and see if the difference lies in features or in classifier, we also computed chebyshev moments and concatenated with Histogram of Oriented Gradients features. After the training and testing results, we saw that the accuracy was lower than the other method.

Firstly, the gradient was simply obtained by filtering it with two one-dimensional filters: horizontal: (-1 0 1) and vertical: $(-1\ 0\ 1)^T$. The second step was to split the image into 4x4 cells and for each cell one histogram is computed according to the number of bins orientation binning. The numbers of bins we used is 9. The result of the feature vector of HOG is a 144 dimensional vector for every image leaf. This vector is a computation of 4x4x9 and that's how we got the 144 dimensional vector. Different normalization schemes are possible for a vector **V**, containing all histograms of a given block. The normalization factor N_f that we used is:

$$\text{L2-norm: } N_f = \mathbf{V}/\sqrt{||\mathbf{V}||_2^2 + e^2} \tag{10}$$

All images were normalized with respect to orientation, so that the major axis appeared vertically. This establishes a common reference for the HOG descriptors.

We computed Zernike Moments up to order $n=20$ and the result was a 121 dimensional vector for every image leaf, which was normalized by computing the complex modulus.

In this paper we used linear SVM as classifier. Before we started the classification we concatenated Zernike Moments (ZM) and Histogram of Oriented Gradients (HOG) arrays and then we normalized our data into range [0, 1]. After obtaining the best *C* parameter for our training model we calculated the overall accuracy of our system.

Using Zernike Moments (ZM) up to order 20 and Histogram of Oriented Gradients (HOG) as features, resulted in a highest accuracy of 97.18% for using only *Flavia* dataset, 98.13% for using only *Swedish Leaves* dataset and 97.65% for using both datasets, which are listed in Table 1. The test and training samples were randomly selected as indicated in Tables 2, 3.

Fig. 5. Overview of the Swedish Leaf Dataset

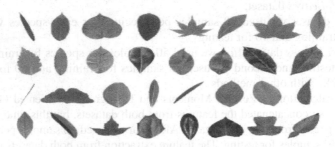

Fig. 6. Overview of the Flavia Leaf Dataset

Table 1.

Dataset	Features	Classifier	Best Accuracy
Flavia	ZM + HOG	Linear SVM	97.18%
Flavia + Swedish Leaves	ZM + HOG	Linear SVM	97.65%
Swedish Leaves	ZM + HOG	Linear SVM	98.13%

Table 2. Comparison based on the Swedish Leaves database

Method	Features	Classifier	Training Data	Testing Data	Best Accuracy
[16]	MDM-CD-C	1-NN	25 samples	50 samples	91.07%
[16]	MDM-CD-A	1-NN	25 samples	50 samples	91.33%
[16]	MDM-CD-M	1-NN	25 samples	50 samples	91.20%
[16]	MDM-RA	1-NN	25 samples	50 samples	91.60%
[15]	TSLA	1-NN	25 samples	50 samples	96.53%
[15]	TSL	1-NN	25 samples	50 samples	95.73%
[15]	SPTC + DP	1-NN	25 samples	50 samples	95.33%
[15]	TAR	1-NN	25 samples	50 samples	90.40%
Our	ZM + HOG	SVM	25 samples	50 samples	95.86%
Our	ZM + HOG	SVM	50 samples	25 samples	98.13%

Table 3. Comparison based on the Flavia database

Method	Features	Classifier	Training Data	Testing Data	Best Accuracy
[11]	Shape Features Vein Features Color Features Texture Features Pseudo-Zernike Moments	RBPNN	40 samples	10 samples	95.12%
[12]	Shape Features Vein Features Color Features Texture Features Zernike Moments	RBPNN	40 samples	10 samples	93.82%
[10]	Geometrical Features Morphological Features	PNN	40 samples	10 samples	90.30%
[14]	Geometrical Features Morphological Features	K-SVM	40 samples	10 samples	96.20%
[14]	Geometrical Features Morphological Features	SVM	40 samples	10 samples	94.50%
Our	ZM + HOG	SVM	40 samples	10 samples	97.18%

Our method seems to outperform other methods on the *Flavia* dataset, which is currently the most popular benchmark and is very close to the best reported in the *Swedish Leaves*. That could be attributed to the fact that we use some of the best descriptors for the shape (contour) and for the internal structure of the leaf (veins). These are actually the essential visual properties that need to be captured. It is expected that the better the state of the art in this representation becomes, the higher the recognition accuracy will be.

6   Conclusion

A new approach of plant classification based on leaves recognition is proposed in this paper. The approach consisted of three phases namely the preprocessing phase, feature extraction phase and the classification phase. We could classify plants via the leaf images loaded from digital cameras or scanners.

Zernike Moments (ZM) and Histogram of Oriented Gradient have been used for feature extraction and Linear SVM has been adopted for classification. Compared to other methods, this approach is of comparable or better accuracy on the *Flavia* and the *Swedish Leaves* databases. To our knowledge it is also the first time that these two databases are combined.

References

1. Chaki, J., Parekh, R.: Plant Leaf Recognition using Shape based Features and Neural Network classifiers. International Journal of Advanced Computer Science and Applications (IJACSA) 2(10) (2011)
2. Pan, J., He, Y.: Recognition of plants by leaves digital image and neural network. In: International Conference on Computer Science and Software Engineering, vol. 4, pp. 906–910 (2008)
3. Cotton Incorporated USA. The classification of Cotton (2005), http://www.cottoninc.com/ClassificationofCotton
4. Singh, K., Gupta, I., Gupta, S.: SVM-BDT PNN and Fourier Moment Technique for Classification of Leaf Shape. International Journal of Signal Processing, Image Processing and Pattern Recognition 3(4), 67–78 (2010)
5. Kumar, N., Pandey, S., Bhattacharya, A., Ahuja, P.S.: Do leaf surface characteristics affect agro bacterium infection in tea. J. Biosci. 29(3), 309–317 (2004)
6. Suard, F., Rakotommamonjy, A., Bensrhair, A., Broggi, A.: Pedestrian Detection using Infrared images and Histograms of Oriented Gradients. In: Intelligent Vehicles Symposium 2006, Tokyo, Japan, June 13-15 (2006)
7. Cristianini, N., Shawe-Taylor, J.: An Introduction to Support Vector Machines. Cambridge University Press (2000)
8. Wu, G., Bao, F.S., Xu, E.Y., Wang, Y.-X., Chang, Y.-F.: A Leaf Recognition Algorithm for Plant Classification Using Probabilistic Neural Network. In: IEEE 7th International Symposium on Signal Processing and Information Technology (2007)
9. Kulkarni, A.H., Rai, H.M., Jahagirdar, K.A., Kadkol, R.J.: A Leaf Recognition System for Classifying Plants Using RBPNN and pseudo Zernike Moments. International Journal of Latest Trends in Engineering and Technology 2, 1–11 (2013)
10. Kulkarni, A.H., Rai, H.M., Jahagirdar, K.A., Upparamani, P.S.: A Leaf Recognition Technique for Plant Classification Using RBPNN and Zernike Moments. International Journal of Advanced Research in Computer and Communication Engineering 2(1), 1–5 (2013)
11. Du, J.-X., Wang, X.-F., Zhang, G.-J.: Leaf shape based plant species recognition. Applied Mathematics and Computation 185(2), 883–893 (2007)
12. Arunpriya, C., Selvadoss Thanamani, A.: An Efficient Leaf Recognition Algorithm for Plant Classification using Kernelized Support Vector Machine. International Journal of Computer Science and Management Research 2(2) (February 2013) ISSN 2278-733X
13. Mouine, S., Yahiaoui, I., Verroust-Blondet, A.: A Shape-based Approach for Leaf Classification using Multiscale Triangular Representation, Thesis. Le Chesnay, France CReSTIC Université de Reims, FRANCE (2013)
14. Hu, R.-X., Jia, W., Ling, H., Huang, D.: Multiscale Distance Matrix for Fast Plant Leaf Recognition. IEEE Transactions on Image Processing 21(11), 4667–4672 (2012)
15. Zhang, D., Lu, G.: Review of shape representation and description techniques. Pattern Recognition 37(1), 1–19 (2004)

16. Belongie, S., Malik, J., Puzicha, J.: Shape Matching and Object Recognition Using Shape Context. IEEE Trans. Pattern Analysis and Machine Intelligence 24(4), 509–522 (2002)
17. Backes, A.R., Bruno, O.M.: Shape classification using complex network and Multi-scale Fractal Dimension. Pattern Recognition Letters 31(1), 44–51 (2010)
18. Dalal, N., Triggs, B.: Histograms of Oriented Gradients for Human Detection. In: CVPR, pp. 886–893 (2005)
19. Mingqiang, Y., Kidiyo, K., Joseph, R.: A Survey of Shape Feature Extraction Techniques. In: Yin, P.-Y. (ed.) Pattern Recognition, p. 25 (2008)
20. Zulkifli, Z.: Plant Leaf Identification Using Moment Invariants & General Regression Neural Network., Master Thesis, University Technology Malaysia (2009)
21. Mukundan, A.: A Comparative Analysis of Radial-Tchebichef Moments and Zernike Moments. In: BMVC 2009, pp. 1–7 (2009)
22. Söderkvist, O.J.O.: "Computer Vision Classification of Leaves from Swedish Trees", Master Thesis, Computer Vision Laboratory Linköping University (2001)

Ground Resistance Estimation Using Feed-Forward Neural Networks, Linear Regression and Feature Selection Models

Theopi Eleftheriadou[1], Nikos Ampazis[1], Vasilios P. Androvitsaneas[2],
Ioannis F. Gonos[2], Georgios Dounias[1], and Ioannis A. Stathopulos[2]

[1] Department of Financial and Management Engineering,
University of the Aegean 41 Kountouriotou Street, 82100 Chios, Greece
g.dounias@aegean.gr, n.ampazis@fme.aegean.gr
[2] High Voltage Laboratory, School of Electrical and Computer Engineering,
National Technical University of Athens, 9 Iroon Polytechniou Street, GR-15780,
Zografou Campus, Athens, Greece
v.andro@mail.ntua.gr, igonos@cs.ntua.gr

Abstract. This paper proposes ways for estimating the ground resistance of several grounding systems, embedded in various ground enhancing compounds. Grounding systems are used to divert high fault currents to the earth. The proper estimation of the ground resistance is useful from a technical and also economic viewpoint, for the proper electrical installation of constructions. The work utilizes both, conventional and intelligent data analysis techniques, for ground resistance modelling from field measurements. In order to estimate ground resistance from weather and ground data such as soil resistivity, rainfall measurements, etc., three linear regression models have been applied to a properly selected dataset, as well as an intelligent approach based in feed-forward neural networks,. A feature selection process has also been successfully applied, showing that features selected for estimation agree with experts' opinion on the importance of the variables considered. Experimental data consist of field measurements that have been performed in Greece during the last three years. The input variables used for analysis are related to soil resistivity within various depths and rainfall height during some periods of time, like last week and last month. Experiments produce high quality results, as correlation exceeds 99% for specific experimental settings of all approaches tested.

Keywords: Ground Resistance, Soil Resistivity, Feed-forward Neural Networks, Linear Regression, Feature Selection.

1   Introduction and Literature Review

Grounding plays an important role in transmission and distribution network for the safe operation of any electrical installation. It is an essential part of the protection system of electrical installations and power systems against lightning and fault currents. Grounding systems are used to divert high fault currents to the earth. Thus, a properly designed grounding system capable of dissipating large currents safely to

A. Likas, K. Blekas, and D. Kalles (Eds.): SETN 2014, LNAI 8445, pp. 418–429, 2014.

earth is required, regardless of the fault type. A grounding system in order to be effective, must have a ground resistance that has to be maintained in low levels during the whole year [1-2]. It is well known that most of the rise of potential of a grounding rod is determined by the soil resistivity surrounding the grounding rod and the magnitude of the applied current. As a result, it is desirable to obtain the lowest feasible ground resistance value, in order to provide the lowest impede path for fault currents to be dispersed into the earth, in the shortest time possible.

However, most of the cases of electrical installations are characterized either by lack of space for the installation of the grounding systems, or the huge cost which often maybe prohibitive for the construction. In the last decades several techniques have developed for reducing the ground resistance value and maintaining it in low levels, with the use of ground enhancing compounds being predominant among them. Research works have been carried out on natural and chemical compounds all over the world.

The objective of this paper is to utilize conventional and intelligent data analysis methodologies in order to estimate ground resistance. Specifically, three linear regression models have been used, as well as an intelligent approach based in feed-forward neural networks, for estimating ground resistance from weather and ground data such as soil resistivity, rainfall measurements, etc., succeeding to achieve high correlation results. A feature selection process has also been tested with success in the grounding estimation problem, showing that features selected for estimation agree with experts' opinion on the importance of the variables considered.

So far, researchers as Salam et al. [3] have successfully used ANNs to model and predict the relationship between the ground resistance and the length of the buried electrode in soil. Amaral et al. [4] attempted to correlate soil resistivity, injection current frequency and peak current with ground resistance value, while Gouda et al. [5] developed an ANN for grounding system designing, consisted of vertical rods. More recent researches [6-7] focused on modeling the correlation among ground resistance, soil resistivity and soil humidity using ANNs and testing several training algorithms on them. This effort has been based on previous ANN architectures, developed in [8-9].

The rest of the paper is organized as follows:

In Section the field measurements of soil resistivity and ground resistance are described. Section 3 refers to the experimental results from the application of linear regression, feed-forward neural networks and feature selection techniques on the data gathered. Finally, Section 4 refers to conclusions and future work.

2   Field Measurements of Soil Resistivity and Ground Resistance

The data needed for the neural network training have been obtained by field measurements performed in the context of an experiment, which is still carried out till nowadays, for the evaluation of ground enhancing compounds performance inside the National Technical University of Athens Campus, Hellas [10], under the supervision and technical support of High Voltage Laboratory, School of Electrical and Computer Engineering. During the experimental procedure, six grounding rods have been tested, five of them embedded in various ground enhancing compounds (e.g. G2 in conductive concrete, G3 in bentonite, etc.) and one of them in natural soil as a reference electrode (G1). All the measurements have been performed according to [2], since February 2011 till now. Soil resistivity was measured by using the 4-point method (Wenner method), at different distances (α) of 2m, 4m, 8m, 12m and 16m as shown in Fig. 1. Four electrodes 0.5m in length are driven in line, at equal distances a each other and in a depth b. A test current (It) is injected at the two terminal electrodes and the voltage (Ut) between the two middle electrodes is measured. The ratio Ut/It results the apparent resistance R (in Ω). Consequently, the apparent soil resistivity ρ is given by the following formula [2]:

$$\rho = \frac{4\pi a R}{1 + \dfrac{2a}{\sqrt{(a^2 + 4b^2)}} - \dfrac{2a}{\sqrt{(4a^2 + 4b^2)}}} = \frac{4\pi a R}{n} \tag{1}$$

where variable n depends on the ratio value b/a and fluctuates between the values of 1 and 2. In the particular case of this experimental array where $b<<a$, the (1) is simplified to:

$$\rho = 2\pi a R \tag{2}$$

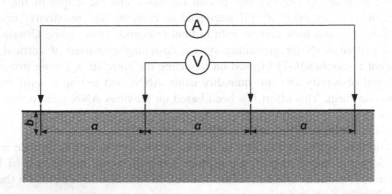

Fig. 1. Wenner method for measurement of apparent resistivity

The 3-pole method, also known as the fall of potential method was used to accurately measure the ground resistance of each main rod, using two probes driven into the soil at the distances of 20m and 40m from main rod, respectively [10] as shown in Figure 2.

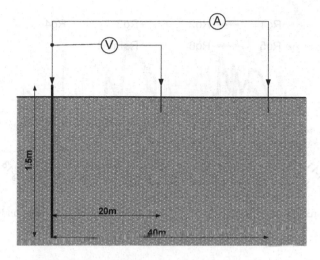

Fig. 2. The fall of potential method for the measurement of ground resistance

The rainfall height data were provided by the Hydrological Observatory of Athens, operated by the National Technical University of Athens. Due to the fact that soil humidity measurements require special and expensive sensors and equipment, rainfall height on the experimental field is used for a collateral estimation of soil humidity. The measurements have been repeated at regular time intervals. The variation of soil resistivity and ground resistance of enhancing compounds, based on experimental results, is presented in Figs. 3 and 4 respectively, so that the reader would be able to have a clear picture of the progress of the phenomenon by the ongoing experiment.

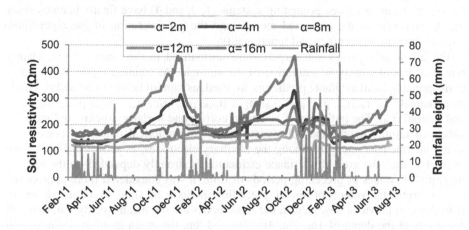

Fig. 3. Soil resistivity versus time and rainfall at various depths

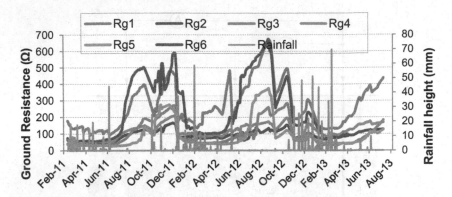

Fig. 4. Ground resistance of natural soil (R_{g1}) and ground enhancing compounds versus time and rainfall

3   Methodologies and Experimental Results

Linear Regression [11], Feed-forward Neural Networks [12] and Feature Selection Techniques [13] were used for modelling the ground resistance estimation from available data measurements. Specifically, in our experiments we initially trained three different linear regression models, and a number of feed-forward neural network configurations (with a different selection on the number hidden nodes) for predicting the three variables of interest (Rg1, Rg2, and Rg4), i.e. the ground resistance value of the grounding systems 1, 2 and 4, under test. The natural and chemical properties of the ground enhancing compounds 3, 5 and 6 did not allow the yield of accurate results with satisfactory convergence, as these materials have been gradually absorbed by the surrounding soil, presenting a remarkable decrease in their performance. Therefore, the results from only three grounding systems (1, 2, and 4) have finally been used for the development of the presented models and the generalization of the algorithms, with no discount in accuracy and functionality.

For all models, inputs and targets were normalized in the range [0 +1], mainly however, in order to avoid saturation of the sigmoid. As training inputs the features corresponding to all available predictors we used, as rainfall height r and soil resistivity ρ, namely r_d, r_w, r_m, $ρ_{2d}$, $ρ_{4d}$, $ρ_{8d}$, $ρ_{12d}$, $ρ_{16d}$, $ρ_{2w}$, $ρ_{4w}$, $ρ_{8w}$, $ρ_{12w}$, $ρ_{16w}$, $ρ_{2m}$, $ρ_{4m}$, and rainfall (r_{ed}). The indicators d, w and m correspond to daily, weekly and monthly values of rainfall height and soil resistivity, while numerical indicators correspond to the intermediate intervals among the auxiliary electrodes, as shown in Fig. 1. Due to the fact that, the ground resistance estimation is strongly depended on the relative magnitudes' values of preceding periods of time, it was considered more appropriate for experimental values of broad preceding periods of time to be used, rather than those of previous day. Hence, the input nodes are the mean weekly value of soil resistivity at the depth of 1m, 2m, 4m, 6m and 8m, the mean monthly value of soil resistivity at depths of 1m and 2m, the total rainfall height of the day the measurement is carried out, the total rainfall height of the previous week and the total rainfall height of the previous month. It should be noted that the mean monthly values of soil resistivity at depths of 1m and 2m were chosen as extra inputs because at greater depths, the soil is quite moist and soil resistivity is not affected in large scale by rainfall. The dataset consisted of 248 points covering the period from 17/02/2011 to 19/07/2013.

Table 1. Correlation averaged over the 10-fold CV splits and on the test set (separated by "/"), for Linear Regression and Feed-forward Neural Network models trained with all prediction variables. In bold we show the best result in terms of correlation on the test set.

Predicted Variable	Linear Regression Correlation (train/test)	Hidden Layer Size	Neural Network Correlation (train/test)
R_{g1}	**0.840/0.831**	2	0.958/0.795
		3	**0.971/0.827**
		4	0.979/0.825
		5	0.985/0.646
		6	0.973/0.763
		7	0.982/0.558
		8	0.984/0.774
		9	0.983/0.751
		10	0.985/0.678
		11	0.987/0.739
		12	0.976/0.825
R_{g2}	0.921/0.747	2	**0.982/0.720**
		3	0.988/0.637
		4	0.990/0.589
		5	0.988/0.402
		6	0.991/0.497
		7	0.991/0.595
		8	0.992/0.549
		9	0.989/0.390
		10	0.989/0.458
		11	0.992/0.504
		12	0.990/0.456
R_{g4}	0.943/0.689	2	0.989/0.463
		3	0.996/0.403
		4	0.995/0.419
		5	0.997/0.422
		6	0.996/0.505
		7	0.997/0.422
		8	0.996/0.415
		9	**0.996/0.620**
		10	0.996/0.457
		11	0.997/0.582
		12	0.997/0.539

For all models the dataset was linearly partitioned into two sets using 70% of the samples for training/validating the models and the last remaining 30% of the samples for testing the results. In turn, the first set was partitioned into k=10 subsets of equal size. Of the k subsets, a single subset was retained as the validation data set and the remaining k − 1 subsets were used as training data. The cross-validation process was repeated k times (k-fold Cross Validation - CV), with each of the k subsets used exactly once as the validation data. The k results from the k train/validation iterations were averaged to produce a single estimation. As a performance measure for the accuracy of the models we used the correlation between the actual and predicted Rg1, Rg2, and Rg4 values on the test set.

Table 2. Linear Regression coefficients for all predicted variables

REGRESSOR / PREDICTION VARIABLE	R_{g1}	R_{g2}	R_{g4}
r_d	-0.0400	-0.1156	-0.0933
r_w	-0.1290	-0.0857	-0.0902
r_m	-0.3074	-0.2375	-0.2625
ρ_{2d}	0.1860	0.3195	0.3079
ρ_{4d}	0.1973	0.3557	0.3571
ρ_{8d}	0.1157	-0.0017	0.0330
ρ_{12d}	0.1439	0.1661	0.1643
ρ_{16d}	-0.0035	0.0727	0.1303
ρ_{2w}	-2.96E+01	-5.83E+01	-2.86E+01
ρ_{4w}	-3.51E+01	-6.90E+01	-3.57E+01
ρ_{8w}	0.0293	0.0218	0.0244
ρ_{12w}	0.0712	0.0523	0.0886
ρ_{16w}	0.0350	0.1298	0.1685
ρ_{2m}	0.0593	0.1590	0.1563
ρ_{4m}	-1.39E+02	-2.53E+01	-2.24E+02
r_{ed}	0.0291	0.0033	0.0072
Intercept (Constant)	0.1002	0.0906	0.0453

The prediction accuracy of the models trained with all input variables is summarized in Table 1. In each cell of this table we report (separated by "/") the averaged correlation over all the 10-fold CV splits, and the correlation for the unseen, during training, 30% of the remaining samples (test set). As it can be seen from the table, the linear regression and neural network models exhibit, on the average, very good (and similar) performances over the CV folds (up to 99.7%). However, the correlation reported for the test set is lower, and is shown to decrease by 1% (for the linear regression model), up to 37% (for the neural network models), compared to the correlation reported for the corresponding CV fold.

For the neural network models, the best correlation on the test set for predicting Rg1 was obtained with a neural network with 3 hidden nodes (82.7%), whereas for Rg2 the best result (72%) was achieved by a network with 2 hidden nodes, and for Rg4 by a network with 9 hidden nodes (62%). The best neural network performances are quite similar to the ones reported by the linear regression models, which indicates that more complex non-linear model are probably unnecessary for this types of predictions, and likely to overfit. The coefficients calculated by the linear regression models are shown in Table 2. Figure 5 displays the graphical plots of the variables Rg1, Rg2, and Rg4 versus their predicted values for the linear regression and the best neural network models.

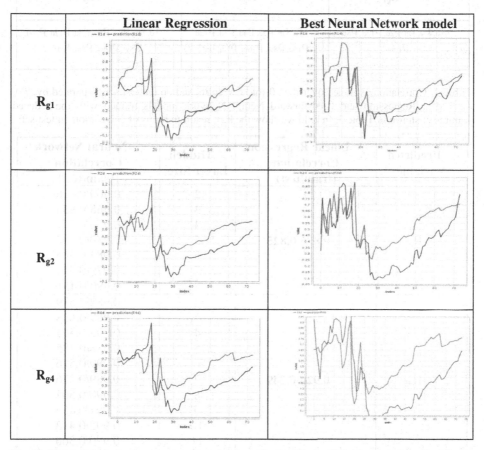

Fig. 5. Plots of the actual versus predicted values for R_{g1}, R_{g2}, and R_{g4} produced by the Linear Regression, and best Neural Network models (as identified in Table 1)

Even though from Table 2 we can infer the relevant importance of each predictor by the value of the corresponding coefficient calculated by the linear regression, this inspection might not necessarily reveal the best attribute set. To this end, we run a second round of experiments in order to determine the most relevant attributes of the whole dataset by trying all possible combinations of attribute selections. We adopted a brute force approach operator, i.e. we selected the best attribute set by trying all possible combinations of attribute selections when fed to a linear regression model. In order to establish a performance measurement, which indicates how well a feature subset would perform on the given data set, we followed the same 10-fold CV approach described above, but this time on the whole dataset. Table 3 shows the most relevant attributes discovered by this process for $R_{g1}, R_{g2},$ and R_{g4}.

Table 3. Most relevant attributes for predicting $R_{g1}, R_{g2},$ and R_{g4}

R_{g1}	R_{g2}	R_{g4}
$r_d, r_w, r_m, \rho_{2d}, \rho_{12d}, \rho_{8w}, \rho_{16w}$	$r_d, r_m, \rho_{2d}, \rho_{4d}, \rho_{8d}, \rho_{12d}, \rho_{16d}, \rho_{8w}, \rho_{16w}, \rho_{2m}, r_{ed}$	$r_d, r_m, \rho_{2d}, \rho_{4d}, \rho_{8d}, \rho_{12d}, \rho_{16d}, \rho_{8w}, \rho_{16w}, \rho_{2m}, r_{ed}$

Table 4. Correlation averaged over the 10-fold CV splits and on the test set (separated by "/"), for Linear Regression and Feed-forward Neural Network models trained with the reduced feature set shown in Table 3. In bold we show the best result in terms of correlation on test set.

Predicted Variable	Linear Regression Correlation (train/test)	Hidden Layer Size	Neural Network Correlation (train/test)
R_{g1}	0.836/0.825	2	0.960/0.816
		3	**0.968/0.856**
		4	0.976/0.677
		5	0.980/0.662
		6	0.984/0.365
		7	0.979/0.544
		8	0.980/0.451
R_{g2}	0.920/0.749	2	0.982/0.589
		3	**0.987/0.628**
		4	0.992/0.504
		5	0.988/0.485
		6	0.989/0.516
		7	0.989/0.376
		8	0.990/0.504
		9	0.991/0.455
		10	0.992/0.412
		11	0.990/0.566
		12	0.991/0.524
R_{g4}	0.942/0.694	2	0.990/0.424
		3	0.993/0.522
		4	0.996/0.541
		5	0.996/0.551
		6	0.996/0.535
		7	**0.995/0.633**
		8	0.995/0.484
		9	0.995/0.521
		10	0.996/0.586
		11	0.995/0.600
		12	0.995/0.571

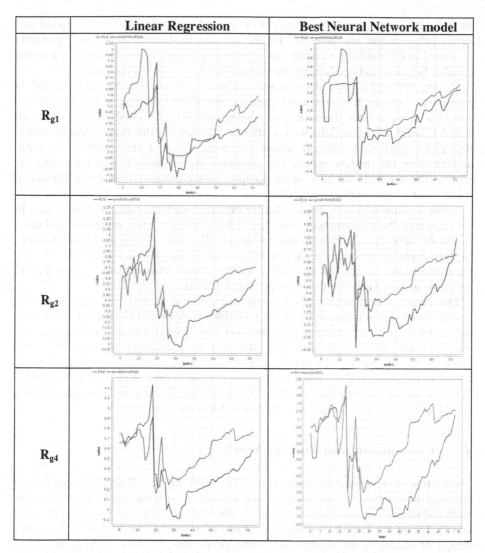

Fig. 6. Plots of the actual versus predicted values for R_{g1}, R_{g2}, and R_{g4} produced by the Linear Regression and best Neural Network models (as identified in Table 4)

Regarding the elements in Table 3 one could draw the conclusion that ground enhancing compounds (in this case R_{g2} and R_{g4}) as chemical materials present more complex attitude than the natural soil (R_{g1}), thus they need more variables for the determination of their performance and the prediction of their behavior. A possible explanation to this fact is that, the soil in the experimental field does not present great non-uniformity, so besides the rainfall height measurements the more representative values of soil resistivity, which determine the behavior of R_{g1}, are the daily value in depths of 1m and 6m and the mean weekly value in depths of 4m and 8m. On the contrary, for the enhancing materials almost all the relevant variables, which cover all the periods of time and all the depths of the ground field under test, effect on the materials behavior and are necessary for the targeted prediction. This fact is probably attributed to the chemical composition of the tested materials, which presents a multi-variable behavior and needs more relevant attributes for a statistical analysis.

Having obtained a new reduced feature set for each of the variables that we wish to predict, we then run the same experiments as described in the beginning of this section, that is, we utilized three linear regression models and a number of feed-forward neural network configurations with a different selection on the number hidden nodes. Again, we split each reduced feature set using 70% of the samples for training/validating the models and the last remaining 30% of the samples for testing the results. The set with the 70% of the samples was partitioned into $k=10$ subsets of equal size for running the 10-fold CV.

Table 4 summarizes the results that we obtained with the reduced feature sets. In this case also, the performances over the CV folds both for linear regression and neural network models are similar to those with the full feature set (up to 99.6%). Similarly, the correlation reported for the test set is lower, is shown to decrease by 1% for the linear regression model, and up to 36% for the neural network models, compared to the correlation reported for the corresponding CV fold.

For the neural network models, the best correlation on the test set for predicting R_{g1} was obtained with a neural network with 3 hidden nodes (85.6%), whereas for R_{g2} the best result (62.8%) was achieved by a network with 3 hidden nodes, and for R_{g4} by a network with 7 hidden nodes (63.3%). Thus, with the reduced features sets, the correlation on the test set for R_{g1} and R_{g4} slightly increases, whereas there's a small decrease in the case of R_{g2}. Figure 6 also displays the graphical plots of the variables R_{g1}, R_{g2}, and R_{g4} versus their predicted values for the linear regression and the best neural network models trained with the reduced features sets.

4   Conclusions and Further Work

The current work applied linear regression, feed-forward neural networks and feature selection techniques for modelling ground resistance with the use of field measurements related to soil resistivity and rainfall. The work reflects extensive expertise and knowledge on the subject of grounding, which is of crucial importance in the proper design of electrical installations in constructions. Results show very good performance of actual versus predicted values of ground resistance for three different ground enhancing compounds like conductive concrete or bentonite. For measuring the performance of the proposed methodologies, correlation averaged over the 10-fold CV splits and on the test set was used, for Linear Regression and Feed-forward Neural Network models trained with either the reduced or the full feature set. Additional experimentation is underway, regarding both (a) the application of other intelligent techniques in the existing dataset, such as wavelet neural networks, inductive machine learning and hybrid intelligent schemes, and (b) the collection of additional data regarding daily and weekly measures for different types of grounding compound and different grounding materials and additives.

References

[1] ANSI/IEEE Std 80-2000: IEEE Guide for safety in AC substation grounding (2000)
[2] ANSI/IEEE Std 81-2012: IEEE guide for measuring earth resistivity, ground impedance, and earth surface potentials of a grounding system (December 28, 2012)
[3] Salam, M.A., Al-Alawi, S.M., Maquashi, A.A.: An artificial neural networks approach to model and predict the relationship between the grounding resistance and the length of the buried electrode in soil. Journal of Electrostatics 64, 338–342 (2006)
[4] Amaral, F.C.L., De Souza, A.N., Zago, M.G.: A novel approach to model grounding systems considering the influence of high frequencies. In: Proc. of 5th Latin-American Congress on Electricity Generation & Transmission (CLAGTEE 2003), Sao Pedro, Brasil, November 16-20 (2003)
[5] Gouda, O.E., Amer, M.G., El Saied, M.T.: Optimum design of grounding systems in uniform and non-uniform soils using ANN. International Journal of Soft Computing 1(3), 175–180 (2006)
[6] Androvitsaneas, V.P., Asimakopoulou, F.E., Gonos, I.F., Stathopulos, I.A.: Estimation of ground enhancing compound performance using artificial neural network. In: Proceedings of 3rd International Conference on High Voltage Engineering and Application, Shanghai, China, September 17-20, pp. 174–178 (2012)
[7] Asimakopoulou, F.E., Tsekouras, G.J., Gonos, I.F., Stathopulos, I.A.: Estimation of seasonal variation of ground resistance using artificial neural networks. Electric Power Systems Research 94(1), 113–121 (2013)
[8] Tsekouras, G.J., Kanellos, F.D., Kontargyri, V.T., et al.: A comparison of artificial neural networks algorithms for short term load forecasting in greek intercontinental power system. In: Proceedings of 7th WSEAS International Conference on Circuits, Systems, Electronics, Control & Signal (CSECS 2008), Puerto De La Cruz, Canary Islands, Spain, December 15-17, pp. 108–115 (2008)
[9] Asimakopoulou, G.E., Kontargyri, V.T., Tsekouras, G.J., et al.: Artificial neural network optimisation methodology for the estimation of the critical flashover voltage on insulators. IET Science, Measurement & Technology 3(1), 90–104 (2009)
[10] Androvitsaneas, V.P., Gonos, I.F., Stathopulos, I.A.: Performance of ground enhancing compounds during the year. In: Proceedings of 31st International Conference on Lightning Protection, Vienna, Austria, September 2-7, pp. 231-1–231-5 (2012)
[11] Guerard Jr., J.B.: Regression Analysis and Forecasting Models. In: Guerard Jr., J.B. (ed.) Introduction to Financial Forecasting in Investment Analysis, ch. 2. Springer Science + Business Media, New York (2013)
[12] Zhang, G.P.: Neural Networks for Time-Series Forecasting. In: Rosenberg, et al. (eds.) Handbook of Natural Computing. Springer, Heidelberg (2012)
[13] Liu, H., Hiroshi, M.: Feature Selection for Knowledge Discovery and Data Mining. The Springer International Series in Engineering and Computer Science, vol. 454 (1998)

Developing a Game Server for Humans and Bots

Nikos Dikaros[1] and Dimitris Kalles[2]

[1] Faculty of Pure and Applied Sciences, Open University of Cyprus, Cyprus
Hellenic Ministry of Interior, Athens, Greece
ndikaros@gmail.com
[2] Hellenic Open University, Patras, Greece
kalles@eap.gr

Abstract. The paper focuses on modern web development tools as a means of implementing a strategy board game in a web environment. We examine various Ajax frameworks in order to create the client side interface and the turn based interaction between players in the web. A rating system is implemented for measuring the skill of human and computer players alike, and a distributed architecture is proposed for aspiring AI researchers and enthusiasts, in order to integrate their game playing bots with the main server of the game.

Keywords: Online board games, rating systems, web systems engineering.

1   Introduction

Over the last 20 years, the World Wide Web has evolved from just a means of requesting formatted text in the form of HTML from a web server, to a means of a bidirectional exchange of information between clients and servers with the use of dynamic web pages. At the same time, technologies for creating visual interfaces on a web browser have improved a lot. Many online games, which traditionally have been played in server-client desktop applications, are now available in web browsers. At the same time, AI in strategy games has boomed to such a degree that computer programs can now beat top human players. Examples of this, are chess, backgammon and checkers whereas poker still poses big challenges to researchers.

RLGame is a relatively new game that resembles checkers. Attempts have been made to create a computer player for RLGame which utilized various artificial intelligence techniques, like reinforcement learning, neural networks, minimax etc [1-4]. As its development is still immature for a computer program to play at a competent level, and the game is not yet widespread so as to investigate high level strategies, we aim to promote the interest towards RLGame by enticing more people to practice and play the game and by allowing AI researchers to experiment with computer bots which might plays the game at top level. For this reason, we created a game server where human players can play against each other from their web browser with a rich visual interface, using modern web development technologies.

We also implemented a rating system, which serves as the measure of a player's ability in the game, using Glicko [11], as it is quite modern and is widely used in chess ratings nowadays. To facilitate AI research, we plan to help researchers by

A. Likas, K. Blekas, and D. Kalles (Eds.): SETN 2014, LNAI 8445, pp. 430–435, 2014.
© Springer International Publishing Switzerland 2014

letting their bots battle against the human players logged in the RLGame server. To this end, the paper describes a distributed architecture which facilitates bot-server integration. We expect and certainly hope that we will be soon seeing humans and bots competing against each other for the highest possible rating.

The rest of this paper is structured in five sections: we first offer some background on RLGame and earlier work, and then we set out describing the architecture of our server and the rating systems we implement for competing agents, before offering some research and development directions and concluding the paper.

2   A Brief Background on Game Playing and Learning

RLGame game is played on a square board of size n, by 2 players. Two square bases of size a are located on bottom left and top right corners. The top left belongs to the white player and the upper right belongs to the black player. At the beginning of the game each player possesses β pawns. The goal is to move a pawn into the opponent's base or to force all of the opponent's pawns out of the board.

Every pawn in the base can move at one step to any of the adjacent to the base free squares. A pawn can move to a vertically or horizontally adjacent and empty square, provided that the maximum distance from its base is not decreased (so, backward moves are not allowed). Distance from the base is measured as the maximum of the horizontal and the vertical distance from the base (and not as a sum of these quantities). A pawn which cannot make a legal move is lost (more than one pawn may be lost in one round). If some player runs out of pawns he loses.

Fig. 1 shows some indicative move examples. The leftmost board demonstrates a legal and an illegal move (for the pawn pointed to by the arrow - the illegal move is due to the rule that does not allow decreasing the distance from the home base). The rightmost boards demonstrate the loss of pawns (with arrows showing pawn casualties), where a "trapped" pawn automatically gets removed from the game. As a by-product of this rule, when all adjacent squares next to a base are occupied, the rest of the pawns inside the base are lost.

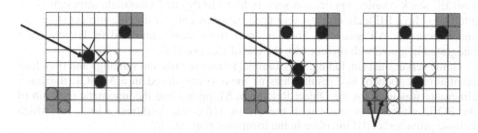

Fig. 1. Some examples of RLGame moves

In earlier work, neural networks were used in combination with reinforcement learning. Instead of just training the bot by letting it play against itself, games against humans were also used to accelerate the learning process [1, 2, 3]; a minimax tutor was also used [4].

An earlier web game server was developed using SCALA and the Lift framework for server side programming, while Javascript and Jquery were used for the game logic and web interface. Comet technology was used for the asynchronous calls from server to client [5]. In that server, a previously created Java applet was integrated [6] to allow human-vs.-computer games, where users play against a trained agent for which neural networks and reinforcement learning were used. Our approach is at the junction of solving games [7], generic engines for game playing [8] and, of course, web game servers.

3   Server Infrastructure Implementation

We reconstructed the web interface of the game server to pursue aesthetics and ergonomics. We used the recently booming Primefaces framework for the web interface and its utilities asynchronous calls from a server to the clients. To rank the players we added an implementation of the Glicko rating system as a measure of the player's capabilities; a player's rating is updated after each game it plays.

To facilitate artificial intelligence research in the game we propose a way, through which, anyone who creates a game playing bot will be able to pit it against human players in the RLGame server, using standard HTTP requests. The bots will connect to an http server, which exchanges requests with the RLGame server (for example, when a human player makes a move, the RLGame server sends an http request with the coordinates of the move, encoded as GET or POST parameters). We want the AI developers to be free to develop in any language and technology they prefer, but a common language of communication with the RLGame server is necessary to achieve interoperability, hence the need to develop an http request interpreter which accepts and parses predefined commands transmitted through HTTP protocol. On top of that, a bot creator would construct a piece of middleware to just map inputs and outputs to the ones required by the HTTP interpreter. An architectural diagram of the proposed infrastructure is depicted in Figure 2.

We used technologies from the Java ecosystem for the implementation of the game server. Tomcat 7 was chosen as the web server, as it is more lightweight than full Java EE stack enabled application servers like JBOSS and Glassfish, although some additional Java EE technologies were used independently inside the project (like JSF and Hibernate). All necessary libraries apart from those contained in Tomcat were integrated in a java web project with the use of Eclipse IDE.

Game server data (including, for example, player details and ranking) and play logs (containing opponent ids, results, lists of moves) are stored in a MySQL database. Hibernate was used for the Object Relational Mapping, and the automatic creation of the POJO classes was made with the use of Hibernate Utilities, a tool, for which Eclipse provides a GUI interface in the form of a plug-in.

Primefaces is an open source Ajax-enabled JSF component library framework, whose features we used to create the web interface of RLGame server, and achieve the asynchronous communication between server and client. For the latter, we used the PrimePush utility, built on top of the Atmosphere framework. Primefaces was chosen over the other Ajax enabled JSF component libraries, due to the multitude of components it offers, the simplicity of integration within the Java web project and the clarity of its documentation.

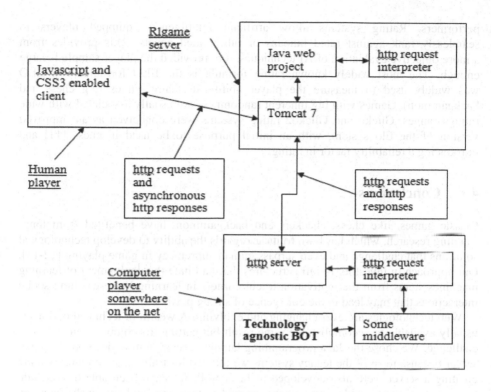

Fig. 2. Architecture of the RLGame server

To implement the web interface of the game server, various features of Primefaces were used, including a chat infrastructure based on the PrimePush utility.

Primefaces offers a component named p:terminal, which is a very good simulation of a command line terminal running into a web browser. The user can type various commands which are parsed and executed at the server side. The developer can create at will its own commands and parse them in a managed (Java) bean method. This component was used to implement player invitations but has substantial further potential. The playing board was created with the use of the p:draggable and p:droppable components, which primefaces offer to allow drag-n-drop functionality for pawn manipulation. A typical board square consists of a p:panel, which contains two p:outputLabel components each of them representing the black and white pawns. One of those components or none of them can be rendered according to if a pawn is occupying the square. The representation of the board is kept on a java structure residing on the server.

Multiplayer online games require asynchronous communication between the client and the server (or, between peers). An umbrella of techniques commonly used to achieve such communication is described by the generic name COMET or Ajax push [9]. Primefaces offers a relevant solution called PrimePush.

Nearly all multiplayer games adopt some form of a rating system. Beyond settling the question of who is best, players are also interested in making it into a list of top performers. Rating systems allow artificial intelligence equipped players to seamlessly rank against rated humans or other rated agents. This provides from a more objective evaluation of AI techniques, too, provided the player sample is large enough. The most widely known rating formula is the ELO formula [10]. ELO was widely used to measure the player ability in many games (e.g chess and backgammon). Games with big inherent randomness are usually associated with wide ratings ranges. Glicko and Glicko2 rating systems were conceived as an improved version of the Elo system, with an initial purpose to be used in chess [11] and introducing a reliability factor in rating.

4   Conclusions

Classic games, like chess, checkers and backgammon, have benefited from long-standing research, which has born fruits as regards the ability to develop technological solutions that challenge and even surpass human supremacy in game playing [12-15]. Our approach in investing in infrastructures that facilitate the deployment of learning machines stems from the motivation to cut corners in learning by researching social interactions that may lead to the emergence of strong players.

Web technologies are ever changing and evolving. A wealth of technical options is usually available to accomplish the same result but getting the combination right is a challenge. We chose the Java programming language ecosystem to develop our game server because most of the legacy systems we utilized for training a computer bot and creating a server were also developed in Java. Still, we have been able to conclude that, earlier work aside, primefaces proved interesting and its web interface components visually pleasing.

Nowadays HTML5 (as well as a set of APIs that accompany it) is on the rise, and since it will most probably dominate the web in the future, we would expect to see the spawning of development efforts towards an implementation of the RLGame server with the use of HTML5.

We are quite confident that the rating system we added to the server will boost the interest of human players into playing more games and devoting some mental energy to improve their strategies.

Finally, we are now implementing the integration of computer bots into the RLGame server, to facilitate its interaction with third parties' playing algorithms. We utilized a low level solution that adopts HTTP requests for this kind of architecture, but it remains to be seen if some higher level, more sophisticated technology, like web services, will eventually be more appropriate.

Acknowledgements. A beta version of the RLGame server now offering a human-vs-human functionality is available at `http://83.212.105.28:8080/rlgameserver/`, with bot integration aspects being under development. The work is carried out in the context of a M.Sc. dissertation project and access has been granted to all earlier dissertations and projects developed at a multitude of learning and research institutions, in Greece and in Cyprus.

References

1. Kalles, D., Kanellopoulos, P.: On Verifying Game Design and Playing Strategies using Reinforcement Learning. In: ACM Symposium on Applied Computing, Special Track on Artificial Intelligence and Computation Logic, Las Vegas (2001)
2. Kalles, D., Ntoutsi, E.: Interactive Verification of Game Design and Playing Strategies. In: IEEE International Conference on Tools with Artificial Intelligence, Washington, D.C. (2002)
3. Kalles, D.: Player co-modelling in a strategy board game: Discovering how to play fast. Cybernetics and Systems 39(1), 1–17 (2008)
4. Kalles, D., Kanellopoulos, P.: A Minimax Tutor for Learning to Play a Board Game. In: 18th European Conference on Artificial Intelligence, Workshop on Artificial Intelligence in Games, Patras, Greece (2008)
5. Dimas, G.: Game web server development and operasion. Msc Dissertation, Hellenic Open University (2011)
6. Vlassi, A.: Systems for Strategy games. Msc Dissertation, Hellenic Open University (2008)
7. Schaeffer, J., Burch, N., Björnsson, Y., Kishimoto, A., Müller, M., Lake, R., Lu, P., Sutphen, S.: Checkers Is Solved. Science 317(5844), 1518–1522 (2007)
8. General Game Playing, http://games.stanford.edu/ (retrieved January 19, 2014)
9. Comet (programming) (January 8, 2014). In : Wikipedia, The Free Encyclopedia, http://en.wikipedia.org/w/index.php?title=Comet_(programming)&oldid=589745306 (retrieved January 19, 2014)
10. Elo rating system (January 16, 2014). In: Wikipedia, The Free Encyclopedia, http://en.wikipedia.org/w/index.php?title=Elo_rating_system&oldid=590943708 (retrieved January 19, 2014)
11. Glicko rating system. In: Wikipedia, The Free Encyclopedia (January 18, 2014), http://en.wikipedia.org/w/index.php?title=Glicko_rating_system&oldid=591203472 (retrieved January 19, 2014)
12. Hsu, F.-H.: Behind Deep Blue: Building the Computer that Defeated the World Chess Champion. Princeton University Press (2002)
13. Schaeffer, J., Bjoernsson, Y., Burch, N., Kishimoto, A., Mueller, M., Lake, R., Lu, P., Sutphen, S.: Checkers is Solved. Science 317(5844), 1518–1522 (2007)
14. Tesauro, G.: Temporal Difference Learning and TD-Gammon. Communications of the ACM 38(3), 58–68 (1995)
15. Papahristou, N., Refanidis, I.: On the Design and Training of Bots to Play Backgammon Variants. In: International Conference on Artificial Intelligence Applications and Innovations, Halkidiki, Greece (2012)

Feature Evaluation Metrics for Population Genomic Data

Ioannis Kavakiotis[1], Alexandros Triantafyllidis[2],
Grigorios Tsoumakas[1], and Ioannis Vlahavas[1]

[1] Department of Computer Science, Aristotle University of Thessaloniki, 54124, Greece
{ikavak,greg,vlahavas}@csd.auth.gr
[2] Department of Genetics, Development and Molecular Biology, School of Biology, Aristotle University of Thessaloniki, 54124, Greece
atriant@bio.auth.gr

Abstract. Single Nucleotide Polymorphisms (SNPs) are considered nowadays one of the most important class of genetic markers with a wide range of applications with both scientific and economic interests. Although the advance of biotechnology has made feasible the production of genome wide SNP datasets, the cost of the production is still high. The transformation of the initial dataset into a smaller one with the same genetic information is a crucial task and it is performed through feature selection. Biologists evaluate features using methods originating from the field of population genetics. Although several studies have been performed in order to compare the existing biological methods, there is a lack of comparison between methods originating from the biology field with others originating from the machine learning. In this study we present some early results which support that biological methods perform slightly better than machine learning methods.

Keywords: Feature selection, Single nucleotide polymorphism, SNPs, Bioinformatics, Machine learning.

1   Introduction

Single Nucleotide Polymorphisms (SNPs) are considered nowadays one of the most important classes of genetic markers in many scientific fields such as human genetics and molecular ecology. At the same time analyses of SNP data are nowadays gaining more popularity in many applications with great medical as well as economic interest, such as food traceability, discrimination between wild and framed population and forensic investigations [1].

In recent years, the advancement of biotechnology has made feasible the genotyping of thousands or even millions of SNPs and consequently the production of very large SNP datasets from a wide range of model and non model organisms. Two important tasks in terms of analyses, performed with SNP datasets are the individual assignment to groups of origin and the selection of the most informative markers (SNPs). In terms of computer science these are the classification and the feature selection tasks respectively.

A. Likas, K. Blekas, and D. Kalles (Eds.): SETN 2014, LNAI 8445, pp. 436–441, 2014.

The importance of feature selection for SNP datasets is beyond dispute either for biology or machine learning. From the computational view, feature selection aims to improve the prediction performance of the predictors through defying the curse of dimensionality, to provide faster and more cost effective predictors and to facilitate data visualization and data understanding [2]. From the biology perspective, the importance of selecting the most informative markers from genome wide datasets has been stated in many scientific projects and publications [1, 3, 4] and are mainly economic. The main drawback in using genome wide datasets is the high cost to produce, in contrast to smaller panels (datasets) which are cheaper and more flexible and can occur through/after the feature selection process.

The methods to measure marker informativeness in population genetics and consequently to select features are not similar to those used in the field of machine learning. More specifically, the two most popular genetic methods depend on the allele frequencies of a particular marker i.e. attribute (explained in subsequent section). Moreover the assignment success of the reduced dataset is evaluated through genetic assignment approaches or software such as GENECLASS2 [5]

The purpose of this study is to compare, for the first time, the frequency based metrics which are used for feature selection purposes in population genetics with established methods from the field of machine learning and data mining and eventually determine which are more appropriate for feature selection when building models for the classification of individuals into groups of origin.

2   Background Knowledge

The Genetic Information: From DNA to Genome
Deoxyribonucleic acid (DNA) is the primary hereditary material of all known living organisms. It is a very large molecule composed of smaller units linked together. These smaller units are four (for DNA) and are called nucleotides named adenine (A), cytosine (C), guanine (G), thymine (T).

Genes are made of nucleotides and each one contains a particular set of instructions. A chromosome is an organized structure of DNA which contains genes as well as many other nucleotide sequences, with gene regulatory or no (known) function. The genome is the entirety of hereditary information possessed by an organism and it is encoded mostly in DNA.

Single Nucleotide Polymorphisms – SNPs
Single nucleotide polymorphism is the most common type of genetic variation. A SNP occurs when a Single Nucleotide (A, T, G or C) in the genome differs between members of a biological species or paired chromosomes. For instance, consider two DNA sequences from different individuals; *seq1:* ATCTG and *seq2:* ATGTG, which differ in the third nucleotide.

An allele is one of the possible alternative forms of the same gene or same genetic locus. In the previous example there were two alleles, which is the most common case in SNP variations. A marker with only two alleles is called biallelic.

Population Genomic Datasets – SNP Datasets
The dimensionality of SNP datasets can vary a lot depending on the number of different SNPs analyzed multiplied by the number of samples analyzed. Animal datasets can reach a hundred thousand attributes (SNPs) whereas human dataset can easily contain over a million SNPs. Each attribute is a genotype which occurs from the combination of two nucleotides in the two chromosomal copies of a diploid organism and thus can have at most three values. For instance, one SNP genotype can have the following values AA, GG and AG (GA is considered same) which occur from the combination of the two alleles adenine and guanine.

The term allele frequency refers to the frequency of each allele in a population. For instance, consider a dataset with five individuals. Assume that the first attribute can have the following values TT, CC, TC. Three individuals have values TT, one CC and one TC. The allele frequencies are 0.7 for the allele T and 0.3 for the allele C.

3   Methods

3.1   Feature Selection via Filter Methods

Feature selection methods are divided in two major categories. The first category comprises of 'filter' methods, which evaluate the attributes based on general characteristics of the data. The second category contains "wrapper" methods which use a machine learning algorithm to evaluate the candidate subset of features [6]. The main advantage of wrappers is that they commonly offer better classification accuracy which is the most important aim. The main disadvantage of wrapper methods is that the algorithm will build a model many times in order to evaluate different subsets, which in some cases, such as SVMs, is too computationally expensive. This is an important drawback especially for SNP datasets which can be very large. On the contrary, the main advantage of filters is that they are much faster than wrapper methods.

3.2   Evaluation Metrics

Allele Frequency Based Methods
In our study we included two methods for evaluation of marker informativeness from the field of population genetics, although until now several methods have been proposed. The first is Delta [7] which is without dispute the most commonly used method. The second one is Pairwise Wright's F_{ST} [8] which is reported to be the most successful one [1]. For the two methods we use the same notations: $p_A{}^i$ is the frequency of the allele A in the ith population, $p_A{}^j$ is the frequency of the same allele A in the jth population and p_A is the frequency of allele A in all populations. The notations with the second allele B occur similarly. Delta and pairwise Wright's F_{ST} are given by calculating the mean of their values out of all possible population combinations.

Delta
For a biallelic marker i.e a marker with two alleles the delta value is given by the following equation:

$$\delta = |p_A{}^i - p_A{}^j|$$

Pairwise Wright's F_{ST}

For a biallelic marker the F_{ST} value is given by the following equation:

$$F_{ST} = (H_t - H_s) / H_t$$

where H_s is the average expected heterogygosity across subpopulations and H_t is the expected heterozygosity of the total population [9] and they are given by the following equations:

$$H_t = 2\, p_A\, p_B$$

$$H_s = p_A^i\, p_A^j + p_B^i\, p_B^j$$

Machine Learning Methods

The following two attribute evaluators from machine learning are implemented in Weka machine learning library [10].

InfoGain

This criterion evaluates features by measuring the information gain with respect to the class [11]. Information gain is given by

$$Infogain = H(Y) - H(Y|X)$$

where

$$H(Y) = -\sum_{y\in Y} p(y) log_2 (p(y))$$

$$II(Y|X) = -\sum_{x\in X} p(x) \sum_{y\in Y} p(y|x) log_2 (p(y|x))$$

ReliefF

The general idea behind ReliefF [12] is that scores features according to their value's ability to distinguish better instances from different classes and group together instances of the same class. This is achieved by sampling instances randomly and checking neighboring instances of the same and different classes.

3.3   Classification Algorithm – Decision Trees

The comparison of the different feature ranking methods was made through the comparison of the classification accuracy of different subset of features, with decision trees (J48). Decision trees have many advantages such as simplicity and high interpretability. Moreover, a feature selection process can aid the algorithm to produce smaller and more predictive trees [11].

4   Evaluation

The experiments were conducted on a dataset [4], which consisted of 59436 attributes/SNPs and 446 instances/individuals that are almost equally distributed between

14 different classes/groups. For every feature selection method we followed the following procedure: We built twelve times the classifier using 10 – fold cross-validation with different number of attributes. Each time we selected the top-k most informative SNPs (20, 40, 60, 80, 100, 120, 160, 200, 300, 400, 500, 1000) from the training folds in order to avoid having upwardly biased results.

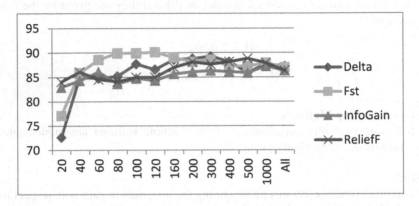

Fig. 1. Comparison of Feature selection methods through classification accuracy

The results clearly show that the best method for selecting the most informative SNPs is Pairwise Wright's F_{ST} which is the only method that reaches 90,1% accuracy so early (120 SNPs). The other methods need many more attributes to reach the same level of accuracy (Delta 89%/300SNPs, InfoGain 87/1000, ReliefF 89/500). Another interesting observation is that the first twenty SNPs selected by the machine learning methods are significantly more informative than those selected by the allele frequency methods.

Table 1. Score with first 20 SNP and best score for each method

	Delta	PairwiseF_{ST}	InfoGain	ReliefF
Best Score	89	90.1	87	89
20 first SNPs	72.6	77.13	82.96	84.08

5   Conclusion and Future Work

Although some studies have been conducted to compare biological methods for selecting the most informative markers from a SNP dataset, none of them compare biological with machine learning methods. In this study we present some early results of our attempt to compare the most successful biological with the most successful machine learning methods and determine which are the most appropriate for the task of informative SNP selection. In the future, we intend to broaden our study in various ways. Firstly, we intent to compare other more sophisticated techniques from the machine learning field. Secondly, we aim to evaluate methods with more classifiers in order to support our conclusions with more confidence and lastly, to run our experiments with more datasets. Those datasets will contain populations/groups with varying degrees of differentiation trying to respond to real life biological problems.

References

1. Wilkinson, S., Wiener, P., Archibald, A., et al.: Evaluation of approaches for identifying population informative markers from high density SNP chips. BMC Genet. 12, 45 (2011)
2. Guyon, I., Elisseeff, A.: An introduction to variable and feature selection. J. Mach Learn Res. 3, 1157–1182 (2003)
3. Nielsen, E., Cariani, A., Mac Aoidh, E., et al.: Gene-associated markers provide tools for tackling illegal fishing and false eco-certification. Nat. Com. 3, 851 (2012), doi:10.1038/ncomms1845
4. Wilkinson, S., Archibald, A., Haley, C., et al.: Development of a genetic tool for product regulation in the diverse British pig breed market. BMC Gen. 13, 580 (2012)
5. Piry, S., Alapetite, A., Cornuet, J.M., Petkau, D., Baudouin, L., Estoup, A.: GENECLASS2: A software for genetic assignment and first generation migrant detection. J. Hered. 95, 536–539 (2004)
6. Witten, I.H., Frank, E., Hall, M.A.: Data Mining: Practical Machine Learning Tools and Techniques, 3rd edn. Morgan Kaufmann, Burlington (2011)
7. Shriver, M.D., Smith, M.W., Jin, L., et al.: Ethnic affiliation estimation by use of population-specific DNA markers. Am. J Hum. Genet. 60, 957–964 (1997)
8. Wright, S.: The genetical structure of populations. Ann Eugenic 15, 323 (1951)
9. Beebee, T., Rowe, G.: An Introduction to Molecular Ecology. Oxford University Press, Oxford (2004)
10. Hall, M., Frank, E., Holmes, G., Pfahringer, B., Reutemann, P., Witten, I.H.: The WEKA Data Mining Software: An Update. SIGKDD Explorations 11, 10–18 (2009)
11. Wang, Y., et al.: Gene selection from microarray data for cancer classification–a machine learning approach. Comput. Biol. Chem. 29, 37–46 (2005)
12. Robnik-Sikonja, M., Kononenko, I.: Theoretical and empirical analysis of relief and relieff. Mach. Lean. 53, 23–69 (2003)

Online Seizure Detection from EEG and ECG Signals for Monitoring of Epileptic Patients

Iosif Mporas[1], Vasiliki Tsirka[2], Evangelia I. Zacharaki[1],
Michalis Koutroumanidis[2], and Vasileios Megalooikonomou[1]

[1] Multidimensional Data Analysis and Knowledge Management Laboratory
Dept. of Computer Engineering and Informatics, University of Patras
26500 Rion-Patras, Greece
{imporas,ezachar}@upatras.gr, vasilis@ceid.upatras.gr
[2] Dept. of Clinical Neurophysiology and Epilepsies
Guy's & St. Thomas' and Evelina Hospital for Children
NHS Foundation Trust, London, UK
{vasiliki.tsirka,michael.koutroumanidis}@gstt.nhs.uk

Abstract. In this article, we investigate the performance of a seizure detection module for online monitoring of epileptic patients. The module is using as input data streams from electroencephalographic and electrocardiographic recordings. The architecture of the module consists of time and frequency domain feature extraction followed by classification. Four classification algorithms were evaluated on three epileptic subjects. The best performance was achieved by the support vector machine algorithm, with more than 90% for two of the subjects and slightly lower than 90% for the third subject.

Keywords: Seizure, electroencephalogram, electrocardiogram, classification.

1   Introduction

The 1% of the world population suffers from seizures [1, 2]. Epilepsy is manifested through recurrent seizures, resulting from an abnormal synchronous activity in the brain involving a large network of neurons [3]. The epileptic seizures are the product of highly non-linear dynamics in the brain circuits evolving over time [4]. The producing mechanism of seizure is not well known yet, thus making it's study a tedious task [4, 5].

Clues to the seizure producing process have began to emerge from the quantitative analysis of the electroencephalogram (EEG) [2, 4]. The epileptic seizures analysis is based on visual investigation of the EEG signal, which is performed manually by expert neurologists for the detection of patterns of interest, such as spikes or spike wave discharges [5]. Manual investigation is difficult, time-consuming and can be performed only by experts. Except this, the EEG signal analysis is highly subjective and thus frequently there is disagreement between expert neuroscientists.

The electrocardiographic (ECG) signals can also offer valuable information related to the seizure discharges [4]. In [4, 6, 7, 8, 9] it has been reported that seizures are

A. Likas, K. Blekas, and D. Kalles (Eds.): SETN 2014, LNAI 8445, pp. 442–447, 2014.

often associated with cardiovascular and respiratory alterations. For the automatic analysis and detection of epileptic events from multimodal recordings (here EEG and ECG) several approaches have been proposed in the literature.

In the general case, the analysis is based on the estimation of the EEG channels' spectral magnitude [4, 5, 6, 7]. Other reported EEG features are the autoregressive filter coefficients, the continuous and discrete wavelet transform, and the energy per brain wave (delta, theta, alpha, beta, gamma) bands [4, 6]. Except the frequency domain, time domain features have been proposed, such as zero-crossing rhythm [3] and statistics of the EEG samples per channel [4, 6]. The ECG features are mainly based on the heart rate estimation (after R-points detection) and statistics of it, i.e. heart rate variability [4, 6, 7, 8, 9].

A number of classification algorithms have been reported for seizure detection. The most widely used are the artificial neural networks [5, 6], the support vector machines [1, 3, 4], the decision trees [10] and other less popular methods [7, 8, 11].

In this paper we evaluate four widely used classification algorithms on the binary seizure detection task. Time and frequency domain EEG and ECG features reported in the literature are used here. The evaluated architecture is part of the ongoing work for constructing online tools for seizure detection and analysis for the needs of the ARMOR project [12].

2   Online Seizure Detection Module

The presented module for seizure detection is part of the ARMOR project's [12] system for monitoring and analysis of brain disorders. Within the ARMOR framework patients suffering from seizures are monitored through sensors and the multimodal data (EEG, ECG, EMG and EOG) are processed automatically (real-time by software tools) or semi-manually (offline with the support of software tools and visualizations) by neurology experts. The purpose of the online tools is to monitor and identify brain abnormalities for alarming. In the presented architecture of the seizure detection module the EEG and ECG recordings are used from the multimodal data, while EMG and EOG which are mainly used for movement/ artifact detection are not part of this study. The block diagram of the seizure detection architecture is illustrated in Fig. 1.

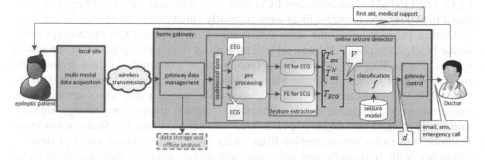

Fig. 1. Block diagram of the online seizure detection module in the ARMOR concept

As can be seen in Figure 1, the captured multimodal data (EEG and ECG) are wirelessly transmitted from a wearable solution to a local gateway for online processing. During online seizure detection, the EEG and ECG signals are initially preprocessed. Preprocessing consists of frame blocking of the incoming streams to epochs of constant length with constant time-shift. Each epoch is a matrix including the corresponding time-frame's samples for the N-dimensional EEG signal appended by the ECG signal. After preprocessing, time-domain and frequency-domain features for the EEG and ECG signals are estimated. In specific, each of the N-dimensions of the EEG signal are processed by time-domain and frequency-domain feature extraction algorithms for EEG, while the ECG signal is processed by time-domain (based on heart rate estimation) feature extraction algorithms dedicated for electrocardiogram. The extracted time-domain and frequency domain features for the EEG, $T^N_{EEG} \in \mathbb{R}^{|T_{EEG}|}$ and the ECG signal, $T_{ECG} \in \mathbb{R}^{|T_{ECG}|}$, are afterwards concatenated to a single feature vector $V \in \mathbb{R}^{N \cdot (|T_{EEG}|) + |T_{ECG}|}$ representing each of the epochs.

During the training phase of the seizure detector a dataset of feature vectors with known class labels (labeled manually from medical experts) are used to train a binary model (two classes: seizure vs. non-seizure). At the test phase the existing seizure model is used in order to decide for each epoch's feature vector the corresponding class. Post-processing of the automatically detected labels can be performed for improving the performance of the architecture.

3   Experimental Setup

The online seizure detection module was evaluated on data collected within the ARMOR project. Specifically, data were collected in the Department of Clinical Neurophysiology from 3 patients (IDs 07, 08 and 09) with diagnosed idiopathic generalized epilepsy manifested with absences. Patients were recruited from the St Thomas' epilepsy clinic and they were investigated with sleep video EEG after partial sleep deprivation, with extended, prolonged recording on awakening with one or multiple sessions of hyperventilation to reveal possible absences. All three patients had one or more clinical events of absences during the recording that were captured by the video EEG. The EEG (21 electrodes) and ECG data were recorded with sampling frequency equal to 500 Hz and the recordings were manually annotated by neurological experts.

During pre-processing the time-synchronized EEG and ECG recordings were frame blocked to epochs of 1 second length, without time-overlap between successive epochs. For each epoch the following features were extracted: (i) time-domain features: minimum value, maximum value, mean, variance, standard deviation, percentiles (25%, 50%-median and 75%), interquartile range, mean absolute deviation, range, skewness, kyrtosis, energy, Shannon's entropy, logarithmic energy entropy, number of positive and negative peaks, zero-crossing rate, and (ii) frequency-domain features: 6-th order autoregressive-filter (AR) coefficients, power spectral density, frequency with maximum and minimum amplitude, spectral entropy, delta-theta-alpha-beta-gamma band energy, discrete wavelet transform coefficients with mother wavelet function Daubechies 16 and decomposition level equal to 8, thus resulting to a feature vector of dimensionality equal to 55 for each of the 21 EEG channels, i.e. 1155 in total. For the ECG channel the following features were estimated: the heart rate absolute value (based on R-peak detection algorithm, implemented as in [13]) and variability statistics of the heart rate, i.e. minimum value, maximum value, mean, variance, standard deviation, percentiles (25%, 50% and 75%), interquartile range, mean absolute deviation, range, thus resulting to a feature vector of dimensionality equal to 12. The dimensionality of the overall feature vector V is 1155+12=1167.

Binary seizure detection models were trained. Specifically, we relied on the support vector machines (SVMs), implemented with the sequential minimal optimization method and polynomial kernel function, a backpropagation multilayer perceptron (MLP) neural network, the k-nearest neighbor (IBK) algorithm and the C4.5 decision tree. All online seizure detection models were implemented using the WEKA machine learning toolkit software [14].

4   Experimental Results

The online seizure detection module described in Section 2 was evaluated following the experimental setup described in Section 3. The recorded data, which consisted of three subjects (sub-07 subj-08 and sub-09) was used for evaluating subject-dependent seizure detection models, i.e. the evaluated training and test data subsets consisted of one subject in each experiment. In order to avoid overlap between the training and the test data ten-fold cross validation was followed. The detection accuracies for the online module for the subjects 07, 08 and 09 are shown in Table 1. The accuracies are presented in percentages and the non-seizure state is denoted as clear.

Table 1. Seizure detection accuracy (in percentages) for the four evaluated algorithms and for the three subjects

Subject	SVM	MLP	C4.5	IBk
sub-07	96.11	92.93	81.91	91.67
sub-08	88.81	82.37	76.02	80.61
sub-09	92.48	87.50	79.34	84.86

As can be seen in Table 1, the best performing algorithm is the SVMs followed by the MLP across all subjects. The C4.5 decision tree achieved the lower seizure detection accuracy for all subjects. Specifically, the detection accuracy per epoch for the best performing SVM algorithm varies from approximately 96% to 88%, while the second more accurate algorithm, i.e. the MLP, presents accuracy from approximately 93% to 88% for the subjects 07-09 respectively. The significantly higher seizure detection accuracy of the best performing SVM algorithm (approximately 3% comparing to the second-best MLP algorithm, more than 10% higher than the C4.5) is mainly owed to the advantage of it when processing feature vectors of high dimensionality. The 1167 length of the feature vector in combination with the limited amount of evaluation data offers advantage to the support vector machine based model, due to the curse of dimensionality effect [14].

The accuracy performance across the three subjects varies approximately 4% for the best performing SVM algorithm. It is worth mentioning that the duration of each idiopathic generalized seizure occurrence was approximately 4 successive epochs, while the available seizure occurrences for subject 08 were significantly fewer than the ones of subject 07, which presented the best seizure detection performance. Although direct comparison with other studies is not possible due to the different specifications of each dataset, the achieved seizure recognition accuracy is competitive to the performance reported in the literature, which in most experimental setups varies from 80% to 95% [1, 5, 6, 7].

In a second step, we applied a post-processing smoothing window filter to the recognized labels of each frame (epoch). This post-processing aims at eliminating sporadic erroneous labeling of the current frame and contributes for improving the overall recognition accuracy. A simple and computationally effective rule for post-processing is smoothing each decision (or score) with respect to its closest neighbors. In particular, when the N preceding and the N successive frames are classified to one of the two classes (seizure or clear) then the current frame is also (re)labeled as of this class. The length w of the smoothing window is subject to investigation and in the general case is equal to $w=2N+1$, where $N \geq 0$. The case $N=0$ corresponds to eliminating the post-processing of the classified labels, while the cases $N=1, 2$ correspond to window size $w=3, 5$. The effect of the smoothing window in the online seizure recognition performance for the best performing SVM algorithm is shown in Table 2.

Table 2. Seizure detection accuracy (in percentages) for the best-performing SVM model and post-processing with different window size

Subject	$w=1$	$w=3$	$w=5$
sub-07	96.11	96.84	92.07
sub-08	88.81	89.45	83.23
sub-09	92.48	93.20	88.44

As can be seen in Table 2, the effect of a smoothing window for $w=3$ (i.e. for $N=1$) improved the detection accuracy for all evaluated subjects. However, the use of smoothing windows with bigger length significantly reduced the performance. The optimal size of the smoothing window will depend on the specifications of the data, which in our case for the seizure events are approximately 4 successive epochs.

5   Conclusion

In this paper, we examined the performance of a seizure detection module for online monitoring of epileptic patients, as part of a framework for monitoring of epileptic patients. The module is using as input data streams from electroencephalographic and electrocardiographic recordings. The architecture of the module consists of time and frequency domain feature extraction followed by classification. Four classification algorithms were evaluated on three epileptic subjects. The best performance was achieved by the support vector machine algorithm, which more than 90% for two of the subjects and slightly lower than 90% for the third subject. The use of a post-processing smoothing filter on the recognized labels showed that slight improvement of the overall performance can be achieved.

Acknowledgement. The reported research was partially supported by the ARMOR Project (FP7-ICT-2011-5.1 - 287720) "Advanced multi-paRametric Monitoring and analysis for diagnosis and Optimal management of epilepsy and Related brain disorders", co-funded by the European Commission under the Seventh' Framework Programme.

References

1. Shoeb, A., Edwards, H., Connolly, J., Bourgeois, B., Treves, S.T., Guttag, J.: Patient-specific seizure onset detection. Epilepsy Behav. 5(4), 483–498 (2004)
2. Corsini, J., Shoker, L., Sanei, S., Alarcón, G.: Epileptic seizure predictability from scalp EEG incorporating constrained blind source separation. IEEE Trans. Biomed. Eng. 53(5), 790–799 (2006)
3. Hunyadi, B., Signoretto, M., Van Paesschen, W., Suykens, J.A., Van Huffel, S., De Vos, M.: Incorporating structural information from the multichannel EEG improves patient-specific seizure detection. Clin. Neurophysiol. 123(12), 2352–2361 (2012)
4. Valderrama, M., Nikolopoulos, S., Adam, C., Navarro, V., Le Van Quyen, M.: Patient-specific seizure prediction using a multi-feature and multi-modal EEG-ECG classification. In: XII Med. Conf. on Medical and Biological Engineering and Computing, vol. 29, pp. 77–80 (2010)
5. Mohseni, H.R., Maghsoudi, A., Shamsollahi, M.B.: Seizure detection in EEG signals: A comparison of different approaches. In: Conf. Proc. IEEE Eng. Med. Biol. Soc., pp. 6724–6727 (2006)
6. Nasehi, S., Pourghassem, H.: Seizure Detection Algorithms Based on Analysis of EEG and ECG Signals: A Survey. Neurophysiology 44(2), 174–186 (2012)
7. Greene, B.R., Boylan, G.B., Reilly, R.B., de Chazal, P., Connolly, S.: Combination of EEG and ECG for improved automatic neonatal seizure detection. Clin. Neurophysiol. 118(6), 1348–1359 (2007)
8. Varon, C., Jansen, K., Lagae, L., Van Huffel, S.: Detection of epileptic seizures by means of morphological changes in the ECG,
   ftp://ftp.esat.kuleuven.be/pub/SISTA/cvaron/13-163.pdf
9. Zijlmans, M., Flanagan, D., Gotman, J.: Heart rate changes and ECG abnormalities during epileptic seizures: Prevalence and definition of an objective clinical sign. Epilepsia 43(8), 847–854 (2002)
10. Polat, K., Gunes, S.: Classification of epileptiform EEG using a hybrid system based on decision tree classifier and fast Fourier transform. Applied Mathematics and Computation 187(2), 1017–1026 (2007)
11. Fazle Rabbi, A., Fazel-Rezai, R.: A Fuzzy Logic System for Seizure Onset Detection in Intracranial EEG. Computational Intelligence and Neuroscience 2012, Article ID 705140, 12 (2012)
12. ARMOR project, http://www.armor-project.eu/
13. Sabarimalai, M., Soman, K.P.: A novel method for detecting R-peaks in electrocardiogram (ECG) signal. Biomedical Signal Processing and Control 7(2), 118–128 (2012)
14. Witten, H.I., Frank, E.: Data Mining: practical machine learning tools and techniques. Morgan Kaufmann Publishing

Towards Vagueness-Oriented Quality Assessment of Ontologies

Panos Alexopoulos[1] and Phivos Mylonas[2]

[1] iSOCO, Avda del Partenon 16-18, 28042, Madrid, Spain
palexopoulos@isoco.com
[2] Ionian University, Department of Informatics,
7 Tsirigoti Square, 49100, Corfu, Greece
fmylonas@ionio.gr

Abstract. Ontology evaluation has been recognized for a long time now as an important part of the ontology development lifecycle, and several methods, processes and metrics have been developed for that purpose. Nevertheless, vagueness is a quality dimension that has been neglected from most current approaches. Vagueness is a common human knowledge and linguistic phenomenon, typically manifested by terms and concepts that lack clear applicability conditions and boundaries such as *high*, *expert*, *bad*, *near* etc. As such, the existence of vague terminology in an ontology may hamper the latter's quality, primarily in terms of shareability and meaning explicitness. With that in mind, in this short paper we argue for the need of including vagueness in the ontology evaluation activity and propose a set of metrics to be used towards that goal.

1 Introduction

Ontologies are formal conceptualizations of domains, describing the meaning of domain-specific data in a common, machine-processable form by means of concepts and their interrelations [6]. Their primary function is to ensure that the meaning of data exchanged between and within systems is consistent and shared, both by humans and machines. Nevertheless, as a given ontology might not always be able to perform this function in a satisfactory way for the domain and/or application scenario at hand, a thorough evaluation of it should always precede its release and usage.

Several ontology evaluation approaches have been proposed during the past years. A typical categorization scheme for these approaches regards the process by which evaluation is performed. Thus, one may find approaches that compare the ontology to some "Gold Standard" ontology and measure the former's fitting degree to the latter [4], or approaches that do the same with data sources that are relevant to the domain an ontology is supposed to cover [5]. There are also evaluation approaches that use an ontology in some concrete application context and evaluate it along with the application [9] and, finally, approaches that have human users judging how well an ontology satisfies a set of predefined criteria and requirements [11]. At the same time, different evaluation approaches define

A. Likas, K. Blekas, and D. Kalles (Eds.): SETN 2014, LNAI 8445, pp. 448–453, 2014.

target different ontology dimensions. Thus, there are criteria and metrics related to the *content* of the ontology (e.g. what entities does it contain), its *structure* (e.g. how are entities related), its *usability* (e.g. how well documented it is) and its *functionality* (e.g. how well can it answer particular queries).

In this paper, we are interested in an ontology evaluation dimension, which, to the best of our knowledge, has not been considered in any existing evaluation framework, namely *vagueness*. Vagueness is a common human knowledge and language phenomenon, typically manifested by terms and concepts like *high, expert, bad, near* etc., and related to our inability to precisely determine the extensions of such concepts in certain domains and contexts. That is because vague concepts have typically blurred boundaries which do not allow for a sharp distinction between the entities that fall within their extension and those that do not [8]. For example, some people are borderline tall: not clearly *"tall"* and not clearly *"not tall"*.

In a previous paper, we have argued that the existence of vague terminology in ontologies and semantic data can affect in a negative way ontology comprehensibility and shareability and limit their value as a reusable source of knowledge [1]. The reason is the subjective interpretation of vague definitions that can cause **disagreements** among the people who develop, maintain or, most importantly, use a vague ontology. With that in mind, in this paper we focus on the problem of assessing if and to what extent vagueness is present in an ontology, as well as to what extent it hampers its quality, mainly in terms of meaning explicitness and shareability. To facilitate this assessment we define a set of vagueness-oriented ontology evaluation metrics and provide some guidelines for measuring them.

The structure of the rest of the paper is as follows. In the next section we explain in more detail the motivation behind our work while in section 3 we describe a set of vagueness-specific ontology evaluation criteria and metrics as well as guidelines for their assessment/measurement. Section 4 describes the process and results of applying the framework for the evaluation of actual ontologies and, finally, section 5 summarizes our work and outlines its future directions.

2 Motivation

The existence of vague terminology in ontologies and semantic data has already been identified by the community [3] [1], as well as the potential negative effects it may have on ontology comprehensibility and shareability [1] The reason is the subjective interpretation of vague definitions that can cause **disagreements** among the people who develop, maintain or, most importantly, use a vague ontology.

Such a situation, for example, arose in a real life application scenario where, while trying to develop an electricity market ontology for an energy-related electronic marketplace, we faced significant difficulties in defining concepts like *"Critical System Process"*, *"Strategic Market Participant"* or *"High Profit Margin"*. The reason was that when, for example, we asked our domain experts to provide exemplar instances of critical processes, there were certain processes for which there was a dispute among the experts about whether they should be regarded as critical or not. As it turned out, the source of the problem was not only that different domain experts had different criteria of process criticality, but also that no one could really decide which of those criteria were sufficient to classify a process as critical. In other words, the problem was the vagueness of the predicate *"critical"*, manifested by the existence of borderline cases regarding its applicability.

More generally, as we have shown in [1], vagueness in ontologies can cause problems in scenarios involving i) the structuring of data with a vague ontology (where disagreements among experts on the validity of vague statements may occur), ii) the utilization of vague facts in ontology-based systems (where reasoning results might not meet users' expectations) and iii) the integration of vague semantic information (where the merging of particular vague elements can lead to semantic data that will not be valid for all its users).

3   Vagueness Metrics for Ontologies

3.1   Vagueness Spread

In an ontology the elements that may be vague are typically concepts, relations, attributes and datatypes. A concept is vague if, in the given domain, context or application scenario, it admits borderline cases, namely if there are (or could be) individuals for which it is indeterminate whether they instantiate the concept. Primary candidates for being vague are concepts that denote some phase or state (e.g., *adult, child*) as well as attributions, namely concepts that reflect qualitative states of entities (e.g., *red, big, broken* etc.).

Similarly, a relation is vague if there are (or could be) pairs of individuals for which it is indeterminate whether they stand in the relation. The same applies for attributes and pairs of individuals and literal values. Finally, a vague datatype consists of a set of vague terms which may be used within the ontology as attribute values. For example, the attribute *performance*, which normally takes as values integer numbers, may also take as values terms like *very poor, poor, mediocre, good* and *excellent*. Primary candidates for generating such terms are gradable attributes such as size or height which give rise to terms such as *large, tall, short* etc.

Given the above, the first vagueness-related metric we propose for an ontology is **Vagueness Spread (VS)**, namely the ratio of the number of ontological elements (classes, relations and datatypes) that are vague (VOE), divided by the total number of elements (OE):

$$VS = \frac{|VOE|}{|OE|} \tag{1}$$

This metric practically reflects the extent to which vagueness is present in the ontology and it provides an indication of the ontology's potential comprehensibility and shareability; an ontology with a high value of vagueness spread is less explicit and shareable than an ontology with a low value.

Calculation of this metric is typically performed in a manual fashion by domain experts who need to identify the elements of the ontology that are vague. This can be done by analyzing the elements' definitions and deciding whether they admit borderline cases. Thus, for example, the definition of the ontology class *"StrategicClient"* as *"A client that has a high value for the company"* is vague while the definition of *"AmericanCompany"* as *''A company that has legal status in the Unites States"* is not. As part of our ongoing work, we are in the process of developing a vague sense classifier that may be help domain experts detect vague ontological definitions in a semi-automatic fashion; nevertheless this is to be reported in a future work.

3.2   Vagueness Explicitness

A vague ontology element that is explicitly identified and documented as such, is more usable than one that's not. The reason is that without such an explicit characterization, ontology users may not realize the fact that the element is vague and use it, thus risking the potential consequences mentioned in the introduction.

Therefore, a second metric we propose is **Vagueness Explicitness (VE)**, namely the ratio of the number of vague ontological elements that are explicitly identified as such (EVOE), divided by the total number of vague elements (VOE):

$$VE = \frac{|EVOE|}{|VOE|} \tag{2}$$

Obviously, the higher the value of this metric is, the better is the ontology. As far as its calculation is concerned, this is done also in a manual fashion by checking the elements' definitions.

3.3   Vagueness Intensity

As suggested in the introduction, vague ontology elements can be problematic because of the disagreement they may cause among the ontology's users. The higher this disagreement is, the more problems the element is likely to cause. Thus, another vagueness-related metric we define is **Vagueness Intensity (VI)**, namely the degree to which the ontology's users disagree on the validity of the (potential) instances of the ontology elements. The exact formula for this metric depends on the way one decides to measure user agreement. Our proposed approach is to i) consider a sample set of vague element instances, ii) ask from a group of potential ontology users to denote whether and to what extent they believe these instances are valid and iii) Measure the inter-agreement between users using Cohen's Kappa (if users simply say "Agree" or "Disagree") or its weighted version (if users rate their agreement in some scale) [10]. For example, the value of kappa for judges who either agree or disagree to a vague statement's validity is given as follows:

$$\kappa = \frac{Pr(a) - Pr(e)}{1 - Pr(e)} \tag{3}$$

where $Pr(\alpha)$ is the proportion of times the judges agree and $Pr(e)$ is the proportion of times they are expected to agree by chance alone. Complete agreement corresponds to $\kappa = 1$, and lack of agreement (i.e. purely random coincidences of rates) to $\kappa = 0$. Then, the value of VI for a set of S vague statements is the average of the disagreements for each statement, namely:

$$VI = \frac{1}{|S|} \sum_{s \in S} (1 - \kappa_s) \qquad (4)$$

4   Vagueness Evaluation Examples

To illustrate how our proposed metrics can be applied in practice, we applied them to two concrete ontologies. The first was the Citation Typing Ontology (or CiTO[1]), a publicly available ontology that enables characterization of the nature or type of citations, both factually and rhetorically, permitting these descriptions to be published on the Web. CiTO consists primarily of relations, many of which are vague (e.g., relations *plagiarizes* and *citesAsAuthority*). In order to measure the vagueness spread of the particular ontology we had two domain experts manually identify the elements that were vague. In the end, we got 27 vague elements and 17 non-vague, resulting in a VS of 0.61. Vagueness explicitness, in turn, was 0, practically because none of the vague elements were identified as such. Finally, vagueness intensity is derived from a CiTO usage experiment [7] where the authors measured the kappa value for 5 raters over 104 relation instances and obtained a kappa value of 0.16.

The second ontology was an enterprise ontology, developed in the context of a decision support system for tender call evaluation [2]. This ontology defined basic concepts and relations regarding an enterprise's internal and external environment (e.g. *Business Function*, *Employee*, *Client*, etc.), several of which were vague (e.g. *Competitor*, *High Potential Employee*, etc.). Vagueness spread in this case was lower than CiTO, (0.25) but its intensity (which we measured by having members of the enterprise assess the validity of sample instances of the vague elements) was significant (0.75). Finally, vagueness explicitness was 1.0, practically because we had developed the ontology ourselves, making sure that vagueness was properly documented.

Table 1. Correspondence of Metamodel Elements to Required Vagueness Aspects

Ontology	VS	VE	VI
CiTO	0.61	0.0	0.84
Enterprise Ontology	0.25	1.0	0.75

---

[1] http://purl.org/spar/cito/

5   Conclusions and Future Work

In this work we considered the phenomenon of vagueness and discussed its role in the ontology evaluation process. We introduced three novel metrics, i.e., Vagueness Spread (VS), Vagueness Explicitness (VE) and Vagueness Intensity (VI) that may be used in recognizing and calculating vagueness early enough within an ontology structure, thus aiding towards its quality optimization. Among our future work is to automate the vague element identification process as well as to apply the metrics to a larger number of publicly available ontologies and semantic datasets.

References

1. Alexopoulos, P., Villazon Terrazas, D., Pan, J.Z.: Towards vagueness-aware semantic data. In: URSW. CEUR Workshop Proceedings, vol. 1073, pp. 40–45. CEUR-WS.org (2013)
2. Alexopoulos, P., Wallace, M., Kafentzis, K., Thomopoulos, A.: A fuzzy knowledge-based decision support system for tender call evaluation. In: Iliadis, Maglogiann, Tsoumakasis, Vlahavas, Bramer (eds.) AIAI. IFIP, vol. 296, pp. 51–59. Springer, Heidelberg (2009)
3. Bobillo, F., Straccia, U.: Fuzzy ontology representation using owl 2. International Journal of Approximate Reasoning 52(7), 1073–1094 (2011)
4. Brank, J., Madenic, D., Groblenik, M.: Gold standard based ontology evaluation using instance assignment. In: Proceedings of the 4th Workshop on Evaluating Ontologies for the Web (EON 2006), Edinburgh, Scotland (May 2006)
5. Brewster, C., Alani, H., Dasmahapatra, S., Wilks, Y.: Data-driven ontology evaluation. In: Proceedings of the Language Resources and Evaluation Conference (LREC 2004), pp. 164–168. European Language Resources Association, Lisbon (2004)
6. Chandrasekaran, B., Josephson, J., Benjamins, R.: What are ontologies and why do we need them? IEEE Intelligent Systems 14(1), 20–26 (1999)
7. Ciancarini, P., Iorio, A.D., Nuzzolese, A.G., Peroni, S., Vitali, F.: Characterising citations in scholarly articles: An experiment. In: AIC@AI*IA. CEUR Workshop Proceedings, vol. 1100, pp. 124–129. CEUR-WS.org (2013)
8. Hyde, D.: Vagueness, Logic and Ontology. Ashgate New Critical Thinking in Philosophy (2008)
9. Porzel, R., Malaka, R.: A task-based approach for ontology evaluation. In: Proceedings of ECAI 2004 Workshop on Ontology Learning and Population, Valencia, Spain (August 2004)
10. Sim, J., Wright, C.C.: The kappa statistic in reliability studies: Use, interpretation, and sample size requirements. Physical Therapy (March 2005)
11. Tartir, S., Arpinar, I.B., Moore, M., Sheth, A.P., Aleman-Meza, B.: OntoQA: Metric-based ontology quality analysis. In: Proceedings of IEEE Workshop on Knowledge Acquisition from Distributed, Autonomous, Semantically Heterogeneous Data and Knowledge Sources (2005)

Vertex Incremental Path Consistency
for Qualitative Constraint Networks*

Michael Sioutis and Jean-François Condotta

Université Lille-Nord de France, Artois, CRIL-CNRS UMR 8188, Lens, France
{sioutis,condotta}@cril.fr

Abstract. The Interval Algebra (IA) and a subset of the Region Connection Calculus, namely, RCC-8, are the dominant Artificial Intelligence approaches for representing and reasoning about qualitative temporal and topological relations respectively. Such qualitative information can be formulated as a Qualitative Constraint Network (QCN). In this framework, one of the main tasks is to compute the path consistency of a given QCN. We propose a new algorithm that applies path consistency in a vertex incremental manner. Our algorithm enforces path consistency on an initial path consistent QCN augmented by a new temporal or spatial entity and a new set of constraints, and achieves better performance than the state-of-the-art approach. We evaluate our algorithm experimentally with QCNs of RCC-8 and show the efficiency of our approach.

1 Introduction

Spatial and temporal reasoning is a major field of study in Artificial Intelligence; particularly in Knowledge Representation. This field is essential for a plethora of areas and domains that include dynamic GIS, cognitive robotics, spatiotemporal design, and reasoning and querying with semantic geospatial query languages [3, 6, 8]. The Interval Algebra (IA) [1, 2] and a subset of the Region Connection Calculus [9], namely, RCC-8, are the dominant Artificial Intelligence approaches for representing and reasoning about qualitative temporal and topological relations respectively.

The state-of-the-art technique to decide whether a set of IA or RCC-8 relations is *path consistent* [13], considers the underlying complete graph of the respective constraint network all at once. However, due to the recent work of Huang [5] who showed that given a path consistent IA or RCC-8 network one can extend it arbitrarily with the addition of new temporal or spatial entities respectively, we could as well decide the path consistency of a constraint network by beginning with a subnetwork comprising a single temporal or spatial entity and extending it with a new entity at each step. This would allow us to work with a smaller underlying graph for each addition of a temporal or spatial entity, as opposed to considering the underlying graph of the entire constraint network for all entities.

---

* This work was funded by a PhD grant from Université d'Artois and region Nord-Pas-de-Calais.

A. Likas, K. Blekas, and D. Kalles (Eds.): SETN 2014, LNAI 8445, pp. 454–459, 2014.

The latter case is well described in the work of Gerevini [4, chapt. 3] for qualitative temporal reasoning who applies path consistency in an edge incremental manner obtaining a time complexity of $O(n^2 \cdot (n-1)) = O(n^3)$, where n is the number of the temporal entities. In short, to decide the path consistecy of a constraint network of n entities, edge incremental path consistency considers $O(n^2)$ constraints and for each contraint applies path consistency on the underlying complete graph of the network which is of degree $n-1$. The edge incremental path consistency described in the work of Gerevini, has been established as the state-of-the-art path consistency approach up to now. We will often refer to it simply as one-shot path consistency, since it can be performed in a single appliance of a path consistency algorithm that uses a queue initialized with all $O(n^2)$ constraints to reason with a network of n entities. Our approach is different and complementary to that of Gerevini, in that we process the constraint network in a vertex incremental manner, deciding or maintaining its path consistency bit by bit. To construct a path consistent network of n temporal or spatial entities, we apply path consistency $n-1$ times, one for every temporal or spatial entity that is added in the initial single-entity subnetwork. At each appliance, the underlying complete graph of the subnetwork along with the new entity has degree 1, ..., $n-1$ respectively, and the new entity also brings $O(1)$, ..., $O(n-1)$ constraints respectively, resulting in $O(1 \cdot 1 + \ldots + (n-1) \cdot (n-1))$ operations. Thus, we increase on average the performance of the path consistency algorithm, but do not improve its worst-case complexity which remains $O(n^3)$. In this paper, we make the following contributions: (i) we present an algorithm that maintains or decides the path consistency of an initial path consistent constraint network augmented by a new temporal or spatial entity and its accompanying constraints, and (ii) we implement our algorithm and evaluate it experimentally with QCNs of RCC-8, showing the efficiency of our approach.

2   Preliminaries

A (binary) qualitative temporal or spatial constraint language [11] is based on a finite set B of *jointly exhaustive and pairwise disjoint* (JEPD) relations defined on a domain D, called the set of base relations. The set of base relations B of a particular qualitative constraint language can be used to represent definite knowledge between any two entities with respect to the given level of granularity. B contains the identity relation Id, and is closed under the converse operation $(^{-1})$. Indefinite knowledge can be specified by unions of possible base relations, and is represented by the set containing them. Hence, 2^B will represent the set of relations. 2^B is equipped with the usual set-theoretic operations (union and intersection), the converse operation, and the weak composition operation. The converse of a relation is the union of the converses of its base relations. The weak composition $\diamond$ of two relations s and t for a set of base relations B is defined as the strongest relation $r \in 2^B$ which contains $s \circ t$, or formally, $s \diamond t = \{b \in B \mid b \cap (s \circ t) \neq \emptyset\}$, where $s \circ t = \{(x,y) \mid \exists z : (x,z) \in s \wedge (z,y) \in t\}$ is the relational composition. As illustration, consider the qualitative temporal constraint language IA [2],

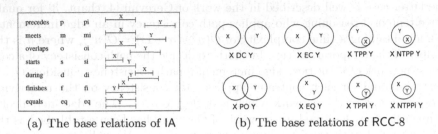

(a) The base relations of IA   (b) The base relations of RCC-8

Fig. 1. IA and RCC-8 constraint languages

and the qualitative spatial constraint language RCC-8 [9]. The set of base relations of IA is the set $\{eq, p, pi, m, mi, o, oi, s, si, d, di, f, fi\}$. These thirteen relations represent the possible relations between *time intervals*, as depicted in Figure 1a. The set of base relations of RCC-8 is the set $\{dc, ec, po, tpp, ntpp, tppi, ntppi, eq\}$. These eight relations represent the binary topological relations between *regions* that are non-empty regular subsets of some topological space, as depicted in Figure 1b (for the $2D$ case). IA and RCC-8 networks are qualitative constraint networks (QCNs), with relation eq being the identity relation in both cases.

Definition 1. *A RCC-8, or IA, network is a pair $\mathcal{N} = (V, C)$ where V is a finite set of variables and C a mapping associating a relation $C(v, v') \in 2^B$ to each pair (v, v') of $V \times V$. C is such that $C(v, v) \subseteq \{eq\}$ and $C(v, v') = (C(v', v))^{-1}$.*

Given a QCN $\mathcal{N} = (V, C)$ and a new temporal or spatial entity α accompanied by mapping C' that associates a relation $C(\alpha, v) \in 2^B$ to each pair (α, v) of $\{\alpha\} \times V$, $\mathcal{N} \uplus \alpha$ denotes the QCN $\mathcal{N}'' = (V'', C'')$, where $V'' = V \cup \{\alpha\}$, and C'' is a mapping that associates a relation $C(v, v') \in 2^B$ to each pair (v, v') of $V \times V$ and a relation $C(\alpha, v) \in 2^B$ to each pair (α, v) of $\{\alpha\} \times V$. In what follows, $C(v_i, v_j)$ will be also denoted by C_{ij}. Checking the consistency of a QCN of IA or RCC-8 is $\mathcal{NP}$-hard in general [7, 12]. However, there exist large maximal tractable subsets of IA and RCC-8 which can be used to make reasoning much more efficient even in the general $\mathcal{NP}$-hard case. These maximal tractable subsets are the sets $\hat{\mathcal{H}}_8, \mathcal{C}_8$, and $\mathcal{Q}_8$ for RCC-8 [10] and $\mathcal{H}_{IA}$ for IA [7]. Consistency checking is then realised by a path consistency algorithm that iteratively performs the following operation until a fixed point $\overline{C}$ is reached: $\forall i, j, k$ do $C_{ij} \leftarrow C_{ij} \cap (C_{ik} \diamond C_{kj})$, where variables i, k, j form triangles that belong to the underlying complete graph of the input network [13]. If $C_{ij} = \emptyset$ for a pair (i, j) then C is inconsistent, otherwise $\overline{C}$ is *path consistent*. If the relations of the input QCN belong to some tractable subset of relations, path consistency implies consistency, otherwise a backtracking algorithm decomposes the initial relations into subrelations belonging to some tractable subset of relations spawning a branching search tree [14]. Thus, the performance of path consistency is crucial for the overall performance of a reasoner, since path consistency can be used to solve tractable networks, and can be run as the preprocessing and the consistency checking step of a backtracking algorithm.

3   iPC+ Algorithm

In this section we present a new algorithm that enforces path consistency in a vertex increment manner. We call our algorithm iPC+, where symbol + is only used to differentiate it from the edge incremental path consistency algorithm of Gerevini [4, chapt. 3], as we consider extensions of a given QCN with a new temporal or spatial entity accompanied by new sets of constraints.

Function iPC+($\mathcal{N} \uplus \alpha$)

    in   : A QCN $\mathcal{N} \uplus \alpha = (V'', C'')$, where $\mathcal{N} = (V, C)$ is the initial path consistent QCN augmented by a new temporal or spatial entity α.

    output : False if network $\mathcal{N} \uplus \alpha$ results in a trivial inconsistency (contains the empty relation), True if the modified network $\mathcal{N} \uplus \alpha$ is path consistent.

1 **begin**
2     $Q \leftarrow \{(i, j) \mid (i, j) \in V \times \{\alpha\}\}$;
3   **while** $Q \neq \emptyset$ **do**
4        $(i, j) \leftarrow Q.pop()$;
5   **foreach** $k \leftarrow 1$ **to** V'', $(i \neq k \neq j)$ **do**
6           $t \leftarrow C''_{ik} \cap (C''_{ij} \diamond C''_{jk})$;
7   **if** $t \neq C''_{ik}$ **then**
8   **if** $t = \emptyset$ **then return** False;
9              $C''_{ik} \leftarrow t$; $C''_{ki} \leftarrow t^{-1}$;
10              $Q \leftarrow Q \cup \{(i, k)\}$;
11           $t \leftarrow C''_{kj} \cap (C''_{ki} \diamond C''_{ij})$;
12   **if** $t \neq C''_{kj}$ **then**
13   **if** $t = \emptyset$ **then return** False;
14              $C''_{kj} \leftarrow t$; $C''_{jk} \leftarrow t^{-1}$;
15              $Q \leftarrow Q \cup \{(k, j)\}$;

16   **return** True;
17 **end**

---

iPC+ receives as input a QCN $\mathcal{N} \uplus \alpha = (V'', C'')$, where $\mathcal{N} = (V, C)$ is the initial path consistent QCN augmented by a new temporal or spatial entity α. The output of algorithm iPC+ is False if network $\mathcal{N} \uplus \alpha$ results in a trivial inconsistency, and True if the modified network $\mathcal{N} \uplus \alpha$ is path consistent. The queue data structure is instatiated by the set of edges $(i, j) \in V \times \{\alpha\}$ (line 2), i.e., the set of edges corresponding to the new temporal or spatial entity α. Path consistency is then realised by iteratively performing the following operation until a fixed point $\overline{C''}$ is reached: $\forall i, j, k$ perform $C''_{ij} \leftarrow C''_{ij} \cap (C''_{ik} \diamond C''_{kj})$, where edges $(i, k), (k, j) \in V'' \times V''$ (line 5).

Theorem 1. *For a given QCN $\mathcal{N} \uplus \alpha = (V'', C'')$ of RCC-8, or IA, where $\mathcal{N} = (V, C)$ is the initial path consistent QCN augmented by a new temporal or spatial entity α, function iPC+ decides the path consistency of QCN $\mathcal{N} \uplus \alpha$.*

If we start with a single-entity QCN and extend it one entity at a time applying iPC+ in total $n - 1$ times, it follows that we will obtain a time complexity of

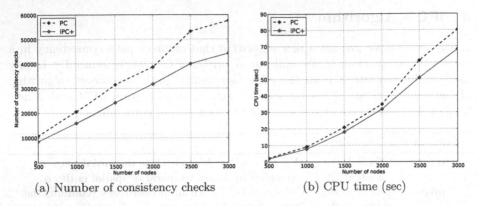

(a) Number of consistency checks   (b) CPU time (sec)

Fig. 2. Performance of iPC+ and PC for QCNs of RCC-8

$O(1 \cdot 1 + \ldots + (n-1) \cdot (n-1)) = O(1/6 \cdot (n-1) \cdot n \cdot (2n-1))$ for constructing a QCN of n temporal or spatial entities, which is an improvement on average over the strict $O(n^3)$ complexity of the one-shot path consistency algorithm (PC).

4   Experimental Evaluation

We generated random RCC-8 networks using the $A(n, d, l)$ model [13]. In short, model $A(n, d, l)$ creates random networks of size n, degree d, and an average number l of RCC-8 relations per edge. We considered network sizes between 500 and 3000 with a 500 step and $l = 4$ $(= |B|/2)$ relations per edge. For each size series we created 70 networks that span over a degree d between 8.0 and 11.0 with a 0.5 step, i.e., 10 network instances were generated for each degree. For model $A(n, d, l)$, a degree d between 8 and 11 belongs to the phase transition of RCC-8 relations, and, hence, guarantees hard and more time consuming, in terms of solubility, instances for the path consistency algorithm [13]. The experiments were carried out on a computer with an Intel Core 2 Duo P7350 processor with a CPU frequency of 2.00 GHz, 4 GB RAM, and the Lucid Lynx x86_64 OS (Ubuntu Linux). The python implementations of iPC+ and PC, were run with the CPython interpreter (http://www.python.org/), which implements Python 2. Only one of the CPU cores was used for the experiments. Regarding iPC+, we begin with a single node and grow the network one node at a time.[1]

A *consistency check* takes place whenever we apply the intersection operator (∩) between two constraints (lines 6 and 11). This parameter is critical as the consistency check operation lies in the core of a path consistency algorithm. Results on the average number of consistency checks that each algorithm performs are shown in Figure 2a. On average, iPC+ performs 22.5% less consistency checks than PC, and 23.2% less in the final step in particular, where the networks of 3000 nodes are considered. Let us now see how all these numbers translate to CPU time. A diagrammatic comparison on the CPU time for each algorithm is

---

[1] All tools and datasets used here can be acquired upon request from the authors or found online in the following address: http://www.cril.fr/~sioutis/work.php

shown in Figure 2b. On average, iPC+ runs 14.4% faster than PC, and 15.0% faster in the final step in particular (68 sec for iPC+ and 80 sec for PC), where the networks of 3000 nodes are considered. Similar results were obtained for IA that we omit to present here due to space constraints.

5 Conclusion and Future Work

In this paper we presented an algorithm, viz., iPC+, for maintaining or deciding the path consistency of an initial path consistent constraint network augmented by a new temporal or spatial entity and its accompanying constraints. Experimental evaluation with QCNs of RCC-8 showed that iPC+ is able to perform better than PC for random networks of model $A(n, d, l)$. Future work consists of evaluating our approach more thoroughly with structured and real datasets, and using chordal graphs to obtain a vertex incremental *partial* path consistency variant of our algorithm.

References

1. Allen, J.F.: An Interval-Based Representation of Temporal Knowledge. In: IJCAI (1981)
2. Allen, J.F.: Maintaining knowledge about temporal intervals. CACM 26, 832–843 (1983)
3. Bhatt, M., Guesgen, H., Wölfl, S., Hazarika, S.: Qualitative Spatial and Temporal Reasoning: Emerging Applications, Trends, and Directions. Spatial Cognition & Computation 11, 1–14 (2011)
4. Gerevini, A.: Incremental qualitative temporal reasoning: Algorithms for the point algebra and the ord-horn class. Artif. Intell. 166(1-2), 37–80 (2005)
5. Huang, J.: Compactness and its implications for qualitative spatial and temporal reasoning. In: KR (2012)
6. Koubarakis, M., Kyzirakos, K.: Modeling and Querying Metadata in the Semantic Sensor Web: The Model stRDF and the Query Language stSPARQL. In: Aroyo, L., Antoniou, G., Hyvönen, E., ten Teije, A., Stuckenschmidt, H., Cabral, L., Tudorache, T. (eds.) ESWC 2010, Part I. LNCS, vol. 6088, pp. 425–439. Springer, Heidelberg (2010)
7. Nebel, B.: Solving Hard Qualitative Temporal Reasoning Problems: Evaluating the Efficiency of Using the ORD-Horn Class. In: ECAI (1996)
8. Open Geospatial Consortium: OGC GeoSPARQL - A geographic query language for RDF data. OGC® Implementation Standard (2012)
9. Randell, D.A., Cui, Z., Cohn, A.: A Spatial Logic Based on Regions and Connection. In: KR (1992)
10. Renz, J.: Maximal Tractable Fragments of the Region Connection Calculus: A Complete Analysis. In: IJCAI (1999)
11. Renz, J., Ligozat, G.: Weak Composition for Qualitative Spatial and Temporal Reasoning. In: van Beek, P. (ed.) CP 2005. LNCS, vol. 3709, pp. 534–548. Springer, Heidelberg (2005)
12. Renz, J., Nebel, B.: Spatial Reasoning with Topological Information. In: Freksa, C., Habel, C., Wender, K.F. (eds.) Spatial Cognition 1998. LNCS (LNAI), vol. 1404, pp. 351–371. Springer, Heidelberg (1998)
13. Renz, J., Nebel, B.: Efficient Methods for Qualitative Spatial Reasoning. JAIR 15, 289–318 (2001)
14. Renz, J., Nebel, B.: Qualitative Spatial Reasoning Using Constraint Calculi. In: Handbook of Spatial Logics, pp. 161–215 (2007)

Being Logical or Going with the Flow?
A Comparison of Complex Event Processing Systems

Elias Alevizos and Alexander Artikis

National Centre for Scientific Research (NCSR) "Demokritos", Athens 15310, Greece
{alevizos.elias,a.artikis}@iit.demokritos.gr

Abstract. Complex event processing (CEP) is a field that has drawn significant attention in the last years. CEP systems treat incoming information as flows of time-stamped events which may be structured according to some underlying pattern. Their goal is to extract in real-time those patterns or even learn the patterns which could lead to certain outcomes. Many CEP systems have already been implemented, sometimes with significantly different approaches as to how they represent and handle events. In this paper, we compare the widely used Esper system which employs a SQL-based language, and RTEC which is a dialect of the Event Calculus.

1 Introduction

As the number of possible sources of information which can feed a system with real-time data increases, so does the need for distributed systems with the ability to efficiently handle flows of data. The most typical scenario is one in which a network of sensors has been installed, with each sensor sending its readings to a (possibly distributed) processing system. The system's goal is to detect (or even learn) in real-time certain patterns present in the incoming data flows, so that the appropriate preventive or reinforcing action be taken. Domains in which such systems could prove helpful are network intrusion detection, traffic management and environmental monitoring, to name but a few.

The usual Database Management Systems (DBMS) have certain features, like the requirement for storing before processing or that of asynchronous processing, which prevent them from being directly transferred to the problem of stream processing and pattern matching. During the last decade, a significant number of the so-called complex event processing (CEP) systems have appeared that attempt to overcome the limitations of typical DBMSs [5], [6]. A CEP system attempts to inverse the human-active database-passive (HADP) interaction model of traditional DBMSs. Instead, its goal is to notify its users "immediately" upon the detection of a pattern of interest. Data flows are seen as streams of events, some of which may be irrelevant for the user's purposes. Therefore, the main focus is on the efficient filtering out of irrelevant data and processing of the relevant. Obviously, for such systems to be acceptable, they have to satisfy certain efficiency and accuracy constraints, such as low latency and robustness.

A. Likas, K. Blekas, and D. Kalles (Eds.): SETN 2014, LNAI 8445, pp. 460–474, 2014.

Numerous CEP systems have already been implemented, with very different approaches to event processing. In this paper we present an initial comparison of the widely used Esper system [1], which relies on a SQL-based language and Java, and the Event Calculus for Run-Time reasoning (RTEC) [2], a logic programming language for representing and reasoning about events and their effects. Both engines consume as their input a number of streams of low-level events, i.e. time-stamped, simple, derived events (SDE) which are themselves the product of previous computational stages on even more basic events, such as those coming from sensors. Based on these SDEs and their event representation language, the user can define the complex events (CE) of interest.

Our intention is not to build a full-scale and general benchmark for CEP systems. As of this time and to the best of our knowledge, there are no such standard benchmarks, although work towards this direction has recently appeared [10], [11]. We are rather focusing on gaining some insights with regards to the possible advantages and shortcomings of applying different event recognition approaches on a specific domain.

The rest of the paper is structured as follows. In Section 2 we present the main features of Esper and RTEC. Section 3 first describes a task for which RTEC has already been tested and then it illustrates how these systems express a class of event patterns for that task. In Section 4, the results from the comparison tests, in terms of similarity and performance, are presented and explained. Finally, in Section 5 we draw some conclusions from our tests and discuss some future work directions.

2   Complex Event Processing Engines

In this section, we briefly present the CEP engines that we investigate.

2.1   Esper

Among the currently available and well-known CEP engines, we have opted for Esper [1] (see [4], [9] and [13] for some application domains in which Esper has been used), since it is free, open-source and has already been the target of previous benchmark studies [10]. Esper is integrated into the Java and .NET languages and can be used in CEP applications as a library. For ease of understanding, one could conceptualize the Esper engine as a database turned upside-down. Traditional database systems work by storing incoming data in disks, according to a predefined relational schema. They can hold an exact history of previous insertions and updates are usually rare events. User queries are not known beforehand and there are no strict constraints as far as their latency is concerned. The Esper engine, on the other hand, lets users define from the very start the queries they are interested in, which act as filters for the streams of incoming data. Events satisfying the filtering criteria are detected in "real-time" and may be pushed further down the chain of filters for additional processing or published to their respective listeners/subscribers.

Esper provides a rich set of constructs by which events and event patterns can be expressed. One way to achieve event representation and handling is through the use of expression-based pattern matching. Patterns incorporate several operators, some of which may be time-based, and are applied to sequences of events. A new event matches the pattern expression whenever is satisfies its filtering criteria. Another method to process events is through the Event Processing Language (EPL) queries which resemble in their syntax that of the well-known SQL. The most usual SQL constructs may also be used in EPL statements. However, the defined queries are not applied to tables but to views, which can be understood as basic structures for holding events, according to certain user demands, e.g. the need for grouping based on certain keys or for applying queries to events up to certain time point in the past.

2.2   RTEC

The Event Calculus for Run-Time reasoning (RTEC) is a logic-based CEP engine that has been successfully used in Big Data applications [3], [2]. Moving away from traditional database-like constructs, it has been written in Prolog, having as its main goal to capture the expressivity of the Event Calculus [8]. The Event Calculus is a logic formalism which extends the expressive power of logic systems so that they can handle events taking place in time. By allowing for the temporal representation of "actions" (or events), a set of rules may be built which make reasoning about time intervals, events and their relationships possible.

RTEC uses a number of techniques for increased performance and scalability. For real-time operation, a windowing mechanism may be used in order to capture events that arrive with a certain delay. Intermediate results from computations are stored in "cache" memory so that their recomputation is avoided and an indexing mechanism tunes the engine to those events that are deemed relevant.

3   Complex Event Definition

The city of Helsinki, Finland, is currently trying to develop a recognition system to support city transport management. Each vehicle of the transport network is equipped with sensors that send measurements such as arrival and departure time from a stop, acceleration information, in-vehicle temperature and noise levels. Information extracted from the sensors constitutes the SDE streams for a CEP engine. Based on these SDEs, CEs are recognized related to the punctuality of a vehicle, passenger and driver comfort, passenger and driver safety and so on. RTEC has already been tested in the domain of city transport management. More details may be found in [2].

In order to compare Esper with RTEC, we translated the main RTEC features into EPL. RTEC provides its users with four basic constructs which allow them to define the required rules for their domain: simple fluents that are subject to the law of inertia, and statically determined fluents defined in terms of three interval manipulation constructs: union, intersection and complement. Our aim is to express the RTEC features into pure EPL statements, without resorting to any Java-implemented algorithms or data structures, except of course for those holding the input streams and managing the output data.

3.1   Law of Inertia

First, we give an example of how a simple fluent is defined in RTEC. The term $F = V$ denotes that fluent F has value V. For a simple fluent F, $F = V$ holds at time-point T if $F = V$ has been *initiated* by an event at some time-point earlier than T (using predicate initiatedAt), and has not been *terminated* in the meantime (using predicate terminatedAt), which implements the *law of inertia*. The occurrence of an event E at time T is modeled by the predicate happensAt(E, T). Interval-based semantics are obtained with the predicate holdsFor$(F = V, I)$, where I is a list of maximal intervals for which fluent F has value V continuously.

Based on the above predicates and the instantaneous SDEs (*enter_stop* and *leave_stop*) about arrival and departure times from a stop, the user can define the simple fluents for public transport vehicle punctuality with the following rules:

$$\text{initially}(punctuality(\_, \_) = punctual) \tag{1}$$

$$\begin{aligned}&\text{initiatedAt}(punctuality(Id, VehicleType) = punctual, \ T) \leftarrow \\ &\quad \text{happensAt}(enter\_stop(Id, VT, Stop, scheduled), \ \_)\end{aligned} \tag{2}$$

$$\begin{aligned}&\text{initiatedAt}(punctuality(Id, VehicleType) = punctual, \ T) \leftarrow \\ &\quad \text{happensAt}(enter\_stop(Id, VT, Stop, early), \ \_)\end{aligned} \tag{3}$$

$$\begin{aligned}&\text{initiatedAt}(punctuality(Id, VehicleType) = non\_punctual, \ T) \leftarrow \\ &\quad \text{happensAt}(enter\_stop(Id, VT, Stop, late), \ \_)\end{aligned} \tag{4}$$

$$\begin{aligned}&\text{initiatedAt}(punctuality(Id, VehicleType) = non\_punctual, \ T) \leftarrow \\ &\quad \text{happensAt}(leave\_stop(Id, VT, Stop, early), \ \_)\end{aligned} \tag{5}$$

where Id is the id of a vehicle, *VehicleType* may be a bus or a tram, *Stop* is the code of a stop, and '_' is an 'anonymous' Prolog variable.

All vehicles are initialized as being punctual. As new SDEs arrive, a vehicle becomes non punctual if it arrives late at a stop or leaves early. It becomes punctual again if it arrives early or on time at a stop. The maximal intervals for which a vehicle is considered continuously (non-) punctual are computed using the built-in/domain-independent RTEC predicate holdsFor from rules (1)–(5).

Initialization of the punctuality fluent (rule (1) in RTEC) is performed in Esper with a special *InitEvent* carrying the appropriate initial value. Rules (2)–(3) can be expressed in EPL with the following statement:

insert into $SFEvent$
select $se.vehicleId$ as $vehicleId$,
    0 as $sfId$,
    $createHash(vehicleId, 0)$ as $hash$,
    $se.timestamp$ as $timestamp$,
    $punctual$ as $sfValue$ (6)
from $StopEvent$ as se
where $se.eventType = eventbean.StopEventType.ENTER$ and
    $(se.punct = eventbean.Punctuality.EARLY$ or
    $se.punct = eventbean.Punctuality.SCHEDULED)$

The above statement "listens" to all the SDEs related to arrivals/departures to/from stops ($StopEvent$) and keeps only the arrival events ($se.eventType = eventbean.StopEventType.ENTER$) in which the vehicle is early or scheduled. When such an event is detected, it essentially notifies the system that the vehicle has become (or remains) punctual (as in rules (2) and (3)). After this initial filtering, the statement forwards the remaining events towards the simple fluent stream ($SFEvent$ in statements (6)–(7)). Each $SFEvent$ is also accompanied by an attribute called $sfValue$ which indicates the value of the detected event.

The statement for non punctuality, expressed in RTEC by rules (4)–(5), is written in EPL as:

insert into $SFEvent$
select $se.vehicleId$ as $vehicleId$,
    0 as $sfId$,
    $createHash(vehicleId, 0)$ as $hash$,
    $se.timestamp$ as $timestamp$,
    $non\_punctual$ as $sfValue$ (7)
from $StopEvent$ as se
where $(se.eventType = eventbean.StopEventType.ENTER$ and
    $se.punct = eventbean.Punctuality.LATE)$
    or
    $(se.eventType = eventbean.StopEventType.LEAVE$ and
    $se.punct = eventbean.Punctuality.EARLY)$

Due to space limitations we do not present here our domain-independent EPL code for computing the maximal intervals of simple fluents, given their starting and ending points. We briefly note that the computation method is relatively simple. A memory is maintained, holding the previously computed intervals as tuples in the form of [$startstamp$, $endstamp$, $sfValue$] and a current interval in the form of [$startstamp$, -1, $sfValue$], where -1 indicates a still open interval. Upon the arrival of a new interval, its $sfValue$ is compared against the $sfValue$ of the current interval. If they are equal, we ignore the new interval. If they are different, the current interval is closed, with the $timestamp$ of the new interval replacing -1. Afterwards, a new open interval is created, beginning with the *timestamp* and the *sfValue* of the last interval. When a new interval arrives delayed, certain extra checks have to be performed as well, which we omit here.

3.2   Interval Manipulation

We now turn our attention to the interval manipulation constructs of RTEC: union, intersection and complement. Among the patterns that we would like to detect within the context of city transport management is the case when a certain vehicle is being driven in a style that is deemed unsafe. The vehicle sensors feed the system with three relevant data streams, one that informs us about the intervals during which a vehicle takes a (very) sharp turn and two more for the intervals of (very) abrupt acceleration and deceleration. The city transport management domain experts define a driving style as unsafe when a vehicle takes a very sharp turn or is in a very abrupt acceleration or deceleration. The RTEC rule for this definition can therefore be written as follows:

$$\text{holdsFor}(driving\_style(Id, VehicleType) = unsafe, \ UDI) : -$$
$$\text{holdsFor}(sharp\_turn(Id, VehicleType) = very\_sharp, VSTI),$$
$$\text{holdsFor}(abrupt\_acceleration(Id, VehicleType) = very\_abrupt, VAAI), \quad (8)$$
$$\text{holdsFor}(abrupt\_deceleration(Id, VehicleType) = very\_abrupt, VADI),$$
$$\text{union\_all}([VSTI, VAAI, VADI], UDI)$$

where *Id* is the vehicle identifier, *VSTI* is the list of intervals for a very sharp turn, *VAAI* and *VADI* the lists of very abrupt acceleration and deceleration respectively and finally *UDI* is the list of intervals for unsafe driving, to be computed as the union of *VSTI*, *VAAI* and *VADI*. The holdsFor predicate can be used in order to define the required domain-dependent rules. *I* in union_all(L, I) is a list of maximal intervals that includes each time-point that is part of at least one list of *L*. Effectively, union is an implementation of OR over intervals. *sharp_turn*, *abrupt_acceleration* and *abrupt_deceleration* are streams of incoming SDEs.

Using the library that we developed for expressing the main RTEC features, rule (8) can be written:

$$
\begin{array}{l}
\text{insert into } UnionEvent \\
\text{select } ste.vehicleId \text{ as } vehicleId, \\
\quad 1 \text{ as } unionId, \\
\quad createHash(ste.vehicleId, 1) \text{ as } hash, \\
\quad ste.startstamp \text{ as } startstamp, \\
\quad ste.endstamp \text{ as } endstamp \\
\text{from } SharpTurnEvent \text{ as } ste \\
\text{where } ste.sharpness = eventbean.Sharpness.VERY\_SHARP
\end{array}
\quad (9)
$$

The above EPL statement consumes events from the stream of *sharp_turn* SDEs, keeps only those denoting a very sharp turn and feeds the resulting output into the stream of Union events. Of course, two similar statements should also be written for the *abrupt_acceleration* and *abrupt_deceleration* streams of SDEs. These three statements together would complete the definition for unsafe driving.

Until now, we have shown how domain-dependent RTEC rules can be expressed as domain-dependent EPL statements. It is worth commenting that RTEC rules can be expressed in a purely declarative and more compact way than EPL statements. Additionally, when writing EPL statements, the user needs to have at least some elementary knowledge of how events are represented.

3.3 EPL Library

In order to better understand the functionality of the *unionId* and *hash* attributes, we take a closer look at the internals of our application-independent EPL library. EPL can use such SQL-like statements to filter event streams and/or to push the results of filtering further down to other streams. Besides this basic functionality, EPL can also make use of the so-called views, which are similar to SQL tables and can hold multiple events. More complex operations can be performed on these views, such as aggregation and grouping. For our present purposes, we are interested in time-based views whose expiry policies (when to remove an event) employ time windows.

The RTEC constructs (inertia, interval union, intersection and relative complement) that were translated to EPL follow the same pattern for computing the maximal intervals of a fluent. For each RTEC construct, we maintain a memory holding the previously computed disjoint intervals up to certain time point in the past. Under the assumption that the incoming event intervals arrive in an orderly manner, such a memory would be redundant, since we would need to maintain only a single interval and update it, in case a new event overlaps with it or simply release it as a final result if there is no overlap. However, there are events which arrive delayed, affecting in this way the previously computed intervals. In order to be able to handle delayed events, we need to store the intermediate results, at least up to a certain time point. RTEC has a sliding window approach to deal with such delayed information. For the same reason, we need to use the time-based views provided by EPL. Whenever a new event arrives (for our union example, a *UnionEvent*, similarly for the other three constructs), we first check whether and how it affects any of the previously computed intervals. Any new insertions, deletions or updates are performed according to the results of this checking step.

An additional memory/view for storing intervals of previous events as well, besides the computed intervals, is required for the operations of intersection and complement. In these cases, the interval of a new event may not only interact with the previously computed intervals but with previous events too.

Consider, for example, intersection. I in intersect_all(L, I) of RTEC is a list of maximal intervals that includes each time-point that is part of all lists of L. In Esper, a new *IntersectionEvent* may not overlap at all with any of the stored intervals but we still cannot deduce that it should be ignored. An overlapping event may have appeared previously which, at the time of its appearance, had no effect and was not involved in the construction of an interval. On the other hand, the union operation is additive and the unionized intervals implicitly take into account all previous events. All time-points included in previous *UnionEvents* (in their intervals of [*startstamp*, *endstamp*)) are also to be found in the stored intervals and there is no need for additional memories.

For the union operation, the definition of its time-based view is shown in statement (10). This statement simply creates a view (*window*), based on the attributes of the *UnionEvent*. Its purpose is to store the currently computed intervals for the union operation. According to this statement alone, it has no expiry policy (.*win* : *keepall*()) and keeps all intervals until they are explicitly deleted.

This view is initially empty. Upon the arrival of a new *UnionEvent*, a merge operation is performed which is the equivalent of the SQL upsert (update and insert) operation. EPL statement (11) performs the merge operation.

The *where* clause of statement (11) compares all the stored intervals of the *UnionWindow* with the new *UnionEvent* in order to determine whether any of the intervals overlap with the new event. If there is no such interval then the new event may simply be inserted as a new interval. If there are affected intervals, then a new event (*CheckAffected*) is created whose purpose is to collect information about those intervals. We omit this step here to save space. We just note that out of the affected intervals (including the newly arrived interval), what we need to know is their minimum *startstamp* and their maximum *endstamp*. Every interval that falls between these two time points is subsequently deleted (we omit the presentation of the deletion statement).

Finally the unionized interval, simply defined as [*minstartstamp*, *maxendstamp*), is stored, according to statement (12) (the *AffectedIntervals* event holds the required information and is triggered by the *CheckAffected* event).

A similar procedure is followed for the other three constructs as well, with a slight difference. In the cases of intersection and complement, besides storing intervals, we also need to store previous events.

```
context UnionContext
create window UnionWindow.win:keepall()
select vehicleId as vehicleId, unionId as unionId, hash as hash,     (10)
    startstamp as startstamp, endstamp as endstamp
from UnionEvent
```

context *UnionContext*
on *UnionEvent ue*
merge *UnionWindow uw*
where $(ue.startstamp >= uw.startstamp$ and $ue.startstamp <= uw.endstamp$
　　　and $ue.endstamp >= uw.endstamp)$ or
　　　$(uw.startstamp >= ue.startstamp$ and $uw.endstamp <= ue.endstamp)$ or
　　　$(ue.endstamp >= uw.startstamp$ and $ue.endstamp <= uw.endstamp$
　　　and $ue.startstamp <= uw.startstamp)$ or
　　　$(ue.startstamp >= uw.startstamp$ and $ue.endstamp <= uw.endstamp)$
when not matched
then insert select *ue.vehicleId* as *vehicleId, ue.unionId* as *unionId,*
　　　　　　　　ue.hash as *hash,*
　　　　　　　　ue.startstamp as *startstamp, ue.endstamp* as *endstamp*
when matched
then insert into *CheckAffected* select *ue.vehicleId* as *vehicleId,*
　　　　　　　　　　　ue.unionId as *unionId,*
　　　　　　　　　　　ue.hash as *hash,*
　　　　　　　　　　　ue.startstamp as *startstamp,*
　　　　　　　　　　　ue.endstamp as *endstamp*

$$\tag{11}$$

context *UnionContext*
on *AffectedIntervals ai*
merge *UnionWindow uw*
where $uw.startstamp = ai.minstartstamp$ and $uw.endstamp = ai.maxendstamp$
when not matched
then insert select *ai.vehicleId* as *vehicleId, ai.unionId* as *unionId,*
　　　　　　　　ai.hash as *hash, ai.minstartstamp* as *startstamp,*
　　　　　　　　ai.maxendstamp as *endstamp*

$$\tag{12}$$

Statements 10–12 make use of contexts, as seen at their first lines. Contexts are an EPL concept for partitioning windows according to a specified key (we have omitted the declaration of the *UnionContext* here). In our case, we have used the hash attribute, created upon the *unionId* and *vehicleId*, as the partitioning key. This has the effect that each unique combination of the *unionId* and *vehicleId* attributes has a separate *UnionWindow* (essentially a separate memory for each combination), although we only need to define it once. Whenever a new event is pushed into the *UnionEvent* stream, as in statement (9), the Esper engine makes a choice as to which *UnionWindow* it should be sent, according to its *hash* value. For example, *UnionEvents* with a value of *vehicleId* equal to 75 and participating in the union operation with identifier equal to 1, giving us a hash value of 18880, are fed only to the *UnionWindow* with the same hash value. If the *UnionWindow* was one and the same for all vehicles and unions, then statement (11) would refer to this single window, holding all union intervals. Its where clause would have to include an extra condition, ($ue.vehicleId = uw.vehicleId$ and $ue.unionId = uw.unionId$) so that the new event is checked only against the intervals related to this specific $vehicleId$ and $unionId$. By creating different windows for each value of the partitioning key, contexts implement a more efficient indexing mechanism than checking in a single window for the right combination of $vehicleId$ - $unionId$. Additionally, contexts are more amenable to parallelization when multiple threads are available.

Of course, for real-time operation, an "infinite" memory that never deletes intervals and/or events would be impractical. To address this issue, we introduced a windowing parameter, called working memory, as in RTEC, and two special events, the $QueryEvent$ and the $ClearEvent$. At each query step (e.g. defined as 1000 time steps), a $QueryEvent$ is first sent to the Esper engine, followed by a $ClearEvent$. The $QueryEvent$ releases all the intervals which fall outside of the working memory window as final results and the $ClearEvent$ deletes those intervals.

3.4 Event Hierarchy Representation

Figure 1 depicts the event hierarchy of the city transport management application, that is, the SDE streams (denoted by incoming arrows on the left), the operations in which they are involved (denoted by boxes) and the CEs to be detected (denoted by outgoing arrows from the operation boxes). The results from a certain operation can be fed into another operation, so that complex chains of rules may be implemented.

An important difference between RTEC and Esper in their functioning is the way in which they process information from new events. RTEC does not perform any computations before a query is "triggered". Being written in Prolog, it essentially employs a pull method for retrieving information from events. At the time of a query, it backtracks in order to satisfy its goals which describe the CEs of interest. On the other hand, Esper employs a push method, performing on-the-fly processing of new events. Even if a $QueryEvent$ has not appeared yet, new SDEs are directly pushed towards their respective windows and the $QueryEvent$ triggers the release of the computed intervals. However, there are some exceptions to on-the-fly processing, whenever there are event hierarchies in which an operation requires the results of a previous operation. In these cases, an operation must wait for the final results of the previous one. For example, in Figure 1, the $uncomfortable$ CE, depends both on two of the SDE streams and on the intermediate $pure\_sharp\_turn$ stream. Before a $QueryEvent$ arrives, the operation for $uncomfortable$ can unionize the two SDE streams but it has to wait for the $QueryEvent$ in order to include the $pure\_sharp\_turn$ stream.

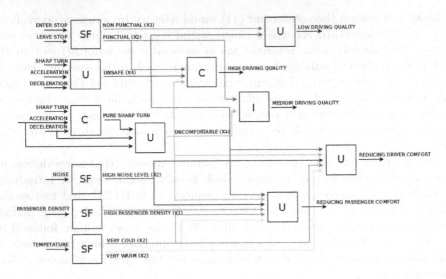

Fig. 1. The event hierarchy of the city transport management application. SF=simple fluent, U=union, I=intersection, C=complement. The number besides each CE stream indicates its fanout.

4   Empirical Evaluation

For the tests that follow, we used three different synthetic datasets of SDEs, based on the city transport management task described above and generated during the PRONTO project (http://www.ict-pronto.org). Each dataset consists of 50.000 SDEs. In the first dataset, all SDEs refer to a single vehicle, the second contains events for 10 vehicles and the third for 100. In total, we have 8 incoming SDE streams and 13 CE streams.

4.1   Similarity Testing

In order to assess the similarity of the results produced by RTEC with those produced by Esper, we ran a series of tests on the City Transport Manaagement datasets. Using the intervals computed by RTEC as a reference point, we compared them with the intervals produced by Esper. The comparison metric for each CE is computed as the division of the intersection of the RTEC and Esper intervals by their union. Figure 2 presents the comparison results for the three different datasets.

For most of the CEs in all datasets, the similarity is near perfect (above 99%), while for all of them it lies above 95%. For a few of them, especially in the dataset with 100 vehicles, it falls to a level of about 95%. These discrepancies are due to a slight difference between RTEC and Esper in the way open intervals are treated, i.e. intervals which, at the time of a query, have not been closed, e.g. when a sharp turn has not finished when a query is triggered. In this case, RTEC produces intervals in the form of $[startstamp, inf)$ which are

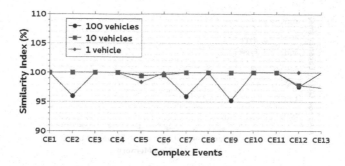

Fig. 2. Esper/RTEC similarity index for three different datasets

ignored during the comparison, whereas Esper produces intervals in the form of [*startstamp, querytime*). In the dataset with 100 vehicles, due to its structure, such open intervals appear more often.

4.2 Performance Comparison

After ensuring that Esper can reproduce the RTEC results with an accepted level of reliability, we ran another series of experiments in order to compare their performance, in terms of average latency per query. All the experiments were conducted on a machine with an Intel Core 2 Duo CPU P8600 @ 2.40 Ghz x 2 processor and 3.0 Gib of memory, running the 32-bit version of Debian 7.3. Esper was run with java-7-openjdk-i386 and RTEC with YAP Prolog 6.2.2. Both engines were tested as single-threaded applications. Figures 3(a) 3(c) depict the results of the performance comparison tests, with each figure referring to a different dataset. In order to assess the impact of the size of the working memory window (how far into the past an operation can look into when computing intervals), we varied its value from 1000 (equal to the query step) to 15000 time-points.

Figures 3(a)–3(c) show that RTEC outperforms Esper significantly, with Esper suffering a worst degradation as the working memory window increases (increased gradient). By separating the time of on-the-fly processing from that of query-time processing (see Section 3 for an explanation of their difference), we discovered that the observed latency is almost exclusively due to query-time processing. In an attempt to isolate the possible bottlenecks, we measured latencies on a per operation basis. The results did not indicate that a specific type of operation is a significant source of delay. We observed that the latency of an operation correlates with its fanout. The operations for the *unsafe* and the *uncomfortable* CEs, both with a fanout of 4 (see Figure 1), were consistently among the most severe bottlenecks. Therefore, we are inclined to assume that one reason behind Esper's lower performance lies in the "communication" overhead between the connected operations.

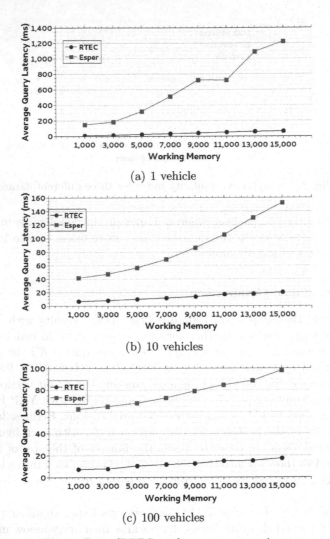

(a) 1 vehicle

(b) 10 vehicles

(c) 100 vehicles

Fig. 3. Esper/RTEC performance comparison

5 Conclusions

We presented a comparison of two CEP engines with significant differences as far as their event representation languages are concerned. As CEP engines mature over time, such comparison tests are expected to become more common. They will allow for the identification of the possible limitations and advantages of one solution over another and will facilitate the classification of event-based systems [12].

For the CEP engines under comparison here —Esper and RTEC—, we showed that the translation of an event hierarchy from one language to the other, although not a trivial task, is certainly possible. In fact, for certain domains, such as city transport management above, the whole process could be delegated to automatic translators. However, when the task of translation is left to the user, EPL statements are longer and require some low-level knowledge of how events are represented, which could make them more susceptible to subtle errors. Contrary to what one might expect, we also showed that a system from the field of Artificial Intelligence, like RTEC, may outperform a state-of-the-art system from the fields of databases and distributed systems.

Our tests are far from being complete and we do not consider the results presented here to be final. RTEC is very well-suited for problems whose main goal is to find those time intervals during which certain conditions hold. Moreover, translating the RTEC constructs directly into EPL statements might very well result in an inefficient implementation from the point of view of Esper. However, this is exactly one of our goals, i.e. to find those domains for which a certain CEP system might be more appropriate than others.

For these reasons, we would like to continue this line of work. We aim to investigate, for example, whether the recently introduced data flow programming model of Esper improves performance for the type of event definitions that were examined in this paper. Additionally, we will compare the two engines using event patterns that are more readily expressed in EPL. We will also compare the two systems, along multiple dimensions, both in terms of semantics and performance (see [14], [10], [7] for examples of studies with a more detailed treatment of these issues).

Acknowledgments. We have benefited from discussions with Matthias Weidlich on the comparison of Esper and RTEC. This work has been funded by the EU SPEEDD project (FP7-ICT 619435).

References

1. Esper reference document,
   http://esper.codehaus.org/esper-4.10.0/doc/reference/en-US/html/index.html
   (accessed: January 21, 2014)
2. Artikis, A., Sergot, M.J., Paliouras, G.: Run-time composite event recognition. In: DEBS, pp. 69–80 (2012)
3. Artikis, A., Weidlich, M., Gal, A., Kalogeraki, V., Gunopulos, D.: Self-adaptive event recognition for intelligent transport management. In: 2013 IEEE International Conference on Big Data, pp. 319–325 (2013)
4. Balis, B., Kowalewski, B., Bubak, M.: Real-time grid monitoring based on complex event processing. Future Generation Computer Systems 27(8), 1103–1112 (2011)
5. Cugola, G., Margara, A.: Processing flows of information: From data stream to complex event processing. ACM Comput. Surv. 44(3), 15 (2012)
6. Etzion, O., Niblett, P.: Event Processing in Action. Manning Publications Company (2010)
7. Grabs, T., Lu, M.: Measuring performance of complex event processing systems. In: Nambiar, R., Poess, M. (eds.) TPCTC 2011. LNCS, vol. 7144, pp. 83–96. Springer, Heidelberg (2012)

8. Kowalski, R.A., Sergot, M.J.: A logic-based calculus of events. New Generation Comput. 4(1), 67–95 (1986)
9. Ku, T., Zhu, Y., Hu, K.: Semantics-based complex event processing for RFID data streams. In: The First International Symposium on Data, Privacy, and E-Commerce, ISDPE 2007, pp. 32–34 (2007)
10. Mendes, M.R.N., Bizarro, P., Marques, P.: A performance study of event processing systems. In: Nambiar, R., Poess, M. (eds.) TPCTC 2009. LNCS, vol. 5895, pp. 221–236. Springer, Heidelberg (2009)
11. Mendes, M.R., Bizarro, P., Marques, P.: Towards a standard event processing benchmark. In: Proceedings of the 4th ACM/SPEC International Conference on Performance Engineering, ICPE 2013, pp. 307–310. ACM, New York (2013)
12. Voisard, A., Ziekow, H.: Architect: A layered framework for classifying technologies of event-based systems. Inf. Syst. 36(6), 937–957 (2011)
13. Weber, S., Lowe, H.J., Malunjkar, S., Quinn, J.: Implementing a real-time complex event stream processing system to help identify potential participants in clinical and translational research studies. In: AMIA Annu Symp Proc., pp. 472–476 (2010), PMID: 21347023 PMCID: PMC3041381
14. Wu, E., Diao, Y., Rizvi, S.: High-performance complex event processing over streams. In: Proceedings of the 2006 ACM SIGMOD International Conference on Management of Data, pp. 407–418. ACM (2006)

Event Recognition
for Unobtrusive Assisted Living

Nikos Katzouris[1,2], Alexander Artikis[1], and Georgios Paliouras[1]

[1] Institute of Informatics & Telecommunications
National Center for Scientific Research 'Demokritos'
[2] Department of Informatics & Telecommunications
National Kapodistrian University of Athens
{nkatz,a.artikis,paliourg}@iit.demokritos.gr

Abstract. Developing intelligent systems towards automated clinical monitoring and assistance for the elderly is attracting growing attention. USEFIL is an FP7 project aiming to provide health-care assistance in a smart-home setting. We present the data fusion component of USEFIL which is based on a complex event recognition methodology. In particular, we present our knowledge-driven approach to the detection of Activities of Daily Living (ADL) and functional ability, based on a probabilistic version of the Event Calculus. To investigate the feasibility of our approach, we present an empirical evaluation on synthetic data.

1   Introduction

Developing intelligent systems towards automated clinical monitoring and assistance for the elderly is attracting significant attention, due to the increase in the ageing population. Age-related demographic trends in most western countries and increasing health-care costs, indicate a need for robust telehealth solutions which shall prolong seniors' independent living. USEFIL[1] is an FP7 project aiming to provide health-care assistance to seniors who live alone. The USE-FIL system relies on a three-layer architecture. The bottom layer consists of an in-house data acquisition platform comprising off-the-self, low cost sensors. A data fusion component in the intermediate layer of the system is responsible for combining data from multiple sources via spatio-temporal reasoning. Fused data are consumed by a Decision Support System in the top-level layer, which provides input to a number of user-friendly, interactive health-care/monitoring apps, designed both for the USEFIL resident and the medical/caregiving stuff. The main objective of the Decision Support System is the identification of early deterioration signs for a plethora of medical cases and behavioural disturbances.

We present our approach to USEFIL's data fusion component. Its role is to interpret the parameters of raw sensor data into a semantic representation of human behaviour and functional ability, while counterbalancing confidence in the sensor measurements by fusing data from multiple sources. Its tasks range

---

[1] http://www.usefil.eu/

A. Likas, K. Blekas, and D. Kalles (Eds.): SETN 2014, LNAI 8445, pp. 475–488, 2014.
© Springer International Publishing Switzerland 2014

from contextualization of sensor measurements to detecting sleep and Activities of Daily Living (ADL), and characterising functional ability.

USEFIL's sensor network is able to provide a wide range of measurements and indications, related both to user's activities and to the environment. The sensors include a depth camera (kinect), a light wrist watch (Wrist Wearable Unit – WWU), a hidden camera installed in a smart-PC, a number of microphones around the house, and so on. A key requirement in most assisted living applications is unobtrusiveness: Monitoring should not intervene with daily activities, so that the user feels comfortable and sensor data are collected naturally and in an unbiased fashion. Thus, rich as may it be, the sensor network does not cover the entire house, nor can it provide indications for all situations of interest. Moreover sensor data may often be corrupted by noise. Thus, in order to increase confidence in the representation of the user status it is necessary to exploit the existing monitoring equipment as much as possible, by combining different sensor resources, while addressing uncertainty. To this end, we employ a Complex Event Recognition methodology, which allows to combine heterogeneous data sources by means of event hierarchies. Our approach is based on a probabilistic version of the Event Calculus [14], which allows for handling noise and modelling uncertainty.

The rest of this paper is structured as follows. Section 2 contains basic background on the Event Calculus and ProbLog, the probabilistic logic programming language on which our implementation relies. Section 3 describes the construction of event patterns related to the detection of ADL and functional ability. In Section 4 we present an empirical evaluation of our approach, and in Sections 5 and 6 we summarise and put our work in context.

2   Event Recognition and Probabilistic Event Calculus

Complex Event Recognition [10] refers to the automatic detection of event occurrences within a system. From a sequence of *low-level events* (LLEs) – such as sensor data, an event recognition system recognizes complex, or *high-level events* (HLEs) of interest, that is, events that satisfy some pattern. Event recognition systems with a logic-based representation of event definitions, are attracting significant attention in the event processing community for a number of reasons, including the expressiveness and understandability of the formalized knowledge and their declarative, formal semantics.

In this paper we follow the standard logic programming notation, so variables start with an upper-case letter, while predicates, function symbols and constants start with a lower-case letter. The Event Calculus is a many-sorted, first-order predicate calculus for representing and reasoning about events and their effects. Its ontology comprises *time points* (integer or real numbers), *fluents* (properties that have values in time) and *events* (occurrences that may affect the values of fluents). In this work, we assume that the time model is linear and integer-valued. For a fluent F, the expression $F = V$ means that F has the value V, and intuitively $F = V$ holds at a particular time point if it has been *initiated* at a previous time point and has not been *terminated* since. The *domain-independent* axioms of the Event Calculus formalize the commonsense law of *inertia*, according to which fluents persist in time unless they are affected by events. The axioms of the dialect employed in this work are as follows:

$$\text{holdsAt}(F = V, T) \leftarrow$$
$$\quad \text{initially}(F), \qquad\qquad (1)$$
$$\quad \text{not broken}(F = V, 0, T).$$

$$\text{holdsAt}(F = V, T) \leftarrow$$
$$\quad \text{initiatedAt}(F = V, T_s),$$
$$\quad T_s < T, \qquad\qquad (2)$$
$$\quad \text{not broken}(F = V, T_s, T).$$

$$\text{broken}(F = V, Ts, T) \leftarrow$$
$$\quad \text{terminatedAt}(F = V, T_f), \qquad (3)$$
$$\quad T_s < T_f < T.$$

not represents "negation by failure", which provides a form of default persistence – inertia of fluents. According to Axiom (1), $F = V$ holds at time T if $F = V$ held initially and has not been broken since. According to Axiom (2), $F = V$ holds at time T if the fluent F has been initiated to value V at an earlier time T_s, and has not been broken since. Axiom (3) dictates that a period of time for which $F = V$ holds is broken at T_f if $F = V$ is terminated at T_f.

In this work we assume that LLEs and HLEs, as defined in an event recognition context, correspond respectively to Event Calculus events and fluents. Given the domain-independent axioms of the Event Calculus, the construction of HLE patterns consists in defining *domain-specific* rules which describe initiation and termination conditions.

Various types of uncertainty exist in event-related domains, such as erroneous or missing LLEs [1]. To address uncertainty, in [18] the Event Calculus has been ported in the probabilistic logic programming language ProbLog [13]. ProbLog is a probabilistic version of Prolog, where standard Prolog facts and rules may be annotated with probabilities. Probabilistic facts are expressions of the form $p_i :: f_i$, where f_i is a Prolog fact and p_i is a real number in the interval $[0, 1]$. Probabilistic facts in ProbLog represent random variables with an independence assumption, thus a rule defined as a conjunction of a set of probabilistic facts, has a probability that is equal to the product of the probabilities of these facts. When a predicate appears in the head of more than one rule, then its probability is computed by calculating the probability of the implicit disjunction created by the multiple rules. ProbLog facts with no probability are implicitly given a probability of 1. In addition to probabilistic facts, ProbLog supports probabilistic rules as well, that is, expressions of the form $p_0 :: h \leftarrow f_1, \ldots, f_n$. Intuitively, such a rule means that if $\wedge_{j=1}^{n} f_j$ is true and each f_j has probability p_j, then h is true with probability $p_h = \prod_{j=0}^{n} p_j$. For a non-ground probabilistic expression $p :: e$ (rule or fact), the probability p applies to all possible groundings of e.

ProbLog supports several forms of probabilistic inference, such as computing the success probability of a query (the overall probability of a query being true) or finding the most likely explanation of a query (the proof with the highest probability). Given a program P and a query q, computing the success probability of q can be achieved by summing the probabilities of all subprograms L that entail q. This is a hard task even for small problems, since it involves a number of summands which is exponential in the size of the Herbrand base of the initial program. Thus in practice, ProbLog uses Binary Decision Diagrams (BDDs) [4] and techniques from dynamic programming to efficiently address computations through different proofs of a query, allowing the implementation to scale to queries containing thousands of different proofs [13].

3   Event Definitions for Activities of Daily Living

In this section we present our approach to detecting activities of daily living (ADL) and characterizing functional ability. ADL typically refers to the fundamental self-care activities, such as getting out of bed, walking around etc. ADL detection is of particular importance in assisted living applications, since the capacity to perform such activities has been confirmed in numerous studies to have broad implications for functioning, reflecting a person's ability to live independently. Given the fact that disability or functional impairment is usually closely related to a person's inability to perform these and other basic tasks without assistance, the requirements of the ADL use-case in USEFIL involve, in addition to ADL detection, estimation of the ADL's score in the *Barthel Index* [8].

The Barthel Index, commonly acknowledged as the "golden standard" for functional ability, consists of 10 items that measure a person's daily functioning. The items include feeding, moving from wheelchair to bed and return, grooming, transferring to and from a toilet, bathing, walking on level surface, going up and down stairs, dressing, and continence of bowels and bladder.

In USEFIL, obtaining a Barthel score for some of these ADL is subject to restrictions/limitations, mainly due to monitoring insufficiency, related to the unobtrusiveness requirement[2]. Table 1 presents three ADL for which the monitoring equipment suffices in order to formulate interesting event patterns, namely *transfer, mobility* and *stairs*. *Transfer* (or "changing position") refers to the ability of a person to get up from bed and lie down, stand up from a chair and sit down. The corresponding scores in the Barthel Index range from 0 to 3, as shown in Table 1. Since the goal is to determine user's level of independence and possibly detect signs of functional decline, we assume that the user is able to perform to some extend. As a result, we do not score *transfer* with a 0. *Mobility* ADL refers to the ability of a person to walk adequately well, while *stairs* ADL refers to a person's ability to walk stairs upwards/downwards. The respective scores in the Barthel Index range are presented in Table 1. Similar to *transfer*, we do not score *mobility* with 0 and 1; we also do not score *stairs* with 0.

3.1   Complex Events

As mentioned in Section 2, an HLE definition consists of Event Calculus rules expressing the conditions in which the HLE is initiated and terminated. Consider

---

[2] For these ADL a surrogate, indirect index is obtained, which measures the increase in frequency of performing the ADL when someone else is in the house, in the long term.

Table 1. ADL, their respective scores in the Barthel Index and sensors which provide relevant LLEs

ADL	Barthel scores	Related sensors
Transfer	0: unsafe - no sitting balance* 1: major help (one or two people, physical), can sit 2: minor help (verbal or physical) 3: independent	WWU Kinect camera Microphones
Mobility	0: immobile* 1: wheelchair independent, including corners, etc.* 2: walks with help of one person (verbal or physical) 3: independent (but may use any aid, e.g., stick)	WWU Kinect camera Microphones
Stairs	0: unable 1: needs help (verbal, physical, carrying aid) 2: independent up and down	WWU Kinect camera Microphones

the event hierarchy presented in Figure 1, developed in collaboration with the USEFIL experts. The leaves in this tree-like hierarchy represent sensor-level data (LLEs), which are obtained by applying various aggregation and transformation techniques on raw sensor measurements, while each node represents an HLE. According to this representation, in order to obtain a Barthel score for the transfer ADL (root node), one should try to infer whether the user changed position, while receiving help for this task, and also take into account the ease and safety with which the user performs.

Position change (ex. from sitting to standing, or from lying to sitting) depends on the corresponding HLEs, which in turn are inferred from sensor-level LLEs. Help is inferred by carer detection, which in turn may be inferred from kinect evidence (more than one persons) or microphone evidence (more than one speakers), and also by user-carer proximity, a value in meters, also provided by the kinect. The ease and safety with which the user transfers serves as a surrogate for the fact that we have no way to discriminate between major and minor help, as required by the Barthel standard (see definitions for Barthel scores of 1

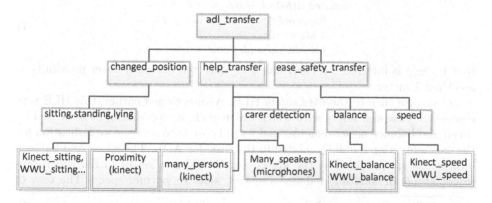

Fig. 1. An event hierarchy for the *transfer* ADL

and 2 in Table 1). Instead, we use the contextual knowledge of the ADL, that is, the user's speed and balance while changing position, as an indirect indication for the user's functional ability, which in turn is utilized in the extraction of the Barthel score for the ADL.

We next describe the construction of an Event Calculus program for Barthel-scoring the *transfer* ADL, starting from the bottom level (sensor data) of the event hierarchy and moving up to the root node of the target event.

The second from the bottom level of the event hierarchy consists of HLEs which result mostly from the combination of sensor-level data. For instance, *sitting* is defined in terms of two sensor-level events, one coming from the kinect and one from the wrist wearable unit, as the following two rules dictate:

$$\text{initiatedAt}(sitting = true, T) \leftarrow \qquad \text{initiatedAt}(sitting = true, T) \leftarrow$$
$$\text{happensAt}(kinect\_sitting, T). \qquad \text{happensAt}(wwu\_sitting, T). \qquad (4)$$

Note that by means of such rules, the probability of an HLE at time T results by the combined probabilities of all related evidence, up to that time. For instance from the following sensor evidence[3]

$$0.8 :: \text{happensAt}(kinect\_sitting, 10)$$
$$0.7 :: \text{happensAt}(wwu\_sitting, 11) \qquad (5)$$

and the two rules in (4), the probability of *sitting* HLE at time 12 (i.e the probability of holdsAt($sitting = true, 12$)) is $0.8 + 0.7 - 0.8 \cdot 0.7 = 0.94$, provided that the HLE has not been terminated in the meantime.

The first HLE in the next level of the event hierarchy (see Figure 1) is recognized once the user changes position:

$$\text{initiatedAt}(changed\_position = true, T) \leftarrow$$
$$\text{initiatedAt}(sitting = true, T),$$
$$\text{terminatedAt}(standing = true, T). \qquad (6)$$

There are similar axioms for the remaining pose combinations. The *help_transfer* HLE definition is as follows:

$$\text{initiatedAt}(help\_transfer = true, T) \leftarrow$$
$$\text{happensAt}(proximity(Value), T),$$
$$Value \leq 1,$$
$$\text{holdsAt}(carer\_detected = true, T). \qquad (7)$$

that is, help is inferred if a carer has been detected and user-carer proximity is less than 1 meter.

Let us now turn to the *ease_safety* HLE. As mentioned earlier, this HLE represents the ease and safety with which the user changes position, as indicated by speed and balance measurements, and its purpose is to serve as an indication for the user's functional ability, related to the *transfer* ADL. The speed and balance indications are provided by the kinect and WWU as a set of LLEs, which represent *steady* or *unsteady* balance and *fast, slow,* or *normal* speed. The task of

---

[3] Recall that a statement of the form $p :: a$ in ProbLog means that a is true with probability p (see Section 2).

combining these LLEs into a single indication for the user's functional abilities is not straightforward. For instance, a *fast* or *normal* transfer speed is an indication for an easy transfer. However, it may be accompanied by *unsteady* balance, an indication of unsafe transfer, in which case there is no interpretation of this contextual knowledge which says something meaningful for the user's functional abilities (in other words, an easy but unsafe transfer does not provide any insight for the user's ability w.r.t the *transfer* ADL). We address this issue as follows: First, we define values for the *ease_safety* HLE, which follow the actual Barthel scores for the *transfer* ADL. Intuitively, a score of 1 for *ease_safety* is to be interpreted as a difficult and unsafe transfer, a score of 3 as an easy and safe one and a score of 2 as something between the extreme cases.

We associate each LLE related to speed and balance to the *ease_safety* HLE in the obvious way according to which *fast* or *normal* speed, or *steady* balance indicates ease and safety (thus a value of 3 for *ease_safety* HLE), while *slow* speed or unsteady balance indicates difficulty or unsafety (thus a value of 1 for *ease_safety* HLE). This can be formulated as a set of rules of the following form (we omit the whole set of rules for brevity):

$$\text{initiatedAt}(ease\_safety = 3, T) \leftarrow$$
$$\text{happensAt}(kinect\_balance\_steady, T). \tag{8}$$

Then the average value of 2 for *ease_safety* is defined by means of a probabilistic rule, which weights the conjunction of the extreme cases at time T, by the confidence value of the most probable one. To do so, we use the concept of a *intentional probabilistic fact* [11] in ProbLog, i.e a probability associated to a rule, which is not defined explicitly, but is calculated at runtime, based on a number of constraints which must be satisfied, as in the following rule:

$$P :: \text{initiatedAt}(ease\_safety = 2, T) \leftarrow$$
$$P_1 :: \text{holdsAt}(ease\_safety = 1, T),$$
$$P_2 :: \text{holdsAt}(ease\_safety = 3, T),$$
$$P \text{ is } \max\{P_1, P_2\}. \tag{9}$$

P in Rule (9) is an intentional probability. By Rule (9) an average score will be attributed (with a significant probability) to the *ease_safety* HLE, only if the extreme scores for the HLE, both have significant probabilities, which means that contradictory evidence w.r.t ease and safety has been received.

For the definition of the top-level HLE in the hierarchy, we use two auxiliary HLEs, *transf_help* and *transf_no_help*, which are initiated by the conjunction of *changed_position* and *help_transfer*, or the negation of the latter. The definitions of the *adl_transfer* HLE is given disjunctively, for each different Barthel score. The definition of a 1-score is as follows:

$$\text{initiatedAt}(adl\_transfer = 1, T) \leftarrow \qquad \text{initiatedAt}(adl\_transfer = 1, T) \leftarrow$$
$$\text{initiatedAt}(transf\_help = true, T), \qquad \text{initiatedAt}(ease\_safety = 1, T), \quad (10)$$
$$\text{holdsAt}(ease\_safety = 1, T). \qquad \text{holdsAt}(transf\_help = true, T).$$

p^1_{max} :: initiatedAt($adl\_transfer = 1, T$) ←
    initiatedAt($transf\_help = true, T$),
    holdsAt($ease\_safety = 2, T$).

p^1_{max} :: initiatedAt($adl\_transfer = 1, T$) ←
    initiatedAt($ease\_safety = 2, T$),
    holdsAt($transf\_help = true, T$).

$$\text{(11)}$$

p^1_{min} :: initiatedAt($adl\_transfer = 1, T$) ←
    initiatedAt($transf\_help = true, T$),
    holdsAt($ease\_safety = 3, T$).

p^1_{min} :: initiatedAt($adl\_transfer = 1, T$) ←
    initiatedAt($ease\_safety = 3, T$),
    holdsAt($transf\_help = true, T$).

$$\text{(12)}$$

The definition consists of a set of crisp and a set of probabilistic rules, which aim to account for the inherent uncertainty of the Barthel scoring task. Rules (10) state that if help was offered and the user's functional abilities as indicated by the *ease_safety* HLE are minimum, then a Barthel score of 1 should be attributed to the *transfer* ADL. On the other hand, Rules (11) state that if the functional abilities are not minimum, then the score may still be 1 (since help was offered), however with a reduced confidence, reflected in the probability p^1_{max}. Similarly, Rules (12) state that if the functional abilities are the highest possible, then a Barthel score of 1 should be attributed to *transfer* with an even smaller confidence (*min* and *max* in the probabilities denote that p_{min} is intended to be smaller than p_{max}). The definition for a 3-score is similar. The difference is that the *transf_no_help* auxiliary HLE is utilized, instead of the *transf_help* one. Finally, Rules (13)-(15) provide a definition for a 2-score in the Barthel index:

p^2_{max} :: initiatedAt($adl\_transfer = 2, T$) ←
    initiatedAt($changed\_position = true, T$),
    holdsAt($ease\_safety = 2, T$).

p^2_{max} :: initiatedAt($adl\_transfer = 2, T$) ←
    initiatedAt($ease\_safety = 2, T$),
    holdsAt($changed\_position = true, T$).

$$\text{(13)}$$

$p^2_{min_1}$ :: initiatedAt($adl\_transfer = 2, T$) ←
    initiatedAt($transf\_no\_help = true, T$),
    holdsAt($ease\_safety = 1, T$).

$p^2_{min_1}$ :: initiatedAt($adl\_transfer = 2, T$) ←
    initiatedAt($ease\_safety = 1, T$),
    holdsAt($transf\_no\_help = true, T$).

$$\text{(14)}$$

$p^2_{min_2}$ :: initiatedAt($adl\_transfer = 2, T$) ←
    initiatedAt($transf\_help = true, T$),
    holdsAt($ease\_safety = 3, T$).

$p^2_{min_2}$ :: initiatedAt($adl\_transfer = 2, T$) ←
    initiatedAt($ease\_safety = 3, T$),
    holdsAt($transf\_help = true, T$),

$$\text{(15)}$$

Recall that the intention in USEFIL is for a 2-score to account for "vague" situations, where help may have been provided or not, but the functional abilities of the user do not allow to classify her as fully independent or not. For example, if the user manages to stand up from the sitting position with no help, but with very low balance, it is unsafe to classify the user as independent. Instead, an intermediate score of 2 is an indication for the medical stuff in USEFIL that the user may need assistance for that particular ADL. Thus Rule (13) attributes a score of 2 by means of functional ability only, without taking help into account. Then, Rules (14) and (15) weight contradicting cases with a 2-score, that is, cases where functional ability is the lowest, but transfer was achieved with no help (Rules (14)) and cases where functional ability is the best possible, but help is inferred with a significant probability (Rules (15)).

The presented rules allow for the possibility that the *adl_transfer* HLE has more than one values at a particular time point. The obvious way to select between competing scores is to keep the one with the highest probability. However, delivering all the inferred Barthel scores allows a broader view of the user's status, which may be useful to the medical personel. In particular, the intended behavior of the formulated knowledge is to provide a dominant Barthel score for the ADL, but also provide additional indications via the less probable scores, particularly in the "vague" cases mentioned earlier.

The probabilities in the knowledge base may be tuned manually or may be learned using ProbLog's parameter learning utilities. For this work the probabilities where defined by experts, while we further tuned the values manually using synthetic data. In future work we will additionally use machine learning techniques to refine the probabilities from data.

The process of constructing event definitions for the other two ADL mentioned earlier, namely *mobility* and *stairs* is similar. Details are omitted due to space limitations.

4   Empirical Evaluation

USEFIL is an ongoing research project and real data is not yet available. Moreover, since ADL Barthel scoring is an empirical task, designed to be carried out by humans (medical personnel), by means of observing a patient, neither normative data, nor annotated datasets are available. Thus in order to validate that the formulated knowledge behaves as expected we performed experiments using synthetic data that simulate particular situations.

We defined a number of scripts, as presented in Table 2 for transfer, in order to annotate the generated datasets. The notation $score_1 \rightarrow score_2$ in Table 2 means that $score_1$ is the dominant score (the one with the highest probability), while $score_2$ is the second best score, which may be used as an additional indication for the user's functional status. For instance $3 \rightarrow 2$ means that the user is able to transfer with no help but there are some indications of functional decline, while a score of $2 \rightarrow 3$ is the opposite, that is, there are serious indications of functional decline, however the user may transfer with no assistance. We refer to such cases as *soft* Barthel scores, in contrast to the *hard* scores of 1 and 3. In Table 2 we order the various cases from the best possible, in terms of functional ability, to the worst possible.

We generated 50 instances of each script in Table 2 (a total of 600 instances) as follows: We defined a temporal window within which we assume that evidence

Table 2. Script definitions for different parameters of the *adl_transfer* HLE

Case	Transfer	Help	Speed	Balance	Barthel score
1	yes	no	fast	steady	3
2	yes	no	normal	steady	3
3	yes	no	slow	steady	$3 \rightarrow 2$
4	yes	no	fast	unsteady	$3 \rightarrow 2$
5	yes	no	normal	unsteady	$3 \rightarrow 2$
6	yes	no	slow	unsteady	$2 \rightarrow 3$
7	yes	yes	fast	steady	$2 \rightarrow 1$
8	yes	yes	normal	steady	$2 \rightarrow 1$
9	yes	yes	slow	steady	$1 \rightarrow 2$
10	yes	yes	fast	unsteady	$1 \rightarrow 2$
11	yes	yes	normal	unsteady	$1 \rightarrow 2$
12	yes	yes	slow	unsteady	1

related to transfer may result to the recognition of the *adl_transfer* HLE. This window was set to 15 seconds. To generate an instance of a script we generated related LLEs, randomly timed across the 15 second window, so that the values of the generated LLEs comply with the particular script. For example the following set of LLEs is an instance of case 1 in Table 2 for changing position from sitting to standing:

0.784 :: holdsAt($kinect\_sitting = true, 10$).
0.854 :: holdsAt($wwu\_sitting = true, 11$).
0.478 :: happensAt($many\_persons, 12$).
0.756 :: holdsAt($proximity = 2.4, 15$).
0.553 :: happensAt($many\_speakers, 16$).
0.786 :: holdsAt($transfer\_speed = fast, 17$).
0.324 :: holdsAt($transfer\_balance = steady, 21$).
0.788 :: holdsAt($wwu\_standing = true, 24$).
0.698 :: holdsAt($kinect\_standing = true, 25$).

Indeed, the above data indicate that the user is sitting at time 10 and standing at time 25 (thus *changed_position* will be recognized). In addition the *many_persons* and *many_speakers* LLEs indicate the presence of a carer and the *proximity* LLE indicates that user-carer distance does not qualify for inferring physical help (it is larger that the threshold of 1 meter). Moreover speed and balance LLEs are valued as in case 1 of Table 2.

Instances were generated in a sorted fashion and between two scripts there is a period of time during which nothing happens, or the user is assumed to walk around the house. Thus the generated data form a (temporally) sorted stream. A large number of random USEFIL LLEs, irrelevant to the *transfer* task, was also added in the data. Time in the data ranges in the interval $[0, 10000]$ with a step of 1 (that is, the temporal distance between two consecutive events is 1). Four different datasets were generated in this manner: In the first one, the generated LLEs are *crisp* (i.e their probability is 1.0). In the second, noise in the form of random probabilities was injected in the speed and balance LLEs, while all other LLEs were crisp (*smooth noise*). In the third dataset all generated LLEs were noisy (*strong noise*).

Table 3. Precision and recall for all identified variations of Barthel scores for the *adl_transfer* HLE, and for 4 different levels of noise

	crisp		smooth		strong		strong_incomplete	
	precision	recall	precision	recall	precision	recall	precision	recall
Transfer								
$transfer_3$	1.0	1.0	0.961	1.0	0.783	0.693	0.723	0.686
$transfer_{3\rightarrow2}$	1.0	1.0	0.975	0.96	0.574	0.568	0.498	0.573
$transfer_{2\rightarrow3}$	1.0	1.0	0.695	0.925	0.407	0.84	0.413	0.764
$transfer_{2\rightarrow1}$	1.0	1.0	0.957	0.926	0.260	0.129	0.218	0.145
$transfer_{1\rightarrow2}$	1.0	1.0	0.988	0.88	0.444	0.24	0.384	0.114
$transfer_1$	1.0	1.0	0.943	1.0	0.944	0.48	0.784	0.426

In the fourth dataset noise was injected to all LLEs as in the *strong noise* case, and additionally, up to 3 LLEs related to a particular script could be randomly omitted, or have different values from the ones required by the script (*strong-incomplete noise*). The purpose of the last dataset was to simulate more realistic cases where data may be missing due to hardware malfunction or delayed delivery, or they may have erroneous values with significant probability. The experiments consisted in evaluating the predictive accuracy of the presented event definitions for the different cases of noise.

As mentioned in Section 3, for these experiments, the parameters (probabilities) of the event definitions were manually determined based on expert knowledge. An HLE is recognized at time T if its probability at time T exceeds a *recognition threshold* p_1. In order to disambiguate between hard and soft Barthel scores, as presented in Table 2, we additionally defined a lower probability threshold p_2. In order to attribute a strong Barthel score $score_1$ to a transfer activity at time T, the probability of $score_1$ at T should be the maximum of the probabilities of all other Barthel scores, and it should exceed the threshold p_1. Moreover, the probability of the second most probable score $score_2$ should be smaller than the threshold p_2. In the opposite case, the activity will be attributed a soft score of $score_1 \rightarrow score_2$. For these experiments the above thresholds were set to $p_1 = 0.5$ and $p_2 = 0.2$ respectively.

Our experimental results are presented in Table 3. The results indicate that the formulated knowledge is able to classify correctly the level of functional dependency related to the *transfer* activity for the crisp case. It also achieves good results in the smooth noise case. Note that a perfect recall is achieved for the hard scores of 1 and 3 in the smooth noise case, that is, all activity instances of scores 1 and 3 were correctly classified. This is because the *help_transfer* HLE is crisply recognized in this case (the relevant LLEs are crisp), thus 1-score and 3-score activity instances are recognized with an increased probability by means of the crisp rules of the form (10) (and respective rules for a 3-score). Noise in the recognition of the *ease_safety* HLE is responsible for the erroneous classifications of activity instances, particularly for the soft score cases, where an activity instance contained contradictory evidence regarding balance and speed. Score 2 $\rightarrow$ 3 has the worst precision due to a large number of false positives (3 $\rightarrow$ 2 and 2 $\rightarrow$ 1 instances incorrectly attributed with a score of 2 $\rightarrow$ 3).

Precision and recall drop significantly in the two remaining cases of noise. Hard scores (3 and 1) are classified relatively well, with the exception of the low recall for 1-scores in the strong noise case, which is attributed to an increased number of false negatives, that is, 1-score activity instances which were incorrectly classified as $1 \rightarrow 2$. Due to the increased noise and contradictory evidence for the *ease_safety* HLE in the generated activity instances, the predictive accuracy for some of the ambiguous (soft) scores is particularly low. This indicates the need for adjustment and refinement of the parameters (weights) of the knowledge base, an issue to be addressed in future work by means of machine learning. The worst recognition results are achieved with the fourth dataset, where in addition to the increased level of erroneous classification of functional ability, a number of transfer activities were not recognized at all, due to missing LLEs.

5   Related Work

A number of logic-based approaches for reasoning support in ambient intelligence and assisted living applications have been proposed. In [9] the authors present an approach based on if-then rules for the detection of elders' activity related to ADL and possible emergency conditions. The knowledge base in [9] was expert-engineered, while its construction was assisted by semi-supervised learning techniques (clustering and mixture models).

In [12] a method is presented for the recognition of HLEs using rules that impose temporal and spatial constraints between LLEs. Some of the constraints in the event definitions are optional, and as a result, an HLE may be recognized from incomplete information, but with lower confidence. The confidence of an HLE increases with the number of relevant (optional) LLEs. Due to noisy or incomplete information, the recognized HLEs may be logically inconsistent with each other. The method resolves these inconsistencies using the confidence, duration and number of involved LLEs.

In [15] the system SINDI (Secure and INDependent lIving) is proposed, which relies on Answer Set Programming (ASP) [2], a logic programming paradigm based on the stable model semantics. SINDI addresses uncertainty by means of a number of ASP features such as non-deterministic choice rules and cardinality constraints. ASP reasoning on sensory evidence extracts a number of "indicators" [15], relevant to interesting cases which are subject to monitoring, as for example ADL and sleep quality. These indicators are correlated in a dependency graph, which is reasoned upon, again with ASP, to deduce signs of improvement or aggravation of the monitored condition.

In [5,6] the authors present a method for reasoning and decision-making support in a smart home setting. They use low-level and high-level ontologies to represent the domain, and interesting "situations" [5] to be recognized, respectively. Description logic reasoners and SWRL[4], which offer the ability to define temporal relations between entities, are utilized to detect target situations. Decision-making is assisted by an influence diagram based on Markov Logic Networks [16]. Ontological

---

[4] http://www.w3.org/Submission/SWRL/

modelling and automata-based reasoning are utilized in [3], towards the detection of potential emergency situations for the elderly, while an ontology/description logic-based approach to seniors' ADL detection is presented in [7].

Common in all the above approaches is a limited/restricted handling of uncertainty. [9], [3] and [7] cannot handle uncertainty whatsoever, while [12] lacks a formal probabilistic semantics. [15] does not support probabilistic reasoning and relies on (crisp) ASP constructs in order to address uncertainty. The approach in [5,6] is not able to handle uncertainty at the level of sensory data.

In contrast, the work presented here addresses uncertainty by means of a formal probabilistic semantics (ProbLog is based on the distribution semantics [17]), while it preserves the power of logic programming. The probabilistic version of the Event Calculus utilized in this paper was recently introduced in [18], in an effort to deal with uncertainty in activity recognition applications. The aim of our work is to evaluate the probabilistic Event Calculus in the context of a large, distributed monitoring system for assisted living.

6 Conclusions

We presented a Complex Event Recognition approach to detecting Activities of Daily Living and the level of functional ability, as defined by the Barthel index. The presented work is part of a real-world, unobtrusive, distributed monitoring system which is being developed in the FP7 project USEFIL, and involves various components such as multimedia processing and decision support. Our work is part of a research agenda that aims at evaluating the use of the Event Calculus in large distributed applications.

Our approach builds on previous work and proposes a logical framework based on the Event Calculus, properly extended in order to account for noise and uncertainty, by means of probabilistic reasoning with ProbLog. This framework exhibits a formal (probabilistic) semantics, and supports the representation of complex temporal phenomena for event recognition.

Further work includes experimentation with the real datasets that will be collected during the pilot studies of USEFIL. Moreover, to improve event recognition accuracy, we will employ techniques for weight learning and refinement (as opposed to setting the weights of rules manually), and abduction to deal with noise in the form of missing LLEs.

Acknowledgement. The research leading to these results has received funding from the European Union, Seventh Framework Programme (FP7/2007- 2013), under grant agreements n° 288532 (USEFIL) and n° 619435 (SPEED). The first author would like to thank the Hellenic Artificial Intelligence Society for additional financial support.

References

1. Artikis, A., Sergot, M., Paliouras, G.: A logic programming approach to activity recognition. In: Proceedings of the 2nd ACM International Workshop on Events in Multimedia, pp. 3–8. ACM (2010)

2. Bonatti, P., Calimeri, F., Leone, N., Ricca, F.: Answer set programming. In: Dovier, A., Pontelli, E. (eds.) GULP. LNCS, vol. 6125, pp. 159–182. Springer, Heidelberg (2010)
3. Botia, J.A., Villa, A., Palma, J.: Ambient assisted living system for in-home monitoring of healthy independent elders. Expert Systems with Applications 39(9), 8136–8148 (2012)
4. Bryant, R.E.: Graph-based algorithms for boolean function manipulation. IEEE Transactions on Computers 100(8), 677–691 (1986)
5. Chahuara, P., Portet, F., Vacher, M.: Context aware decision system in a smart home: Knowledge representation and decision making using uncertain contextual information. In: ARCOE 2012, p. 52 (2012)
6. Chahuara, P., Portet, F., Vacher, M.: Making context aware decision from uncertain information in a smart home: A markov logic network approach. In: Augusto, J.C., Wichert, R., Collier, R., Keyson, D., Salah, A.A., Tan, A.-H. (eds.) AmI 2013. LNCS, vol. 8309, pp. 78–93. Springer, Heidelberg (2013)
7. Chen, L., Nugent, C.D., Wang, H.: A knowledge-driven approach to activity recognition in smart homes. IEEE Transactions on Knowledge and Data Engineering 24(6), 961–974 (2012)
8. Collin, C., Wade, D.T., Davies, S., Horne, V.: The barthel ADL index: a reliability study. Disability & Rehabilitation 10(2), 61–63 (1988)
9. Dalal, S., Alwan, M., Seifrafi, R., Kell, S., Brown, D.: A rule-based approach to the analysis of elders activity data: Detection of health and possible emergency conditions. In: AAAI Fall 2005 Symposium (2005)
10. Etzion, O., Niblett, P.: Event processing in action. Manning Publications Co. (2010)
11. Fierens, D., Van den Broeck, G., Renkens, J., Shterionov, D., Gutmann, B., Thon, I., Janssens, G., De Raedt, L.: Inference and learning in probabilistic logic programs using weighted boolean formulas. To Appear in Theory and Practice of Logic Programming, TPLP arXiv preprint arXiv:1304.6810 (2013)
12. Filippaki, C., Antoniou, G., Tsamardinos, I.: Using constraint optimization for conflict resolution and detail control in activity recognition. In: Keyson, D.V., et al. (eds.) AmI 2011. LNCS, vol. 7040, pp. 51–60. Springer, Heidelberg (2011)
13. Kimmig, A., Demoen, B., De Raedt, L., Costa, V.S., Rocha, R.: On the implementation of the probabilistic logic programming language problog. Theory and Practice of Logic Programming 11(2-3), 235–262 (2011)
14. Kowalski, R., Sergot, M.: A logic-based calculus of events. In: Foundations of Knowledge Base Management, pp. 23–55. Springer (1989)
15. Mileo, A., Merico, D., Bisiani, R.: Reasoning support for risk prediction and prevention in independent living. Theory and Practice of Logic Programming 11(2-3), 361–395 (2011)
16. Richardson, M., Domingos, P.: Markov logic networks. Machine Learning 62(1-2), 107–136 (2006)
17. Sato, T.: A statistical learning method for logic programs with distribution semantics. In: Proceedings of the Twelfth International Conference on Logic Programming (ICLP 1995), pp. 715–729 (1995)
18. Skarlatidis, A., Artikis, A., Filippou, J., Paliouras, G.: A probabilistic logic programming event calculus. Journal of Theory and Practice of Logic Programming, TPLP (2014)

Declarative Reasoning Approaches
for Agent Coordination

Filippos Gouidis, Theodore Patkos,
Giorgos Flouris, and Dimitris Plexousakis

Institute of Computer Science, FO.R.T.H
Heraklion, Crete, Greece
{gouidis,patkos,fgeo,dp}@ics.forth.gr

Abstract. Reasoning about Action and Change (RAC) and Answer Set Programming (ASP) are two well-known fields in AI for logic based reasoning. Each paradigm bears unique features and a possible integration can lead to more effective ways to address hard AI problems. In this paper, we report on implementations that embed RAC formalisms and concepts in ASP and present the experimental results obtained, building on a graph-based problem setting that introduces casual and temporal requirements.

Keywords: Answer Set Programming, Event Calculus, Reasoning about Action and Change, Multi-Agent Action Coordination.

1 Introduction

Planning within a multi-agent setting is a challenging task in terms of computational capacity and representational demand, involving coordination of actions under constraints of diverse complexity. The practical impact of this kind of planning problems is evident in a multitude of domains ranging from logistics to robotics, and others [1]. Over the last decades, research in AI has contributed a repertoire of methodologies to approach multi-agent classical planning. Among them, theories for reasoning about action and change (RAC) stand out as a prominent approach. Building on the progress of classical first-order logic (FOL), formalisms such as the Situation Calculus [2] and the Event Calculus (EC) [3,4] have been applied successfully to reasoning in dynamic domains. Nonetheless, one of the great benefits of FOL, its high expressiveness, is also one of its main limitations when confronted with the demands of practical domains. Much effort has been placed in appropriately restricting FOL, as for instance to Horn clause reasoning to allow for efficient theorem proving.

In the last decade, the progress achieved in the field of Answer Set Programming (ASP) has grown at a fast pace. ASP is a form of declarative programming oriented towards difficult, primarily NP-hard, search problems [5]. It uses alternative semantics than standard and logic programming, based on default reasoning and the notion of stable models [6], while relying on constructs that resulted in powerful and efficient systems. Moreover, recent advancements in

A. Likas, K. Blekas, and D. Kalles (Eds.): SETN 2014, LNAI 8445, pp. 489–503, 2014.
© Springer International Publishing Switzerland 2014

the underlying theoretical models (e.g., [7]) and a better understanding on their basic properties managed to close significantly the conceptual gap that exists between ASP and FOL [8], offering the opportunity for the one to harness features from the other.

In this paper, we build on a setting that introduces challenging features to both fields of ASP and FOL and develop two approaches that use EC as specification language and ASP as implementation language, as well as a third approach relying exclusively on state-of-the-art ASP constructs. Consider the following example.

Example 1.1 The Intelligent Operations Center Domain: We imagine the case of a centrally-managed operations center (OC) of a smart city. The OC's dashboard receives requests from citizens that can be treated by different public services (Emergency Medical Service, Fire Department, Police Department etc). Each request requires the presence of a unit (agent) of one or more services in a certain location, in order to perform a specific activity.

The capabilities among agents may vary significantly. For example, a hospital can have both helicopters and ambulances, and these two types of agents have totally different travel times between locations in the city. Moreover, the presence of agents of one service or their operations may affect the agents of other services. For example, once a vehicle of the civil protection finishes clearing a road from rubble it will speed up the travel time of an ambulance that wants to pass this road; on the contrary, the presence of a fire fighter in a certain location may cause delays and traffic jams, hampering the speed of the ambulance.

The main responsibility of the OC is to manage the city services and decide how to effectively deploy and plan the actions of the available agents, in order to provide optimum and timely assistance to citizens. Apart from the financial gains achieved by optimizing everyday operations, the system becomes valuable during emergency response scenarios (e.g., following a major earthquake), where there is an overflow of requests and coordinating operations becomes critical. □

While non-declarative approaches have extensively been applied in problem settings similar to the one described above, extending their representational models with new dimensions is non-trivial. Furthermore,they are often prone to domain-dependent performance [9]. Our targeted objectives aim at demonstrating how expressive RAC formalisms, which are able to reason about complex phenomena, such as temporal and causal constraints, inertia, triggered events, coordination of actions, can be harmonized with the recent progress in ASP on theoretical and practical aspects. The paper reports on initial results towards comparing strong and weak points of RAC and ASP theories both from the point of view of representation and from the point of view of computational efficiency. The current and future results of this line of research aim at contributing towards a better coupling of state-of-the-art formalisms covering real-world, computationally intensive requirements. Encodings and execution guidelines are available online[1].

---

[1] F2LP website (last accessed 4/3/2014): http://www.ics.forth.gr/isl/MACPDRA/

The rest of this paper is structured as follows. After a brief introduction in Section 2 to the languages involved, we formally characterize the problem setting of Example 1.1 in Section 3. In Section 4, we elaborate on the strong and weak points of modeling this problem under different methodologies. Section 5 presents experimental results and the paper concludes with a discussion on future steps.

2   Background

2.1   Event Calculus

Action theories are logical languages for reasoning about the dynamics of changing worlds, having played a pivotal role in the development of non-monotonic logics and in formalisms to represent knowledge. The EC [3,4] is a narrative-based many-sorted first-order language for reasoning about action and change, where the sort $\mathcal{E}$ of *events* (or *actions*) indicates changes in the environment, the sort $\mathcal{F}$ of *fluents* denotes time-varying properties and the sort $\mathcal{T}$ of *time-points* is used to implement a linear time structure. The calculus implements the *principle of inertia* for fluents, which captures the property that things tend to persist over time unless affected by some event, and applies the technique of *circumscription* to solve the frame problem and support default reasoning.

Different dialects have been proposed over the years; in this study, we axiomatize our domains based on the Discrete-time Event Calculus (DEC) [10] and the recently proposed Functional Event Calculus (FEC) [11]. DEC defines a set of predicates to express which fluents hold when ($HoldsAt \subseteq \mathcal{F} \times \mathcal{T}$), which events happen ($Happens \subseteq \mathcal{E} \times \mathcal{T}$), which their effects are ($Initiates$, $Terminates$, $Releases \subseteq \mathcal{E} \times \mathcal{F} \times \mathcal{T}$) and whether a fluent is subject to the law of inertia or released from it ($ReleasedAt \subseteq \mathcal{F} \times \mathcal{T}$).

FEC, on the other hand, generalizes the EC to include non-binary (i.e. non-truth-valued) fluents taking values from the sort $\mathcal{V}$. In accordance to DEC, the key predicates and functions are $Happens \subseteq \mathcal{E} \times \mathcal{T}$, $ValueOf : \mathcal{F} \times \mathcal{T} \rightarrow \mathcal{V}$, $CausesValue \subseteq \mathcal{E} \times \mathcal{F} \times \mathcal{V} \times \mathcal{T}$, $PossVal \subseteq \mathcal{F} \times \mathcal{V}$. Non-determinism and triggered actions are supported by both formalisms. Along with the set of domain-independent rules that axiomatize the notions of inertia, causality and effect, the execution of reasoning tasks is performed with a set of domain-dependent axioms expressing the dynamics of the world.

2.2   Answer Set Programming

Answer set programming (ASP) is a recently developed programming technique combining declarativeness, modularity and expressiveness. It is founded on logic programming answer sets semantics, which drive the computation of stable models (answer sets). The procedure followed on most of ASP solvers is an enhanced version of DPLL algorithm. ASP is gaining increasing popularity due to its ability to combine an expressive, non-complex language over powerful solvers.

An Answer Set Program is a set of rules of the form:

Rule: $A_0 \text{:-} L_1 , \dots , L_{k-1}, \text{not } L_k, \dots, \text{not } L_n$.

where L_j are atoms and *not* represents negation-as-failure. The set of literals $\{L_1, \dots, L_n\}$ are called the body of the rule and A_0 the head. Intuitively, the head of a rule has to be true whenever all its body literals are true in the following sense: a non negated literal L_i is true if it has a derivation and a negated one, $\text{not } L_i$, is true if the atom L_i does not have one. According to stable model semantics, only atoms appearing in some head can appear in answer sets. Furthermore, derivations have to be acyclic, a feature that is important to model reachability. Rules with an empty body are called facts and their head is unconditionally true, i.e., it appears in all answer sets. Rules with an empty head are called integrity constraints and are used to reject answer set candidates.

ASP has already proven its potential in expressiveness in comparison to other declarative approaches, enabling the representation of phenomena for commonsense and nonmonotonic reasoning ([12,13]), while its solvers outperform satisfiability-based and constraint-programming solvers in many domains [14,15]. The success of ASP is demonstrated in a wide variety of fields that spans from hardware design and phylogenetic inference to the Semantic Web. In this study, we use the most recent ASP implementation developed by Potsdam Answer Set Solving Collection (Potassco), named Clingo[2]. It combines the grounder Gringo and solver Clasp and encompasses many utilities, such as detailed tuning of grounding and solving, utilization of useful built-in functions and also the ability to integrate scripts written in Lua and Python languages, through which high flexibility to the developer is possible.

3   Smart City Operations Center: Formal Definition

We assume a set $\mathcal{AG} = \{\alpha_1, \alpha_2, \dots\}$ of *agents* having different *types*, denoted by $\mathcal{TP} = \{\tau_1, \tau_2, \dots\}$. Each type represents different capabilities (such as cars or helicopters). Agents also belong to different *services* $\mathcal{SV} = \{\sigma_1, \sigma_2, \dots\}$, representing agencies in the smart city, such as the Police or the Fire Brigade. We denote by τ^α and σ^α the type and service, respectively, that agent α belongs to.

The smart city contains a set $\mathcal{LC} = \{\lambda_1, \lambda_2, \dots\}$ of *locations*. Each location is associated with a (possibly empty) set of services, representing the fact that this location requires agents from said services to visit it; this set of services is denoted by $Srv^{\lambda_i} \subseteq \mathcal{SV}$ for some location λ_i.

The conceptual model for the operations center system is a state-transition system described by the 4-tuple $\mathcal{OC} = \langle \mathcal{S}, \mathcal{AC}, \mathcal{EV}, \gamma \rangle$, where:

- $\mathcal{S} = \{s_1, s_2, \dots\}$ is a finite set of states that capture the assignment of agents and services to specific locations and also the connections between locations with specific costs[3];

---

[2] Clingo website (last accessed 4/3/2014): http://potassco.sourceforge.net/

[3] Due to space limitations, we leave implicit certain aspects, such as the propositions that characterize each state; these are formally defined in subsequent sections.

- $\mathcal{AC} = \{move\}$ is the set of possible actions, with $move : \mathcal{AG} \times \mathcal{LC} \to \mathcal{LC}$ being the only action that an agent can perform, i.e., move between locations;
- $\mathcal{EV} = \{changeCost\}$ the set of possible events, with $changeCost : \mathcal{TP} \times \mathcal{LC} \times \mathcal{TP} \times \mathcal{LC} \times \mathcal{LC} \to \mathbb{Z}^+$ a function expressing that when some agent type is at a specific location, it changes the cost of the connection between two locations for a given type of agent. Such events may be triggered by the change in location in each state;
- $\gamma : \mathcal{S} \times 2^{\mathcal{AC}} \to 2^{\mathcal{S}}$ is a state transition function. Multiple actions may occur concurrently, but we implicitly assume only one action for each agent.

Note that we model no specific agent action for the servicing of tasks at a location. In the future, we will also include servicing actions with durations and order (priorities) among them; for the time being, the arrival of an agent at a location causes also the successful execution of the task required. The system $\mathcal{OC}$ is fully observable (i.e., the initial state is fully known), deterministic and no exogenous actions or events can occur (i.e., the only changes to its state are due to agent actions or events triggered by these actions).

As explained above, the $\mathcal{OC}$ will issue a set of orders to the agents, essentially creating a path that each agent should follow (i.e., a sequence of locations). Given $\mathcal{OC} = \langle \mathcal{S}, \mathcal{AC}, \mathcal{EV}, \gamma \rangle$, an initial state s_0 and a set of goal states $S_g \subset S$, a plan π is defined as usual, as a sequence of nonempty sets of actions $(\{c_1^1, ...\}, ..., \{c_1^k, ...\})$ corresponding to a sequence of state transitions $(s_0, s_1 ..., s_k)$, such that $\gamma(s_0, \{c_1^1, ...\}) = s_1$, $\gamma(s_1, \{c_1^2, ...\}) = s_2$, ..., $\gamma(s_{k-1}, \{c_1^k, ...\}) = s_k$ and $s_k \in S_g$. In our case, a plan π_{acc} is called *acceptable* iff for all locations λ_j in the smart city, and for all $\sigma \in Srv^{\lambda_j}$, there exists an agent α and a state s_i ($0 \geq i \geq k$) produced by π_{acc}, such that $\sigma^\alpha = \sigma$ and the agent is at location λ_j at state s_i.

The objective of the $\mathcal{OC}$ is to develop a plan that will service all nodes in the least possible time. Let $T^\pi(i, \alpha)$ denote the time required for agent α to execute the ith $move(\alpha, \lambda_j)$ action of its own plan, i.e., the time it spent at λ_j plus the time required to travel from λ_j to the destination dictated by the action. The *service time* for a plan π, denoted by $\hat{\pi}$, is defined as $\hat{\pi} = max_\alpha \{\sum_i T^\pi(i, \alpha)\}$. Now, a plan π_{opt} is called *optimal* iff it is acceptable and there is no acceptable plan π'_{acc} such that $\widehat{\pi}'_{acc} < \hat{\pi}_{opt}$. We denote as $\mathcal{SCOC}$ the problem of finding an optimal plan for a given $\mathcal{OC}$ instance of a smart city.

Example 2.1 Simple Action Coordination: Consider the graph presented on Fig. 1a. In the initial state agent α_1 is located at λ_1 and needs to reach λ_4, while agent α_2 located at λ_2 needs to reach λ_5. Moreover, the arrival of α_2 at λ_2 reduces the cost of traveling from λ_1 to λ_2 from 9 to 3 time units, i.e., it increases the speed of agents traveling through this edge by a factor of 3.

Fig. 1b presents the situation that would occur if all agents acted towards minimizing the time required to execute their own plan: α_2 would go directly to λ_5 resulting in a total overall execution time of 11 time units. Given our definition of an optimum plan, the objective of agents is to minimize the overall servicing time. According to this scheme, α_2 first visits λ_3, affecting the travel time of α_1, as shown in Fig. 1c. Notice that when α_2 arrives at λ_3, agent α_1

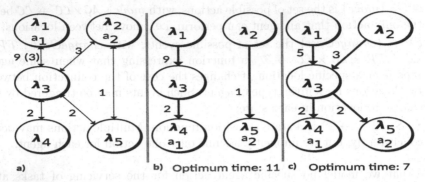

Fig. 1. Agent α_1 must reach λ_4 and α_2 λ_5. The presence of α_2 at λ_3 causes the cost of traveling from λ_1 to λ_3 to decrease from 9 to 3 time units.

already covered one third of the distance to λ_3. As such, this plan yields an overall servicing time of 7 time units and is the optimal one. ☐

4 Representation and Reasoning

The general structure of the $\mathcal{SCOC}$ setting requires planning with a combination of features, such as temporal and causal constraints. The problem incorporates characteristics of simpler frameworks, such as variations of the Traveling Salesman Problem, distance graphs and temporal reasoning with precedence ordering. Furthermore, it extends them in various ways, as for instance with dynamically changing edge costs. While the individual problems are extensively studied in relevant literature, their interplay in a unified framework still remains an open problem which attracts the interest of research community, mainly due to their impact in many real-world domains [9]. Such a setting requires expressive formalisms, in order both to support the complex phenomena that emerge and to allow for a formal verification of their properties. In this section, we describe how the EC and ASP can be applied to approach representational and practical issues related to the problem of $\mathcal{SCOC}$, revealing strong and weak points of each.

4.1 Representing $\mathcal{SCOC}$ with Event Calculus Axiomatizations

The $\mathcal{SCOC}$ planning problem formulates a demanding domain; while RAC theories are well suited to express some of its aspects, others prove to be more challenging, as we discuss next. We chose the EC as the specification language to describe the domain, not only due to its ability to model a multitude of commonsense phenomena, but also because of the availability of tools that can support our reasoning tasks.

Both FEC and DEC have been used to model the setting; we concentrate in this subsection on FEC, whose ability to model functional fluents offers greater flexibility, even though both theories are comparable for the given domain. We picture the smart city as a graph, whose edges have weights that may change dynamically as a result of occurring events. To simplify the presentation we assume one service and one agent type; the axiomatization can trivially be extended to the more general case, by simply using a different graph per agent type/service. In compliance with the notation introduced in the previous sections, let $ag, ag_1, ...$ denote variables of the $\mathcal{AG}$ sort, $l, l_1, ...$ variables of the $\mathcal{E}$ sort, while variables $num, num_1, ...$ denote positive reals[4].

The following domain closure axioms define all fluents and actions needed to model $\mathcal{SCOC}$, in order to reason about the state of agents (i.e., being at a location or moving), the state of locations (i.e., served or not) and the distance traveled:

$$f = At(ag) \vee f = Moving(ag) \vee f = RemDist(ag, l_1, l_2) \vee f = Step(l_1, l_2) \vee f = Served(l).$$
$$e = Departs(ag, l_1, l_2) \vee e = Arrives(ag, l) \vee UpdateRemDist(ag, l_1, l_2, num).$$

Fluent $Step$ denotes how much distance the agent can cover in one timepoint along the edge (l_1, l_2), while $RemDist$ captures the distance that remains to be traveled. $Step$ is subject to change, as it depends on the state of the world. We further assume uniqueness of names axioms for actions and fluents. The possible values for these fluents are appropriated restricted:

$$PossVal(At(ag), l). \ PossVal(Step(l_1, l_2), num). \ PossVal(RemDist(ag, l_1, l_2), num).$$
$$PossVal(Moving(ag), v) \equiv v = True \vee v = False.$$
$$PossVal(Served(l), v) \equiv v = True \vee v = False.$$

Certain predicates are also defined. For instance, $Connected(l_1, l_2, num)$ denotes edges and the corresponding distance between locations.

In comparison to other action theories, the explicit representation of time inside EC predicates facilitates the developer in expressing complex temporal expressions, necessary in $\mathcal{SCOC}$ to model for instance *actions with durations*, such as traveling for a given amount of time. Moreover, the calculus has established solutions to the frame, ramification and qualification problems, relieving the developer from the tedious work of explicitly writing frame or minimization axioms. Many aspects of the domain can easily be described by axioms expressing *context-dependent effects of actions*, *action preconditions* and *state constraints*, with existentially quantified variables whenever needed:

$$CausesValue(Arrives(ag, l), at(ag), l, t) \leftarrow ValueOf(Moving(ag), t) = True.$$
$$Happens(Departs(ag, l_1, l_2), t) \rightarrow ValueOf(At(ag), t) = l_1.$$
$$ValueOf(At(ag), t) = l_1 \wedge ValueOf(At(ag), t) = l_2 \rightarrow l_1 = l_2.$$
$$Happens(Departs(ag, l_1, l_2), t) \rightarrow \exists num Connected(l_1, l_2, num).$$

In order to handle metric distances between locations or calculate traveled distances, $\mathcal{SCOC}$ calls for extensive use of *numerical operations* to be incorporated in the domain description. For instance, we have to recalculate the $Step$ fluent every time certain agent actions affect it, such as when some agent arrives

---

[4] All variables in formulae are implicitly universally quantified, unless stated otherwise. Moreover, we assume $\mathcal{E} \supseteq \mathcal{AC} \cup \mathcal{EV}$, i.e., events axiomatized by the Event Calculus refer both to agent actions and triggered events.

at, serves or leaves a particular location. We use the predicate $AffectsCost(ag, l, l_1, l_2, num, v)$ to model different variations of the $costChange$ event introduced in Section 3. For instance, when $v = 1$ (resp. $v = 2$, $v = 3$) $AffectsCost$ denotes that the cost of traveling from l_1 to l_2 becomes num when agent ag arrives at (resp. is present at, departs from) location l. The following axiom models the case when $v = 3$ (the rest are similarly defined):

$$CausesValue(Departs(ag, l), Step(l_1, l_2), (num_1/num), t) \leftarrow$$
$$[Connected(l_1, l_2, num_1) \wedge ValueOf(At(ag), t) = l \wedge affectsSpeed(ag, l, l_1, l_2, num, 3)].$$

Despite the simplicity of such axioms, the introduction of numerical variables leads to an explosion of grounded terms having tremendous impact in performance, as discussed in Section 5, calling for special measures to be adopted.

Finally, *triggered events*, i.e., events that occur when the world is in a particular state, are a significant leverage in modeling real-world domains [16]. In our case, we use triggered events to keep track of the distance that an agents needs to travel before reaching the destination location:

$$Happens(UpdateRemDist(ag, l_1, l_2, (num_1 - num_2)), t) \leftarrow ValueOf(Moving(ag), t) = True \wedge$$
$$ValueOf(RemDist(ag, l_1, l_2), t) = num_1 \wedge ValueOf(Step(l_1, l_2), t - 1) = num_2.$$

Note that, in contrast to most benchmark problems in action theories, in our case the duration of certain actions, such as the agent's travel is not known beforehand, rather it needs to be calculated on-the-fly. Our modeling adopts the simple solution of recalculating the remaining distance at every timepoint according to the distance the agent has traveled in the previous timepoint (notice that *Step* refers to $t - 1$ in the previous axiom). A variation of this problem with static edge weights has also been implemented to show the difference in performance when action duration is known *a priori*. ASP constructs can provide radical solutions, as we argue in the next section.

Finally, the axiomatization needs also to include the description of the initial state, specifying the location and state of all agents, as well as the goal state, i.e., $ValueOf(Served(n), T_{opt}) = True$ for some timepoint T_{opt}. Note that since the problem we solve is a planning problem, we do not specify completion of the *Happens* predicate, letting the reasoner produce all combinations of event occurrences that can lead to the satisfaction of the goal state. Of course, T_{opt} is not known beforehand.

4.2 Representing $\mathcal{SCOC}$ in Answer Set Programming

This subsection describes an alternative modeling that uses ASP as specification language for describing $\mathcal{SCOC}$, aimed at exploiting the potential of state-of-the-art ASP solvers. Given the structure of the problem, we based our representation on standard methods found in literature for encoding graph traversal, as given for instance in [17]. Due to the dynamic nature of the problem, we extended the methodology with a treatment of time. In this way, atoms representing dynamic attributes contain a variable accounting for time. As before, we simplify the setting and assume only one agency and every node of the graph has to be visited at least by one of the agents.

To accommodate planning, Clingo offers a special functionality where reasoning progresses incrementally. Specifically, a special variable, which denotes timepoints in our case, is acting as a place-holder that increases by a constant step number to perform grounding and solving in consecutive steps, until an answer set satisfying the goal state is found. To accomplish this, the program is divided into 3 independent parts: the basic, the cumulative and the volatile part. The former contains the definitions that are used throughout the execution, as well as the initial state, while the latter specifies the goal condition. The cumulative part, on the other hand, incorporates all rules and constraints that have to be grounded every time the reasoning progresses by one step.

The state of the graph is specified by predicates, such as $in(Ag1,Nd1,1)$ and $edge(Nd1,Nd2,W,1)$ contained in the basic part. In order to represent the displacement of the agents, rules able to express cardinality constraints are used:

$$0\{on\_the\_road(AG,X,Y,C,t) : edge(X,Y,C,t)\}1 : -agent(AG), in(AG,X,t).$$

This rule states that an agent located at a node at a certain time-point can initiate *at most* one movement and this movement should have as destination a node that is connected (i.e., $edge$) to the node that is currently located at. Such rules give significant leverage to the developer, offering a compact way to introduce various types of restrictions.

In order to avoid the overload of grounded terms introduced in the Event Calculus encodings when numerical operations are in place, we embedded in our ASP encodings *external predicates*, a special functionality offered by Clingo. The truth value of these predicates can be decided by scripts written in the Lua language, without requiring grounding or disturbing execution during reasoning. Such an external predicate is @*new_cost* appearing in the following rule:

$$on\_the\_road(AG,X,Y,C\_NEW,t) : -on\_the\_road(AG,X,Y,C\_OLD,t-1), 0 < C\_OLD,$$
$$e(X,Y,W\_OLD,t-1), e(X,Y,W\_NEW,t), C\_NEW = @new\_cost(W\_NEW,W\_OLD,C\_OLD,t).$$

The rule calculates the remaining distance for agents on the move. The performance gains obtained when executing such computationally demanding tasks in parallel with reasoning is depicted in the evaluation discussed in Section 5.

While the built-in constructs described before offer enhanced functionalities to support declarative reasoning, certain aspects of $SCOC$ were not handled as conveniently as with the EC encodings. The representation of inertia, which had to be explicitly defined in all time-dependent rules, and the treatment of time in general, are characteristic examples:

$$-edge(X,Y,C2,t) : -edge(X,Y,C,t), edge(X,Y,C2,t-1), C2! = C.$$
$$edge(X,Y,C2,t) : -edge(X,Y,C2,t-1), not -edge(X,Y,C2,t).$$

These rules model the weight of edges at each timepoint, having the law of inertia explicitly expressed. The first rule implies that if for two consecutive time moments an edge has different weights, the earlier value must become obsolete the next time moment, while the second rule indicates that if an edge's value has not become obsolete, it is conserved for the next time moment ("−" denotes strict negation). Similar behavior has to be designed for other atoms, whose value may change over time. The ease of accommodating such phenomena with the EC and their direct application to new features with minumum effort, often referred to as elaboration tolerance, becomes easily evident.

Finally, the constraint expressing the goal condition, i.e., whether all nodes have been visited, is expressed as follows and added in the volatile part:

$$: -not\ reached(X, t), node(X), query(t).$$

We additionally made use of Clingo's built-in function *minimize*, in order to achieve a second-level of optimization:

$$\#minimize\{C : on\_the\_road(AG, X, Y, C, t)\}$$

With this expression we can define a secondary criterion to classify optimal plans, when more than one are found. Specifically, we choose the one with minimum distances traveled by all agents, denoted by variable C. Special treatment of such expressions allows the Clingo solver to calculate solutions effectively.

5   Experimental Evaluation

5.1   Preparation

Recent progress in generalizing the definition of stable model semantics used in ASP [7] has opened the way for highly expressive formalisms to be reformulated in ASP encodings and take advantage of the several efficient implementations that are available. Specifically, the precise characterization of the correspondence between stable models and circumscription used by many theories for reasoning about action and change, such as the Situation and the EC, has permitted the reformulation of the latter in ASP. For that purpose, we used the F2LP[5] tool to transform our circumscriptive DEC-based axiomatization into a logic program that can be executed with ASP reasoners. This is important since not all first-order formulae can be transformed into the clausal form used in ASP solvers while preserving stable models. F2LP applies the translation developed in [18] that guarantees that the ASP encoding created as output is equivalent to the circumscription-based axiomatization.

While the FEC-based axiomatization can also become input to F2LP, we preferred to use the dedicated reasoner and encoding style for FEC theories developed in [19]. The importance of this tool relies on its capacity to support reasoning with very expressive classes of problems with minimum effort on the developer's side. Specifically, it can execute the epistemic extension of FEC [11], which we plan to integrate in future variations of the $\mathcal{SCOC}$ setting, when for instance not all agent locations will be known initially.

---

[5] F2LP website (last accessed 4/3/2014): http://reasoning.eas.asu.edu/f2lp/

Due to the fact that FEC and DEC are implemented in a non-incremental way, we created a non-incremental version of the ASP implementation (ASP-non), in addition to the incremental one (ASP-inc), to study the differences and allow for a more direct comparison. In particular, we first executed each problem instance with ASP-inc in order to find optimal times and then we used those times to ran with the rest of the programs.

Our results are given in terms of overall time for solution (analyzed further in grounding and solving time) and atoms produced. All experiments were conducted on a workstation having 2 Intel eight-core CPU of 2.30 GHZ and 384 GB of RAM memory. For the computation of the answer sets version 4.2.1 of Clingo was used. A time limit of 15 minutes held for each test; if a solution was not found within the time limit the result was considered unknown. Also, all implementations were tuned to generate only one answer set. All encodings, results and a script for executing the encodings are available online.

5.2   Results

We designed 2 sets of experiments, one for a simple problem variation where the topology of the graphs remained unchanged during planning (s-$SCOC$) and another where edge costs could changed dynamically according to agents' locations (d-$SCOC$). Tables 1 present relevant statistics for both variations. Each experiment considered graphs of size 5, 10 and 15 nodes with an increasing number of agents scattered randomly in each case. A set of rules also assigned random values to edges (ranging from 1 to 10), and also dictated how the location of agents could affect those values in the d-$SCOC$ case.

At first glance, it is evident that d-$SCOC$ is a much harder problem than s-$SCOC$, as reflected on the times required to find optimal plans. We also noticed that for more complex problem instances, the incremental approach to problem solving is generally more expensive than the non-incremental one, requiring the reasoner to interchange between grounding and solving while converging to a solution. As already mentioned, the incremental approach is the only way of finding a plan when the number of necessary steps is unknown. Therefore, one important conclusion is to incorporate in future executions the functionality offered by Clingo to manually set lower and upper bounds for initiating and terminating the incremental reasoning process; approximate values for these bounds can easily be determined given the initial state.

It is interesting to notice also that increasing the number of agents available to serve tasks manages to reduce significantly plan finding times, even though this is not always reflected in the number of atoms produced. This is related to the length of the produced plans, which is shorter when more agents are available, despite the fact that more alternative routes need to be considered. In fact, what we found considering bigger, as well as less complex graphs than cliques, is that this performance gain converges to a number of agents specific for each topology, after which no significant profit is measurable.

Table 1. Experimental Results for the s-$\mathcal{SCOC}$ and d-$\mathcal{SCOC}$ case. (times are in seconds).

		Graph Size	5			10			15		
		# of agents	1	3	5	1	6	10	1	8	15
s-$\mathcal{SCOC}$	ASP-inc	T†	0.035	0	0	1.82	0.01	0.01	46.98	0.01	0.01
		G°	0.01	0	0	1.80	0	0	46.96	0	0
		S△	0.025	0	0	0.02	0.01	0.01	0.02	0.01	0.01
		A°	894	539	401	2691	1989	2310	4462	2856	2889
	ASP-non	T†	0.02	0	0	7.27	0.01	0.02	85.35	0.06	0.05
		G°	0.01	0	0	7.25	0	0	85.33	0.01	0.01
		S△	0.01	0	0	0	0.01	0.02	0.02	0.05	0.04
		A°	1717	1029	742	6019	4473	5241	11205	6805	6730
	FEC	T†	0.34	0.03	0.02	8.70	0.17	0.20	431.44	0.06	0.52
		G°	0.11	0	0	8.02	0	0	429.28	0.01	0.01
		S△	0.23	0.03	0.02	0.68	0.17	0.20	2.16	0.05	0.51
		A°	10533	4847	4224	31578	14965	18241	58184	6805	34812
	DEC	T†	0.05	0.02	0.02	0.68	0.22	0.47	21.76	0.99	2.46
		G°	0.01	0	0	0.59	0.04	0.19	21.45	0.23	1.06
		S△	0.04	0.02	0.02	0.09	0.18	0.28	0.31	0.76	1.40
		A°	3526	4049	4497	14559	22663	30368	33566	51821	74032
d-$\mathcal{SCOC}$	ASP-inc	T†	0.03	0.01	0.01	0.71	0.02	0.03	473.43	0.20	0.10
		G°	0.01	0	0	0.61	0	0	473.08	0	0
		S△	0.02	0.01	0.01	0.10	0.02	0.03	0.35	0.20	0.10
		A°	1179	1629	2359	10966	3363	6260	43174	4355	8094
	ASP-non	T†	0.01	0.01	0.01	0.07	0.03	0.01	90.46	0.06	0.08
		G°	0	0	0	0.02	0	0	89.72	0	0.01
		S△	0.01	0.01	0.01	0.05	0.03	0.01	0.74	0.06	0.07
		A°	1120	1490	2282	7530	3020	5799	34862	5732	7360
	FEC	T†	230.31	135.92	132.50	N/A	284.80	460.90	N/A	408.86	N/A
		G°	0	0	0	N/A	0.07	0.13	N/A	0.07	N/A
		S△	230.31	135.92	132.50	N/A	284.73	460.77	N/A	408.79	N/A
		A°	406064	347891	327901	N/A	677987	948587	N/A	1080183	N/A
	DEC	T†	230.31	135.92	29.30	N/A	86.65	146.59	N/A	116.60	228.99
		G°	0.01	0.14	0.03	N/A	0.11	0.50	N/A	0.45	2.22
		S△	20.03	27.69	29.27	N/A	86.54	146.09	N/A	116.15	226.77
		A°	60868	89823	114522	N/A	277090	445634	N/A	528443	947717

† Total Time   ° Grounding Time   △ Solving Time   ° Atoms Produced

Noticeable also is the difference in performance between the EC and the pure ASP implementations. This difference is primarily attributed to the cost of handling the numerical manipulations by the former. Specifically, in order to model edge traversal, we considered as the smallest distance that an agent can travel in one timepoint to be a a tenth of the unit distance. That is, if the maximum cost of any edge in a graph is 8, the smallest distance covered in one step is 0.1, requiring number variables to range between 80 possible values. For the ASP case though, we relied on external predicates to model and calculate such values, significantly reducing the number of grounded atoms. As depicted in the tables, these are orders of magnitude fewer in the ASP encodings with respect to the EC encodings. This conclusion will play key role in our future implementations that will be driven by the goal of seamlessly combining the structures offered by state-of-the-art ASP tools into EC encodings.

Finally, we notice that in the majority of cases the dominant factor affecting performance is the time spent by the grounder to instantiate the problem, whereas solving time is usually negligible. We note here that our encodings did not emphasize on performance and the solutions adopted leave space for further improvements. We expect that the incorporation of heuristics along with modelings more tailored to the specific execution style of Gringo will achieve better results. Nevertheless, we wish to stress that the recently released reactive ASP solver oClingo is expected to have enormous impact in problems such as the one studied here. oClingo is able to perform online reasoning without having to re-initialize the solving process every time new information arrives. This facility will be harnessed to provide replanning capabilities for future variations of $SCOC$ that will additionally allow for unpredictable occurrences of external events to change the state of the system.

6   Discussion and Conclusion

In this paper, we contrasted contemporary and prominent approaches of the fields of RAC and ASP, both from the representational and the practical standpoint. We initiate a line of research that focuses on those aspects where a synergetic application can prove more fruitful, building on recent theoretical and applied advancements in both fields.

Closest to ours is the work conducted in the context of the housekeeping robotics domain [20,21]. Research there investigates collaborative planning by considering ASP and the high-level action description language $C+$ for domain specification, leaning towards the former as more appropriate to formalize the concepts involved. Yet, temporal relations, which are inherent in this kind of settings, are much more conveniently handled with the EC than with $C+$ or domain-specific solutions. This type of problem can be addressed by other techniques, such as graphplan or integer linear programming. But, as $SCOC$ will expand to include more features in the future, with non-deterministic events (stochastic and unpredictable), durational, prioritized tasks, and the capability of re-planning being the most imminent ones, the broadness of the tools and theories we presented in this study will be the first candidates to resolve them. For this reason, we also plan to consider other EC dialects, such as the Cached Event Calculus [22], and study their performance.

Furthermore, the problem bears strong similarities to the general construct of the Traveling Salesperson Problem and its many variations. The progress that has been and still is being made in analyzing their theoretical properties and developing efficient procedural algorithms, as for instance in [9], may provide inspiration for developing more efficient, real-world implementations for $SCOC$. As we showed, the use of external predicates and the strong coupling of declarative reasoning with scripting languages may achieve significant performance gains.

References

1. Ghallab, M., Nau, D., Traverso, P.: Automated Planning: Theory and Practice. Morgan Kaufmann (2004)
2. Reiter, R.: Knowledge in Action: Logical Foundations for Specifying and Implementing Dynamical Systems. MIT Press (2001)
3. Kowalski, R., Sergot, M.: A Logic-based Calculus of Events. New Generation Computing 4(1), 67–95 (1986)
4. Miller, R., Shanahan, M.: Some alternative formulations of the event calculus. In: Kakas, A.C., Sadri, F. (eds.) Computational Logic: Logic Programming and Beyond. LNCS (LNAI), vol. 2408, pp. 452–490. Springer, Heidelberg (2002)
5. Lifschitz, V.: What is answer set programming? In: Proceedings of the Twenty-Third AAAI Conference on Artificial Intelligence, 1594–1597. AAAI (2008)
6. Gelfond, M., Lifschitz, V.: The stable model semantics for logic programming. In: International Logic Programming Conference and Symposium, pp. 1070–1080 (1988)
7. Ferraris, P., Lee, J., Lifschitz, V.: Stable models and circumscription. Artificial Intelligence 175(1), 236–263 (2011)
8. Denecker, M., Vennekens, J., Vlaeminck, H., Wittocx, J., Bruynooghe, M.: Answer set programming's contributions to classical logic. In: Balduccini, M., Son, T.C. (eds.) Logic Programming, Knowledge Representation, and Nonmonotonic Reasoning. LNCS, vol. 6565, pp. 12–32. Springer, Heidelberg (2011)
9. Kumar, T.S., Cirillo, M., Koenig, S.: On the traveling salesman problem with simple temporal constraints. In: 10th Symposium of Abstraction, Reformulation, and Approximation (SARA 2013), pp. 73–79 (2013)
10. Mueller, E.: Commonsense Reasoning, 1st edn. Morgan Kaufmann (2006)
11. Miller, R., Morgenstern, L., Patkos, T.: Reasoning about knowledge and action in an epistemic event calculus. In: 11th International Symposium on Logical Formalizations of Commonsense Reasoning, Commonsense 2013 (2013)
12. Eiter, T., Ianni, G., Krennwallner, T.: Reasoning web. semantic technologies for information systems, 40–110 (2009)
13. Coban, E., Erdem, E., Ture, F.: Comparing ASP, CP, ILP on two Challenging Applications: Wire Routing and Haplotype Inference. In: Proc. of the 2nd International Workshop on Logic and Search, LaSh 2008 (2008)
14. Kim, T.-W., Lee, J., Palla, R.: Circumscriptive event calculus as answer set programming. In: 21st International Joint Conference on Artificial Intelligence (IJCAI 2009), pp. 823–829 (2009)
15. Celik, M., Erdogan, H., Tahaoglu, F., Uras, T., Erdem, E.: Comparing ASP and CP on four grid puzzles. In: Proc. of the 16th International Workshop on Experimental Evaluation of Algorithms for Solving Problems with Combinatorial Explosion, RCRA 2009 (2009)
16. Tran, N., Baral, C.: Reasoning about Triggered Actions in AnsProlog and Its Application to Molecular Interactions in Cells. In: 9th International Conference on the Principles of Knowledge Representation and Reasoning (KR 2004), pp. 554–564 (2004)
17. Gebser, M., Kaminski, R., Kaufmann, B., Schaub, T.: Answer Set Solving in Practice. In: Synthesis Lectures on Artificial Intelligence and Machine Learning. Morgan & Claypool Publishers (2012)
18. Lee, J., Palla, R.: Reformulating the situation calculus and the event calculus in the general theory of stable models and in answer set programming. Journal of Artificial Intelligence Research 43(1), 571–620 (2012)

19. Ma, J., Miller, R., Morgenstern, L., Patkos, T.: An epistemic event calculus for asp-based reasoning about knowledge of the past, present and future. In: Proc. of the 19th International Conference on Logic for Programming, Artificial Intelligence, and Reasoning, LPAR-19 (2013)

20. Erdem, E., Aker, E., Patoglu, V.: Answer set programming for collaborative house-keeping robotics: Representation, reasoning, and execution. Intelligent Service Robotics 5(4), 275–291 (2012)

21. Aker, E., Erdogan, A., Erdem, E., Patoglu, V.: Causal reasoning for planning and coordination of multiple housekeeping robots. In: Delgrande, J.P., Faber, W. (eds.) LPNMR 2011. LNCS, vol. 6645, pp. 311–316. Springer, Heidelberg (2011)

22. Chittaro, L., Montanari, A.: Efficient temporal reasoning in the cached event calculus. Computational Intelligence 12(3), 359–382 (1996)

Reasoning about Actions with Loops

Jiankun He, Yuping Shen, and Xishun Zhao*

Institute of Logic and Cognition
Department of Philosophy
Sun Yat-sen University
Guangzhou, China, 510275
{hejiank,shyping,hsszxs}@mail.sysu.edu.cn

Abstract. Plans with *loops* (or *loop-plans*) are more *general* and *compact* than classical *sequential* plans, and gaining increasing attention in AI. While many existing approaches focus on *algorithmic* issues, few work has been devoted to the *semantical* foundations of planning with loops. In this paper we develop a tailored action language $\mathcal{A}_K^L$ for handling domains with loop-plans and argue that it posses a "better" semantics than existing work and could serve as a clean, solid semantical foundation for reasoning about actions with loops.

1 Introduction

Consider the example [1,2]: An agent is instructed to chop down a tree with an axe. The tree is initially *up* and the agent *knows* that. The *nondeterministic* action *chop* hits the tree once and the tree will be either down or still up, the *sensing* action *check* makes the agent to know whether the tree is down.

Sequential planning is unable to solve the problem because the number of chops to get the tree down is not known in advance. However, it is not hard to see that the problem can be solved by a loop-plan π: **while** *up* **do** *chop*; *check* **od**. The semantics behind can be given by the corresponding *transition system* in Fig. 1. Simply speaking, each node in Fig. 1 is called a *c-state*, which consists of two parts: one is a *single* interpretation representing the (physical) *world state*, the other is a set of interpretations representing the agent's *belief state*. It follows that the agent's knowledge can be described in terms of typical epistemic approach [3]. E.g., in c-state σ_1 the world state and the belief state are the same (i.e., $\{U\}$, the tree is *up*), so σ_1 means the tree is up and the agent knows that. On the other hand, the c-state σ_2 means that the tree is *down* (i.e., $\emptyset$) and the agent *does not* know about that (there are two possibilities in the agent's belief). The nondeterministic action *chop* may lead σ_1 to σ_2 or σ_3 and makes the agent to *lose* knowledge, while *sensing* action *check* may lead σ_2 to σ_4 and makes the agent to *obtain* knowledge about the tree. One may (informally) verify that there exists a path from σ_1 to σ_4 by executing the plan π, in other words, π is a loop-plan which leads the system from its initial node to the goal.

---

* Corresponding Author.

A. Likas, K. Blekas, and D. Kalles (Eds.): SETN 2014, LNAI 8445, pp. 504–509, 2014.

Our action language $\mathcal{A}_K^L$ is an extension of [3,4], which incorporates nonde-terministic actions, sensing actions, and loop-plans. In the rest of the paper, we shall first introduce the syntax and semantics of $\mathcal{A}_K^L$, and then compare it with existing approaches, moreover, we point out that it posses a "better" seman-tics and could serve as a clean, solid semantical foundation for reasoning about actions with loops.

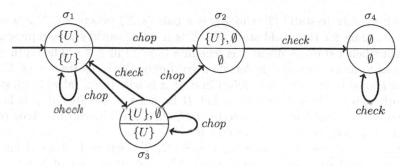

Fig. 1. Transition system of the tree chopping example

2   Syntax of $\mathcal{A}_K^L$

Let F and A be two *disjoint non-empty* sets of symbols, called *fluent (symbols)* and *action (symbols)* respectively. An action $a \in A$ is either a *sensing* or *non-sensing* one. A *(fluent) literal* l is either a fluent f or its negation $\neg f$. We do not distinguish between $\neg\neg f$ and f.

Let l be a literal, φ and ψ be *(fluent) formulas* (boolean combinations of fluents), a *domain description* D is a set of the following kinds of propositions: *value* propositions of the form "**initially** l", describing the initial state, *knowl-edge* propositions of the form "a **determines** f", saying that *sensing* action a makes the value of f be known, *effect* propositions of the form "a **cause** ψ **if** φ", describing the effects of a *non-sensing* action a. Particularly, effect propositions of the form "a **cause** $\bot$ **if** φ" can be rewritten as "**nonexecutable** a **if** φ", where $\bot$ is a classical contradiction. If φ is a tautology $\top$, then we drop the **if** part in the above propositions.

Definition 1. *A plan π in $\mathcal{A}_K^L$ is inductively defined as follows:*

$$\pi := \epsilon \mid a \mid \pi_1; \pi_2 \mid \varphi?\pi_1 : \pi_2 \mid \textbf{while } \varphi \textbf{ do } \pi_1 \textbf{ od}$$

in which ϵ is the empty sequence of actions, $a \in A$ an action, $\varphi?\pi_1 : \pi_2$ a conditional plan[1] and **while** φ **do** π_1 **od** *a loop-plan.*

A *query* is an expression of the form "**Knows** φ **after** π", where φ is formula and π is plan. Intuitively, a query asks whether φ is known to be true after executing π. The tree chopping example can be formalized as the domain:

---

[1] Reads "If φ then execute π_1 else execute π_2".

$$D_{TC} = \left\{ \begin{array}{l} \textbf{initially } U, \; chop \textbf{ causes } U \vee \neg U \textbf{ if } U, \\ check \textbf{ determines } U, \textbf{ nonexecutable } chop \textbf{ if } \neg U \end{array} \right\}$$

Under the domain D_{TC}, it is natural to give a *positive* answer to the query **Knows** $\neg U$ after π, where π is the loop-plan **while** U **do** $chop$; $check$ **od**.

3   Semantics of $\mathcal{A}_K^L$

A *combined state* (c-state) [3] σ in $\mathcal{A}_K^L$ is a pair $\langle s, \Sigma \rangle$, where $s \in \Sigma$ is a set of fluents standing for the world state and Σ is a set of world states representing the agent's belief state. A fluent f is *true* in s ($s \models f$) iff $f \in s$. The truth value of a fluent formula φ under s is defined accordingly. For a c-state $\sigma = \langle s, \Sigma \rangle$, we say φ is *known to be true* (resp. *false*) in σ, if φ is true (resp. false) in all states of Σ; otherwise, φ is *unknown* in σ. Let B be a set of c-states, if φ is known to be true (resp. false) in *every* c-state of B, then φ is known to be true (resp. false) in B; otherwise, φ is unknown in B.

A transition system is a tuple $\langle F, A, S, S^b, \mathcal{R}, \mathcal{R}^b \rangle$, where F, A are defined as above, $S \subseteq \mathscr{P}(F)$ is a set of world states, $S^b \subseteq \mathscr{P}(S)$ is a set of belief states, $\mathcal{R} \subseteq S \times A \times S$ is the transition relation for world states, and $\mathcal{R}^b : S^b \times \mathcal{R} \to S^b$ is a transition function for belief states.

The *signature* $sig(D)$ (resp. $sig(\varphi)$) of a domain description D (resp. a formula φ) is the set of fluents mentioned in D (resp. φ). Given a domain description D, the following notations are adopted (and slightly modified) from [3,4]:

- $F(a, s) = \{ \psi \mid \exists ``a \textbf{ causes } \psi \textbf{ if } \varphi" \in D \text{ s.t. } s \models \varphi \}$.
- $I(a, s) = sig(D) \backslash \{ f \mid f \in sig(\psi), \text{where } \psi \in F(a, s) \}$, denotes the set of fluents that are not possibly affected by action a in s.
- $\mathcal{R}_D = \{ \langle s, a, s' \rangle \mid (s' \cap I(a, s)) = (s \cap I(a, s)) \text{ and } \forall \varphi \in F(a, s), s' \models \varphi \}$. Roughly speaking, each transition says that inertia is applied to not possibly affected fluents, and formulas in $F(a, s)$ are true in s' after the action. Note that if a is a sensing action, then $\langle s, a, s \rangle \in \mathcal{R}_D$.

- $F^b(a) = \{ f \mid \exists ``a \textbf{ determines } f" \in D \}$.
- $V(\Theta, s) = \{ f \in \Theta \mid s \models f, \text{where } \Theta \text{ is a set of fluents} \}$.
- $\mathcal{R}_D^b(\Sigma, \langle s, a, s' \rangle) = \{ s_1 \in S \mid s_0 \in \Sigma, \langle s_0, a, s_1 \rangle \in \mathcal{R}_D, \text{ and } V(F^b(a), s_1) = V(F^b(a), s') \}$, where Σ is a belief state and $\langle s, a, s' \rangle \in \mathcal{R}_D$. Intuitively, if a is a non-sensing action, then each state in Σ evolves according to $\mathcal{R}_D$. If a is a sensing action, then states in Σ which do not agree on $F^b(a)$ with the physical world state are removed.

Definition 2 (Transition Function). *Let D be a domain description in $\mathcal{A}_K^L$, B be a set of c-states and $\langle \bot, \{\bot\} \rangle$ be a specialized c-state (every formula is false in state $\bot$). The associated transition function Φ is a function that maps a plan and a set of c-states to a set of c-states, defined as follows:*

1. $\Phi(\epsilon, B) = B$;
2. $\Phi(a, B) = \{ \langle s', \Sigma' \rangle \mid \langle s, \Sigma \rangle \in B, \mathcal{R}_D(\langle s, a, s' \rangle), \mathcal{R}_D^b(\Sigma, \langle s, a, s' \rangle) = \Sigma' \}$
   $\cup \{ \langle \bot, \{\bot\} \rangle \mid \langle s, \Sigma \rangle \in B, \forall s' \neg \mathcal{R}_D(\langle s, a, s' \rangle) \}$;

3. $\Phi(\pi_1; \pi_2, B) = \Phi(\pi_2, \Phi(\pi_1, B));$

4. $\Phi(\varphi?\pi_1 : \pi_2, B) = \Phi(\pi_1, \{\langle s, \Sigma \rangle \in B \mid \varphi \text{ is known to be true in } \langle s, \Sigma \rangle\})$
$$\cup \Phi(\pi_2, \{\langle s, \Sigma \rangle \in B \mid \varphi \text{ is known to be false in } \langle s, \Sigma \rangle\})$$
$$\cup \{\langle \perp, \{\perp\} \rangle \mid \varphi \text{ is unknown in some } \langle s, \Sigma \rangle \in B\};$$

5. if $\pi = $ **while** φ **do** π_1 **od**, then

$$\Phi(\pi, B) = \begin{cases} \bigcup_{k=0}^{\infty} \Phi(\pi^k, B) \setminus & \text{if } \bigcup_{k=0}^{\infty} \Phi(\pi^k, B) \setminus \\ KT_\varphi(\bigcup_{k=0}^{\infty} \Phi(\pi^k, B)) & KT_\varphi(\bigcup_{k=0}^{\infty} \Phi(\pi^k, B)) \neq \emptyset \\ \\ \{\langle \perp, \{\perp\} \rangle\} & \text{otherwise} \end{cases}$$

where $KT_\varphi(B) = \{\langle s, \Sigma \rangle \in B \mid \varphi \text{ is known to be true in } \langle s, \Sigma \rangle\}$ and (i) $\pi^0 = \epsilon$; (ii) $\pi^{n+1} = \varphi?(\pi_1; \pi^n) : \epsilon$.

A world state s is called an *initial state* of a domain description D, if $s \models l$ for every value proposition "**initially** l" $\in D$, in which l is a literal comes from $sig(D)$. A c-state $\langle s, \Sigma \rangle$ is an *initial c-state* of D, if s is an initial state and Σ is a set of initial states of D.

Definition 3 (Entailment). *Let B_0 be the set of all initial c-states of D, then $D \models_{\mathcal{A}_K^L}$ Knows φ after π iff φ is known to be true in $\Phi(\pi, B_0)$.*

Example 1. Consider the tree chopping example. Let $s_1 = \{U\}$ and $s_2 = \emptyset$, then the set of all initial c-states of D_{TC} is $B_0 = \{\langle s_1, \{s_1\} \rangle\}$. Recall that $\pi = $ **while** U **do** *chop*; *check* **od**. Then we have

- $\Phi(chop, B_0) = \{\langle s_1, \{s_1, s_2\} \rangle, \langle s_2, \{s_1, s_2\} \rangle\};$
- $\Phi(chop; check, B_0) = \Phi(check, \Phi(chop, B_0)) = \{\langle s_1, \{s_1\} \rangle, \langle s_2, \{s_2\} \rangle\};$
- $\bigcup_{k=0}^{\infty} \Phi(\pi^k, B_0) = \{\langle s_1, \{s_1\} \rangle, \langle s_2, \{s_2\} \rangle\};$
- $\Phi(\pi, B_0) = \bigcup_{k=0}^{\infty} \Phi(\pi^k, B_0) \setminus KT_U(\bigcup_{k=0}^{\infty} \Phi(\pi^k, B_0)) = \{\langle s_2, \{s_2\} \rangle\}.$

It follows that $D_{TC} \models_{\mathcal{A}_K^L}$ **Knows** $\neg U$ **after** π, which means that the tree will eventually go down and the agent will know that after executing the plan π.

Example 2. [2] Now consider the action *chop* has a non-deterministic effect that may make the axe broken (Br) and extend D_{TC} to D'_{TC} with:

$\{chop$ **cause** $Br \vee \neg Br$, **nonexecutable** *chop* **if** Br, *check* **determines** $Br\}$

Let $s_1 = \{U\}, s_2 = \emptyset, s_3 = \{Br\}, s_4 = \{U, Br\}$ and $s_5 = \perp$, by executing the same plan π in D'_{TC}, we have:
$\bigcup_{k=0}^{\infty} \Phi(\pi^k, B_0) = \{\langle s_1, \{s_1\} \rangle, \langle s_2, \{s_2\} \rangle, \langle s_3, \{s_3\} \rangle, \langle s_4, \{s_4\} \rangle, \langle s_5, \{s_5\} \rangle\}$, and thus

$$\Phi(\pi, B_0) = \bigcup_{k=0}^{\infty} \Phi(\pi^k, B_0) \setminus KT_U(\bigcup_{k=0}^{\infty} \Phi(\pi^k, B_0))$$
$$= \{\langle s_2, \{s_2\} \rangle, \langle s_3, \{s_3\} \rangle, \langle s_5, \{s_5\} \rangle\}$$

It follows that $D'_{TC} \not\models_{\mathcal{A}_K^L}$ **Knows** $\neg U$ **after** π due to $\langle s_5, \{s_5\} \rangle \in \Phi(\pi, B_0)$. This is intuitive, because the axe may be broken before the tree getting down. Actually, there is no feasible solution to the problem under the $\mathcal{A}_K^L$ semantics.

---

[2] Suggested by the anonymous reviewers.

4   Related Work

Lobo's Approach. J. Lobo [5] proposed a similar action language with nondeterministic actions, sensing actions and loops. We denote the entailment relation of Lobo's semantics by $\models_{LB}$ and illustrate the difference by two examples.

Example 3. The tree chopping example can be rewritten in Lobo's language as:

$D''_{TC} = \{$**initially** U, *chop* **may affect** U **if** U, *check* **causes to know** $U\}$

By Lobo's semantics, $D''_{TC} \not\models_{LB}$ **Knows** $\neg U$ **after** π. Simply speaking, this is because in [5] $D \models_{LB}$ **Knows** φ **after** π holds iff φ is known to be true in *all* evolution branches of the plan π under initial *situations* of D. However, in the above example, $\neg U$ is known to be false in one of the resulting situations. Therefore, $\pi =$ **while** U **do** *chop*; *check* **od** is not a solution to tree chopping under Lobo's semantics.

Example 4. A coin is showing the heads and the agent knows that. The goal is to toss the coin until it shows the tails. The domain in Lobo's language is:

$D_{tail} = \{$**initially** H, *toss* **may affect** H **if** H, *check* **causes to know** $H\}$

Intuitively, a solution to this example could be: $\pi' =$ **while** H **do** *toss*; *check* **od**. However, $D_{tail} \not\models_{LB}$ **Knows** $\neg H$ **after** π', that is, the plan π' never gives rise to the tails. In contrast, π' is a solution to this example in $\mathcal{A}_K^L$.

Our work differs from Lobo's in that we use an idea similar to the operational semantics of nondeterministic computation: the transition system accepts the input (i.e., the plan) if there exists *at least one* accepting branch (providing that no branch is leading to a failure state). E.g., in Fig. 1, the loop-plan π leads a branch from the initial c-state σ_1 to (the accepting) c-state σ_4, thus we regard π as a feasible plan. However, Lobo's semantics requires that the system accepts only if *all* branches reach the accepting states, therefore π is not a feasible solution.

Other Work. Y.Lespérance *et al* [1] extended situation calculus to handle domains with unbounded iterations like the Tree Chopping example. However, their approach does not allow loosing knowledge and thus requires a rather complicated framework to treat loop plans. H. Levesque studied planning with loops on top of the so-called *robot program*, whose semantics is just *informally* given in [6], moreover, to make the planning algorithm feasible, Levesque adopted a weak correctness guarantee, i.e., the algorithm is generally *not* sound. S. Srivastava *et al* [7] regarded loop-plans as a kind of *generalized programs* and studied the termination conditions of executing loop-plans together with planning algorithms. A. Cimatti *et al* [8] considered planning on nondeterministic domains, which involve the so-called *strong cyclic plans* that resemble loop-plans discussed in this paper. E. Winner *et al* [9] proposed a LoopDISTILL algorithm for automatically acquiring loop-plans from existed solutions to example plans. Nevertheless, most of these approaches mainly focus on algorithmic aspects of generalized planning, and pay few attention to inventing well-suited semantics for planning with loops.

5   Conclusion

Although lots of work has been contributed to the algorithmic aspects of planning with loops, in our opinion, a clean and solid semantics should also be contributed to this area. E.g., in the early days of AI, the STRIPS language was observed leading incorrect planning results for seemingly trivial domains, due to lacking of a "good" semantics [10,11]. In this paper, we present an action language $\mathcal{A}_K^L$ together with a transition function based semantics for reasoning about actions with loops. Compared to related work like Lobo's action language, our semantics appears to be more natural and intuitive for some domains. In future work, we will propose an underlying logical framework for $\mathcal{A}_K^L$ together with soundness and completeness and implement the language for plan generation and verification.

Acknowledgement. We are grateful to the anonymous reviewers for their valuable comments. The research was partially supported by NSFC Grant 61272059, MOE Grant 11JJD720020, NSSFC Grant 13&ZD186 and the Fundamental Research Funds for the Central Universities Grant 1409025.

References

1. Lespérance, Y., Levesque, H.J., Lin, F., Scherl, R.B.: Ability and knowing how in the situation calculus. Studia Logica 66(1), 165–186 (2000)
2. Sardina, S., Giacomo, G.D., Lespèrance, Y., Levesque, H.: On the semantics of deliberation in indigolog - from theory to implementation. Annals of Mathematics and Artificial Intelligence 41(2-4), 259–299 (2004)
3. Son, T.C., Baral, C.: Formalizing sensing actions: A transition function based approach. Artificial Intelligence 125(1-2), 19–91 (2001)
4. Amir, E.: Planning with nondeterministic actions and sensing. In: AAAI 2002 Workshop on Cognitive Robotics (2002)
5. Lobo, J., Mendez, G., Taylor, S.R.: Knowledge and the action description language $\mathcal{A}$. Theory and Practice of Logic Programming 1(2), 129–184 (2001)
6. Levesque, H.J.: Planning with loops. In: Proceedings of 19th International Joint Conference on Artificial Intelligence (IJCAI 2005), pp. 509–515 (2005)
7. Srivastava, S., Immerman, N., Zilberstein, S.: Applicability conditions for plans with loops: Computability results and algorithms. Artificial Intelligence 191, 1–19 (2012)
8. Cimatti, A., Pistore, M., Roveri, M., Traverso, P.: Weak, strong, and strong cyclic planning via symbolic model checking. Artificial Intelligence 147(1), 35–84 (2003)
9. Winner, E., Veloso, M.: LoopDISTILL: Learning domain-specific planners from example plans. In: Proceedings of ICAPS 2007 Workshop on AI Planning and Learning (2007)
10. Lifschitz, V.: On the semantics of strips. In: Georgeff, M.P., Lansky, A. (eds.) Reasoning about Actions and Plans. Morgan Kaufmann, San Mateo (1987)
11. Fikes, R.E., Nilsson, N.J.: Strips, a retrospective. Artificial Intelligence 59(1-2), 227–232 (1993)

Computer Aided Classification of Mammographic Tissue Using Shapelets and Support Vector Machines

George Apostolopoulos[1], Athanasios Koutras[1,2],
Ioanna Christoyianni[1], and Evaggelos Dermatas[1]

[1] Wired Communications Lab.,
Electrical and Computer Engineering Department, University of Patras, Greece
{gapost,ioanna,dermatas}@george.wcl2.ee.upatras.gr
[2] Informatics and Mass Media Department,
Technical Educational Institute of Western Greece, Greece
koutras@teipat.gr

Abstract. In this paper a robust regions-of-suspicion (ROS) diagnosis system on mammograms, recognizing all types of abnormalities is presented and evaluated. A new type of descriptors, based on Shapelet decomposition, derive the source images that generate the observed ROS in mammograms. The Shapelet decomposition coefficients can be used efficiently to detect ROS areas using Support-Vector-Machines (SVMs) with radial basis function kernels. Extensive experiments using the Mammographic Image Analysis Society (MIAS) database have shown high recognition accuracy above 86% for all kinds of breast abnormalities that exceeds the performance of similar decomposition methods based on Zernike moments presented in the literature by more than 8%.

Keywords: Shapelets, support vector machines, mammogram, breast cancer, computer-aided diagnosis (CAD), feature extraction.

1   Introduction

Breast cancer has been a major cause of fatality among all cancers for women [1]. However, mortality rates have been decreasing during the last years due to better diagnostic facilities and effective treatments [2]. Screening mammography using X-ray imaging of the breast is the most effective, low-cost, and highly sensitive technique for detecting early, clinically unsuspected breast cancer [3]. The radiographs are searched for signs of abnormality by expert radiologists but complex structures in appearance and signs of early disease are often small or subtle. That's the main cause of many missed diagnoses that can be mainly attributed to human factors [3,4]. Studies have shown an error rate between 10% - 30% for detection of cancer in screening studies [5], [6]. Of these, a percentage of 52% can be attributed to breast cancer signs misinterpretation while another 43% is mainly due to sheer overlook of signs in abnormal scans [6] by expert radiologists. The consequences of errors in detection or classification are costly, so there has been a considerable interest in developing

A. Likas, K. Blekas, and D. Kalles (Eds.): SETN 2014, LNAI 8445, pp. 510–520, 2014.
© Springer International Publishing Switzerland 2014

methods for automatically classifying suspicious areas of mammography tissue, as a means of aiding radiologists in double reading screening mammograms and improving the efficacy of screening programs thus avoiding unnecessary biopsies.

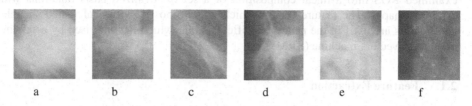

a   b   c   d   e   f

Fig. 1. Types of breast cancer on mammograms

Among the various types of breast abnormalities, clustered microcalcifications and mass lesions are the most important ones. Masses and clustered microcalcifications often characterize early breast cancer [7] that can be detectable before a woman or the physician can palp them. Masses appear as dense regions of varying sizes and properties and can be characterized as circumscribed (Fig 1a), spiculated (Fig 1b), or ill defined (Fig 1c). On the other hand, microcalcifications (Fig 1f), appear as small bright arbitrarily shaped regions on the large variety of breast texture background. Finally, asymmetry and architectural distortion (Fig 1e-d), are also very important yet difficult abnormalities to detect.

Computer-aided methods in the field of digital mammography are divided into two main categories; *computer aided detection* methods [8-11] that are capable of pinpointing regions of suspicion (ROS) in mammograms for further analysis from an expert radiologist and *computer aided diagnosis* methods [12-16] which are capable of making a decision whether the examined ROS consist of abnormal or healthy tissue. Sampat et al. [17], and Rangayyan et al. [18], provide an extensive review on different stages of CAD methodology for breast cancer.

In this study, we propose a method to classify regions of suspicion (ROS) that contain abnormal or healthy tissue using a novel feature extraction technique based on *shapelets* and a SVM classifier. The proposed method linearly decomposes each tested ROS into a series of localized basis functions with different shapes, which are called *shapelets*. The basis set that is chosen consists of the weighted Hermite polynomials which correspond to the perturbations about a circular Gaussian and in their asymptotic form to the Edgeworth expansion in several dimensions [19-20]. The coefficients of the linear decomposition are used as features that are fed into the classifier. Extensive experiments have shown great accuracy of over 86% in recognizing normal and abnormal breast tissue in mammograms which outperforms by 8% similar features based on Zernike moments [21].

The structure of this paper is as follows: In the next section, a detailed description of the features extracted from mammograms using *Shapelet* analysis as well as Zernike moments is given. Additionally a description of the utilized classifier based on Support Vector Machines is also given. In section 3 we present the data set and the experimental results and finally, in section 4 some conclusions are drawn.

2   The Proposed Method

The proposed system consists of a feature extraction module that decomposes each examined ROS into a linear composition of a set of localized basis functions with different shapes. The feature vectors which are composed by the calculated shapelet coefficients are used in the neural classifier module which is comprised by a scheme of support vectors machine (SVM) [22].

2.1   Feature Extraction

Shapelet Based Feature Extraction

Shapelets in the Cartesian Domain

The Shapelet image decomposition method was introduced in [19], providing an efficient method for the estimation of discrimination data for accurate detection of ROS areas, based on several expressions of the spatial pixels distribution of an object as a linear sum of orthogonal 2D functions,

$$f(x,y) = \sum_{n_1=0}^{\infty} \sum_{n_2=0}^{\infty} f_{n_1,n_2} \cdot \Phi_{n_1,n_2}(x,y;\beta) \tag{1}$$

where f_{n_1,n_2} are the Shapelet coefficients to be determined, whereas the Shapelet basis functions $\Phi_{n_1,n_2}(x,y;\beta)$ are

$$\Phi_{n_1,n_2}(x,y;\beta) = \frac{H_{n_1}\left(x \cdot \beta^{-1}\right) \cdot H_{n_2}\left(y \cdot \beta^{-1}\right) \cdot e^{-\frac{|x|^2+|y|^2}{2\cdot\beta^2}}}{\beta \cdot 2^n \cdot \sqrt{\pi \cdot n_1! n_2!}} \tag{2}$$

where $H_n(.)$ is a Hermite polynomial of order n, and β is the scaling factor of each Shapelet. The Hermite polynomials form an orthonormal basis set, ensuring that the features which are extracted from any image can be determined by:

$$f_{n_1,n_2} = \iint_{\mathbb{R}} f(x,y) \cdot \phi_{n_1,n_2}(x,y;\beta) \cdot dx \cdot dy \tag{3}$$

Shapelets in the Polar Domain

Polar shapelets have been introduced in [19]. They include all the major properties of the Cartesian Shapelets with a scaling β in spite of the polar shapelets are separable in r and θ. For this reason, the polar shapelets coefficients are easier to comprehend in terms of rotational symmetries, are simpler and more intuitive. A function $f(r,\theta)$ in polar coordinates is decomposed as a weighted sum:

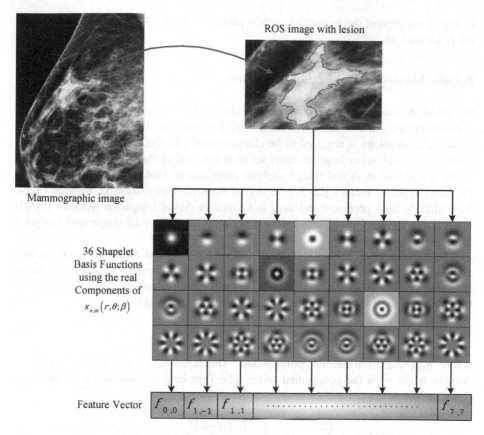

ROS image with lesion

Mammographic image

36 Shapelet
Basis Functions
using the real
Components of
$x_{n,m}(r,\theta;\beta)$

Feature Vector $\quad f_{0,0} \quad f_{1,-1} \quad f_{1,1} \quad \cdots\cdots\cdots\cdots\cdots\cdots\cdots\cdots \quad f_{7,7}$

Fig. 2. The feature extraction process using the real parts of the polar shapelets basis functions

$$f(r,\theta) = \sum_{n=0}^{\infty} \sum_{m=-n}^{+n} f_{n,m} \cdot x_{n,m}(r,\theta;\beta) \tag{4}$$

where $x_{n,m}(r,\theta;\beta)$ are the polar basis functions related to Laguerre polynomials $L_{\frac{n-|m|}{2}}^{|m|}$

$$x_{n,m}(r,\theta;\beta) = \frac{(-1)^{\frac{n-|m|}{2}}}{\beta^{|m|+1}} \cdot \left[\frac{[(n-|m|)/2]!}{\pi[(n+|m|)/2]!} \right]^{1/2} \cdot r^{|m|} \cdot L_{\frac{n-|m|}{2}}^{|m|}\left(\frac{r^2}{\beta^2}\right) \cdot e^{-\frac{r^2}{2\cdot\beta^2}} \cdot e^{-i\cdot m\cdot\theta} \tag{5}$$

with n and m both even or odd, respectively.

The polar shapelets coefficients of order n and m are calculated using the overlap integral

$$f_{n,m} = \iint_{\mathbb{R}} f(r,\theta) \cdot x_{n,m}(r,\theta;\beta) \cdot r \cdot dr \cdot d\theta \tag{6}$$

In Fig. 2 we present the feature extraction process with the 36 estimated shapelets in the polar domain.

Zernike Moments Based Feature Extraction

In optical systems, which are constructed using lenses, optical fibers or other optical components are often circular, therefore when the structure of the measured deformations and aberrations is required to be characterized efficiently the Zernike functions forming a complete, orthogonal basis set over the unit circle. The Zernike moments firstly introduced in digital image analysis problems in 1980 [23, 24] and evaluated for many types of images [25-27]. In digital mammography, Zernike moments have been already been proposed and used in Computer Aided Diagnosis Systems (CAD) for the diagnosis of breast masses as descriptors (features) of shape and marginal characteristics [21].

The Zernike moments defined as a family of orthogonal functions over the unit disk, ensuring that there is minimum correlation among the moments and consequently, minimum redundancy of information, invariant both to rotation and displacement. In polar coordinates the Zernike function $Z_n^m(r, \theta)$ is defined by:

$$Z_n^{\pm m}(r, \theta) = R_n^m(r) \cdot e^{jm\theta} \tag{7}$$

where $R_n^m(r)$ are the Zernike polynomials. The index n is the degree of the polynomial, while m is the polynomial order. The Zernike polynomials are defined as a finite sum of powers of r^2:

$$R_n^m(r) = \sum_{k=0}^{(n-|m|)/2} \frac{(-1)^k \cdot (n-k)!}{k! \left(\dfrac{n+|m|}{2} - k \right)! \left(\dfrac{n-|m|}{2} - k \right)!} \cdot r^{n-2k} \tag{8}$$

where $n = 0,1,2,\dots,\infty$ and $m = -n, -n+2, -n+4, \dots, +n$, with $n - |m| = even$ and $|m| \le n$.

2.2   The SVM Classifier

The main idea behind SVMs, when dealing with a real life pattern classification problem, is to find an *optimal* hyperplane in a vector space called, feature space, where the original data are embedded via a nonlinear mapping. By the term *optimal*, it is suggested that for a separable classification task (linear separable in feature space), the hyperplane (w, b) with the maximum margin from the closest data points belonging to the different classes is selected among the infinite choices of hyperplanes.

Using mathematical notation, having a data set $D = \{(x_i, y_i)\}_{i=1}^n$ of labeled examples $y_i \in \{-1,1\}$ and a nonlinear mapping from the input space into a high dimensional feature space $\varphi(.)$ where the data samples are linearly separable we are seeking for the vector $\mathbf{w}_0$ that minimizes $\frac{1}{2}\|\mathbf{w}\|^2$ subject to the constraints

$$y_i\left(\mathbf{w}^T\varphi(\mathbf{x}_i)+b\right)\geq 1 \quad i=1,...,n .$$
(9)

However, the mapping into a higher feature space through a nonlinear function does not guaranty perfect separation of the classes for many real-life problems. Therefore we have to introduce slack-variables ξ_i that measure the deviation of a data point from the ideal condition of pattern separability and relax the hard margin constraints as follows:

$$y_i\left(\mathbf{w}^T\varphi(\mathbf{x}_i)+b\right)\geq 1-\xi_i, \ \xi_i\geq 0, \ i=1,...,n .$$
(10)

From the above formulation it is obvious that data with $1\geq\xi_i\geq 0$ are correctly classified while data with $\xi_i > 1$ are classified incorrectly. With the introduction of the slack variables the goal is to maximize the margin and at the same time to keep the number of data samples with $\xi > 0$ as small as possible (for $\xi_i - 0$ for all i we have the linear separable case and all the data have at least maximum margin from the separating hyperplane). Therefore the quantity that has to be minimized is

$$\frac{1}{2}\|\mathbf{w}\|^2 +C\sum_{i=1}^{n}g(\xi_i)$$
(11)

$$\text{where } g(\xi_i)=\begin{cases}0, & \xi_i=0\\1, & \xi_i>0\end{cases}$$

The above problem is a combinatorial problem, which is difficult to solve and as a result an alternative approach is required. A mathematical tractable implementation of the previous two demands is given by minimizing

$$\frac{1}{2}\|\mathbf{w}\|^2 +C\sum_{i=1}^{n}\xi_i$$
(12)

which corresponds to the so called L1 soft margin SVMs. The parameter C is a positive constant that controls the relative influence of the two competing terms. The solution to this optimization problem subject to the constraints is given by the saddle point of the primal Lagrangian equation:

$$L_p\left(\mathbf{w},b,\xi,\alpha,\beta\right)=\frac{1}{2}\|\mathbf{w}\|^2 +C\sum_{i=1}^{n}\xi_i -\sum_{i=1}^{n}\alpha_i\left(y_i\left(\mathbf{w}^T\varphi(\mathbf{x}_i)+b\right)-1+\xi_i\right)-\sum_{i=1}^{n}\beta\xi_i$$
(13)

This leads to the dual maximization problem of the dual Langrangian equation:

$$L_d\left(\alpha\right)=\sum_{i=1}^{n}\alpha_i -\frac{1}{2}\sum_{i,j=1}^{n}\alpha_i\alpha_j y_i y_j\left(\varphi^T(\mathbf{x}_i)\varphi(\mathbf{x}_i)\right)$$
(14)

subject to the constraints

$$\sum_{i=1}^{n} \alpha_i y_i = 0 \text{ and } C \geq \alpha_i \geq 0 \quad , \; i = 1, ..., n \tag{15}$$

The solution of the above optimization problem leads to the *optimal* discriminating function:

$$f(\mathbf{x}) = sign\left(\sum_{i=1}^{n} y_i a_i \left(\boldsymbol{\varphi}^T(\mathbf{x}_i) \boldsymbol{\varphi}(\mathbf{x}) \right) + b \right) \tag{16}$$

with $b = \dfrac{1}{|I|} \sum_{i \in I} \left(y_i - \sum_{j=1}^{n} y_j a_j \left(\phi^{\mathrm{T}}(x_i) \phi(x_j) \right) \right), \; i \in I := \{i : 0 < \alpha_i < C\}.$

The points for which $a_i > 0$ are called Support Vectors and they are usually a small portion of the original data set. Especially those support vectors that have $a_i = C$ are those that lie within the margin or in the wrong side of the separating hyperplane have the strongest influence on the solution $\mathbf{w}_0$. The choice of C which is done a-priori by the user heavily affects the width of the margin.

In this formulation, if the nonlinear mapping function is chosen properly, the inner product in the feature space can be written in the following form

$$\phi^T(x_i) \cdot \phi(x_j) = K(x_i, x_j) \tag{17}$$

where K is called the inner-product kernel. A kernel function is a function in input space and, therefore, we do not explicitly perform the nonlinear mapping $\varphi(.)$. Instead of calculating the inner product in a feature space $\varphi^T(x_i) \cdot \varphi(x_j)$, one can indirectly calculate it using the kernel function $K(x_i, x_j)$. Different kernels produce different learning machines and different discriminating hypersurfaces.

Among others the most popular are the polynomial learning machines, the radial basis function networks and the two-layer perceptrons. In our experimental procedure we have employed radial basis function machines (the width σ^2, which is common to all kernels is specified also a priori by the user)

$$K(\mathbf{x}, \mathbf{x}_i) = e^{\left(-\frac{1}{2\sigma^2} \|\mathbf{x} - \mathbf{x}_i\|^2 \right)}, \quad i = 1, ... n \tag{18}$$

for recognizing healthy and abnormal mammographic tissue testing all kinds of abnormalities.

3   Experimental Results

3.1   The MIAS Data Set

In our experiments the MIAS MiniMammographic Database [28], provided by the Mammographic Image Analysis Society (MIAS), was used. The mammograms are digitized at 200-micron pixel edge, resulting to a 1024 × 1024 pixel resolution. In the MIAS Database there is a total of 119 ROS containing all kinds of existing abnormal tissue from masses to clustered microcalcifications. The smallest abnormality extends to 3 pixels in radius, while the largest one to 197 pixels. These 119 ROS along with another 119 randomly selected sub-images from entirely normal mammograms were used throughout our experiments. A database of 238 ROSs of 35×35 pixels size is used. The image database has been designed to include all types of different ROS areas abnormalities, i.e. circumscribed, spiculated, ill defined masses, microcalcifications, asymmetry and architectural distortion as well as regions with normal (healthy) tissue.

3.2   Training and Evaluation of the SVM Classifier

From a total number of 238 ROS included in the MIAS database, 119 regions are used for the training procedure: 60 groundtruthed abnormal regions along with 59 randomly selected normal ones. In the evaluation procedure, the remaining 119 regions are used that contain 59 groundtruthed abnormal regions together with 60 entirely normal regions. Therefore, no ROS was used both in the training and testing procedure. The above procedure was repeated 10-times using randomly chosen ROSs in the training and testing sets in order to get the unbiased classification performance of the SVM.

Each ROS image is converted in polar coordinates and the inner product among images and each mask of the polar Shapelets basis functions is obtained. In this research, basis functions of order $n = 7$ and $-n \leq m \leq n$ have been chosen. The feature vector is composed by the real parts of the polar Shapelets resulting to 36 coefficients (SH-Features), defining the image information used for detection of ROS areas. Therefore, each ROS image is described by a feature vector with 36-dimensionality. In the classification experiments, the features derived by the polar Shapelets are used to train the SVM scheme. In order to find the SVM configuration for maximum recognition accuracy the values of (σ^2, C) for the RBF machine, a *grid-search* approach was used in a systematic manner with different values for the parameters followed by a cross validation.

For comparison reasons we have also estimated the Zernike moments of an image $I(r, \theta)$ in polar coordinates, by projecting the image onto the orthogonal basis of the Zernike functions, thus resulting to the following complex numbers:

$$a_n^{\pm m} = \frac{n+1}{\pi} \cdot \sum_{n=0}^{\infty} \sum_{\substack{m=-n, \\ n-|m|=even, \\ |m| \leq n}}^{+n} I(r, \theta) \cdot Z_n^m(r, \theta) \tag{19}$$

The factor $\frac{n+1}{\pi}$ is used to normalize the moment's expression. In this research, Zernike functions of degree $n = 6$ and order $m = -n, -n + 2, -n + 4, \cdots, +n$ have been chosen. The feature vector is composed by the real parts of the Zernike moments $a_n^{\pm m}$ resulting to 28 coefficients.

In Fig. 3 we present the recognition accuracy when different values of the shapelet scaling factor β where used. It is clear that the best results were achieved when using a scaling factor equal to 0.2 that results to the best overall true positive identification rate of over 86% for RBF machines.

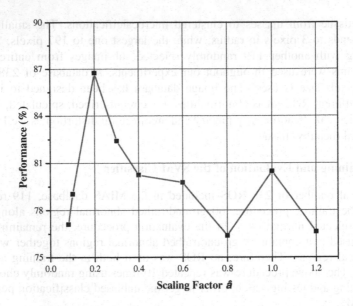

Fig. 3. The performance of the Shapelet features using different values of scaling factor β

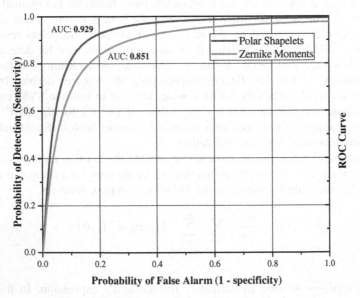

Fig. 4. The ROC curve of the proposed method

In Fig. 4 a ROC curve, is presented visualizing the relative trade-offs between benefits (true positives) and costs (false positives). As it is shown, the closer the ROC curve follows the left-hand and the top border of the ROC space, the more accurate the classification result will be. Additionally, a quantitative comparison of the proposed feature extraction method's accuracy is shown in Fig. 4 where the ROC curve is compared with the corresponding ROC calculated using Zernike moments (ZE-features) based features described in the previous section. As it is shown, the proposed features outperform Zernike based features resulting in 86% classification accuracy compared to 78.5% obtained by ZE-Features for RBF support machines.

4   Conclusions

In this paper we investigated the performance of a classifier based on Support Vector Machines and a novel set of features based on Shapelet image decomposition, in the problem of recognizing breast cancer in ROS of digital mammograms. It is well known that the disease diagnosis on mammograms is a very difficult task even for experienced radiologists due to the great variability of the mass appearance. The experimental results showed superior performance and accuracy of the proposed feature set compared to similar features that have already been proposed when used to recognize all different types of breast abnormalities. However further studies will address the problem of automatic selection of the shapelet scaling β and order in more complex tasks such as the discrimination between different types of abnormalities.

References

1. Feuer, E.J., Wun, L.M., Boring, C.C., Flanders, W.D., Timmel, M.J., Tong, T.: The lifetime risk of developing breast cancer. Journal of the National Cancer Institute 85(11), 892–897 (1993)
2. Sirovich, B.E., Sox, H.C.: Breast cancer screening. Surgical Clinics of North America 79(5), 961–990 (1999)
3. Martin, J.E., Moskowitz, M., Milbrath, J.R.: Breast cancer missed by mammography. American Journal of Roentgenology 132(5), 737–739 (1979)
4. Kalisher, L.: Factors influencing false negative rates in xero-mammography. Radiology 133, 297 (1979)
5. Kerlikowske, K., Carney, P.A., Geller, B., Mandelson, M.T., Taplin, S.H., Malvin, K., Ballard-Barbash, R.: Performance of screening mammography among women with and without a first-degree relative with breast cancer. Annals of Internal Medicine 133(11), 855–863 (2000)
6. Bird, R.E., Wallace, T.W., Yankaskas, B.C.: Analysis of cancers missed at screening mammography. Radiology 184(3), 613–617 (1992)
7. Tabar, L., Dean, B.P.: Teaching Atlas of Mammography, 2nd edn. Thieme, NY (1985)
8. Sampaio, W.B., Diniz, E.M., Silva, A.C., Cardoso de Paiva, A., Gattass, M.: Detection of masses in mammogram images using CNN, geostatistic functions and SVM. Computers in Biology and Medicine 41(8), 653–664 (2011)
9. Pereira, D.C., Ramos, R.P., Zanchetta do Nascimento, M.: Segmentation and detection of breast cancer in mammograms combining wavelet analysis and genetic algorithm. Computer Methods and Programs in Biomedicine (2014)
10. Oliver, A., Freixenet, J., Martí, J., Pérez, E., Pont, J., Denton, E., Zwiggelaar, R.: A review of automatic mass detection and segmentation in mammographic images. Medical Image Analysis 14(2), 87–110 (2010)

11. Wang, D., Shi, L., Heng, P.A.: Automatic detection of breast cancers in mammograms using structured support vector machines. Neurocomputing 72(13-15), 3296–3302 (2009)

12. Eltoukhy, M.M., Faye, I., Samir, B.B.: A statistical based feature extraction method for breast cancer diagnosis in digital mammogram using multiresolution representation. Computers in Biology and Medicine 42(1), 123–128 (2012)

13. Eltoukhy, M.M., Faye, I., Samir, B.B.: A comparison of wavelet and curvelet for breast cancer diagnosis in digital mammogram. Computers in Biology and Medicine 40(4), 384–391 (2010)

14. Buciu, I., Gacsadi, A.: Directional features for automatic tumor classification of mammogram images. Biomedical Signal Processing and Control 6(4), 370–378 (2011)

15. Ren, J.: ANN vs. SVM: Which one performs better in classification of MCCs in mammogram imaging. Knowledge-Based Systems 26, 144–153 (2012)

16. Zanchetta do Nascimento, M., Martins, A.S., Neves, A.L., Ramos, R.P., Flores, E.L., Carrijo, G.A.: Classification of masses in mammographic image using wavelet domain features and polynomial classifier. Expert Systems with Applications 40(15), 6213–6221 (2013)

17. Sampat, M.P., Markey, M.K., Bovik, A.C.: Computer-Aided Detection and Diagnosis in Mammography. In: Handbook of Image and Video Processing. Elsevier, London (2003)

18. Rangayyan, R.M., Ayres, F.J., Leo Desautels, J.E.: A review of computer-aided diagnosis of breast cancer: Toward the detection of subtle signs. Journal of the Franklin Institute 344(3), 312–348 (2007)

19. Refregier, A.: Shapelets–I. A method for image analysis. Monthly Notices of the Royal Astronomical Society 338(1), 35–47 (2003)

20. Refregier, A., Bacon, D.: Shapelets—II. A method for weak lensing measurements. Monthly Notices of the Royal Astronomical Society 338(1), 48–56 (2003)

21. Tahmasbi, A., Saki, F., Shokouhi, S.B.: Classification of benign and malignant masses based on Zernike moments. Computers in Biology and Medicine 41(8), 726–735 (2011)

22. Scholkopf, B., Burges, C.J.C., Smola, A.J.: Advances in Kernel Methods. Support Vector Learning. The MIT Press, London (1999)

23. Zernike, F.: Diffraction theory of the cut and its improved form, the phase contrast method. Physica 1, 689–704 (1934)

24. Teague, M.: Image analysis via the general theory of moments. J. Opt. Soc. Am. 70, 920–930 (1980)

25. Teh, C., Chin, R.: On image analysis by the methods of moments. IEEE Transactions on Pattern Analysis and Machine Intelligence 10, 496–513 (1988)

26. Bailey, R., Srinath, M.: Orthogonal moment feature for use with parametric and nonparametric classifiers. IEEE Transactions on Pattern Analysis and Machine Intelligence 18, 389–399 (1988)

27. Khotanzad, A., Hong, Y.: Classification of invariant image representations using a neural network. IEEE Transactions on Acoustics and Speech Signal Processing 38, 1028–1038 (1990)

28. http://peipa.essex.ac.uk/info/mias.html

Discriminating Normal from "Abnormal" Pregnancy Cases Using an Automated FHR Evaluation Method

Jiří Spilka[1], George Georgoulas[2], Petros Karvelis[2], Václav Chudáček[1],
Chrysostomos D. Stylios[2], and Lenka Lhotská[1]

[1] Department of Cybernetics, Czech Technical University, Prague, Czech
[2] Laboratory of Knowledge and Intelligent Computing,
Technological Educational Institute of Epirus,
Department of Computer Engineering Arta, Greece

Abstract. Electronic fetal monitoring has become the gold standard for fetal assessment both during pregnancy as well as during delivery. Even though electronic fetal monitoring has been introduced to clinical practice more than forty years ago, there is still controversy in its usefulness especially due to the high inter- and intra-observer variability. Therefore the need for a more reliable and consistent interpretation has prompted the research community to investigate and propose various automated methodologies. In this work we propose the use of an automated method for the evaluation of fetal heart rate, the main monitored signal, which is based on a data set, whose labels/annotations are determined using a mixture model of clinical annotations. The successful results of the method suggest that it could be integrated into an assistive technology during delivery.

Keywords: Electronic fetal monitoring, Fetal Heart Rate, Random Forests, Classification.

1 Introduction

Fetal heart rate (FHR) monitoring has become an indispensable part of fetal assessment during pregnancy and, more importantly, during the delivery. It most commonly refers to the monitoring of fetal heart rate and uterine contractions (UC). These two signals comprise what is also known as the Cardiotocogram (CTG). CTG monitoring provides obstetricians with insight into fetal well-being acting as the main source of information for the fetus which is obviously not amenable to direct observation.

Since its introduction, the goal of fetal monitoring is to detect potential adverse outcomes and provide information about fetal well-being. However, the initial enthusiasm was followed by skepticism since the CTG was accused for the increased rate of cesarean sections [1] while high intra- and inter-observer variability was also reported [2],[3]. Despite the skepticism, CTG remains the most prevalent method for intrapartum fetal surveillance [4], often supported by ST-analysis, which nonetheless does not diminish the need for a correct interpretation of CTGs.

A. Likas, K. Blekas, and D. Kalles (Eds.): SETN 2014, LNAI 8445, pp. 521–531, 2014.

International Federation of Gynecology and Obstetrics (FIGO) guidelines [5] introduced in 1986 serve as the basis for CTG interpretation although several national updates have also been released – see e.g. [6] for references. The guidelines were meant to assure the lowest number of asphyxiated neonates as possible while avoiding false alarms (which leads to unnecessary cesarean sections). An additional goal of the guidelines is to lower the high inter and intra-observer variability.

In an attempt to reach a more objective interpretation of the CTG, computerized systems appeared, some of them being as old as the FIGO guideline themselves. Beginning with the work of [7] the automated analysis of CTG was based upon clinical guidelines [8]. Additionally, beyond the morphological features used in the guidelines, new features were introduced. These were primarily based on research in adult heart rate variability [9]. Therefore, time domain [10],[11], frequency domain [12], time-frequency [13], and nonlinear descriptors/features [14] were proposed over the past years and combined with various machine learning paradigms such as Support Vector Machines (SVMs) [15] and artificial neural networks (ANNs) [16],[17] to name just a few.

In this work we use for the first time a Random Forest (RF) classifier along with a sophisticated model for the definition of classes based on the latent class analysis (LCA). The results are promising indicating that this kind of modelling is probably more suitable for building a decision support system compared to systems that rely on information coming from the pH. Such a decision system would be closer to clinical reality than a system based solely on pH.

The rest of this paper is structured as follows: Section 2 provides the necessary background for FHR preprocessing and feature extraction as well as a short description of the RF classifier. In section 3 the data set along with the LCA are presented in brief, followed by a description of the experimental procedure and the respective results. Finally section 4 summarizes the findings offering also some hints for future work.

2   The Automatic FHR Analysis Method

2.1   FHR Preprocessing

The FHR could be contaminated by large amount of artefacts, especially when it is recorded using ultrasound probe. An example of FHR with artefacts can be seen in Fig. 1. Therefore preprocessing aims at removing these artefacts before proceeding to the feature extraction stage. Our preprocessing methodology employed a simple artefact rejection scheme: let $x(i)$ be a FHR signal in beats per minute (bpms), where N is the number of samples and $i = 1,2, ..., N$, whenever $x(i) > 50$ or $x(i) < 210$ we interpolated $x(i)$ using cubic Hermite spline interpolation implemented in MATLAB version 7.14.0.739.

2.2   Feature Extraction

The FIGO guidelines' morphological features were the first features used to describe the FHR and further used as inputs to classification schemes. Later, in order to examine FHR in more detail, other features originating from different domains were introduced. These were essentially based on adult heart rate variability analysis and mostly included frequency and nonlinear methods. Since all features used in this work are described in our previous works [14], [15] for the sake of brevity we present the features in Table 1 and provide necessary information to be able to repeat the analysis. We refer the interested reader to the referenced works in Table 1 for a more detailed description of the used features. In total we worked with 21 features such that different parameter settings yielded a total number of 49 features.

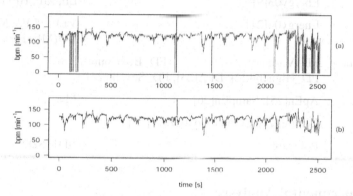

Fig. 1. Artefacts rejection. (a) Raw signal with artefacts, (b) signal after artefacts removal.

2.3   Random Forest Classification

Most classification tasks after the feature extraction stage include a feature selection stage [28] in order to alleviate the often encountered curse of dimensionality. Feature selection methods are usually divided into filter, wrapper, and embedded methods [29]. Decision Trees (DT) classifiers are of the last variety having the feature selection part inherently encoded during their construction process.

RFs are a learning paradigm that as it is implied by its name are comprised by a set of DTs that act together in order to reach a classification decision. RFs were introduced by Breiman [31] and since then they have been employed in many classification as well as regression tasks [32]-[34]. RFs are very competitive compared to other state of the art classification algorithms, such as boosting. Unlike boosting RFs provide fast training.

Each member of the ensemble of trees operates on a bootstrapped sample of the training data. Moreover at each node of a tree random feature selection is performed. More specifically, a subset S with M features from the original set of n features is selected and then the best feature among M is selected to split the node. With this mechanism there is no need for explicitly excluding a set of features before the classification process.

Table 1. Features involved in this study

Feature set	Features	parameters
FIGO-based [5]	baseline	mean, standard deviation
	number of accel. and decel, Δ_{total}	
Statistical	STV, STV-HAA[18], STV-YEH[19], Sonicaid[20], SDNN [9],Δ_{total}[10], LTI-HAA[18]	
Frequency	Energy03[9]	LF, MF, HF, LF/HF
	Energy04[21]	VLF, LF, MF, HF, LF/(MF+HF)
Fractal dim.	FD_Variance, FD_BoxCount, FD_Higuchi[22], DFA[23], FD_Sevcik[24]	
Entropy	ApEn[25], SampEn[26]	M= 2, r = 0.15,0.2
Complexity	Lempel Ziv Complexity (LZC) [27]	
Other	Poincaré	SD1, SD2

3   Experimental Analysis

For the experimental evaluation of the proposed approach, we employed a newly released CTG database [35] and a multiple trial resampling method. The database, the evaluation procedure and the results are presented in the rest of this section.

3.1   Database

The CTU-UHB database [35] consists of 552 records and it is a subset of 9164 intrapartum CTG records that were acquired between years 2009 and 2012 at the obstetrics ward of the University Hospital in Brno, Czech Republic. The CTG signals were carefully selected with clinical as well as technical considerations in mind. The records selected were as close as possible to the birth and in the last 90 minutes of labor there is at least 40 minutes of usable signal. Additionally, since the CTG signal is difficult to evaluate in the second (active) stage of labor, we have included only those records which had second (active) stage's length at most 30 minutes. The CTGs were recorded using STAN and Avalon devices. The acquisition was done either by scalp electrode (FECG 102 records), ultrasound probe (412 records), or combination of both (35 records). For three records the information was not available. All recordings were sampled at 4Hz. The majority of babies were delivered vaginally (506) and the rest using cesarean section (46). A more detailed description of the CTU-UHB is provided in [35].

3.2   Latent Class Analysis

In this work we used clinical annotations from 9 clinicians. All clinicians are currently working in delivery practice with experience ranging from 10 to 33 years (with a median value of 15 years). Clinicians evaluated the CTG recordings into three classes: normal, suspicious, and pathological (FIGO classes). Since there is a large inter-observer variability in evaluation the simple majority voting among clinicians cannot be used. Therefore we employed a more powerful approach - the latent class analysis (LCA) [36]. The LCA is used to estimate the true (unknown) evaluation of CTG and to infer weights of individual clinicians' evaluation. The LCA and its advantages over majority voting were described in [37]. For other examples on LCA in machine learning see, e.g. [38] and [39]. The clinical evaluations were considered as coming from mixture of multinomial distribution with unknown parameters and unknown mixing proportions. The Expectation Maximization (EM) algorithm [40] was used to estimate the unknown parameter and proportions. The EM algorithm was restarted several times with different starting values to avoid local maximum. The limit of log-likelihood convergence was set to 10e−3. The resulting class for individual examples was determined by the largest posterior probability.

The application of LCA leads to different labeling compared to the majority voting annotation as it is summarized in the following cross (Table 2), which corresponds to the data set described in Section 3.1. For the calculation of this table four cases from the original 552 CTGs were removed because the majority voting was inconclusive. This is a situation which is unlikely to occur with the LCA.

Table 2. Cross table (contingency table) of the annotations resulting from applying the majority voting (MV) and the (LCA)

	Normal by LCA	Suspicious by LCA	Pathological by LCA
Normal by MV	168	50	0
Suspicious by MV	7	185	66
Pathological by MV	0	3	69

In this preliminary study,we merged the suspicious and pathological class (according to the LCA) for simplicity reasons into a "super class" of abnormal cases. Thus we are interested in those records that deviate from normality.

3.3   Evaluation Procedure

For evaluating our approach we employed 5 trials of 2 fold cross validation (5x2 CV) [41], [42]. In other words we divided the available data into two sets and we used one for training the random forest classifier and the other one (testing) for estimating its performance and then we reversed their roles (the training became the testing set). The whole procedure was repeated 5 times with reshuffling taking place between each one of the five different trials.

Since RFs are not a parameter free algorithm, some parameter tuning needs to take place which however should be decoupled from the performance estimation process [42],[43]. Therefore during each training phase we performed a grid search increasing the number of trees from 100 to 1000 with a step increment of 50 and the number of features from 1 to 10 with a step increment of 1 (Breiman suggested a value for the feature equal to $\lfloor \log_2 n+1 \rfloor$ where n is the number of features, while also other suggested values can be found in the literatures ($\sqrt{n}$ or even as low as 1 [44]), so we tried a search in the vicinity of these suggested values). To perform this grid search each time the training set was divided again into a training and testing set (2/3 of the original training set comprise the new training) a performance metric was evaluated (see paragraph bellow) and the procedure was repeated five times (not to be confused with the 5 repetitions of the 5x2 CV procedure) after reshuffling the cases. The averaged performance metric over these five trials was used for selecting the "best" set of parameters. Using this set of parameters a new random forest was trained using the original training set and its performance was tested using the test set.

The "best" set of parameters was selected using two different criteria, which were derived from the elements of the confusion matrix (Table 3). Following the standard practice in the medical field we labeled the abnormal cases as positive and the normal cases as negative:

Table 3. Confusion matrix for a typical dichotonomous (2-class) problem

		predicted class	
		Positive	Negative
True	Positive	True Positive (TP)	False Negative (FN)
class	Negative	False Positive (FP)	True Negative (TN)

a) Balanced Error Rate (BER) [45]:

$$BER = \left(FP / (FN + TP) + (FN / (FP + TN))\right) / 2$$

b) Geometric mean (G-Mean) [46]:

$$G - Mean = \sqrt{TPrate \cdot TNrate}$$

Where:
True Positive Rate (TPrate) also known as Sensitivity or Recall:
$$TPrate = TP / (TP + FN)$$

True Negative Rate (TNrate) also known as Specificity:
$$TNrate = TN / (TN + FP)$$

The aforementioned criteria were selected instead of the more common accuracy measure due to the slight imbalanced of the data set, since these criteria are not affected by the distribution of cases into the different classes.

3.4   Results

Tables 4 and 5 summarize the results for the two different performance metrics that were used during the random forest tuning process and Fig. 2 includes the respective specificity and sensitivity values in a box plot format, which reveals that under this setting the two approaches are very similar.

Table 4. Aggregated Confusion matrix using BER for tuning

		predicted class	
		abnormal	normal
True	abnormal	1365	520
class	normal	189	686

Table 5. Aggregated Confusion matrix using g-mean for tuning

		predicted class	
		abnormal	normal
True	abnormal	1359	526
class	normal	187	688

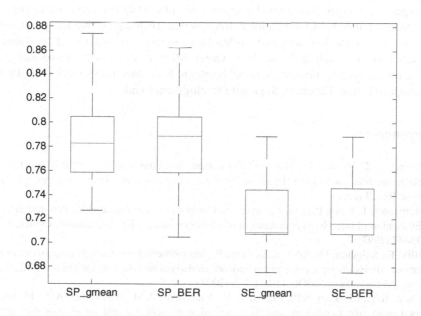

Fig. 2. Boxplot of the specificities and the sensitivities for the 2 different criteria used during tuning

4   Conclusions

This research work integrates a method for combining experts' evaluation of CTG recording with an automatic approach that attempts to reproduce their decision. The automated method uses a number of diverse features, coming from different domains, along with an advanced ensemble method, the RF paradigm. Our preliminary results indicate that the "latent" labeling approach creates different annotations compared to simple majority voting and that the resulting classification problem can be tackled by an automated method, even though the performance should be further improved before it can be adopted into clinical practice.

Moreover the sensitivity (~72%) and specificity (~78%) values achieved are higher (even though there is no one-to-one correspondence) than those achieved using the pH value for labeling [47] indicating that the proposed data model (features-LCA labeling) may provide more consistent approach than the one relying on the pH level.

In future work we will continue testing of the proposed three class setting approach (normal, suspicious, and pathological) and especially with in an ordinal classification setting. This way we will exploit the natural ranking of categories which in most cases leads to higher classification performance [48] compared to a scheme that does not take into account the natural ordering of the classes.

Acknowledgments. This research work was supported by the joint research project "Intelligent System for Automatic CardioTocoGraphic Data Analysis and Evaluation using State of the Art Computational Intelligence Techniques" by the programme "Greece-Czech Joint Research and Technology projects 2011-2013" of the General Secretariat for Research & Technology, Greek Ministry of Education and Religious Affairs, co-financed by Greece, National Strategic Reference Framework (NSRF) and the European Union, European Regional Development Fund.

References

1. Alfirevic, Z., Devane, D., Gyte, G.M.: Continuous cardiotocography (CTG) as a form of electronic fetal monitoring (EFM) for fetal assessment during labour. Cochrane Database Syst. Rev. 3 (2006)
2. Bernardes, J., Costa-Pereira, A., Ayres-de-Campos, D., van Geijn, H.P., Pereira-Leite, L.: Evaluation of interobserver agreement of cardiotocograms. Int. J. Gynaecol. Obstet. 57(1), 33–37 (1997)
3. Blix, E., Sviggum, O., Koss, K.S., Oian, P.: Inter-observer variation in assessment of 845 labour admission tests: comparison between midwives and obstetricians in the clinical setting and two experts. BJOG 110(1), 1–5 (2003)
4. Chen, H.Y., Chauhan, S.P., Ananth, C.V., Vintzileos, A.M., Abuhamad, A.Z.: Electronic fetal heart rate monitoring and its relationship to neonatal and infant mortality in the United States. Am. J. Obstet. Gynecol. 204(6), 491.e1–491.e10 (2011)
5. FIGO, Guidelines for the Use of Fetal Monitoring. Int. J. Gynaecol. Obstet. 25, 159–167 (1986)

6. ACOG: American College of Obstetricians and Gynecologists Practice Bulletin. No.106: Intrapartum fetal heart rate monitoring: nomenclature, interpretation, and general management principles. Obstet. Gynecol. 114(1), 192–202 (2009)
7. Dawes, G.S., Visser, G.H.A., Goodman, J.D.S., Redman, C.W.G.: Numerical analysis of the human fetal heart rate: the quality of ultrasound records. Am. J. Obstet. Gynecol. 141(1), 43–52 (1981)
8. de Campos, D.A., Ugwumadu, A., Banfield, P., Lynch, P., Amin, P., Horwell, D., Costa, A., Santos, C., Bernardes, J., Rosen, K.: A randomised clinical trial of intrapartum fetal monitoring with computer analysis and alerts versus previously available monitoring. BMC Pregnancy Childbirth 10(71) (2010)
9. Task-Force. Heart rate variability. Standards of measurement, physiological interpretation, and clinical use. Task Force of the European Society of Cardiology and the North American Society of Pacing and Electrophysiology. Eur. Heart J. 17(3), 354–381(1996)
10. Magenes, G., Signorini, M.G., Arduini, D.: Classification of cardiotocographic records by neural networks. In: Proc. IEEE-INNS-ENNS International Joint Conference on Neural Networks, IJCNN 2000, vol. 3, pp. 637–641 (2000)
11. Goncalves, H., Rocha, A.P., de Campos, D.A., Bernardes, J.: Linear and nonlinearfetal heart rate analysis of normal and acidemic fetuses in the minutes precedingdelivery. Med. Biol. Eng. Comput. 44(10), 847–855 (2006)
12. Van Laar, J.O.E.H., Porath, M.M., Peters, C.H.L., Oei, S.G.: Spectral analysis of fetal heartrate variability for fetal surveillance: Review of the literature. Acta Obstetricia et Gynecologica Scandinavica 87(3), 300–306 (2008)
13. Georgoulas, G., Stylios, C.D., Groumpos, P.P.: Feature Extraction and Classiffication of Fetal Heart Rate Using Wavelet Analysis and Support Vector Machines. International Journal on Artiffical Intelligence Tools 15, 411–432 (2005)
14. Spilka, J., Chudáček, V., Koucký, M., Lhotská, L., Huptych, M., Janků, P., Georgoulas, G., Stylios, C.: Using nonlinear features for fetal heart rate classification. Biomedical Signal Processing and Control 7(4), 350–357 (2012)
15. Georgoulas, G., Stylios, C.D., Groumpos, P.P.: Predicting the risk of metabolic acidosis for newborns based on fetal heart rate signal classification using support vector machines. IEEE Trans. Biomed. Eng. 53(5), 875–884 (2006)
16. Czabanski, R., Jezewski, M., Wrobel, J., Jezewski, J., Horoba, K.: Predicting the risk of low-fetal birth weight from cardiotocographic signals using ANBLIR system with deterministic annealing and epsilon-insensitive learning. IEEE Trans. Inf. Technol. Biomed. 14(4), 1062–1074 (2010)
17. Georgieva, A., Payne, S.J., Moulden, M., Redman, C.W.G.: Artiffical neural networks applied to fetal monitoring in labour. Neural Computing and Applications 22(1), 85–93 (2013)
18. De Haan, J., Van Bemmel, J.H., Versteeg, B., Veth, A.F.L., Stolte, L.A.M., Janssens, J., Eskes, T.K.A.B.: Quantitative evaluation of fetal heart rate patterns. I. Processing methods. European Journal of Obstetrics and Gynecology and Reproductive Biology 1(3), 95–102 (1971)
19. Yeh, S.Y., Forsythe, A., Hon, E.H.: Quantification of fetal heart beat-to-beat interval differences. Obstet. Gynecol. 41(3), 355–363 (1973)
20. Pardey, J., Moulden, J., Redman, C.W.G.: A computer system for the numerical analysis of nonstress tests. Am. J. Obstet. Gynecol. 186(5), 1095–1103 (2002)
21. Signorini, M.G., Magenes, G., Cerutti, S., Arduini, D.: Linear and nonlinear parameters for the analysis of fetal heart rate signal from cardiotocographic recordings. IEEE Trans. Biomed. Eng. 50(3), 365–374 (2003)

22. Higuchi, T.: Approach to an irregular time series on the basis of the fractal theory. Phys. D 31(2), 277–283 (1988)
23. Peng, C.K., Havlin, S., Stanley, H.E., Goldberger, A.L.: Quantification of scaling exponents and crossover phenomena in nonstationary heartbeat time series. Chaos 5(1), 82–87 (1995)
24. Sevcik, C.: A Procedure to Estimate the Fractal Dimension of Waveforms. Complexity International 5 (1998)
25. Pincus, S.: Approximate entropy (ApEn) as a complexity measure. Chaos 5(1), 110–117 (1995)
26. Richman, J.S., Moorman, J.R.: Physiological time-series analysis using approximate entropy and sample entropy. Am. J. Physiol. Heart Circ. Physiol. 278(6), H2039–H2049 (2000)
27. Lempel, A., Ziv, J.: On the complexity of finite sequences. IEEE Transactions on Information Theory IT-22(1), 75–81 (1976)
28. Theodoridis, S., Koutroumbas, K.: Pattern recognition, 4th edn. Academic Press (2009)
29. Guyon, I., Gunn, S., Nikravesh, M., Zadeh, L.A.: Feature extraction: foundations and applications. STUDFUZZ, vol. 207. Springer (2006)
30. Liu, H., Motoda, H.: Computational methods of feature selection. Chapman & Hall/CRC (2007)
31. Breiman, L.: Random forests. Machine Learning 45, 5–32 (2001)
32. Athanasiou, L., Karvelis, P., Tsakanikas, V., Naka, K., Michalis, L., Bourantas, C., Fotiadis, D.: A novel semi-automated atherosclerotic plaque characterization method using grayscale intravascular ultrasound images: Comparison with Virtual Histology. IEEE Transactions on Information Technology in Biomedicine 16(3), 391–400 (2012)
33. Liaw, A., Wiener, M.: Classification and Regression by random Forest. R News 2(3), 18–22 (2002)
34. Díaz-Uriarte, R., De Andres, S.A.: Gene selection and classification of microarray data using random forest. BMC Bioinformatics 7(1), 3 (2006)
35. Chudáček, V., Spilka, J., Burša, M., Janků, P., Hruban, L., Huptych, M., Lhotská, L.: Open access intrapartum CTG database. BMC Pregnancy and Childbirth 14 (2014)
36. Lazarsfeld, P.F.: The Logical and Mathematical Foundations of Latent Structure Analysis. In: Samuel, A., Stouffer (eds.) Measurement and Prediction, pp. 362–412. John Wiley & Sons, New York (1950)
37. Spilka, J., Chudáček, V., Janků, P., Hruban, L., Burša, M., Huptych, M., Zach, L., Lhotská, L.: Analysis of obstetricians' decision making on CTG recordings. Journal of Biomedical Informatics (2014) (manuscript submitted for publication)
38. Dawid, A.P., Skene, A.M.: Maximum likelihood estimation of observer error-rates using the EM algorithm. Applied Statistics 28, 20–28 (1979)
39. Raykar, V.C., Yu, A.: Eliminating Spammers and Ranking Annotators for Crowd sourced Labeling Tasks. Journal of Machine Learning Research 13, 491–518 (2012)
40. Dempster, A.P., Laird, N.M., Rubin, D.B.: Maximum likelihood from incomplete data via the EM algorithm. Journal of the Royal Statistical Society. Series B (Methodological), 1–38 (1977)
41. Dietterich, T.G.: Approximate statistical tests for comparing supervised classification learning algorithms. Neural Computation 10(7), 1895–1923 (1998)
42. Japkowicz, N., Shah, M.: Evaluating learning algorithms: A classification perspective. Cambridge University Press (2011)
43. Salzberg, S.L.: On comparing classifiers: Pitfalls to avoid and a recommended approach. Data Mining and knowledge discovery 1(3), 317–328 (1997)

44. Hastie, T.J., Tibshirani, R.J., Friedman, J.H.: The elements of statistical learning: data mining, inference, and prediction. Springer (2009)
45. Xuewen, C., Wasikowski, M.: Fast: A roc-based feature selection metric for small samples and imbalanced data classification problems. In: Proceedings of the 14th ACM SIGKDD International Conference on Knowledge Discovery and Data Mining, pp. 124–132. ACM (2008)
46. Kubat, M., Stan, M.: Addressing the curse of imbalanced training sets: one-sided selection. In: ICML, vol. 97, pp. 179–186 (1997)
47. Spilka, J., Georgoulas, G., Karvelis, P., Oikonomou, V.P., Chudáček, V., Stylios, C.D., Lhotská, L., Janků, P.: Automatic evaluation of FHR recordings from CTU-UHB CTG database. In: Bursa, M., Khuri, S., Renda, M.E. (eds.) ITBAM 2013. LNCS, vol. 8060, pp. 47–61. Springer, Heidelberg (2013)
48. Frank, E., Hall, M.: A simple approach to ordinal classification. In: Flach, P.A., De Raedt, L. (eds.) ECML 2001. LNCS (LNAI), vol. 2167, pp. 145–156. Springer, Heidelberg (2001)

Semi-Automated Annotation of Phasic Electromyographic Activity

Petros Karvelis[1], Jacqueline Fairley[2], George Georgoulas[1], Chrysostomos D. Stylios[1], David B. Rye[2], and Donald L. Bliwise[2]

[1] Laboratory of Knowledge and Intelligent Computing,
Technological Educational Institute of Epirus, Department of Computer Engineering
Arta, Greece
[2] Emory University, School of Medicine Department of Neurology,
Atlanta, USA

Abstract. Recent research on manual/visual identification of phasic muscle activity utilizing the phasic electromyographic metric (PEM) in human polysomnograms (PSGs) cites evidence that PEM is a potentially reliable quantitative metric to assist in distinguishing between neurodegenerative disorder populations and age-matched controls. However, visual scoring of PEM activity is time consuming-preventing feasible implementation within a clinical setting. Therefore, here we propose an assistive/semi-supervised software platform designed and tested to automatically identify and characterize PEM events in a clinical setting that will be extremely useful for sleep physicians and technicians. The proposed semi-automated approach consists of four levels: A) Signal Parsing, B) Calculation of quantitative features on candidate PEM events, C) Classification of PEM and non-PEM events using a linear classifier, and D) Post-processing/Expert feedback to correct/remove automated misclassifications of PEM and Non-PEM events. Performance evaluation of the designed software compared to manual labeling is provided for electromyographic (EMG) activity from the PSG of a control subject. Results indicate that the semi-automated approach provides an excellent benchmark that could be embedded into a clinical decision support system to detect PEM events that would be used in neurological disorder identification and treatment.

Keywords: Phasic Electromyographic Metric, PEM, EMG, Clinical Decision Support Systems, Graphical User Interfaces, GUIs.

1   Introduction

The movement disorders literature in sleep medicine contains a plethora of schemes (visual [1-4] and computerized [5-10]) to characterize electromyographic (EMG) activity during sleep, providing evidence differentiating between healthy and neurodegenerative patient populations. Notwithstanding the relevant clinical benefit of early diagnosis of neurodegenerative conditions from implementation of these schemes a standardized EMG processing methodology has yet to be adopted in clinical practice [11].

A. Likas, K. Blekas, and D. Kalles (Eds.): SETN 2014, LNAI 8445, pp. 532–543, 2014.
© Springer International Publishing Switzerland 2014

Impediments to the adaptation of a standardized methodology to measure EMG activity during sleep for clinical assessment have been outlined by Neikrug and Ancoli-Israel [12], with concerns relevant to our study summarized below:

   a.   Consistency in scoring and defining pertinent EMG activity metrics are lacking, preventing valid comparisons between studies across different labs.

   b.   Major drawbacks in visual scoring methods (laborious time consumption and mislabeling) and absence of rigorous validation of computerized approaches with prevalence values of patient populations equal to that encountered clinically.

   c.   Delineation of amount, duration, and level of phasic EMG activity required for pathological classification.

Addressing the concerns posed by Neikrug and Ancoli-Isreal are crucial in order to efficiently translate research findings regarding EMG activity in sleep for clinical benefit. Therefore we present a quantitative methodology, within a user friendly computerized approach,that will establish standards required tackle the issues mentioned in a) and b). The proposed system builds upon our previous work [9] to define quantitative features which efficiently compare to validated visual scoring techniques for phasic EMG metric (PEM) identification, established by Bliwise *et al.* [4]. We utilize the validated quantitative features to develop an assistive/semi-supervised graphical user interface (GUI) that reduces scoring time in labeling phasic EMG events. The major aim of this work is the design and development of a user friendly GUI for automatic phasic EMG identification that will be used in both healthy and neurodegenerative patient populations, so there is not included any classification of pathological cases that will be future work. Therefore, the evaluation of the proposed approach is obtained by comparing clapsed times of expert scoring using our GUI for manual and semi-supervised labeling of phasic EMG leg events from a human control data set. Our work represents an excellent benchmark for the development of a clinical decision support system to detect PEM events for future use in neurological disorder identification and treatment within a clinical setting.

2   Methods

2.1   Data Collection

All data collected in this study followed Institutional Review Board guidelines outlined by Emory University (Atlanta, Georgia, USA) under the approved protocol IRB00024934. Overnight polysomnogram (PSG) data were recorded from one 72 year old male subject (S001), not meeting ICSD criteria for neurodegenerative disease diagnoses, using the Embla Model N7000 data acquisition unit and the proprietary software program RemLogic^{TM}. Electromyogram (EMG) data was recorded, digitized at a sampling rate of 200Hz with impedance values<10,000 Ohms, from bilateral electrodes located on the left anterior tibialis (left leg). EMG signals were exported from RemLogic using the European Data Format (.edf). The proprietary numerical computing software program MATLAB® (version 8.2 R2013b) and the open source software library for biomedical signal processing BioSig Toolbox (http://biosig.sourceforge.net/), MATLAB® compatible, version 2.88 (Schloegl A-Graz University of Technology, Graz, Austria) were utilized to convert .edf files into a .mat format for quantitative processing and GUI scoring. Data segments containing artifacts were manually excluded from the final data set, which consisted of ~4.5 hours of EMG data from Rapid Eye Movement (REM) and Non-REM sleep, approximately distributed equally.

2.2   Graphical User Interface (GUI)

The proposed semi-automated approach consists of four levels: A) Signal parsing to segment the signal into 1 sec windows, B) Calculation of quantitative features on candidate PEM events, C) Classification of PEM and non-PEM events using a linear classifier, and D) Post-processing/Expert feedback to correct/remove automated misclassifications of PEM and Non-PEM events. Details regarding pertinent aspects of each level of our semi-automated PEM annotator are delineated below:

2.3   Level A: Signal Parsing

Unlike our previous work [9,14] in order to detect candidate PEMs we parse the signal using a non-overlapping sliding window. The size of the window is chosen as 1 sec.

2.4   Level B: Calculation of Quantitative Features on Candidate PEM Events

Expanding upon our previous work we automated, within the GUI, the calculation of 15 features on the candidate PEM and Non-PEM events obtained from Stage A using a 1 sec non-overlapping moving window. Feature descriptions and corresponding mathematical equations were described in detail in our previous work [9] and are reprinted below, for the reader's convenience:

1. Relative EMG Frequency Power (Prel): a frequency domain feature that provides a sub-band analysis of the high frequency EMG signal components (frequency band [12.5 to 32 Hz]) [15] (sampled at 200 Hz) with the power spectra density ($P(f)$) extracted using the Fast Fourier Transform (FFT) [16,17]

$$\text{i. } \text{Prel} = \frac{P([12.5-32Hz])}{P([8-32Hz])} = \frac{\int_{12.5}^{32} P(f)df}{\int_{8}^{32} P(f)df} . \tag{1}$$

2. Spectral Edge Frequency 95th Percentile (SEF 95): the frequency up to which 95 percent of the total signal power is accumulated [18].

$$\int_0^{SEF\,95} P(f)df = 0.95 \int_0^{f_s/2} P(f)df , \tag{2}$$

where f_s, is the sampling frequency.

3. Skewness ($Skew$): a time domain feature that measures the asymmetry of the probability distribution of the EMG signal amplitude [19].

$$Skew = \frac{\frac{1}{M}\sum_{i=1}^{M}(x(i)-\bar{x})^3}{\left(\frac{1}{M}\sum_{i=1}^{M}(x(i)-\bar{x})^2\right)^3} , \tag{3}$$

with M representing the number of data samples contained in the processing window and $\bar{x}$ symbolizing the sample mean $\bar{x} = \frac{1}{M}\sum_{i=1}^{M} x_i$ within that interval.

4. Variance (s^2) [19]:

$$s^2 = \frac{1}{M-1}\sum_{i=1}^{M}(x(i)-\bar{x})^2 . \tag{4}$$

5. Kurtosis (Kurt): a measure of the peakedness or flatness of the probability distribution of the signal amplitude [20]

$$Kurt = \frac{\frac{1}{M}\sum_{i=1}^{M}(x(i)-\bar{x})^4}{\left(\frac{1}{M}\sum_{i=1}^{M}(x(i)-\bar{x})^2\right)^2} . \tag{5}$$

6. Entropy (Ent): an information domain feature that calculates the amount of uncertainty or unpredictability of the EMG signal amplitude

$$Ent = -\sum_{i=1}^{n}\frac{bin_i}{M}\log\left(\frac{bin_i}{M}\right), \tag{6}$$

with M symbolizing the length of the data signal, n representing the number of bins, with the optimal number of bins obtained using the Freedman–Diaconis rule [21], to estimate the histogram of the data signal with bin_i indicating the number of data samples from EMG signal contained in the ith histogram bin [22].

7. Mobility (*Mobi*): a time domain feature that measures the relative average slope of the EMG signal. It is expressed as the standard deviation (*std*) of the slope (signal's first derivative *dx / dt*) with reference to the *std* of the signal amplitude [22].

$$Mobi = \frac{std\left(\frac{d(x)}{dt}\right)}{std(x)}, \tag{7}$$

where, the EMG signal is symbolized by the discrete variable x for $std(x) = s$ (See equation 4) and a first order approximation is used to calculate the derivative such that,

$$std\left(\frac{d(x)}{dt}\right) = sqrt\left(\frac{1}{M-2}\sum_{i=1}^{M-1}\left(f_{sampl}(x(i+1) - x(i)) - \frac{1}{M-1}\sum_{i=1}^{M-1}f_{sampl}(x(i+1) - x(i))\right)^2\right). \tag{8}$$

8. 75th Amplitude Percentile (75_Amp): the amplitude value below which 75% of the total EMG signal amplitude resides [22]. So, the value separates lowest 75% and highest 25% of the data. It is also called upper quartile or third quartile.

$$card\{x(i) \mid x(i) < 75\_Amp\} = \frac{75 \cdot M}{100}, \tag{9}$$

where M is the number of samples $x(i)$ of the EMG signal in one epoch and card represents the number of elements within the sample set (set's cardinality).

9. Complexity (Comp): the ratio of the mobility (*Mobi*) of the first derivate of the signal to the mobility of the signal amplitude. Complexity expresses the average EMG wave-shape in relation to a pure sine wave [22].

$$Comp = \frac{Mobi(dx / dt)}{Mobi(x)}. \tag{10}$$

10. Mean Absolute Amplitude (*MAA*): a time domain feature that measures the absolute value of the mean EMG amplitude [23].

$$MAA = \frac{1}{M}\sum_{i=1}^{M}|x(i)|. \tag{11}$$

11. Curve Length (L): the sum of the value of the first order differences of the EMG signal amplitude values [24].

$$L = \sum_{i=1}^{M} |x(i+1) - x(i)|. \tag{12}$$

12. Mean Energy (MnE): a time domain feature that measures the squared EMG signal amplitude [24].

$$MnE = \frac{1}{M} \sum_{i=1}^{M} x(i)^2. \tag{13}$$

13. Zero Crossings (ZC): defined as the number of crossings of the EMG signal over the ordinate, where the axis equals zero [24].

$$ZC'(i) = \begin{cases} 1, & x(i) \leq 0 \cap x(i+1) > 0 \\ 1, & x(i) \geq 0 \cap x(i+1) < 0 \\ 0, & otherwise \end{cases},$$

$$ZC(i) = \sum_{i=1}^{M-1} ZC'(i). \tag{14}$$

14. Average Nonlinear Energy (NE): a non-linear feature that is sensitive to signal fluctuations in the time and frequency domain, with respect to the following non-linear operator (NLO):

$$NLO[i] = x(i)^2 - x(i-1)x(i+1), \tag{15}$$

the NLO is weighted with a Hanning window and then the NE is calculated as follows:

$$NE = \frac{1}{M} \sum_{i=1}^{M} NLO_w[i], \tag{16}$$

where, NLO_w is the Hanning windowed version of the nonliner operator, NLO, with M being the data epoch [24].

15. Spectral Entropy (SE): defined as the amount of uncertainty or unpredictability of the EMG signal in the frequency domain [24],

$$SE = -\sum P(f) \log_2 P(f). \tag{17}$$

2.5 Level C: Classification of PEM and Non-PEM Events Using a Linear Classifier

Supervised classification of one second epochs as PEM versus Non-PEM events were conducted using a linear classifier [25]. The feature vector y obtained from Level B is represented as $y \in \mathfrak{R}^{15}$, such that the linear discriminant function, $\delta_k(y)$, with respect to the class k is defined by the following:

$$\delta_k(y) = y^T \Sigma^{-1} \mu_k - \frac{1}{2} \mu_k^T \Sigma^{-1} \mu_k + \log \pi_k, \tag{18}$$

where, $k = 1, 2$ represents the two classes describing the PEM and Non-PEM events respectively, μ_k is the 15 component mean vector, Σ is the 15×15 feature covariance matrix, Σ^{-1} is the inverse of the feature covariance matrix, and prior probabilities are defined by π_k such that:

$$\pi_k = \frac{N_k}{N_1 + N_2}, \ k = 1, 2, \tag{19}$$

and N_k is the number of samples within the k class training data set.

The mean vector and covariance matrix for each class k are estimated during the training phase and are described by the following:

$$\mu_k = \frac{1}{N_k} \sum_{i=1, y_i \in k}^{N_k} y_i, \ k = 1, 2, \tag{20}$$

$$\Sigma = \frac{1}{N-2} \sum_{k=1}^{2} \sum_{i=1}^{N} (y_i - \mu_k) \cdot (y_i - \mu_k)^T. \tag{21}$$

As for the evaluation of the linear algorithm we used the PEM and Non-PEM events annotated by a phasic EMG expert scorer from the data set of S002. Lastly, to obtain PEM and Non-PEM labeling, the function is maximized using the classification rule k^* where,

$$k^* = \arg\max_{k=1,2} \delta_k(y). \tag{22}$$

2.6   Level D: Post-processing/Expert Feedback to Correct/Remove Automated Misclassifications of PEM and Non-PEM Events

Level D includes the semi-automated portion of our GUI. This stage permits the user/scorer to provide feedback within the classification scheme by correcting any automated misclassifications, from Level C, of PEM and Non-PEM events. Figure 1 summarizes all the aforementioned levels included within the proposed semi-automated phasic EMG annotator using a flowchart. A screen shot of the visual interface produced by the developed GUI is shown in Figure 2. Lastly Figure 3 displays the output of the GUI following Level C.

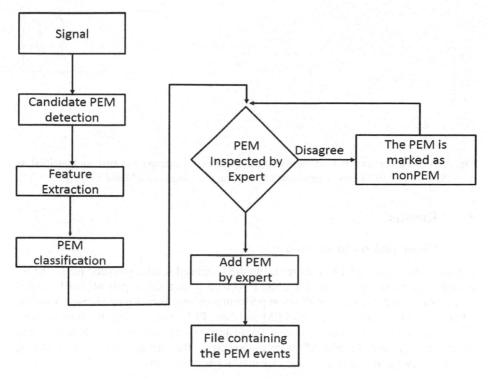

Fig. 1. Flowchart of Semi-Automated PEM Annotator Methodology

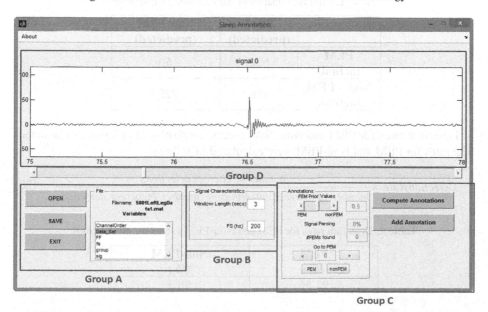

Fig. 2. Screenshot of the left leg EMG data from S001, displayed within our semi-automated phasic EMG activity GUI annotator

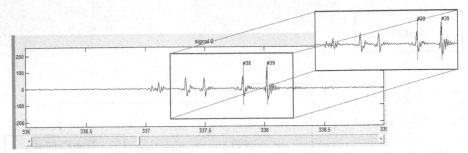

Fig. 3. Four PEM events two are correctly classified and annotated and two are classified as non- PEM events (PEM events demarcated by vertical read lines and #38 and #39)

3   Results

3.1   Classification and Speedup

In this study one expert PEM scorer using the proposed semi-automated phasic EMG activity GUI annotated the left leg EMG PSG data from a single patient, S001. Tables 1 through 3 comprise the classification performance results and time elapsed from the latter. Classification results for all PEM and Non-PEM events using the linear discriminant algorithm are provided in a confusion matrix in Table 1. Results from the linear algorithm "predicted" were compared to the "actual" labels of PEM and Non-PEM events obtained from the expert EMG activity scorer.

Table 1. Confusion matrix of our classification scheme

	PEM (predicted)	**Non-PEM (predicted)**
PEM (actual)	622	50
Non – PEM (actual)	126	7289

Detection rates for PEM and Non-PEM events are displayed in Table 2. The detection rates for PEM and Non-PEM were calculated as follows:

$$Detection\ Rate = \frac{number\ of\ correct\ detections}{number\ of\ correct\ detections\ +\ number\ incorrect\ detections} \tag{20}$$

Table 2. Detection rates for PEM and Non-PEM events for patient S001

PEM (%)	**Non-PEM (%)**
92.56	98.3

Lastly, the time elapsed while the expert labels PEM and Non-PEM events with/without use of our semi-automated phasic EMG activity scheme are shown in Table 3.

Table 3. Time spent by an expert annotating data from a single subject, S001 with or without use of our semi-automated phasic EMG activity annotator

	Time in secs
Annotation time without semi-automated labeling	4hr 26min 2sec
Annotation time with semi-automated labeling	58min 30sec

4   Conclusions

Here we developed and describe a software tool for semi-automated classification of phasic EMG events recorded from surface electrodes in an overnight human PSG. The semi- automated software tool provides to the user the opportunity to add PEM events that are not detected or to remove PEM events that the software incorrectly detected, easily and quickly using a simple point and click operation. Accurate and timely computerized PEM annotation will aid in addressing all the concerns posed by Neikrug and Ancoli-Israel [12] and assist in establishing standardized EMG processing methodologies for future use in neurological disorder identification and treatment.

Future work will incorporate more sophisticated classifiers which provide confidence intervals on the detected events. Also, since PEM events are less prevalent than Non-PEM events we will concentrate on avoiding false dismissals/false negatives (type II errors). The latter will reduce the need for the user to review excessive incorrectly automated-annotations of PEM segments (False Negatives). This will minimize the time spent by the user/scorer for annotation. Moreover, to determine user-friendliness and clinical relevance of the GUI, we will investigate GUI robustness with respect to training levels of scorers (e.g. beginner, intermediate, and expert) and different data sets/patient populations (e.g. neurodegenerative disorder patients and age matched-controls). Lastly, investigation of the proposed future work will aid in meeting the long-term goal to develop a supportive technology for the efficient annotation of EMG events within a clinical decision support system platform.

Acknowledgements. This work was supported in part by the National Institute for Neurological Disorders and Stroke (NINDS) under Grant Nos. 1 R01 NS-050595; 1 R01 NS-055015; 1 F32 NS-070572, 3 R01 NS-079268-02W1; 1P50NS071669 and the National Science Foundation sponsored program Facilitating Academic Careers in Engineering and Science (FACES), Grant Nos. 0450303 and 0450303, at the Georgia Institute of Technology and Emory University. Acknowledgments

This research work was partially supported by the joint research project "Intelligent System for Automatic CardioTocoGraphic Data Analysis and Evaluation using State of the Art Computational Intelligence Techniques" by the programme "Greece-Czech Joint Research and Technology projects 2011-2013" of the General Secretariat for Research & Technology, Greek Ministry of Education and Religious Affairs, co-financed by Greece, National Strategic Reference Framework (NSRF) and the European Union, European Regional Development Fund.

References

1. Montplaisir, J., Gagnon, J.F., Fantini, M.L., Postuma, R.B., Dauvilliers, Y., Desautels, A., Rompré, S., Paquet, J.: Polysomnographic diagnosis of idiopathic REM sleep behavior disorder. Movement Disorders 25, 2044–2051 (2010)
2. Consens, F.B., Chervin, R.D., Koeppe, R.A., Little, R., Liu, S., Junk, L., Angell, K., Heumann, M., Gilman, S.: Validation of a polysomnographic score for REM sleep behavior disorder. Sleep 28(8), 993–997 (2005)
3. Frauscher, B., Iranzo, A., Höghl, B., Casanova-Molla, J., Salamero, M., Gschliesser, V., et al.: Quantification of electromyographic activity during REM sleep in multiple muscles in REM sleep behavior disorder. Sleep 31, 724–731 (2008)
4. Bliwise, D.L., He, L., Ansari, F.P., Rye, D.B.: Quantification of electromyographic activity during sleep: a phasic electromyographic metric. Journal of Clinical Neurophysiology 23, 59–67 (2006)
5. Burns, J.W., Consens, F.B., Little, R.J., Angell, K.J., Gilman, S., Chervin, R.D.: EMG variance during polysomnography as an assessment for REM sleep behavior disorder. Sleep 30(12), 1771–1778 (2007)
6. Mayer, G., Kesper, K., Polch, T., Canisius, S., Penzel, T., Oertel, W., Stiasny-Kolster, K.: Quantification of tonic and phasic muscle activity in REM sleep behavior disorder. Journal of Clinical Neurophysiology 25, 48–55 (2008)
7. Ferri, R., Manconi, M., Plazzi, G., Vandi, S., Poli, F., Bruni, O., et al.: A quantitative statistical analysis of the submental muscle EMG amplitude during sleep in normal controls and patients with REM sleep behavior disorder. Journal of Sleep Research 17, 89–100 (2008)
8. Kempfner, J., Sorensen, G., Zoetmulder, M., Jennum, P., Sorensen, H.B.: REM Behaviour Disorder detection associated with neurodegenerative diseases. In: 2010 Annual International Conference of the IEEE Engineering in Medicine and Biology Society (EMBC), Buenos Aires, pp. 5093–5096 (2010)
9. Fairley, J.A., Georgoulas, G., Mehta, N.A., Gray, A.G., Bliwise, D.L.: Computer detection approaches for the identification of phasic electromyographic (EMG) activity during human sleep. Biomedical Signal Processing and Control 7(6), 606–615 (2012)
10. Fairley, J.A., Georgoulas, G., Smart, O.L., Dimakopoulos, G., Karvelis, P., Stylios, C.D., Rye, D.B., Bliwise, D.L.: Wavelet analysis for detection of phasic electromyographic activity in sleep: Influence of mother wavelet and dimensionality reduction. Computers in Biology and Medicine (in press, available online January 11, 2014)
11. Iranzo, A., Santamaria, J., Tolosa, E.: The clinical and pathophysiological relevance of REM sleep behavior disorder in neurodegenerative diseases. Sleep Medicine Reviews 13(6), 385–401 (2009)
12. Neikrug, A.B., Ancoli-Israel, S.: Diagnostic tools for REM sleep behavior disorder. Sleep Medicine Reviews 16(5), 415–429 (2012)
13. Bliwise, D.L., He, L., Ansari, F.P., Rye, D.B.: Quantification of electromyographic activity during sleep: A phasic electromyographic metric. Journal of Clinical Neurophysiology 23(1), 59–67 (2006)
14. Zoubek, L., Charbonier, S., Lesecq, S., Buguet, A., Chapotot, F.: Feature selection for sleep/wake stages classification using data driven methods. Biomedical Signal Processing and Control 2(3), 171–179 (2007)
15. Hayes, M.H.: The DFT and FFT, the periodogram. In: Statistical Digital Signal Processing and Modeling. John Wiley & Sons, Inc., New York (1996)

16. Proakis, J.G., Manolakis, D.G.: Digital Signal Processing: Principles, Algorithms and Applications, 4th edn. Prentice Hall, New York (2006)
17. Long, C.W., Shah, N.K., Loughlin, C., Spydell, J., Bedford, R.F.: A comparison of EEG determinants of near-awakening from isoflurane and fentanyl anesthesia. Spetral edge, median power frequency, and delta ratio. Anesth. Analg. 69(2), 169–173 (1989)
18. Wasserman, L.: Statistical functionals. In: All of Statistics. A Concise Course in Statistical Inference. Springer, New York (2004)
19. Filliben, J.: Measures of skewness and kurtosis. Quantitative techniques. In: NIST/SEMATECH e-Handbook of Statistical Methods. U.S. Department of Commerce, Washington, DC (2003)
20. Freedman, D., Diaconis, P.: On the histogram as a density estimator-L2 Theory. Probability Theory and Related Fields 57(4), 453–476 (1981)
21. Zoubek, L.: Automatic classification of human sleep recordings combining artifact identification and relevant features selection, PhD dissertation. University of Ostrava, Grenoble (2008)
22. Agarwal, R., Gotman, J., Flanagan, D., Rosenblatt, B.: Automatic EEG analysis during long-term monitoring in the ICU. Electroencephalogr. Clin. Neurophysiol. 107(1), 44–58 (1998)
23. Alessandro, M.: The utility of intracranial EEG feature and channel synergy for evaluating the spatial and temporal behavior of seizure precursors, PhD dissertation, Georgia Institute of Technology, Atlanta (2001)
24. Duda, R., Hart, P., Stork, D.: Pattern Classification, 2nd edn. Wiley Interscience (2000)

Time Dependent Fuzzy Cognitive Maps
for Medical Diagnosis

Evangelia Bourgani[1], Chrysostomos D. Stylios[2], George Manis[1],
and Voula C. Georgopoulos[3]

[1] Dept. of Computer Science & Engineering, University of Ioannina, Ioannina, Greece
ebourgani@gmail.com, manis@cs.uoi.gr
[2] Dept. of Computer Engineering, TEI of Epirus, Artas, Greece
stylios@teiep.gr
[3] School of Health and Welfare Professions, TEI of Western Greece, Patras, Greece
voula@teipat.gr

Abstract. Time dependence in medical diagnosis is important since, frequently, symptoms evolve over time, thus, changing with the progression of an illness. Taking into consideration that medical information may be vague, missing and/or conflicting during the diagnostic procedure, a new type of Fuzzy Cognitive Maps (FCMs), the soft computing technique that can handle uncertainty to infer a result, have been developed for Medical Diagnosis. Here, a method to enhance the FCM behaviour is proposed introducing time units that can follow disease progression. An example from the pulmonary field is described.

Keywords: Fuzzy Cognitive Map, time evolution, medical diagnosis.

1 Introduction

In medicine, the capability of immediate diagnosis and treatment is always a necessity and under constant investigation. Doctors have to make immediate decisions and determine the appropriate treatment. Pulmonary diseases include a set of different and complementary cases/diagnosis that cannot be easily discerned due to their similar characteristics. Differentiating diseases that have common or similar symptoms and/or missing information based on the first symptoms may lead to a wrong decision. Thus, differential diagnosis is a highly complex procedure that demands the incorporation of many factors, with missing or conflicting information and taking into consideration various aspects from seemingly unrelated factors. To overcome ambiguity, omissions and imprecision which can infer misleading results, computational intelligence methods has been proposed to solve many complex problems by developing intelligent system. Fuzzy logic has proved to be a powerful tool for decision-making systems [1].

Medical Decision Support Systems (MDSS) are planned to support human decision making successfully by evaluating information from different sources, combining it to support clinicians' decisions concerning diagnosis, therapy planning and monitoring

A. Likas, K. Blekas, and D. Kalles (Eds.): SETN 2014, LNAI 8445, pp. 544–554, 2014.

of the disease and treatment processes. Medical Decision Systems have to consider a high amount of data and information from interdisciplinary sources (patient's records and information, doctors' physical examination and evaluation, laboratory tests, etc.) and, in addition, information may be vague, missing or not available. Thus, MDSS are complex systems involving inexact, uncertain, imprecise and ambiguous information [2]. These systems can provide assistance in crucial clinical judgments, particularly for inexperienced medical professionals.

The method of differential diagnosis that is presented in this work is based on Fuzzy Cognitive Maps (FCMs). Here a new type of FCMs is introduced where the values of concepts and the values of weights are changed according to the time interval. This is in accordance to the real world problems where the influence from one concept to another is not instant and it differs from one interconnection to another one, so here time influence is considered and introduced. A FCM tool is developed and used for medical differential diagnosis of two pulmonary diseases: acute bronchitis and common-acquired pneumonia.

The main contribution of this paper is the introduction of the temporal aspect, which is essential for cases where time is significant because time evolution highly influence the final result. Such a field is medical applications and here the proposed approach is successfully applied for differential diagnosis of pulmonary diseases. In the following sections, the FCM-Medical Decision Support Tool (FCM-MDST) is introduced and described including the time dependent features because the progression of diseases are influenced by the time and so SCM-MDST is able to lead to a decision per time unit. Specifically, section 2 refers to the principles of FCM, section 3 describes the need for using MDSS, section 4 describes the proposed tool and how it was developed, while in section 5 results and comments are stated.

2   Fuzzy Cognitive Map

Fuzzy Cognitive Map belongs to the soft computing approaches and it originated from the combination of Fuzzy Logic and Neural Networks. It is a modelling method for complex decision systems. An FCM is illustrated as a causal graphical representation, consisting of interrelated concepts. It was introduced by Kosko [3] as an extension to Cognitive Maps [4]. The general graphical illustration of FCM is a signed, weighted graph with feedback. Nodes of the graph are concepts, which correspond to variables, states, factors and other characteristics that are used in the model and describe the behaviour of the system [5]. FCM nodes constitute the set of concepts $C = \{C_1, C_2, \ldots, C_n\}$. Arcs (C_j, C_i) represent the causal link between concepts (how concept C_j causes concept C_i). The weights of arcs form the weighted values of the matrix (w_{nxn}). Each element of the weight matrix w_{ji} belongs to $[-1,1]$.

The value A_i of the concept C_i expresses the degree of its corresponding physical value. At each simulation step, the value A_i of a concept C_i is calculated by computing the influence of other concepts C_j's on the specific concept C_i following the calculation rule:

$$A_i^{k+1} = f(A_i^k + \sum_{\substack{j \neq i \\ j=1}}^{n} A_j^k w_{ji}) \tag{1}$$

where A_i^{k+1} is the value of concept C_i at simulation step k+1, A_j^k the value of the interconnected concept C_j at simulation step k, w_{ji} is the weight of the interconnection between concept C_j and C_i, and f is a sigmoid threshold function:

$$f = \frac{1}{1+e^{-\lambda x}} \tag{2}$$

where $\lambda > 0$ is a parameter that determines its steepness

The graph that illustrates the FCM consists of nodes and weighted interconnections. Signed and weighted arcs connect various nodes. This connection represents the causal relationships among the concepts. Fig. 1 illustrates a simple FCM with different aspects in the behaviour of the system, showing its dynamics and allowing the systematic causal propagation [6].

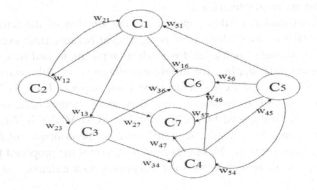

Fig. 1. The fuzzy cognitive map model

The sign of the weight show the causal relationship between concepts. That is, if $w_{ji}>0$ then concept C_j increases C_i, if the weight is $w_{ji}<0$ then concept C_j decreases C_i, while if $w_{ji}=0$ concept C_j has no causal effect on C_i. Moreover, the values of the weight indicate the strength of the influence between the concepts. The direction of causality (forward and backward) shows which concept causes another concept. For optimizing the behaviour of the system, various learning methods have been developed [7], enhancing the basic FCM and succeeding in better results.

3   FCMs for Medical Decision Support Systems

Medical Decision Support Systems follow the general nature of medical interventions: predict (predictive machine), prevent (preventive medicine), heal (curative medicine), or at least comfort (medical assistance) [8]. For this goal, a patient's particular situation must be considered and supplemented with an appropriate examination to give a more certain result. Complexity of MDSS is increased as they are consisted of irrelevant and relevant subsystems and elements, taking into consideration many factors that may be complementary, contradictory, and competitive;

these factors influence each other and determine the overall diagnosis with a different degree. A MDSS usually extracts causal knowledge from the appropriate medical domain; it builds a causal knowledge base and makes inference with it. Fuzzy Cognitive Map is a model that can give this opportunity.

When medical experts have to make a decision, they should take into consideration a variety of factors (concepts) giving to them a particular degree of importance (weight) on how much influence the other concepts. They have a conceptual model in their mind with interconnected factors until finally reach to a decision. FCMs are highly applicable in medicine. They are used for medical decision making, reasoning, differential diagnosis, prediction and/or treatment purposes. In general, medical decision is a complex procedure as many factors and functions should be taken under consideration before the final decision. However, the interest of using MDSS is not only on the accuracy and prediction of the results but also into the transparency and interpretability from the professional that use the MDSS during his daily work.

FCMs can model any real world system as a collection of concepts and causal relation between concepts. Fuzzy Cognitive Maps have been successfully used to develop Decision Support Systems (FCM-DSS) for various cases such as diagnosis, prediction, treatment etc. Georgopoulos et al. used successfully the FCM-DSS for differential diagnosis [9]. FCM-DSS has been also used in radiotherapy for determining the success of the radiation therapy process by estimating the final dose that delivered to the target tumor [10]. As a diagnostic support system, FCM-DSS has been used for labor modelling giving promising results [11]. FCM proved to be a simple and transparent way for representing and useful to describe any system in many fields such as engineering, medicine, and business and so on.

4   FCM System for Pulmonary Differential Diagnosis

Acute bronchitis and common-acquired pneumonia [12] are two pulmonary disorders that have many factors (symptoms) in common. FCM construction for these two pulmonary diseases demands four stages: the definition of the factor-concepts (symptoms) and decision concepts, definition of time unit that important changes can be noticed, the determination of weights and the definition of weight change according to time unit and additional parameters.

- Concepts: Factor concepts (symptoms) can be derived both from literature and experts in order all possible cases to be taken under consideration from the system. Thus, concepts can be collected from literature taking every possible and rare circumstance into account that experts do not usually find during their daily incidents. Experts can also add other concepts from their experience and knowledge. In this way, every possible concept, even the rarest, contribute to the final result.
- Time unit definition: Experts have to define the time unit (interval) which is the time that experts regard as adequate and capable to change the weights in a remarkable degree. This time can be ranged according to the under investigation differential diagnosis and speciality.

- Weight determination: Experts will set the weights during the whole progression of a disease, taking into consideration their theoretical background and their experience knowledge. They define the degree of interconnections linguistically and through a defuzzification process a numerical value is given.
- Weight per time unit determination: Pulmonary diseases may need one day to few days in order a patient to present the most symptoms. For this reason, experts have to determine the new weights taking into consideration not only the initial interconnections among the concepts but also how the degree of this relationship is changing as the time goes by. This weight evolution depends on additional factors, which finally determine the direction of change.
- Simulation: The cycle of simulation for each time interval stops when there is achieved a sufficient difference between two decisions. The suggested difference is defined by experts and it is dependent on each case and application area.

Regarding to the weight definition, experts will set the weights during the whole progression of a disease, taking into consideration their theoretical background and their experience knowledge. Experts determine the interconnections using fuzzy rules; a linguistic variable that describes the relationship between the two concepts is inferred according to each expert who also determines the grade of causality between the two concepts. That is, after the definition of concepts, experts are asked to propose the degree of influence among all the concepts, using IF- THEN rules. These rules are according to the statement:

For time unit 0...N: " IF a { none, very-very low, very low, low, negatively medium, positively medium, high, very high, and very very high} change in concept value C_i occurs THEN a { none, very-very low, very low, low, negatively medium, positively medium, high, very high, and very very high} change in value Cj is caused THUS the influence of C_i to C_j is a T_{Cij}{influence}". In this way each influence is determined. The inferred fuzzy weights across experts are aggregated and deffuzified giving an initial numerical weight in the interval [-1, 1]. Thus, basic weights and weight matrix are defined.

In addition to the initial weights, experts have to determine which concepts' dependencies (weights) have lower or bigger influence during the progression of the disease. The direction of this change depends on contribution of some other parameters, such as the age, if the patient smokes (how many years and the amount of cigarettes) or not and if there is another co-morbidity. That is, as the days pass the interdependences among some symptoms have different evolution in time compared to others and this change depends on both time and the additional parameters; interconnections can become weaker or stronger. Taking these changes into account during the simulation process, experts need to define the change for each time unit. Thus, for each interconnection influenced by the time, new values on each additional parameter will lead to the appropriate weight change. Linguistic degrees are used to indicate the direction of change (such as none, very-very low, very low, low, negatively medium, positively medium, high, very high, and very very high). These degrees correspond to negative or positive direction.   In this case the statement will be:

For time unit 0 ....N: "IF (Additional Factor 1=TRUE (AND/OR Additional Factor 2...3 =TRUE) AND IF a { none, very-very low, very low, low, negatively medium, positively medium, high, very high, and very very high} change in concept value C_i occurs THEN a { none, very-very low, very low, low, negatively medium, positively medium, high, very high, and very very high} change in value C_j is caused THUS the influence of C_i to C_j is a T'_{Cij} {influence} ELSE {keep the time unit 0 influence value (T_{Cij} {influence}).The inferred new fuzzy weights, for each time unit and for each parameter, aggregated and defuzzified giving new numerical weight($w_{ij}' = w_{ij}/t$) in the interval [-1,1] to the correspondent interconnections. This procedure can approximate better real life situations, as the weights can change per time unit incorporating more elements and parameters that characterize each one patient.

Experts should also set the correspondent weights, following the way that each disease is evolving. Apart from that, disease progression includes activation and/or deactivation of specific concepts and as a result, activation and/or deactivation of their correspondent weight-values (interconnections).Thus, each patient case is a different case and the progression of symptoms depends on time and additional factors. For example, the symptoms for the same disease for two different patients follow different evolution and some of them may obtain less or bigger meaning in case of patient's smoking or not. It is generally a multiple-aspect process. The use of weights per time unit and per relative additional factor tries to make the FCM able to more accurately represent a wide variety of patient profiles.

Figure 2 illustrates the FCM model for the differential diagnosis of the two pulmonary diseases: acute bronchitis and common-acquired pneumonia. It should be underlined that some interconnections are omitted as the high complexity makes it unreadable.

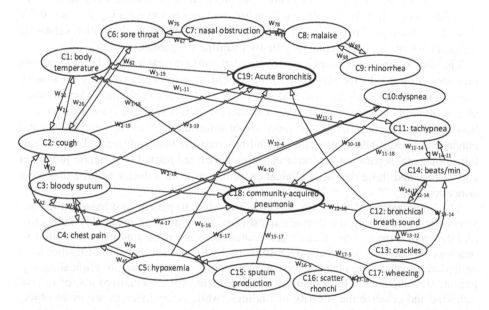

Fig. 2. FCM for pulmonary differential diagnosis

Figure 2 illustrates the factor-concepts (concepts C1 till C17) and the two decision concepts for differential diseases (concepts C18 and C19) which are in bold circles. The direction of the illustrated arrows shows the direction of dependence and the weights are the weights according to experts for each time unit. The FCM model is characterized by high complexity and many factors should be combined both from the patient's history and the clinical examination in order to have the final result.

4.1   FCM-Medical Decision Support Tool Description

Acute Bronchitis and Community-acquired pneumonia are two severe lung diseases that have some common concepts-factors, especially in their non-typical or first appearance. The following example is based on the previous described methodology. Table 1 contains the factor concepts which are symptoms that can be retrieved from patient's answers and other that demand doctor's examination (such as bronchical breath sound, crackles, rhonchi, wheezing, hypoxemia and so on) and the diagnosis concepts. The severity of each factor-concept, the appearance time and the duration of each symptom may differ from day to day, rendering the insertion of a time interval necessary, such time can be one day for those disorders. As progression of pulmonary disorders depend on time, it is possible concepts that are not presented as first symptoms of a disease will be initially deactivated (equal to zero), while the deactivated ones can become activated in the following days. Thus, the correspondent interconnections may be zero or have a different value for a time unit, while they can be changed or activated for another. Time unit will be the time interval that experts will have judged as critical and capable to provoke a change to the factor/concepts and, as a consequence, to the weights of interconnections. In the described case, we will regard this time unit to be one day, as hour-intervals do not make a big difference for these two diseases. The physician has to insert in addition to the initial values of concepts and the time (day) that they firstly examine the patient.

The factor-concepts (symptoms) are divided into two categories: factor-concepts that are set by the doctor according to the patient's answers and from his/her history records and those which are activated according to clinical examination's results such as auscultation, measurement of oxygen and so on. In this way, the system is trying to handle the human uncertainty, the omission of information derived from patients and enhance the result adding the clinical findings into the final judgment. Table 1 contains concepts' separation as: factor concepts which are related to patients' judgment and history and those that need clinical examination from a doctor and the diagnosis concepts.

The initialization of the factor concepts according to patients are based on the answers they give during the doctor's questions. These answers are highly subjective and depend on many other factors that characterize the patient as individual, that is, many symptoms may have been overestimated by the patient (because of his/her fear) or underestimated. The other factor-concepts, which are according to clinical examination, are subjected to the capability and judgment of the specialized doctor to characterize and criticize the severity of findings, while other concepts are more objective, such as tachycardia, hypoxemia, tachycardia and fever, as they are based on

Table 1. Concepts' separation

Factor Concepts		Diagnosis Concepts
According to patient's answers	**According to doctor's clinical exam**	
C1: body temperature		
C2: cough	C5: hypoxemia	
C3: bloody sputum	C12: bronchical	
C4: chest pain	breath sound	
C6: sore throat	C13: crackles	C18:Acute Bronchitis
C7: nasal obstruction	C14: beats/min	C19:Community-
C8: malaise	C11: tachypnea	acquired pneumonia
C9: rhinorrhea	C16: scatter rhonchi	
C10: dyspnea	C17: wheezing	
C15: sputum	C1:body temperature	
production		

medical equipments' results. The system is trying to give the appropriate values for each symptom, handling the uncertainty and multi-influenced symptoms.

The gradation of severity of each symptom, as it is illustrated to the user interface and can be used by the physician, is linguistic and represents the degrees that each concept can take. For example, fever gradation can be: hypothermia ($<35.6°$), normal ($35.7-37.3°$), slight fever ($37.4-37.8°$), high fever ($37.9-39.0°$), very high fever ($39.1-40.9°$), hyperpyrexia ($>41°$). Cough degrees can be: no cough, productive cough, non-productive cough. Similarly, the rest symptoms are defined according to their possible degrees.

Doctor has to insert the time (day) of starting the simulation. In relation to this day the weights of some concepts have less or more interference to the final result, in proportion to the existing additional factors. Thus, the system can use the appropriate weights according to each case. The use of the correspondent to the time weights, make the system able to take these changes into account. This adaptation enhances the system and allows it to reach more confident results. The system can run as many times as the number of time units specifies.

In fig.3 we can see an interface of the proposed tool which includes the factor concepts of the FCM model and the results for each time interval. The user interface allows the doctor to insert the values, define the patients' additional factors based on his/her history. The results are presented in another window. The results are presented per day and specify whether a clinical examination was performed or not, in order to be able to give the appropriate significance. Based on the results illustrated in the results window the doctor will infer his final diagnosis / decision.

The results will be an estimation of the possible final diagnosis, taking into consideration many factors during each time interval /day. The simulation results through the time interval/days may enhance the first diagnosis or lead to the opposite one as more specific patient's characteristics can be added and change the result. The doctor can judge the simulated results through the days and decide if they are accepted or not, forming his final decision.

When the doctor does not insert values at a time unit this means that there is no other concept triggering. Then, the system updates the weighted interconnection according to the experts' definition and there will be produced a new diagnosis based on the existing concept values. In the following time units, new concepts may be triggered while other may be deactivated. Thus, using the updated weights another decision is reached.

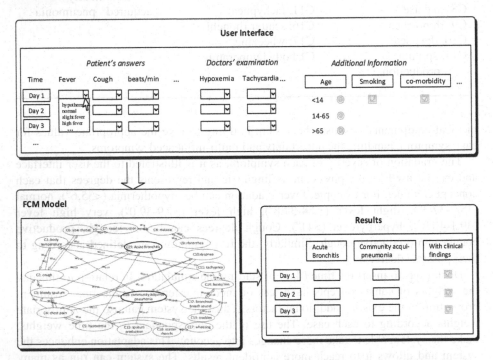

Fig. 3. Tool for differential diagnosis of acute bronchitis and community-acquired pneumonia

5   Conclusion - Comments

In this work, there was proposed a new Fuzzy Cognitive Map model that takes into consideration the time dependence among concept and a Medical Decision Support tool for pulmonary diseases was developed. This tool provides to the doctor a first estimation of the patient's situation. The user of the tool is the doctor who asks the patient to recall and refer the symptoms during the previous days and insert the values to the appropriate concepts. For each day the patient may present some of the symptoms (concept-factors), so the doctor can activate the correspondent concepts with values that ensue from the answers of the patient. The following days some of the symptoms may recede or not, which means change of their value, while others can be presented. Thus, the doctor can activate and deactivate other concepts and/or change their values. If the doctor examines the patient, s/he should insert the values to the system by activating the correspondent concepts. In this case, if a concept-factor which is referred to the concepts that demand clinical examination is activated, then the correspondent check box will be activated, underlining that the result incorporates clinical examination and findings. Also, the weights change according to the symptoms' duration (days), allowing the system to reach faster to clearer decisions. Thus, the system can make an estimation for each time interval (day) and the doctor will be able to judge the results, taking into consideration the disease progress and making the final decision administering the necessary drugs.

As these two diseases are easily confused and they need different prescription, this tool can enhance or support the final decision. It is a dynamic and easily adaptable to changes tool, which allows triggering and/or activation of concepts.

Acknowledgements. This research work was supported by the joint research project "Intelligent System for Automatic CardioTocoGraphic Data Analysis and Evaluation using State of the Art Computational Intelligence Techniques" by the programme "Greece-Czech Joint Research and Technology projects 2011-2013" of the General Secretariat for Research & Technology, Greek Ministry of Education and Religious Affairs, co-financed by Greece, National Strategic Reference Framework (NSRF) and the European Union, European Regional Development Fund.

References

1. Phuong, N., Kreinovich, V.: Fuzzy logic and its applications in medicine. Inter J. Med. Inf. 62, 165–173 (2001)
2. Sprogar, M., Lenic, M., Alayon, S.: Evolution in medical decision making. Journal of Medical Systems 36, 479–489 (2002)
3. Kosko, B.: Fuzzy Cognitive Maps. International Journal of Man-Machine Studies 24, 65–75 (1986)
4. Axelrod, R.: Structure of Decision: The cognitive maps of political elites. Princeton, NJ (1976)
5. Dickerson, J., Kosko, B.: Virtual Worlds as Fuzzy Cognitive Maps. Fuzzy Engineering, 125–141 (1997)
6. Xirogiannis, G., Glykas, M.: Fuzzy cognitive maps in business analysis and performance-driven change. IEEE Transactions on Engineering Management 13(17), 111–136 (2004)
7. Stach, W., Kurgan, L., Pedrycz, W.: A Survey of Fuzzy Cognitive Map Learning Methods. In: Grzegorzewski, P., Krawczak, M., Zadrozny, S. (eds.) Issues in Soft Computing: Theory and Applications, pp. 71–84 (2005)
8. Oja, E.: Simplified neuron model as a principal component analyzer. Journal of Mathematical Biology 16, 267–273 (1982)

9. Georgopoulos, V., Malandraki, G., Stylios, C.: A Fuzzy Cognitive Map Approach to Differential Diagnosis of Specific Language Impairment. Journal of Artificial Intelligence in Medicine 29, 221–278 (2003)
10. Papageorgiou, E., Stylios, C., Groumpos, P.: An Integrated Two-Level Hierarchical System for Decision Making in Radiation Therapy Based on Fuzzy Cognitive Maps. IEEE Transactions on Biomedical Engineering 50(12), 1326–1339 (2003)
11. Stylios, C.D., Georgopoulos, V.C.: Fuzzy Cognitive Maps for Medical Decision Support – A Paradigm from Obstetrics. In: 32nd Annual International Conference of the IEEE EMBS, Buenos Aires, Argentina, August 31 - September 4 (2010)
12. Pulmonary Disorders. In: The Merck Manual of Diagnosis and therapy, pp. 432–436. Merck Research Laboratories (2006)

Flexible Behavior for Worker Units in Real-Time Strategy Games Using STRIPS Planning

Ioannis Vlachopoulos[1], Stavros Vassos[2], and Manolis Koubarakis[1]

[1] Department of Informatics and Telecommunications,
National and Kapodistrian University of Athens, Greece
{johnvl,koubarak}@di.uoa.gr
[2] Department of Computer, Control, and Management Engineering,
Sapienza University of Rome, Italy
vassos@dis.uniroma1.it

Abstract. In this paper we investigate how STRIPS planning techniques can be used to enhance the behavior of worker units that are common in real-time strategy (RTS) video games. Worker units are typically instructed to carry out simple tasks such as moving to destinations or mining for a type of resource. In this work we investigate how this interaction can be extended by providing the human player with the capability of instructing the worker unit to achieve simple goals. We introduce the "Smart Workers" STRIPS planning domain, and generate a series of planning problems of increasing difficulty and size. We use these problem sets to evaluate the conditions under which this idea can be used in practice in a real video game. The evaluation is performed using a STRIPS planner that is implemented inside a commercial video game development framework.

1   Introduction

In real-time strategy RTS video games the human player is, more or less, in charge of a kingdom over a large game map where other kingdoms also co-exist and fight over resources and domination. This amounts to controlling a variety of buildings, units, and resources that are located in the map, with the aim to expand their territory and eliminate the other kingdoms in the map.

Worker units are a special type of units that are typically instructed to carry out simple tasks such as moving to destinations and mining for a type of resource. Such tasks are completely specified by the human player using direct commands that instruct the worker unit to perform each of the atomic actions separately. In this work we investigate how this can be extended by providing the human player with the capability of instructing the worker unit to achieve simple goals. The idea is to employ worker units with an appropriate STRIPS representation [8] of the game-world so that these commands-goals can be resolved by taking advantage of methods for real-time planning.

This practical application domain seems well-suited for experimenting with real-time planning techniques as i) it features a variety of objects that the worker units may need to interact with, including different types of buildings, resources, as well as other units, ii) it requires that the worker unit performs a different sequence of actions for

A. Likas, K. Blekas, and D. Kalles (Eds.): SETN 2014, LNAI 8445, pp. 555–568, 2014.

achieving the same objective in the variety of situations that may occur in the game-world, and iii) the gameplay is such that an instantaneous reactive response is not a strong requirement; some upgraded worker units with deliberation capabilities may take even a couple of seconds to "think" before executing the command given by the human player without this breaking the believability of the characters.

In order to explore this idea we developed the "Smart Workers RTS mini-game". The game-world of this conceptual game is slightly more refined than usual RTS video games, in that some actions require the worker unit to hold a specific tool so that to be able to perform the action. Different buildings provide different tools and resources, and, similar to usual RTS games, depending on which buildings the human player decides to build consuming ones resources, different tools are provided for worker units to use. For instance, food rations (which are necessary for feeding the units of the king-dom) can be produced in various ways: by hunting for animals and then cooking the raw-meat, by harvesting a rice farm, etc. For each of these actions the worker unit may need to visit a building first to acquire the specific tool needed, e.g., getting some weapon from the armory before going to hunt for animals.

We investigated how flexible behavior for worker units can be handled via planning using heuristic state-space search. A usual concern among game developers against using sophisticated approaches for decision making is that it is often faster to customize the domain specification so that a simpler approach can be applied. In order to explore this, we experimented with the idea of ordering the action types with which applicable actions are generated so that to help simple search methods find the goal. Our results show that even in this relatively simple domain this practical approach is very unstable in its performance: there are scenarios where it actually performs better than a planning approach but also others where it performs very poorly. On the other hand, it becomes obvious that for domains like this where there is a significant level of variety in the game-world specification, the sophisticated academic AI methods prove to be more robust and practical.

2   STRIPS Planning

In a classical planning we are given i) an initial state, ii) a goal condition, and iii) a set of available actions in terms of preconditions and effects, and we want to find a sequence of actions such that if we execute each action in sequence starting from the initial state, we will result in a state that satisfies the goal condition. In this work we will focus on the most basic type of planning problems and the STRIPS formalism which allows us to model a planning problem using first-order logic literals in a practical way [8].

In STRIPS, a state is represented as a set of ground first-order logic literals following a closed world assumption (CWA). That is, no variables or function symbols can be mentioned in a literal, only constants. Also, by the CWA principle, the presence of a ground literal in the set implies that the literal holds in the state while its negative version does not hold in the state, and absence of a ground literal in the set means that the literal does not hold in the state while its negative version holds in the state. In the Smart Workers domain that we describe in Section 3, the following literals may be used to represent that (from the perspective of a particular worker unit), the worker unit is holding a sword, there is a wild boar in the forest, and the fact that raw meat can be converted into food:

$$holding(sword_2), \; lives\text{-}in(boar_2, forest_1)$$
$$is\text{-}converted\text{-}to(raw\text{-}meat, food\text{-}ration),$$

The available actions are represented by action schemas, each of which characterize a set of possible ground actions using variables as parameters. An action schema specifies the preconditions and effects of all possible ground actions based on sets of literals that use the parameters of the action. The intuition is that the action schema functions as a template that specifies for each ground version of the action three sets of ground literals: one that captures the preconditions of the action, and two that capture the positive and negative effects of the action. For a ground action, the corresponding set of ground precondition literals must hold in current state in order for the ground action to be applicable. Similarly, the corresponding set of ground positive effects are added to the current state after the action is executed, while the corresponding set of ground negative effects are removed from the current state. This will become more clear in Section 3, where we give specific examples of action schemas in detail.

One way to solve STRIPS planning problems is performing state-space search. This is similar to performing a search method over a given graph, except that the nodes of the graph are implicitly specified by the available predicates and constants of the domain, while the vertices of the graph are implicitly specified by the action schemas. Similar to informed search algorithms, a forward-chain state-space planner can use heuristic functions that give an estimate about how far each state is from one that satisfies the given goal, in order to guide the search toward the most promising actions.

The STRIPS representation of states, goals, and actions as sets of literals, allows for investigating domain-independent heuristic functions, that is, functions that can be applied in any STRIPS planning domain to guide the search. The idea is that these heuristic functions exploit some aspect of the structure of the problem that can be identified just by looking at the decomposition of states to literals and the correlation of literals in the sets that specify the preconditions and effects of the action schemas. For example, a very simple domain independent heuristic function is one that counts the goal state literals that are not included in current state, and reports this number as the estimation for the number of actions that are required to reach the goal. We will refer to this heuristic function as the Goal Count heuristic (GC).

A much more sophisticated heuristic function that has proven to be very successful in many application domains is the Fast Forward heuristic (FF) [11]. This heuristic is based on building a relaxed version of the given problem by removing all negative effects from the available action schemas, and finding a solution for the relaxed problem using a simplified version of the Graphplan algorithm over planning graphs [3]. The heuristic value returned is the length of the plan that is extracted for the relaxed problem.

As a means of presenting the STRIPS domains and problems in a formal and common syntax, we will appeal to the Planning Domain Definition Language (PDDL) [9]. In PDDL a planning task is specified in two parts: i) the planning domain specifies the available predicates and action schemas, and ii) the planning problem specifies the available objects (constants) as well as the initial state and goal condition. Literals are represented in a prefix notation, e.g., literal $holding(raw\text{-}meat)$ is written as

Fig. 1. Screenshot of the Smart Workers RTS domain

(holding raw-meat) in PDDL. Special keywords are used to specify preconditions and effects as lists of literals as we will see in the next section where we specify the Smart Workers domain using PDDL.

3 The Smart Workers Domain

The Smart Workers domain follows the typical setting of real-time strategy (RTS) video games where the user manages various resources, structures, and units with the aim to eliminate all other kingdoms. Worker units are a special type of unit that are typically instructed to carry out simple tasks such as moving to places or mining for a type of resource. Such tasks are normally specified by the human player using direct commands that instruct a worker unit to perform each of the atomic actions separately.

In the Smart Workers domain the game-world is slightly more detailed in that these simple tasks also require that the worker unit uses or holds a particular resource in order to execute them. For example, in order to hunt for food the worker unit first needs to get some weapon from the armory, provided that such a structure is available. As different structures provide different tools and resources, the capabilities of the worker units depend heavily on the structures that the human player has chosen to build.

In this setting we explore the possibility that worker units are given *goals* as instructions, instead of *direct action execution commands*, and investigate how this behavior can be practically and effectively implemented. The idea is that a worker unit has an appropriate STRIPS representation of the game-world so that these advanced commands can be resolved taking advantage of methods for real-time planning. In particular, we will be focusing on one specific goal for worker units, namely bringing a food ration to the kingdom, and our intention is to identify which method is more appropriate for handling this problem given that there are various ways that this could be pursued in the Smart Workers domain. We now proceed to specify the Smart Workers planning domain using PDDL syntax.

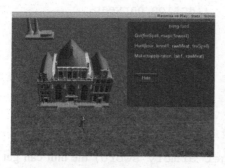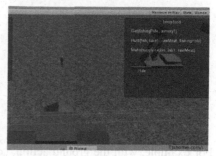

Fig. 2. Left: Plan extracted with all buildings available. Right: Alternative plan extracted with warehouse and farm disabled.

3.1 The Predicates of the Domain

The following predicates capture the properties of the available structures, objects, and resources in an abstract way. Note that in PDDL variables are denoted with a preceding question mark.

- (holding ?o): The worker unit holds object ?o.
- (provides ?s ?o): The worker unit may get or harvest object ?o from structure ?s.
- (is-converted-to ?o1 ?o2): Object ?o1 may be converted to object ?o2 through an appropriate convert action. For instance, raw meat from hunting can be converted into a food ration.
- (sells ?s ?a): Structure ?s sells object ?o.
- (accepts ?s ?o): Object ?o can be used in structure ?s in order to produce a new object.
- (lives-in ?s ?a): Animal ?a is located in structure ?s. For example, lives-in(forest, boar).

We also use the following predicates to specify the type of objects.

- (building ?b): Object ?b is a building.
- (natural-place ?n): Object ?n is a mine that can be harvested for resources or a lake or a forest.
- (weapon ?w): Object ?w is a weapon.
- (tool ?t): Object ?t is a harvesting tool.

We now proceed to present the available actions in the Smart Workers domain, in the form of PDDL action schemas.

3.2 The Actions of the Domain

An action schema specifies the preconditions and effects of actions in terms of sets of literals that take as arguments the parameters of the action schema. The following two characterize the simple actions with which the worker unit gets an object from a building, and harvests for a resource.

```
                                    (:action harvest
     (:action get                    :parameters (?n ?o ?t)
      :parameters (?b ?o)            :precondition (and
      :precondition (and                (natural-place ?n)
        (building ?b)                    (tool ?t)
        (provides ?b ?o))                (holding ?t)
      :effect (                          (provides ?n ?o))
        (holding ?o))              :effect (
     )                                   (holding ?o))
                                    )
```

For example, with the ground action (get armory sword) the unit can get a
sword from the armory as long as the literal (provides armory sword) is in
present in the set representing the current state. The effect of such an action would be
that the fact (holding sword) is added to the representation of the state. For the
other action schema ?o is a type of resource, ?n a structure, and ?t a tool. Apart from
the requirement that ?n is of the appropriate type and provides the resource ?o, the unit
need also hold a harvesting tool. Similar to the previous action the appropriate literal is
added to the representation of the state after the execution of the action.

The domain also includes actions fish, hunt, buy, as well as actions
craftResource, and craftWeapon for creating new objects from more basic resources. These can be used in various ways to generate food rations, depending on the
literals in the currents state. Some of these ways include getting rice from a windmill
farm, using a weapon to go for hunting and then converting the raw-meat, producing a
magic spell to go for hunting, as well as harvesting for gold, generating gold coins, and
buying food from the market.

3.3 Implementation in the Unity Game Engine

We implemented the Smart Workers domain in the popular Unity[1] game engine, also
making use of the so-called "iThink" STRIPS planner library that has been developed
in the C# programming environment of Unity [1]. Note that the planner does not take
PDDL code as input. Instead, the planning domain and the planning problem are specified using special functions of the iThink planner library, in a similar way as in PDDL.
In particular, ground literals and ground actions are formed using directly the actual C#
objects (in the programming sense) of the game-world as arguments. This allows for
a more practical correlation of the actual objects in the game-world and the symbolic
literals of STRIPS planning. Along the same lines, another feature of the planner is that
it takes advantage of the functionality of Unity that allows to put a tag on objects of the
game-world, as a means to specify a type for each object.

Also, unlike academic planners which typically perform first a pre-processing step
that generates a propositional version of the problem (essentially building a structure
similar to the search graph for the planning problem), iThink performs search in a text-
book fashion following a closed list and an open list of visited states that are generated
during the search. Some basic forward-chaining search methods and heuristics are supported, and as a means of further controlling the way that new states are generated

---

[1] http://unity3d.com/

the iThink planner provides a simple language for specifying how the search methods should generate candidates for applicable actions. This is done by means of a list of action prototypes that make use of the action schemas and the in the domain such as the following: `get-2-tag::armory-tag::weapon`. Apart from implementing the role of object types as in typed STRIPS, the order of the prototypes in the list plays a crucial role in uninformed search.

Except for the planning aspect, the Smart Workers domain was implemented as a functional mini-game. Figure 1 is a screenshot that shows part of the domain.

3.4 An Example Scenario

In a simple usage example of the "Smart Workers RTS" domain, initially the worker unit stands idle on the virtual kingdom waiting for a goal to be assigned to. Depending on the available buildings that the unit can use, the goal "bring a food ration" may be realized by different types of hunting as depicted in Figure 2 and Figure 2. Several types of goals may be assigned, and a vast amount of different configurations of available resources require a flexible worker behavior in order to meet the orders. For example, depending on the stage of the game only some buildings may be build already, while some others may become unavailable any time due to enemy kingdom attacks

In reality, in a real game not all workers would have this type of capability. After a certain upgrade though, worker units may also accept goals instead of direct orders, and obtain the capability of planning for a minimal depth. A second upgrade may allow some worker units to become even more flexible considering a longer search depth. A final upgrade may allow some smart workers to accept joint goals or give them the ability to order other units to perform direct commands.

4 Evaluation of Planning Methods in the Smart Workers Domain

As mentioned earlier, we will be focusing on one specific goal for worker units, namely bringing a food ration to the kingdom, with the intention to identify which method is more appropriate for handling this problem given that there are various ways that this can be achieved in the Smart Workers domain. For this purpose we specified a series of planning problems over the Smart Workers domain, and evaluated the performance of some basic informed and uninformed state-space search methods using the planner iThink.

4.1 Problems Sets of Increasing Levels of Difficulty

The presence of specific types of buildings in the current state of the game-world allows the worker unit to perform actions that it may not be able to perform otherwise. For instance, if there is no armory in the domain the worker cannot get a weapon. Essentially, the available structures in the current state determine to a great extent the available actions of the worker unit. Following this observation we developed a series of planning problems of increasing difficulty, which differ in the types of structures that are available.

We start with Level 1 which is the easiest as all buildings are available and the goal can be reached by performing one action, and go up to Level 6 removing one type of structure each time. As the available actions of the worker unit get limited, the optimal plan becomes longer making it more challenging to identify a solution fast. Also, to investigate how the number of literals affect the difficulty of the planning problem, for each type of problem we also considered larger instances by increasing the number of buildings of each type.

4.2   Search Methods Considered

A usual concern among game developers against using sophisticated approaches for decision making is that it is often faster to customize the domain specification so that a simpler domain-dependent approach can be applied. In order to investigate whether this concern applies for the Smart Workers domain, we focused on some approaches that attempt to explore the spectrum between the two extremes of i) applying a sophisticated domain-independent academic method and ii) applying a domain-specific approach tailored specifically for the problem of planning for food rations in this domain.

We chose to experiment with three search methods: i) basic uninformed depth-first search (DFS) with a maximum depth limit, ii) A* heuristic search (Astar), and heuristic depth-first search (H-DFS) with a maximum depth limit, a variation of DFS which uses a heuristic function to order the nodes that are inserted into the open list in every iteration. For the informed search methods we experimented with the goal count (GC) and the Fast Forward (FF) heuristic that we mentioned in Section 2.

In order to investigate whether a domain-dependent approach would be more effective, we tweaked the action templates of the iThink planner so that action generation considers actions that are more promising first (according to our experience with the domain). In this way, the uninformed search essentially runs on what we call an "empirically optimized" action odering. We also tried the same methods with a random action ordering to examine how it affects the results.

4.3   Results

Below, we present some diagrams that compare the performances of the search methods considered with their heuristic functions, in the subsection before. Indicatively, we discuss Levels 2,3, and 4.

Level 2. In Figure 3(a), the execution time of these methods is compared, in the second level of difficulty, where the worker has to execute at least two actions to reach the goal, for example getting rice from a windmill and converting it into a food ration. By optimizing the action ordering, DFS, although a blind search method, seems to work best along with A* with the goal count heuristic (GC). Heusristic DFS goal count works also well, but methods using FF slower. This is can be explained by the amount of time needed to produce the planning graphs since each state contains many literals and numerous actions are applicable. For this difficulty of the problem, all search methods needed almost the same number of nodes to visit. The differences in execution time had to do more with the implementation of each method, such as the sorting that A*

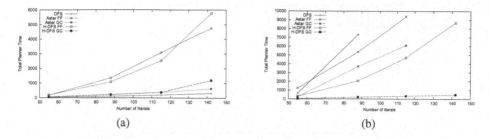

(a)   (b)

Fig. 3. Level 2 and Level 3 Total planner time in msec

uses, or FF mentioned before. It is interesting to note that by providing a random action ordering, the situation changes completely. DFS now is unable to return a plan in a reasonable amount of time, thus being the slowest, and algorithms that use goal count, delay greatly too, but not to the same extent as DFS. However, the FF heuristic, seems to be little affected, as expected.

Level 3. We removed some buildings from the domain of the game, resulting in fewer actions available for the worker to execute. In this level of difficulty, to reach the goal, we need at least 3 actions, meaning that the minimum depth of search is 3. A candidate optimal plan, may involve a sequence, like getting a weapon, hunting an animal in a forest for raw meat and converting it into food in the slaughterhouse. In Figure 3 we present some results about the execution time of the search methods we considered before. DFS now is the slowest to return a plan-solution, despite having provided an helping action ordering for the current goal. A* algorithm, regardless of heuristic function delays to extract solution, although the solution is optimal and being at least faster than DFS. Heuristic Depth FS proves to be the fastest one for this difficulty of the problem, especially when using the goal count heuristic, which returns a solution almost instantly and optimal. H-DFS consumes also the fewest nodes, meaning that it seems to be more accurate for the current difficulty. DFS and A* using the GC heuristic consume a large and unnecessary amount of state space, while A* using FF is more accurate, but a bit less accurate than heuristic DFS. Finally, if we alter the action ordering, DFS will be unable to return a solution in each size of the initial state, but still Heuristic Depth FS with GC function is still the fastest search method with heuristic DFS FF following.

Level 4. In order to make the current planning problem even more difficult, we removed some more buildings from the domain, limiting the actions of the worker unit and forcing him to devise more complex plans. For level 4 of difficulty, the optimal plan to satisfy the goal consists of four actions. The optimal plan is even more complicated than previous levels; the worker now has to harvest gold from a mine and produce money from it and use the money to buy a food ration from the market building. Depth First Search is still a very slow, along with A* goal count, thus being unable to return

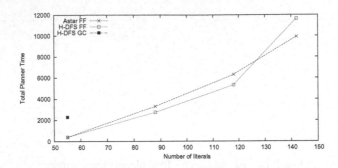

Fig. 4. Level 4 - Total planner time in msec

a solution in an acceptable time. Heuristic Depth FS using GC function is unable to solve the problem, even for the smallest initial state, while in previous level was the fastest. The algorithms using FF heuristic seem to be efficient enough as they work quite well even for the largest size of the initial state where we have four buildings of each available type.

Results. It is important to note how the increasing levels of difficulty mentioned before are produced by removing buildings from the planning domain. The domain may be thinned, resulting in smaller state space, but at the same time we "lose" actions that could lead directly to the goal we set. This means that the search algorithm has to look for more complicated sets of actions that could lead to the goal state, meaning greater search depth and thus larger search space consumed. For example, if we remove the warehouse from the domain, the latter will look smaller but the agent can no longer simply get a food ration and as a result, it has to find ingredients from other structures to produce one. Consequently the new plan has more than one actions.

It is also important to note that we were not able to find an optimal action ordering that will work well for DFS in all levels of difficulty. Levels such as 3 and 4 are indications as of why this is true. As we see, our "empirically optimized" action ordering fails to provide DFS with information that helps perform well. Nonetheless, we can devise another ordering that is specifically optimal for level 3 by moving up to the list those actions that are needed to solve the planning problems in Level 3. In Figure 5, we report on the running time of the different approaches with this new ordering. DFS now seems to work extremely well, even though it does not extract the optimal solution-plan.

As we anticipated though there other scenarios where this new ordering cannot cope well. In particular, in Figure 6 we report on the running time of the different approaches with this new ordering. DFS was not able to solve any problem in this Level with the new ordering.

Finally, note that search methods using the FF heuristic are not affected from the change of orderings (as expected) and that have the most consistent behavior overall.

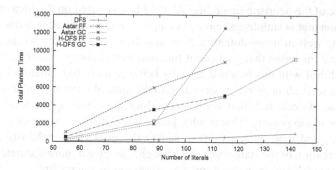

Fig. 5. Level 3 - Total planner time in msec, Optimal action ordering for Level 3

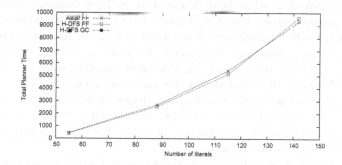

Fig. 6. Level 4 - Total planner time, Optimal action ordering for Level 4

5 Discussion

Judging from the previous results, we conclude the following. First of all, for simple problems, such as level 2 of the previous problem, simple search algorithms like depth first search can be quite efficient though the solution extracted is not always optimal. Adding also some optimizations, like altering the ordering of actions in a manner to manipulate DFS towards the solution, can render sometimes such search methods even more efficient and comparable with more sophisticated algorithms that use heuristic mechanisms. Using heuristic functions, and especially computationally involved such as FF, may prove ineffective for these simple problems as the state space is quite small. In the case of FF, it takes a lot of time to produce the planning graph given that the initial state contains numerous literals as well as numerous actions are applicable. However, as the problem difficulty increases, there is also a proportional increase in the need of using more sophisticated techniques. Simple algorithms are less efficient as their search field is vast and choose blindly the next node/state to expand, resulting often in an unacceptable execution time and quality of solution. This cannot be avoided even using domain-specific knowledge such as the optimization of action ordering.

The choice of the heuristic functions GC and FF was based on the idea of trying out both a function that is simple and easy to compute, and a sophisticated one that seems to be working well in many domains. Note also that the goal state we set, contained only one literal, meaning that goal count function would always return 1. This means, that A* combined with this function actually behaves more like Breadth First Search. A* algorithm sorts all open states according to the sum of current plan actions and the heuristic value. We conclude that, open states which are in the highest level of the state space tree are in top priority. That is why, goal count function proves ineffective when we need more and more plan actions to satisfy the goal as A* exhausts a great and unnecessary portion of the state space. FF, though, can give a more accurate estimation of the expected plan length in this domain as observed by the results.

In order for Heuristic DFS to work efficiently, it must be accompanied with a very accurate heuristic function, like FF. Using the goal count heuristic proves ineffective in many cases, especially when the difficulty of the problem increases. Even though it is classified among heuristic search algorithms, due to the fact that goal count always returns 1 value for the specific goal, it is greatly affected by the action ordering but in a completely irregular manner. For example, there are cases where this algorithm is unable to return a solution in a reasonable amount of time even when the action ordering is optimal, while with a random ordering may work quite well. This unreliability renders this algorithm with goal count heuristic inappropriate for meeting the needs of a demanding video game. However, using FF, heuristic DFS proves to be the best because as mentioned before, in most cases the function often leads straightforward to the solution, zeroing the need for backtracking.

Even when the domain of the game becomes vast, potentially due to a large number of buildings, there are various ways to simplify it though not implemented within the demo. For instance, the workers' behavior can be modified so that they can sense game objects in a specific radius instead of sensing the whole game world. Alternatively, if there are more than one buildings of each type, the worker can sense one object of each available type, in other words, providing a representative domain, of course according to what the worker is able to do or not. Consequently, by using such methods, the search domain can be simplified greatly, and judging from the diagrams in the previous section, we can always find a search method and heuristic function that work extremely well for average sizes of the domain, especially, for lower difficulties of the problem where the search depth does not exceed 5.

6   Related Work

To the best of our knowledge planning methods have not been explored before in the genre of RTS video games for the purposes of guiding the worker units in the game. There are, though, other cases where planning has been used to guide the *AI opponents* in RTS games, such as for example the work of in [4]. In this approach, the authors look for means of creating an AI opponent that can produce efficiently large quantities of specific resources (food, gold, lumber) under some time constraints using a specific planner. In order to prove the effectiveness of this approach, a human extracted plan and a plan extracted by the authors' planner are put into comparison regarding time, under the same goal of producing a specific quantity of resources. In contrast, in this work *we extend the available interactions in typical RTS domains* and focus on an agent-based approach for achieving flexible behavior for worker units in the new richer domain under the command of the human player. Note that the two approaches solve different problems.

Also, there are other cases where off-line or on-line planning has been used to guide the behavior of NPCs in other genres. A popular example of a game using such techniques is the first-person shooter game called "F.E.A.R" [17]. It uses Goal Oriented Action Planning (G.O.A.P) which is inspired by similar to classical STRIPS regarding state and action representation. Agents, being able to sense their environment decide which goal is the best to execute and plans a sequence of actions in order to achieve it. There are various other games that adopted a similar goal-oriented planning technique, including the following titles: Fallout 3, Empire: Total War, Condemned: Criminal Origins, F.E.A.R. 2: Project Origin, Deux Ex: Human Revolution, Demigod and Ghost Buster.

Another technique that is similar in spirit to classical planning is the use of Hierarchical Task Networks (HTN). In order to reach the goal, it is divided into smaller ones, easier to solve, until it is decomposed into simple actions that can be executed directly. A well-known game that uses HTN planning is the first-person shooter game Unreal Tournament [10,15]. In Unreal Tournament, HTNs are used to coordinate the behavior of various non-player characters to execute goals collaboratively.

An interesting approach that falls in this category is the development and evaluation of an HTN planning library which used as a testbed a well known Role Playing Game, "The Elder Scrolls VI: Oblivion". This system exported as a planning solution behavior scripts for agents, scripted in the language of this game. One main the main motives of this approach was also the increasing need to produce dynamic and automated behavior for agents according to the plan extracted given that there are numerous states in which the game environment is [13]. Some other related work that has been performed in the planning community is reported in [14,16,2].

Finally, on a different direction the work of [6] investigates search methods for finding good action sequences for a group of units engaged in combat with enemy units. Also, [5] looks into the problem of employing search algorithms in RTS games.

7 Conclusions

In this work we were interested in extending the game play of real-time strategy video games, by providing a more realistic domain by allowing human players to instruct the worker units to perform high-level commands that involve finding an appropriate sequence of actions to execute. To realize this idea, we evaluated various STRIPS planning techniques inside a real video game environment so that we can extract conclusions with respect to which extent each method performs well and under which circumstances. We conclude that even in small problems like the ones in the Smart Worker domain, the sophisticated heuristic methods are the only ones reliable, compared to approaches we tried that focus on simple search methods and exploiting domain-dependent customizations, even though sometimes for small problems some unnecessary overhead is added. Finally, as future work we intend to investigate how similar goals may be handled by more than one worker units in collaboration.

References

1. Anastassiou, V.M., Diamantopoulos, P., Vassos, S., Koubarakis, M.: iThink: A library for classical planning in video-games. In: Maglogiannis, I., Plagianakos, V., Vlahavas, I. (eds.) SETN 2012. LNCS, vol. 7297, pp. 106–113. Springer, Heidelberg (2012)
2. Bartheye, O., Jacopin, E.: Connecting PDDL-based off the shelf planners to an arcade game. In: AI in Games Workshop at ECAI 2008 (July 2008)
3. Blum, A., Furst, M.: Fast Planning Through Planning Graph Analysis. In: Proceedings of the 14th International Joint Conference on Artificial Intelligence, IJCAI 1995 (1995)
4. Chan, H., Fern, A., Ray, S., Wilson, N., Ventura, C.: Online planning for resource production in real-time strategy games. In: Proceedings of the International Conference on Automated Planning and Scheduling (ICAPS). AAAI Press (2007)
5. Churchill, D., Buro, M.: Incorporating search algorithms into rts game agents (2012)
6. Churchill, D., Buro, M.: Portfolio greedy search and simulation for large-scale combat in starcraft. In: CIG, pp. 1–8. IEEE (2013)
7. Edmund, L.: Enhanced npc behavior using goal oriented action planning (2007)
8. Fikes, R.E., Nilsson, N.J.: Strips: A new approach to the application of theorem proving to problem solving. Artificial Intelligence 2 (1971)
9. Ghallab, M., Howe, A., Knoblock, C., Mcdermott, D., Ram, A., Veloso, M., Weld, D., Wilkins, D.: PDDL—The Planning Domain Definition Language (1998)
10. Hoang, H., Lee-urban, S., Muñoz Avila, H.: Hierarchical plan representations for encoding strategic game ai. In: Proc. Artificial Intelligence and Interactive Digital Entertainment Conference, AIIDE 2005 (2005)
11. Hoffmann, J., Nebel, B.: The FF planning system: Fast plan generation, through heuristic search
12. James, W.: Artificial intelligence in games: A look at the smarts behind lionhead studios black and white and where it can and will go in the future. In: Spring Simulation Multiconference (2008)
13. Kelly, J.P., Botea, A., Koenig, S.: Offline Planning with Hierarchical Task Networks in Video Games. In: Proceedings of the Fourth International Conference on Artificial Intelligence and Interactive Digital Entertainment, AIIDE 2008 (2008)
14. Michael, B.: Call for AI Research in RTS Games. In: Proceedings of the AAAI Workshop on AI in Games (2004)
15. Munoz-Avila, H., Fisher, T.: Strategic planning for unreal tournament bots. In: AAAI Workshop on Challenges in Game AI. AAAI Press (2004)
16. Ontanon, S., Mishra, K., Sugandh, N., Ram, A.: Online case based planning. Computational Intelligence 26
17. Orkin, J.: Three States and a Plan: The AI of F.E.A.R. In: Proceedings of the Game Developer's Conference, GDC (2006)
18. Smith, M.: Game ai for domination games
19. Vassos, S., Papakonstantinou, M.: The SimpleFPS Planning Domain: A PDDL Benchmark for Proactive NPCs. In: Intelligent Narrative Technologies IV, Papers from the 2011 AIIDE Workshop, Technical Report WS-11-18. AAAI Press (October 2011)

Opening Statistics and Match Play
for Backgammon Games

Nikolaos Papahristou and Ioannis Refanidis

Dept. of Applied Informatics, University of Macedonia
Egnatia 156, Thessaloniki, 54006, Greece
nikpapa@gmail.com, yrefanid@uom.gr

Abstract. Players of complex board games like backgammon, chess and go, were always wondering what the best opening moves for their favourite game are. In the last decade, computer analysis has offered more insight to many opening variations. This is especially true for backgammon, where computer rollouts have radically changed the way human experts play the opening. In this paper we use Palamedes, the winner of the latest computer backgammon Olympiad, to make the first ever computer assisted analysis of the opening rolls for the backgammon variants Portes, Plakoto and Fevga (collectively called Tavli in Greece). We then use these results to build effective match strategies for each game variant.

Keywords: Monte Carlo, Game Statistics, Match play, Backgammon, Plakoto, Fevga.

1   Introduction

Backgammon is a perfect information, turn-taking game of two players, where the outcome is influenced both from skill and the roll of the dice. At each turn, the available candidate moves are computed according to the roll of two six-sided dice, resulting in 21 possible rolls. Standard backgammon opening rolls have been thoroughly analyzed in [6]. To the best of our knowledge, this kind of analysis has not been made in other backgammon variants. In this paper we attempt to computationally analyze the opening rolls of the backgammon variants Portes, Plakoto and Fevga, using our Palamedes bot[1]. We then use these results to extract useful statistical information about the games.

Our methodology is similar to the one used in [6]: The most promising continuations after each roll are analyzed using rollout analysis, a Monte Carlo method that is commonly used in backgammon. Starting from the resulting position after each candidate move, a fixed number of games is played until a terminal position is reached. Counting the results of these games we can finally get the probabilities of single wins (WS), double wins (WD), single losses (LS) and double losses (LD). Bases on these

---

[1] Palamedes can be freely downloaded from http://ai.uom.gr/nikpapa/Palamedes

A. Likas, K. Blekas, and D. Kalles (Eds.): SETN 2014, LNAI 8445, pp. 569–582, 2014.
© Springer International Publishing Switzerland 2014

probabilities, we can then compute the estimated equity of each position using the following equation:

$$E = WS - LS + 2 * (WD - LD) \tag{1}$$

This kind of evaluation is considered to offer accurate results in backgammon, despite the fact that the move selection algorithm of the rollout phase is not so strong in terms of performance [12]. Rollouts can also be truncated, which means that they could stop after a fixed amount of plies (instead of going till the end of the game) and average together the estimates of the resulting positions, with a negligible change in their estimates.

The rest of the paper is structured as follows: First we briefly discuss the related work and the three backgammon variants, then we present our experimental results, we discuss them and, finally, we conclude the paper and identify some challenges for future research.

2   Background

2.1   Related Work

Monte Carlo methods have recently gained increased interest by game AI researchers due to the success of the MCTS algorithm in the game of Go [3, 5], as well as in other games [4, 7, 14]. In MCTS and it's most popular variant UCT, rollouts (usually called playouts) are used to simulate a trajectory, whereas its outcome is used to build and update a tree from the starting position. The rollouts can be random or based on heuristics. Recent advances in computer Go indicate that adding domain knowledge in the rollouts is critical for producing state of the art performance.

More relevant to our setup are the MCTS variants that attempt to solve the game-theoritic value of positions. MCTS-Solver [13] and Monte Carlo Proof-Number Search (MC-PNS) [10] are two such algorithms that are based on Proof Number Search [1]. Score bounded MCTS [2] is another technique for proving the game theoretic value of games of multiple outcomes. However, all three algorithms are suitable for determinist games only. To the best of our knowledge we are not aware of similar enhancements for non-deterministic, perfect information games with chance nodes such as backgammon.

2.2   Rules of Backgammon Variants Examined

Most backgammon variants are usually conducted in a board containing 24 *points* divided in 4 quadrants of 6 points each. Each player starts the game with a number of checkers or stones at his disposal (usually 15) placed in a fixed starting position. The players take turns playing their checkers forward using an element of chance in the form of two six-sided dice. The checkers can be moved only to an *open point* according to the game rules. When all checkers of a player are inside his last quadrant of the board (called his *home* board), he can start taking them out of the board; this is called bearing off. The player that clears all his checkers first is the winner of the game.

At the end of the game, if the losing player has borne off at least one checker, he loses only one point. However, if the loser has *not* borne off any of his checkers, he loses a double game or *gammon* and two points. In standard backgammon, if the loser has not borne off any of his checkers and still has a checker in the winner's home board, he loses a triple game or *backgammon* and three points.

Portes   Plakoto   Fevga

Fig. 1. Starting position and direction of movement for Tavli games

There are hundreds of backgammon variants played around the world, however most of them can be classified into three categories, according to the rule that defines a player's *made point*, that is a point where only the player that has "made" it can move into:

- The *hitting games* (e.g. Backgammon, Portes, Accy-deucey), where players can "hit" lone checkers of the opponent, placing them on the *bar,* forcing the opponent to re-enter them in his home board before playing any other move. A *made point* in this type of games is a point containing two or more checkers.
- The *pinning games* (e.g. Plakoto, Tapa), where players can "pin" lone checkers of the opponent, thus preventing the movement of the pinned checker. A made point in this type of games is a point where two or more checkers of the same player exist or one checker that has pinned an opponent checker.
- The *running* games (e.g Fevga, Narde, Gul-bara), where no pin or hit is possible. A single checker in a point constitutes a "made point". In this type of games, movement of checkers is in the same direction for both players (Fig. 1, right), further complicating matters.

Fig. 1 shows the starting positions and the direction of checker movement for the three variants that we examine in this paper. As can be easily seen, Plakoto and Fevga have starting positions where all player checkers are stacked in their first point. On the other hand, Portes (and her almost twin backgammon) have a special crafted starting position. We examine the importance of the starting position later in the discussion section.

The rules mentioned above are the most important for the variants Portes, Plakoto and Fevga that we examine in this paper. There are some other details about the rules of Plakoto and Fevga that can be found in [2]. Portes is identical to backgammon, with the following changes: a) No cube² is used; b) no triple wins (backgammons); and c) a double roll is allowed in the first move.

2.3   Match Play and Tavli

Backgammon games can be played individually, in which case they are called *money games*; however, more often they are played in a match, where each player accumulates points (one point for single wins, two points for double wins) until a player reaches a predefined number of points. In Greece, the most popular way of playing backgammon games is a Tavli match (Fig. 2), where Portes, Plakoto and Fevga are played one after the other, until a player reaches five or seven points.

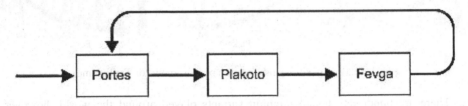

Fig. 2. Flow of a Tavli match. (Source: http://www.bkgm.com/variants/Tavli.html)

2.4   Palamedes

All the experiments in this paper are made using our latest Palamedes bot. Palamedes, originally started as a project aimed at developing expert-playing bots at Tavli games, currently supports Portes, Plakoto, Fevga, Narde, Hypergammon, Nackgammon, Takhteh, with more variants planned for the future. At the core of the evaluation function of each game is a Neural Network trained by TD(λ) [11] and millions of self-play games. The training procedure that we used [8, 9] is inspired by the early successes of TD-Gammon in backgammon [12]. Palamedes is the current world champion in computer backgammon, after taking the first place at the latest Backgammon Computer Olympiad held in Tilburg, Netherlands, 2011.

3   Experimental Setup and Results

We used our latest and best Neural Networks (NN) game evaluation functions for selecting each move on the rollouts. For Portes we used Portes_ACG13 NN, for Plakoto we used Plakoto5, and for Fevga we used Fevga6 [8]. The rollouts were performed using 1-ply playing mode, which means that Palamedes looked ahead only at the current roll for each play during the rollouts, selecting the best play of each trial. After the opening roll we rolled out the five most promising candidate moves

---

² When the doubling cube is used the stakes of the game can be increased by the players. Using the cube speeds up match play and provides an added dimension for strategy.

(selected using 2-ply evaluation), using 100,000 games per position. The standard error of the estimated equity E (1) when performing this number of trials is less than 0.02. Rollouts were performed using **cubeless untruncated money play**. *Cubeless* means that games are played without a doubling cube. *Untruncated* means that rollouts were played out until the end of the game. *Money play* means that each game is played individually and not as a part of a match.

Opening rolls were split in two groups, single and double, in order to shed more light into the effect of rolling a double at the start of the game. This is most useful in standard backgammon, which does not allow a double opening roll like the Portes variant does. The move selected for each roll was picked as the best after rolling out the most promising candidate moves available. These figures were constructed by singling out the move with best equity after each roll. The actual moves selected can be seen in Appendix B.

Figs. 3-5 summarize the results for each roll and game variant and compares the games. All numbers shown are with regard to the first player making the move. Averages of all single rolls are marked with the word 'SINGLE'. Averages of all double rolls are marked with the word 'DOUBLE'. Finally the word 'ALL' is the weighted (according to the probability of each roll) average of all 21 rolls.

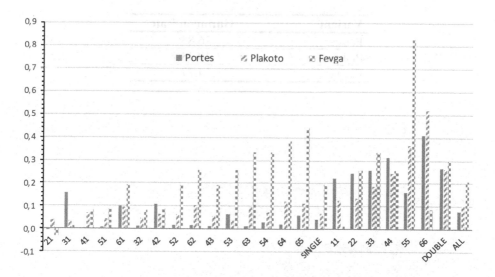

Fig. 3. Comparison of estimated equity of all opening rolls

In Fig. 3 the estimated equity of all opening moves for all games is presented. The starting roll with the greatest equity is by far the 55 in Fevga, while the least useful roll is the 21 in Fevga.

Fevga All Rolls	47,31%	10,22%	38,42%	4,05%
Fevga Double Rolls	47,39%	12,89%	36,06%	3,66%
Fevga Single Rolls	47,30%	9,69%	38,89%	4,12%
Plakoto All Rolls	29,90%	22,77%	29,62%	17,71%
Plakoto Double Rolls	27,85%	28,91%	27,30%	15,95%
Plakoto Single Rolls	30,31%	21,55%	30,09%	18,06%
Portes All Rolls	38,18%	14,62%	34,87%	12,31%
Portes Double Rolls	41,84%	17,57%	30,68%	9,73%
Portes Single Rolls	37,45%	14,03%	35,70%	12,82%

0%   100%

■ Single Wins (WS)   ◌ Double Wins (WD)   ╲ Single Losses (LS)   ∵ Double Losses (LD)

Fig. 4. Expected outcome (%) of the first player

Fig. 4 summarizes the outcome of all rolls to produce the expected result of the first player. From this figure we can derive the percentage of games that result in doubles, also called "gammon rate", by adding WD and LD (Table 1).

Table 1. Gammon rates of Tavli variants

Variant	Gammon Rate
Portes	26.85%
Plakoto	40.48%
Fevga	14.27%

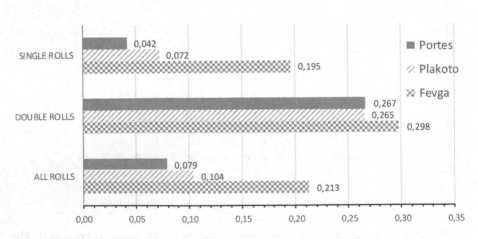

Fig. 5. Total estimated equity of the first player

Perhaps the most interesting result of this study is the total estimated equity of the first player shown in Fig. 5. Ideally, a perfectly designed backgammon game would give zero equity to the first player. This would mean that the opening roll does not favor one player over the other. Our study shows that the "best" variant in that regard is Portes, closely followed by Plakoto. On the other hand, Fevga gives a significant advantage to the first player.

4   Discussion

This section discusses and compares the results of the three games to each other, as well as to previous similar studies. We also attempt to explain some of the results found from a strategic point of view.

4.1   Portes

The results for the single rolls of the Portes variant are very similar to a previous study on standard backgammon openings [6]. In that study, the rollouts were performed by GnuBG[3], a very strong open source backgammon program at a 2-ply depth. The estimated equity of all single rolls in [6] is 0.039, ours is 0.042. Almost all best opening moves coincide with our best selected moves. The gammon rate is estimated in [6] at 27.6%. If we count the backgammons, which according to Portes rules are counted as gammons, this rate is increased to 28.8%. Our results estimate this at a more modest 26.9%, almost a 2% difference. We give two possible explanations for this behavior: a) 1-ply rollouts are not accurate enough, and b) the playing style of Palamedes is more conservative compared to that of GnuBG, resulting in somewhat fewer gammons.

Since the analysis of the single opening rolls is nothing new, we concentrate the discussion around the effect of the double rolls. The inclusion of doubles in the opening roll gives more advantage to the first player. The average equity of all double rolls is 0.267 (Fig. 5), six times larger than the equity of the single rolls. This was expected, since a) doubles usually result in more distance travelled than the average single roll, and b) even small doubles like 11 give the opportunity to construct strategically made points without risking getting hit by the opponent. The best double roll is 66 with 0.41 equity; even the worst double roll (11, E=0.22) is better than the best single roll (31, E=0.16). The effect of doubles can be seen in the weighted average of all rolls (Fig. 5, E=0.079), which is almost twice that of the single rolls.

4.2   Plakoto

Plakoto results, compared to the other games, demonstrate an increased gammon rate. 41% of Plakoto games are won as doubles, 14% more than the rate we calculated in Portes. This rate can be explained by the strategic strength of pinning an opponent checker inside his home board. It is well known that this kind of pin can result in double games because if the pinning player manages not to get pinned himself, he can place his checkers in such a way that during bear off most of his pieces will be borne off before the pinning checker is unpinned. This places the pinned player at a great

---

[3] http://www.gnubg.org

disadvantage, because usually he does not have enough time to return the last checker to his home board and avoid the double loss. Of course, one can play a very conservative game and avoid leaving lone checkers in his home board at all costs. However, this can lead to other problems: building large stacks of checkers, that are extremely inflexible and also minimize the chances of hitting lone checkers of the opponent. For this reason, Palamedes and most expert players prefer a "restrained aggressive approach" during the opening, leaving some lone checkers open when there is a small chance that the opponent can pin them. This strategy however, inevitably falls victim to a lucky pinning roll by the opponent, which may be enough to result in a double loss. This reasoning strongly suggests that the starting position of Plakoto (Fig. 1, middle) greatly influences the gammon rate and the equity of the first player.

In order to test the hypothesis above, we made another experiment changing the starting position: Instead of having all 15 checkers at the starting point, the checkers are distributed evenly in the first three points. This variant is known in some regions as the *Tapa* variant and we will use this naming also in this paper. The starting position of Tapa makes the pinning of checkers inside the home board during the opening more difficult, because the players can construct made points more easily during the start of the game. We used the same methodology and the same Neural Network (Plakoto-5) for the rollouts. Even if this NN was not trained for this specific variant, we believe that it is sufficient to produce strong play, because the type of positions resulting from a Tapa game are well within the range of positions the NN has seen during self-play training[4].

Table 2. Comparison of Tapa and Plakoto estimated results for the first player

Variant	WS (%)	WD (%)	LS (%)	LD (%)	EQUITY	GAMMON RATE (%)
Plakoto	29.89	22.77	29.62	17.71	0.104	40.48
Tapa	37.40	13.12	37.91	11.55	0.026	24.67

The results of the Tapa experiment (Table 2) confirm our hypothesis. The gammon rate is reduced from 40.48 to 24.67%. Also the equity of the first player is reduced to 0.026, which is even lower than the equity of the single rolls in the Portes variant (Fig. 5).

Another notable point that can be seen in Table 2 is that the first player wins about the same amount of single games as the second player (29.9% vs 29.6%). Consequently all the advantage that the first player has can be attributed to the difference in double games won which is 22.77% compared to 17.71% of the second player.

---

[4] The opposite situation could be problematic: a Tapa trained NN may not evaluate correctly Plakoto's opening positions with early home board pins in points 2 and 3, because this kind of experience would have been extremely rare in its self-play training.

4.3   Fevga

The first interesting result in the Fevga experiments is that the expected equity of the first player (0.213) is the highest amongst all games examined, more than twice that of the Plakoto (0.104). Winning 57.5% of the games gives the player who plays first a distinctive advantage. Fevga also has the roll with the most gained equity in all games, the 55 roll at 0.84 equity. We also observe that all high sum rolls (e.g. 63, 64, 65) give very high equity for the first player, with 65 (E=0.44), even surpassing the best Portes roll (66, E=0.41). However, unlike the two other variants, doubles do not increase the equity of the single rolls that much (from 0.19 to 0.21). This can be attributed to the fact that apart form 55, the other two large doubles (44 and 66) that typically have increased equity, have a reduced effect because of Fevga's starting rule [2]. Overall, we note that the further the starting checker is able to move during the first roll, the better the chances are for the first player. This observation fully justifies the name of the game ('Fevga' means 'run' in Greek).

Another surprising observation is that the gammon rate (14.27%) is very low compared to the other variants. The greatest factor that affects this statistic is the very small chance of the second player winning a double game. With 4.05% the second player wins less than half doubles that the first player does (10.22%).

5   Match Play

In this section we show how we can use the statistics from Table 1 to construct effective match strategies for Tavli variants. When playing a match, the goal of the players is to win the match and not to maximize their expected reward at the individual games. For this reason all strong backgammon programs select the best move by approximating the Match Winning Chance (MWC) at each move selection. We present a simple method, similar to the one used in backgammon, for approximating MWC, using the estimates of the NN evaluations and the gammon rate computed in Table 1. For simplicity, we examine only matches of the same game type where the player that starts each game is determined randomly.

First, we build a table estimating MWC before the start of the game for all possible score differences during the course of the match. In the most simple case, that is, when the score is tied, the players have the same chance of winning the match. The table is calculated using the following recursive definition:

$$mwc(A,B) = S * mwc(A-1, B) + D * mwc(A-2, B) + S * mwc(A, B-1) + D * mwc(A, B-2) \quad (2)$$

where A is the remaining points left for player A to win the match, B is the remaining points left for player B to win the match, mwc(A,B) is the table entry specifying the probability of winning the match for the A player when the current score is A points away – B points away, S is the probability each player has of winning a single game (= (1 - gammon rate) / 2), D is the probability each player has of winning a double game (=gammon rate / 2). Appendix A show the tables computed with this method for the games Portes, Plakoto, Fevga and match away scores up to 9.

Finally, for move selection, a similar equation is used for determining the MWC of each move:

$$MWC = WS * mwc(A-1, B) + WD * mwc(A-2, B) + LS * mwc(A, B-1) + LD * mwc(A, B-2) \ (3)$$

where WS, WD, LS and LD are the output estimations of our neural network evaluation function.

5.1   Experiments in Match Play

In order to test the above method, we made an experiment playing 10000 5-point matches in the three variants examined where one player uses the "match" strategy and the other player uses the "money play" strategy that tries to maximize the value of each individual games. The match started half the time by the "match" player and the other half by the "money" player. The results along with some useful statistics that we stored during the course of the matches are shown in Table 3. All results are from the point of the match player.

Table 3. Performance of match strategy vs money play strategy in 10000 5-point matches

Variant	Match Wins	Diff. moves	Games WS	Games WD	Games LS	Games LD	Total game points
Portes	5144±98	7.1%	22937	7094	19558	9066	-565
Plakoto	5103±98	4.6%	15994	10627	15238	11007	-4
Fevga	5067±98	5.3%	28395	4453	27358	5401	-635

The performance of the match strategy is better than the money-play strategy in all games, in terms of matches won by the match player, although the total points won by the match player is less than the points won by the money player. In other words, the match player is able to win the points when they are more important in order to win the current match. This observation is clearer in Portes and Plakoto, and less significant in Fevga, due to the low gammon rate of Fevga that does not give many opportunities for the players to take justified risks for a gammon. We also kept counters whether the money player would play the same move with the match strategy in a non trivial decision (number of possible moves > 1) when it was the turn of the match player (column Diff. moves). As it can be seen in this column the two strategies differ very slightly and this can be an explanation why the match strategy is only better by a small margin.

Finally, we also measured the result of each game (columns: WS, WD, LS, LD) and the total game points from the point of the match player. Interestingly, the match player wins more single games and less double games in all three variants. This can be explained with the following reasoning: when the match player is ahead on the score, it will play more conservatively trying to keep its lead and not take unnecessary chances to win a gammon that could give also winning chances to the opponent. On the other hand, when he is behind he will go more aggressively for a gammon in order to try to close the gap before it is too late. This risky strategy some times will be successful, but most of the times it will result in gammons for the opponent.

6   Conclusions and Future Work

In this paper we used Palamedes bot to conduct rollout experiments on the opening moves of the first player for three popular backgammon games: Portes, Plakoto and Fevga. Our findings for Portes without the double rolls are very close to those found in the literature. To the best of our knowledge, this is the first time that an analysis of the opening moves was conducted for the other two variants, Plakoto and Fevga.

Our results show that the advantage of the first player is significant in the Fevga variant, small in Plakoto and very small in Portes. The superiority of the Portes variant in this statistic was expected because Portes (and backgammon) has the advantage of a specially crafted starting position which is not present in the other variants. Another interesting result is that the gammon rates of the three games fall in completely different ranges. The smallest gammon rate is for the Fevga variant (14.27%), followed by Portes/Backgammon (26.9%), whereas Plakoto has the largest rate (at 41%).

We also showed the effect of the starting position on the statistics examined in the Plakoto variant. Changing only slightly the starting position (Tapa variant), we managed to lower significantly the gammon rate and the advantage of the first player, making Tapa the most "fair" backgammon variant examined so far. It would be interesting to try the opposite procedure in the backgammon/Portes variant: what would be the gammon rate and equity of a variant with the same rules as backgammon but a starting position where all starting checkers are placed in the player's first point? If the results of our Plakoto/Tapa experiments are any indication, we suspect that we would see an increase in both of these measurements. We could have tried out an experiment using the Portes NN in this variant. However, unlike the Plakoto/Tapa case, here the change of the starting position is significant, so we feel that the Portes NN will not generalize well. A new NN-based evaluation function should be self-trained, but as this is not trivial, we leave it for future work.

Finally, as a practical application, we used the computed gammon rates to construct a match strategy that outperformed our previous money play strategy when playing 5-point matches in Portes and Plakoto. In the future we plan to extend this method in matches where the starting player of the game is the one that wins the previous game, and in matches that consist of different game types like a Tavli match.

Acknowledgements. The first author was partially supported by a Hellenic Artificial Intelligence Society (EETN) scholarship.

References

1. Allis, L.V., van der Meulen, M., van den Herik, H.J.: Proof-Number Search. Artificial Intelligence 66, 91–124 (1994) ISSN 0004-3702
2. Cazenave, T., Saffidine, A.: Score Bounded Monte-Carlo Tree Search. In: van den Herik, H.J., Iida, H., Plaat, A. (eds.) CG 2010. LNCS, vol. 6515, pp. 93–104. Springer, Heidelberg (2011)
3. Coulom, R.: Efficient selectivity and backup operators in Monte-Carlo tree search. In: van den Herik, H.J., Ciancarini, P., Donkers, H.H.L.M(J.) (eds.) CG 2006. LNCS, vol. 4630, pp. 72–83. Springer, Heidelberg (2007)
4. Finnsson, H., Björnsson, Y.: Simulation-based approach to general game playing. In: Fox, D., Gomes, C.P. (eds.) Proceedings of the Twenty-Third AAAI Conference on Artificial Intelligence, AAAI 2008, pp. 259–264 (2008)
5. Gelly, S., Silver, D.: Achieving master level play in 9 x 9 computer Go. In: Fox, D., Gomes, C.P. (eds.) Proceedings of the Twenty-Third AAAI Conference on Artificial Intelligence, AAAI 2008, pp. 1537–1540. AAAI Press (2008)
6. Keith, T.: Backgammon openings. Rollouts of opening moves (2006), http://www.bkgm.com/openings/rollouts.html (accessed August 26, 2013)
7. Lorentz, R.J.: Amazons discover Monte-Carlo. In: van den Herik, H.J., Xu, X., Ma, Z., Winands, M.H.M. (eds.) CG 2008. LNCS, vol. 5131, pp. 13–24. Springer, Heidelberg (2008)
8. Papahristou, N., Refanidis, I.: On the Design and Training of Bots to Play Backgammon Variants. In: Iliadis, L., Maglogiannis, I., Papadopoulos, H. (eds.) AIAI 2012. IFIP AICT, vol. 381, pp. 78–87. Springer, Heidelberg (2012)
9. Papahristou, N., Refanidis, I.: Training Neural Networks to Play Backgammon Variants Using Reinforcement Learning. In: Di Chio, C., et al. (eds.) EvoApplications 2011, Part I. LNCS, vol. 6624, pp. 113–122. Springer, Heidelberg (2011)
10. Saito, J.T., Chaslot, G., Uiterwijk, J.W.H.M., van den Herik, H.J.: Monte-Carlo proof-number search for computer Go. In: van den Herik, H.J., Ciancarini, P., Donkers, H.H.L.M(J.) (eds.) CG 2006. LNCS, vol. 4630, pp. 50–61. Springer, Heidelberg (2007)
11. Sutton, R.S., Barto, A.G.: Reinforcement Learning: An Indroduction. MIT Press (1998)
12. Tesauro, G.: Programming backgammon using self-teaching neural nets. Artificial Intelligence 134, 181–199 (2002)
13. Winands, M.H.M., Björnsson, Y., Saito, J.T.: Monte-Carlo tree search solver. In: van den Herik, H.J., Xu, X., Ma, Z., Winands, M.H.M. (eds.) CG 2008. LNCS, vol. 5131, pp. 25–36. Springer, Heidelberg (2008)
14. Winands, M.H.M., Björnsson, Y.: Evaluation Function Based Monte-Carlo LOA. In: van den Herik, H.J., Spronck, P. (eds.) ACG 2009. LNCS, vol. 6048, pp. 33–44. Springer, Heidelberg (2010)

Appendix A: Precomputed Match Winning Chance (MWC) Tables for Tavli Games

The following tables are calculated according to Section 5 and equation (2).

Table 4. MWC (%) for player A on Portes variant

A away		MATCH WINNING CHANCE (MWC)								
	B away	1	2	3	4	5	6	7	8	9
1		50.00	68.28	81.68	89.04	93.53	96.16	97.73	98.65	99.20
2		31.73	50.00	65.85	76.78	84.56	89.83	93.37	95.72	97.25
3		18.32	34.15	50.00	62.91	73.20	80.98	86.72	90.84	93.75
4		10.96	23.22	37.09	50.00	61.39	70.85	78.41	84.26	88.69
5		6.47	15.44	26.80	38.61	50.00	60.25	69.07	76.36	82.23
6		3.84	10.17	19.02	29.15	39.75	50.00	59.41	67.68	74.71
7		2.27	6.63	13.28	21.59	30.93	40.59	50.00	58.74	66.56
8		1.35	4.28	9.16	15.74	23.64	32.32	41.26	50.00	58.20
9		0.80	2.75	6.25	11.31	17.77	25.29	33.44	41.80	50.00

Table 5. MWC (%) for player A on Plakoto variant

A away		MATCH WINNING CHANCE (MWC)								
	B away	1	2	3	4	5	6	7	8	9
1		50.00	64.88	79.43	86.77	91.90	94.91	96.85	98.03	98.78
2		35.12	50.00	65.87	75.78	83.47	88.67	92.34	94.84	96.55
3		20.57	34.13	50.00	61.90	71.98	79.55	85.33	89.56	92.65
4		13.23	24.22	38.10	50.00	60.91	69.87	77.20	82.97	87.43
5		8.10	16.53	28.02	39.09	50.00	59.69	68.13	75.17	80.93
6		5.09	11.33	20.45	30.13	40.31	50.00	58.94	66.82	73.60
7		3.15	7.66	14.67	22.80	31.87	41.06	50.00	58.29	65.75
8		1.97	5.16	10.44	17.03	24.83	33.18	41.71	50.00	57.79
9		1.22	3.45	7.35	12.57	19.07	26.40	34.25	42.21	50.00

Table 6. MWC (%) for player A on Fevga variant

A away		MATCH WINNING CHANCE (MWC)								
	B away	1	2	3	4	5	6	7	8	9
1		50.00	71.43	84.18	91.18	95.09	97.27	98.48	99.15	99.53
2		28.57	50.00	66.69	78.37	86.25	91.39	94.68	96.74	98.02
3		15.82	33.31	50.00	63.91	74.72	82.70	88.39	92.33	95.00
4		8.82	21.63	36.09	50.00	62.19	72.20	80.03	85.93	90.26
5		4.91	13.75	25.28	37.81	50.00	60.98	70.32	77.92	83.88
6		2.73	8.61	17.30	27.80	39.02	50.00	60.07	68.85	76.19
7		1.52	5.32	11.61	19.97	29.68	39.93	50.00	59.35	67.65
8		0.85	3.26	7.67	14.07	22.08	31.15	40.65	50.00	58.77
9		0.47	1.98	5.00	9.74	16.12	23.81	32.35	41.23	50.00

Appendix B: Best Move of All Opening Rolls Per Variant Examined

	PORTES		PLAKOTO		FEVGA	
ROLL	BEST MOVE	EQ	BEST MOVE	EQ	BEST MOVE	EQ
SINGLE ROLLS						
21	24/23 13/11	0.006	24/22 24/23	0.042	24/21	-0.030
31	8/5 6/5	0.155	24/21 24/23	0.037	24/20	0.012
41	24/23 13/9	0.002	24/20 24/23	0.070	24/19	0.086
51	24/23 13/8	0.011	24/19 24/23	0.043	24/18	0.090
61	13/7 8/7	0.108	24/18 24/23	0.097	24/17	0.194
32	24/21 13/11	0.017	24/21 24/22	0.050	24/19	0.086
42	8/4 6/4	0.110	24/20 24/22	0.065	24/18	0.090
52	24/22 13/8	0.015	24/19 24/22	0.066	24/17	0.194
62	24/18 13/11	0.017	24/18 24/22	0.106	24/16	0.259
43	24/20 13/10	0.015	24/20 24/21	0.056	24/17	0.194
53	8/3 6/3	0.059	24/19 24/21	0.039	24/16	0.259
63	24/18 13/10	0.018	24/18 24/21	0.096	24/15	0.336
54	24/20 13/8	0.029	24/19 24/20	0.073	24/15	0.336
64	8/2 6/2	0.016	24/18 24/20	0.121	24/14	0.385
65	24/18 18/13	0.072	24/18 24/19	0.117	24/13	0.440
DOUBLE ROLLS						
11	8/7 (2) 6/5(2)	0.213	24/23 (4)	0.129	24/20	0.012
22	13/11(2) 6/4(2)	0.240	24/20 24/22 (2)	0.137	24/16	0.259
33	8/5 (2) 6/3 (2)	0.259	24/18 24/21 (2)	0.187	24/15	0.336
44	24/20(2) 13/9(2)	0.348	24/16 (2)	0.247	24/16	0.259
55	13/8 (2) 8/3 (2)	0.160	24/14 24/19 (2)	0.361	24/9 24/19	0.831
66	24/18(2) 13/7(2)	0.398	24/12 (2)	0.521	24/18	0.090

Story Generation in PDDL Using Character Moods:
A Case Study on Iliad's First Book

Andrea Marrella and Stavros Vassos

Sapienza University of Rome, Italy
{marrella,vassos}@dis.uniroma1.it

Abstract. In this paper we look into a simple approach for generating character-based stories using planning and the language of PDDL. A story often involves modalities over properties and objects, such as what the characters believe, desire, request, etc. We look into a practical approach that reifies such modalities into normal objects of the planning domain, and relies on a "mood" predicate to represent the disposition of characters based on these objects. A short story is then generated by specifying a goal for the planning problem expressed in terms of the moods of the characters of the story. As a case study of how such a domain for story generation is modeled, we investigate the story of the first book of Homer's Iliad as a solution of an appropriate PDDL domain and problem description.

1 Introduction

In this work we present some preliminary results toward modeling stories as solutions of automated planning problems [6]. Planning systems are problem-solving algorithms that operate on explicit representations of states and actions [3]. We focus on the standardized Planning Domain Definition Language (PDDL) [5]; it allows one to formulate a *planning problem* $\mathcal{P} = \langle I, G, \mathcal{P}_D \rangle$, where I is the initial state, G is the goal state, and $\mathcal{P}_D$ is the planning domain. In turn, a planning domain $\mathcal{P}_D$ is built from a set of *propositions* describing the state of the world (a state is characterized by the set of propositions that are true) and a set of *operators* (i.e., actions) that can be executed in the domain. Each operator is of the form $o = \langle Pre_o, Eff_o \rangle$, where Pre_o and Eff_o specifies the preconditions and effects of o, in terms of the set of domain propositions. A solution for a PDDL planning problem is a sequence of operators—a *plan*—whose execution transforms the initial state I into a state satisfying the goal G. In this paper we focus on the STRIPS subset of PDDL 2.1 [2], which also makes use of the common features of typing and (possibly quantified) conditional effects.

By representing the underlying dynamics of the world in which a story unfolds as a planning domain and the characteristics of the specific target story instance that we intend to generate as a planning problem, then we can use an off-the-shelf planner to generate a story according to the given description. One motivation for this approach is that a wide range of story alternatives can be handled by a concise representation, while these stories can be adapted and tweaked both at design time and real-time in order to satisfy requirements that arise during the execution, e.g., in a video game context.

As a case study, we investigate the knowledge representation and modeling task of generating the story of the first book of Homer's classic work Iliad. Figure 1 shows a

A. Likas, K. Blekas, and D. Kalles (Eds.): SETN 2014, LNAI 8445, pp. 583–588, 2014.

- *Apollo's priest Chryses comes to the Achaian camp and asks to ransom back his daughter Chryseis, who has been captured by Agamemnon.*
- *Chryses, is insulted and sent away. He prays to Apollo to punish the Greeks, which Apollo does by sending a plague upon them.*
- *Achilleus calls an assembly to deal with the plague, and the prophet, Kalchas, reveals that Apollo was angered by Agamemnon's refusal to return the daughter of his priest.*
- *Agamemnon agrees to give her back, but demands compensation. This provokes Achilleus' anger, and, after they exchange threats and angry words, Agamemnon decides to take Achilleus' "prize", the captive woman, Briseis.*
- *The goddess, Athene, prevents Achilleus from killing Agamemnon by promising that he will one day be compensated with three times as many prizes.*
- *Agamemnon's men take Briseis from Achilleus, and Achilleus prays to his divine mother, Thetis, for help. He says he will not fight, and he asks her to persuade Zeus to make the battle go badly for the Greeks so they will see that they should not have dishonored him.*
- *Odysseus leads a group of Greeks to Chryse to return Chryseis to Chryses. Meanwhile, Achilleus isolates himself from the other Greeks.*
- *Thetis, begs Zeus to honor her son, Achilleus, by turning the battle against the Greeks so they will see that they need him.*

Fig. 1. An abstract of the first book of Iliad

high-level summary of its content. We will focus on modeling the underlying facts and dynamics so that these events are generated as an action sequence that solves a planning problem expressed in PDDL. As we will see next, the emphasis is on the disposition that characters have with respect to each other and how this drives their actions.

2   Modeling the First Book of Iliad in PDDL

One immediate observation is that PDDL focuses on an action-centered representation that models single aspects of the world, namely which properties are *true* at a given moment, while stories such as the war described in Iliad involve many *modalities* over these properties. In other words, while PDDL is typically used to model facts like:

"Agamemnon is at the Greek camp," "Chryseis is kept captive by Agamemnon,"

in the narrative of Iliad perhaps the statements most crucial to the plot are those about what the heros of the story *believe, desire, request*, for example:

"Chryses desires that Chryseis is not kept captive by Agamemnon."

There is a vast amount of work in the literature for representing and reasoning with such modalities, but our intention here is to investigate a practical way to do so while remaining in the simple representation of the STRIPS subset of PDDL. The statements

```
(:action interact-mood
 :parameters (?c1 - character ?c2 - character ?t - types_of_interaction
              ?c3 - character ?loc - location)
 :precondition (at ?c1 ?loc)
 :effect (and
  (when (and (mood ?c2 ?c1 neutral) (= ?t request_release) (related ?c1 ?c3)
             (captured ?c3 ?c2) (at ?c2 ?loc) (at ?c3 ?loc))
        (and (mood ?c1 ?c2 request_release) (mood ?c2 ?c1 bad)))
  (when (and (mood ?c1 ?c2 bad) (mood ?c2 ?c1 request_release) (= ?t refuse_release)
             (captured ?c3 ?c1) (at ?c2 ?loc) (at ?c3 ?loc))
        (mood ?c2 ?c1 bad))
  ... ))
```

Fig. 2. Part of the specification of the action capturing mood interaction between characters

above can of course be directly represented by means of normal predicates, as for instance, having both a normal $HeldCaptive(x, y)$ predicate and a pair of predicates capturing the desire modality of a person p in the story: $DesiresHeldCaptive(p, x, y)$ and $DesiresNotHeldCaptive(p, x, y)$.[1] It becomes then interesting to identify some common patterns and a representation methodology so that this type of information can be specified in a way that is both intuitive and concise, and can be effectively maintained and extended in order to capture the intended stories that we would like to generate.

In this work we look into an approach that *reifies* such modalities into *objects* in the domain, and relies on a predicate to represent the disposition or *mood* of characters toward the each other with respect to an object reified in this way. We call this predicate mood and, for example, the following PDDL literal can be used to model that Agamemnon has a negative disposition toward Achilleus:

(mood agamemnon achilleus bad),

while the following can be used to model that the mood of Agamemnon toward Chryses is particularly related to a former request that Agamemnon has accepted:

(mood agamemnon chryses accept_release).

A number of objects similar to `accept_release` are used to model the (abstracted and overloaded) moods of characters in the first book of Iliad as we will see next, such as `request_release`, `refuse_release`, and `desire_capture`. These reified objects are just syntactic terms that need to be handled appropriately in the actions that are available in the domain in order to make sense and generate the intended outcomes. Moreover, it becomes important that as many as possible of such objects can be used to identify general interactions that may happen in the story, so that we get a concise representation that can be easily adapted and maintained.

The idea then about available actions is that they fall in two categories: i) *physical* actions that modify only physical properties of the world, e.g., the typical move action, and ii) *interaction* actions that modify the mood disposition between two characters with respect to a context and possibly with another character, e.g., the action of asking to release a prisoner which may change the mood between the persons involved.

---

[1] Note that $\neg DesiresHeldCaptive(p, x, y)$ is different than $DesiresNotHeldCaptive(p, x, y)$.

For the first type of actions, the PDDL modeling includes an abstraction of the physical activities that are described in the summary of Figure 1 in terms of appropriate action schemas for go, capture, release, punish (by means of a disaster), and cease_disaster. As it is easy to observe in the summary of Figure 1, these actions are a small part of what is really happening in the story. A lot more has to do about who requests what, and how this affects the relationships of the heros and the gods in the story. This form of interaction is captured by means of an interact-mood action that operates on the level of the mood disposition between characters.

Part of the action schema for the action interact-mood is shown in Figure 2. This action takes 5 arguments as follows: i) the character which initiates the interaction, ii) a second character that participates in the interaction, iii) the type of interaction in terms of a mood or a reified modality, iv) a character which is the object of the interaction, and v) the location where the interaction takes place (there is also action interact-self that does not include an object for the interaction as an argument).

In the effects of interact-mood, the possible cases for interactions are modeled which depend mostly on the moods of the participating characters and result in updating them accordingly. The cases are modeled based on PDDL conditional effects; here the first case models that when a character $c1$ requests from $c2$ the release of character $c3$ and some conditions hold about the moods between the characters, then the mood of $c2$ about $c1$ becomes request_release and $c1$ become angry with $c2$. In the second case, something similar is modeled about refusing to release interaction. A number of cases like this can be specified, and one can think of a table that depending on the moods between $c1$ and $c2$ and the type of interaction, a different outcome takes place.

Action instances of interact-mood may be driven by physical properties of the world and the mood disposition between characters, but the important thing to note though is that we require they *always modify only the mood disposition between characters participating to the interaction*. This provides a layer for representing the gist of the story as a game between the relationships of characters, while physical actions are just ways to materialize the tensions expressed in the moods.

The goal of the planning problem is then expressed also solely in terms of the moods of the characters, which in the case of the first book of Iliad could be the following:

```
(and (mood Achilleus Agamemnon bad) (mood Zeus Agamemnon accept_punish)
     (mood Chryses Agamemnon good))
```

I.e., at the end of the first book Achilleus is upset with Agamemnon, Zeus is in the mood of punishing Agamemnon, and Chryses is happy with the former captor of his daughter.

Figure 3 shows a plan that is obtained using version 6 of SGPlan [1].[2] Note that variants of the actual story can be obtained by planning for different goals, tweaking the initial state, or altering the action schemas.

3 Discussion

There is a lot of related work in the literature in employing planning for generating narrative or interactive stories, also taking advantage of the increasing expressiveness

---

[2] The full PDDL specification and the required instructions to run SGPlan planner can be found at https://code.google.com/p/the-iliad-project/

```
(GO CHRYSES APOLLO_TEMPLE GREEKS_CAMP)
(INTERACT-MOOD CHRYSES AGAMEMNON REQUEST_RELEASE CHRYSEIS GREEKS_CAMP)
(INTERACT-MOOD AGAMEMNON CHRYSES REFUSE_RELEASE CHRYSEIS GREEKS_CAMP)
(GO CHRYSES GREEKS_CAMP APOLLO_TEMPLE)
(INTERACT-MOOD CHRYSES APOLLO REQUEST_PUNISH AGAMEMNON APOLLO_TEMPLE)
(INTERACT-SELF APOLLO ACCEPT_PUNISH AGAMEMNON APOLLO_TEMPLE)
(PUNISH APOLLO GREEKS_CAMP PLAGUE)
(INTERACT-MOOD KALCHAS AGAMEMNON REQUEST_RELEASE CHRYSEIS GREEKS_CAMP)
(INTERACT-SELF AGAMEMNON ACCEPT_RELEASE CHRYSEIS GREEKS_CAMP)
(RELEASE AGAMEMNON CHRYSEIS GREEKS_CAMP)
(INTERACT-MOOD AGAMEMNON ACHILLEUS DESIRE_CAPTURE BRISEIS GREEKS_CAMP)
(INTERACT-SELF ACHILLEUS ATTEMPT_TO_KILL AGAMEMNON GREEKS_CAMP)
(INTERACT-MOOD ATHENE ACHILLEUS BLOCK_THE_ATTEMPT_TO_KILL AGAMEMNON GREEKS_CAMP)
(GO ODYSSEUS GREEKS_CAMP APOLLO_TEMPLE)
(GO CHRYSEIS GREEKS_CAMP APOLLO_TEMPLE)
(INTERACT-MOOD ODYSSEUS CHRYSEIS MEET CHRYSES APOLLO_TEMPLE)
(INTERACT-MOOD CHRYSES ODYSSEUS DESIRE_CEASE_DISASTER APOLLO APOLLO_TEMPLE)
(CEASE_DISASTER APOLLO GREEKS_CAMP PLAGUE)
(INTERACT-MOOD ACHILLEUS THETIS REQUEST_PUNISH AGAMEMNON GREEKS_CAMP)
(INTERACT-MOOD THETIS ZEUS REQUEST_PUNISH AGAMEMNON GREEKS_CAMP)
(INTERACT-SELF ZEUS ACCEPT_PUNISH AGAMEMNON OLYMPUS)
```

Fig. 3. The planning solution for the first book of Iliad

of the evolving versions of PDDL, e.g., [7] that makes use of constraints to specify requirements on the sequencing of events. There are only a few approaches that look into the modalities we discussed. In particular, Riedl and Young [8] look into the case of representing the *intentions* of characters and finding stories that are believable in that characters behave intentionally. They introduce a planning formalism that goes beyond PDDL and demonstrate its power with a specialized planning system. Haslum [4] later showed that this type of representation can in fact be compiled into PDDL.

In this work we decided to take a practical approach that allows to represent any type of modality over facts and events, but leaving the semantics of these events to be also specified by means of preconditions and effects given by the person modeling the planning domain. For example, when the object `desire_capture` is used in the planning domain description, there is no guarantee by the framework that it relates to the predicate `captured` in any way or that a character will act based on this desire. Nonetheless, all objects of this sort get their intended meaning by means of the `mood` predicate that specifies how they change by the available interactions, while they also trigger physical actions by being used in their preconditions.

So, in a sense our approach is not really an approach to knowledge representation and reasoning, rather than a simple methodology for expressing the intended meaning of modalities over facts using a separate "moods" layer. This indeed has many drawbacks, the most obvious being that there is no way to verify that the modalities actually get their intended meaning, as this completely relies on the PDDL programmer. Nonetheless, as it is often the case in game developing, simple programming methodologies can go a long way compared to knowledge representation systems, and one reason for this is that the former are easier to understand and control. So, in a sense our approach can be seen as a kind of programming methodology for PDDL programs for generating stories based on two layers: a moods layer and a physical layer.

4   Conclusions

In this work we present a simple idea for modeling stories via planning, and show how this could works for the case of the first book of Iliad, the classic work of Homer. We look into a simplistic approach that reifies modalities over facts (e.g., related to desires and requests) into objects in the domain, and relies on a "mood" predicate to represent the disposition of characters toward the each other and with respect to such objects. Except for physical actions, we introduce a pair of and particular mood interaction actions which affect only the mood of characters. The goal of the planning problem can then be expressed in terms of the moods of the characters of the stories, which in order to be satisfied will drive physical action. Our experimentation with modeling the first book following these ideas showed that it is intuitive and practical, but may also lead to similar stories than the one that is intended. We do not consider this to be a major problem in the sense that these stories are still reasonable and in general would be perhaps welcome as possible alternative outcomes in a video game scenario (unlike here where we were interested in modeling a very specific sequence of events). Finally, we note that this approach is not intended to be thought of as a proper framework for representing modalities, rather than a practical approach that would be intuitive to the story developers as a kind of programming methodology. Finally, we note that this work is inspired by the PDDL modeling challenge in the 6th edition of the Intelligent Narrative Technologies Workshop.

References

1. Chen, Y., Wah, B.W., Hsu, C.W.: Temporal planning using subgoal partitioning and resolution in SGPlan. J. of Artificial Intelligence Research 26 (2006)
2. Fox, M., Long, D.: Pddl2.1: An extension to pddl for expressing temporal planning domains. J. Artif. Intell. Res. (JAIR) 20, 61–124 (2003)
3. Geffner, H., Bonet, B.: A Concise Introduction to Models and Methods for Automated Planning. Morgan & Claypool Publishers (2013)
4. Haslum, P.: Narrative planning: Compilations to classical planning. J. Artif. Int. Res. 44(1), 383–395 (2012)
5. Mcdermott, D., Ghallab, M., Howe, A., Knoblock, C., Ram, A., Veloso, M., Weld, D., Wilkins, D.: PDDL - The Planning Domain Definition Language. Tech. rep., CVC TR-98-003, Yale Center for Computational Vision and Control (1998)
6. Nau, D., Ghallab, M., Traverso, P.: Automated Planning: Theory & Practice. Morgan Kaufmann Publishers Inc., San Francisco (2004)
7. Porteous, J., Cavazza, M.: Controlling narrative generation with planning trajectories: The role of constraints. In: Iurgel, I.A., Zagalo, N., Petta, P. (eds.) ICIDS 2009. LNCS, vol. 5915, pp. 234–245. Springer, Heidelberg (2009)
8. Riedl, M.O., Young, R.M.: Narrative planning: balancing plot and character. J. Artif. Int. Res. 39(1), 217–268 (2010), http://www.cc.gatech.edu/~riedl/pubs/jair.pdf

A Novel Probabilistic Framework to Broaden the Context in Query Recommendation Systems

Dimitris Giakoumis and Dimitrios Tzovaras

Information Technologies Institute, Centre for Research and Technology Hellas (CERTH/ITI),
6th Km Charilaou-Thermi Road, 57001 (PO Box 361), Thermi-Thessaloniki, Greece
{dgiakoum,tzovaras}@iti.gr

Abstract. This paper presents a novel probabilistic framework for broadening the notion of context in web search query recommendation systems. In the relevant literature, query suggestion is typically conducted based on past user actions of the current session, mostly related to query submission. Our proposed framework regards user context in a broader way, consisting of a series of further parameters that express it more thoroughly, such as spatial and temporal ones. Therefore, query recommendation is performed herein by considering the appropriateness of each candidate query suggestion, given this broadened context. Experimental evaluation showed that our proposed framework, utilizing spatiotemporal contextual features, is capable to increase query recommendation performance, compared to state-of-art methods such as co-occurence, adjacency and Variable-length Markov Models (VMM). Due to its generic nature, our framework can operate on the basis of further features expressing the user context than the ones studied in the present work, e.g. affect-related, toward further advancing web search query recommendation.

Keywords: context-aware, web search, query recommendation, spatiotemporal features, probabilistic framework.

1 Introduction

Automatic query recommendation is essential for modern web search systems. Typically, such systems (e.g. Google) take as input keywords expressing the user's search intent. However, user queries are often extremely concise, consisting of few (1-2) words [1], and are significantly prone to ambiguity [2]. As a result, it is common for the initial query to be refined several times by the user [3], until a "proper" query is submitted, that is, a query expressing user intent in a way enabling the search engine (SE) to provide results optimally matching that intent, satisfying the user. The capability of the SE interface to assist the user in this process, through query recommendations, is highly significant [3]; in essence, by inferring the user's search intent, the SE can provide query recommendations so as to assist the user to find easier and earlier what s/he is looking for. It has been reported that a reduction of only 1% in the time spent from a user searching in Google could lead to saving more than 187.000 person-hours (21 years) each month [4]. Automatic query recommendation has thus become one of the most fundamental features of modern web search engines [5].

A. Likas, K. Blekas, and D. Kalles (Eds.): SETN 2014, LNAI 8445, pp. 589–602, 2014.

To this end, a plethora of automatic query recommendation systems have been proposed in the past (e.g. [2],[3],[6-9]). This line of research typically focuses on providing recommendations by comparing the queries that have been issued so far in the present user session, to queries of search sessions that have been recorded in the search engine's query logs. For instance, in [6], query recommendations were provided on the basis of the user input query's *co-occurrence* with other queries within sessions of the server's log. In [7], instead of taking into account all queries that co-occurred in logged sessions with the user's query, query substitution/expansion was performed on the basis of the queries that were found in the server's log to immediately follow the user input query (*adjacency* method). Extending this approach and building upon a Markovian Prediction Suffix Tree (PST) [15], the authors of [3] presented a query recommendation method based on Variable-length Markov Models (*VMM*), where the user input query, as well as the queries preceding it within the present user session were taken into account. In [17], a similar approach, based on variable length HMMs was proposed. Further recent query suggestion studies include [18], which focused on frequency of occurrence, keyword similarity measures and modification patterns of queries, and [19], where the focus was on the identification of conceptually related queries through click-through graphs. In general, methods like the above provide suggestions by calculating the probability of each candidate suggestion to be issued next by the user, given the user context in terms of the so far issued queries, under the model defined through the server's query logs [3]. Moreover, user actions related to clicks on URLs provided as search results have also been utilized [9],[19].

As sometimes denoted within the above approaches, their aim is to infer query recommendations on the basis of the "user context" [3],[9]; however, they operate on only a limited view of context, which regards only queries and clickthrough data. These methods will be referred in the rest of the paper as SoA (State-of-Art) methods. Their limited view of context results to recommendations that are same for a given query (or query sequence, clickthrough actions), regardless for e.g. the temporal or spatial context of different user sessions. Focusing on the early provision of helpful recommendations (e.g. optimally provided right after the first query submission), the issue of same recommendations regardless the spatiotemporal user context becomes of even higher importance. The same query may be used to express different information needs in the morning than in the evening, during weekdays or weekends [10], in the summer or winter, in different locations [11]. By not taking into account such information, a query recommender will always provide the same recommendation for a given input query or query sequence. Thus, although this limited view of user context can lead to recommenders that are effective up to an extent, it may as well lead to sub-optimal results in practical application scenarios.

As such a scenario, let us suppose the case of a tourist, using a web search system through his smartphone during midday, so as to find information regarding nearby restaurants in a town he is visiting (e.g. Thessaloniki), while being at a museum located at a suburb of that city. While wandering in that suburb, prior to visiting the museum, he has noticed that a number of fine-dining restaurants exist therein. Unfortunately, he recalls neither the names of those restaurants, nor the name of the suburb. Therefore, he provides "Thessaloniki restaurants" as a query to the search engine. The

SE web interface provides a large number of results, along with recommendations assisting the user in refining the query, so as to easier find what s/he is looking for.

However, if the above recommendations are based only on the query-oriented context of the user's web search session, they would be the same, regardless the time (e.g. midday, night) or specific location (e.g. city centre, a city suburb) of the user. Thus, since the "Thessaloniki restaurant" searches recorded in the SE log typically focus on taverns located at the city center, the recommendations will be rather irrelevant to the present user's actual needs. Suppose now that the above recommender system operated on the basis of a broadened view of context, taking into account, apart from the queries submitted in the present session, also the time of day, as well as the location of the user, boosting in the recommendations list, queries that have been provided to the SE from similar location and time as the one of the user. In this case, the name of the suburb would be highly probable to appear in the recommendations, along with terms such as "fine-dining restaurants", significantly reducing the time and effort needed from the user to find what he is looking for.

In the latter case of the above example, the recommender system, by operating on a broadened notion of the user context, would have been enabled to provide more personalized results, better suited to the present user's needs. Web search is highly important for tourists, whereas more personalized search, better adapted to their needs at the time of search engine usage are essential, given that relevant use cases typically regard searching information about places that the SE user visits for the first time. The above may as well hold in more generic use cases, where, by utilizing spatial, temporal and even further characteristics of the user context, a query recommender system could provide results better tailored to the user needs.

To this end, although context-aware recommender systems is a highly active research field [13], only few past works have studied a broadened notion of context in web search query recommendation, focusing for instance on location metadata [11] or temporal information [20]. However, the significance of broadening the context in query recommendation calls for novel methods that would allow incorporating spatial, temporal, as well as further types (e.g. affect-related) of contextual features.

1.1   Contribution

Following the above, the present work introduces a novel framework that allows spatiotemporal and potentially further (e.g. affect-related) features describing the user context to be included in the process of automatic query suggestion. To this end, it utilizes as a basis SoA query recommendation approaches that predict user search intent from past queries of the present search session, refining their results by taking into account a broader view of the user context. At its current implementation, our framework has been experimentally tested using spatial and temporal contextual features, so as to augment SoA query suggestion approaches such as co-occurrence, adjacency and VMM. Through experimental evaluation, our framework was found capable to increase the initial performance of the SoA methods. Due to its generic nature, our proposed framework can be potentially used in conjunction with practically any SoA query suggestion method that is based solely on session query terms or clickthrough data. Moreover, it can be extended toward incorporating further spatial, temporal or other contextual features, describing the user's context in a more thorough way.

1.2   Paper Outline

In the rest of the paper, Section 2 describes our probabilistic framework for broadening the context in query suggestion and Section 3 describes the process that was followed for experimental evaluation, along with the obtained results. Conclusions are drawn in Section 4.

2   The Query Recommendation Context Broadening Framework

If viewed as a black box, our proposed framework (Fig. 1) receives as input past queries of the present user session, as well as parameters that describe the session's spatiotemporal context. As shown in Fig. 1, by incorporating a SoA query recommendation method, it obtains candidate suggestions (SoA query suggestions), along with the probability that they would stand for the user's next submitted query. Thereafter, prior to providing the candidate suggestions to the user, ranking them via their probability score (as would have been typically done at this point in SoA query suggestion), our framework fuses for each candidate its current probability with the probability that the specific query would have been submitted to the search engine given the present spatiotemporal context (SoA query suggestions refinement). This final joint probability is eventually used so as to rank candidate suggestions and provide them to the search engine user (Final Query Suggestions).

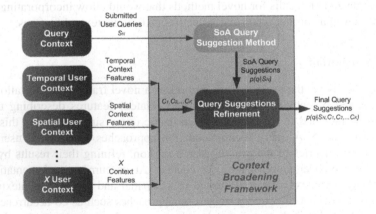

Fig. 1. Conceptual Architecture of the proposed context-broadening framework

For describing our approach in more detail, let us suppose a currently active user session in a web search system, which consists of N queries submitted so far. Let $S_N = \{q_1, q_2,...,q_N\}$ be this submitted query sequence and a probabilistic query suggestion method (e.g. co-occurrence), which recommends M candidate queries q_i, $1<i<M$, on the basis of S_N. At this, typically concluding point of SoA query recommendation methods, the result is a list of the candidate queries, ordered by the probability that they will be issued next by the user given S_N, that is $P(q_i)=p(q_i/S_N)$.

Taking now a step forward from SoA, instead of providing query recommendations on the basis of the conditional probability $p(q_i/S_N)$, our framework takes into account S_N and also further features describing the user context. Therefore, if K is the number of the utilized contextual features C_k, the probability of q_i to be issued next is estimated within our framework as:

$$p(q_i \mid S_N, C_1, C_2,...,C_K) \tag{1}$$

Equation 1 calculates the probability that q_i will be issued next by the user, on the basis of her/his past queries and also a series of further parameters that could potentially describe user context in a thorough way. For instance, C_k's can be parameters related to the spatial, temporal, or even the affective context of the user. They could also be used to encode user actions during search engine usage, i.e. clickthrough results selection data.

Using the Bayes theorem and assuming conditional independence between S_N, $C_1,...,C_K$ for a given q_i, from Equation 1 it holds:

$$p(q_i \mid S_N, C_1, C_2,...,C_K) = \frac{p(q_i)p(S_N, C_1,...,C_K \mid q_i)}{p(S_N, C_1,...,C_K)} =$$

$$\frac{p(q_i)p(S_N \mid q_i)p(C_1 \mid q_i)...p(C_K \mid q_i)}{\sum_{j=1}^{M} p(q_j)p(S_N \mid q_j)p(C_1 \mid q_j)...p(C_K \mid q_j)} =$$

$$\frac{p(q_i)\dfrac{p(q_i \mid S_N)p(S_N)}{p(q_i)}p(C_1 \mid q_i)...p(C_K \mid q_i)}{\sum_{j=1}^{M} p(q_j)\dfrac{p(q_j \mid S_N)p(S_N)}{p(q_j)}p(C_1 \mid q_j)...p(C_K \mid q_j)} = \tag{2}$$

$$\frac{p(q_i \mid S_N)p(S_N)p(C_1 \mid q_i)...p(C_K \mid q_i)}{\sum_{j=1}^{M} p(q_j \mid S_N)p(S_N)p(C_1 \mid q_j)...p(C_K \mid q_j)} ... \Rightarrow$$

$$p(q_i \mid S_N, C_1, C_2,...,C_K) = \frac{p(q_i \mid S_N)p(C_1 \mid q_i)...p(C_K \mid q_i)}{\sum_{j=1}^{M} p(q_j \mid S_N)p(C_1 \mid q_j)...p(C_K \mid q_j)} \tag{3}$$

In Equation 3, $p(q_i/S_N)$ describes the conditional probability that q_i will be issued next, given the so far user submitted queries S_N, which, as explained above, can be obtained through any probabilistic state-of-art query suggestion method, such as co-occurrence, adjacency etc. The terms $p(C_1/q_i),\ldots p(C_K/q_i)$ describe the conditional probabilities that the current value of each contextual parameter $C_1,\ldots C_K$ (describing the present session's context) is expected to hold, given that query q_i is submitted by the user to the search engine. For each candidate query q_i, the $p(C_k/q_i)$ terms, can derive from histograms expressing the distribution of q_i occurrences within the server's log, in respect of the possible values of each C_k parameter.

As mentioned above, Equations 2 and 3 are formed following Equation 1, under the assumption of conditional independence between the parameters for a given q_i. In essence, this means that optimally, knowledge over one's parameter value for a given query should have absolutely no effect over the probability distribution of the other parameters. This assumption calls for careful selection of the contextual parameters to be used in our framework. However, cases of suboptimal conditional independence between the parameters can as well be tolerated as an approximation [16], keeping in mind that they might induce negative effects on our framework's performance.

In the present study, the contextual parameters shown in Table 1 were considered, expressing aspects of the spatiotemporal context of the user during the web search session. The prior probabilities of queries, regarding the specific parameters, were estimated herein as described in the following.

Table 1. Contextual parameters used in the present study

Parameter Name	Description
TD	Time of Day [0-23]
DW	Day of Week [1-7]
DM	Day of Month [1-28]
MY	Month of Year [1-12]
LOC (CI, CO)	Location (City, Country)

2.1   Contextual Parameter Priors for Candidate Query Suggestions

Focusing first on temporal features of the user context, in the present study we considered the contextual parameters "time-of-day" (TD), "day-of-week" (DW), "day-of-month" (DM) and "month-of-year" (MY). For each temporal context parameter, we first calculated for each query (q_i) existing in the database, the histogram of query occurrences in respect of the different possible parameter values. From each histogram, we then estimated the *pdf* of the specific parameter, as a mixture of Gaussians, fitted to the priors through Expectation-Maximization (EM). In the present implementation, six GMM components were used for modeling the TD parameter, three for the DW, seven for the DM and three for the MY. An example of a query's histogram, related to the TD (time of day) temporal context parameter, as well as the respective resulted *pdf* are shown in Fig. 2. Fig. 2b shows the six GMM components of the TD parameter, which have been fitted through EM to the histogram of Fig. 2a. Fig. 3c shows the cumulative *pdf* of the Fig. 2b GMM components, which is the result of the components summation.

The amount of GMM components, as well as their initial distribution, was selected so as to provide EM with initial clusters that covered the entire span of the given parameter's values. It should be noted at this point that, as shown in Table 1, the DM parameter was defined to have its allowed values in the span [1, 28], by normalizing the actual month-dependent span of this parameter (e.g. 1-31 for January, 1-30 for April) in this, common for all months span, so as to consider day-of-month values over a common, month-independent reference.

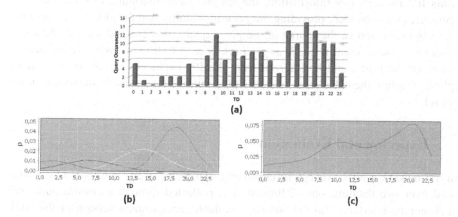

Fig. 2. (a) Example of query histogram from AOL dataset for the time-of-day (TD) parameter, (b) GMM components after EM, (c) cumulative *pdf*

In the context of query recommendation, data sparseness in the server query logs is a typical problem; the same query may have only a few (e.g. less than ten) occurrences. In our case, this issue can affect the afore-described pdf estimation process. The generation of smoother *pdfs* for queries of low occurrence, is achieved in the present study by employing Laplacian (add-one) smoothing. This leads, in cases of queries with low amount of occurrences, to *pdfs* which in fact describe a tendency of a query to appear more in specific times-of-day, days-of-month etc., without being over-fitted to the specific time-of-day etc. of the limited occurrences that have appeared in the logs. Of course, as the amount of query occurrences becomes higher, the role of this smoothing is suppressed, allowing the resulting *pdf* to depict the occurrence tendencies of queries in a more precise way. At this point, it should be noted that Laplacian smoothing can be considered as a rather simple approach to deal with data sparseness in probability density estimation. However, it was used herein so as to compare our framework to SoA methods, without boosting its performance with more sophisticated smoothing approaches. Nevertheless, more sophisticated smoothing approaches could as well be employed in the future within our proposed framework.

From the resulting *pdfs*, the conditional probabilities of Eq. 3 related to our temporal contextual features are estimated for any given query that is provided as suggestion from the utilized SoA method, expressing the probability of the current contextual parameter's value to hold, given the specific query. Therefore, for each candidate query q_i, the probabilities $p(C_{TD}/q_i)$, $p(C_{DW}/q_i)$, $p(C_{DM}/q_i)$, $p(C_{MY}/q_i)$ are calculated in respect of the TD, DW, DM and MY context parameters, so as to provide input to Eq. 3, toward determining the final, context-aware probability of each query suggestion.

In respect of spatial context parameters, the present study focused on the location (LOC) of the user during the web search session, in terms of her/his city (CI) and country (CO). To this end, the "MaxMind Geolite" country and city IP geolocation database[1] was utilized, enabling the detection of the user's country and city from her/his IP. Through this information, the geographical distribution of each query's occurrences was obtained, providing the prior probability that the city of the currently logged-in user could be the source of the given query; this enabled the calculation of the $p(LOC/q_i)$ term used in Eq. 3, as $p(CI/q_i)$, or as $p(CO/q_i)$ in cases where only the country of the user could be inferred from the IP. Laplacian smoothing was again applied, enabling the calculation of query probabilities for locations inexistent in the train set.

3   Experimental Evaluation

Our framework's effectiveness in enhancing automatic query suggestion was evaluated over two datasets, one of limited size, collected through a custom built web search engine interface, and the publicly available, anonymized version of the AOL query logs dataset [14]. Our aim was to compare our framework against baseline query suggestion methods, i.e. co-occurrence [1], adjacency [7] and VMM [15],[3], so as to examine whether the use of spatiotemporal contextual features would increase query suggestion performance. The datasets, experimental evaluation and the results obtained are explained in the following of the present section.

3.1   Datasets and Evaluation Process

CUBRIK Dataset. The "CUBRIK dataset" was collected through a custom built web search engine interface (Fig. 3), which had as purpose to provide users with fashion-oriented web images related to the user query. This interface allowed recording time-stamped user actions (submitted queries) along with their IPs during search engine usage. The dataset consisted of more than 1300 queries provided by 50 different users from 11 cities of 6 countries. Through this dataset, we were capable to evaluate both SoA query suggestion methods, as well as our framework, in a case of a small-size dataset. Moreover, by recording user IPs, we were capable to evaluate, apart from temporal, also spatial contextual features, over their capability to enhance automatic query suggestion through our proposed framework.

---

[1] http://dev.maxmind.com/geoip/legacy/geolite/

Fig. 3. The "CUBRIK fashion dataset" search engine interface

AOL Dataset. The publicly available, anonymized version of the AOL dataset [14] that was used in the present work, consists of web search query logs that were collected in 2006; it contains a sum of over 36 million queries, where the user IP has been replaced by an anonymous user ID.

Evaluation Process. In order to evaluate our method, we used it in order to re-rank, on the basis of several contextual features, the suggestion results of three state-of-art query suggestion methods, namely the co-occurrence, the adjacency and the VMM. In this context, our aim was to compare the effectiveness of our method, to the one of the SoA methods that were used to provide in each case the $p(q_i/S_N)$ term of our method's Eq. 3.

To this end, the first step was to split the queries of both our datasets into sessions. Sessions were identified based on changes on the username and by utilizing a temporal distance threshold between queries of the same user; herein, a five-minute threshold was used for splitting sessions, following [1] and [12], leading to over 2 million and 350 sessions for the AOL and CUBRIK datasets respectively.

In our experiments, following past works such as [11], we used the Mean Reciprocal Rank (MRR) as evaluation metric of query suggestion performance. The MRR expresses the inverse of the rank of the relevant query suggestion provided to the user, calculated as $MRR=1/rank(q_i)$, where, supposing that q_{i-1} is the last query submitted from the user in the present session (after which, a suggestion will be provided), q_i is the next query that is known (through the database log) to have been submitted from the user, serving as the ground truth of the test case and $rank(q_i)$ is the rank of q_i within the suggestions list provided from the query suggestion algorithm.

Since our framework operates on the basis of a SoA method, in essence re-ranking its results through contextual features, we omitted from the evaluation of both the

SoA methods and our proposed one, the cases for which the SoA method failed to provide a result relevant to the ground truth (q_{i+1}) within its suggestions list, as in [11]. The AOL dataset results presented below were obtained after randomly splitting the whole database into two equally sized parts, one used as the training set and the other for evaluation. Due to the limited size of the CUBRIK dataset, the respective results presented below were obtained through leave-one-out cross validation over the dataset's sessions. In order to reduce the noise that is introduced in the datasets from significantly rare queries and sessions, we followed the rationale of [3] and kept in the train and test sets respectively only those sessions that had more than one occurrence.

3.2   Experimental Results

CUBRIK Dataset. Table 2 presents the results that were obtained for the CUBRIK dataset through the co-occurrence (coOcc) and adjacency (Adj) methods, along with the results from using coOcc or Adj as the SoA method of our framework, for different combinations of utilized features of the temporal context. In particular, for a more thorough overview of the contextual features effect, Table 4 (as well as the rest of this section's tables) shows, apart from the results obtained by using all the spatiotemporal features (TD, DW, DM, MY and LOC) together and each one alone, also the best results taken by trying all different combinations of these features in pairs, triples or quadruples.

Table 2. Results (MRR) of the **co-occurrence** (coOcc) and **adjacency** (Adj) methods on the CUBRIK dataset, used alone and in conjunction with spatiotemporal features through our proposed framework

Method	MRR	Method	MRR
CoOcc	*16,56%*	*Adj*	*20,24%*
CoOcc {TD, DW, DM, MY, LOC}	16,16%	Adj {TD, DW, DM, MY, LOC}	16,24%
CoOcc {TD, DM, MY, LOC}	16,54%	Adj {TD, DM, MY, LOC}	18,49%
CoOcc {TD, MY, LOC}	16,96%	Adj {TD, MY, LOC}	21,31%
CoOcc {TD, LOC}	17,08%	Adj {MY, LOC}	21,34%
CoOcc {TD}	***17,96%***	**Adj {TD}**	***23,42%***
CoOcc {DW}	17,34%	Adj {DW}	15,81%
CoOcc {DM}	15,50%	Adj {DM}	19,54%
CoOcc {MY}	16,48%	Adj {MY}	21,13%
CoOcc {LOC}	16,50%	Adj {LOC}	17,05%

As shown inTable 2, by using a triplet of spatiotemporal contextual features, consisting of TD, MY and LOC, our framework provided an increase in MRR performance, for both the CoOcc and Adj methods. The best performance in both the coOcc and Adj cases was obtained by using our framework, so as to enhance query suggestion with information over the time-of-day context of the user (TD); the initial performance of coOcc and Adj was increased through our framework by 1.4% and 3.18% respectively.

Table 3 shows the respective results obtained over the CUBRIK dataset for the VMM method. By comparing the first row of Table 4 and Table 3, it is clear that in accordance to the results of [3], the VMM method outperformed both the Adj and coOcc in terms of MRR over our limited-sized CUBRIK dataset. Moreover, by augmenting through our framework the VMM-based query suggestion with the TD, DM, MY and LOC contextual features, an increase in MRR of 1.46% was obtained. The use of less contextual features further increased performance, whereas, the best result was again obtained by using our framework so as to augment VMM with information regarding the session's time-of-day.

Table 3. Results (MRR) of the VMM method on the CUBRIK dataset, used alone and in conjunction with temporal features through our proposed framework

Method	MRR
VMM	22,76%
VMM {TD, DW, DM, MY, LOC}	22,69%
VMM {TD, DM, MY, LOC}	24,22%
VMM {TD, DM, MY}	24,49%
VMM {TD, MY}	24,50%
VMM {TD}	**27,13%**
VMM {DW}	20,55%
VMM {DM}	21,81%
VMM {MY}	24,78%
VMM {LOC}	22,14%

As shown from the above results, due to the limited size of this dataset, all MRR results obtained were relatively low. However, in all the coOcc, Adj and VMM cases, significant increase in query suggestion performance was introduced by augmenting through our framework, their query suggestion process with spatiotemporal contextual features.

AOL Dataset. Table 4 presents the results that were obtained for the AOL dataset through the co-occurrence an the adjacency methods, along with the results obtained by using coOcc or the Adj as the SoA method of our framework, for different combinations of utilized features of the temporal context.

As shown in Table 4, by using all features of the temporal context within our framework, the average MRR for CoOcc was increased from 47.94% to 48.23%. By trying different combinations of features, the best result was obtained from using the time-of-day (TD) alone, which was 48.52%. In the adjacency method case, by using all features of the temporal context, a slight decrease in performance was obtained, at the level of 0.02%, however by omitting the DW parameter an increase of 0.09% was noticed and omitting also DM lead to further increase in performance. Again, the TD parameter alone led to the best MRR, which was 51.55%.

Table 4. Results (MRR) of the **co-occurrence** and **adjacency** methods on the AOL dataset, used alone and in conjunction with temporal features through our proposed framework

Method	MRR	Method	MRR
CoOcc	*47,94%*	*Adj*	*51,32%*
CoOcc {TD, DW, DM, MY}	48,23%	Adj {TD, DW, DM, MY}	51,30%
CoOcc {TD, DM, MY}	48,37%	Adj {TD, DM, MY}	51,41%
CoOcc {DM, MY}	48,42%	Adj {DM, MY}	51,49%
CoOcc {TD}	**48,52%**	**Adj {TD}**	**51,55%**
CoOcc {DW}	48,36%	Adj {DW}	51,40%
CoOcc {DM}	48,04%	Adj {DM}	51,27%
CoOcc {MY}	48,10%	Adj {MY}	51,23%

Finally, Table 5 shows the respective results obtained by using the VMM method as basis. Similarly to the above, by using all features of the temporal context, a slight decrease in performance was obtained, at the level of 0.01%, however by omitting the DW parameter an increase of 0.11% was noticed and omitting also DM lead to further increase (of 0.18%) in performance. Again, the TD parameter alone led to the best result for the VMM case, which was 51.72%. This was the best result that was obtained for this study's AOL dataset –based evaluation of automatic query suggestion.

Table 5. Results (MRR) of the **VMM** method on the AOL dataset, used alone and in conjunction with temporal features through our proposed framework

Method	MRR
VMM	*51,50%*
VMM {TD, DW, DM, MY}	51,49%
VMM {TD, DM, MY}	51,61%
VMM {DM, MY}	51,68%
VMM {TD}	**51,72%**
VMM {DW}	51,57%
VMM {DM}	51,44%
VMM {MY}	51,41%

Discussion. The above results, first of all confirm, in line with [3], the increased performance that can be obtained in query suggestion through the VMM method, compared to adjacency and co-occurrence. In both our datasets, the limited-sized one and the AOL, VMM outperformed the other SoA methods examined. Thereafter, through our proposed context-broadening framework, query suggestion performance, in terms of MRR, was found to further improve.

In the limited-size (CUBRIK) dataset, an increase of 4.37% in MRR was found by incorporating information regarding the session's time-of-day in query suggestion, compared to the VMM. In relative measures, the initial MRR of VMM (22,76%) was increased by a maximum of 19,20%. In the large dataset (AOL), an increase of 0.22% was obtained by incorporating this time only temporal contextual features in the VMM-based query suggestion process.

From the above analysis, the most important of our examined contextual features was found to be the TD, since its integration in the query suggestion process constantly led to the best MRR performance. This indicates that since the interests of web search engine users vary among different hours of the day [10], it is essential for query recommendation systems to augment their operating context with such information. Moreover, as shown from the CUBRIK dataset results, in accordance to [11], the user location parameter (LOC) was found also capable to enhance query suggestion performance in a number of cases, being used along with features of the temporal context. Unfortunately, the anonymized nature of the AOL dataset did not allow for features of the spatial context to be evaluated over it, however, the CUBRIK dataset results demonstrate a strong query suggestion enhancement potential for such features. Finally, focusing again on the AOL dataset results and the individual performance of temporal contextual features, the potential of the DW (day-of-week) parameter to enhance query suggestion performance is also evident, in accordance to differences that have been reported in search engine user interests between weekdays and weekends [10].

4   Conclusions

The present study introduced a novel probabilistic framework for broadening the context in automatic query suggestion. Our proposed framework takes a step forward from SoA methods that regard user context only in terms of queries that are submitted to the search engine, providing recommendations dependant also on spatiotemporal user context parameters. By evaluating our approach against the co-occurrence, the adjacency and VMM methods, we found increase in query recommendation performance, in terms of MRR. These results first of all demonstrate that our proposed framework, by broadening the context of query recommendation systems, has potential to increase their performance in future practical applications. In line with past works [10][11], the results of the present study further highlight the importance of incorporating spatiotemporal features in the query suggestion process. Moreover, due to its generic nature, our framework can incorporate in the future further contextual parameters than only spatiotemporal ones, e.g. affect-related, toward query recommendation systems that will operate in an even more broadened notion of the user context.

Acknowledgments. The present study was supported by the EU-funded research project CUBRIK.

References

1. Wen, J.-R., Nie, J.-Y., Zhang, H.-J.: Clustering user queries of a search engine. In: Proceedings of the 10th International Conference on World Wide Web (2001)
2. Cui, H., Wen, J.-R., Nie, J.-Y., Ma, W.-Y.: Probabilistic query expansion using query logs. In: Proceedings of the 11th International Conference on World Wide Web (2002)

3. He, Q., Jiang, D., Liao, Z., Hoi, S.C.H., Kuiyu, C., EePeng, L., et al.: Web Query Recommendation via Sequential Query Prediction. Paper presented at the IEEE 25th International Conference on Data Engineering, ICDE, March 29-April 2 (2009)
4. Qiu, F., Cho, J.: Automatic identification of user interest for personalized search. In: Proc. Fifteenth Int'l Conf. on World Wide Web (WWW 2006), pp. 727–736. ACM, New York (2006)
5. Kato, M., Sakai, T., Tanaka, K.: When do people use query suggestion? A query suggestion log analysis. Information Retrieval 16(6), 725–746
6. Huang, C.-K., Chien, L.-F., Oyang, Y.-J.: Relevant term suggestion in interactive web search based on contextual information in query session logs. Journal of the American Society for Information Science and Technology 54(7), 638–649 (2003)
7. Jones, R., Rey, B., Madani, O., Greiner, W.: Generating query substitutions. In: ACM WWW, pp. 387–396 (2006)
8. Meij, E., Bron, M., Hollink, L., Huurnink, B., de Rijke, M.: Learning Semantic Query Suggestions. In: Bernstein, A., Karger, D.R., Heath, T., Feigenbaum, L., Maynard, D., Motta, E., Thirunarayan, K. (eds.) ISWC 2009. LNCS, vol. 5823, pp. 424–440. Springer, Heidelberg (2009)
9. Cao, H., Jiang, D., Pei, J., He, Q., Liao, Z., Chen, E., et al.: Context-aware query suggestion by mining click-through and session data. Paper Presented at the Proceedings of the 14th ACM SIGKDD Int'l. Conf. on Knowledge Discovery and Data Mining (2008)
10. Mei, Q., Church, K.: Entropy of search logs: how hard is search? with personalization? with backoff? Paper Presented at the Proceedings of the 2008 International Conference on Web Search and Data Mining (2008)
11. Bennett, P.N., Radlinski, F., White, R.W., Yilmaz, E.: Inferring and using location metadata to personalize web search. In: Proceedings of the 34th International ACM SIGIR Conference on Research and Development in Information Retrieval (2011)
12. Silverstein, C., Marais, H., Henzinger, M., Moricz, M.: Analysis of a very large web search engine query log. SIGIR Forum 33(1), 6–12 (1999)
13. Adomavicius, G., Tuzhilin, A.: Context-Aware Recommender Systems. In: Ricci, F., Rokach, L., Shapira, B., Kantor, P.B. (eds.) Recommender Systems Handbook, pp. 217–253. Springer, US (2011)
14. Pass, G., Chowdhury, A., Torgeson, C.: A picture of search. In: InfoScale 2006, p. 1 (2006)
15. Ron, D., Singer, Y., Tishby, N.: Learning probabilistic automata with variable memory length. In: COLT, pp. 35–46 (1994)
16. Zhang, H.: The optimality of naive Bayes. In: Proceedings of the 17th International FLAIRS Conference (FLAIRS2004). AAAI Press (2004)
17. Liao, Z., Jiang, D., Pei, J., Huang, Y., Chen, E., Cao, H., Li, H.: A vlHMM approach to context-aware search. ACM Trans. Web 7(4), Article 22 (2013)
18. Qumsiyeh, R., Ng, Y.K.: Assisting web search using query suggestion based on word similarity measure and query modification patterns. In: World Wide Web, pp. 1–20 (2014)
19. Goyal, P., Mehala, N., Bansal, A.: A robust approach for finding conceptually related queries using feature selection and tripartite graph structure. Journal of Information Science 39(5), 575–592 (2013)
20. Miyanishi, T., Sakai, T.: Time-aware structured query suggestion. In: Proc. of the 36th Int'l ACM SIGIR Conf. (SIGIR 2013) (2013)

iGuide: Socially-Enriched Mobile Tourist Guide for Unexplored Sites

Sofia Tsekeridou[1], Vassileios Tsetsos[2], Aimilios Chalamandaris[3],
Christodoulos Chamzas[4], Thomas Filippou[5], and Christos Pantzoglou[4]

[1] Athens Information Technology – AIT, Peania Attikis, Greece
sots@ait.gr
[2] Mobics, Athens, Greece
btsetsos@mobics.gr
[3] Innoetics Ltd., Marousi, Athens, Greece
aimilios@innoetics.com
[4] Athena R.I.C., Xanthi Branch & Democritus University of Thrace, Greece
chamzas@ceti.gr
[5] Vodafone Greece, Chalandri, Greece
thomas.filippou@vodafone.com

Abstract. The paper presents iGuide, a system that aims at enabling a *socially enriched mobile tourist guide service*, with the aim to address a much wider range of sites and attractions than existing solutions cover, including historic and traditional settlements, sites of natural beauty or unattended sites of cultural heritage where access to information is unavailable or not directly provided. The casual visitor will obtain information and guidance while personally contributing to content enrichment of the visiting places by uploading user-generated media (images, videos) along with personalised views about the acquired experience (comments, ratings). At the same time, users will receive supplementary location-based services and recommendations to enhance their visiting experience and facilitate their wandering in places of interest and their direct interaction with local provisions. iGuide targets to offer text-to-speech (narration), rich multimedia content including real time 3D graphics, augmented reality services and a backend Web 2.0 informational portal and recommender tool.

Keywords: Mobile tourist guide, recommender tool, personalization, social media, 3D cultural content, augmented reality.

1   Introduction

E-tourism services that enhance visitor's experiences by providing in situ timely validated information are still inexistent or insufficient. The visit is usually affected by severe content issues such as: inadequate or outdated content, inaccessibility introduced by language barriers and misinformation. Most of the existing e-tourism systems mainly provide Web-based access to tourist information and services. In most

A. Likas, K. Blekas, and D. Kalles (Eds.): SETN 2014, LNAI 8445, pp. 603–614, 2014.
© Springer International Publishing Switzerland 2014

cases, this is experienced prior to the visit while only a few provide in situ services. The latter are usually limited to specific sites (museums, or popular archaeological sites). Thus, there is an imminent need for developing e-tourism services and associated digital cultural content that will be available on the spot for places of interest while the tourist is visiting a cultural site, a scene of natural beauty or mainly unattended cultural attractions where no other source of valid information is directly available. Furthermore, social networking and social media applications have already large user penetration. They are utilised in various contexts (business and pleasure) as they allow content co-creation and sharing by setting users as active content contributors and reviewers.

The paper presents the iGuide system that focuses on dynamic e-tourism service provisioning offering contextualised cultural exploration on the move. It aims to enhance user experience by enabling the provision of dynamic location-based tourist information and recommendations while allowing active users to contribute in terms of content, ratings, tags, etc. Evidently, cultural heritage and tourism are domains that can benefit in terms of accessibility and economic development from the advances of information and communication technologies [1]. Currently, human-computer interaction applications such as virtual mobile guides are evolving into a standard tool [1][2]. This is also a result of the Web 2.0 technology trends as social networking mechanisms and processes like tagging or geo-tagging, allow users with similar interests to share experiences and become a part of a community [3]. The use of smartphones may change tourist experience by changing both timing and information searching patterns [4]. G. Ghiani et al. [5] proposed a smartphone-based museum guide system with edutainment features. Kathayat et al. [6] proposed a collaborative learning platform that facilitates interactive games performed in urban environments. Weber et al. [7] demonstrated the potential of location-based applications in tourism and cultural heritage. Additionally, Google presented the Latitude service which allows people to access information on where, when and what their friends are doing [8]. The Wiketude World Browser [8] provides details on prominent locations. The Mobile Tourguide System uses panoramic image collections to recognise the content of an uploaded image [10]. On the other hand, DBpedia mobile [11] is one of the few applications that take advantage of the Semantic Web.

Furthermore, the importance of managing content and metadata of tourist and cultural heritage content is depicted by the number of existing standards. Amongst the most notable are: CIDOC [12], Core Data Index to Historic Buildings and Monuments of the Architectural Heritage [19], CIDOC CRM [14], MIDAS Heritage [15], LIDO [16], Dublin Core [17] and Spectrum [18]. They have designed to assist the production of record systems, to facilitate archaeological research, to classify individual heritage assets in terms of location, functional types, architectural features, physical conditions, protection status, activities, geospatial-temporal information and other bibliographic sources,. The EU is currently funding projects that focus on harvesting metadata of 2D and 3D cultural heritage content [19] [20] and on developing information provisioning systems for cultural sites [21]. The interoperability of a metadata schema is one of the most vital aspects and hence its creation has to comply with the current best practices.

During the last five years, social media applications have become very popular. This has led many companies to consider such services in various application contexts, including education, e-government, tourism, etc. Social media applications such as YouTube, Flickr and other have been enriched in millions with tourist and cultural content. Tourists consult Web sites that offer visitors comments and ratings, to decide on their destinations prior to their visit and share their own views. Trip advisor is such an example. A distinct example of exploiting social media applications in the tourism domain is Empedia [22]. The importance of social media applications towards boosting a country's tourism economy though branding is vital.

Nowadays, Recommender systems are an essential research area [23]. Current systems identify the target user's neighbours based on profile similarities, and then suggest items that neighbours have liked in the past. User profiling is a challenging task. User profiles are usually based on data of limited relevance that are too simple to produce quality recommendations [24]. Massive quantities of User Generated Content (UGC) on social networks are now available - UGC warehouses can be mined and analysed to expand user profiles based on which more reliable recommendations can be made. The methodology of incorporating new Web 2.0 features and practices in personalised recommender applications becomes an important and urgent research topic that will be investigated in the context of e-tourism.

Furthermore, feature and capability multiformity found in devices that access digital information necessitates the provisioning of content adaptation and personalisation mechanisms. Content adaptation is interlinked with mobile devices that differentiate in terms of computational power, network bandwidth, display size, constrained text input as well as dynamic user contexts (location, preferences, etc.). Examples of browsing content adaptation systems are: Everyplace Mobile Portal [25], Cocoon [26], MyMobileWeb [27], Alembik [28], Dilithium Content Adapter [29]. The W3C consortium has been documenting the challenges in building Web content and applications that are accessed by mobile devices [30]. Apart from content adaptation, iGuide will conduct research on providing 3D content to mobile devices. Currently, X3DOM technology can be seen as a unified carrier of accelerated 3D graphics. Recently, Jung et al. [31] demonstrated the capabilities of X3DOM-WebGL technologies on different platforms.

iGuide differentiates from existing solutions as it advances the state-of-the-art by offering:

- A mobile tourist and cultural heritage virtual guide that provides dynamically contextualised, timely and validated information, enhanced with visualisation and narration capabilities. The information is adapted to the end user's context while being complemented with personalised recommendations. Its content adaptation mechanism takes under consideration the smartphone hardware capabilities. iGuide allows access to social media applications for content- and experience-sharing. User-generated content can be filtered and used for the enrichment of the provided content. The goal is to innovate through the integration and interoperation of a number of value-added technological capabilities and services, offered as a personalised and contextualised package to the tourist.

- A universal e-tourism solution that is focused on unattended cultural heritage sites, natural environment routes and historic-traditional settlements. iGuide will provide content and metadata management tools to upload and manage tourist and cultural information of new places of interest and the interoperation with existing cultural-content archives and digital libraries. The content enrichment through iGuide's interoperation with social media applications will add value to the on-site but also to the pre- and post-visit experience of the end user.

In the sequel, Section 2 presents the envisioned use cases of iGuide against which its fully-featured functionalities will be evaluated. Section 3 presents the conceptual architecture definition of iGuide and provides a more detailed technical description of each iGuide component. Finally, Section 4 outlines the conclusions and discusses on the future work.

2   The iGuide Use Cases

The feasibility of the iGuide system and its envisioned services will be evaluated in terms of properly defined use cases. The latter further present the diversity of the iGuide usage contexts according to the interests, actions and/or context of the end user. These use cases of iGuide are listed and briefly described below:

2.1   Pre-scenario - Pre-visit Experience

The user visits the iGuide social media portal and collects information about his/her destination, reads and exchanges information about the experiences other users had or requests from others to comment on his/her visiting choices. The system dynamically updates the user profile based on chosen locations, places of interest, travel times, number of visitors, etc. By the time the user visits his/her destination, content is being filtered based on the user profile updates. Further advanced personalisation takes place on the spot during the visit based on dynamic contextual user information leading to dynamically produced recommendations. Moreover, prior to the actual visit, the user can download an offline map that will be available during the visit, so that network connectivity is not a prerequisite for enjoying advanced tourist experience.

2.2   1st Scenario - Touring in Urban Areas of Cultural Importance

The visitor approaches a settlement in an urban area of cultural importance, like the old town of Xanthi (Figure 1), having initiated the iGuide mobile application. Information about the surroundings (buildings of architectural and historical interest, museums, shopping options, current or future events) appear on the smartphone device following an easy-to-follow thematic structure. As visitors can access different types of information, this is dynamically adapted based on user's current location and pre-defined filters or the filters the system has dynamically enabled by extracting user profile information. The information covers multimedia content such as images, video, 3D models, audio (e.g. local folklore music), augmented reality elements and the ability to listen to all of the textual information using the text-to-speech technology. The system will also propose trails and points-of-interest, classified according to the visitor's profile. It will recommend visiting experiences of prior visitors with similar interests that have been published on the social media portal. As an example, a preliminary selection of the points of cultural/historic interest in the old town of Xanthi are shown with red numbers on its map (Figure 1).

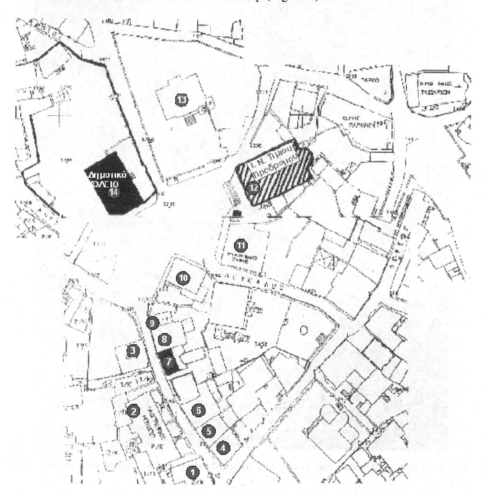

Fig. 1. A map of the old town of Xanthi with numbered points of cultural/historic interest

2.3   2nd Scenario - Touring in Open Unattended Archaeological Sites

The visitor approaches an unattended archaeological site where handy information is missing and initiates the iGuide mobile application. Such a site has been selected to be the village of Maroneia and its surrounding archaeological sites, like its ancient theatre (Figure 2). Information about the site (both archaeological and historical) appears on the smartphone following a user-friendly thematic structure. Similar experience as in the 1st scenario follows with respect to adapted content, narration and recommendations.

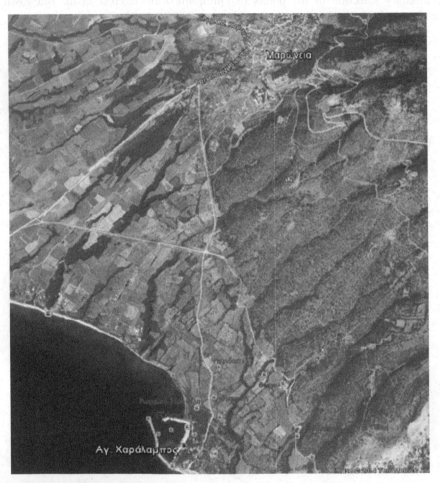

Fig. 2. A map of the Maroneia village and its surrounding archaeological sites shown in red text

2.4   3rd Scenario - Touring in Open Nature Sites

The visitor approaches a site of natural beauty using any means of transport while the iGuide mobile application is already running. Such a site is the Nestos river in a segment that its width is minimal (Figure 3) that attains many points of natural beauty. The system dynamically pop-ups information about the specific area and all textual information can be listened to (narrated). Assuming that the visitor requires all types of information related to the area, the application brings up a note about an archaeo-logical site that is nearby, about the accessible nature observation points and about a waterfall. The user decides to visit the waterfall. The application accompanies the visitor throughout the chosen trail and provides information about the flora and fauna, the water springs and all other important points-of-interest.

Fig. 3. A map of the segment of Nestos river where its width is minimal, with many points of natural beauty

2.5   Post-Scenario - After-Visit Experience

The user may use the social media portal to upload comments, tagged videos and photos, after he/she has completed his/her visit in order to share the experience, to further promote the visited sites. Other users of the application will be notified accordingly so that social interaction between this virtual community starts over.

3   The iGuide System

The presented iGuide system integrates a significant number of technologies ranging from wireless communications, optimised multimedia content (2D/3D) visualisation, mobile application software engineering up to location-based and context aware data processing, digital content and metadata management, mobile social media and social networking software development and content recommendation and personalisation. The iGuide system will provide content depending on geo-location and filtering crite-ria given by users or retrieved by a smartphone. The application will construct perso-nalised and contextualised virtual tour guides presenting dynamic content in urban areas of cultural importance, unattended archaeological sites and natural beauty sites, in addition to providing value added content and services such as mobile social soft-ware, personalised advertisements and offers, according to user preferences, location and context. Semantically annotated geo-locations will be exploited for constructing dynamic tour guides.

Figure 2 depicts the basic components that in an integrative and interoperate mode lead to the provision of the iGuide service. Within iGuide, the dynamic context information collection is of vital importance for adapting all envisioned services and providing accurate and timely recommendations to the end user. Context information may include: user profile, mobile platform capabilities, wireless network status, financial data (costs per use, etc.), location and place of interest, service time request, activity, media and information from other users of the service (collaborative filtering). The recommendation approach will thus benefit from a hybrid method combining both content filtering and collaborative filtering approaches and deploying powerful dynamic user profiling functionalities.

In addition, a complementary Web-based and Mobile-friendly tourism and social media portal will be researched upon and developed to service not only the on the spot tourist experience as an alternate information channel accessed through the mobile Web browser, but also to allow prior or after the visit information provisioning, experience sharing, rating and commenting in an attempt to provide a complete end-to-end service and associated experience to the user.

The fundamental components of the iGuide System, composed of the iGuide Server and Social Media Portal, the iGuide Mobile Application and the Visitor Awareness System, are conceptually illustrated in Figure 4.

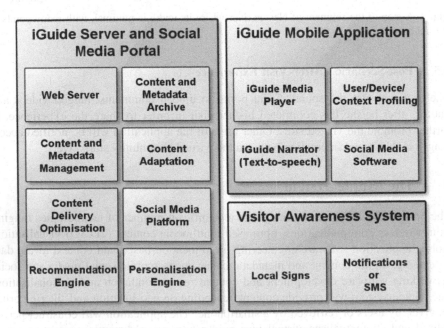

Fig. 4. Conceptual Architecture of the iGuide System

The description and functionalities of each illustrated component of the iGuide Server and Social Media Portal in Figure 1 are briefly described below:

- **Web Server:** It serves Web content to both mobile and desktop clients. Several content management tools and services can be deployed in the server as Web applications.
- **Content and Metadata Archive:** The system's persistence store where both cultural content and metadata settings are kept.
- **Content and Metadata Management:** It manages (insert, delete, update, semantically tag) the content and metadata handling.
- **Content Adaptation:** It adapts content to an appropriate, for the user's mobile device, format. This may imply content transcoding, filtering, etc. The basic difference in preparation and adaptation is their time of occurrence. The former takes place before content delivery, while the latter occurs during service execution and content delivery. The latter is also affected by the recommendation and personalisation engines.
- **Content Delivery Optimisation:** Several techniques can be used under challenging conditions, to optimise the content delivery to mobile devices. Content prefetching based on user's movement or location-based content caching will be considered.
- **iGuide Portal and Social Media Platform:** iGuide is inherently a social media platform. Thus, all possible interactions between (location-based) social media applications will be investigated.
- **Recommendation Engine:** It will provide context-aware recommendations of cultural content and added value services (targeted advertisements and offers) based on state of the art techniques. Content, user and environment semantics will be exploited where available.
- **Personalisation Engine:** Is a fundamental component of content adaptation that constitutes a substrate for all context-aware functionality. Content delivery or recommendations may be affected by the engine's results. Knowledge engineering approaches (e.g. rules, ontologies etc.) will be deployed for its implementation.

Furthermore, the fundamental components of the iGuide Mobile Application are the following:

- **iGuide Media Player:** The fundamental component of the mobile client application used for the provision and visualisation of the contextualised and adapted information to the end-user. A prototype will be developed on an open platform (Android). However, the design of the client will be platform-agnostic. The media player will consist of User Interface elements (for browsing-rendering of cultural content), a Text-to-Speech (TTS) system interface, a local Location-based Services (LBS) engine, an augmented reality player, user device persistence managing and other local components necessary for the desired functionality.
- **User/Device/Context Profiling:** The component will register and/or dynamically collect context information with respect to device capabilities, user profile and preferences not already available at the iGuide server, location, network connectivity status, etc. The logging and use of such context data enables service adaptation and personalisation as well as provisioning of targeted recommendations in addition to such contextual data gathered in the iGuide server.

- **Mobile Social Media Software:** The goal is to enable location-based mobile social applications, develop a respective community and provide services to users to bookmark and thus receive personalised information for visiting places and recommendations over a smartphone.
- **iGuide Narrator:** A Text-to-Speech (TTS) system will be adapted for mobile platforms (specifically Android) in order to provide Greek and English narration during the guiding phase. An initial web-based prototype of the system can be accessed at [34].

4   Conclusions and Future Work

The paper has presented the iGuide system, a Socially Enriched Mobile Tourist Guide targeted mainly, but not only, to Unexplored Sites. Existing solutions and state-of-the-art research and technologies have been discussed, while the innovations brought around by iGuide have been emphasized. The use cases that iGuide facilitates and provisions for have been presented, demonstrating the diversity of usage contexts of iGuide along with its multi-component and multi-functional system architecture, which has also been presented. Major components of the iGuide system architecture are the Recommendation and Personalization Engines along with the Dynamic User/Device/Context Profiling Module, components that enable dynamic and timely recommendations on touristic content to end users according to their preferences, the preferences of their peers, their context (location) and their device characteristics.

Future work will include finalization of the sites of interests and guidance scenarios as well as modes of presentation of the respective content to end users, requirements engineering and system architectural specification. It will further involve research and development of the innovative methodologies for each identified system module, along with integration of the developed components, as well as testing and evaluation under real-life use contexts. The utmost goal is to achieve enhanced user experience in a natural way.

Acknowledgment. The current work has been partially funded by national and European Commission funds from NSRF 2007-2013, OP Competitiveness and Enterpreneurship, Cooperation 2011, in the context of the project iGuide: Socially Enriched Mobile Tourist Guide for Unexploited Cultural and Natural Monuments, 11ΣΥΝ_10_1205.

References

1. Pletinckx, D.: The Integration of Location Based Services in Tourism and Cultural Heritage. EPOCH Publication,
   http://www.epoch-net.org/
   index.php?option=com_content&task=view&id=198&Itemid=304
2. Floch, J.: A Framework for User-Tailored City Exploration. In: Procs. of the Third International Symposium on End-User Development, June 7-10, pp. 239–244 (2011)

3. Schneider, F., Feldmann, A., Krishnamurthy, B., Willinger, W.: Understanding online social network usage from a network perspective. In: Procs. of the 9th ACM SIGCOMM Conference on Internet Measurement Conference, Chicago, Illinois, USA, pp. 35–48 (2009)
4. Kramer, R., Modsching, M., Hagen, K., Gretzel, U.: Behavioural impacts of mobile tour guides. In: Procs. of the Information and Communication Technologies in Tourism, pp. 109–118 (2007)
5. Ghiani, G., Paternò, F., Spano, L.D.: Cicero designer: An Environment for End-User Development of Multi-Device Museum Guides. In: Pipek, V., Rosson, M.B., de Ruyter, B., Wulf, V. (eds.) IS-EUD 2009. LNCS, vol. 5435, pp. 265–274. Springer, Heidelberg (2009)
6. Kathayat, S.B., Braek, R.: Platform Support for Situated Collaborative Learning. In: Procs. of Int. Conf. on Mobile, Hybrid, and On-line Learning (eL&mL). IEEE Press, Los Alamitos (2009)
7. Weber, M., Stan, A., Ioannidis, G.: Location-Aware and User-Centric Touristic Media. User Centric Media Journal 40, 247–254 (2010)
8. Google Latitude, http://www.google.com/latitude
9. Wikitude, http://www.wikitude.com
10. Yow, K.C., Lee, J.: Mobile tourguide system. Singaporean-French IPAL Symposium (2009)
11. Becker, C., Bizer, C.: DBpedia Mobile: A Location-Enabled Linked Data Browser. In: Procs. of Linked Data on the Web (LDOW), Beijing, China, April 22 (2008)
12. CIDOC: International Committee for Documentation, http://cidoc.mediahost.org
13. Core Data Index to Historic Buildings and Monuments of the Architectural Heritage, http://archives.icom.museu/object-id/heritage/core.html
14. CIDOC Conceptual Reference Model (CRM), http://www.cidoc-crm.org
15. MIDAS Heritage, http://www.english-heritage.org.uk/professional/archives-and-collections/nmr/heritage-data/midas-heritage
16. LIDO - Lightweight Information Describing Objects, http://www.lido-schema.org/schema/v1.0/lido-v1.0-schema-listing.html
17. Dublic Core Metadata Initiative, http://dublincore.org
18. SPECTRUM: The UK Museum Documentation Standard, 2nd edn. Cambridge, UK (1997)
19. The CARARE Project, http://www.carare.eu
20. Yeates, R.: COVAX: making visible the culture of Europe, Cultivate Interactive (July 2002), http://www.cultivate-int.org/issue7/covax
21. Vlahakis, V., Karigiannis, J., Ioannidis, N.: Augmented Reality Touring of Archaeological Sites with the ARCHEOGUIDE System, Cultivate Interactive (2003), http://www.cultivate-int.org/issue9/archeoguide
22. Empedia – Interactive Guide to the East Midlands, http://empedia.info
23. Resnick, P., Iacovou, N., Suchak, M., Bergstrom, P., Riedl, J.: Grouplens: An open architecture for collaborative filtering of netnews. In: CSCW, pp. 175–186 (1994)
24. Adomavicius, G., Tuzhilin, A.: Toward the next generation of recommender systems: A survey of the state-of-the-art and possible extensions. IEEE Trans. on Knowledge and Data Engineering 17(6), 734–749 (2005)
25. Everyplace Mobile Portal, http://www-01.ibm.com/software/pervasive/ws_everyplace_mobile_portal_enable

26. Apache Cocoon, `http://cocoon.apache.org`
27. MyMobileWeb, `http://mymobileweb.morfeo-project.org`
28. Alembik – Media Transcoding Server,
    `http://alembik.sourceforge.net/overview.html`
29. Dilithium Content Adapter (DCA), `http://www.dilithiumnetworks.com`
30. W3C - Authoring Challenges for Device Independence,
    `http://www.w3.org/TR/2003/NOTE-acdi-20030901`
31. Jung, Y., Behr, J., Graf, H.: X3DOM as carrier of the virtual heritage. In: Procs. of the
    4th ISPRS Workshop 3D-ARCH 2011: 3D Virtual Reconstruction and Visualization of
    Complex Architectures, p. 8 (2011)
32. Cultural Heritage Assets through X3DOM, `http://www.x3dom.org/?p=1989`
33. 3DSSE – A 3D Scene Search Engine Prototype, `http://www.ceti.gr/3dsse`
34. Innoetics Text-to-speech prototype,
    `http://www.spellcastcloud.com/ttsotf/form_iguide.htm`

MYVISITPLANNER[GR]: Personalized Itinerary Planning System for Tourism

Ioannis Refanidis[1], Christos Emmanouilidis[2], Ilias Sakellariou[1],
Anastasios Alexiadis[1], Remous-Aris Koutsiamanis[2,3], Konstantinos Agnantis[1],
Aimilia Tasidou[2,3], Fotios Kokkoras[4], and Pavlos S. Efraimidis[3]

[1] University of Macedonia, Greece
[2] ATHENA Research & Innovation Centre, Greece
[3] Democritus University of Thrace, Greece
[4] Technological Educational Institution of Thessaly, Greece

{Yrefanid,iliass}@uom.gr, chrisem@ceti.gr, Lalen@java uom.gr,
{akoutsia,pefraimi}@ee.duth.gr, {kagnadis,atasidou}@gmail.com,
fkokkoras@teilar.gr

Abstract. This application paper presents MYVISITPLANNER[GR], an intelligent web-based system aiming at making recommendations that help visitors and residents of the region of Northern Greece to plan their leisure, cultural and other activities during their stay in this area. The system encompasses a rich ontology of activities, categorized across dimensions such as activity type, historical era, user profile and age group. Each activity is characterized by attributes describing its location, cost, availability and duration range. The system makes activity recommendations based on user-selected criteria, such as visit duration and timing, geographical areas of interest and visit profiling. The user edits the proposed list and the system creates a plan, taking into account temporal and geographical constraints imposed by the selected activities, as well as by other events in the user's calendar. The user may edit the proposed plan or request alternative plans. A recommendation engine employs non-intrusive machine learning techniques to dynamically infer and update the user's profile, concerning his preferences for both activities and resulting plans, while taking privacy concerns into account. The system is coupled with a module to semi-automatically feed its database with new activities in the area.

1   Overview

Undoubtedly the Web has revolutionized the way visitors obtain information regarding activities they can attend during their trip and how they form their itinerary. A number of services, such as Yahoo Trip Planner, Trip Advisor and Lonely Planet aim at assisting the discovery of such information and visit organization, however, they fail to provide more intelligent services such as personalized recommendations and automatic itinerary generation. This results to the user manually selecting activities and forming plans, a process that might prove to be time consuming and error-prone.

A. Likas, K. Blekas, and D. Kalles (Eds.): SETN 2014, LNAI 8445, pp. 615–629, 2014.

This paper presents MYVISITPLANNER[GR1], a web-based recommendation and activity planning system, aiming at providing the visitor or the resident of Northern Greece with personalized plans concerning available activities. A broad range of activities that might be of his interest are considered, such as visiting museums, archaeological sites, churches and galleries, attending a concert or a performance, walking through interesting urban and rural paths, mountaineering, rafting or swimming, and many others. Personalization in the system has three aspects: preferences regarding the type of activities that are of the visitors' interest; preferences with respect to the scheduling of activities; and, finally, constraints imposed by other tasks already scheduled within the visitors' calendar. Preferences are described by user profiling, dynamically customized in a non-intrusive, user-specific manner, by monitoring user interaction with the system. Weighted activity types and soft scheduling constraints impact on the plan definition. Scheduling preferences concern the preferred time of day to schedule an activity and the tightness of the plan. Other profile aspects taken into account include age, gender and spoken languages. A set of default profiles has been created, to facilitate initialization of a visit plan. Finally, constraints imposed by other tasks are defined by integrating information from the user's calendar.

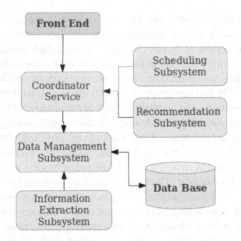

Fig. 1. MYVISITPLANNER[GR] System Architecture

A typical use case consists of three steps: setting the visit framework; selecting activities; and, finally, forming the plan. In the first step the user defines the time period, the geographical areas and the user profile. In the second step the system recommends activities, taking into account the user's profile and the constraints imposed by the activities such as location, availability, estimated visit duration, as well as user-related constraints. The user can edit the recommended list, by removing and/or adding activities. Finally, in the third step, the system presents to the user an ordered list of distinct alternative plans for the selected activities.

---

[1] MYVISITPLANNER[GR] is currently available at http://mvp.gnomon.com.gr/

Since the success of MYVISITPLANNER^{GR} heavily depends on making valid recommendations, a semi-automatic process for information extraction from web sites feeds the database on a regular basis, besides information manually entered by the cultural activity providers. In all cases, a system administrator validates new entries. MYVISITPLANNER^{GR} adopts a service oriented architecture (Fig.1), with services providing the data management, recommendation and scheduling functionalities.

The rest of the paper is organized as follows: First related work concerning other trip management systems is briefly discussed, taking also into account their capacity to offer personalized recommendations and planning capabilities. The activity types ontology is presented next, followed by a description of the recommendation module. The scheduling engine of the system is then presented and the information extraction mechanisms are outlined. Next privacy concerns are highlighted and finally the paper concludes with a discussion of challenges for future work.

2 Related Work

There are several available web-based systems supporting trip organization. The motivation behind our work was Yahoo!'s Trip Planner (http://travel.yahoo.com/trip). After defining the trip dates as well as the geographical area covered by it, Yahoo!'s Trip Planner suggests activities and the user selects the ones to be included in the trip. For each activity, information is given about open hours and cost (in text form), as well as reviews. It is the user's responsibility to schedule manually each selected activity in time, with the risk of violating constraints imposed by the selected activities or by his other tasks.

Trip Advisor (http://www.tripadvisor.com.gr/), Lonely Planet (http://www.lonelyplanet.com/) and Travel Muse (http://www.travelmuse.com/) offer similar functionalities like Yahoo!'s Trip Planner. Other sites, like Expedia (http://www.expedia.com/) and Travelocity (http://www.travelocity.com/), focus on booking flights, hotels, cars and activities, thus suggesting only activities that have some cost. In all the aforementioned cases, there is no personalization concerning the suggested activities or user's preferences about the way the activities are placed in his calendar. Furthermore, there is no support for retrieving and updating the user's calendar and no automated scheduling functionality is offered.

plnnr (pronounced 'planner', http://plnnr.com/) is a recent web application offering similar functionality to MYVISITPLANNER^{GR}. By the time of writing this paper it covers 20 cities all over the world. After selecting the trip dates, the user can select one of four predefined themes (i.e., profiles), that is, 'family', 'outdoors', 'first time' and 'culture'. The user also selects one out of five levels of plan intensity, as well as a luxury level (e.g., hotel stars). Finally, the system creates a plan for each day of the visit, with the user being able to add or remove activities to/from the plan. The user can print the plan in the form of an agenda, similar to other web based trip planning applications. To the best of our knowledge, plnnr is the only system that offers some customization, in the form of predefined profiles used to suggest activities, as well as automated scheduling of the selected activities. Compared to MYVISITPLANNER^{GR}, it lacks deep and broad activity ontology and a user profiling mechanism for personalization; it does not support a rich model of preferences over the way activities are scheduled in time; it does not encompass collaborative filtering for the recommendation module; and, finally, it does not integrate with the user's calendar.

There are many other systems that support automated scheduling of personal activities, most of them focusing on meeting scheduling. To the best of our knowledge, SELFPLANNER [15, 14], is the only one that focuses on scheduling personal individual activities, while encompassing a rich model of activities, with unary and binary constraints and preferences. It also exploits a rich scheduling engine based on deterministic and stochastic greedy search algorithms to schedule user's activities in time and space. Since SELFPLANNER is a general system, it could be used in principle to schedule tour activities as well. However, without a coupled information system providing data, mainly location and temporal availability of each activity, it would be impractical to use the system to create itineraries.

Other systems cope with the problem of automated meeting scheduling [7, 8, 17, 18]. RCal [19], an intelligent meeting scheduling agent, supports parsing and reasoning about semantically annotated schedules over the web[13].PTIME [5], developed under the CALO project [12], learns user's preferences about the way meetings are scheduled.

Tour planning and personalization is particularly useful for mobile guidance applications, which offer a rich, ubiquitous and interactive user experience, which may be personalized by exploiting context-adaptive features. The opportunities offered by adding such high-added value futures, such as planning/scheduling and information harvesting in a privacy preserving manner have not been well-explored yet [6].

3   The Ontology

MYVISITPLANNER^{GR} employs a dedicated ontology to describe activity types in a structured manner. The simplicity of the ontology was a design requirement, since it is intended to be directly handled by activity providers to input activity descriptions. Since these users will not generally be familiar with formal ontological descriptions, rather than defining a formal cultural activities ontology, the choice was to define a simple tour activities structure employ commonly perceivable terms. A representative subset of the employed activity ontology is presented in Fig. 2 and Fig. 3.

The main hierarchy contains the types of available activities, such as "Monument" or "Archaeological Site". The activity types are further analyzed at deeper hierarchy levels. An activity provider, thus, has the flexibility to either stay at the more abstract hierarchical level, or provide more accurate categorizations of provided activities. The rest of the hierarchies express auxiliary cross-cutting categorizations of the main activity type hierarchy and help mitigate a potential combinatorial explosion of activity types that would have otherwise been introduced by a categorization of very fine granularity. More specifically, the theme hierarchy allows the expression of the thematic category of the activity; the historical era (epoch) hierarchy enables a categorization according to the historical period of interest; and the target group hierarchy assists in linking activities with different target groups.

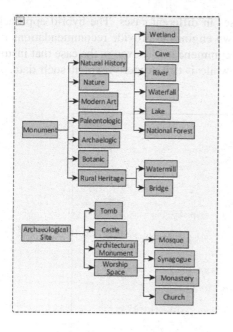

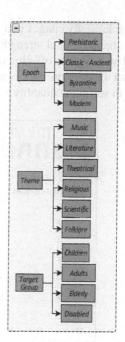

Fig. 2. Activity Type Hierarchy

Fig. 3. Auxiliary Hierarchies (Epoch, Theme and Target Group)

A key target of the defined ontology usage is for describing activities and user profile preferences. In the former case, the description allows sets of ontology entries to be specified. For example, in describing a castle on the shore of a lake, the set {Castle, Lake} can be specified. In the latter case, the description requires sets of weighted ontology entries. For example, in describing a user who is interested in caves, does not like castles and is indifferent to bridges, the set {(Cave, 1.0), (Castle, 0.0), (Bridge, 0.5)} can be specified. The simplicity in profiling is served by defining preferences over the activity type rather than the auxiliary hierarchies.

An evident advantage of the adopted ontological approach is that it combines simplicity towards the user with the ability to handle more complex associations by employing a composite similarity metric, to achieve improved performance in the recommendation results.

4   The Recommendation Subsystem

The recommendation subsystem in MYVISITPLANNER^GR assists the users in selecting the set of activities they wish to engage with during their trip (Fig.4). It is implemented as a hybrid collaborative filtering recommendation system [16]. It comprises two independent recommendation engines whose output is fed into a fusion function in order to derive a final ordered list of activities (Fig.5). Each recommendation engine displays advantages and weaknesses in different cases. The hybrid approach builds on the individual strengths of the two engines to provide recommendations of improved quality, thus offering relevant recommendations, even in the case that insufficient user interaction data is available, while it can properly exploit such data, if available in sufficient quantity.

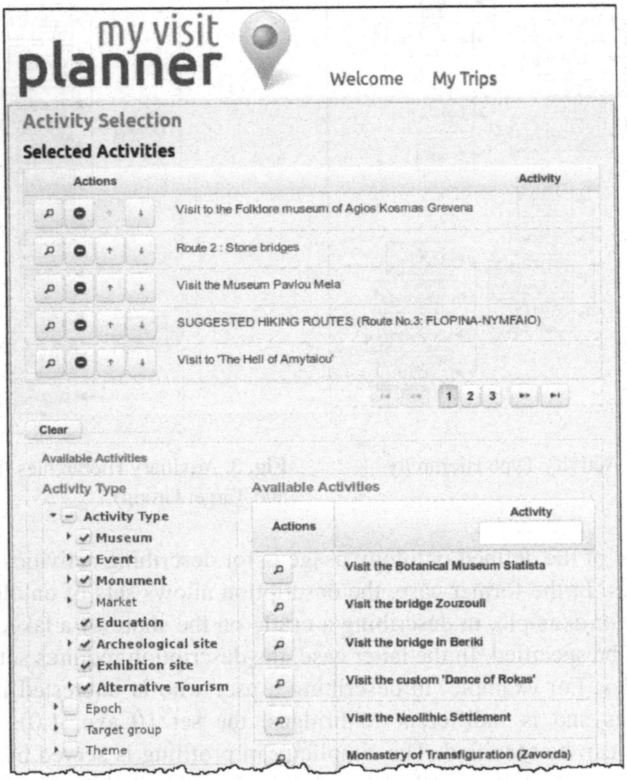

Fig. 4. Selecting Activities

The first engine performs recommendation by suggesting user activities which are similar to the activities that have already been rated by the same user. The similarity of the activities is calculated via the Hausdorff distance (Eq. 1) between the ontological description of each activity, where the description is represented as a non-empty set of tree nodes taken from the activity type ontology. This distance expresses the greatest of all distances of a given activity from an activity type, described by a set of activity types to the closest activity type of the other activity. This metric has been selected as it effectively expresses the maximum dissimilarity between two activities, while having low computational requirements.

$$d_H(A, B) = \max \left\{ \sup_{a \in A} \inf_{b \in B} d(a, b), \sup_{b \in B} \inf_{a \in A} d(a, b) \right\}$$

(1)

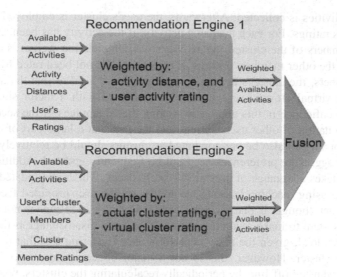

Fig. 5. Hybrid Recommendation Subsystem

The distance between the individual activity types, denoted d(a, b) above, is equal to the length of the shortest path between them, when the activity types are taken as tree nodes in the hierarchical ontology. This engine takes advantage of the ontological information available for each activity, as well as the user's ratings for activities. Initially, the available activities are collected, consisting of all the activities which conform to the trip's time and location restrictions and the user's language restrictions. Then, the user's past activity ratings are fetched. For each of the available activities, the most similar set of rated-by-the-user activities is estimated. Each of the available activities' recommendation weight is calculated as a function of the Hausdorff distance between itself and the most similar rated activities and the mean rating of the rated activities. One advantage of this approach for generating recommendations is that ratings for activities are not required from other users, since only the user's own ratings are used. Another advantage is that a large part of the calculations can be pre-computed off-line, since the activity descriptions change infrequently and as a result the distance between the activities remains unchanged. The disadvantages are that the user needs to provide ratings for some activities and that the other users' ratings are not taken advantage of. The former can be improved by deducing ratings from a user profile, albeit with somewhat limited accuracy. The latter is addressed by the second recommendation engine.

The second engine performs a variation of collaborative filtering recommendation. It suggests user activities by clustering users via top-down clustering and suggesting activities rated by other cluster members to members of the cluster. The similarity of the users is calculated via the distance between the ontological description of the user profile preferences and the similarities in age, gender, spoken languages and scheduling preferences. This engine takes advantage of the ontological information available for each user profile as well as the activity ratings of other users. As before, the set of available activities is collected. Afterwards, the user's cluster is employed as a proxy for the user's ratings. For each available activity, if the activity has been rated by one or more members of the cluster, the activity's recommendation weight is assigned as the mean of the other members' ratings. If an activity has not been rated by any of the cluster members, the cluster's aggregate preferences are used to rate the activity, behaving as a virtual cluster-average user, but weighted with a factor signifying the diminished confidence in this approach. Among the advantages of the second engine are the exploitation of other users' ratings and the fact that a large part of the calculations, but not all, can also be pre-computed as clusters should be relatively stable and the cluster's aggregate preferences need not be frequently updated. Additionally, this engine also takes advantage of user profile preferences, which are updated from their initial values using machine learning techniques on the user provided feedback. The most important, though, is that the prior availability of user ratings is not a prerequisite for the system to make recommendations. The main disadvantage is the increased computational load, given the need to perform user clustering and that users need to belong to a cluster. However, this is not a major concern, since user clusters are formed and adjusted off-line, by periodically recalculating the clusters, while the prior definition of default representative user profiles enables usage by new users.

In the final merging stage the outputs of each of the two engines are combined. Each engine produces an independent list of (Activity, Weight) tuples. The merging function expresses the confidence in each engine by examining the richness of the information processed by each engine, such as user profile preferences generality, ratings, cluster size, cluster virtual profile preference generality, and weighs the two lists accordingly. Finally, the list is returned ordered from the most to the least recommended activity. Some parts of the user model are also used in an auxiliary manner to filter recommended activities out before inputting them into the recommendation engines. Age will filter age-inappropriate activities and spoken languages will filter out activities performed in unfamiliar languages. Scheduling preferences are forwarded to the scheduling engine.

One of the problems many systems with explicit user profile preferences have is the lack of user engagement in defining their preferences. Therefore, user profile preferences tend to be generic, neither strongly preferring nor strongly disliking anything. A remedy to this adopted by the present approach is to perform non-intrusive learning of these preferences by logging user choices during system usage, such as selecting, deselecting and viewing activities as a proxy for actual ratings. Obviously, direct user feedback in the form of plan and activity ratings is considered more significant, therefore the information gleamed in this manner is appropriately weighted such that the low confidence in these measurements is appropriately represented.

The recommendation subsystem executes the off-line calculations using the Apache Mahout[2] machine learning library on the Apache Hadoop[3] MapReduce framework.

---

[2] http://mahout.apache.org/
[3] http://hadoop.apache.org/

5   The Scheduling Engine

MYVISITPLANNER^{GR} exploits the planning engine of SELFPLANNER[14, 15]. This gives advantage to users of the latter system, since rescheduling of their non-cultural activities is possible, provided that these activities have been added to their calendars through SELFPLANNER; otherwise, activities manually inserted into a user's calendar are never rescheduled in order to accommodate new activities originated by MYVISITPLANNER^{GR}.

There are many types of cultural activities, from a scheduling point of view. An activity may have a fixed time and location. For example, a one-time concert may be of this type. Most activities however, e.g. a visit to a museum, are flexible, in the sense that the user is able to select when to perform them, within some specified time window. Similarly, some activities (e.g., concert) have a fixed duration, whereas others (e.g., museum visit) have a variable duration, depended on the user's profile.

Most activities have a specific location, however there might exist activities that are offered in several locations, like, e.g., watching a movie in any of the cinemas in the area. Furthermore, there are activities that have a different starting and ending location; for example, walking through the city does not require necessarily returning back to the starting point on foot, before performing any other activity. Locations are taken into account by the scheduling engine, in order to ensure that there is enough time for the visitor to move from the location of each activity to the location of the next one in his plan.

Bundles of activities are also supported. A bundle encompasses many elementary activities that are usually offered in reduced price as a bundle than when bought individually. Activities of a bundle may have ordering constraints among them.

Defining the temporal domain of an activity can be a laborious task for the cultural activity provider. MYVISITPLANNER^{GR} supports a structured and, at the same time, intuitive way to define temporal domains, based on an ordered list of statements concerning periods when the activity is provided or not [2]. Each statement has priority over the previous ones. For example, the following statements:

```
Every MoTuWeThuFri 09:00 to 21:00
Every Sat 10:00 to 18:00
Every Sun 10:00 to 17:00
Except every December 25th
```

define that an activity is offered 09:00 to 21:00 from Monday to Friday, 10:00 to 18:00 the Saturdays, 10:00 to 17:00 the Sundays, but is not offered the Christmas day.

A rich model of constraints and preferences is supported. Each activity is characterized by a wishfulness for the user. Furthermore, the user can express his preferences over the activity's temporal domain, that is, when he prefers the activity to be scheduled. Although the scheduling engine supports arbitrary preferences over the temporal domain, MYVISITPLANNER^{GR} offers only a limited set of options to the user, such as scheduling the activity in the morning or in the evening of any day. Binary preferences are supported as well. The user can express that he prefers two activities to be scheduled temporarily close or away to each other. Furthermore, the user can state his preferences not over specific activities but over activity classes in the ontology. In that case, unary and binary preferences are applied to single activities and to pairs of activities respectively, unless they are overwritten by specific preferences.

Fig. 6. An automatically generated visit plan

In order to solve the scheduling problem, the scheduling subsystem calls the scheduling engine of SELFPLANNER, which is offered as an external TCP/IP server. The scheduling engine works in two phases: In the first phase it finds a good enough solution using Squeaky Wheel Optimization (SWO) [9], whereas in the second phase it employs Simulated Annealing, using SWO's solution as the starting state, in order to rich the nearest local optimum, defined across an extensive set of local transformations [3, 1]. After obtaining the first schedule, the user can ask for alternative schedules (Fig.6). In that case, the scheduling engine attempts again to solve the problem, while trying simultaneously to maximize a metric of the distance between the already found plans and the new one [4].

The scheduling engine supports more features than these exploited by the current version of MYVISITPLANNER^{GR}. Interruptible are the activities that can be accomplished in parts. For example, writing a paper is an interruptible activity. Having collected data of real cultural activities, we did not encounter any one requiring interruptible execution; hence there is no need to support them. Similarly, concurrent are the activities that can be executed concurrently with others, that is, they do not require the user's full attention. For example, attending a teleconference while working on a presentation might be possible. Although one could imagine cases when a cultural activity could be accomplished concurrently with others, we do not offer this option to MYVISITPLANNER^{GR} users. So, all cultural activities are considered as requiring the user's full attention; hence no concurrency is possible for them. However, for users of both MYVISITPLANNER^{GR} and SELFPLANNER systems, interruptibility and concurrency are important, since each time MYVISITPLANNER^{GR} is asked to produce a plan, all user's activities (from both systems) are taken into account.

6   Information Extraction from Semi-structured Data

Being a data intensive application, MYVISITPLANNER^{GR} requires a constant feed of fresh information regarding cultural events. To handle this requirement the system uses DEiXTo [10], a web content extraction suite that includes a GUI application for designing extraction rules (wrappers) and a command line executor that applies these rules to target URLs and stores the retrieved content into a database. The exact role of DEiXTo is threefold: a) extract classified-at-the-source cultural events, b) extract non-classified-at-the-source events, and c) detect new sources.

6.1   Extracting Classified Events

This task is based on the availability of local information sites that post cultural events in a classified manner, that is, they have their content organized in categories such as theater, music, etc. Additionally, these sites are built with modern content management systems and, as a result, they are excellent targets for extraction tasks. This is due to their web pages being template based, thus, one can easily detect HTML patterns reappearing in every event page and design accurate extraction rules based on those patterns. These sites typically organize the posted events in a master-detail fashion, where a master page includes a list of links to individual pages presenting the details of a single event. As a result there are also master and detail extraction rules, usually one pair for every event category of interest, in every site. DEiXTo uses a greedy (first occurrence matching), tree-matching algorithm which is described in detail in [10]. It matches the tree pattern of the extraction rule against the DOM tree of the page under consideration. The system works as described in the following paragraphs.

Master wrappers are executed periodically and extract URLs of pages containing cultural event descriptions. These URLs are the targets of the detail wrappers that extract the title, the body and the category of the event. The reader should recall that the category of the event is already known by design. The body text of the event is stored without any modifications and later is parsed with regular expressions and heuristic based techniques for metadata related to the event (location, time, cost, etc). The complete metadata set extracted for an event is finally presented to a human expert (along with the original page) who ensures that the correct information will be headed to the database.

Duplicate entries are currently detected and removed, based on the URL of the detail page. A similarity measure over the title and possibly over the body text is under consideration, since it is possible to have the same event posted in two or more different sites.

Finally, the extracted body text is cleared up from junk words, is passed to a Greek stemmer and the result is stored to serve as train instance for the classifier.

Currently, there are 12 sites monitored with a total of 54 extraction rules.

6.2   Extracting Non-Classified Events

This case is similar to the previous except that the class of the extracted events is not known because the target site does not provide such event separation. This introduces one extra step in the metadata extraction procedure: the event should be classified. This is done using the stemmed body text (as described at the end of Section 6.1) and the classifier of the system. The result is verified by a human operator.

6.3   Detecting New Sources

The web is constantly changing as new technologies and services emerge. This is more intensive in the Greek web in which the transition to second or third generation sites is still in progress. As a result, MYVISITPLANNER^{GR} requires a way to detect new potential sources of cultural events.

There are currently two subsystems for new source detection. The first one queries the Google search engine with well-designed queries regarding specific cultural events in the geographical region of interest. The first ten unseen results are extracted using DEiXTo, their URLs are visited and their content is stemmed and classified as relevant cultural event or not. Relevant pages are checked by a human expert to see if they probably belong to a new site that should be wrapped properly with extraction rules and added to the list of the sources that provide classified events.

The second subsystem for new source detection is a crawler that aims at supporting the human exert mentioned earlier, in the task of detecting new sites that can serve as sources of cultural events. The crawler starts from the domain root address of pages detected using the Google search methodology and classified as relevant. It then crawls the target site at a certain depth and classifies the pages visited with the help of the body text extractor, the Greek stemmer and the classifier. If the percentage of the related pages of the crawled site is above a certain threshold, the site is considered interesting and is forwarded to the human expert for further examination.

7   Privacy Concerns

Storage of large amounts of data concerning user interests, travels, preferences and behaviors is a significant problem for both the user and the service provider who stores this data. The users risk having their private and potentially sensitive data misused. The service provider incentivizes more attacks against itself since more data are to be gained by unlawfully acquiring it and is also potentially liable for any data theft. At the same time, the recommendation subsystem requires the availability of large amounts of data to be able to function. We have attempted to reach a trade-off which allows the recommendation subsystem to deliver its intended functionality effectively, while at the same time increasing the users' privacy protection and diminishing the potential for large-scale data exfiltration. The penalty for this decision lies in increased implementation complexity, higher computational overheads and optionally, shifting some of the privacy protection burden to the users.

To enhance data protection, apart from the obvious security measures (e.g. access control, logging, auditing), user data which is deemed sensitive is kept in encrypted form in the database. The data is transparently decrypted whenever the user logs into the system, and is kept decrypted for the duration of the user's session and then re-encrypted automatically. The data in the database is encrypted using the symmetric cipher. The symmetric key is itself encrypted using another cipher, using the KEK (Key Encryption Key) scheme [11], to allow changing user encryption keys without needing to decrypt the data and re-encrypt with the new key. The data which is considered sensitive and thus protected by the privacy mechanism in MYVISITPLANNER^GR is shown in Table 1 against the main processes where it is accessed and the entities that need access to the data. At this stage the system allows access to the user data to all entities, when the user is logged in. An additional protective measure could be to limit the access of each entity to the data needed for the processes they perform.

Table 1. Data usage in MYVISITPLANNER^GR processes

Data Item	User Profile Editing (UI)	Recommendation Activity Similarity Based Recommendation	Recommendation User Clustering	Recommendation User Cluster Based Recommendation	Scheduler Scheduling
Demographic Data	■		■		
Activity Type Preferences (in User Profile)	■		■		
System Preferences (in User Profile)	■				■
Detailed User Interaction Log	■				
Activity Ratings	■	■	■		

8   Conclusions

This paper presented MYVISITPLANNER^GR, an ongoing work aiming at helping visitors and residents of the Northern Greece area to include cultural activities, such as visiting museums churches and archaeological sites, attending performances or doing outdoor activities (walking, swimming, climbing, etc.), in their calendars. In order to schedule the activities, the system takes into account user preferences concerning the types of the activities and the way they are scheduled, as well as constraints imposed by the selected activities and the user's other commitments. A search engine employing greedy search followed by stochastic local search is employed to produce plans, while alternative plans with noticeable differences to the already suggested ones are provided, upon a user's request. The system is supported by a hybrid recommendation engine providing personalized activities recommendations, and by a semi-automated information extraction module to feed the system's database with fresh data. MYVISITPLANNER^GR is now entering the deployment and evaluation phases.

Acknowledgements. The reported work is financially **supported by** the General Secretariat for Research & Technology (Grant 09SYN-62-129). The collaboration with all project partners is gratefully acknowledged.

References

1. Alexiadis, A., Refanidis, I.: Post-Optimizing Individual Activity Plans through Local Search. In: ICAPS 2013 Workshop on Constraint Satisfaction Techniques for Planning and Scheduling Problems (COPLAS), Rome (2013)
2. Alexiadis, A., Refanidis, I.: Defining a Task's Temporal Domain for Intelligent Calendar Applications. In: Iliadis, Maglogiann, Tsoumakasis, Vlahavas, Bramer (eds.) Artificial Intelligence Applications and Innovations III. IFIP, vol. 296, pp. 399–406. Springer, Boston (2009)
3. Alexiadis, A., Refanidis, I.: Meeting the Objectives of Personal Activity Scheduling through Post-Optimization. In: First International Workshop on Search Strategies and Non-standard Objectives (SSNOWorkshop 2012). CPAIOR, Nantes, France (2012)
4. Alexiadis, A., Refanidis, I.: Generating Alternative Plans for Scheduling Personal Activities. In: ICAPS 2013 Workshop on Scheduling and Planning Applications (SPARK), Rome (2013)
5. Berry, P., Conley, K., Gervasio, M., Peinter, B., Uribe, T., Yorke-Smith, N.: Deploying a Personalized Time Management Agent. In: 5th Inter. Joint Conference on Autonomous Agents and Multi Agent Systems (AAMAS-2006) Industrial Track, pp. 1564-1571 (2006)
6. Emmanouilidis, C., Koutsiamanis, R.-A., Tasidou, A.: Mobile Guides: Taxonomy of Architectures, Context Awareness, Technologies and Applications. Journal of Network and Computer Applications 36(1), 103–125 (2013)
7. Garrido, L., Sycara, K.: Multi-agent meeting scheduling: Preliminary experimental results. In: 1st International Conference on Multi-Agent Systems, ICMAS (1995)
8. Jennings, N.R., Jackson, A.J.: Agent based meeting scheduling: A design and implementation. IEE Electronic Letters 31(5), 350–352 (1995)
9. Joslin, D.E., Clements, D.P.: "Squeaky Wheel" Optimization. Journal of Artificial Intelligence Research 10, 375–397 (1999)
10. Kokkoras, F., Ntonas, K., Bassiliades, N.: DEiXTo: A web data extraction suite. In: Proc. of the 6th Balkan Conference in Informatics, Thessaloniki, Greece, pp. 9–12 (2013)
11. Landrock, P.: Key Encryption Key. In: Encyclopedia of Cryptography and Security, US, pp. 326–327. Springer (2005)
12. Myers, K.: Building an Intelligent Personal Assistant. AAAI Invited Talk (2006)
13. Payne, T.R., Singh, R., Sycara, K.: Calendar Agents on the Semantic Web. IEEE Intelligent Systems 17(3), 84–86 (2002)
14. Refanidis, I., Alexiadis, A.: Deployment and Evaluation of SELFPLANNER, an Automated Individual Task Management System. Computational Intelligence 27(1), 41–59 (2011)

15. Refanidis, I., Yorke-Smith, N.: A Constraint Based Programming Approach to Scheduling an Individual's Activities. ACM Transactions on Intelligent Systems and Technologies 1(2) (2010)

16. Ricci, F., Rokach, L., Shapira, B., Kantor, P.B.: Recommender Systems Handbook. Springer, New York (2010)

17. Sen, S., Durfee, E.H.: On the design of an adaptive meeting scheduler. In: 10th International Conference on Artificial Intelligence for Applications, pp. 40–46 (1994)

18. Sen, S., Durfee, E.H.: A formal study of distributed meeting scheduling. Group Decision and Negotiation 7, 265–289 (1998)

19. Singh, R.: RCal: An Autonomous Agent for Intelligent Distributed Meeting Scheduling. Technical Report CMU-RI-TR-03-46. Robotics Institute, Carnegie Mellon University (2003)

Simultaneous Image Clustering, Classification and Annotation for Tourism Recommendation

Konstantinos Pliakos and Constantine Kotropoulos

Department of Informatics, Aristotle University of Thessaloniki
Box 451, Thessaloniki, 54124, Greece
{kpliakos,costas}@aiia.csd.auth.gr
http://www.aiia.csd.auth.gr

Abstract. The exponential increase in the amount of data uploaded to the web has led to a surge of interest in multimedia recommendation and annotation. Due to the vast volume of data, efficient algorithms for recommendation and annotation are needed. Here, a novel two-step approach is proposed, which annotates an image received as input and recommends several tourist destinations strongly related to the image. It is based on probabilistic latent semantic analysis and hypergraph ranking enhanced with the visual attributes of the images. The proposed method is tested on a dataset of 30000 images bearing text information (e.g., title, tags) collected from *Flickr*. The experimental results are very promising, as they achieve a top rank precision of 80% for tourism recommendation.

Keywords: Probabilistic Latent Semantic Analysis (PLSA), Clustering, Image Classification, Image Annotation, Recommendation systems, Hypergraph.

1 Introduction

Nowadays, the continuously rising popularity of photo-sharing web applications leads to a huge amount of uploaded images. Browsing through this volume resorts to search engines, which exploit mainly the text information in tags, titles, etc. Image tags are keywords, which are added to an image by a user of a social media platform, describing the image content from this user's point of view. The aforementioned image annotation is a very critical procedure, as it is responsible for search engine retrieval accuracy and contributes to the organization of the images uploaded to the web. It aims at bridging the gap between the semantic and visual content of an image. However, it suffers from several limitations, such as spam, lack of uniformity, and noise. Several times, the tags given to an image by a user are far from being accurate, containing much redundancy, or even false information. Therefore, an automated annotation system is of paramount importance. Recently, besides annotation, much progress has been made toward developing new recommendation systems. However, achieving satisfactory efficiency or accuracy remains still an open problem.

Tourism is a vital economic sector for Greece and many other countries. Nowadays, the way people decide their tourist destination differs from the past. It is

A. Likas, K. Blekas, and D. Kalles (Eds.): SETN 2014, LNAI 8445, pp. 630–640, 2014.
© Springer International Publishing Switzerland 2014

no longer solely based on brochures or simple search on the web. The sectors of e-tourism and marketing are thriving and the need for developing efficient tourism recommendation systems is indisputable. Here, a tourism related recommendation system is presented and experimental results are disclosed, demonstrating its great potential.

Our work was motivated by [1] where the problem of vast amount of images was handled by building an Internet landmark recognition engine, resorting to efficient object recognition and unsupervised clustering techniques. In [2], a cluster-based landmark and event detection scheme was presented that was based on clustering performed on both visual and tag similarity graphs. More relevant to our approach are the methods presented in [3] and [4]. A worldwide tourism recommendation system was implemented based only on visual matching and minimal user input in [3] and a probabilistic model was developed in [4] that was based on Latent Dirichlet Analysis (LDA) for simultaneous image classification and annotation.

The novel contribution of this paper is in the development of a complete image annotation and tourism recommendation system. In particular, the GPS coordinates (latitude, longitude) of a dataset of 30000 geo-tagged images crawled from *Flickr* were clustered by means of hierarchical clustering to form 2993 clusters. Hereafter, these clusters are referred to as geo-clusters. From them, the 100 most dense geo-clusters were selected as places of interest (POI). Indeed, popular tourist destinations attract more visitors, who upload more geo-tagged images on social media sharing platforms. The text information (e.g., titles, tags) of the images that belong to each geo-cluster was concatenated, forming a geo-cluster derived document. Next, probabilistic latent semantic analysis (PLSA) [5], [6], [7] properly initialized was employed to build an image annotation sub-model. PLSA performs a probabilistic mixture decomposition, which associates an unobserved class variable to co-occurrence of terms and documents. That is, the PLSA is used to represent documents as probability distributions of topics treated as unobserved class variables. By applying PLSA to a term-document matrix the relations between the terms and the documents are captured by observing the probability distribution between the documents and the generated topics and between the topics and terms. Here, the PLSA is applied in a term-document (geo-cluster) matrix and the annotation is performed by assigning the geo-cluster derived document and all the images belonging to the geo-cluster the most strongly related terms to it. The annotation sub-model of the proposed system is also enhanced by exploiting the visual attributes of images. Such an approach is more complete than that in existing methods, such as [3] and [4]. Next, a hypergraph was constructed, capturing the relations computed by the PLSA between the geo-cluster derived documents and the topics as well as the vocabulary terms. A hypergraph is defined as a set of vertices made by concatenating different kind of objects (e.g., documents, topics, terms) and hyperedges linking these vertices. In contrast to simple graphs, multi-link relations between the vertices are captured in hypergraphs. Tourism recommendation is treated as a hypergraph ranking problem and the 5 top ranked geo-clusters are recommended as tourist destinations. For evaluation purposes, 200 images were removed from the dataset along with their text information to be used for recommendation assessment. The experiments demonstrate the merits of the proposed system. Both classification and annotation results are very promising. A top rank precision of 80% is disclosed for tourism recommendation.

The remainder of this paper is organized as follows. In Section 2, the image annotation is detailed. The hypergraph ranking model is analyzed in Section 3. The dataset and the term-document matrix are described in Section 4. Hypergraph construction is explained in Section 5. The outline of the proposed system is presented in Section 6. In Section 7, experimental results are presented demonstrating the effectiveness of the proposed method. Conclusions are drawn and topics for future research are indicated in Section 8.

2   Image Annotation

2.1   Image Annotation Using Semantic Topics

In text processing, PLSA models each term in a document as a sample from a mixture model. The mixture components are multinomial random variables that can be interpreted as topic representations. The data generation process can be described as follows: 1) select a document d with probability $P(d)$, 2) pick a latent topic z with probability $P(z|d)$ and 3) generate a term t with probability $P(t|z)$. The joint probability model is defined by the mixture:

$$\left.\begin{aligned} P(t,d) &= P(d)P(t|d) \\ P(t|d) &= \sum_{z \in Z} P(t|z)P(z|d) \end{aligned}\right\} \tag{1}$$

where $t \in T = \{t_1, t_2, \cdots, t_k\}$ and $d \in D = \{d_1, d_2, \cdots, d_m\}$ represent the vocabulary terms and documents, respectively, while $z \in Z = \{z_1, z_2, \cdots, z_n\}$ is an unobserved class variable representing the topics. As it is indicated in (1), the document specific term distribution $P(t|d)$ is a convex combination of the n topic conditional distributions $P(t|z)$. The annotation procedure is performed as follows:

1 PLSA is applied to a term-document matrix $\mathbf{A} \in \mathbb{R}^{k \times m}$.
2 For each document to be annotated, the most related topic is chosen, that with the highest probability.
3 The 30 most related terms to that topic are employed to annotate the document.

Terms providing geographical information are identified using geo-gazetteers[1]. Thus, a complete annotation model, which provides, geographic and semantic information is obtained.

---

[1] http://www.geonames.org

2.2 PLSA Initialization

PLSA depends on proper initialization method. In addition to the common random initialization, there are many other schemes, e.g., the Random C (RC) [6]. A variant of RC is the Dense Random C (DRC) summarized in Algorithm 1. The DRC treats the columns of **A** unequally. Only the densest columns are chosen, as they provide more valuable information. The reduction of the number of the columns makes the method less time consuming. The DRC was found to be more effective than the RC in the experiments conducted.

Algorithm 1. Dense Random C Initialization

Input: matrix $\mathbf{A} \in \mathbb{R}^{k \times m}$ with $A(i, j,) \geq 0$.
Output: matrix $\mathbf{S} \in \mathbb{R}^{k \times n}$, containing the conditional probabilities $P(t|z)$.

1 Count the non-zero elements of each column of **A**.
2 Compute the mean document vector $\bar{\mu}$.
3 Find the c columns of **A**, having more non-zero elements than $\bar{\mu}$.
4 Average x randomly chosen columns out of the c and set the average column vector as a column of **S**. Repeat 3-4 for all columns of **S**.

2.3 Classification-Based Visual Content Annotation

The visual features of an image provide valuable, complementary, information about its content. Image annotation is strongly related to image classification, considering the class label as a global description of the image, while the tags are treated as local description of the individual image parts. Here, 13 seed images, which represent 13 different visual topics were chosen manually from the dataset. For each of them, the 5 nearest neighbor images in the dataset were located by means of the k-Nearest Neighbor algorithm (k-NN), resorting to the distance between GIST descriptors [8] of the seed image and any image in the dataset. This way, 13 classes were formed, each of them containing 6 images. The average GIST descriptor among the 6 images that belong to each class defines a template for each class. Each visual topic (class) was assigned manually one label and a few representative tags, e.g., clouds, sky, sea, sunset, defining the image visual content. Each test image is classified into one of the 13 classes by finding the minimum distance between its GIST descriptor and the templates of the 13 classes. Representative images assigned to different classes are shown in Fig. 1.

3 Tourism Recommendation

The second part of the proposed system consists of a hypergraph model representing the multi-link relations between terms of the vocabulary, documents (geo-clusters), and topics as they were computed in Sec. 2.1.

Fig. 1. A sample of 12 images, representing different classes

Hereafter, set cardinality is denoted by $|\cdot|$, the ℓ_2 norm of a vector appears as $\|.\|_2$ and $\mathbf{I}$ is the identity matrix of compatible dimensions. A hypergraph $\mathbf{H}$ is a generalization of a graph with edges connecting more than two vertices. $\Psi(V, E, w)$ denotes a hypergraph with set of vertices V and set of hyperedges E to which a weight function $w : E \rightarrow \mathbb{R}$ is assigned. V consists of sets of objects of different type (documents, topics, terms). A $|V| \times |E|$ incidence matrix is formed having elements $H(v, e) = 1$ if $v \in e$ and 0 otherwise. Based on $\mathbf{H}$, the vertex and hyperedge degrees are defined as:

$$\left. \begin{array}{l} \delta(v) = \sum_{e \in E} w(e) H(v, e) \\ \delta(e) = \sum_{v \in V} H(v, e) \end{array} \right\}. \tag{2}$$

The following diagonal matrices are defined: the vertex degree matrix $\mathbf{D}_u$ of size $|V| \times |V|$, the hyperedge degree matrix $\mathbf{D}_e$ of size $|E| \times |E|$, and the $|E| \times |E|$ matrix $\mathbf{W}$ containing the hyperedge weights.

Let $\Theta = \mathbf{D}_u^{-1/2} \mathbf{H} \mathbf{W} \mathbf{D}_e^{-1} \mathbf{H}^T \mathbf{D}_u^{-1/2}$, then $\mathbf{L} = \mathbf{I} - \Theta$ is the positive semi-definite Laplacian matrix of the hypergraph. The elements of Θ, $\Theta(u, v)$, indicate the relatedness between the objects u and v. In order to compute a real valued ranking vector $\mathbf{f} \in \mathbb{R}^{|V|}$, one minimizes

$$\Omega(\mathbf{f}) = \frac{1}{2} \mathbf{f}^T \mathbf{L} \mathbf{f}, \tag{3}$$

requiring all vertices with the same value in the ranking vector $\mathbf{f}$ to be strongly connected [9]. The aforementioned optimization problem was extended by including the ℓ_2 regularization norm between the ranking vector $\mathbf{f}$ and the query vector $\mathbf{y} \in \mathbb{R}^{|V|}$ in music recommendation [10]. The function to be minimized is expressed as

$$\tilde{Q}(\mathbf{f}) = \Omega(\mathbf{f}) + \vartheta \|\mathbf{f} - \mathbf{y}\|_2^2 \tag{4}$$

where ϑ is a regularizing parameter. The best ranking vector $\mathbf{f}^* = \arg\min_{\mathbf{f}} \tilde{Q}(\mathbf{f})$ is [10]:

$$\mathbf{f}^* = \frac{\vartheta}{1+\vartheta} \left(\mathbf{I} - \frac{1}{1+\vartheta}\Theta\right)^{-1} \mathbf{y}. \tag{5}$$

4   Dataset and Term-Document Matrix

Popular tourist destinations attract more visitors, who upload more geo-tagged images on social media sharing platforms. To properly organize such geo-tagged images into geographical clusters, an hierarchical clustering algorithm, based on geographical distances computed with the "Haversine formula"[2] was applied. Thus, from 30000 geo-tagged randomly selected images related to Greece, that were collected from *Flickr*, 2993 geo-clusters were formed. The 100 most dense geo-clusters were considered as places of interest. Next, a document was created of each geo-cluster comprising the concatenation of all text information (e.g., title, tags) available for all the images assigned to the geo-cluster.

A vocabulary was defined by processing the text information contained in a dataset of 150000 images, in order to properly capture the context of the tourism application. Prior to vocabulary extraction, all characters were converted to lower case and unreadable or redundant information was removed. A vocabulary of unique words was generated along with their frequencies and terms with frequency less than 100 were removed from the vocabulary. By doing so, a vocabulary of 1901 terms was finally retained.

Next, having created 100 documents and having set the vocabulary of terms, a term-document matrix $\mathbf{A}$ was formed with size 1901×100. Each element $A(i,j)$ corresponds to the number of occurrences of a term i in a document (geo-cluster) j. In order to proceed to the image annotation, the PLSA was applied to $\mathbf{A}$.

5   Hypergraph Construction

The vertex set is defined as $V = Doc \cup Top \cup Ter$, where Doc, Top, Ter correspond to documents (geo-clusters), topics, and vocabulary terms, respectively. The hypergraph $\mathbf{H}$ is formed by concatenating the hyperedge set. It has a size of 2201×100 elements. It is formed by the concatenation of 100 documents, 200 topics, and 1901 vocabulary terms capturing the multi-link relations among the 100 geo-cluster derived documents. The weights of the hyperedge set are set equal to one.

As was mentioned in Sec. 2.1, each document is represented by a probability distribution on a set of topics. For accuracy and simplicity reasons, although each document can be related to more than one topics, only the relation between the document and the topic corresponding to the highest probability $P(z|d)$ is represented in the hypergraph. Then, the relations between any topic and the 15 most strongly related terms to that topic are retained.

---

[2] http://www.movable-type.co.uk/scripts/latlong.html

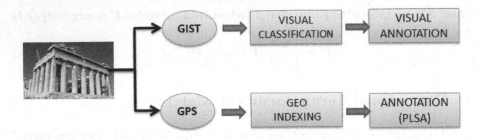

Fig. 2. Annotation system

The query vector **y** is initialized by setting the entry corresponding to the target document (geo-cluster) g, where the input image was assigned, to 1 and all other objects v connected to the specific document to $\Theta(g, v)$. It is underlined, that $\Theta(i, j)$ is the element of Θ which corresponds to the objects i and j and it is a relatedness measure of the 2 connected objects. The query vector **y** has a length of 2201 elements.

The ranking vector $\mathbf{f}^*$ is derived by solving (5), after setting the values of the query vector **y**. It has the same size and structure as **y**. The values corresponding to documents (geo-clusters) are used for tourist destination recommendation with the top ranked geo-clusters being recommended as tourist destinations to the user, who has imported the input image.

6 System Outline

Fig. 2 demonstrates the proposed system annotation. Given an image as input, the distances between image geo-location captured using GPS technology and the geo-cluster centers are computed. The input image is then assigned to the nearest geo-cluster. Simultaneously, the image visual content is classified by means of a nearest neighbor algorithm fed by the image GIST descriptor [8]. Next, the class label and the predefined representative tags offer a visual content annotation. Simultaneously, the vocabulary terms assigned to the closest geo-cluster derived document by the PLSA, offer geographic and semantic annotation for this image, as was demonstrated in Sec. 2.1. Proceeding to tourism recommendation, the query vector **y** is initialized, as was mentioned in Sec. 5. Hypergraph ranking is applied and the 5 top ranked geo-clusters are recommended as tourist destinations.

7 Experimental Results

The averaged Recall-Precision curve is used as figure of merit. Precision is defined as the number of correctly recommended objects divided by the number of all recommended objects. Recall is defined as the number of correctly recommended objects divided by the number of all objects.

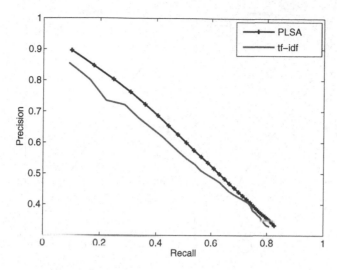

Fig. 3. Recall-precision of PLSA compared to that of tf-idf

For evaluation purposes, a test set containing 200 images was randomly chosen and removed from the training set along with their text information. As is demonstrated in Fig. 3, the PLSA outperforms the term frequency-inverse document frequency (TF-IDF) method [11]. TF-IDF is a classical global weighting scheme for vector space model, where terms appearing in documents are weighted proportionally to term frequency and inversely proportional to the document frequency.

In Fig. 4, recall-precision curves are plotted for the PLSA, having been initialized by the RC and the DRC for 5 and 10 iterations. The results indicate the superiority of DRC over RC for the same number of iterations. For evaluation purposes, the average recall precision curves over 1000 repetitions of the PLSA training for each initialization are shown.

Furthermore, it was noted that better results are obtained by increasing the number of topics, as can be seen in Fig. 5. This may be attributed to the fact that geo-cluster derived documents may contain multiple topics. Indeed, these documents consist of the tags of many photos taken by several people and each one may possess multiple semantic topics. The recall-precision curves were obtained by averaging recall-precision pairs in 100 repetitions.

Fig. 6 discloses the classification rates obtained for the 13 visual topic classes. It is seen that the proposed classification method performs extremely well for scenes of flying birds or cloudy sky. Good results are also obtained for all other classes. Clearly, the GIST features reaffirm the reputation of being the most effective features for scene matching tasks. However, their performance is not at the same level as in object recognition tasks.

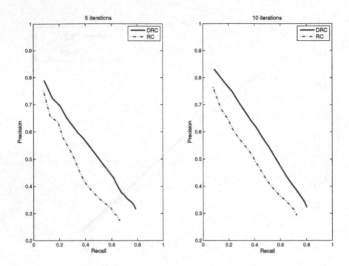

Fig. 4. RC and DRC recall-precision curves for 5 and 10 iterations

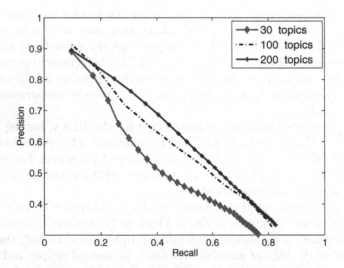

Fig. 5. PLSA recall-precision curves for 30, 100, 200 topics

Fig. 7 demonstrates the accuracy of tourism recommendation for the 5 top ranking positions. The best results are obtained for the 1st ranking position. The precision does not degrade, falling below 60%, when additional ranking positions are taken into account, indicating the effectiveness of the proposed method.

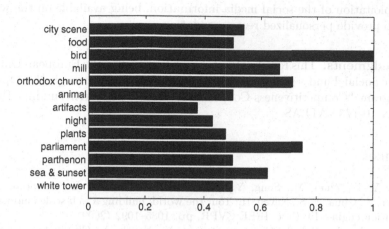

Fig. 6. Accuracy results of the visual image classification

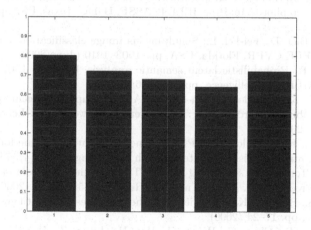

Fig. 7. Recommendation precision for the top 5 ranking positions

8 Conclusions and Future Work

Here, a novel and efficient annotation and recommendation system was proposed. A method to organize large collections of images was developed based on clustering and classification. PLSA was enhanced by an effective initialization method and used in order to extract semantic information from image metadata. The annotation procedure was also supplemented, exploiting image visual attributes. Thanks to hypergraph learning, tourism recommendation has been implemented. The dataset used in the experiments can be expanded to cover the entire Greek territory. Several online updating methods can be applied to PLSA, improving system performance. Finally, the proposed system could be favored

by the exploitation of the social media information, being available on the web
in order to provide personalized recommendation.

Acknowledgments. This research has been co-financed by the European Union
(European Social Fund - ESF) and Greek national funds through the Operation Program "Competitiveness-Cooperation 2011" - Research Funding Program: SYN-10-1730-ATLAS.

References

1. Zheng, Y.-T., Zhao, M., Song, Y., Adam, H., Buddemeier, U., Bissacco, A.,
   Brucher, F., Chua, T.-S., Neven, H.: Tour the world: building a web-scale landmark
   recognition engine. In: Proc. IEEE CVPR, pp. 1085–1092 (2009)
2. Papadopoulos, S., Zigkolis, C., Kompatsiaris, Y., Vakali, A.: Cluster-based landmark and event detection on tagged photo collections. Multimedia, 52–63 (2011)
3. Cao, L., Luo, J., Gallagher, A.: A worldwide tourist recommendation system based on
   geotagged web photos. In: Proc. IEEE ICASSP, Dallas, Texas, USA, pp. 2274–2277
   (2010)
4. Wang, C., Blei, D., Fei-Fei, L.: Simultaneous image classification and annotation.
   In: Proc. IEEE CVPR, Florida, USA, pp. 1903–1910 (June 2009)
5. Hofmann, T.: Probabilistic latent semantic analysis. In: Proc. 15th Conf. Uncertainty in Artificial Intelligence, pp. 289–296 (1999)
6. Bassiou, N., Kotropoulos, C.: On-line PLSA: Batch updating techniques including
   out of vocabulary words. IEEE Trans. Neural Networks and Learning Systems
   (to appear, 2014)
7. Bassiou, N., Kotropoulos, C.: RPLSA: A novel updating scheme for probabilistic
   latent semantic analysis. Computer, Speech, and Language 25(4), 741–760 (2011)
8. Oliva, A., Torralba, A.: Building the GIST of a scene: The role of global image
   features in recognition. Progress in Brain Research 155, 23–36 (2006)
9. Agarwal, S., Branson, K., Belongie, S.: Higher order learning with graphs. In: Proc.
   23rd ICML, pp. 17–24 (2006)
10. Bu, J., Tan, S., Chen, C., Wang, C., Wu, H., Lijun, Z., He, X.: Music recom-
    mendation by unified hypergraph: Combining social media information and music
    content. In: Proc. ACM Conf. Multimedia, pp. 391–400 (2010)
11. Salton, G., Wong, A., Yang, C.S.: A vector space model for automatic indexing.
    Commun. ACM, 613–620 (1975)

Author Index